THE
UNIFICATION OF
SOUTH AFRICA
1902–1910

THE
UNIFICATION OF
SOUTH AFRICA
1902-1910

BY

L. M. THOMPSON
PROFESSOR OF HISTORY
UNIVERSITY OF CAPE TOWN

OXFORD
AT THE CLARENDON PRESS

Oxford University Press, Amen House, London E.C.4

GLASGOW NEW YORK TORONTO MELBOURNE WELLINGTON
BOMBAY CALCUTTA MADRAS KARACHI KUALA LUMPUR
CAPE TOWN IBADAN NAIROBI ACCRA

FIRST PUBLISHED 1960

REPRINTED LITHOGRAPHICALLY IN GREAT BRITAIN
AT THE UNIVERSITY PRESS, OXFORD
FROM SHEETS OF THE FIRST EDITION
1961

PREFACE

THE unification of South Africa was one of the last creative expressions of the age of optimism which was brought to a close by the First World War. This decisive step towards the elimination of imperial authority in South Africa, in favour of the white settlers of Afrikaner and British stocks, was considered to be justified by the hopes that the Anglo-Boer feud would disappear, that white South Africans would grow increasingly humane in their dealings with their non-white fellow countrymen, and that the Union would become a liberal democracy on the British pattern. Today it can hardly be said that those hopes have been realized. Most white South Africans have been actuated by racial sentiment rather than by the liberal traditions of their countries of origin. Consequently, besides being a striking example of the operation of political forces in a multi-racial society, the story of the unification of South Africa provides a salutary reminder of the limitations of human foresight.

Fortunately there is a wealth of private papers, most of them still unpublished, which help one to discover the motives and unravel the tactics of the men who played the leading parts in the story, and on many of the key issues I have been able to let them speak for themselves. Although the last word cannot yet be said on the policy of the British Government, since the official British records of the period, including the dispatches between the Colonial Secretary and the South African High Commissioner and Governors, have not been made available to the historian, the general tenor of that policy is clear enough from other sources.

Many previous publications bear upon the subject of this book. Some are essentially tendentious; a large proportion are biographies, which inevitably give an incomplete picture; and none appears to have been based upon a study of more than a fraction of the primary material which is listed in the bibliography at the end of this volume.

I have thought it desirable to provide thorough documentation, and to reserve comment upon the main assumptions of the period for a brief concluding section. Most of the issues which aroused strong feelings fifty years ago are still the stuff of political controversy in South Africa today.

One of the pleasures of historical research is the co-operation one receives from the owners of private papers, from librarians and archivists, and from scholars. Lord Brand, himself the author of a lucid analysis of the South African Constitution (*The Union of South Africa*, published by the Clarendon Press in 1909), generously placed his South African papers at my disposal. The Dowager Lady de Villiers allowed me to use the papers of the first Lord de Villiers; Mr. Patrick and Mr. John Duncan, those of Sir Patrick Duncan; Mrs. Niven, those of Sir Percy Fitzpatrick; Mrs. Ruffel, those of Sir Walter Stanford; and Mr. R. Silburn, those of Colonel P. A. Silburn. Mr. J. C. Smuts, as literary executor of his father, and the Trustees of the Smuts Archive gave me access to the relevant parts of the Smuts Papers; the Trustees of the South African Public Library, to the papers of J. H. Hofmeyr, Sir James Rose Innes, and J. X. Merriman; and the Honourable Richard Feetham supplied me with a key document. I am most grateful to all of them.

The staff of the Jagger Library, University of Cape Town, responded kindly and efficiently to my many requests. So did the staffs of the South African Public Library and the Library of the Union Parliament, Cape Town; of the archives in Cape Town, Pretoria, Bloemfontein, and Pietermaritzburg; and of the libraries of Chatham House, the Institute of Historical Research, and the Royal Empire Society (now the Royal Commonwealth Society), London, and Rhodes House and New College, Oxford. Special thanks are due to Mr. G. D. Quinn of the Jagger Library, who was most helpful with bibliographical problems.

I am very deeply indebted to four historians—Professor Sir Keith Hancock, Professor H. J. Mandelbrote, Professor J. S. Marais, and Dr. Jean van der Poel. Each of them gave me invaluable encouragement while the work was in progress, and generously set aside time to read the entire manuscript and supply me with cogent comments. Without the benefit of their wide knowledge this book would have emerged with more blemishes than it has.

Many others have been consulted on particular points. I would specially mention Mr. R. F. Currey, formerly headmaster of St. Andrew's College, Grahamstown; Professor B. Beinart, Mr. T. R. H. Davenport, Dr. S. I. M. du Plessis, Mr. G. B. Nourse, Professor H. M. Robertson, Professor J. du P. Scholtz, Professor H. J. Simons, Dr. Sheila T. van der Horst, and Mrs. M. A. Williams, of this University; and Professor and Mrs. G. H. Le May of the University of the Witwatersrand, Johannesburg, who provided me with an analysis of the results of the South African general election of 1910.

My warm thanks are also due to the candidates for the honours degree in history who, during the last five years, have taken The Unification of

South Africa as a special subject. I have gained much from our seminar discussions and some of their research essays have been of real value.

I am very grateful to Professor M. J. Pollard, who checked the mathematics of the statistical appendix; the staff of the Oxford University Press, Cape Town, who gave me valuable advice; my daughter Caroline, who made the first draft of the map; Miss M. A. Hennings, who made the index; and Mrs. E. Gal, who typed the manuscript with unflagging energy and efficiency.

It is, too, my pleasant duty to acknowledge the financial assistance received from the South African Department of Education, Arts, and Science (National Council for Social Research) towards the costs of my visits to England and to Pretoria, Bloemfontein, and Pietermaritzburg.

For any opinions expressed or conclusions reached, however, the responsibility is, of course, entirely mine. They are not to be regarded as representing those of any other person, nor those of the Department of Education, Arts, and Science.

Finally, I cannot refrain from expressing my gratitude to the Delegates and staff of the Clarendon Press, who have done so much to mitigate the difficulties which confront an author living six thousand miles away from his publisher.

L. M. T.

University of Cape Town
February 1959

CONTENTS

CONTENTS

(7) Parliament — 203
(A) Form and Powers — 203
(B) The Senate — 204
(C) The House of Assembly — 212
(i) The Franchise — 212
(ii) The Constituencies — 226
(iii) General — 242
(D) Miscellaneous — 242
(8) The Provinces — 248
(9) The Supreme Court — 260
(10) The Civil Service — 265
(11) Rhodesia and the High Commission Territories — 269
(12) The Amending Section — 279
(13) Finance and Railways — 284
(14) The Capital — 294
(15) The Report of the Convention — 305

CHAPTER VI. SOUTH AFRICA APPROVES OF THE CONSTITUTION — 309
(1) Initial Reactions to the Report of the Convention — 309
(2) The Reactions of the Colonial Parliaments — 327
(A) The Transvaal — 327
(B) The Orange River Colony — 331
(C) The Cape Colony — 336
(D) Natal — 348
(3) The Bloemfontein Session of the National Convention — 362
(4) South Africa Approves — 384

CHAPTER VII. THE CONSTITUTION ENACTED IN ENGLAND — 398
(1) The British Background — 398
(2) The Failure of the Schreiner Mission — 402
(3 The Colonial Secretary's Conference — 407
(4) The South Africa Bill in the House of Lords — 416
(5) The South Africa Bill in the House of Commons — 423

CHAPTER VIII. SOUTH AFRICA UNITED — 433
(1) A Fresh Start *versus* the Old Party Lines — 433
(2) The Governor-General, the Prime Minister, and the Cabinet — 448
(3) The General Election — 460
(4) Conclusion — 480

CHRONOLOGY

1902

31 May   Treaty of Vereeniging

1903

March   Intercolonial Conference, Bloemfontein
2 July   Transvaal Boers' Meeting at Heidelberg
6 October   Lyttelton succeeds Chamberlain as Colonial Secretary

1904

10 February   Transvaal Legislative Council passes Labour Importation Ordinance
22 February   Jameson forms Progressive Ministry in Cape Colony
23 May   Transvaal Boers' Congress in Pretoria
June   First Chinese labourers arrive on Witwatersrand
November   Formation of Transvaal Progressive Association and Transvaal Responsible Government Association
4 December   Orange River Colony Boers' Congress at Brandfort

1905

28 January   Botha announces formation of Het Volk
February   Intercolonial Railway Conference, Johannesburg
2 April   Selborne succeeds Milner as High Commissioner and Governor of Transvaal and Orange River Colony
25 April   Publication of Lyttelton Constitution providing representative government for Transvaal
May   Smythe forms Ministry in Natal
April–June   Gustav Preller's articles launch Afrikaans language movement
5 December   Campbell-Bannerman forms Liberal Ministry in Britain

1906

January   British general election results in overwhelming Liberal victory
7 February   Smuts interviews Campbell-Bannerman
February   Start of Natal Native Rebellion
March   Intercolonial Conference, Pietermaritzburg
April–June   West Ridgeway Committee in South Africa
3 May   Announcement of formation of Orangia Unie

10 June	Defeat and death of Bambata at Mome Gorge: beginning of end of Natal Native Rebellion
28 November	Moor forms Ministry in Natal
28 November	Jameson asks Selborne to review the relations between the South African colonies
6 December	Publication of Letters Patent instituting responsible government in Transvaal

1907

7 January	Selborne Memorandum sent to South African Governments
4 March	Botha forms Het Volk–Nationalist Ministry in Transvaal
April	Colonial Conference assembles in London
5 June	Publication of Letters Patent instituting responsible government in Orange River Colony
June	Transvaal Government gives notice of intention to withdraw from Customs Union
3 July	Publication of Selborne Memorandum
27 November	Fischer forms Orangia Unie Ministry in Orange River Colony
9 December	Dinizulu arrested
December	Language congress at Paarl: agreement between advocates of Afrikaans and advocates of Dutch

1908

3 February	Merriman forms South African Party Ministry in Cape Colony
6 April	Asquith succeeds Campbell-Bannerman as Prime Minister of Britain
May	Intercolonial Conference, Pretoria and Cape Town
June–July	Closer Union Resolutions approved by South African Parliaments
24 August	Hertzog's Education Bill pased by Orange River Colony Parliament
29 August	Smuts's 'Suggested Scheme for South African Union' sent to de Villiers, Merriman, and Steyn
September–March 1909	Trial of Dinizulu
30 September–6 October	Meetings of Transvaal delegates to National Convention
12 October–5 November	National Convention, Durban session
22 November–18 December	National Convention, Cape Town session

1909

11 January– 3 February	National Convention, Cape Town session (continued)
30 March–16 April	Draft South Africa Act considered by South African Parliaments
3–11 May	National Convention, Bloemfontein session
2–4 June	Amended draft South Africa Act approved by Parliaments of Cape Colony, Transvaal, and Orange River Colony
10 June	Amended draft South Africa Act approved in Natal by referendum
6 July	*The Times* publishes 'An Appeal to the Parliament and Government of Great Britain and Ireland' signed by Schreiner, &c.
20–21 July	Colonial Secretary confers with South African delegates
22 July–3 August	South Africa Bill in House of Lords
16–19 August	South Africa Bill in House of Commons
20 September	South Africa Act receives royal assent

1910

March	Last Chinese labourers leave South Africa
17 May	Gladstone arrives in Cape Town
21 May	Gladstone invites Botha to form a Ministry
24 May	Jameson announces formation of Unionist Party of South Africa
31 May	Inauguration of Union of South Africa
14 June	Botha announces his Government's policy
19 August	Hertzog's Smithfield speech
15 September	General election
31 October	Opening of Union Parliament

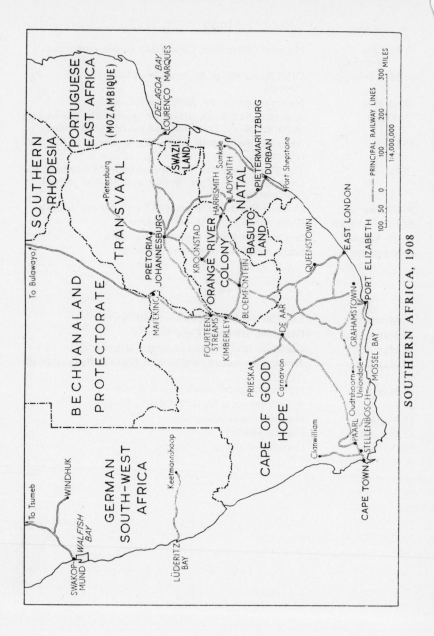

SOUTHERN AFRICA, 1908

CHAPTER I

SOUTH AFRICA DIVIDED

1. THE ELEMENTS OF THE SOUTH AFRICAN PROBLEM

ON 31 May 1902 the representatives of the Boer commandos decided to lay down their arms.

For nearly a century Britain had been confronted with a problem of exceptional difficulty in South Africa, where the Afrikaners[1] continued to outnumber the British settlers, the Bantu-speaking Africans were several times as numerous as the Afrikaners and the British settlers combined, and nearly every European person used Coloured, or African, or Indian labourers.[2] If there was a satisfactory answer to this problem, Britain had never found it. She had conquered the Cape to obtain control of the sea route to India and the preservation of that control had been the one fixed purpose of her South African policy. In other respects she had been inconsistent, because her evangelical, economic, and imperial inclinations were incompatible with one another. In the second quarter of the century she had been largely concerned to raise the status of the non-whites, in the third quarter to reduce the burden on the British taxpayer, and in the last quarter to establish British supremacy throughout southern Africa; but any advance towards one of those objectives had been to the detriment of both the others.

In the late 1820's and the 1830's, spurred on by the evangelicals, she had relieved the Coloured people of their legal disabilities and made tentative efforts to devise a liberal policy towards the Africans on the eastern frontier of the Cape Colony. Unfortunately, however sound this approach may have been in principle, in practice it was not accompanied by adequate safeguards for the security of the lives and property of the white farmers, with the result that many of the Boers trekked away, convinced that Britain was opposed to their welfare, and determined to establish their own independent states. Britain annexed Natal, their first republic, in 1843, mainly for strategic reasons, but soon afterwards

---

[1] The words Africander, Afrikaander, Afrikaner, &c., were used almost indiscriminately in the nineteenth century. The modern form, Afrikaner, is used throughout this book.

[2] See below, Appendix A. i–v, for analyses of the population of the Union of South Africa in 1911 ; and the note to Appendix A. i for an explanation of the racial categories used in South African censuses.

separatist opinion became dominant in Britain and she granted the Voor-trekkers their independence in the South African Republic and the Orange Free State by the conventions of Sand River (1852) and Bloem-fontein (1854).

Nevertheless, the schism in South Africa was never complete. Until late in the century the main channels of trade to both the republics were from the British colonial ports, and there were always many people who spoke and thought of South Africa as a single country, differing only as to whether it should be under British or Afrikaner control. Afrikaners formed a majority of the white population of the Cape Colony as well as the republics, and they were conscious of their kinship, their common language, and their common religion; British settlers dominated the finance and the commerce of all South Africa; and Bantu-speaking Africans were in a large majority in every territory. The Africans were gradually conquered and subjected to white domination, when many became labour tenants on farms owned by Europeans, but still more continued to live on attenuated tribal lands, where their culture began to be transformed by the impact of traders, missionaries, and government officials.

British high commissioners soon found that the conventions of 1852 and 1854 did not provide a durable basis for harmony in South Africa. In particular, conflicts between Boers and Africans caused instability on the colonial frontiers. Consequently, in 1858 Sir George Grey, an imaginative and resourceful High Commissioner, conceived the idea of joining the colonies and republics together in a federation under the British Crown. He obtained some support in the Orange Free State, which needed help in its struggles with the Basuto, but he failed to carry the British Government with him.

The next attempt to create a British South African federation was made by a Colonial Secretary, Lord Carnarvon, at the time when separatism was beginning to give way to imperialism in England. In 1875 he summoned a conference to consider the question, but the Orange Free State, smarting under the recent British annexations of Basutoland (1868) and Griqualand West (1871), would have nothing to do with it; nor would the Cape Colony, which had recently become self-governing and was resentful that the initiative had come from without. Carnarvon then adopted the expedient of commissioning Sir Theophilus Shepstone to annex the South African Republic, which was bankrupt and seemed near to anarchy. Although there was no resistance to Shepstone's proclama-tion of annexation (April 1877), the administration that was then set up in the Transvaal failed to take account of Boer sentiment, and there was a rebellion in 1881. After the Boers had won a victory at Majuba the Gladstone Government granted the Transvaal a qualified form of independence and three years later full autonomy, except that Britain retained control over its treaties with foreign countries, other than the Orange Free State. Carnarvon's project had miscarried and the Act for the creation of a self-governing federation under the crown of 'such of the South African Colonies and States as may agree thereto' was stillborn.[3]

Before 1870 South Africa had lacked the facilities of a modern country and nearly all her inhabitants, white as well as non-white, were farmers. Then, however, as a result of the opening of the diamond mines at Kimberley (1870) and the gold-mines of the Witwatersrand (1886), capital flowed in, railways were built, and South Africa took a significant place in the world economy as the source of over half the world's annual supply of diamonds and about a quarter of its gold. Most of the mining companies were British. Their skilled work was done by white men—mainly immigrants from Britain—and their unskilled work by Africans, who came from all over southern Africa on short-term contracts, leaving their families behind them. In 1898 the gold-mining industry employed 9,476 white men at an average monthly wage of £26, and 69,797 Africans at an average monthly wage of 49s. 9d. plus food and accommodation. Thus the mines, with their voracious appetite for cheap unskilled labour, accentuated the trend towards the disintegration of tribalism.

Griqualand West, including Kimberley, was annexed by Britain in 1871; but the Witwatersrand was situated in the heart of the South African Republic and its gold was beginning to be mined at the very time when the competition between the European powers for African territories was reaching its climax. The results were explosive. President Kruger strove to keep the Republic under Boer control, using the gold-mines as his main source of revenue, but denying the Uitlanders (as the immigrants were called) any effective say in the Government; whereas Britain sought to establish her supremacy throughout South Africa. Of the mining magnates none was more powerful than the English-born Cecil Rhodes. He was the dominant figure in De Beers Consolidated Mines (which controlled nearly the entire diamond industry), Consolidated Gold Fields (one of the greatest gold-mining corporations), and the British South Africa Company (which obtained a royal charter for the development of the country north of the Limpopo); and in 1890 he also became Prime Minister of the Cape Colony. In 1895 Rhodes tried to take a short cut for Britain by organizing a conspiracy: the Uitlanders

---

[3] The South Africa Act, 1877. The quotation is from the preamble. In terms of s. 60 the Act lapsed on 1 Aug. 1882.

were to rise, an armed force under L. S. Jameson was to come to their
aid, and the High Commissioner was to hurry to Pretoria to 'restore
order'. In spite of the fact that the Uitlander rising failed to materialize,
Jameson's force invaded the Republic, only to be surrounded and captured. This fiasco enhanced Kruger's standing among his own people and
increased his intransigence. It also compromised the British case, especially as it was widely (and correctly) suspected that Joseph Chamberlain,
the Colonial Secretary, had been privy to the plot. Thereafter the relations
between Britain and the South African Republic went from bad to worse.
In March 1899, Kruger having rejected several petitions for reform, many
of the Uitlanders appealed to the Queen. They declared not only that
they had no share in the Government, but also that the administration
was corrupt, the courts had lost their independence, the juries were
packed, the police were arbitrary, and the press was muzzled. By that
time an Anglo-German agreement had removed the likelihood of German intervention, and Chamberlain and Sir Alfred Milner, the High
Commissioner, decided to take up the Uitlander cause. The last chance
of a settlement was lost in August, when J. C. Smuts, Kruger's young
State Attorney, offered a five-years' franchise and Chamberlain rejected
the conditions which were attached to it. Britain then took steps to
augment her forces in South Africa, and the two Boer republics, who
had made a military alliance and had been arming furiously, issued an
ultimatum which expired on 11 October 1899.

The result of the war was that all white South Africans were brought
under the British Crown for the first time since the Great Trek. But other
elements of the South African problem were unchanged: Afrikaners
remained a clear majority of the white population and many of them still
cherished a republican ideal; Africans continued to be an overwhelming
majority of the total population, and their tribal structure was inexorably
disintegrating. Moreover, South Africa was still disunited—divided
between the self-governing Cape Colony and Natal, the newly annexed
Transvaal and Orange River Colony, and other territories administered
by the High Commissioner and the British South Africa Company. Such
a situation called for statesmanship of the highest order.

2. LORD MILNER AND THE POST-WAR SETTLEMENT

The man who assumed the chief responsibility for framing and applying British policy in South Africa after the war was Lord Milner, High
Commissioner for South Africa and Governor of the Transvaal and the

Orange River Colony until April 1905.[4] Joseph Chamberlain, who remained Colonial Secretary until he resigned to campaign for tariff reform in October 1903, shared his general outlook and endorsed most, but not quite all, of the points in his programme, while Alfred Lyttelton, Chamberlain's successor, gave him his complete support.

Selecting able subordinates and inspiring them with unquestioning devotion, Milner built up strong and efficient administrative machines in both the new colonies. He had a remarkable flair for finance and a prodigious capacity for work, and he was logical and lucid to a fault. Indeed, he was that somewhat rare phenomenon, an Englishman with a doctrinaire cast of mind. Whether this was the result of influences exerted on him by his half-German father, or during his schooling at Tübingen, or his service as Under-Secretary for Finance under Lord Cromer in Egypt, one cannot be sure, but by the time he arrived in South Africa in 1897 the rigidity was there, and in the South African milieu it became more and more pronounced.

Milner described himself as 'an Imperialist out and out'.[5] It was his basic premiss that 'the British race' had a special mission to perform in the world. To him 'the racial bond . . . is fundamental'; 'deeper, stronger, more primordial than . . . material ties is the tie of common blood, a common language, common history and traditions'.[6] He considered, however, that the British 'race' was in the process of disintegrating through the drift towards autonomy of the great colonies of settlement in North America, Australia, and New Zealand. It was of paramount importance to him that this drift should be checked by the creation of a central imperial institution, superior to all the existing institutions in the Empire, including the Parliament at Westminster. He therefore gave a fresh impetus to the imperial federation movement, which had been in decline since its hey-day in the 1880's. What was wanted, he declared, was 'a real Imperial Council', which should have control of 'all our *world business*', while the existing parliaments should only control matters of local concern.[7]

---

[4] Milner received his peerage in May 1901. He was High Commissioner for South Africa from May 1897 to Apr. 1905. From May 1897 to Mar. 1901 he was also Governor of the Cape Colony; and from Aug. 1901 to Apr. 1905 Governor of the Transvaal and of the Orange River Colony.

[5] Address to the Navy League, Johannesburg, 28 May 1904. Cecil Headlam (ed.), *The Milner Papers (South Africa) 1897–1905* (London, 1931–3, 2 vols.), ii. 503.

[6] *The Nation and the Empire: being a collection of speeches and addresses: with an introduction by Lord Milner, G.C.B.* (London, 1913), p. xxxv. That Milner was actuated by a 'racial' premiss was apparent throughout his career in South Africa, though it was not until he wrote this introduction to a collection of his speeches that he formulated it so clearly.   [7] Milner to Sir George Parkin, 13 Sept. 1901. Headlam, ii. 267.

Implicit in Milner's doctrine was a concept of a hierarchy of races. White communities of non-British stock who lived in the colonies were to be treated with tolerance. They should have the same political rights as British settlers; and no attempt should be made 'to disintegrate them, or to rob them of their individuality'[8] (but in practice this was always subject to the proviso that they were loyal to the Empire). Non-whites, on the other hand, were in a completely different category. 'A political equality of white and black is impossible', he declared.[9] 'The white man must rule, because he is elevated by many, many steps above the black man; steps which it will take the latter centuries to climb, and which it is quite possible that the vast bulk of the black population may never be able to climb at all.'[10]

Milner regarded it as his mission to transform South Africa from 'the weakest link in the imperial chain'[11] into a strong and effective link. He played a leading part in the events which led to the outbreak of war in October 1899, and soon afterwards he began to devise his plans for the post-war settlement. In November 1899 he was reasoning as follows:

The *ultimate* end is a self-governing white Community, supported by *well-treated* and *justly governed* black labour from Cape Town to Zambesi. There must be one flag, the Union Jack, but under it equality of races and languages. Given *equality* all round, English must prevail, though I do not think, and do not wish, that Dutch should altogether die out. I think, though all South Africa should be *one Dominion* with a common government dealing with Customs, Railways, and Defence, perhaps also with Native policy, a considerable amount of freedom should be left to the several States. But though this is the ultimate end, it would be madness to attempt it at once. There must be an interval, to allow the British population of the Transvaal to return and increase, and the mess to be cleared up, before we can apply the principle of self-government to the Transvaal. . . . How long the period of unrepresentative government may last, I cannot say. I, for one, would be for shortening it as much as possible, but not before a loyal majority is assured. As for the Boer himself, provided I am once sure of having broken his political predominance, I should be for leaving him the greatest amount of individual freedom. First beaten, then fairly treated, and not too much worried on his own 'plaats' in his own conservative habits, I think he will be peaceful enough.[12]

[8] *The Nation and the Empire*, p. xxxviii.
[9] Milner to the Rev. James Green, Dean of Pietermaritzburg, 12 Dec. 1901, Headlam, ii. 314.
[10] Address to the Municipal Congress, Johannesburg, 18 May 1903, ibid. 467.
[11] Milner to Sir George Parkin, 28 Apr. 1897, ibid. i. 42.
[12] Milner to Sir Percy Fitzpatrick, 28 Nov. 1899, ibid. ii. 35–36.

In December 1900 he set out his intentions in a lucid memorandum.[13] First of all, it was essential that the British element should be increased to the point where there would be a permanent British majority in the white population of South Africa:

On the political side, I attach the greatest importance of all to the increase of the British population. British and Dutch have to live here on equal terms. If, ten years hence, there are three men of British race to two of Dutch, the country will be safe and prosperous. If there are three of Dutch to two of British, we shall have perpetual difficulty. . . . We not only want a majority of British, but we want a fair margin, because of the large proportion of 'cranks' that we British always generate, and who take particular pleasure in going against their own people. . . .

A healthy social and political condition of South Africa would be the following: Assuming that 60 per cent. of the white population will shortly be industrial and commercial, and 40 per cent. agricultural, then I should like to see 45 out of the 60 British and 15 Dutch, 15 out of the 40 British and 25 Dutch. The former proportion will accomplish itself. It will not be long, with the influx of the new population to the Mines and elsewhere, before three-fourths of the industrial and commercial population are British. But to make even as much as two-fifths of the agricultural population British will take some working. It is only to be done by bringing British settlers, through Government Agency, in considerable numbers into the districts I have specified.

Secondly, the Afrikaners were to be exposed to the full force of modern Western cultural influences, transmitted in the English language:

Next to the composition of the population, the thing which matters most is its education. . . . Dutch should only be used to teach English, and English to teach everything else. Language is important, but the tone and spirit of the teaching conveyed in it is even more important. Not half enough attention has been paid to school reading books. To get these right would be the greatest political achievement conceivable. I attach especial importance to school *history books*. A good world-history would be worth anything. At present children are only taught the history of South Africa, with at most a little English history, of the narrowest purely English type, thrown in. Everything that makes South African children look outside South Africa and *realize the world* makes for peace. Everything that cramps and confines their views to South Africa only (limits their historical reading, for instance, to Slagter's Nek and Dingaan's Day, and Boomplaats and Majuba) makes for Afrikanderdom and further discord.

Thirdly, the Transvaal and the Orange River Colony should be governed

13 Milner to Major Hanbury Williams, 27 Dec. 1900, ibid. 242–4.

as crown colonies for an indefinite period, though some services, such as railways, might be reorganized on an intercolonial basis. Only when there was a secure British majority in the white population of South Africa and the Afrikaners had been brought out of their cultural isolation, would it be safe to join the South African colonies together in a self-governing dominion:

> Generally speaking, our political aim should be to work *towards* Federation, by making, or keeping, as many branches of Government as possible common to two, or more, or all the Colonies. . . . I believe a great deal can be done to federate *practically and in detail*, before we embark on the discussion of a federal constitution, just as I believe in a lot of *virtual self-government* in the new Colonies, without letting the supreme control out of Imperial hands. We must be very sure of our ground before we part with executive authority. Indeed, I hope that there may never be 'responsible Government' in the two Colonies as separate States, but that we shall always keep Imperial control over them till we can with safety grant 'responsible government' to a Federated South Africa.

In many respects this programme was remarkably similar to the programme which Lord Durham had drawn up in 1839 for the elimination of French Canadian nationalism. Not only was there the same insistence on the need for British immigration and for the anglicization of a local settler community of non-British stock, but with Milner, too, there was a belief that material progress would promote his political objectives. He planned to accelerate the recovery and development of the gold-mining industry of the Witwatersrand and to encourage the Afrikaners to adopt more scientific methods of agriculture and stock-raising, largely because he considered that the atmosphere of an expanding and 'modern' economy would be inimical to the survival of Afrikaner nationalism.

The first important occasion on which Milner tried to promote his post-war plans was in May 1902, when he publicly advocated the suspension of the Constitution of the Cape Colony. Since 1900 the Cape Parliament had not been summoned, lest it should oppose the pro-British policy of the Government of Sir Gordon Sprigg, and the expenditure of money raised under governors' warrants. As the war drew to a close Milner feared that the Cape Parliament would prove a serious obstacle to the fulfilment of his objectives, and he decided that the Constitution should be suspended and the colony reduced to crown colony status, so that the three territories with large Afrikaner populations could be moulded in the same pattern. Milner was aware, however, that it would be difficult to persuade the Colonial Secretary to give effect to his wishes, for Chamberlain had already rejected similar proposals, pointing out that the suspension of the Cape Constitution would arouse opposition not only in the British Parliament, but also from other self-governing colonies.[14] Accordingly, being 'absolutely convinced . . . of the necessity of intervention from home to put the Cape Colony straight',[15] Milner tried to force Chamberlain's hand. He arranged for a petition for suspension to be drawn up and signed by Progressive members of the Cape Parliament and presented to Sir Walter Hely-Hutchinson, the Governor. Hely-Hutchinson forwarded it to Milner as High Commissioner and Milner replied that he agreed with its contents and had his reply published in the press on 19 May. But the plan miscarried. The Cape Opposition reacted with vigour, and so did Sir Henry de Villiers, the Chief Justice, and Sir Gordon Sprigg, the Prime Minister; and when Chamberlain consulted the prime ministers who were in England for the 1902 Colonial Conference he found that they were unanimously opposed to suspension. The petition was therefore dismissed by the British Cabinet and Milner was rebuked—but he was not recalled. When the Cape Parliament met in August, Sprigg contrived to remain in office by steering a middle course between the Progressives[16] and the Afrikaner Bond:[17] the necessary indemnity acts were passed and a resolution was adopted deploring the agitation for the destruction of 'the rights and privileges enjoyed by the inhabitants of this colony'. Milner was bitterly disappointed that his *coup* had failed, but he had some cause for satisfaction in February 1904 when Sprigg resigned after a general election in which the Progressives, aided by the temporary disfranchisement of some 10,500 Afrikaner voters for assisting the republican commandos during the war, obtained a majority of one in the Legislative Council and a majority of five in the House of Assembly; and Dr. L. S. Jameson, Rhodes's former lieutenant, became Prime Minister.[18]

Milner was more successful in his efforts to ensure that the peace treaty at the end of the war should not impede him in applying his plans to the Transvaal and the Orange River Colony.[19] He had his way in the three

[14] Milner to Chamberlain, 17 Jan. 1900, 22 Aug. 1900, and 5 Dec. 1900, and Chamberlain to Milner, 10 Sept. 1900, 22 Dec. 1900, and 7 Feb. 1901, Headlam, ii. 55–58, 121–5, 171–3, 180–2, 202–3.

[15] Milner to Sir Walter Hely-Hutchinson, 5 Mar. 1902, ibid. 408.

[16] The Progressives were the Imperialist Party in the Cape Colony. At the end of 1907 they changed their name to Unionist. See below, pp. 39–40.

[17] On the Afrikaner Bond see below, pp. 37–39.

[18] On the abortive attempt to suspend the Constitution of the Cape Colony see Cd. 1162 (1902); Headlam, ii. 404–26; Julian Amery, *The Life of Joseph Chamberlain* (London, 1951, vol. iv), lxxx; Eric A. Walker, *Lord de Villiers and his Times: South Africa 1842–1914* (London, 1925), xii; L. S. Amery (ed.), *The Times History of the War in South Africa, 1899–1902* (London, 1900–9, 7 vols.), v. iii.

[19] On the origins of the Treaty of Vereeniging see Cd. 528, 546, 663, 1096 (1901–2);

most important articles, dealing with language, constitutional advance, and the franchise. On 28 February 1901, during an abortive parley at Middelburg, Kitchener, the British commander-in-chief, had told Botha that he was prepared to recommend that the English and Dutch languages should be placed on an equal official footing, but Milner had objected and in the terms offered to the Boers on 7 March 1901 the language provision had read: 'Both the English and Dutch languages will be used and taught in public schools where parents of the children desire it, and allowed in Courts of Law.'[20] Milner had still been dissatisfied, and after the Boers had rejected the British offer he had set himself to provide more definitely for the predominance of the English language in any terms that might subsequently be offered. He had advised Chamberlain that 'we should be somewhat stiffer on . . . language. It should be clearly understood that . . . we do not promise equality of the two languages. English must be the official language and the principal medium of instruction.'[21] Chamberlain had consented to this.[22] Accordingly article 5 of the Treaty of Vereeniging read:

The Dutch language will be taught in public schools in the Transvaal and Orange River Colony where the parents of the children desire it, and will be allowed in courts of law when necessary for the better and more effectual administration of justice.[23]

Furthermore, Milner made it quite clear to the Boer commissioners that English would be the only medium of instruction in the schools.[24] As regards constitutional development, failing the retention of some form of republican independence, the Boer leaders had hoped to include in the treaty a provision that the Transvaal and Orange River Colony should be granted self-government under the Crown by a specified date. Kitchener supported this request, but both Chamberlain and Milner set their faces against it,[25] and article 7 of the Treaty of Vereeniging left the timing of the constitutional evolution of the new colonies completely open:

Headlam, ii. 207–34, 324–66; Julian Amery, lxxviii; L. S. Amery, v. vii, xxi; Ds. J. D. Kestell and D. E. van Velden, *De Vredesonderhandelingen tusschen de regeeringen der twee Zuid-Afrikaansche republieken en de vertegenwoordigers der Britische regeering . . . 1902 . . .* (Pretoria, 1909) (English translation, Pretoria, 1912); C. R. de Wet, *Three Years War* (London, 1902), xxviii, xxxv–xxxvii, appendices A–C; Sir George Arthur, *Life of Lord Kitchener* (London, 1920, 3 vols.), ii. xliv, li, liv–lvi; C. M. van den Heever, *Generaal J. B. M. Hertzog* (Johannesburg, 1943), pp. 142–75.

[20] Headlam, ii. 210–13.   [21] Ibid. 334–5.
[22] Ibid. 336.   [23] Cd. 1096 (1902), p. 12.
[24] Kestell and van Velden, p. 114; van den Heever, p. 170.
[25] Headlam, ii. 328, 336–8; Arthur, ii. 87.

Military administration in the Transvaal and Orange River Colony will at the earliest possible date be succeeded by Civil Government, and, as soon as circumstances permit, representative institutions, leading up to self-government, will be introduced.[26]

Thus Milner secured the things that mattered most to him. On the other hand, he caused Britain to yield to the Boers on the franchise question. It had originally been Chamberlain's intention that non-whites should acquire the franchise in the new colonies on the same terms as in the Cape Colony, where there was no political colour-bar.[27] On 28 February 1901 Botha had told Kitchener at Middelburg that the Boers were strongly opposed to a *Kaffir* suffrage and would agree to leave the question to be settled after the grant of *representative* government.[28] Chamberlain had accepted this, but added: 'we cannot consent to purchase peace by leaving the *coloured* population in the position in which they were before the war, with not even the ordinary civil rights which the Government of the Cape Colony has long conceded to them'.[29] Accordingly, the terms offered by the British Government on 7 March 1901 had included the following: 'As regards the extension of the franchise to Kaffirs in the Transvaal and Orange River Colonies, it is not the intention of H.M. Government to give such franchise before representative government is granted to those Colonies, and if then given, it will be so limited as to secure the just predominance of the white race. The legal position of coloured persons will, however, be similar to that which they hold in the Cape Colony.'[30] Nevertheless, in the version of the treaty drafted in Pretoria on 20 May 1902 the article read simply: 'The question of granting the franchise to natives will not be decided until after the introduction of self-government.'[31] No reference was made to Coloured people as distinct from 'natives'. Chamberlain promptly queried this draft article: 'Seems to be worded so that we should actually have to exclude natives from the Franchise in any constitution establishing a self-governing Colony. Would it not be enough to leave out from after "until" to end, and insert "the introduction of representative government"?'[32] Milner replied: 'Yes. That would be the object of the clause. Clause suggested by you would defeat that object. . . . I think there is much to be said for leaving question of political rights of natives to be settled by Colonists themselves.'[33] Apparently Chamberlain made no further comment. The

---

[26] Cd. 1096, p. 12.
[27] Headlam, ii. 41.
[28] Cd. 528 (1901), p. 2. Here and in the next sentence the italics are mine.
[29] Headlam, ii. 212.
[30] Ibid. 213.
[31] Ibid. 351.
[32] Ibid. 356.
[33] Ibid. 357.

result was that article 8 of the Treaty of Vereeniging followed the draft of 20 May.[34] Britain thereby undertook not to admit any Africans to the franchise in the Transvaal or the Orange River Colony while she had the power to do so, and she ignored the Coloured inhabitants of those colonies. Milner had persuaded Chamberlain to change his original intentions to the detriment of the non-Europeans, with whom Britain had had no quarrel, to make the treaty more palatable to the Boers, with whom she had been waging war.

Once the treaty was signed, the most pressing problem confronting Milner was the repatriation and resettlement of the Boers. Kitchener's methods of dealing with the guerrilla warfare had caused widespread devastation and depopulation. At the end of the war about 31,000 Boers were prisoners-of-war (24,000 of them in St. Helena, Ceylon, and elsewhere overseas), about 110,000 men, women, and children were away from their homes in 'concentration camps',[35] and farmhouses had been burnt, stock killed, and crops destroyed in many parts of both colonies. This problem was handled humanely and expeditiously. By March 1903 nearly all the Boers were back on the land, and they had been provided with food, implements, stock, seed, and building materials to enable them to resume farming.[36] In clause 10 of the treaty Great Britain had undertaken to make a free grant of £3 millions for distribution among the people of the new colonies who were unable to provide for themselves owing to war losses. In fact Great Britain made free grants totalling about £7 millions in partial compensation for war losses, in addition to about £2½ millions which were paid out against receipts issued by the

[34] Cd. 1096, p. 12. According to Headlam, Milner subsequently 'bitterly regretted that he had yielded to the Boers over the Native Franchise . . . regarding this as the greatest mistake he had ever made', though 'He never dreamed, of course, of putting natives on a par with whites in respect of political power.' Headlam quotes from a letter written by Milner to Selborne on 10 May 1905 as follows: 'If I had known as well as I know now the extravagance of the prejudice on the part of almost all the whites—not the Boers only—against any concession to any coloured man, however civilized, I should never have agreed to so absolute an exclusion, not only of the raw native, but of the whole coloured population from any rights of citizenship, even in municipal affairs.' Headlam, ii. 353.

[35] The British had placed Boer men, women, and children in 'concentration camps' to prevent them from assisting the commandos and to save them from starvation. About 1,200 men, 4,000 women, and 16,000 children died in the camps. This high mortality occurred because on their arrival many of the Boers were sick and undernourished and because the British administration of the camps was inefficient. Subsequently it has been alleged that the British wilfully tried to exterminate the inhabitants of the camps: this is quite untrue. Headlam, ii. 225–31; L. S. Amery, v. 86–88, 251–6; A. C. Martin, *The Concentration Camps 1900–1902 (Facts, Figures and Fables)* (Cape Town, 1957).

[36] W. Basil Worsfold, *The Reconstruction of the New Colonies under Lord Milner* (London, 1913, 2 vols.), ii. iii; Headlam, ii. x; L. S. Amery, vi. ii.

military during the war, while the colonial governments spent another £9 millions on grants and loans for resettlement.[37] Notwithstanding Boer complaints over such matters as delays in completing the payments and the high cost of commodities (which was inevitable in a period of dearth), the treatment of the Boers compared very favourably with the treatment meted out to the defeated sides in other modern wars. At Versailles in 1919 Botha recalled that it had been 'a generous peace that the British people made with us'.[38]

The capital required by the Transvaal and Orange River Colony governments for resettlement and reconstruction came from a loan of £35 millions which was guaranteed by the British Government. Over £18½ millions of this loan was used to purchase the railways in the Transvaal from the Netherlands Railway Company and to construct new lines. The total railway mileage of the Transvaal and Orange River Colony rose from 1,331 in 1901 to 1,761 at the end of 1907 and 2,710 on 31 May 1910. To administer the guaranteed loan Milner created an Intercolonial Council under which the railways of the Transvaal and the Orange River Colony were united as the Central South African Railways. In 1903 Milner also convened a conference which led to the creation of a South African Customs Union, embracing all the British colonies and protectorates south of the Zambesi.[39]

The key to Milner's plans for material development in South Africa lay in the Witwatersrand gold-mining industry, which he wished to vitalize the entire South African economy. Until 1904, however, its recovery was retarded by a shortage of unskilled labour. Milner did everything he could to help the companies recruit sufficient Africans. In 1901 he negotiated with the Portuguese authorities a *modus vivendi*,[40] under which the mines were entitled to resume recruiting in Portuguese East Africa. He also issued regulations to improve the quality of the food, sanitation, and accommodation in the compounds. Nevertheless, in November 1903 a Commission reported that there was a shortage of 129,364 unskilled labourers in the gold-mining industry. The mines had become unpopular among Africans in consequence of an attempt to reduce their wages, and some Africans had saved enough money from their war-time earnings to tide them over the next few years. Experiments were made in some mines to overcome the crisis by using white men as unskilled labourers, but they did not succeed, because whites demanded

<hr>

[37] Worsfold, I. v; and appendix.
[38] Headlam, ii. 364. It should be borne in mind, however, that unlike many defeated sides, the Boers had had their territories annexed by the victor.
[39] Cd. 1599 (1903).   [40] Cd. 3564 (1907), pp. 61–63.

much higher wages than Africans and were no more efficient. The result was that in December 1903 the Chamber of Mines, the Chamber of Commerce, and the nominated Legislative Council recommended that labourers should be imported from China on short-term contracts, terminating with compulsory repatriation. Early in 1904 the Legislative Council passed a Labour Importation Ordinance, which was approved by the Colonial Secretary, and in June 1904 Chinese labourers began to arrive on the Witwatersrand. They had contracted to perform unskilled work in the mines, under conditions similar to those applying to Africans from Portuguese East Africa, for three years, at the end of which, or, in the event of re-engagement, at the end of the new term, they were to be returned to China. In the year starting in July 1906 the gold-mining industry employed an average of 17,513 whites, 102,420 Africans, and 53,062 Chinese; and the average monthly wages were £26. 15s. for whites, 52s. 3d. for Africans, and 41s. 6d. for Chinese. Thereafter the number of Africans coming to the mines rapidly increased, and after the Transvaal received responsible government the industry continued to expand, notwithstanding the Government's decision to prohibit further importations from China. Consequently the Chinese fulfilled the purpose for which they had been brought to the Transvaal. The value of the gold output rose sharply from £12,628,057 in 1903 to £27,400,992 in 1907 and it continued to rise, though more slowly, in the following years. Without Chinese labour the recovery and expansion of the gold-mining industry would have been much less rapid and it might have become necessary to modify the labour structure: with it, the industry became the sheet-anchor of the entire South African economy and it was re-established on the pre-war basis of a relatively small number of highly paid white men and a relatively large number of non-whites, who left their families behind them and were confined to unskilled tasks and paid low wages.[41]

To Milner these material achievements were important not only in themselves but also as steps towards his political objectives. But those objectives were not achieved. British immigration did not take place on a scale sufficient to cause a significant increase in the British proportion of the white population of South Africa. At the end of the war several thousand men who had come to fight in South Africa from Britain, Australia, New Zealand, and Canada remained in the country, but the shortage of unskilled labour, the depression, and the political uncertainties caused many of them to leave again. In April 1904 the white popula-

[41] On the Chinese labour question see Worsfold, I. xi–xiv; Sheila T. van der Horst, *Native Labour in South Africa* (London, 1942), pp. 167–72. For statistics of the gold-mining industry see below, Appendix A. xii.

tion of Johannesburg, which had been 76,500 before the war, had only increased to 83,363. Although it increased more rapidly in the next few years, the white population of the towns in the coastal colonies actually decreased, and in May 1911 only 51·7 per cent. of the white population of the Union of South Africa was urban instead of the 60 per cent. which Milner had confidently anticipated. Furthermore, although Milner put a great deal of effort into schemes for British settlement on the land in the Transvaal and Orange River Colony, their results were not of major importance. In spite of an expenditure of about £2½ millions from the guaranteed loan for buying land and advancing cash and goods, only about 1,200 settlers, representing a population of between two and three thousand men, women, and children, were established on the land[42]— about half as many as had formed the 1820 settlement in the Cape Colony and about an eighth as many as Milner had wanted—not nearly enough to form an effective leavening to the rural Afrikaner population, except in a few small areas. Consequently Milner failed to create a British majority in the white population of South Africa. In May 1911 the Afrikaners were not 40 per cent. of the total, as Milner had hoped, but more than 54 per cent.[43]

Milner also displayed great zeal in furthering his educational projects. While the war was still in progress schools were established in the concentration camps and teachers were imported from Britain and other parts of the Empire. After the Treaty of Vereeniging an elaborate system of government schools was created in the new colonies and ordinances were passed making English the sole medium of instruction, allowing Dutch to be taught as a subject for not more than five hours a week, and giving the officials wide powers, including the power of appointing teachers. Whether, if this policy had been persisted in over a long period, the Afrikaner inhabitants of the Transvaal and Orange River Colony would have been drawn out of their cultural isolation, as Milner had hoped, must remain an open question. In fact it was only applied for a few years, during which, as will be shown in the next section, it acted as a stimulus for an Afrikaner reaction.

On 2 April 1905 Milner retired from South Africa. In his farewell speeches he reiterated the main points of his imperialist policy to the applause of Transvaal urban audiences:

[42] Worsfold, ii. 91–117.

[43] There is no means of making an exact assessment of the Afrikaner proportion of the total white population, but a close approximation is obtained from the religious tables of the 1911 census report. 54·37 per cent. of the white inhabitants of the Union of South Africa are shown as belonging to the Dutch Reformed Churches. See below, Appendix A. iii.

If you believe in me, defend my works when I am gone. . . . I shall live in the memories of people here, if I live at all, in connection with the great struggle to keep this country within the limits of the British Empire. Certainly I engaged in that struggle with all my might, because I was from head to foot one mass of glowing conviction of the rightness of our cause. But a frightfully destructive conflict of that kind is at the best a sad business to look back upon. I should prefer to be remembered for the tremendous effort, wise or unwise in various particulars, made after the war, not only to repair its ravages, but also to restart the new Colonies on a far higher plane of civilization than they had ever previously attained.[44]

In a private letter to his successor, Lord Selborne, Milner explained that the war had not decided that South Africa would remain permanently in the Empire: it had only made that possible. He warned Selborne that no Afrikaner politician was to be trusted. Every one of them, he wrote, had the same ideal of 'a separate Afrikander nation and State, comprising, no doubt, men of other races, who are ready to be "afrikanderized," but essentially autochthonous, isolated and un-British'. Every one of them used the same weapons of 'duplicity and deceit'. To ensure the permanent attachment of South Africa to the Empire would require 'years of strong, patient policy', without interference from the 'tomfoolery' of British party politics.[45]

It is, of course, conceivable that if Milner had had his way—if British immigration had been persistently encouraged, if the Cape constitution had been suspended, and if the Transvaal, the Orange River Colony, and the Cape Colony had been ruled as crown colonies over a long period, with Dutch banned as a medium of instruction in the government schools —the Afrikaner people would eventually have been swamped and anglicized. It is also arguable that their descendants, and the other inhabitants of South Africa, white and non-white, would have benefited from such a process. But a liberal democracy, such as Britain was by the twentieth century, inevitably lacked the ruthlessness and the will to see such a policy through to conclusion. Milner's plans were therefore fatally unrealistic. And worse. To attempt to denationalize a people, and to fail, is to produce the very opposite to the result intended. 'Milnerism' became to the Afrikaner the epitome of 'British oppression' and sowed seed for a nationalism more bitterly anti-British than anything that had existed before the war.

On balance, therefore, there can be little doubt that Lord Milner and the Unionist Government wrought harm in South Africa. Encouraging

[44] Speech in Johannesburg, 31 Mar. 1905, Headlam, ii. 546–7.
[45] Milner to Selborne, 12 Apr. 1905, ibid. 550–8.

unattainable aspirations among British South Africans, increasing anglophobia among Afrikaners, and doing little to improve the prospects of
the non-whites, they made it immeasurably more difficult for the peoples
of South Africa to establish for themselves a stable and humane society.

3. THE REACTION AGAINST IMPERIALISM

At the end of the war it might have seemed likely that Afrikaner
nationalism had been shattered once and for all. The republics were
overthrown and their former ruling race was impoverished and dispirited.
Moreover, the events of the war had left a bitter legacy of divisions
within Afrikanerdom—between Transvaalers, Free Staters, and Cape
colonials, and between *bittereinders* (bitter-enders) who had fought to
the end, *hensoppers* (hands-uppers) who had passively accepted British
rule, and National Scouts who had actively assisted the British forces.
Smuts expressed the general feeling in March 1904 when he wrote:
'South Africa is on the downward grade in every sense, and at present
I see no ray of light in the future.'[46]

Nevertheless, there was a rapid Afrikaner revival. On the material
level, although the war had accentuated the poor white problem, which
had originated a few years earlier as a result of the gradual closing of
the frontiers of white settlement in southern Africa,[47] the British Administration, as we have seen, made every effort to rehabilitate the Boers and
within a few years most of them were successfully re-established on the
land. On the other hand, on the cultural level the Afrikaners themselves
developed a powerful response to the challenge of Milnerism, and on the
political level they became organized to take full advantage of the swing
of the pendulum in Britain.

The Afrikaner revival was initiated by the Dutch Reformed Church,
the most powerful Afrikaner institution which survived the war intact.[48]
Its theology was still the strait Calvinism of the *Christianae Religionis*

[46] Smuts to Emily Hobhouse, 6 Mar. 1904, Smuts Papers.

[47] T.G. 13 (1908), *Report of the Transvaal Indigency Commission*; Carnegie Commission, *Report on the Poor White Problem in South Africa* (Stellenbosch, 1932, 5 vols.).

[48] There were, in fact, several Dutch Reformed Churches in South Africa. The parent
church was the *Nederduits Gereformeerde Kerk in Suid-Afrika* (N.G.K.). Since the
Great Trek off-shoots of the N.G.K. had been created in Natal, the Orange Free State,
and the Transvaal. They remained linked in spirit with the Cape N.G.K., but each had
its own autonomous synod and the church in the Transvaal had a different name—the
Verenigde Kerk. In the Transvaal—and there alone—there was also the *Nederduits
Hervormde Kerk van Afrika*, which did not differ significantly from the N.G.K. or the
Verenigde Kerk in doctrine. Finally, there was the *Gereformeerde Kerk in Suid-Afrika*
(the 'Dopper' Church to which Paul Kruger belonged), which was the most fundamen-
talist of the Dutch Reformed Churches in South Africa.

Institutio and the Heidelberg Catechism, unyielding before the liberal winds which had modified the theology of most Calvinist churches in other countries in the eighteenth and nineteenth centuries. Its predikants included some of the ablest and most highly educated Afrikaners, whose influence in secular as well as spiritual affairs was as great as that of the clergy in Catholic peasant communities. Predikants had ministered to the commandos in the field during the war, and after the peace many of them used their immense prestige to resist all tendencies towards the anglicization of the Boers and to preserve their language and their culture as well as their religion, not only from patriotic motives, but also because the power and prestige of the Church depended on the maintenance of Afrikanerdom, exclusive and unsullied. They demanded of National Scouts and *hensoppers* a public confession of guilt before they readmitted them to *nagmaal* (communion).[49] They also expounded a mystique of a people chosen of God, who would be purified by their sufferings and led to fulfil God's mission. For example, on Dingaan's Day (16 December) 1903 Ds. J. D. du Toit adjured his people to re-establish the lines 'which fix the boundary between us and all uitlanders', for the power of Afrikanerdom lay in 'the isolation of our principle'.[50] A year later, at the burial of President Kruger in Pretoria, Ds. H. S. Bosman, the Moderator of the Dutch Reformed Church in the Transvaal, delivered himself as follows:[51]

Then referring particularly to the words [Psalm 137]: 'By the waters of Babylon there we sat down; yea, we wept when we remembered Zion,' he said the Afrikander people grieved, but not as those who had no hope. . . .

As the people of Jerusalem had never lost faith in their God, but had prayed continually for deliverance, so must they be constant in their faith, and acknowledge their sins because when sin was acknowledged so did deliverance follow the sins of the people of Jerusalem. Having been forgiven their sins they were brought back to the land from which they were taken. . . .

The speaker then likened the people of this country to those men of God and urged them to keep to that word, which remained for-ever. . . . He urged them, by the God of Paul Kruger, not to let that national feeling die out. . . .

[49] J. A. Coetzee, *Politieke Groepering in the wording van die Afrikanernasie* (Johannesburg, 1941), p. 322.

[50] *Volksstem*, 19 Dec. 1903, cited by Coetzee, pp. 346–7. Du Toit urged 'dat opnieuw in hart en leven de lijnen getrokken worden, die de grens aanwijzen tussen ons en alle uitlanders' and that the power of Afrikanerdom lay 'in het isolement van ons beginsel'.

[51] *Cape Times*, 17 Dec. 1904, cited by Jan Kirstein, 'Some Foundations of Afrikaner Nationalism' (unpublished essay), pp. 26–27. Kirstein's penetrating essay also directed me to the earlier quotations in this paragraph.

Paul Kruger was dead, but his people were not dead. Neither was his spirit dead, and they could go along the lines that he had laid down under the flag that now waved over them, and still be true to it, but they would always remain Afrikanders, God helping them.

It was predikants who organized opposition to Milner's educational policy in the Transvaal and the Orange River Colony. At first they contended that article 5 of the Treaty of Vereeniging meant that Dutch was to be used as the medium of instruction (and not merely taught as a subject) in government schools where the parents desired it, and when that argument had been rejected they founded private schools for *Christelijk-Nationaal Onderwijs* (Christian National Education). In these C.N.O. schools the Calvinist tradition was emphasized, Afrikaner national consciousness was promoted, and both English and Dutch were used as media of instruction at the primary level, though at the secondary level most of the instruction was in English because there was no provision for the writing of examinations in the Dutch medium in South Africa. Although the C.N.O. movement was seriously hampered by lack of funds, it had the moral support of very many Afrikaners.[52]

Resistance to anglicization was also fostered by Afrikaner journalists and poets. Unlike other white settler communities who have established themselves outside Europe, the Afrikaners had developed a vernacular which differed so much from the language of their ancestors as to be a new language. But in 1902 Afrikaans was still only a spoken language: it had no standard written form and virtually no literature. An attempt which had been made in the 1870's to establish Afrikaans as a written language had failed and written deviations from Dutch were still regarded as somewhat contemptible by most educated Afrikaners, including the predikants, for Dutch was the language of the Church. Such a dichotomy was a major cultural weakness. It promoted illiteracy, since it was doubly difficult for the Boer to learn to read and write Dutch, and it left him open to anglicization. To combat this weakness the *Zuid-Afrikaanse Taalbond* (South African Language Union) adopted a simplified spelling of Dutch in 1904 and the new spelling was soon recognized by the educational authorities in all the four colonies. However, there were some who believed that the simplification of Dutch was not enough and revived the ambition of rendering Afrikaans itself into writing. J. H. H. de Waal tried

[52] On the educational question see H. Gunn, *The Language Question in the Orange River Colony, 1902–1910* (Johannesburg, 1910); E. G. Malherbe, *Education in South Africa, 1652–1922* (Cape Town, 1925); E. Botes, *Die Taalmediumvraagstuk* (Johannesburg, 1941); J. C. Coetzee, *Onderwys in Transvaal, 1838–1937* (Pretoria, 1941); and M. A. Basson, *Die Voertaalvraagstuk in die Transvaalse Skoolwese* (Johannesburg, 1944).

to do this in the *Goede Hoop* and so did editors in Pretoria and Bloemfontein. Then in March 1905 J. H. Hofmeyr, the dominant figure in the
Afrikaner Bond, made an eloquent appeal to Afrikaners not to use
English, but Dutch; to which Gustav Preller, sub-editor of the Pretoria
Volksstem, replied with the assertion that Dutch as well as English was
alien to the Afrikaner. 'As a transitional measure, until Afrikaans is
universally written [in South Africa]', he declared, 'our line of action
will be: write and talk Afrikaans, learn Dutch, read both.'[53] Preller's
request met with a ready response. Organizations were founded in the
Cape Colony, the Orange River Colony, and the Transvaal to promote
the writing of Afrikaans, to convince Afrikaners that it should be used
as their written as well as their spoken language, and to obtain official
recognition for it. Furthermore, Eugène Marais, Louis Leipoldt, Totius
(J. D. du Toit), and Jan Celliers began to publish poetry of a quality
which showed that Afrikaans had a high literary potential. Much of this
poetry dwelt on the war-time sufferings of the Afrikaner people. That of
Totius was permeated by the Calvinist spirit, while Celliers was a self-
conscious nationalist.

> But it is clear to every Afrikaner [wrote Celliers in 1907] that only our
> own literature, steeped in the Afrikaner spirit and intelligible to Afrikaners,
> through and through in language and content, that only such a literature is
> really calculated to hit the mark here. Who wants to help us build up such
> a literature for our people? We have a people to serve, we have a nation to
> educate; we cannot wait![54]

The rivalry within Afrikanerdom between the advocates of Dutch and
the advocates of Afrikaans persisted until at a conference at Paarl in
December 1907 both sides agreed to form a united front against anglicization. For the time being they would work together to obtain for Dutch
an equal position with English on the understanding that eventually
Afrikaans would replace Dutch.[55]

It was also not long after the war that the Boers in the Transvaal and

[53] Cited by G. S. Nienaber and P. J. Nienaber, *Die Geskiedenis van die Afrikaanse
Beweging* (Pretoria, 1941), p. 132: 'Als overgangsmaatregel, totdat het Afrikaans
algemeen geschreven wordt, omschrijven we onze gedragslijn: Afrikaans schrijven en
spreken, Hollands leren, albei lezen.'

[54] Cited in C. M. van den Heever and P. de V. Pienaar (eds.), *Kultuurgeskiedenis van
die Afrikaner* (Cape Town, 1945–50, 3 vols.), iii. 172: 'Maar dit is voor elke Afrikaner
duidelik dat slegs 'n eige letterkunde, deurtrokke van die Afrikaanse gees en vir
Afrikaners verstaanbaar, deur en deur in taal en inhoud, dat so 'n letterkunde alleen
bereken is om hier werkelik doel te tref. Wie wil ons help om so 'n letterkunde voor
ons mense op te bouw? Ons het 'n volk om te behou, ons het 'n nasie om op te voed;
ons kan nie wag nie!'

[55] On the Afrikaans language movement see the works mentioned in the two preceding
footnotes and J. H. H. de Waal, *My Herinnerings van ons Taalstryd* (Cape Town,

the Orange River Colony became organized for political action. Before they dispersed from Vereeniging in 1902 the representatives of the commandos appointed a committee to organize relief for war widows and orphans and instructed three of its members, generals Louis Botha, C. R. de Wet, and J. H. de la Rey, to collect money in Europe. The generals' mission was not very fruitful, for they raised less than £125,000 on the European continent. They then decided to fall back on attempting to obtain concessions from Britain. In London, however, Chamberlain refused to change the terms of the Treaty of Vereeniging, and he reaffirmed this decision when he toured South Africa between December 1902 and February 1903. Thereafter the leading Boer generals, notably Botha and Smuts in the Transvaal and Hertzog in the Orange River Colony, made persistent and vehement criticisms of the Milner régime.

Until May 1903 all the members of the Executive and Legislative Councils in both the ex-republics were nominated officials. The Legislative Council of the Transvaal was then reconstituted to contain fourteen unofficial nominees as well as sixteen officials. Botha, Smuts, and de la Rey were offered seats in the enlarged council, but they declined and all the seats were filled by men who were favourably disposed towards the régime. Soon afterwards, as the campaign for the importation of Chinese labour got under way on the Witwatersrand, the Boer generals in the Transvaal held a series of public meetings, starting in July 1903 at Heidelberg, and in February 1904 Botha and fourteen others sent a telegram to the Colonial Secretary, protesting in the name of the Transvaal Boers against the decision to import Chinese. Lyttelton replied that the Legislative Council had agreed to the importation and that he could not accept their claim to represent Transvaal Boer opinion. Botha and his friends then decided to found a political movement, so that there could be no doubt in the future as to who represented Boer opinion in the Transvaal. After preliminary meetings, a congress was held in Pretoria under Botha's chairmanship in May 1904. It passed resolutions criticizing the Government and demanding full self-government for both the Transvaal and the Orange River Colony and it appointed a committee to create a permanent organization. The committee completed its task in January 1905, when Botha announced the foundation of Het Volk (The People), under a Head Committee consisting of Louis Botha (Chairman), Schalk Burger, J. H. de la Rey, C. F. Beyers, and J. C. Smuts

1932); E. C. Pienaar, *Die Triomf van Afrikaans* (2nd ed., Cape Town, 1946); G. Dekker, *Afrikaanse Literatuurgeskiedenis* (4th ed., Cape Town, 1947); A. J. H. Van der Walt, J. A. Wiid and A. L. Geyer (eds.), *Geskiedenis van Suid-Afrika* (Cape Town, 1951, 2 vols.), ii. 634–703. I have also made use of an unpublished essay, Joan Bradley, 'Section 137 of the South Africa Act'.

(all of whom had been generals during the war), and A. D. W. Wolmarans and Ewald Esselen. Within a very short time branches of Het Volk were established in every village in the Transvaal.

Meanwhile three other bodies were soliciting the support of the British people in the Transvaal. The Transvaal Progressive Association, led by Sir George Farrar (President), Sir Percy Fitzpatrick, Drummond Chaplin, and other directors of gold-mining companies and financial houses, stressed the value of the British connexion and stood for Chinese labour, for representative, but not responsible, government, and for equal voting rights for all white men; the Transvaal Responsible Government Association, led by E. P. Solomon, criticized the Milner régime and demanded responsible government; and several labour groups gradually drew together to form an Independent Labour Party in the interests of white labour. Thus while nearly all the Transvaal Boers were united in a monolithic party led by the *bittereinder* generals, the other potential voters were divided between the Progressives, the Responsibles, and Labour.[56]

In July 1904 Lyttelton had announced in the House of Commons that it had been decided to introduce an elective element in the Transvaal legislature. Letters Patent to give effect to this decision were agreed to by the Cabinet on 25 March 1905, but their publication was delayed until Milner had been succeeded by Selborne. This Constitution, which became known as the Lyttelton Constitution, provided for a predominantly elective legislature, but it kept executive power in the hands of British officials. There was to be a Legislative Assembly consisting of between six and nine officials and between thirty and thirty-five elected members. The franchise was to be given to white men who had been burghers of the South African Republic entitled to vote for members of the First Volksraad, or who occupied property in the Transvaal worth £100, or who earned wages in the Transvaal at the rate of £100 a year. This included most of the white townsmen, but excluded a number of young landless Boers, all women, and all non-Europeans (Coloured and Asiatic as well as African). Every four years a commission was to divide the colony into single-member constituencies, which were to contain an equal number of voters, with a latitude of not more than 5 per cent. either way, and in making their divisions the commissions were to pay due regard to four factors—existing boundaries, community or diversity of interest,

---

[56] On Transvaal politics to the grant of responsible government see B. Spoelstra, 'Die Bewindsaanvaarding van die Botha-Regering oor Transvaal as Selfregerende Britse Kolonie in 1907', *Archives Year Book for South African History, 1953*, ii. 307–88. I have also found very useful D. A. Etheredge, 'The Grant of Responsible Government to the Transvaal in 1906' (unpublished essay).

means of communication, and physical features. It would not be lawful for the assembly to pass money Bills unless they had been recommended by the Governor; and there was to be a reserved civil list of £48,000, covering the salaries of the Lieutenant-Governor, the judges, and the members of the Executive Council. English was to be the language of debate in the assembly, but with the permission of the president a member would be able to address it in Dutch.[57]

The Lyttelton Constitution was still-born. British support for the Unionists had been declining continuously since the khaki election of 1900. The imperialism of Chamberlain and Milner had become discredited by the prolongation of the war into an expensive and inglorious attempt to round up Boer guerrillas, by revelations of the mortality rate in the concentration camps, and by the Government's approval of the Transvaal Labour Importation Ordinance of 1904, which was misrepresented by Liberals as creating conditions akin to slavery in the British Empire. Moreover, Chamberlain's campaign for tariff reform split the Unionists and united the Liberals in defence of free trade. In these circumstances the Government suffered a series of defeats in by-elections, until in December 1905 Balfour resigned and was succeeded by Sir Henry Campbell-Bannerman, who promptly obtained a dissolution and was confirmed in office by the general election of January 1906, in which the Liberals won 377 seats, the Unionists 157, and the Irish Nationalists 83, and there were 53 successful Labour candidates. The Liberals, with a majority of 84 over all other parties in the House of Commons, were in a position to apply their own policy to South Africa, for they could circumvent the Unionist majority in the House of Lords by issuing constitutions for the Transvaal and the Orange River Colony under Letters Patent, as the Unionists had done in the case of the Lyttelton Constitution.

The Liberals were no less anxious than the Unionists to preserve the British Empire and British paramountcy in South Africa, but most of them differed radically from the Unionists as to how those objectives were to be attained. They believed that liberty, not force, was the cement of the Empire; that the cardinal principle of the Empire was the principle of self-government for all settler communities who could stand on their own feet; and that this principle should be applied equally to white settler communities of non-British stock. The cordial acceptance of the imperial connexion by French Canadians under the leadership of Sir Wilfrid Laurier seemed to vindicate their belief. They considered that Chamberlain and Milner, through impatience, bad diplomacy, and a

[57] Cd. 2400 (1905).

spirit of coercion, had involved Britain in an unnecessary and unjust war, which seriously prejudiced the prospects of harmony between Boer and Briton in South Africa and between South Africa and the Empire, and they conceived it to be their duty, when returned to power, to make amends to the Boers for the errors of their predecessors in the hope of reconciling them to their status as British subjects. Furthermore, so obsessed had they become with this aspect of South African affairs that they had no hesitation in regarding its solution as their first priority, although they were somewhat vaguely aware that the results might be detrimental to the interests of the non-European majority in South Africa.

Campbell-Bannerman had had a difficult task in holding the party together during the war, for it included in men like H. H. Asquith, Sir Edward Grey, and R. B. Haldane, a small but influential group of Liberal imperialists, as well as a larger number of ardent 'pro-Boers'. Nevertheless, he had succeeded in retaining the support of the Liberal imperialists by accepting the annexation of the republics as a *fait accompli*, and the support of the pro-Boers by dissociating himself from the Government's handling of the negotiations which had led to the outbreak of war, and by applying the strong phrase 'methods of barbarism' to the policy of burning farms and placing women and children in concentration camps. He and his colleagues had approved of the Treaty of Vereeniging, praising its generosity towards the Boers and refraining from criticizing the colour-bar provision in article 8.

At the time of Balfour's resignation the Unionists believed with Milner that the time was still far off when it would be safe to grant the Transvaal and the Orange River Colony self-government. Campbell-Bannerman, on the other hand, believed that only if that was done immediately was there a hope of obtaining Boer co-operation and loyalty, and he had already committed himself to immediate self-government for the Transvaal in a speech at Dundee on 14 November 1904. His colleagues, however, were hesitant. It was easy to criticize the Unionist Government on liberal premises from the Opposition benches: it would be a very bold decision indeed actually to grant self-government to the Transvaal and the Orange River Colony four years after they had been forcibly incorporated in the Empire. The Liberal imperialist members of the Cabinet were averse to so drastic a change, and Campbell-Bannerman was himself perhaps inclined to hang back for fear of splitting his party in the hour of its great electoral victory.[58]

[58] In describing the South African policy of the Liberal Government I have drawn heavily on G. B. Pyrah, *Imperial Policy and South Africa 1902–10* (Oxford, 1955).

J. C. Smuts, who had contacts in the Liberal Party, was aware of this hesitation. He was also extremely anxious lest the new Government should merely amend the Lyttelton Constitution to make the executive responsible to the legislature, leaving the electoral provisions untouched, because in that event it seemed likely that the Progressives would obtain a majority in the assembly. He therefore hastened to England early in 1906 to interview members of the Government and distribute among them copies of a memorandum in which he played upon their principles and prejudices with consummate skill. The Boers (his memorandum assured them) did not wish to question the annexation of the republics: they accepted that as an accomplished fact. But they did wish to have fair treatment as members of the British Empire. Tranquillity could only be obtained in South Africa by 'the removal of all just grounds of discontent and the unreserved application of Liberal principles to the government of the new colonies, by showing a statesmanlike trust in the people of the land, of whatever race [sic], and granting them a fair and equitable constitution under which they can work out their own salvation.' And again: 'I can conceive of no nobler task for Liberal statesmanship than that it may inaugurate in South Africa such an era of trust and goodwill and reliance on the people on the land, and bring healing to the wounds which the errors of the past have inflicted.' It would be disastrous to preserve the electoral system provided in the Lyttelton Constitution, because it favoured the 'mine-owners' at the expense of 'the permanent population of the land, English as well as Dutch', and 'every precaution ought to be taken to safeguard the interests of the people' against the influence of the mine-owners. In place of the economic qualifications for the franchise in the Lyttelton Constitution there should be white manhood suffrage. In place of redistribution every four years there should be redistribution every ten years. And in place of equal constituencies —an 'undemocratic' system which was not used anywhere else in the Empire except in Australia—the colony should be divided empirically, with regard mainly to the white population basis, so that although each Member of Parliament would be elected by white men he would also in a sense represent the white women and children. Moreover, 'the large native population in the outlying districts' and 'territorial extent' should also count for something in the allocation of seats. As a start the Witwatersrand should have twenty-one seats, Pretoria town and district six, and the rest of the colony twenty-three. If that were done, wrote Smuts, the Boers would win twenty-three of the fifty seats 'on the most sanguine view', so that there could not possibly be a Boer majority.[59]

[59] There is a copy of the Smuts memorandum in the Merriman Papers, No. 240/1906.

After indecisive talks with other members of the Government, including Lord Elgin, the Colonial Secretary, and Winston Churchill, the Under-Secretary, Smuts saw the Prime Minister on 7 February. This discussion has usually been represented as having been limited to the single issue of whether the Transvaal should be granted responsible government or not.[60] In fact it is quite clear from his memorandum that Smuts was at least as concerned to ensure that the electoral system laid down in the Lyttelton Constitution should be revised: and he gained his way on both points. On 8 February Campbell-Bannerman carried the entire Cabinet with him and soon afterwards the Lyttelton Constitution was revoked and a committee was appointed to go to South Africa to investigate the electoral question. After spending two months in South Africa hearing evidence from all interested parties, this committee, under the chairmanship of Sir J. West Ridgeway, recommended a compromise between the wishes of Het Volk and the wishes of the Progressives.[61] The Government accepted its recommendations and on 31 July the new Constitution for the Transvaal was outlined in both Houses, where the Unionists denounced it with acrimony, Balfour showing unwonted heat in describing it as 'the most reckless experiment ever tried in the development of a great colonial policy'.[62] But the Government stood firm and the new Constitution was promulgated as Letters Patent on 6 December 1906.[63]

The Transvaal Parliament was to consist of a Legislative Council of fifteen members and a Legislative Assembly of sixty-nine. In the first instance all the members of the council were to be nominated by the Governor, but vacancies were to be filled by the Governor-in-Council (i.e. by the Governor acting on the advice of his Transvaal ministers) and after five years all the members of the council were to be appointed by the Governor-in-Council. All the members of the assembly were to be elected. Every white man over the age of twenty-one was to have the vote, but no women and no non-Europeans. In the first assembly there were to be thirty-four seats for the Witwatersrand district, six for Pretoria town and suburbs, and twenty-nine for the rest of the colony. A commission was to divide each of these three regions into single-member constituencies, so that every constituency in a region would contain the same number of voters, but a latitude of up to fifteen per cent. either way

[60] Even Pyrah, who expounds and discusses the Smuts memorandum at length (pp. 164–71), seems to imply that this was so (pp. 171–4).

[61] The report of the West Ridgeway Committee has not yet been published nor made available to historians.

[62] *Parl. Deb.*, 4th Ser., clxii. 801–4 (cited in Pyrah, p. 181).

[63] Cd. 3250 (1906).

was allowed to enable the commission to use existing administrative boundaries as far as possible, and the commission was also enjoined to give 'due consideration' to existing boundaries, community or diversity of interest, means of communication, and physical features. Subsequently a new voters' roll was to be compiled every two years, and every fourth year another commission was to be appointed, firstly, to divide the seats between the Witwatersrand district, Pretoria town and suburbs, and the rest of the colony, in proportion to their numbers of registered voters, and, secondly, to subdivide each of these three regions into single-member constituencies in accordance with the same rules which had been laid down for the first commission. English was to be the official language of Parliament, but Dutch could be used in debate and bills and votes and proceedings were to be printed in both languages. Bills amending the constitution, or placing restrictions on non-Europeans only, or providing for the importation of indentured labourers from outside South Africa were to be reserved; and no more licences were to be issued for the importation of indentured labour under the 1904 ordinance.

This remarkable instrument was a bold and generous bid for the confidence and loyalty of the Transvaal Boers. It was also a decisive step towards the triumph of the political colour-bar throughout South Africa. The Liberals defended this aspect of the constitution by appealing to the binding nature of the Treaty of Vereeniging,[64] but their defence was inadequate. Article 8 of the treaty was certainly a major obstacle to the creation by Britain of a non-racial franchise in the Transvaal, but there was nothing in it to prevent her from laying down educational and economic qualifications for the franchise and admitting at the outset Coloured and Asiatic men, as well as white men, who possessed the qualifications. Furthermore, she could at least have tried to obtain from the leaders of the Transvaal political parties an undertaking that qualified Africans also would be able to vote within a given period. The Liberals did neither of these things, because they feared, with reason, that they would not gain the confidence of the Boers if they departed one iota from an absolute political colour-bar; and their humanitarian sentiments were satisfied by a policy of generosity towards the Boers.[65]

---

[64] Above, pp. 11–12.

[65] Pyrah discusses this question in ch. iv, especially pp. 100–4. He does not make it clear, however, that the Treaty of Vereeniging in no way bound the British Government not to admit to the franchise Coloured and Asiatic men, as distinct from Natives.

The reservation of discriminatory legislation meant scarcely anything in practice. Transvaal Acts Nos. 2 and 15 of 1907 blatantly discriminated against Indians, but they were not disallowed because the Liberal Government 'did not feel justified in resisting the expressed will of united white opinion in a self-governing colony'. Pyrah, p. 105.

The general election took place in the Transvaal on 20 February 1907. It was essentially a contest between the Progressives and an alliance of Het Volk and the Transvaal National Association (the Responsibles under a new name), though there were also several labour and independent candidates. Het Volk and the Nationalists had agreed not to nominate candidates for the same seats and it was understood between them that the premiership should go to Sir Richard Solomon, who had had parliamentary and cabinet experience in the Cape Colony and who stood as a Nationalist. In the event Het Volk won thirty-seven seats, the Nationalists six, the Progressives twenty-one, Labour three, and Independents two, so that Het Volk had a clear majority of five; and Sir Richard Solomon was defeated by Sir Percy Fitzpatrick. Selborne then invited Botha to form a Government. He did so, giving four places to Het Volk—Louis Botha (Prime Minister and Agriculture), J. C. Smuts (Colonial Secretary), J. de Villiers (Attorney-General and Mines), and J. Rissik (Lands and Native Affairs)—and two to Nationalists—H. C. Hull (Colonial Treasurer) and E. P. Solomon (Public Works); while Sir Richard Solomon became the Transvaal Agent-General in London. Thus less than five years after he had been commanding the military forces of a republic at war with Britain, Botha became Prime Minister of a self-governing British colony.

Meanwhile the Orange River Colony Afrikaners had also become organized for political action. In September 1904 a group of Boers met at Brandfort and appointed a committee to summon a people's congress. The congress met at Brandfort and Bloemfontein in December 1904 and March 1905, and in May 1906 a party called the Orangia Unie (Orange Union) came into being, with J. B. M. Hertzog, Abraham Fischer, and C. R. de Wet as its principal leaders. The Orangia Unie gained the support of nearly all the Afrikaners, who formed an overwhelming majority of the white population of the colony. Most of the British inhabitants supported the Constitutional Party, led by Sir John Fraser, an old Free State burgher of Scottish origin.

The leaders of Het Volk had always maintained that the Orange River Colony should be given self-government as well as the Transvaal, and Smuts had included the request in the memorandum he presented to members of the British Government early in 1906. Indeed, Britain could hardly have withheld self-government from the Orange River Colony once she had decided to grant it to the Transvaal and the West Ridgeway Committee was instructed to include in its report recommendations for an electoral system for the smaller colony. This was done, and in December 1906, soon after the publication of the Transvaal Letters Patent, the

Government announced that the Orange River Colony, too, would soon receive self-government. The Letters Patent were issued on 5 June 1907.[66] They created a Constitution similar to the Transvaal Constitution. As in the Transvaal, there was to be white manhood suffrage. The electoral sections provided for a primary division of the seats in the assembly between the rural areas (whose voters were nearly all Afrikaners) and the towns and villages (some of whose voters were British). In the first assembly the rural areas were to have twenty-seven seats and the towns and villages eleven seats, and in all subsequent assemblies each of the two regions would receive its due proportion of seats on the voters' basis. The commissions which were to divide the two regions into single-member constituencies were to act upon the same rules as those laid down for the Transvaal commissions.

In the general election, which was held in November 1907, the Orangia Unie won a sweeping victory, obtaining thirty out of the thirty-eight seats in the assembly. On 27 November Abraham Fischer became Prime Minister and Colonial Secretary, J. B. M. Hertzog Attorney-General and Minister of Education, A. E. W. Ramsbottom Colonial Treasurer, C. H. Wessels Minister of Public Works, Lands, and Mines, and C. R. de Wet Minister of Agriculture.

Soon afterwards there was also a change of Government in the Cape Colony. The prestige of the Progressive administration had been undermined by the depression[67] and in September 1907, following a defeat in the Legislative Council, Jameson obtained a dissolution of both Houses and the cumbersome machinery for a general election was set in motion. By that time the rebels had been re-enfranchised. The council elections were held first and the South African Party[68] won sixteen of the twenty-two seats. Jameson then resigned, and on 3 February 1908 J. X. Merriman, the leader of the South African Party, formed a Ministry, consisting of himself as Prime Minister, Treasurer, and Minister of Native Affairs, J. W. Sauer, Commissioner of Public Works, F. S. Malan, Secretary for Agriculture, N. F. de Waal, Colonial Secretary, H. Burton, Attorney-General, and D. P. de Villiers Graaff and H. L. Currey, ministers without portfolio. The assembly elections followed in March and gave the new Government a large majority. The South African Party won sixty-nine seats, the Unionist Party (as Jameson's party was now called) won thirty-three seats, and there were five independents, including two former premiers—Sir Gordon Sprigg and W. P. Schreiner.

This was the culmination of a remarkable anti-imperialist reaction. In

---

[66] Cd. 3526 (1907).   [67] See below, pp. 52–54.
[68] See below, pp. 37–39.

March 1905 Milner had been ruling the Transvaal and the Orange River Colony as crown colonies and a pro-imperialist party had been in power in the Cape: in February 1908 all these three colonies had self-government and all three governments owed their existence to the support of Afrikaners.

4. BRITISH SOUTH AFRICA: POLITICAL

A. *The Transvaal, the Orange River Colony, and the Cape Colony*

Louis Botha, Prime Minister of the Transvaal, had immense personal charm and could win the confidence of all sorts and conditions of people. He was a successful progressive farmer, a military leader of proved capacity, an effective platform speaker, and an astute politician. His ideas were simple and he would persevere doggedly in giving effect to them. He was not a zealous member of the Dutch Reformed Church, and he defied some aspects of its puritanical code, liking nothing better than a game of bridge for stakes. A realist, he found it easy to forget the bitterness of the past and to make the best of things as they were rather than to hanker after some problematical ideal; but he was no extrovert, for he was extremely sensitive to criticism. Serving his political apprenticeship in the republican volksraad in the 1890's, he had naturally gravitated towards those who sought to come to terms with the Uitlanders. When the war came he unhesitatingly threw in his lot with the republics, and after the death of Joubert he succeeded him as Commandant General. By March 1901, however, it was clear to him that victory was unobtainable and he entered into peace negotiations with Kitchener at Middelburg; and at Vereeniging in May 1902 he was the first to declare that further resistance would be suicidal and to advise the representatives of the commandos to obtain the best terms possible. From then onwards he never doubted that the destiny of the Transvaal and the Orange River Colony lay within the British Empire. This attitude came naturally to a man of his temperament. It was also a calculated attitude. If the British could be convinced of his sincerity, they might be persuaded to accelerate the grant of responsible government. Furthermore, since nearly half of the white men in the Transvaal were of British descent, it was wise to gain the support of some of the British, so that he would have a good chance of victory at the polls when self-government was granted. Accordingly, from the time when he began to organize the Transvaal Boers, he described his policy as a policy of conciliation. This involved four things. Firstly, a veil was to be drawn over the wartime divisions within Afrikanerdom by welcoming the *hensoppers* and

National Scouts back into the fold. Secondly, the antipathies between Boer and Briton in the Transvaal were to be broken down and they were to be encouraged to think in terms neither of an Afrikaner nation nor of a British nation, but of a single white nation derived from the spontaneous fusion of the two stocks. Thirdly, this fusion of the white races was not to be confined to the Transvaal: it was to be pan-South African. The British South African colonies were to be united and the ideal of Anglo-Boer nationhood was to prevail throughout the union. Finally, the union was to be a loyal member of the British Empire, like Canada and Australia. In his opening address to the Boer Congress in Pretoria on 23 May 1904 Botha prayed 'that it may please the Almighty Father to inspire all the whites of South Africa with likemindedness, that thence one nation may be born';[69] at President Kruger's funeral he declared that 'From his grave he [Kruger] called to them to say that all white people in this land should be reconciled';[70] and in May 1905 he said that the policy of Het Volk was 'to bring Boer and Briton together'.[71] Such was the constant refrain of all his political pronouncements.[72]

Botha's indispensable colleague was Jan Smuts, who had crowned a fine academic career with a first in the law tripos at Cambridge and possessed precisely those qualities of intellectual distinction and capacity for sustained work which Botha lacked. As Kruger's State Attorney he had made a last-minute effort to avert the war by negotiating a compromise on the franchise question in the South African Republic. When the war broke out, he wrote *A Century of Wrong*, an acrid anti-British propaganda pamphlet, and later, as a commando leader, his operations in the Cape Colony were among the greatest republican successes of

[69] '. . . dat het den Almagtige Vader moge behagen alle blanken van Suid-Afrika met eensgesindheid te bezielen, opdat daaruit een natie geboren word.' Cited in Spoelstra, p. 324.

[70] *Cape Times*, 17 Dec. 1904. Botha's exposition of Kruger's ideas on this occasion contrasted sharply with that of the other speakers: the speech of Ds. H. S. Bosman is cited on pp. 18–19 above.

[71] '. . . Boer en Brit te zamen te brengen.' *Volksstem*, 20 May 1905, cited in J. A. Coetzee, p. 335.

[72] For summaries of the careers of the men who became members of the National Convention, see below, Appendix B. For a list of biographies in alphabetical sequence of their subjects' surnames, see below, Appendix C. iii. *a*. The best of the biographies of South Africans are those of Botha by F. V. Engelenburg; of Hertzog by C. M. van den Heever (the Afrikaans version is to be preferred as the fuller); of Hofmeyr by J. H. Hofmeyr in collaboration with F. W. Reitz; of Schreiner and de Villiers by Eric A. Walker; and of Steyn by N. J. van der Merwe. Pending the publication of Sir Keith Hancock's biography, there is no reliable life of Smuts; and pending the publication of Phyllis Lewsen's biography, there is no reliable life of Merriman. On Botha I am also indebted to Norman Bromberger, 'General Botha and the Conciliation Policy, 1902–1910' (unpublished essay).

1901. For some time after Vereeniging Smuts was prone to acute depression, but eventually Botha persuaded him to adopt his conciliation policy. He played a major part in building up Het Volk, and his superb grasp of political realities was shown in his negotiations with the Liberal leaders in England at the beginning of 1906. Botha was so impressed by his talents that he leaned on him very heavily. It was Smuts who drafted much of Botha's official correspondence and who did the lion's share of the work of the Transvaal Cabinet: and he revelled in it. The exercise of power was most congenial to him. Neverthless, Botha was the leader of Het Volk in fact as well as in name. Smuts did not succeed in inspiring confidence in Boer or Briton to anything like the same extent as Botha.[73]

Botha and Smuts were deeply impressed by the British decision to give the Transvaal responsible government with an electoral system which enabled Het Volk to gain power. In his first speech as Prime Minister of the Transvaal Botha said:

British interests would be absolutely safe in the hands of the new Cabinet. The world would see that the Transvaal Ministry was as jealous for the honour of the flag as any Ministry could be. The honour and interest of the old population was concerned therein. Moreover, they in the Transvaal were actuated by motives of deep gratitude, because the King and the British Government and people had trusted the Transvaal people in a manner unequalled in history by the grant of a free Constitution. Was it possible for the Boers ever to forget such generosity?[74]

In April and May 1907 he attended the Colonial Conference in London where, with other colonial premiers, he was sworn of the Privy Council and received the Freedom of the City of London, and in all his public speeches he expounded his conciliation policy: 'He had but one message from the Transvaal. That was that all the people of the Transvaal wished to draw closer the bond between the Transvaal and the Empire.'[75] And again: 'I have the fullest faith that I shall be able . . . to make of those two great races of South Africa one solid, united and strong race.'[76] Back in South Africa he showed his faith in conciliation by deeds as well

---

[73] The impression made by Smuts on Duncan in this period was as follows: 'I only wish I thought that his fine sentiments were more intimately hitched on to the springs which govern his actions. They do sometimes get turned on but they spend much of their time in the cupboard of his soul.' Duncan to Lady Selborne, 24 June 1908, Duncan Papers. Botha realized that many Afrikaners were suspicious of Smuts, but he always defended him. For example, writing to Steyn on 17 Sept. 1909 he said that nothing gave him more difficulty than the feeling against Smuts, but that although Smuts might be abrupt and tactless he was completely reliable. Steyn Papers.

[74] *The Times*, 12 Mar. 1907.

[75] Ibid., 19 Apr. 1907.   [76] Ibid., 2 May 1907.

as words. His Government bought and presented to King Edward for inclusion in the crown jewels the 3,106 carat Cullinan diamond—the largest diamond yet discovered. It resisted the temptation to disrupt the Milner bureaucracy or to flood the civil service with Afrikaners, irrespective of quality. And although it gave offence to the mining industry in announcing that the Labour Importation Ordinance would not be re-enacted and that the Chinese would be repatriated directly their contracts expired, it met the wishes of the Opposition in its handling of the educational question. Smuts refused to subsidize the C.N.O. schools and drafted and piloted through Parliament a studiously moderate Bill dealing with the government schools. In the early standards instruction was to be in the mother-tongue, Dutch or English, and if the mother-tongue was Dutch, English was gradually to be introduced as a medium, until in and after standard IV English was to be the sole medium of instruction, except that the Director of Education might allow the use of Dutch in not more than two subjects. Furthermore, proficiency in English was to be a condition of promotion to all standards above standard III, whereas Dutch was merely to be taught as a subject, and then only to children whose parents did not object. This Act was a considerable step forwards for the Afrikaners, but it did not put Dutch on anything like the same footing as English.[77] Campbell-Bannerman's great decision seemed therefore to have been vindicated.

It would, however, have been astonishing if the majority of the Transvaal Boers had really believed in the gospel of conciliation so soon after the war. Isolationism and anglophobia were too deeply rooted to be summarily expunged in favour of fusion with the British. Nevertheless, Botha's war record caused many Transvaalers to look up to him as their natural leader and he had a large personal following. Moreover, Het Volk was organized on lines which made it easy for the Head Committee to stifle opposition from below—it could, for example, dissolve local committees which it deemed to be under 'influences . . . detrimental or hostile to the principles or interests' of Het Volk[78]—and most of the members of the Head Committee were Botha men. One who was not was A. D. W. Wolmarans, formerly a close associate of President Kruger, but he was not a serious danger for he was past his prime and he became a member of the nominated Legislative Council and not of the assembly. Another was C. F. Beyers, a war hero and an able lawyer, who made a

[77] Transvaal Act No. 25 of 1907. For the literature on the educational question see above, p. 19, n. 52.

[78] Article 14 of the statutes of Het Volk, official English version, *Volksstem*, 28 Jan. 1905 ; cited in Etheredge, p. 15.

series of fiery speeches during the election. Conciliation, he said, was extinguishing the national flame from the hearts of the people. They would always find that the British were their enemies. They should act as true Afrikaners, for God had brought them into the world as Afrikaners for a definite purpose.[79] After the election Botha managed to neutralize Beyers by having him elected Speaker of the Legislative Assembly. Although isolationist sentiment was thus excluded from the Cabinet and had little effective expression in Parliament, it was certainly not extinguished from the hearts of all the Transvaal Boers. Early in 1908 Botha met with sharp criticisms when he toured the country districts,[80] and at the annual Het Volk congress in April 1908 several delegates urged that the Education Act should be amended, and Wolmarans spoke nostalgically of Krugerism. Nevertheless, the Head Committee was re-elected by a large majority and for the post of Chairman Botha received 134 votes against the 2 given for Wolmarans and 1 for de la Rey.[81]

In the Orange River Colony, on the other hand, conciliation was not the policy of the Government. Unlike Het Volk, the Orangia Unie had no incentive to woo English-speaking voters, for the overwhelming majority of the Orange River Colony electorate was Afrikaner. Furthermore, there was no Botha in the smaller colony. The Prime Minister, Abraham Fischer, owed his position to seniority and experience and it was not he, but ex-President M. T. Steyn and ex-Judge J. B. M. Hertzog who moulded public opinion and formulated policy. Steyn was a Free Stater born and bred. His ideal had always been a pan-South African Afrikaner Republic. As President he had sought to resist the anglicizing forces in the Orange Free State and to strengthen its ties with its sister Republic, and although he had not been uncritical of Kruger's administration, he had regarded the war as a crusade and remained in the field until the bitter end. In 1902 he regretted that the Transvaalers had initiated the peace negotiations and would have preferred to continue the struggle, for to him a promise of self-government under the Crown was no substitute for republican independence. However, his health was shattered and he was too ill to take part in the public discussions at Vereeniging. After a long period under medical supervision in Europe, he returned to his farm 'Onzerust', near Bloemfontein in March 1905, but he had not fully regained his strength and he was unable to take office in the Orangia Unie or the Government. Nevertheless, he was the

---

[79] Spoelstra, pp. 369–70; G. D. Scholtz, *Generaal Christiaan Frederik Beyers, 1869–1914* (Johannesburg, 1941), pp. 121–5, 136–7.

[80] *The Times*, 17 Feb. and 4 Mar. 1908.

[81] Ibid., 11 Apr. 1908.

moral force behind them both. He was consulted on important issues and he spoke in public from time to time, when his impact was tremendous. With his vast flowing beard, his weak eye-muscles, and his shaky hands, he was the personification of the sufferings of the Boers. Living in isolation and rarely encountering English-speaking people, he tended to brood over the past and to harbour grievances against the former National Scouts and *hensoppers*, and those *bittereinders* who, like Botha and Smuts, had recommended acceptance of the British terms at Vereeniging. An ardent Calvinist, he regarded Afrikanerdom as an organic unit with a divine mission, and believed that only when Afrikaner morale had recovered from the onslaughts of British imperialism would there be a secure basis for co-operation with British South Africans. He therefore supported the C.N.O. schools and urged his people 'to avoid foreign ways' and 'to teach their children the story of the concentration camps'.[82] To such a man Botha's conciliation policy seemed extremely dangerous.

Hertzog was the ablest member of the Cabinet. Brought up in the Cape Colony, he had proceeded from Victoria College, Stellenbosch, to Amsterdam University to qualify in law, and for the last four years before the war he was a judge of the Free State High Court. A shy man of scholarly tastes, in a stabler environment he would probably have remained on the bench and left a reputation as a sound jurist. As it was he became a commando leader in the war and soon afterwards, shocked by the poverty and inferiority complex of the Afrikaners in the Orange River Colony, he conceived it to be his mission to help them to regain their self-respect. He then threw himself heart and soul into the political awakening, presiding over the Brandfort and Bloemfontein congresses. The chairmanship of the Orangia Unie (and with it the premiership) would have been his if he had wished, but he preferred that Fischer should take it.[83] By the time the colony received self-government, Hertzog had worked out a theory of the relations which should exist between Boer and Briton in South Africa. Krugerism, he considered, had erred in allowing no place for the British, although it was clear that they had come to South Africa to stay. Milnerism had erred outrageously in repressing the Afrikaners. The proper policy was to foster the creation of a white South African nation composed of two sections, Afrikaner and British, each maintaining its own distinctive culture and its group identity, but co-operating with the other on a basis of complete equality. The touchstone of this equality was the language question. Once the Dutch language had a position of absolute equality with English, especially in the schools, Boer and Briton would grow to trust and respect

---

[82] *Cape Times*, 23 Jan. 1906.   [83] J. A. Coetzee, pp. 328–9.

each other and the Boer could safely co-operate. But first the position of equality had to be attained. Otherwise Afrikaner culture would be submerged and the Afrikaner people would disintegrate. Smuts's Education Act was therefore a bitter disappointment to Hertzog. Like Steyn, he believed that the Transvaalers had let the Free State down at Vereeniging and that they now seemed to be imperilling the very survival of Afrikanerdom for the sake of support from English-speaking voters.[84]

Soon after he took office, Hertzog began to draft an Education Bill embodying his own philosophy. It provided that up to the end of standard IV instruction would be in the language which the child spoke and understood best, English or Dutch, and that the other language would be taught as a subject and gradually introduced as a subsidiary medium; and that after standard IV at least three subjects would be taught in English and at least three in Dutch. Here, then, was absolute equality. What could be more just in a colony where most of the white population were Afrikaners? What better guarantee could there be of mutual respect than a system under which Afrikaner and British children would attend the same schools and become thoroughly conversant with both languages? Nevertheless, the Bill was severely criticized by the Opposition in the Orange River Colony Parliament and by the English medium press throughout South Africa. This was because it went so much farther than Smuts's Act, which had seemed to confirm the hope that English would always be the dominant language of the country. After long debates, however, it passed through both Houses of the Colonial Parliament in August 1908.[85] Hertzog's attempt to apply his Act then gave rise to serious practical difficulties, because many of the teachers and school inspectors were ignorant of Dutch, and 'Hertzogism' became a major political issue throughout South Africa. To his astonishment, Hertzog found himself regarded by the British as an extreme Afrikaner nationalist, Kruger reincarnate, while Afrikaners, including not only those who agreed with his philosophy of equality but also those who actually did nourish extreme ambitions, looked up to him as a national hero. As the tension mounted, Hertzog, convinced of his own rectitude, became bitter and allowed himself to be carried away into vitriolic public denunciations of his critics.[86] Thus the Hertzog Education Act, conceived in a spirit of equity, led to a deepening of the rift between the leaders of Het Volk and the leaders of the Orangia Unie and checked the spread of the doctrine of conciliation.

[84] I have profited from A. E. G. Trollip's unpublished thesis, 'The First Phase of Hertzogism', as well as from the biographies of Hertzog.
[85] Orange River Colony Act No. 36 of 1908.   [86] See below, pp. 467–8.

Unlike the Transvaal and the Orange River Colony, the Cape Colony had had a century of continuous evolution within the British Empire. Its oldest and most powerful political organization was the Afrikaner Bond, which had been dominated by J. H. Hofmeyr since 1884, three years after its inception. Hofmeyr had always accepted the Cape's status as a British colony without question. Within that framework he had striven for greater official recognition of the Dutch language and obtained step by step concessions, which still, however, left Dutch far short of equality with English in the administration and the schools, since many of the senior civil servants and school inspectors were ignorant of Dutch and all the public examinations were conducted in the English medium. Hofmeyr believed in a colonial nationalism, shared by Boer and Briton alike, and even during the palmy days of President Kruger he had hoped that South Africa would become a federal dominion, with full internal autonomy, but under the British flag for defence and for trade. Isolationist sentiment had always existed in parts of the colony and it had become more pronounced since the rise of British imperialism—in 1905 the Burghersdorp *Stem*, for example, dismissed conciliation as pure 'bogt' (nonsense).[87] Nevertheless, Hofmeyr's policy remained the policy of the Bond. So did Hofmeyr's tactics. He had never been willing that an exclusively Bond Ministry should be formed and had himself declined the premiership on several occasions. Consequently, although nearly every member of the Bond was an Afrikaner, it never lacked English-speaking allies. In 1890 Cecil Rhodes had been able to form a Cabinet which relied on Bond support and contained two Bondsmen. After the Jameson Raid, however, the Bond had rejected Rhodes and imperialism had become the determinant of political divisions. The anti-imperialist Schreiner Ministry of 1898–1900 had included Bondsmen and non-Bondsmen. Then in 1903 several leading independent anti-imperialist politicians, of British as well as Afrikaner descent, joined with the Bondsmen at the parliamentary level to form the South African Party, while the Bond retained its own elaborate organization and, indeed, complete autonomy. The South African Party Ministry, which took office on the fall of Jameson in February 1908, contained three men of British descent (Merriman, Burton, and Currey), two Bondsmen (Malan and de Waal), and two others (Sauer and Graaff).

Merriman, the Prime Minister, was a man of independent views and exceptional integrity. Born in England, he had moved to South Africa as a child when his father became Archdeacon of Grahamstown. He returned to England for part of his schooling, but from 1861 onwards he

[87] Cited in the *Cape Times*, 30 Nov. 1905.

lived in South Africa. Entering the Cape Parliament in 1869 he quickly made his mark in debate and in administration, gaining a place in the first Cape Cabinet—Molteno's Ministry of 1872–8. He was a voracious reader of history and he accepted the interpretation of the Whig historians. To him, as to Gladstone, whom he greatly admired, politics were a struggle between right and wrong. The imperialism of Rhodes, Chamberlain, and Milner was, he was sure, a catastrophic departure from the true lines of British policy. During the war he caused the fall of the Schreiner Ministry, of which he was a member, by opposing the introduction of a Treason Bill; he spoke on pro-Boer platforms in England, and he led the agitation against Milner's attempt to suspend the Cape Constitution. Once the war was over he considered that South Africa should be left to manage her own affairs without interference from Britain. Although he was aware that there were isolationist and illiberal forces operating upon the Afrikaners—and he deplored them[88] —he hoped that they would gradually subside, that the differences between Boer and Briton would disappear, and that parties would not evolve on a racial basis but on the basis of town *versus* country. To a great extent, therefore, Merriman's outlook was similar to Botha's. Nevertheless, Merriman never endorsed Botha's conciliation policy. British imperialism was such a bogy to him that even after the fall of the Unionists he remained intensely suspicious of imperialist influence in Britain, of the British officials in South Africa, and of the mining magnates of the Witwatersrand. In these respects he was closer to Steyn, for whom he had an immense personal regard, than to Botha and Smuts, who, he feared, had become too trusting.[89]

Merriman's conduct during the war had earned him the admiration of the Cape Afrikaners and, with his fine parliamentary and administrative record, he was the natural leader of the South African Party from its

[88] For example, on 24 Oct. 1903 Merriman wrote to Ds. J. H. Hofmeyr, moderator of the N.G.K. in the Cape Colony, deploring what was reported to have been said in the synod during a debate on martial law: 'It is with dismay that I find the church whose influence and authority is so great . . . by the violence . . . of some of the utterances during the debate on the question blowing up those embers of strife which all wellwishers of S Africa hoped to see extinguished. . . . I say with all respect that I have been amazed by the interpretation of the New Testament and of the doctrines of the divine founder of our religion that were laid down by some speakers during the debate. If followed to their legitimate conclusion they would lead us far indeed from the doctrine of the sermon on the mount. . . .' Merriman Papers (copy).

[89] For example, commenting to Smuts on Botha's decision to go to the Colonial Conference in London, Merriman wrote: '. . . I always had a sort of feeling that he [Botha] was rather inclined to our great South African fault of leaning over too much to the conciliation of enemies. . . . I hope I may see him before he gets to England. They want to bird lime him there for their Imperial circus.' 8 Mar. 1907, Smuts Papers.

foundation.[90] His position as Prime Minister was, however, insecure. His political majority was mainly derived from the Bond, of which he was not a member. The cement of his party was anti-imperialism, but that was no longer enough. Merriman expected that in the long run English would inexorably become the only language of South Africa,[91] and he stood quite outside the Afrikaner cultural movement. Moreover, he considered that it was his first duty as Prime Minister and Treasurer to stabilize the colony's finances, even though that meant imposing additional taxation upon all sections of the community, whereas the Bond was loth to accept fresh taxation upon its members. There were also personal tensions. Merriman was never able to establish cordial relations with Malan, who was thirty years his junior, and he resented the fact that Hofmeyr continued to exert a great influence over the Bond Members of Parliament and to control the Bond organization through his chairmanship of its *Kommissie van Toezicht* (Supervisory Committee), even though he had retired from Parliament in 1895. The Merriman Cabinet was therefore unstable and subject to recurring crises.

In comparison with Het Volk, the Unie, and the Bond, the Opposition parties were weakly organized and poorly led. Milner had failed to create political solidarity among British South Africans. They belonged to different religious denominations, they pursued different occupations. The Progressives had to reconcile the rival claims of capital and labour, of mining, industry, and commerce, and the Unionists had the additional problem of balancing the local interests of Cape Town, Port Elizabeth, East London, and Kimberley. In the materialistic atmosphere of the Witwatersrand almost the only men of standing who were able and willing to devote much time to politics were company directors and none of them was an accomplished politician. Sir George Farrar, Sir Percy Fitzpatrick, and Drummond Chaplin had all held the office of President of

[90] Nevertheless, Bettie Cloete, *Die Lewe van Senator F. S. Malan* (Johannesburg, 1946), pp. 206–7, gives Malan's account of an interview with the Governor of the Cape Colony in Jan. 1907, according to which Hely-Hutchinson asked him 'if he would accept the premiership when Dr. Jameson resigned' ('of hy die Premierskap sou aanneem wanneer dr. Jameson bedank') and Malan replied that 'it would be a mistake to overlook Merriman') ('dit sou 'n fout wees om meneer Merriman oor die hoof te sien'). It is probable that Hely-Hutchinson actually inquired whether Malan and the Bond would support Merriman if he asked him to form a Cabinet. Hely-Hutchinson would naturally seek information on this point from the leader of the Bondsmen in the House of Assembly.

[91] 'I had much interesting talk with Domine Vorster who is extreme but clever and sensible. He said among many things that impressed me much "I know our grandchildren will speak English and think English but they will not be English they will be S. African." Quite true I think.' Merriman to Mrs. Merriman, 14 Mar. 1903, Merriman Papers.

the Chamber of Mines. Farrar, Chairman of East Rand Proprietary Mines, was conscientious and hard-working but he was a poor speaker and had little imagination. Fitzpatrick, a partner in H. Eckstein & Co. until he retired in 1907, was capable of sudden bursts of political activity and had a ready pen, but the day-to-day grind of party management and parliamentary debate was beyond him. Chaplin, manager of Consolidated Goldfields, though efficient in preparing an argument, was too cold in manner and narrowly British in outlook to be effective in the conditions created by the grant of responsible government. Moreover, these Progressive leaders did not get on well together. They had formerly looked to Milner for guidance and his departure had left them rudderless. There was a similar vacuum in the Cape Colony, where Dr. L. S. Jameson—Rhodes's former lieutenant and the leader of the filibustering raid into the South African Republic—had been pressed into service in default of others. Although he had exceptional personal magnetism and could cast a spell over a public meeting with emotional oratory, he was a creature of impulse and intuition and he lacked intellectual depth. Furthermore, by 1908 he was chronically unwell and his heart was not in political life. He preferred England to South Africa, Rhodesia to the Cape Colony, and he was often absent from the Cape.

Before 1907 the Progressives had regarded Botha's conciliation policy as no more than a clever device for extracting concessions from the British Liberals and electoral support from the Witwatersrand. They had felt sure that if he came into power he would pursue a racialistic policy. Their apprehensions gradually subsided, however, as Botha's Government showed its hand. Above all, Smuts's Education Act went a long way towards modifying their views. Farrar considered that Smuts looked at education 'from the highest point of view',[92] and in December 1907 H. L. Lindsay, the Progressive whip, went so far as to declare in public that the Government was a progressive Government.[93] Meanwhile, Jameson and Botha had met at the Colonial Conference in London, where they found that they had many tastes in common and struck up a warm friendship, and Jameson, who was a follower rather than a leader by temperament, grew to regard Botha as the best hope for South Africa. There were some who deprecated these developments. Farrar was prone to doubts and Chaplin continued to view Botha with profound mistrust. But by the time that Hertzog's Education Act was passed in August 1908 a new pattern was beginning to emerge in South African politics. Since there was no prospect of reversing the electoral victories

[92] Farrar to Patrick Duncan, 22 July 1907, Duncan Papers.
[93] Lady Selborne to Patrick Duncan, 14 Dec. 1907, ibid.

of Het Volk, the Unie, and the South African Party in the foreseeable future, Jameson and Fitzpatrick would endorse the conciliation policy and proclaim their faith in Botha, while denouncing Hertzog and Afrikaner isolationism.[94]

B. *Natal*[95]

Natal politics were completely different from the politics of the other self-governing South African colonies because most of the whites in Natal were of British stock and very anxious to preserve the British character of their colony. Since Natal acquired responsible government in 1893, the colony had been controlled by shifting groups of British colonists, nearly all of whom represented the farming interest and had much the same outlook. As one of them put it: 'We have strictly speaking no parties and we divide up on personalities and not on questions of principle.'[96]

Responsible government in Natal had a fairly good start under the leadership of two men of considerable talents and vision—Sir John Robinson and Harry Escombe—but their successors were lesser men. In May 1905 C. J. Smythe, a Nottingham Road farmer, became Prime Minister and an Opposition formed round F. R. Moor, an Estcourt farmer who had been Secretary for Native Affairs from 1893 to 1897 and again from 1899 to 1903. In a general election held in September 1906 there were no clear cut differences between the policies of the rival leaders and the result of the election was ambiguous, because, although a majority of the successful candidates was believed to be opposed to Smythe, the balance appeared to lie with four Labour men—and neither Smythe nor Moor cared to rely on their support. Smythe resigned on 22 November, and after a week's negotiations Moor managed to form a Ministry which was independent of Labour by including men who had previously supported Smythe. Besides Moor, who took the portfolio of Native Affairs, it consisted of Dr. C. O'Grady Gubbins (Colonial Secretary), W. A. Deane (Agriculture), T. F. Carter (Justice and Public Works), E. A. Brunner (Treasurer), and C. Hitchins (Railways and Harbours). This was the Ministry which, with two changes in July 1908,[97] remained

[94] See below, p. 465.

[95] Here, and in other passages dealing with Natal down to the start of the National Convention, I follow rather closely my article 'The Colony of Natal and "The Closer Union Movement"', *Butterworths South African Law Review, 1955*, pp. 81–106.

[96] T. Hyslop to Steyn, 23 Feb. 1910, Steyn Papers.

[97] On 13 July 1908 A. T. Oliff succeeded Brunner and E. M. Greene succeeded Hitchins.

in office until May 1910. Even for Natal it was an exceptionally rural Ministry: none of its members represented Durban Borough or the adjacent counties. It was also an exceptionally inexperienced Ministry: the Prime Minister was the only member who had previously held office. And it was a Ministry which never inspired confidence in the Natal electorate or the Natal Parliament.

During Natal's first decade as a self-governing colony the electorate was more concerned with the Indian than with the Native question. Since 1860 Natal had been importing labourers from India to work on the sugar estates and elsewhere, on conditions which entitled them to remain in Natal, if they wished, when their contracts expired. By 1893 there were nearly as many Indians as whites in Natal and some were competing successfully with white traders, with the result that the Natal Parliament passed a series of laws preventing Indians from acquiring the franchise, restricting the entry of non-indentured Indians, and imposing a special tax on non-indentured Indians. A number of Indians had migrated from Natal to the Transvaal, where a similar situation developed. The Botha Government became embroiled in an effort to enforce differential legislation against them and they reacted by applying the new technique of passive resistance, led and inspired by a young man named M. K. Gandhi.

Most of the Natal witnesses who appeared before the South African Native Affairs Commission of 1903–5 contended that their own system of native administration was far the best in South Africa. 'We rather congratulate ourselves', said F. R. Moor, 'that our Natives are the best-mannered, and the best behaved, and the most law-abiding people that we have got in South Africa.'[98] As the post-war depression deepened, however, a clamour arose for an increase in the direct African contribution to the revenue, and in 1905 Parliament imposed a poll tax, at the rate of £1 a head, on every man in the colony except indentured Indians and married Africans.[99] In the brief debates on the Poll Tax Bill nobody ventured to suggest that it would lead to trouble, but when the magistrates began to collect the tax from the Africans early in 1906 they met with a hostile reception. On 7 February the Umgeni magistrate was defied and the next day a small force of mounted police which had been sent to support him was attacked about twenty miles south-west of Pietermaritz-

[98] *South African Native Affairs Commission, 1903–05, Report and Appendices* (Cape Town, 1905, 5 vols.), iii, answer 20790.

[99] Natal Act No. 38 of 1905. Standing rules and orders were suspended in both Houses to speed its passage. The Africans exempted were those who paid hut tax—that is to say, roughly speaking, the married men. In the year ending 30 June 1906 the poll tax yielded a revenue of £125,142 of which £76,490 was paid by Africans.

burg and two of the police were killed. Complacency then gave way to something approaching panic. Martial law was proclaimed, the militia was mobilized, and sweeps were made through the southern districts to overawe the tribes. By the end of March all seemed quiet, but a few days later still more startling events occurred farther north. Bambata, a petty chief of the Greytown district, who had been deposed for ignoring official instructions, attacked and seized the man who had been appointed chief in his stead, ambushed a police force, and withdrew across the Tugela river to the Nkandhla forest. Several thousand Africans rallied to his side and he remained at large until his forces were defeated and he was killed in a battle at Mome Gorge on 10 June. A month later the last flickers of resistance had been stamped out. Altogether 30 Europeans and something like 3,000 Africans had been killed in this last serious opposition which was offered on a tribal basis to white supremacy in southern Africa.[1]

By that time the Natal Government had appointed a strong Native Affairs Commission, which soon became aware that the rebellion was a symptom of misgovernment.[2] The system of native administration which Theophilus Shepstone had improvised in Natal in the middle of the nineteenth century had, at the outset, been tolerably benevolent and efficient. Enough land had been set aside for the exclusive use of the Africans to enable them to continue to practise their traditional economy and, with it, to preserve many of the essentials of their tribal culture; and Shepstone had taken pains to gain and keep the confidence of the chiefs, on whose co-operation the system depended for success. After his retirement from the Secretaryship for Native Affairs in 1876, and more particularly after Natal acquired responsible government in 1893, the system degenerated into a despotism that was neither benevolent nor efficient. The increase in the African population led to an acute shortage of land and the officials lost contact with the chiefs. The Africans therefore experienced real hardships and had no constitutional means of redress. Over half of those south of the Tugela lived, not in the locations (reserves), but on land which they leased from white owners; their rents were high in relation to the wages which they could earn, so that many

---

[1] The rebellion and its aftermath, including the arrest and trial of Dinizulu, led to the publication of a sheaf of command papers between 1906 and 1909—Cd. 2905, 2927, 3027, 3247, 3563, 3888, 3889, 3998, 4001, 4194, 4195, 4328, 4403, 4404, and 4585. There is additional material on the subject in the Natal Archives, notably Prime Minister, CI–CV. J. Stuart, *A History of the Zulu Rebellion, 1906, and of Dinizulu's Arrest, Trial and Expatriation* (London, 1913), is a semi-official account.

[2] *Natal Native Affairs Commission, 1906–1907, Report and Evidence* (Pietermaritzburg, 1907, 2 vols.). The first volume, containing the report but not the evidence, was also published as a command paper, Cd. 3889 (1907).

of them fell into debt to white money-lenders; and the rate of interest
which they were charged on such loans was normally about 60 per cent.
per annum and often higher. The poll tax therefore came as the final
straw to many of the Africans, in much the same way as the poll tax levied
by the English Parliament over 500 years earlier had been regarded as
the final straw by English peasants who were experiencing the strains of
the transition to a money economy. Bambata himself, for example, was
a tenant who was in debt and harassed by his creditors. How could he
hope to re-establish himself if his young men—his natural wage-earners
—were to pay an extra tax? The Africans of Zululand, which had been
incorporated in Natal in 1897, were not so hard pressed, because nearly
all of them still lived on their own land, but they were alarmed by a
recent decision of the Government to open up part of their country to
white settlement. Among the Africans throughout Natal there was, indeed, a widespread feeling of dissatisfaction, bordering on despair, and
one of them was speaking for many when he told the commission: 'If we
Natives could only have feathers we would put on our wings and fly to
another country.'[3]

These facts, and others besides, were exposed by the commission,
whose report was a gloomy commentary on the relations between the
races in Natal. But by the time the report was presented in July 1907
the Moor Ministry was contemplating further aggressive action. African
chiefs who had been loyal to the Government during the rebellion were
being mysteriously murdered in Zululand, and the Government was
coming to the conclusion that Dinizulu, the head of the Zulu royal house,
had fomented the rebellion, was responsible for the murders, and was
actively engaged in organizing a further outbreak. Since 1898 Dinizulu
had been living near Nongoma as the chief of the small Usutu tribe and
receiving a salary of £500 a year as a government *induna*. His position
was difficult, because the Government had neglected him while the rebels
had looked to him for leadership and given it out that he was behind
them. He was a somewhat pathetic figure, confused and weak, more
sinned against than sinning. By the end of November 1907 the Government became convinced that its suspicions were well-founded and that
there would be no real peace until Dinizulu had been removed. Martial
law was again proclaimed in Zululand and the northern districts of
Natal, the militia was again mobilized, 3,000 men moved towards
Nongoma, and their commander was instructed to prevent Dinizulu
from having access to lawyers before or after his arrest.[4] On 9 December

[3] Evidence of Nduku, Klip River Division, *Natal N.A. Commission*, ii. 736.
[4] This instruction was decided on at a Cabinet Meeting held on 5 Dec. 1907. Moor at

Dinizulu gave himself up without resistance. He was taken to Pieter-maritzburg where, under an old Natal law (Ordinance No. 14 of 1845), he was subjected to a preliminary examination by a magistrate, lasting from 23 December 1907 until 30 July 1908, throughout all of which period martial law was maintained in Zululand and the northern districts and his legal advisers were not allowed to go there to prepare the case for his defence. Eventually he was committed for trial on twenty-three counts of treason. The trial took place in Greytown before a special court, constituted under Act 8 of 1908, presided over by Sir William Smith of the Transvaal bench. T. F. Carter, K.C., the Natal Minister of Justice and Attorney-General, personally conducted the prosecution, and W. P. Schreiner, K.C., a former Prime Minister of the Cape Colony, led the defence. Sir William Smith delivered judgment on 3 March 1909. He acquitted Dinizulu on all the more serious charges and indulged in considerable irony at the expense of the Natal Government. On the charge that he had fomented the rebellion he remarked: 'I think the probabilities of the case are so overwhelmingly against the theory that the prisoner incited Bambata to commence the rebellion that it seems to me to be incredible. . . . If, under the circumstances I find to have existed in this case, the prisoner did incite him to rebel, I should be inclined to say that he deserves to be acquitted on the ground of insanity. As it is, I think he is entitled to be acquitted upon the facts.' On the charge that during 1907 Dinizulu was conspiring to raise a further rebellion, the Judge said bluntly: 'I do not find any evidence which would warrant the conclusion that any further insurrection or rebellion was contemplated.' However, finding him guilty of having harboured rebels during and after the rebellion, the court sentenced Dinizulu to four years' imprisonment and a fine of £100.[5]

These events had widespread repercussions. Natal still looked to Great Britain as the final guarantee of her internal security, and under the Natal Constitution and his royal instructions the Governor was entitled to act independently of his ministers in the field of native affairs. British Liberals, who had denounced the excesses committed under martial law by the imperial forces during the war, were not disposed to ignore reports that the Natal militia was committing similar excesses against the Africans. Moreover, Natal received a very bad press in Britain. The

first opposed it, but he yielded to the wishes of T. F. Carter, Minister of Justice. Natal Archives, Prime Minister, CIV.

[5] Cd. 4585 (1909). See also Eric A. Walker, *W. P. Schreiner: a South African* (London, 1937), xiii; R. C. A. Samuelson, *Long, Long Ago* (Durban, 1929), xxviii; Stuart, op. cit. xxii.

result was that there were two serious clashes between the British
Government and the Government of Natal.

The first of these clashes occurred in March 1906. The militia had
captured twenty-six Africans who were believed to have taken part in the
breach of the peace on 8 February. The first two to be captured were
given a summary trial by a drum-head court-martial and shot on 13 February. The other twenty-four were tried by a regular court-martial during
March. Twelve of them were sentenced to death and their sentences were
confirmed by the Governor-in-Council. By the time the Secretary of State
received this information a question had been asked in the House of
Commons about the shootings that had taken place on 13 February, and
a battalion of the Queen's Own Cameron Highlanders had been sent
from Pretoria to Pietermaritzburg at the request of the Natal Government to calm the whites and intimidate the Africans. In these circumstances Lord Elgin ordered the Governor to suspend the executions until
he had sent him further information, but Smythe, the Prime Minister,
refused to suspend the executions when asked to do so. Sir Henry
McCallum then fell back on his prerogative powers and himself ordered
the suspension, whereupon all the ministers tendered their resignations
on the ground that the Secretary of State had interfered with the decision
of the Executive Council of a self-governing colony, consenting, however, to remain in office until a further communication had been received
from Whitehall. Elgin gave way before this threat and assured Natal
that he had had no intention of interfering with the action of its responsible Government. The ministers then withdrew their resignations and
the executions were carried out on 2 April. Natal had won the first
round.[6]

In her second clash with Britain Natal was less successful. In September 1907 Moor asked for British military support in the projected operations against Dinizulu, but he withdrew his request when Elgin indicated
that Britain would claim a hand in the settlement of native affairs in
Natal if her troops were used for such a purpose. When Natal decided
to proceed against Dinizulu on her own account, Elgin informed the
Governor that 'As your Ministers have made no appeal for Imperial
assistance the determination of their policy rests entirely with them and
His Majesty's Government cannot interfere', but he went on to remind
him that under the terms of his appointment Dinizulu could not be

---

[6] On the clash described in this paragraph there is unpublished material in the Natal
Archives, Prime Minister, CI; but most of the important documents are published in
Cd. 2905 (1906). See also Stuart, vi, and the comment of Arthur Berriedale Keith,
Responsible Government in the Dominions (2nd ed., Oxford, 1928, 2 vols.), i. 214–17.

removed from his position as a salaried *induna* without his permission.[7]
In spite of this warning the Natal Government decided to suspend
Dinizulu's salary from the date of his arrest, thereby depriving him of
the means of paying for his defence. The Ministry persisted in this attitude until it had lost the sympathy of all parties in Britain and was being
attacked by several of the Natal newspapers. In July 1908 the Unionist
members of the House of Commons joined with the Liberals in deploring
its conduct; and although the Natal Government then yielded, it did so
with such an ill grace that it did not remove the bad impression it had
created in England.[8]

That impression was shared by the Natal governors of the period. It
was Sir Henry McCallum's private opinion that Natal had been granted
responsible government too soon and that she lacked the men to work it
efficiently.[9] His successor, Sir Matthew Nathan, signed the proclamations
of martial law in December 1907 under protest,[10] and was indignant
when the commandant of the militia and the Minister of Agriculture
tried to stop him from visiting Zululand on the pretexts that his presence
would confuse the minds of the Africans and that he might catch
malaria.[11] Even the High Commissioner, Lord Selborne, who was the
most charitable of men, made a pungent private comment after reading
the report of the Natal Native Affairs Commission: 'Natal', he wrote, 'is
bankrupt in policy and in finance.'[12]

The leaders of the South African Party, the Unie, and Het Volk were
also critical. Merriman had never been sympathetic towards Natal, and
he considered that her native policy had been designed 'to keep the
Natives in a state of barbarism'.[13] His opinion of the Natal militia was
extremely cynical: 'As one volunteer officer remarked', he wrote, '"This
is better than farming."'[14] Steyn regretted 'the hysterical manner [in
which] Natal is dealing with the Native question'.[15] Smuts described the
1906 campaign as 'simply a record of loot and rapine'.[16] Even Botha,
who was usually disposed to take a lenient view of the colony of his

[7] Cd. 3888 (1908), Nos. 73 and 81.

[8] On this clash, also, there is unpublished material in the Natal Archives, Prime
Minister, CIII–CV; but most of the important documents are published in Cd. 3888, 3998,
4001, 4194, and 4328.

[9] Stanford's Diary, 5 Sept. 1906.

[10] Cd. 3888, Nos. 74 and 82.

[11] Minutes by W. A. Deane, Minister of Agriculture, 30 Dec. 1907, and Col. Sir
Duncan McKenzie, Commandant, 31 Dec. 1907, Natal Archives, Prime Minister, CV.

[12] Selborne to Duncan, 30 Nov. 1907, Duncan Papers.

[13] Merriman to Prof. Goldwin Smith, 12 Jan. 1908, Merriman Papers.

[14] Merriman to Mrs. Julia Merriman, 18 Mar. 1906, ibid.

[15] Steyn to Merriman, 7 May 1906, ibid.

[16] Smuts to Merriman, 5 May 1906, ibid.

birth, had grave misgivings about Moor's conduct. In September 1907 Moor told him of his suspicions of Dinizulu and Botha replied that he intended to find out for himself if Dinizulu had been loyal.[17] Accordingly he sent to Dinizulu's kraal a certain Conrad Meijer, an old Boer who had been used by the South African Republic in its dealings with the Zulus and who knew Dinizulu well. After spending six days at the kraal Meijer reported to Botha that he was sure that Dinizulu had been responsible neither for the rebellion nor for the subsequent unrest in Zululand. He added: 'Dinizulu has only one object and that is to live on friendly terms with his Government. . . . I would strongly recommend that the Government of Natal, I mean the Ministers themselves, come into more direct contact with Dinizulu and am convinced if this were done that the condition of affairs will speedily improve.' Botha at once sent a copy of this report to Moor.[18] He was therefore shocked when Moor disregarded it and the militia was mobilized against Dinizulu, and he wrote Moor a letter full of reproaches.[19] Thus the rebellion and its aftermath created a widespread lack of respect for Natal—among the British people and politicians of all parties, among the British officials in South Africa, and among those South Africans who were in the seats of power in Cape Town, Bloemfontein, and Pretoria.

The rebellion also caused Natal Europeans to favour new schemes of political engineering, designed to make their position more secure. One such scheme emanated from Major P. A. Silburn, a Natal imperialist. Ever since 1904 he had been warning Natal that there was a danger of a native rebellion and recommending that the existing colonial forces should be combined to form a single intercolonial militia, controlled by a South African Defence Council. Such a 'defence federation' would be a first step towards a full 'political federation' of South Africa, which in turn would promote the imperial federation of Milner's dreams.[20] When the rebellion he had prophesied actually took place, he warmed to his theme and gained support from the Natal press.[21] The result was that an Intercolonial Defence Conference was held in Johannesburg in January 1907, but the Cape representatives would have nothing to do with a

[17] Botha to Moor, 11 Sept. 1907; Botha to Sir Richard Solomon, 12 Sept. 1907 (copy of telegram). Natal Archives, Prime Minister, CIII.

[18] 24 Oct. 1907, ibid. Although Meijer's report was published in Cd. 3888, it was not revealed that Meijer had been acting on behalf of Botha.

[19] 6 Dec. 1907, ibid.

[20] P. A. Silburn, 'Federation of the South African Colonial Forces', *Empire Review*, viii. 378–86 (Nov. 1904); 'The Political Element in Imperial Defence', ibid. ix. 36–43 (Feb. 1905); *Natal Mercury*, 5 May 1905.

[21] P. A. Silburn, 'Colonial Defence', *African Monthly*, i. 3–12 (Dec. 1906); *Natal Mercury*, 2 May 1906; *Natal Witness*, 20 June 1906.

'defence federation', because they were unwilling to recommend the voting of public money for an organization which would not be controlled by the Cape Parliament, and the conference achieved nothing substantial.[22] The other scheme that was canvassed during 1906 was that Natal and the Transvaal should be amalgamated. What a neat solution this seemed to offer! By a simple action Natal would solve both her economic and her military problems. As the *Natal Mercury* put it: 'Natal has been an agent for the Transvaal, and it has done its work so efficiently that it is high time it became a partner.'[23] In the Natal Parliament W. McLarty argued with touching naïvety: 'It would settle this Native question to a great extent. . . . If they were too troublesome we could break up the locations and distribute the Native population throughout the inland colonies.'[24] Amalgamation also gained some support in Transvaal Progressive circles, based on the hope that the Natal British people, voting Progressive, would turn the scales against Het Volk, but, not unnaturally, it was frowned on by the leaders of Het Volk.[25] In the Natal general election of September 1906 C. J. Smythe at first showed signs of flirting with it, but Moor denounced it on the grounds that, being a unitary scheme, it would entail the loss of Natal's independence and individuality and, being a partial scheme, it would tend to divide British South Africa into two opposed camps and postpone a more complete federation. Smythe then hastened to explain that he was no less anxious to preserve Natal's identity and no more was heard of the proposal to amalgamate Natal with the Transvaal.[26]

C. *The High Commission Territories and Southern Rhodesia*

The other British territories in southern Africa were Basutoland, Bechuanaland Protectorate, and Swaziland, which were administered by the High Commissioner; Southern Rhodesia, North-western Rhodesia, and North-eastern Rhodesia, which were administered by the British South Africa Company; and Nyasaland Protectorate, administered by a Governor.

The first three were often described collectively as the 'Protectorates',

[22] 'Report of the Natal Representatives on the Inter-Colonial Conference on Defence', Natal Archives, Prime Minister, CIV.

[23] 5 Sept. 1906.

[24] *Natal Leg. Ass. Deb.* xl. 25–28 (8 May 1906).

[25] E. J. Edwards, *The Amalgamation of the Transvaal and Natal* (Johannesburg, 1906): a pamphlet, reprinting articles published in the *Transvaal Leader* in Aug. and Sept. 1906 with comments by South African politicians.

[26] *South Africa*, 15 Sept. 1906.

E

although Basutoland was in fact an annexed and not a protected territory. They were landlocked countries inhabited mainly by Bantu-speaking Africans. Basutoland, about the size of Belgium, was the watershed of South Africa. In 1904 its population of about 350,000 included 895 whites. It had been annexed in 1868 at the request of Moshesh, the founder chief of the Basuto people, following his defeat by the Boers of the Orange Free State at the end of a series of land wars. After a period of unsuccessful rule by the Cape Colony, it had been administered by the High Commissioner as a separate colony since 1884. No land had been alienated to whites and the white population consisted of officials, missionaries, and traders. Bechuanaland Protectorate was larger than France. Most of it was too arid for human habitation and in 1904 its total population was only about 120,000, of whom 1,004 were whites. Unlike the homogeneous Basuto, the Bechuana comprised several distinct tribes. The sector from 22° S. southwards had been taken under British protection at the request of the chiefs in 1885, primarily to safeguard them from freebooters from the South African Republic, and the boundary had been extended northwards in 1890 and 1891. Blocks of land had been alienated to the British South Africa Company and the Tati Concession and Exploration Company, but the bulk of the land was reserved for the Africans. In 1904 Swaziland, which was smaller than Wales, had a population of about 85,000, including 890 whites. The Swazi, like the Basuto, were a homogeneous people, recognizing a single paramount chief, but they had been less ably led, and towards the end of the nineteenth century numerous concessions had been granted to speculators and farmers. In 1894 Britain rejected the paramount chief's request for protection, and Swaziland then became a protectorate of the South African Republic. After the war it was administered separately from the Transvaal, and when the Transvaal received self-government it was placed under the control of the High Commissioner and the land was partitioned between the Swazi people and the concessionaires.

None of these territories produced much wealth, and their revenues, amounting to about £220,000 per annum, were derived mainly from a head or hut tax imposed on adult Africans. Each year considerable numbers of men left the territories to work on the farms or in the mines in the self-governing colonies. In 1908, for example, about 4,500 Basuto, 1,200 Bechuana, and 1,500 Swazi were employed in the Transvaal mining industries. The handful of white officials ruled the Africans indirectly through their chiefs, and the other European inhabitants had no say in the administration. In Basutoland, unlike the other territories, the Resident Commissioner consulted a National Council, composed mainly of nominees of the chiefs, on matters of concern to the Africans. Having acquired British protection, the chiefs and their advisers were most anxious to keep it rather than to allow their territories to fall under the control of white South Africans, for in that direction, their memories and instincts told them, lay danger to their continued possession of their lands.

Under its royal charter of 1889 the British South Africa Company was empowered to promote trade, commerce, civilization, and good government in the area between the Transvaal, German South-west Africa, Nyasaland, and Portuguese East Africa, subject to the supervision of the High Commissioner. In 1887 Rhodes's agent, Charles Rudd, had obtained a concession from the Matabele chief Lobengula to exploit the mineral resources of what became Southern Rhodesia, and in 1890 a pioneer column occupied Mashonaland. Conflicts developed with the Matabele, and in 1894 Matabeleland, also, was occupied. In 1908 Southern Rhodesia contained about 590,000 Africans, 12,623 whites, and 1,944 Coloured people. The company appointed the Administrator and Executive Council, subject to the approval of the Secretary of State for the Colonies, and the Secretary of State appointed a Resident Commissioner, who had a considerable say in the conduct of native affairs. The Administrator presided over a Legislative Council comprising seven nominees of the company and seven persons elected by those inhabitants who possessed the qualifications which were required for the parliamentary franchise in the Cape Colony. In 1907 there were about 2,000 voters, all of whom except about fifty were white men. There had been no African risings since 1897, but hopes of great and easily exploitable mineral wealth had not been realized. The settlers were mainly of British origin and sentiment. They owned large landholdings and assumed that in time Southern Rhodesia would become a self-governing British colony under their control: but that time had clearly not yet come. For the present they were involved in a series of disputes with the company, which claimed to be the owner of all unalienated land and insisted on the right to raise and expend revenue even if the assembly failed to pass the Administrator's estimates. The company justified its attitude on the grounds that it was administering the country at an annual deficit of £250,000 and that it had never been able to pay a dividend to its shareholders. Effective exploitation of north-western Rhodesia (Barotseland) and north-eastern Rhodesia had scarcely commenced and their combined populations of about 700,000 people included less than 1,000 whites. Neither they nor Nyasaland enter into the story of the unification of South Africa.

5. BRITISH SOUTH AFRICA: ECONOMIC

The South African War had been a period of prosperity for the coastal colonies and for those parts of the inland colonies which came under effective British occupation owing to the presence of up to 200,000 British soldiers and the expenditure of large sums of money by the Imperial Government. In 1902 it was generally expected that peace would be followed by a dramatic expansion of the gold-mining industry and, with it, of the entire South African economy. There was a building boom in nearly every town and village in South Africa and Kaffirs (Witwatersrand gold shares) rose to unprecedented heights on the London Stock Exchange. But these hopes were not fulfilled. The departure of most of the British troops caused a drastic decline in the cash market for local produce, and political uncertainties and the labour shortage in the gold-mining industry retarded the rate of expansion. The years 1903–8 were therefore a period of instability and depression. Property values dropped, mortgages were called up, forced sales took place. Many white workmen were unemployed and many immigrants returned to their countries of origin. Kaffirs dropped steeply in 1903, and although they rose during 1904 (after the arrival of the first Chinese labourers) they fell again during 1905 and continued to fall until recovery set in during 1908 and 1909.[27]

The impact of this depression was uneven in two respects. Firstly, the farming communities were comparatively unaffected and the brunt was borne by the townsmen. Secondly, the inland colonies weathered it more successfully than the coastal colonies, as will now be demonstrated.

The gold-mining industry of the Transvaal did expand, even though its rate of expansion fell short of expectation. The quantity and value of gold produced increased each year, reaching the pre-war figure of £16 millions in 1904 and nearly double that figure in 1910.[28] Although many recent immigrants left the Transvaal disillusioned, still more entered the Transvaal from the coastal colonies and from overseas, and the white population of the colony rose from 297,277 in 1904 to 420,562 in 1911.[29] The balances due to depositors in the Transvaal Post Office Savings Bank increased each year.[30] The annual number of cables and

[27] On the depression see M. H. de Kock, *Selected Subjects in the Economic History of South Africa* (Cape Town, 1924), pp. 124–6; C. G. W. Schumann, *Structural Changes and Business Cycles in South Africa, 1806–1936* (London, 1938), pp. 93–96; *The Economist*, lxvii. 564–5.

[28] See above, pp. 13–14, and below, Appendix A. xii.

[29] See below, Appendix A. i.

[30] T.G. 28 (1909), *Statistics of the Transvaal Colony for the Years 1903–08*, p. 59.

telegrams handled by the Transvaal Post Office remained fairly constant until the financial year 1907/8, when it fell by about one-eleventh.[31] The value of imports rose to a peak in 1905, fell slightly in 1906 and more sharply in 1907, and began to rise again in 1908.[32] Although the revenue fell from £5,427,509 in 1902/3 to £4,411,990 in 1904/5, and then steadied at just over £4,650,000 for the next three years, before rising to £5,735,524 in 1908/9, there was a surplus in each of the years 1902–10, amounting to an accumulated surplus of £5,758,539.[33] Furthermore, the Central South African Railways (comprising the railways of the Transvaal and the Orange River Colony) yielded large profits each year, totalling nearly £16 millions between July 1902 and December 1909.[34]

In the Orange River Colony, also, the white population increased significantly, from 142,679 in 1904 to 175,189 in 1911.[35] Although the Orange River Colony's revenue fell from £956,536 in 1902/3 to £740,453 in 1907/8, there was a surplus in each of those years amounting to an accumulated surplus of £215,662. In the next two years the revenue increased, reaching £952,860 in 1909/10, but deficits totalling £42,108 were incurred, largely because the revenue had become responsible for paying interest on the colony's share of the 1903 guaranteed loan.[36] However, these deficits were more than offset by the colony's share of the large profits of the Central South African Railways, which were not shown in the ordinary accounts.

In Natal, on the other hand, it was estimated that the white population, which numbered 97,109 in 1904, had fallen to 91,443 in 1908,[37] and in 1911 it had risen to only 98,114.[38] Bank deposits fell from £5½ millions at the end of 1902 to £4 millions at the end of 1908.[39] The annual number of telegrams handled fell from over 3 millions in 1902 to under 2 millions in 1908.[40] The value of imports fell from £16½ millions in 1903 to barely half that figure in 1908.[41] Year after year the Natal treasurers overestimated the revenue, which fell from £4,334,175 in the financial year 1902/3 to £3,510,350 in 1907/8, and there were

[31] Ibid., p. 79.   [32] Ibid., p. 69.
[33] See below, Appendix A. viii.
[34] See below, Appendix A. xi. The surplus of nearly £16 millions is the difference between the earnings and the *total* working expenditure of the C.S.A.R. during this period.
[35] See below, Appendix A. i.
[36] See below, Appendix A. ix.
[37] *Natal Statistical Year Book for 1909* (Pietermaritzburg, 1910), p. 3.
[38] See below, Appendix A. i.
[39] *Natal Statistical Year Book for 1909*, p. 8.
[40] Ibid., p. 4.
[41] Ibid., p. 5.

deficits in five of these six years, which produced a net deficit of £1,507,143.[42]

The depression was even more prolonged in the Cape Colony, because the market for its most important export industry—the diamond-mining industry of Kimberley—collapsed during 1907 owing to a financial crisis in Europe and America.[43] The white population, which numbered 579,741 in 1904, almost certainly decreased during the next five years and in 1911 it had risen to only 582,377.[44] Bank deposits fell from nearly £17 millions at the end of 1902 to £9½ millions at the end of 1909.[45] The annual number of telegrams handled by the post office dropped by half in the same period.[46] The value of imports fell from over £32 millions in 1902 to under £14 millions in 1908.[47] Like the Natal treasurers, in most of these years the Cape treasurers grossly overestimated the revenue, which fell from £11,701,150 in 1902/3 to £6,981,873 in 1907/8, and there were deficits in five of the six years ending in June 1909, which produced a net deficit of £3,630,216.[48]

The coastal colonies had two main sources of revenue: customs, which formed 32 per cent. of the revenue of the Cape Colony and 24 per cent. of the revenue of Natal in the year ending in June 1903, and railway receipts, which formed 48 per cent. of the revenue of the Cape Colony and 53 per cent. of the revenue of Natal in the same year.[49] From 1903 onwards both these sources declined sharply, but the means of checking the falls were largely outside the control of the Cape and Natal governments. The customs tariff could not be altered without the consent of the other members of the Customs Union, and the decline in railway receipts was caused to a great extent by the diversion of the Transvaal import trade to the Mozambique port of Lourenço Marques. The financial straits of the coastal colonies were therefore a potent cause of inter-colonial friction.

Already before the war there had been keen competition for the Transvaal trade between Lourenço Marques, Durban, and the Cape

[42] See below, Appendix A. vii. Note that in Natal and the Cape Colony (unlike the Transvaal and the Orange River Colony) the ordinary revenue and expenditure included the receipts and expenditure of the public railways.

[43] See below, Appendix A. xii, for the resultant fall in the diamond output.

[44] See below, Appendix A. i. According to the *Cape Statistical Register, 1909* (Cape Town, 1910), p. 3, the estimated white population of the Cape Colony on 31 Dec. 1907 was 610,680; but this was certainly a gross overestimate.

[45] *Cape Statistical Register, 1909*, p. xviii.

[46] Ibid., p. xvii.

[47] Ibid., p. xix. In 1902, however, the Cape imports were swollen by the war.

[48] See below, Appendix A. vi.

[49] See below, Appendix A. vi–vii.

ports. After the railway line from Delagoa Bay reached the Witwatersrand in 1894, Lourenço Marques began to assert a natural ascendancy, and by 1898 its share of the tonnage of the Transvaal imports had risen to 40 per cent. and the shares of Durban and the Cape ports stood at about 30 per cent. each.[50] Had there been no war the Lourenço Marques share would inevitably have continued to rise, but the war caused a boom for the British colonial ports, and the Cape Colony and Natal assumed that the British conquest of the Transvaal would be to their permanent advantage. Surely a British Transvaal would prefer to trade with British ports! Their hopes were not realized, largely for geographical reasons. The Lourenço Marques route was the shortest route from the coast to the Witwatersrand; and it was also the most profitable route for the Central South African Railways because 85 per cent. of it lay within the C.S.A.R. system.[51] A further reason lay in the *modus vivendi* of 1901, under which, in return for the grant to the gold-mining companies of the right to recruit African labour in Mozambique, the Transvaal undertook that the railway rates from Lourenço Marques to the Witwatersrand would be considerably less than the rates from the British ports, so that the Delagoa Bay route was the cheapest route from Europe to the Witwatersrand for most classes of traffic.[52] The pre-war trend therefore reasserted itself. The Lourenço Marques share of the tonnage of traffic from the ports to the so-called competitive zone in the Transvaal rose from about 34 per cent. in 1903 to 63 per cent. in 1908, Durban's share fell from about 42 per cent in 1903 to 24 per cent. in 1908, and the share of the Cape ports fell from about 24 per cent. in 1903 to 13 per cent. in 1908.[53] As this trend became evident the Cape Colony and Natal protested against the *modus vivendi*. Milner sympathized with them and convened an Intercolonial Conference, which met in Johannesburg in February 1905 and decided that the Mozambique Government should be asked to accept a reduction in the preference granted to Lourenço Marques. But the representations were fruitless, for the Portuguese were naturally unwilling to surrender their advantage. Nor could the Transvaal afford to denounce the *modus vivendi*, which provided the gold-mines with over two-thirds of their African labourers.[54]

---

[50] Cd. 3564 (1907), pp. 19–26; Jean van der Poel, *Railway and Customs Policies in South Africa, 1885–1910* (London, 1933), i–v.

[51] See below, Appendix A. xi.

[52] Under the *modus vivendi* the rates from Lourenço Marques to Johannesburg were between 10s. and 15s. less than the rates from Durban and East London, and between 15s. and 21s. 8d. less than the rates from Port Elizabeth. Cd. 3564, pp. 61–63.

[53] See below, Appendix A. xi.

[54] See below, Appendix A. xii.

The 1905 conference also came to the conclusion that

the only satisfactory solution of questions relating to through rates and other matters in which the interests of the several Railway systems conflict, is to be found in the common management of at least the through lines and the pooling of their receipts with a division of profits on a fixed basis.[55]

Lord Selborne's first essay into the thorny field of intercolonial relations was an attempt to expand and apply this resolution. In September 1906 he addressed letters to the heads of the governments of the British South African colonies, predicting that friction would be 'continuous, and continuously more serious' if their railways were not united into a single system, and proposing that a conference should be convened to consider the subject.[56] This proposal was still-born. Whereas it had been a simple matter to combine the railways of the Transvaal and the Orange River Colony while they were crown colonies, any attempt to unite all the railways in British South Africa raised a difficult problem. What machinery could be devised for the administration of the united railways which would satisfy the parliaments of the self-governing colonies that they would have sufficient control? Selborne soon became aware that this problem was insoluble and he allowed his proposal to be dropped.

Meanwhile Natal had given notice of her intention to withdraw from the customs union, hoping thereby to force the inland colonies to approve of an increase in the tariff. But the inland colonies did not wish to do this. On the contrary, it was their interest to reduce the tariff and to compel the coastal colonies to abandon their practice of applying differential railway rates to the advantage of their own produce, for they had no difficulty in balancing their budgets, and the high cost of imported commodities was causing discontent on the Witwatersrand. Consequently, when an Intercolonial Customs and Railway Conference met at Pietermaritzburg in March 1906 to consider the position created by Natal's announcement, the differences of opinion ran so deep that the discussions were often acrimonious and on three occasions when motions were put to the vote the Cape Colony and Natal sided against the Transvaal and the Orange River Colony. Thomas Hyslop, the Natal Treasurer, explained Natal's need for an increase in the customs tariff. Patrick Duncan, for the Transvaal, replied with an attack upon the coastal colonies, contending that their differential railway rates were contrary to the spirit of the customs convention. With considerable difficulty the conference came to a compromise based on the principles of protection, imperial preference, and free internal trade, with the rider that they

[55] *Minutes of the Inter-Colonial Conference, February, 1905*, p. 18.
[56] *Cape Times*, 22 Nov. 1905.

'should whenever practicable be effected through the Customs Tariff and not through the instrumentality of preferential railway rates'. The general tariff was raised from 10 per cent., with a rebate of $2\frac{1}{2}$ per cent. on British imports, to 15 per cent., with a rebate of 3 per cent., and a few South African products were given additional tariff protection. The through railway rates on imported corn, grain, and flour were reduced to the level of the local rates, and the through rates on imported sugar, coal, and building materials were reduced but not equalized. It was also agreed that no railway administration should change its rates without first consulting the others.[57]

The new Customs Union Convention[58] was confirmed by the colonial legislatures in May and June 1906, but nobody was really satisfied. Natal and the Cape Colony disliked the *modus vivendi* as much as ever, and in the Transvaal adverse resolutions were adopted by the Johannesburg and Pretoria chambers of commerce and the convention was only carried in the Legislative Council by the official vote,[59] which made it evident that as soon as the Transvaal obtained responsible government she would be likely to give notice of her intention to withdraw from the Customs Union. Moreover, unlike Natal, the Transvaal could afford to carry out such a threat.

Meanwhile a series of bitter railway disputes had flared up between the colonies.[60] In the middle of 1906 two new railway lines were completed which disturbed the distribution of traffic between the ports. Previously, Durban had secured the lion's share of the trade of the southwestern Transvaal, via Johannesburg and Klerksdorp. In April 1906, however, Klerksdorp was connected with Fourteen Streams, which was on the main line from the Cape ports to Rhodesia, and in fulfilment of an agreement made with the Cape Colony in 1904 the C.S.A.R. reduced the through rates from the Cape ports over the new line in proportion to the reduction in the mileage, with the result that the Cape ports were able to replace Durban as the principal outlet for the south-western Transvaal. On the other hand, the Cape ports had previously been able to dominate the trade of the northern part of the Orange River Colony, along their main line to Johannesburg, but in June 1906 Harrismith,

---

[57] The Customs and Railway Conferences of Mar. 1906 were regarded as two branches of one body, but technically separate. The *Minutes* and the *Report of Proceedings* of the Customs Conference and the *Minutes and Annexures* of the Railway Conference were subsequently printed and issued to the delegates. Brand Papers.

[58] Cd. 2977 (1906).

[59] *Transvaal Leg. Co. Deb., 1906*, col. 207. The motion for the approval of the convention was carried by 12 votes to 8. Of the Ayes, 6 were officials and 6 non-officials; the 8 Noes were all non-officials.

[60] Van der Poel, pp. 131–6.

which was already connected with Durban, was connected with the line from the Cape to Johannesburg at Kroonstad, and in fulfilment of an agreement made with Natal in 1905 the C.S.A.R. reduced the through rates from Durban over the new line to the northern Orange River Colony with the result that Durban was able to acquire control of the trade of that area. Natal protested against the effect of the new rates from the Cape ports to the south-western Transvaal. The Cape Colony went further, threatening to apply rebates on traffic from her ports to the northern Orange River Colony to offset the reduction in the rates from Durban—a flagrant breach of the agreement which had been made in Pietermaritzburg that there would be no unilateral alteration of rates.

By this time the Cape Colony was also becoming involved in a quarrel with the C.S.A.R., whom she accused of applying rates which were contrary to the resolutions of the Pietermaritzburg Conference. The C.S.A.R. were not impressed by the Cape arguments and the Cape announced her intention to apply rebates to offset the alleged errors.

On two other issues the Cape Colony and Natal joined forces against the C.S.A.R. They contended, firstly, that the *modus vivendi* should be construed as meaning that in applying the reductions in the through rates which had been agreed upon at Pietermaritzburg, proportionate reductions could have been made in the preference accorded to Delagoa Bay; and, secondly, that Delagoa Bay traffic was not entitled to a preference over traffic along the routes which were opened after the *modus vivendi* was signed—that is to say, the routes from the Cape via Fourteen Streams and Klerksdorp and from Durban via Harrismith and Kroonstad. On these points Selborne took legal opinion, which was in support of the contentions of the coastal colonies, who then demanded that the C.S.A.R. should give effect to them. This the C.S.A.R. would not do because the Portuguese were entitled at any time to denounce the *modus vivendi* and thereby to put an end to the recruiting of Mozambique labour for the Transvaal gold-mines.[61]

The result was that by August 1906 the fragile balance of the economic relations between the colonies had been broken and a rates war had commenced. The Cape was giving rebates to offset the effect of the new rates from Durban to the northern Orange River Colony; Natal was about to retort by giving similar rebates on her traffic to the Orange River Colony; and both the Cape and Natal were threatening rebates to offset the C.S.A.R.'s 'misinterpretation' of the Pietermaritzburg

---

[61] *Modus vivendi*, art. XIII: '. . . As soon as the *modus vivendi* is denounced by either of the parties, the engagement of natives in the Province of Mozambique will be *ipso facto* suspended.'

decisions. However, the last word lay with the C.S.A.R., which threatened to nullify the effects of all such rebates by imposing countervailing rates over the C.S.A.R. sections of the through lines. Protesting vigorously but vainly, the Cape and Natal then yielded, and in December 1906 a conference of railway managers met at Bloemfontein to patch up an agreement, which gave Natal the advantage in the northern Orange River Colony and the Cape a concession in the C.S.A.R. rates, but preserved the Delagoa Bay preference in its entirety. The fire was thus temporarily brought under control: but it was obvious that it might break out again in any direction at any moment.

It did break out in a totally new quarter in the middle of 1907. The competition between the ports was affected not only by the railway rates but also by the sea freights from Europe. When, therefore, F. R. Moor, the Prime Minister of Natal, announced that he had obtained from the shipping ring which monopolized the South African trade a reduction in the sea freights to Durban, as from 1 July 1907, there was consternation in the Transvaal and the Cape Colony. The Transvaal protested that the reduction would overthrow the whole of the rates concordat and diminish the revenues of the C.S.A.R., and announced her intention to impose countervailing railway rates. It then transpired that the reduction in the freights was to apply to Delagoa Bay as well as to Durban, so that only the Cape ports would be placed at a disadvantage. This crisis was eventually overcome on 6 July 1907, when Moor, Jameson, and Botha met in Bloemfontein and managed to preserve the *status quo* by allowing the Cape a rebate on railway rates equivalent to the reduction in the sea freights to Durban and Delagoa Bay.[62]

By that time the Botha Government had given notice that the Transvaal intended to withdraw from the Customs Union—notice which was due to expire on 1 July 1908. The events of the past few years had shown, however, that there was no way of regulating the customs tariff and the railway rates to the satisfaction of all the colonies. The high tariff need of the coastal colonies clashed with the low tariff need of the Transvaal. The coastal colonies' appetite for the Transvaal trade clashed with the Transvaal's interest in the Delagoa Bay route. Recent events had also shown that the Transvaal held the whip hand. Thanks to her possession of the one great industry in all South Africa, the coastal colonies had become dependent upon her; and thanks to the position of Delagoa Bay, she could afford to be independent of them. Economic factors therefore pointed to two possibilities. Either the four colonies could go their

[62] *Cape Hansard, 1907*, pp. 91, 175; *Transvaal Leg. Ass. Deb., 1907*, cols. 1009–11; Transvaal Archives, Prime Minister, LVIII; Natal Archives, Prime Minister, CIII.

separate ways, in which case the Transvaal (in association, no doubt, with the Orange River Colony) would be able to prosper by setting up a customs barrier against Natal and the Cape and concentrating her trade through Delagoa Bay, and the coastal colonies would be hard put to make ends meet; or the four colonies could join in a political union and thus bury the causes of their disputes. But one thing was clear: the half-way house of a customs union, buttressed by railway agreements, between independent administrations, had been tried and found wanting.

CHAPTER II

THE IMPULSE TOWARDS UNION

1. THE KINDERGARTEN TAKE THE INITIATIVE

AFTER Lord Milner's departure from South Africa in April 1905, most of the men he had brought out from England to occupy the key posts in the Transvaal Administration continued to serve under Lord Selborne until the introduction of responsible government. They included Patrick Duncan, the Colonial Secretary, Lionel Curtis, the Assistant Colonial Secretary, Lionel Hichens, the Colonial Treasurer, Richard Feetham, the Town Clerk of Johannesburg, John Dove, the Assistant Town Clerk, Robert Brand, the Secretary of the Intercolonial Council, and Philip Kerr, the Assistant Secretary. In addition, Geoffrey Robinson, Milner's former private secretary, remained in the country as editor of the Johannesburg *Star*, and Dougal Malcolm, Lord Selborne's private secretary, became accepted by the others as one of themselves. That these men had exceptional and diverse talents is shown by their subsequent careers.[1] At that time they were still very young—when Milner left South Africa Patrick Duncan, the oldest, was 34 and Philip Kerr, the youngest, was not quite 23—and the appellation, 'the Kindergarten', which had originally been a gibe, had passed into common usage. They were all bachelors and some of them lived together in 'Moot House' in Johannesburg, where they would talk freely when the day's work was over. During 1906 the imminence of self-government in the Transvaal and the Orange River Colony, the growth of isolationist sentiment in the Transvaal, and, above all, the intensity of the economic friction between the colonies caused them serious anxiety. They feared that South Africa

[1] Sir Patrick Duncan (1870–1943) was Governor-General of the Union of South Africa from 1937 until his death. Lionel Curtis (1872–1955) became an influential writer on imperial and international affairs. The Hon. Richard Feetham (b. 1874) was a Judge of the Appellate Division of the Supreme Court of South Africa and is now Chancellor of the University of the Witwatersrand. John Dove (1872–1934) became editor of the *Round Table*. Lord Brand (b. 1878) is a leading British financier. Philip Kerr, Marquis of Lothian (1882–1940), was British Ambassador to Washington at the time of his death. Geoffrey Robinson (Dawson) (1872–1944) became editor of *The Times*. Sir Dougal Malcolm (1877–1954) was President of the British South Africa Company from 1937 until his death. On the Kindergarten see Basil Williams, introduction to *The Selborne Memorandum* (Oxford, 1925); Lionel Curtis, *With Milner in South Africa* (Oxford, 1951), pp. 344–6; and Vladimir Halpérin, *Lord Milner and the Empire* (London, 1952), pp. 198–220.

was drifting apart into two or more mutually hostile groupings and they came to the conclusion that it was essential, both for the Empire and for South Africa, that the centrifugal forces should be checked before they became irrevocably triumphant.

Richard Feetham was the first to record these thoughts systematically. He did so in a paper which he read to his colleagues and some of their Johannesburg business friends on 4 October 1906.[2]

His main point was

that the time has come when federation can no longer be left to adorn the perorations of after-dinner speeches, and the preambles of political pro-grammes: it is no longer to be treated merely as a vague and pious aspira-tion, the fulfilment of which we may leave to some political genius of the next century: it is rather something for which we have to think out at once a concrete plan—a definite goal to which it is our business to find the best and shortest way, and to start at once.

Feetham considered that there had been 'a general advance to this point of view during the past few months' due to the combined action of Trans-vaal and Natal forces against 'a common peril', the Natal Native rebels, and to 'an unmistakeable demonstration, afforded by the railway rate war, of the difficulties and dangers which are inseparable from the present condition of disunion'. He then went on to list four reasons 'which make it our business to worry about the difficulties of federation now, instead of comfortably waiting for them to settle themselves. . . .'

The first was that

The longer we wait, the greater will be the difficulties, because the greater the estrangement between the different Colonies, the greater the growth of incompatible vested interests, [and] the stronger the forces of Colonial as opposed to National sentiment.

The second,

Disunion in South Africa means a weakening of the Imperial tie, because on the one hand intervention of the Imperial Government is demanded in inter-colonial disputes, and its action or inaction is equally a source of com-plaint and resentment; on the other, the Imperial Government is itself tempted or driven to intervene in local questions in a manner which would be unthought of if there was a Federal Government which could speak and act for the whole of South Africa. . . .

---

[2] Richard Feetham, 'Some Problems of South African Federation and Reasons for Facing Them', being a paper read to the Fortnightly Club, Johannesburg, on 4 Oct. 1906.

The third,

The present state of affairs makes for a South Africa which will be Dutch rather than British in sentiment and character, because the quarrels between the Colonies affect in the main the interests of the British commercial communities, and do not disturb to anything like the same extent the natural solidarity of the agricultural population. . . . There is the further consideration that, once their representatives meet in the same Parliament, the influence of British communities, on those points on which they are disposed to think alike because they are British, will be able to make itself felt with new force throughout South Africa.

And, lastly,

Under present conditions we cannot expect to reach economic stability. We may patch up customs conventions for short periods, but, as long as the negotiators have to act as the delegates of five or six different States instead of as representatives of one people, it is extremely improbable that any durable fiscal arrangements can be arrived at. . . .

Feetham's colleagues agreed with this analysis and from then onwards they all gave their unqualified support to the closer union movement[3] which culminated in the creation of the Union of South Africa. They realized that they would have to tread extremely warily, for they knew that the attempt of Lord Carnarvon to federate South Africa in the 1870's had failed largely because it had been organized and directed from Britain. Closer union would not be promoted by any overt action or initiative from the Colonial Office or from the British officials in South Africa. It must be an indigenous product. The Kindergarten could, however, give an immense fillip to the centripetal forces inside South Africa by pointing out the consequences of continued disunion.

Late in October 1906 Lionel Curtis resigned from his official appointment to devote himself to this task. Curtis was probably not the wisest member of the Kindergarten, but he had the sort of mind which produces powerful propaganda once it is convinced that a cause is important because it becomes obsessed by it. From 1906 to 1910 closer union in South Africa was Curtis's passion.[4] First he toured the four colonies, sounding out opinion and collecting information. Next he wrote a draft memorandum rehearsing the arguments for closer union. The draft was then discussed and slightly amended by other members of the Kinder-

---

[3] At this stage the words 'union', 'federation', and 'closer union' were used almost indiscriminately in South Africa. The question whether the Constitution should be unitary or federal is dealt with in Chapter III (2) below.

[4] Thereafter Curtis devoted himself successively to imperial federation and world federation.

garten and towards the end of December 1906 it was printed and a copy was handed to the High Commissioner.[5]

Selborne had been kept informed of the trend in Kindergarten thinking and he, too, agreed with the views which Feetham had outlined in October. His experience as High Commissioner had convinced him that the railway and customs agreements between the colonies could not be patched up much longer, and to the argument that a prematurely united South Africa might fall under Afrikaner domination he replied that only a united country could acquire enough economic stability to attract a large and continuous stream of British immigrants, so that closer union was the surest way of creating a British political majority in South Africa.[6] Moreover, Selborne probably knew that the British Government was beginning to regard an Anglo-German conflict as likely—and it was obviously desirable to consolidate the British position in South Africa before such a war broke out.[7] Accordingly he welcomed the draft memorandum. He approved of most of it as it stood and made a number of amendments.

The memorandum started with a section on the 'Historical Cause of South African disunion'. Its central argument was as follows: The two white races of South Africa were destined to fuse with one another on account of their similar Teutonic origin and the widespread distribution of members of each race in all parts of the country. South Africa had not become disunited because of racial differences between Boer and Briton, but rather because the colonists had had no say in the government of the Cape Colony in the first half of the nineteenth century. Thanks to men like Lord Durham and Lord Elgin it had subsequently become an 'axiom of British policy that any attempt to manage the domestic affairs of a white population by a continuous exercise of the direct authority of the Imperial Parliament, in which the people concerned are not represented, is, save under very special circumstances, a certain path to failure'.[8] Each of the four main British colonies in South Africa now had (or soon would have) independence in respect of its strictly internal affairs, but that did not mean that they had independence in respect of the internal affairs of South Africa as a whole. Their disunion led to intercolonial disputes,

---

[5] On the circumstances of the compilation of what became known as the Selborne Memorandum, see Basil Williams, op. cit., pp. xvi–xxi. The printer's proofs of the draft, dated 19 and 21 Dec. 1906, are in the library of Rhodes House, Oxford.

[6] He stated this very clearly in a private letter to Duncan, dated 30 Nov. 1907, Duncan Papers. This letter is quoted below on p. 80.

[7] The attitude of the British Government is discussed below in Chapter VII (1).

[8] Cd. 3564 (1907), *Papers relating to a Federation of the South African Colonies*, p. 13.

which were referred to the High Commissioner, who was subject to the control of the British Government and the British Parliament. Only through closer union could South Africans acquire full control of their own affairs. The next two parts of the memorandum showed at some length that closer union was the only adequate solution of the railway and customs problems. Part IV dealt with the Native and Labour questions. The white people of South Africa, it declared, were committed to the exceptionally difficult task of establishing 'a self-contained and self-governing society on the base of a race utterly removed from themselves in descent, habits, and civilisation'.[9] Self-governing colonies should be fully responsible for their own internal security: but it was open to question whether each South African colony, separately, could assume this responsibility, although there was no doubt that united South Africa could do so. Moreover, continued disunion would mean the continuation of different native policies by the different colonies, and sooner or later they would clash, whereas union would enable the people of South Africa to devise and apply a single policy, and it would also cause the necessary qualities of wisdom, courage, and endurance to 'be summoned into action' for this purpose. What that policy would or should be the memorandum did not suggest, beyond the general affirmation that

History will record no nobler triumph than that of the people of South Africa if they extend the hand of sympathy to the coloured people, who are differentiated from the natives by their infusion of white blood, and to the educated native, and if they succeed in peacefully leading on the upward path of Christianity and of civilization the vast tribes who are beginning to emerge from barbarism.[10]

Only a Central Government, furthermore, would be in a position to make the most effective use of the native labour resources of South Africa, on which every industry in the country relied, and only such a Government would be able to decide in the interests of the country as a whole whether to continue to import Indian, Chinese, or other labour from overseas. The next sections predicted that the establishment of a Central Government would also give a tremendous impetus to the material progress of South Africa and provide the means whereby the people would be able to control the development of their hinterland—the territories to the north of the Limpopo. The matter was urgent, however. The disputes arising from the completion of the railway lines between Klerksdorp and Fourteen Streams and between Bethlehem and Kroonstad had only been temporarily patched up. Soon a railway conference would have to be held and then the political situation of South Africa as a whole would be the subject of deliberate discussion by all the governments of South Africa. If the conference broke up, there would be a rate war. The British ports would lower rates to compete with Delagoa Bay. The Central South African Railways would then be obliged, under the *modus vivendi*, either to reduce rates from Delagoa Bay or to impose countervailing rates against the coastal colonies. This would make the British South African ports face ruin. The Cape Colony and Natal governments would be financially embarrassed and they would appeal to the High Commissioner—and so the imperial power would become the arbiter between contending British colonies on a matter of strictly domestic concern to South Africa. The leaders of South Africa should therefore postpone all subsidiary questions 'until by a great constitutional reform they have secured to her people the means of considering and deciding them as a whole'.[11] When the people of Canada had been confronted with a similar problem, they had been able to unite within three years from the time when the movement first began. The people of South Africa could do the same, provided that they acted wisely.

South Africans may well ask themselves from what calamities would not their country have been saved, if fifty or even thirty years ago, by a movement born of the soil and nurtured by their own statesmen, the federation of South Africa had been accomplished. Shall it fall to the lot of your children hereafter to have to ask themselves the same question?[12]

This memorandum was strong in its analysis of the economic problems confronting South Africa, but it contained little that was original or profound in the field of political philosophy. The arguments for colonial self-government and federation which Lord Durham had enunciated for the Canadian colonists in 1839 and which had become a commonplace in the intervening years were applied without qualification to other white communities in an entirely different context where they were greatly outnumbered by native Africans. It was naïve to assert that Boer and Briton would easily fuse into a single nation without weighing the effects of their linguistic and other differences. It was also naïve to assume—as appears to have been assumed in the section on the native question—that if they were united white South Africans would deal wisely with the non-white majority of the inhabitants of the country. Apart from an occasional flourish, the document was exclusively concerned with the interests of white South Africans. This was a far cry from the attitude which had prevailed in former times, when a British

---

[11] Cd. 3564, p. 59.   [12] Ibid., p. 61.

Colonial Secretary had expressed doubts about the wisdom of granting representative institutions to a colony with a heterogeneous population like the Cape of Good Hope:

When I bear in mind how powerful, indeed how nearly irresistible, is the authority of an elected Legislature in the colony which it represents, I cannot regard as a matter of secondary concern the adjustment and balance of that authority in such a manner as may prevent its being perverted into a means of gratifying the antipathies of a dominant caste, or of promoting their own interests or prejudices, at the expense of those of other and less powerful classes.[13]

The memorandum also carefully soft-pedalled the imperial objectives which its authors had in mind,[14] because the authors realized that they would be anathema to many white South Africans. Nevertheless—indeed for these very reasons—it was a skilful piece of propaganda, containing precisely the sort of argument that was likely to appeal to a majority of the voters and politicians in South Africa, including the Afrikaners whose support was essential if a united and loyal white South African State was to be created. It was a call to white South Africans to unite in their own interests.[15]

Selborne and the Kindergarten had decided that the memorandum would have most effect if it was issued under the authority of the High Commissioner himself; but in that event they realized that it was necessary to take pains to avoid giving the impression that he was trying to interfere. Accordingly, Curtis visited Jameson, the Prime Minister of the Cape Colony, in November 1906, and told him what was afoot.[16] Jameson at once fell in with the idea, and on 28 November he addressed a Minute to the Governor of the Cape Colony, drawing attention to the intercolonial friction and recommending that the High Commissioner should be asked 'to review the situation in such a manner that the public may be informed as to the general position of affairs throughout the country', with the object of giving 'the people of South Africa . . . a timely opportunity of expressing a voice upon the desirability, and, if acknowledged, the best means, of bringing about a central national Government embracing all the Colonies and Protectorates under British

[13] Lord Stanley to Sir George Napier, Governor of the Cape of Good Hope, 15 Apr. 1842; quoted in K. N. Bell and W. P. Morrell, *Select Documents on British Colonial Policy, 1830–1860* (Oxford, 1928), p. 51.

[14] See above, pp. 61–63.

[15] Comparison of the December proofs with the final version of the memorandum shows that it was Curtis who had almost completely ignored the humanitarian strand in the British imperial tradition and that Lord Selborne had sought to introduce it.

[16] Information conveyed to the author by Lionel Curtis in a letter dated 18 Jan. 1952.

South African administration'.[17] On receiving this Minute Lord Selborne sent copies of it to the governments of Natal, the Transvaal, the Orange River Colony, and Southern Rhodesia, asking them for their views.[18] They all agreed that the High Commissioner should review the situation, but the crown colony governments of the Transvaal and the Orange River Colony tactfully added that they could not bind their successors to any particular line of action.[19] With the ground thus prepared Selborne addressed a dispatch to the Governor of the Cape Colony on 7 January 1907.[20] At the outset he disclaimed any intention of interfering in the internal affairs of South Africa:

To review the present situation in South Africa in such a manner that the public may be informed as to the general position of affairs throughout the country is a task which I should never have undertaken had I not been requested to do so by those who have a right to demand my services—the Ministers of the responsible governing Colonies of Cape Colony and Natal. It is my dearest conviction that no healthy movement towards federation can emanate from any authority other than the people of South Africa themselves; but, when I am called upon by those occupying the most representative and responsible positions in the country to furnish such material as is in my possession, for the information of the people of South Africa, it is clearly my duty to comply with the request.

He then proceeded to draw attention to the main points in the memorandum.

Three choices, therefore [he wrote] lie before the people of South Africa, the make-shift régime of the High Commissioner, the jarring separatism of the States of South America, the noble union of the States of North America. . . .

What South Africa requires more than anything else is stability—stability in political conditions, stability in economic conditions, stability in industrial conditions. . . . But true stability will remain impossible so long as there are five separate governments in South Africa, each developing a different system in all branches of public life and each a potential antagonist of the other, but no one national government with authority to harmonise the whole.

He concluded with an explanation that the memorandum was based on the work of others, but that he personally had edited it and accepted 'the entire responsibility'. He enclosed the memorandum itself, which he called 'A Review of the Present Mutual Relations of the British South

---

[17] Cd. 3564, pp. 4–5.   [18] Ibid., p. 9.

[19] Ibid., pp. 10–12.   [20] Ibid., pp. 5–9.

African Colonies',[21] and at the same time he sent copies of his dispatch and the memorandum to the governments of Natal, the Transvaal, the Orange River Colony, and Southern Rhodesia.[22] Later in January he sent to the same authorities a supplementary memorandum on 'South African Railway Unification and its effect on Railway Rates', which had been prepared by Philip Kerr, the Assistant Secretary of the Inter-colonial Council.[23]

The memorandum having thus been placed in the hands of the South African governments, it remained to decide when and how to release it for publication. At first Lord Selborne was inclined to publish it at once, in the hope that it would stem the drift towards isolationism in the Transvaal,[24] but the Natal Government advised him to hold it over until the new Transvaal Government had taken office and settled down, lest it should become 'the medium of electioneering eloquence',[25] and the advice was accepted. Meanwhile, an effort was made to pave the way by preliminary propaganda and by winning the support of leaders of both the main parties in the Transvaal. Already, on 30 November 1906, Patrick Duncan had spoken at length at a St Andrew's night banquet in Johannesburg of the troubles that beset South Africa and asserted that 'the cure is union'.[26] During January 1907 Lionel Curtis broached the subject in discussion with Smuts; and Abe Bailey, a leading Witwaters-rand mine-director and Progressive politician, tried to arrange a dinner party for the delegates to the Intercolonial Defence Conference,[27] and for Botha, Smuts, and others. Inviting Botha to attend, Duncan explained that the guests would be asked 'to consider whether a movement can be made at the present time in which men of all political parties can join to help forward the cause of union'.[28] Writing to Smuts, Curtis more explicitly outlined a scheme for the foundation of a national organization, to be presided over by the chief justices of the four colonies, to spread the gospel of closer union, to collect and disseminate relevant facts, and to publish a South African *Federalist*.[29] However, the Het Volk leaders declined to be drawn to Bailey's table for reasons which will appear later, and Bailey was left with the lesser satisfaction of public oratory in

[21] Ibid., pp. 12–61.   [22] Ibid., p. 3.
[23] Ibid., pp. 64–108.
[24] Selborne to Duncan, 31 Dec. 1906, Duncan Papers.
[25] Sir Henry McCallum, Governor of Natal, to Selborne, 2 Feb. 1907, Natal Archives, Prime Minister, CIII (copy).
[26] *Star*, 1 Dec. 1906.
[27] On the Intercolonial Defence Conference held in Johannesburg on 21–24 Jan. 1907, see above, pp. 48–49.
[28] Duncan to Botha, 8 Jan. 1907, Duncan Papers (copy).
[29] Curtis to Smuts, 7 Jan. 1907, Smuts Papers.

favour of closer union.[30] The search for bi-partisan support was then switched to the Cape Colony where F. S. Malan, the rising star of the Afrikaner Bond, had already come out for federation in six articles published in *Ons Land*.[31] Sir Percy Fitzpatrick advocated closer union to a packed meeting in the City Hall in Cape Town on 15 March 1907,[32] and Curtis scraped up an acquaintance with Malan and eventually gave him a copy of the Selborne Memorandum, arranging to meet him three days later to receive his verdict. Let Curtis explain what then transpired:

I found Malan sitting on Rhodes's bench with the Selborne Memorandum in his hand. He said nothing for five minutes. When I could bear it no longer I said, 'Well?' 'Publish it,' he said. That was all that passed, and I hastened back to Groot Schuur and told Dr. Jim [Jameson] what Malan had said.[33]

It was then arranged that at the beginning of the next session of the Cape Parliament, in June 1907, Malan would move for the tabling of the memorandum and the dispatch, which would then be published. To appreciate what followed it is necessary to consider the thoughts of the leaders of the South African Party, the Orangia Unie, and Het Volk.

2. THE SOUTH AFRICAN RESPONSE

The policy of uniting the British South African colonies was also uppermost in the thoughts of J. X. Merriman, J. C. Smuts, and M. T. Steyn—three of the most prominent leaders of the anti-imperialist parties of the Cape Colony, the Transvaal, and the Orange River Colony. Since they lived in different parts of South Africa, the development of their ideas and their tactics is clearly revealed in their correspondence, most of which has fortunately been preserved. Merriman was a prolific letter-writer. He wrote freely, and rarely attempted to conceal his prejudices. Already, before the outbreak of the South African War, he had exchanged letters with Steyn and Smuts, and after the Peace of Vereeniging he embarked on a correspondence with both of them which became extensive and intimate. Steyn responded cordially, although his weak eyes and shaky hands made him rely on his wife for most of his writing and much of his reading. His letters were briefer than Merriman's, but

[30] *Rand Daily Mail*, 11 Jan. 1907.

[31] Malan's articles were originally published in *Ons Land* on 30 Aug. and 1, 4, 6, 8, and 11 Sept. 1906. English translations appeared in the *Star* on 17, 19, and 22 Sept. and 3 Oct. 1906. The Dutch version has been republished in Johann F. Preller (ed.), *Die Konvensie-Dagboek van sy edelagbare François Stephanus Malan, 1908–1909* (Cape Town, 1951), pp. 252–69.   [32] *Cape Times*, 16 Mar. 1907.

[33] Curtis to the author, 18 Jan. 1952.

they convey a deep sincerity. He and Merriman were drawn to one another by respect for each other's conduct during the war and by a common conviction that the 'Imperialists' and the 'Magnates' were at the root of all evil in South Africa. Smuts, clear-sighted, ambitious, and logical to a fault, also shared that conviction until responsible government had been introduced into the Transvaal, and he and Merriman derived intellectual stimulation from each other's letters. On the other hand, although the relations between their families were cordial, Steyn and Smuts do not appear to have confided in one another as freely as they did with Merriman on political issues.

These three men determined the timing of the unification movement. They prevented it from becoming dynamic before their parties had assumed office in all three colonies, and directly that political swing had been completed in February 1908 they accelerated and controlled it, while the members of the Kindergarten adopted the subordinate role of expert advisers and propagandists.

It was Smuts who first elaborated the idea that South Africa should be united as a means of reducing the weight of the imperial factor in South Africa. To Merriman as early as 30 May 1904 he wrote:[34]

I look upon the Jingo fever as a moral and political distemper which must work its way. . . . But the renovating influences are at work, the fever has even now passed its crisis, and the future improvement may be more rapid than we think. . . . I believe thoroughly in liberty, in patriotism and in those who are faithful to South Africa; the future is with them—and sooner than we think we shall find that Imperialism has spent its force and has come down never to rise again in South Africa.

After describing the recent Boer congress in Pretoria, he continued:

We must now try to lay the common foundation for the politics of the future, when Federation would have consolidated the popular party in South Africa just as it has consolidated the labour party in Australia; and I am sincerely anxious that that foundation shall be a durable one in all respects. Don't you think that as soon as the liberals get into power we ought to make a move in the direction of federation? That would perhaps take us out of the narrow rut into which we have been getting and supply a larger and ampler ideal for South African patriotism. You know with the Boers 'United S.A.' has always been a deeply-felt political aspiration and it might profitably be substituted for the Imperialism which imports Chinese, a foreign bureaucracy, and a foreign standing army.

During the following two and a half years Smuts concentrated his

[34] Merriman Papers.

energies on organizing Het Volk, securing the Transvaal Constitution, and winning the Transvaal elections, but each of these steps he regarded as a stepping-stone to union. On 13 March 1906 he informed Merriman:[35]

It seems to me that in Federation or Unification lies the solution of our and your troubles. If Hoggenheimer has to do, not only with the crippled population of the Transvaal, but with the people of South Africa, there will be some chance of keeping him in his right place politically. But the only way of bringing about that consummation is to introduce into the Transvaal such a Constitution as will give the general population and not the mining population the balance of power.

On 30 August he added:[36]

As I gauge the situation in South Africa, the currents are slowly but steadily setting in the right direction. . . . But after all I come round to my conviction that unless the power of the magnates in the Transvaal is broken by our entry into a Unified or Federal South Africa, the danger of their capturing supreme power here and so over the rest of South Africa (which they will rout piecemeal) will continue to exist. . . . We must checkmate them by working for the only real and possible Union—viz. of all South Africa.

And again, on 23 December 1906:[37]

Believe me, as long as we stand divided and separated in S.A. the money power will beat us in the Transvaal first and as a consequence over the rest of South Africa. I know the practical difficulties. . . . But once we are convinced that that way alone lies the true solution and the triumph of the people's interest all over South Africa we should go that way and not be deterred by practical difficulties . . . let us . . . proceed to lay the foundation of a united South African people.

Merriman and Steyn, older than Smuts and more suspicious and pessimistic by nature, did not at first view the project with enthusiasm. Replying to Smuts's first letter on the subject on 4 June 1904, Merriman indeed wrote:[38]

I am extremely glad that you are taking up the question of Federation or Union. . . . I quite agree with you that the time has come for discussion which should be by a convention of *elected* delegates.

But he hastened to add:

The danger is that we may have some scheme evolved from a packed nominated 'Conference.' Such a body in fact as those which have done much

35 Merriman Papers.   36 Ibid.
37 Ibid.   38 Smuts Papers.

harm already. I must say that no doubt with the best intentions Lord Milner in his attempts at federation by means of material interests reminds me of the famous projector in the Lagado academy who had a plan for building a house from the roof downwards.

In October 1905 (before the change of Government in England), he was inclined to despair of the Transvaal and counselled Steyn:[39]

The only prospect that I can see lies in a rapprochement between the O.F. Colony and the Cape—when we could isolate the elements that are non S. African and leave them to stew in their own juice. I have long since mentioned the matter to A. Fischer and I am convinced that some union between the O.R.C. and the Cape Colony will be the only chance to set up some sort of barrier against the demoralisation of the whole of S. Africa on the Joberg model.

Steyn, too, took a long time to emerge from his mood of post-war depression, and in June 1905 he was still wondering 'if happiness will ever return to this land again'.[40] By November that year, however, he was becoming more sanguine and he asserted that the ultimate solution lay in a general South African Union.[41] Soon afterwards, when the Liberals had come into power in England, Merriman suggested to Steyn that a National Convention should be elected to take the settlement of South African affairs out of the hands of Downing Street, and Steyn agreed in principle, though he doubted whether the Free Staters were ready for radical changes.[42]

During 1906, however, Merriman became deeply suspicious that Selborne and the Kindergarten were trying to push through a partisan scheme of union from above. This suspicion was in the centre of his thoughts until 1908, and he did his best to implant it in the minds of Steyn and Smuts. The unification of South Africa, he warned Steyn, 'can only be effected by S. Africans and "Gàre au Selborne"! he is in some ways more dangerous than Milner'.[43] 'Festina lente', he cautioned Smuts.[44] And again, replying to Smuts's enthusiastic letter of December 1906:[45]

I was greatly interested in what you write about federation. Do not think

[39] 27 Oct. 1905, Steyn Papers.
[40] Steyn to Merriman, 27 June 1905, Merriman Papers.
[41] Steyn to Merriman, 10 Nov. 1905, ibid.
[42] Merriman's letter has not been preserved, but its tenor is clear from Steyn's reply, dated 5 Jan. 1906, ibid.
[43] Merriman to Steyn, 9 Feb. 1906, Steyn Papers.
[44] Merriman to Smuts, 6 Dec. 1906, Smuts Papers.
[45] Merriman to Smuts, 30 Dec. 1906, ibid.

me luke warm in wishing to unite. Only—timeo Danaos—I do not want to
see any union hastily patched up with a view of serving the ends of Imperialism, that the whole of S. Africa may have one neck in order to fit the yoke
easier on to it.

To his intense relief, they came to agree with him and by the end of
January 1907 the position had been reached where Merriman, Steyn, and
Smuts accepted the need for an early union, but agreed that it should not
be pushed before Het Volk were in power in the Transvaal, the Unie in
the Orange River Colony, and the South African Party in the Cape
Colony. That was why Smuts and Botha refused the invitation to attend
Abe Bailey's dinner. Reporting to Merriman, Smuts wrote:[46]

one cannot shut one's eyes to the fact that there are sinister influences at
work—submarine operations which will have to be carefully watched.
Bailey wants to run Federation as a sort of Barnum policy to advertise himself; some other highly placed persons want to achieve their ambitious hopes,
and others no doubt have purely personal ends to serve. Still, the thing itself
is very good, and if it is initiated in the proper spirit and from and on the
right basis, a tremendous step in advance will be achieved. I would however
wait until there is Selfgovernment in the O.R.C. and a general election at
the Cape has given the quietus to the Jameson crowd.

Steyn agreed:[47]

I see no reason why we should rush the settlement of this delicate question. . . . Whatever happens I do not think that any steps ought to be taken
before the new Governments are in full working order.

And in February 1907 Smuts reiterated:[48]

I hope your party will soon be victorious at the Cape, so that a great
forward start could be made all over South Africa. There will be a great
chance which we ought never to miss.

This was the strategy which Merriman feared would be ruined by
Malan's 'leaning to compromise'.[49] Obsessed by the spectre of an imperialist plot, Merriman did all he could to prevent any immediate move
towards union, persuading Steyn to put pressure on Malan and issuing
a public warning against 'hasty and premature federation'.[50] Nevertheless, Malan decided to make a cautious move in that direction. At his
instigation the Bond Congress, meeting at Middelburg on 25 March

[46] Smuts to Merriman, 25 Jan. 1907, Merriman Papers.
[47] Steyn to Merriman, 30 Jan. 1907, ibid.
[48] Smuts to Merriman, 25 Feb. 1907, ibid.
[49] Merriman to Steyn, 31 Jan. 1907, Steyn Papers.
[50] Speaking at Stellenbosch, 17 Mar. 1907, Cape Times, 18 Mar.

1907, unanimously resolved that 'no practical steps ought to be taken towards the political union of South Africa until responsible government has been put into force in the Transvaal and Orange River Colony, and that the Bond should actively cultivate a favourable feeling towards this end and should endeavour during the forthcoming session to obtain an Intercolonial Commission of Enquiry into the matter'.[51] Even this was too much for Merriman, who feared Malan would 'run us all into a mess by adopting some of Selborne's ideas on Federation' and cause South Africans to be 'dragged at the wheels of the Imperial Chariot or the mine owners' mud cart'.[52] To Steyn he explained his fears at length in a characteristic letter written on 21 June:[53]

Of course if the same parties who brought on the war can divert attention from their misgovernment to the broader *and vaguer* issue of Federation they will be charmed but for us to assist them seems to me as wise as if a commando were to go off hare hunting. Find out what your enemy wants and don't do it is a wise maxim. I think in the present juncture all our energies should be concentrated on getting South African governments in the Cape, O.R.C. and Transvaal—Natal is past praying for—then we may proceed to a National Convention on elected lines to consider this great and complicated question. To begin by a series of nominated conferences under the auspices of Lord Selborne seems to me foolish and likely to defeat its end. Any union to be strong and lasting must proceed from the people and be founded on a broad South African spirit not on the imperial ambition of those who care not one jot for this country. If you agree with me I wish you would utter a word of caution. Malan . . . is too good a fellow and too great a South African asset to be swallowed by the Capitalist boa-constrictor who is now engaged in besliming him previous to deglutition.

When the Cape Parliament met, Malan's question duly led, on 3 July, to the tabling of the Selborne Memorandum, together with the related correspondence.[54] At the same time the documents were released to the press. They included a Minute by the Transvaal Government, pointing out that the correspondence had preceded their assumption of office, emphasizing their friendly feelings towards Portugal, and expressing the hope that the question of South African federation would be solved in such a way as to 'extend the comity of South African co-operation to the province of Mozambique'.[55] The Transvaal Government was in fact

[51] Ibid., 26 Mar. 1907.
[52] Merriman to Steyn, 20 Apr. and 14 June 1907, Steyn Papers.
[53] Ibid.
[54] The question was asked by N. F. de Waal for F. S. Malan (who was absent) on 25 June and the papers were tabled on 3 July. *Cape Hansard, 1907*, pp. 14, 83.
[55] Cd. 3564, p. 108.

anxious not to jeopardize the Mozambique labour supply and even hoped it might contrive to include Mozambique in a South African federation.[56]

The memorandum had a cordial reception from the South African press, which considered that it arrayed the facts lucidly and temperately, crystallized ideas which had previously been vaguely expressed, and gave a stimulus to the adoption of closer union as an immediate policy, instead of merely leaving it as a remote ideal. English-medium newspapers such as the *Natal Mercury* went so far as to liken it to the Durham Report. The only dissenting voice came from the *South African News*, the Cape Town newspaper which was under Merriman's influence, and which considered that the memorandum breathed 'a spirit of panic and precipitation'.[57] Merriman also tried privately to turn his friends against it:[58]

Now comes in Lord Selborne's windy effusion [he informed Smuts]. Surely the price of flunkeyism can go no further than the attempt to compare it with Lord Durham's report. I do not think that it will do much to help the cause of union forward but it is useful as a warning of the spirit that is abroad that seeks to unite communities not on the basis of national aspirations but on that of material and trade interests with a strong Imperial bias. It will be a misfortune for all of us if we allow ourselves to be 'rushed' on those lines.

In the South African Party caucus he fought desperately to prevent Malan from giving effect to the resolution of the Bond Congress, but he failed, and on 23 July Malan moved:[59]

That in the opinion of this House it is desirable that the Government of this colony should, during the recess, approach the Governments of the other self-governing British colonies in South Africa to consider the advisability of taking preliminary steps to promote the union of British South Africa, the result of such negotiations to be laid before the next session of Parliament.

Malan paid a tribute to the Selborne Memorandum, which, he said, had made the question 'a practical and a non-party one', and he explained that he looked to the appointment of an Intercolonial Commission of

[56] Selborne to Duncan, 8 July 1907: 'I do not know what those words mean. I invented them on the spur of the moment. What my Ministers want is to include the Province of Mozambique within a South African Federation, though how they can do that without going to war and conquering that Province I cannot conceive.' Duncan Papers.
[57] *South African News*, 5 July 1907.
[58] 7 July 1907, Smuts Papers.   [59] *Cape Hansard, 1907*, p. 227.

Enquiry after the new Government had taken office in the Orange River Colony, to be followed by a 'conference of delegates from the different colonies', and that he did not expect that union would be consummated for at least five years. Jameson seconded the motion and referred to the same sort of procedure. The only other speaker was T. L. Schreiner, who sounded a note of caution. The Cape Colony, he said, should not 'purchase federation at the cost of the sacrifices of the civil and political rights of His Majesty's civilised and coloured people'. The motion was then carried without a division.[60]

These proceedings were, in fact, innocuous from Merriman's point of view, but he could not bring himself to think so and for a while he was estranged from Malan and distressed by his defeat in the caucus. Then Smuts and Steyn urged him not to throw cold water on the movement towards union, assured him that no action was contemplated before the new Orange River Colony Government was firmly in the saddle, and reminded him of the supreme importance of keeping the South African Party united,[61] while Malan was conciliatory; so that by October the damage had been repaired.[62] Merriman's attitude, however, had earned him the reputation of being an obstructor of union and Selborne had himself reached the conclusion that he was one of 'the narrowest minded men I have ever had to deal with', a man who 'would rather wreck Federation than co-operate with Jameson in any way'.[63]

Steyn agreed with Merriman about the Selborne Memorandum. 'The whole pamphlet', he wrote, 'is crude, full of rhetoric and bad history.'[64] Nevertheless, he was becoming aware that Canada and Australia were moving in the direction of national autonomy, and the knowledge was whetting his appetite for the unification of South Africa so that South Africa could move in the same direction. It is possible that he read Richard Jebb's *Studies in Colonial Nationalism*, in which Jebb contended that the advocates of imperial federation were unrealistic in failing to take account of colonial opinion and declared that the British Empire was becoming 'an alliance of independent nations'.[65] It is certain that he read André Siegfried's *The Race Question in Canada*.[66] Merriman had sent him a copy and he commented as follows:[67]

[60] Ibid., pp. 227–31.

[61] Smuts to Merriman, 15 July and 1 Aug. 1907; Steyn to Merriman, 10 Aug. 1907. Merriman Papers.

[62] Merriman to Smuts, 3 Oct. 1907: 'Malan's conduct has been beyond all praise.' Smuts Papers.   [63] Selborne to Duncan, 8 July 1907, Duncan Papers.

[64] Steyn to Merriman, 11 Sept. 1907, Merriman Papers.

[65] Richard Jebb, *Studies in Colonial Nationalism* (London, 1905), p. 273.

[66] André Siegfried, *The Race Question in Canada* (London, 1907).

[67] Steyn to Merriman, 4 Oct. 1907, Merriman Papers.

If Mr. Siegfried gives us a correct picture of the political state of Canada then it seems to me the trend of events is not making for the consolidation of the Empire, but rather for its peaceful dissolution. I am strengthened in this opinion by one of the latest speeches of Sir Wilfrid Laurier in which he advocated that Canada should be given [the] right to make treaties—in other words her own foreign office. If that is granted there will be only one step left to Complete Independence i.e. the election of her own Governor General.

The result was that at the end of 1907, with the Fischer Cabinet installed in the Orange River Colony and the general election in progress in the Cape, Steyn's usual caution became mixed with expectancy:[68]

We here all hope that . . . the S.A. party will soon be in office with a large majority. We feel it will not help much for us to be in power if you are not. I am not inclined to be in a hurry and yet when I think what a golden opportunity there will be for S.A. with our people in power all over S.A. I feel restless and would like if possible to hurry on events but now more than ever the old S. African adage 'zoetjes oor de klippe'[69] must be our watchword.

As for Smuts, he kept a clear grasp of the tactical situation throughout. It was he who discerned that the breakdown of the Customs Union provided not only a motive but also the occasion for a decisive step towards closer union. In July 1907 he summarized the prospects as follows:[70]

The problem of Federation is a great and noble one. . . . But we shall do nothing till affairs are straighter in the O.R.C. and at the Cape. That is why I am so anxious for an early change at the Cape. You know that early next year a fresh railway and customs conference will have to be held; that conference will be of the greatest importance and I could have wished that a new Cape Government could have taken part in it.

Towards the end of September, as the election campaign began in the Cape, he elaborated his ideas:[71]

Our wishes and prayers go with you, for much, very much for South Africa depends on your victory. By good fortune and hard work we have got together a majority here, which though apparently large is by no means stable. You will win at the Cape—and a unique opportunity will present itself for righting the situation in South Africa, an opportunity such as may not recur in our lifetime. The O.R.C. is all right, Natal also has a well-

[68] Steyn to Merriman, 27 Dec. 1907, Merriman Papers.
[69] Gently over the stones.
[70] Smuts to Merriman, 15 July 1907, Merriman Papers.
[71] Smuts to Merriman, 28 Sept. 1907, ibid.

disposed government. There is the chance to neutralize all the evil effects of the war, to weld South Africa into a compact South African nation, and to rid ourselves of the internal discords which always and inevitably invite Downing Street interference. . . . The Conference on Railway and Customs policy to be held next year will mark the cross-roads; if by any possibility we could make that the starting-point for a united South Africa, no consummation could be better. Otherwise I am afraid we shall drift further apart and develop vested rights alien to the establishment of Union.

During November Merriman visited the Transvaal and the Orange River Colony for discussions with Botha and Smuts and with Steyn and Fischer—discussions which increased the understanding between them. Merriman was 'immensely impressed' with Botha and he found Steyn 'wise and calm and a lesson to all of us'.[72] Then at the end of January, as the Cape Legislative Council election results showed a decisive victory for the South African Party, Smuts sent Merriman his congratulations and added:[73]

I do hope that it will be possible for the South African governments to do a great day's work. Such a chance does not occur in a lifetime. Let us try on sound lines to unite this land of ours and so safeguard its future autonomy and independent development along natural lines.

By that time the general public throughout South Africa were becoming seriously interested in the prospects of union. The press was serving a regular diet of information on the subject and it had become the stock in trade of politicians of all parties. In Progressive circles in the Transvaal two arguments were especially popular: the argument favoured by Bailey and Farrar that union was the only way of enabling the white population of South Africa to deal with the Native question as a whole and without the interference of Downing Street, and the economic argument, which was given more stress by Lionel Phillips.[74] Fitzpatrick, on the other hand, sounded a note of warning. Unlike many other Progressives, he had not been convinced by the Selborne Memorandum. He regarded Curtis as a bore and he feared that South Africa might be united on terms which would reduce the British population to permanent helotry.[75] He therefore declared that there was a danger that union would result in 'the perpetual domination of a party which . . . regards itself as

[72] Merriman to Mrs. A. Merriman, 15 Nov. 1907; Merriman's Diary, 16 Nov. 1907. Ibid.
[73] Smuts to Merriman, 27 Jan. 1908, ibid.
[74] *The Times*, 21 Oct., 25 Nov., and 11 Dec. 1907.
[75] Fitzpatrick to Lionel Phillips, 5 Oct. 1907, Fitzpatrick Papers (copy).

a privileged and exclusive caste'.[76] These sentiments were echoed by Major Silburn in Natal.[77] Selborne deprecated them:[78]

Those who urge delay about Federation on the ground of the present political preponderance of the Dutch are most short-sighted [he wrote to Patrick Duncan]. While the general instability of South Africa continues, all real prosperity will be impossible and all expansion, and the Dutch will continue to preponderate ad eternam . . .: there can be no expansion without stability; and there can be no stability without Federation. Q.E.D.

The members of the Kindergarten agreed with Selborne and continued to support the unification movement, hoping that it would 'be carried out by the qualities of British go and Idealism as opposed to the ignorance, reaction and selfishness of Boerdom'.[79] Curtis, with the encouragement of Smuts, was gathering information about the South African colonies which would be useful when it came to drafting a Constitution, and he and Duncan collected money in England with a view to starting a journal devoted exclusively to the cause of union. In addition to this, Sir Pieter Bam, a Progressive member of the Cape House of Assembly, founded a 'South African Organisation Union' with the object of promoting the federation of South Africa and strengthening the political and commercial ties between South Africa and Great Britain.[80] In such ways powerful propaganda was being prepared to influence the South African people, more particularly the English-speaking and Progressive South Africans.

Meanwhile, however, there was a serious recrudescence of isolationist sentiment in the Transvaal. Touring the country early in 1908, Botha found that economic protectionism was being advocated by a large number of Afrikaner farmers and that it was associated with a feeling that the Government was not sufficiently true to the Kruger tradition. Botha spoke out strongly against protectionism[81] and sent a circular letter to Het Volk Members of Parliament appealing to them to resist it.[82] Nevertheless, the movement gathered weight. On 2 March, according to the *Star*, Botha had an unsatisfactory meeting with some of the leading farmers of the Pretoria district. They opposed the policy of preserving the Customs Union and working towards political union, they wanted protection against the neighbouring colonies, 'such as had existed before the war', and they complained that the Government did not listen to the

[76] *The Times*, 18 Nov. 1907.   [77] *Natal Mercury*, 21 Feb. 1908.
[78] Selborne to Duncan, 30 Nov. 1907, Duncan Papers.
[79] Curtis to Duncan, 26 Nov. 1907, ibid.
[80] *The Times*, 25 Dec. 1907.
[81] e.g. speaking at Middelburg on 5 Feb. 1908, *Star*, 6 Feb.
[82] 17 Feb. 1908, Steyn Papers (copy).

people as Kruger had done and that it did not represent their will.[83] On account of this development, a new note of urgency entered into Smuts's letters. He informed Merriman on 18 February:[84]

For the last few months a very dangerous movement has been growing in the Transvaal—a movement of Separation similar to that which existed before the war. Farmers and individuals clamour for protection against the rest of South Africa, for putting a ring fence round our border and for forced development of our own industries and agricultural production and for protecting local markets. For some months now General Botha and myself have been stumping the country in order to combat this insane retrograde movement; but there is no denying that it is strong and becoming stronger, and that it may possibly yet sweep us off our feet. The fact is the Transvaal is now at the parting of the ways: henceforth we must move either in the direction above indicated or we must hurry on Union. There is no middle course. Perhaps we who are now at the head of affairs are still strong enough to carry the day for Union; but much delay would be fatal, for very powerful and sinister influences are secretly at work among every section of the population.

Merriman, having assumed office as Prime Minister of the Cape Colony on 3 February, promptly replied that he was now prepared to use shock tactics:[85]

I quite agree with you as to the necessity for pushing the question of Union. There is just a probability that if we three States—the Transvaal, O.R.C. and Cape—insist, we can carry the thing by a *coup de main*; while if we wait, I can quite foresee that it may be a very long business; and in the interval we may be crushed by the financial situation.

Steyn, replying to a similar appeal, expressed grave concern lest the Afrikaner people should be weakened by divisions in the hour of their political triumph. They were now in a position, he told Smuts, to follow a policy of uniting all South Africa and consolidating the Afrikaner nationality. Would they seize the opportunity or would the Afrikaner devil of discord again drive them apart?[86]

What, then, was the position in February 1908, when the political swing had been completed? Whereas some of the British South Africans were anxious lest South Africa should be united only to fall under

[83] *Star*, 2 Mar. 1908.   [84] Merriman Papers.
[85] Merriman to Smuts, 24 Feb. 1908, ibid. (copy).
[86] 'Wij zijn nu in staat om een politiek te volgen om geheel Zuid Afrika te vereenigen en de Afrikaansche Nationaliteit te bevestigen — zullen wij nu van die gelegenheid gebruik maken! of zal de Afrikaansche duivel van verdeeldheid ons wederom uit elkander jagen?'
Steyn to Smuts, 23 Feb. 1908, Smuts Papers.

Afrikaner domination, and some of the Transvaal Afrikaners would have preferred to work for the re-establishment of a Krugerist State in the Transvaal alone, the majority of the white population was hoping for the early achievement of some form of political union. The governments of the four colonies were eager to give effect to these hopes and in this they had the cordial support of Selborne and the Kindergarten. Among the advocates of closer union, however, there were many different shades of opinion, of which it will be sufficient to mention three. To the British officials it seemed to be attractive because they believed that it would consolidate and strengthen the British position in South Africa, ensure the loyalty of South Africa in the event of a war with the Triple Alliance, and, perhaps, form a stepping-stone towards imperial federation. To Afrikaners like Steyn closer union seemed to be attractive because it would bring the entire Afrikaner people together in one state which they could hope to control and which might move rather rapidly towards full national independence. It was Botha and Smuts who formed the bridge between these two schools of thought. They had been deeply impressed by the magnanimity of the Campbell-Bannerman Government, they were convinced that without union intercolonial friction was inevitable and strife likely, and they had become imbued with the ideal of a white South African nation derived from the merging of the Afrikaner and the British stocks. To a great extent, therefore, they were in accord with the British officials, but they also believed that their ideal was in the best interests of the Afrikaner people, because they judged that British imperialism had shot its bolt and that the legitimate aspirations of the Afrikaners could be fully satisfied within the framework of the evolving British Empire.

3. THE INTERCOLONIAL CONFERENCE, MAY 1908

In June 1907 the Botha Government gave notice of the Transvaal's intention to withdraw from the Customs Union in its present form, adding that it was prepared to consider proposals for a new agreement. This meant that the withdrawal would take effect on 30 June 1908, under article 33 of the Customs Union Convention of 1906, unless a new agreement had been made by then; so that another Intercolonial Conference was necessary during the first half of 1908. This was the conference to which Smuts was looking forward as 'the starting-point of a united South Africa'.

Towards the end of 1907 the Transvaal Government began to make arrangements for the conference and a storm immediately blew up over the question of the chairmanship. The High Commissioner had presided over all previous customs conferences since the war and the Botha Government, anxious not to offend the High Commissioner and the Progressives, proposed that the custom should be continued. Hull, the Transvaal Treasurer, wrote privately to Merriman, as the man who would 'in all probability be in power in the Cape Colony' when the conference met, to explain the proposal. Selborne, he said, would make 'an exceedingly able and impartial Chairman', and in any case he would not be a member of the conference nor would he have a vote.[87] Moor and Jameson readily agreed, but Merriman replied to Hull that he regarded it as vital that the High Commissioner should be excluded from the conference. Had not Milner abused his chairmanship of the Bloemfontein Conference of 1903 by forcing through imperial preference against the wishes of the Cape Parliament? Was it not the purpose of the 1908 conference to impose taxation upon the people of South Africa? Why, then, should an imperial officer have any place in it? The correct procedure, he contended, was for the conference to elect one of the delegates as chairman or for the colonial Governments to agree in advance that the senior Prime Minister would preside.[88] Botha then made a personal appeal to Merriman to reconsider his attitude. Selborne, he wrote, 'will, I feel sure, abstain most carefully from influencing in any way our proceedings', whereas a chairman drawn from the delegates would inevitably be partisan.[89] But Merriman was obdurate. 'Government of South Africa by South Africans', he retorted, 'seems to me to be a wholesome ideal', and it would be vitiated if Botha's proposal were adopted.[90] He also turned to the Orange River Colony for support:[91]

I have no hesitation in saying that the presence of Lord Selborne would make this conference as abortive as the two last if not as mischievous but of course if the majority are against me I must submit though I shall do so very reluctantly.

Steyn and Fischer agreed with him.[92] Jameson, on the other hand, informed Botha that his Cabinet was unanimous in wanting the High Commissioner to preside[93] and it is probable that if he had remained in power he would have had his way. However, Jameson's days as Prime Minister of the Cape Colony were numbered, and one of Merriman's

[87] 25 Nov. 1907, Merriman Papers.   [88] 29 Nov. 1907, ibid. (copy).
[89] 12 Dec. 1907, ibid.   [90] 20 Dec. 1907, ibid. (copy).
[91] Merriman to Steyn, 31 Dec. 1907, Steyn Papers.
[92] Fischer to Merriman, 2 Jan. 1908; Steyn to Merriman, 7 Jan. 1908. Merriman Papers.
[93] Smuts to Merriman, 17 and 27 Jan. 1908, ibid.

first actions after he assumed office was to have his attitude endorsed by
his Cabinet. Botha then yielded and suggested that Moor, as senior Prime
Minister, should preside over the conference. Moor regretted that the
appointment of the High Commissioner seemed to be out of the question,
but he accepted the chairmanship on the understanding that he would be
able to take part in debate.[94] Thus Merriman had eliminated the imperial
factor from the conference and established a precedent which would be
followed in the National Convention.

The rest of the official preparations for the conference presented no
serious difficulties. It was agreed that the conference should meet in
Pretoria from 4 to 9 May, after the new Cape Parliament had had a brief
session, and that it would then adjourn until 26 May to enable the Natal
and Orange River Colony parliaments to meet. Each of the four self-
governing colonies would be represented by three cabinet ministers and
each colony would have one vote, as in previous conferences. Southern
Rhodesia and the Portuguese Province of Mozambique would also be
represented, but their delegates would not be able to discuss or vote on
items which did not directly concern them or with which they were not
competent to deal—a formula which was designed to debar Rhodesia
as well as Mozambique from participating in the customs and railways
discussions, since her railways were privately owned and she was
restricted in customs matters by the Charter of the British South Africa
Company. Official advisers would be admitted to the conference room
during the discussions on railways and customs, and R. H. Brand would
be secretary to the conference with Philip Kerr as his assistant.[95] The
agenda paper grew to considerable dimensions, and before the conference started all four self-governing colonies had agreed to discuss
many topics besides railways and customs and 'South African National
Union'.[96]

Seeing the list grow, Smuts cautioned Merriman:[97] 'Perhaps we shall
find that Federation is so near that we had better address ourselves to the
greater issue without too much waste of time.' He proposed, therefore,
that the customs convention should be cobbled up to last another year,
with modifications in detail but not in principle, in the hope that the
colonies would be united before the year was out. In his reply Merriman

[94] Botha to Moor, 7 and 14 Mar. 1908 (telegrams); replies, 11 and 17 Mar. (copies of
telegrams). Natal Archives, Prime Minister, CIV.
[95] The relevant agreements were formally adopted as resolutions by the conference
at its first session on 4 May. *Minutes of the Inter-Colonial Conference, Pretoria and
Cape Town, May 1908* (Pretoria, 1908), pp. 7–8.
[96] Ibid., pp. 2, 5.
[97] Smuts to Merriman, 18 Feb. 1908, Merriman Papers.

embarked on a discussion of constitutional principles,[98] but Smuts quickly cautioned him to put first things first:[99] 'I think at the Conference we ought to settle the procedure which the S.A. Governments ought to follow in trying to bring about Union. A wrong procedure will lead us to a blind alley and delay or wreck the cause.' He then summarized the procedures which had been used to bring about the federations of Canada and Australia, explaining that the Canadian Constitution had never been referred to the colonial electorates, whereas the Australian Constitution was approved by the colonial electorates before it was submitted to the British Parliament.

Are we going to adopt the Canadian or Australian procedure or combine the two? It will be a question of nice calculation whether the Parliaments or the peoples of the colonies will be more favourable and that time alone can show. I would favour the idea (as a first stage) of delegates being chosen by parliaments in our forthcoming sessions to a convention which will sit after the prorogation of parliaments and report before the sessions of 1909. The Constitution will be published and if favourably received might be pushed through parliaments, or referred to another Convention of Parliamentary delegates for ratification. If parliaments are hostile and peoples more favourable, a referendum to the electorate might be taken for final confirmation.

From then until the Intercolonial Conference met in May, Merriman, like Smuts, devoted considerable attention to the procedure for achieving union. Writing to Smuts early in March[1] he suggested that the conference should be asked 'to approve the principle of union in a resolution' and to invite the four colonial parliaments to nominate delegates to a convention, which should be composed, not on the basis of colonial equality, but 'on the basis of the European population in each state' (which would have given the Cape Colony fifteen members, the Transvaal eight, the Orange River Colony four, and Natal three in a convention of thirty members). The convention should 'proceed to draft a Constitution' which should be submitted to the colonial parliaments 'for acceptance or amendment' and 'such amended Constitution should be again considered by a Convention and then submitted for ratification to a plebiscite of states'.[2] He also threw out the suggestion that the Constitution should finally be enacted by the colonial parliaments and approved by the Crown without recourse to the Parliament at Westminster, explaining that this procedure seemed to him to be practicable

---

[98] 24 Feb. 1908, Smuts Papers.   [99] 3 Mar. 1908, Merriman Papers.
[1] The day of the month is indecipherable. Smuts Papers.
[2] Summarizing these proposals in a letter to Steyn on 12 Mar. 1908, Merriman wrote that the Constitution should be 'finally ratified by an European plebiscite'. Steyn Papers.

because the existing colonial constitutions were not Acts of the British Parliament but royal Letters Patent and the King 'has no power except with our consent to revoke his gift'.

On 24 March Merriman and Smuts met at Port Elizabeth and discussed these matters. Meanwhile Merriman had sent Smuts's letter and his reply on the procedural questions to Sir Henry de Villiers, the Chief Justice of the Cape Colony, who made cogent comments in reply.[3] In general de Villiers thought that Merriman's proposals 'seem to open up the way to a practical solution of the question of Union', but he differed from Merriman on three points. Firstly, he considered that each colony should have the same number of representatives in the convention:

In regard, however, to the number of delegates to be nominated by each Colony for the proposed Convention, would it not be better to have the same number of delegates for each Colony rather than to proportion the number to the European population of each Colony? In the decision of the question whether there shall be a Union, and, if so, what its Constitution shall be each Colony has an equal interest and should, I am inclined to think, have an equal vote. It would certainly render it less unpalatable for Natal and the O.R.C. to agree to the Meeting of a Convention if they are to have an equal voice with their more powerful neighbours in deciding whether the individuality of the smaller States is to be practically extinguished. The Convention, in framing the Constitution, would of course have to proportion the Parliamentary representation of the different States to their respective wealth, area and population, but until the new Constitution is established each State, as a separate entity, stands on a perfect equality with its neighbours. I would suggest that each Colony should nominate either three or five delegates and, in order to invest the Convention with a perfectly representative and national character it would be well that the Parliamentary Opposition of each Colony should be fully represented. If each Colony sends three delegates there would, I presume, be only one member of the opposition nominated and I would therefore suggest that the number should be five so that any Colony, if so advised, may appoint two representatives of its opposition as delegates.

Secondly, de Villiers criticized and amplified Merriman's rather shadowy ideas on what should happen after the convention had drafted a Constitution:

Your proposal is that the Convention should draw up the Constitution which instrument should be submitted to the several Parliaments for acceptance or amendment. As you do not provide for the third alternative viz. that of rejection by one or more of the Parliaments I presume that, in

---

[3] 30 Mar. 1908, Merriman Papers.

your opinion, the acceptance by any Colony of the principle of Union would prevent it afterwards from altogether rejecting any Constitution framed by the Convention. It is possible, however, that the different Parliaments may make different amendments in which case there will not be, as you anticipate, one but several amended Constitutions to be considered by the second Convention. If all the Colonies are in earnest they could, by conferring plenary powers on the second Convention, expedite the Union and dispense with the proposed ratification by a 'plebiscite of States.' I confess indeed that I do not quite know what you mean by a 'plebiscite of States.' Perhaps you mean that each State is to ascertain by means of a plebiscite of its own electors whether a majority is in favour of the Constitution as finally amended by the second Convention but, if so, the machinery by which this is to be done should be indicated. The Constitutional Mouthpiece of each Colony is its Parliament and I would not advise that the different Parliaments should be passed by for the purpose of ascertaining the opinions of the electors. The wiser course would be to exercise the greatest care in the selection of delegates for both Conventions and to entrust to the second Convention plenary powers to settle the Constitution and submit it to the Imperial Government for acceptance or rejection by the Imperial Parliament.

Thirdly, de Villiers expressed the opinion that, in the light of the limitations which still remained upon the competence of colonial legislatures under the Colonial Laws Validity Act, 1865 (28 & 29 Vict. c. 63), the Constitution would have to be enacted by the Parliament at Westminster:

I do not see how a scheme of Union could be carried through without the assistance and intervention of the Imperial Parliament. That is the only Legislature which in theory has the power of legislating for South Africa as a whole. It is a power which would not be exercised except at the request of the Colonies of S. Africa and it may be taken for granted that a Constitution approved of by them would be sanctioned by the Imperial Parliament. You say that we should consider carefully 'whether the Constitution should not be our own Act approved of by the Crown,' but, without the intervention of the Imperial Parliament, there would have to be several identical Colonial Acts of Parliament and the fatal objection would remain that, in order to effect the Union each of these Acts, by dealing with the affairs of other Colonies, would be *ultra vires* of the Legislature which passes it. No such objection would exist to an Imperial Act of Parliament.

In conclusion he offered 'at any time to discuss the whole subject' of union with Merriman, as he considered it to be 'quite outside party politics', and he said that he agreed with Smuts that 'a wrong procedure might greatly delay and even wreck the cause of Union'.

In spite of de Villiers's lucid reasoning Merriman held to his belief that the Constitution should be submitted to a plebiscite in each of the colonies, and he included words to that effect in his statement about the forthcoming conference in the Cape Parliament on 23 April.[4] He evidently believed that it would be wise to ensure that the South African Constitution should have the greatest possible moral authority over white South Africans and that that would be achieved if it were approved directly by the voters as well as by the parliaments of South Africa. On the other hand, no previous colonial or republican constitution in South Africa had been adopted in that way, so that there was nothing in the South African tradition to make a plebiscite necessary. Furthermore, Smuts was anticipating serious opposition from the Transvaal isolationists, and he continued to wish to leave it open for the Constitution to be adopted by the voters or by the colonial parliaments, whichever seemed to promise the more favourable result. Merriman also continued to hope that it would be unnecessary for the Constitution to run the gauntlet of debate at Westminster, so that it might become an exclusively South African product in form as well as in substance. For the time being he did not press his views on these points, but he felt very strongly about representation in the convention and did his utmost to persuade Smuts to agree with him. Forwarding the Chief Justice's letter to Smuts on 3 April, he explained:[5]

I confess that I am not convinced on that point. The reasons for my position I think we discussed at Port Elizabeth, and the more I reflect on it the stronger is my opinion that a course which ignored the relative proportion of States would open the door to opposition in this Colony—and perhaps in yours—that might wreck the prospect of union. But by fixing a minimum and by adopting your suggestion as to voters a modus vivendi may I hope be arrived at. I confess that in any constituent convention to give satisfaction the Cape Colony ought to have the following represented 1. The Government. 2. The Opposition. 3. The West. 4. The East. 5. The Agricultural. 6. The Commercial element. I suppose something of the kind would obtain in your country. We must before all things avoid the idea that the Convention is to be a mere hole and corner meeting of a few politicians. It is a great national issue in which the whole of South Africa is concerned.

And again in his last letter to Smuts before the conference met:[6]

The only or rather the chief point on which I differ from the C.J. is the one as to whether the Constituent Convention should be elected proportionately or not in each state. I still adhere most strongly to this view and I think that a departure from this principle will certainly endanger the acceptance of any plan by a population like ours. As to the exact basis upon

[4] *Cape Hansard, 1908*, pp. 11–13.   [5] Smuts Papers.
[6] 28 Apr. 1908, ibid.

which proportional representation should be founded I have an open mind, but if we are to be one people we ought to adopt some such basis from the start.

Smuts yielded and accepted the proposition that the number of each colony's representatives in the National Convention should bear some relation to its white population.

The Orangia Unie leaders had been kept informed of these preparations. Merriman outlined his proposals in a letter to Steyn on 12 March,[7] and during April he met him and handed him copies of his correspondence with Smuts and de Villiers, while Smuts talked the matter over with Fischer and some of his colleagues at the end of March. The Unie leaders do not seem to have raised any serious objection to the proposal that the smaller colonies should have fewer representatives at the convention than the larger ones. Mrs. Steyn informed Merriman[8] that her husband had read his correspondence with Smuts and de Villiers 'with great interest and he says there is only one remark he wishes to make' and that was that 'although not in love with a plebiscite he yet thinks that something of the sort will be necessary, unless the governments consider that they have already got a mandate to bring about the Union of South Africa'. She said that Steyn had discussed the matter briefly with Hertzog, who seemed to think that a general election should be held in the Orange River Colony 'before the final Act can be entered into', but Hertzog, she added, was deeply concerned lest the conference should be marred by racialism.

The delegates of the Cape Colony, the Transvaal, and the Orange River Colony therefore went to the Intercolonial Conference resolved to set in train a procedure for unifying South Africa, and had exchanged views on what that procedure should be. The Natal delegates, on the other hand, seem to have been completely in the dark about what was intended. Although they had approved of the item 'South African National Union' being placed on the agenda, they do not seem to have given any particular thought to it or to have been confided in by any of the members of the other colonial Governments. Thus Moor, writing a friendly personal letter to Sir Henry McCallum, the former Governor of Natal, ten days before the conference started, said nothing else about it than that he hoped it would manage 'to place matters, both as regards Customs and Railways, on a more satisfactory footing than is the case at present'.[9]

[7] Steyn Papers.   [8] 19 Apr. 1908, Merriman Papers.
[9] Moor to Sir Henry McCallum, Governor of Ceylon, 24 Apr. 1908, Natal Archives, Prime Minister, CII (copy). I have found nothing in the Natal Archives to suggest that

On the afternoon of Sunday, 3 May, Botha gave a reception to the delegates in Pretoria.[10] There Smuts drew Merriman aside and showed him some draft resolutions which he proposed to move the next day in the conference, providing for a convention of twenty-five members— eleven from the Cape Colony, seven from the Transvaal, four from the Orange River Colony, and three from Natal. Merriman persuaded him to increase the number to thirty—twelve from the Cape Colony, eight from the Transvaal, and five each from Natal and the Orange River Colony.[11]

At ten o'clock the following morning the conference started in the Transvaal Government Buildings. Moor was elected President and, after rules of procedure had been adopted and a few minor matters had been disposed of, the conference decided, on the motion of J. W. Sauer, to deal with the item, 'South African National Union'. Smuts then moved his resolutions and in doing so he stressed the dangers of the existing con- ditions and explained the need for initiating a wise procedure for the attainment of union.[12] Nobody opposed the principle that the four self- governing colonies should join together in some form of political union, or the proposal that a National Convention, composed of delegates appointed by the colonial parliaments, should be convened to draft a Constitution, but the allocation of the seats in the convention caused serious difficulties. Merriman argued strongly for the proposal that he had worked out with Smuts the previous day and was supported by his colleagues, Sauer and Malan. They made much of the fact that it would give Natal one delegate for every 20,000 white inhabitants and the Cape

the Natal Government made any preparations for the item, 'South African National Union'.

[10] The delegates were: J. X. Merriman, J. W. Sauer, F. S. Malan (Cape Colony), F. R. Moor, Dr. C. O'Grady Gubbins, C. Hitchins (Natal), Louis Botha, J. C. Smuts, H. C. Hull (Transvaal), A. Fischer, J. B. M. Hertzog, Dr. A. E. W. Ramsbottom (Orange River Colony), Sir Lewis Michell, F. J. Newton, E. C. Baxter (Rhodesia), T. A. G. Rosado, and B. M. d'Almeida (Mozambique).

[11] Merriman to Sir Henry de Villiers, 31 May 1908, Merriman Papers (copy). Accord- ing to an undated and unsigned typed draft in the Smuts Papers, the Cape Colony would have 10 delegates, the Transvaal 7, and Natal and the Orange River Colony 4 each.

[12] The official *Minutes of the Inter-Colonial Conference, Pretoria and Cape Town, May 1908* (Pretoria, 1908) are a bare record, containing little more than the terms of the resolutions carried. The only accounts which I have found of the debates on the item 'South African National Union' are: (a) A typescript, dated 21 May 1908, initialed A. C. G. L. and headed 'Debate on "Closer Union" Resolutions'. This document was evidently typed by A. C. G. Lloyd, Merriman's private secretary, from Merriman's notes. Merriman Papers, No. 60/1908. (b) A copy of Merriman's letter to de Villiers, dated 31 May 1908, containing a brief summary of the debate. Merriman Papers. (c) A letter from Sir Lewis Michell to Dr. L. S. Jameson, 6 May 1908, cited in Michell's unpublished 'Reminiscences', pp. 349–51. Cape Archives, Michell Papers, No. 28.

Colony only one for every 50,000, and they contended that it was the Cape Colony that was being discriminated against. For Natal, Moor and Gubbins deplored the proposal. With the Transvaal supporting Smuts, much depended on the attitude of the Orange River Colony. At first Fischer and Hertzog supported Natal, but then they weakened, and eventually Moor bowed to the wishes of the majority without calling for a division, though he observed that 'after all Natal might have to stand out'.[13] The only other question that gave rise to long discussion was that of the future of the non-self-governing British territories in southern Africa—Rhodesia, Basutoland, Bechuanaland Protectorate, and Swaziland. Smuts's motions provided for the inclusion of Rhodesia at a later stage, which was approved by the conference, but they made no reference to the other three territories. From the discussion it emerged that the conference was unanimous in not wishing to incorporate them in the Union on its foundation and in hoping that they would be absorbed 'as a matter of course' later on. It was, however, thought to be 'advisable and discreet not to make any special mention of them for fear of raising a dangerous question, viz.—the treatment of Natives by independent African Administrations'.[14] The motions also provided that the convention should proceed with its work even if only two of the self-governing colonies appointed delegates, and left the procedure to be adopted after the convention reported for the convention itself to determine in consultation with the governments of the four self-governing colonies. Eventually the conference unanimously accepted all Smuts's motions, with only one or two verbal alterations, in the following form:[15]

(a) That in the opinion of this Conference the best interests and the permanent prosperity of South Africa can only be secured by an early union, under the Crown of Great Britain, of the several self-governing Colonies;

(b) that to the union contemplated in the foregoing resolution Rhodesia shall be entitled to admission at such time and on such conditions as may hereafter be agreed upon;

(c) that the members of this Conference agree to submit the foregoing resolutions to the Legislatures of their respective Colonies, and to take such steps as may be necessary to obtain their consent to the appointment of delegates to a National South African Convention, whose object shall be to consider and report on the most desirable form of South African Union and to prepare a draft constitution;

---

[13] 'Debate on "Closer Union" Resolutions.'

[14] Ibid. According to Michell ('Reminiscences', pp. 349–51) Merriman said that Swaziland should in due course go to the Transvaal, Bechuanaland Protectorate to the Cape, and Basutoland to the Orange Free State.   [15] Minutes, p. 9.

(d) the Convention shall consist of not more than (12) twelve delegates from the Cape Colony, not more than (8) eight delegates from the Transvaal, not more than (5) five delegates from Natal and the Orange River Colony respectively, and it shall meet as soon as convenient after the next Sessions of all the Parliaments; provided that as soon as at least two Colonies shall have appointed their delegates the Convention shall be considered as constituted;

(e) the Convention shall publish the draft constitution as soon as possible, and shall, in consultation with the Governments of the self-governing Colonies, determine the further steps to be taken in reference thereto;

(f) in the Convention the voting shall be *per capita* and not by States. A Chairman shall be elected from the members who shall have the right of speaking and voting, and in the event of an equality of votes shall have a casting vote.

Merriman then moved the following resolution, which was also carried without a division:[16]

That the above resolutions be published at an early date to be mutually agreed upon by the Governments of the self-governing Colonies after the rising of the Conference, and that the following *communiqué* be issued to the press at once:

'The delegates from the self-governing Colonies have adopted the principle of closer union and undertake to submit certain resolutions to their Parliaments in reference thereto. They also undertake to recommend to their Parliaments the appointment of delegates to a National Convention for the purpose of framing a draft Constitution.'

The conference then turned to consider the customs and railway problems and it quickly ran into heavy weather.[17] The Transvaal delegates, like their crown colony predecessors at Pietermaritzburg in 1906, had come armed with a brief to abolish preferential railway rates, to stop the railways being used as instruments for 'the taxation of the inland colonies by the coast colonies',[18] to reduce the cost of living in the Transvaal, and to obtain lower railway rates for Transvaal farm produce and for raw materials used by Transvaal manufacturers. They received general support from the Orange River Colony delegates. The Natal and Cape Colony delegates, on the other hand, like their 1906 predecessors, were briefed to obtain more revenue by increasing the customs duties and by

[16] *Minutes*, p. 10.

[17] The fullest account of this part of the work of the conference is that given by Hull, the Transvaal Treasurer, to his Parliament on 25 June 1908 (*Transvaal Leg. Ass. Deb., 1908*, cols. 227–37). See also the reports of Moor (*Natal Leg. Ass. Deb.* xliv, pp. 137–8) and Merriman (*Cape Hansard, 1908*, pp. 84–85).

[18] *Minutes*, p. 3.

securing a greater share of the Witwatersrand traffic for their ports. The Cape proposed to do the latter by adjusting the railway rates so as to give the Cape ports, Durban, and Delagoa Bay each one-third of the Witwatersrand traffic; while Natal proposed to fix the rates in such a way that the total transport costs from European ports to the Witwatersrand should be the same via East London, Port Elizabeth, Durban, and Delagoa Bay and to distribute the profits between the railway administrations on a percentage basis. Natal also explicitly demanded that effect should be given to the recent British legal interpretation of the *modus vivendi* by abolishing the rates preferences accorded to the Delagoa Bay route over the recently opened lines from Durban and the Cape ports, and by reducing its preference over the older lines. An attempt was made to find a compromise between these divergent views. On 6 May the conference instructed the customs and railway advisers to devise a means of abolishing the preferential railway rates and of raising the customs tariff to offset the loss of revenue without causing any increase in the cost of living.[19] After the conference adjourned on 9 May the advisers continued with their work, but they were unable to produce a unanimous report because the Cape Colony, faced with long haulages from her ports to the Witwatersrand, was not prepared to accept the principle of equal rates.[20] During the adjournment the Portuguese delegates sent the Transvaal Government a statement in which they roundly criticized the attitude of the Cape Colony and Natal to the *modus vivendi*.[21] They pointed out that Mozambique labour was 'an essential factor for the prosperity of the Transvaal and indirectly rendered an enormous service to the Cape and Natal', that the difference in railway rates was less than it would be if the rates were proportional to mileage, and that the complaints of the Cape and Natal were based 'exclusively on the decrease of their revenue and on the difficulties resulting therefrom for the restoration of their finances'. Their protest concluded with the observation that the Cape and Natal proposals were 'not based on considerations of justice or equity'.

After the conference reassembled in Cape Town on 26 May it soon came to a complete deadlock. Perhaps, indeed, no very serious effort was made to reach a lasting agreement. Merriman, at any rate, realized that the more blatant the failure the stronger would be the argument for union, and he subsequently told the Cape Parliament that 'after the Closer Union resolutions had been passed, most of the representatives present made up their minds it was no use going into the tariff question

[19] Ibid., p. 12.   [20] Ibid., pp. 27 ff.
[21] Natal Archives, Prime Minister, cv (copy).

because after all they could only carry out a temporary matter'.[22] The outcome was that on 28 May the conference passed a resolution moved by Merriman, admitting that it was a 'practical impossibility under existing conditions' to reconcile 'the financial requirements and economic policies of the various South African Governments', and continuing the existing Customs Convention with 'minor modifications' for another year, and thereafter for annual periods, subject to each member having the right to withdraw on 30 June of any year on giving three months' notice, because 'if a satisfactory settlement results from the proposal for Closer Union any alterations now made in the Customs and Railway Tariffs must of necessity be temporary and provisional'.[23] The next day the conference terminated after approving a protocol which made a few trifling amendments to the 1906 convention.[24]

Meanwhile on 27 May the Natal delegates had reopened the question of representation in the National Convention, in a desperate attempt to obtain as many representatives for Natal as for the larger colonies. But they failed. To sweeten the pill for Natal, however, the conference decided that the National Convention should open its sittings in Durban.[25]

Smuts and Merriman had reason to be satisfied with the achievements of the conference, which had panned out exactly as they had hoped. Their Closer Union Resolutions had been adopted *nem. con.* without substantial amendment, and the customs and railway deadlock had made it clear to the world that 'we must either unite or break'.[26]

---

[22] *Cape Hansard, 1908*, p. 84.   [23] *Minutes*, p. 24.
[24] Ibid., pp. 26, 107–9.   [25] Ibid., p. 23.
[26] Merriman to J. Rose Innes, Chief Justice of the Transvaal, 31 May 1908, Innes Papers.

CHAPTER III

THE ORIGIN OF THE PRINCIPAL FEATURES OF THE SOUTH AFRICAN CONSTITUTION

1. THE PERSONAL FACTOR

BESIDES controlling the timing of the unification movement and the procedure by which South Africa was to be united, Merriman and Smuts shared the main responsibility for the principal features of the South African Constitution. Even before the Intercolonial Conference met in Pretoria in May, they had considered many of the basic problems and reached agreement on the handling of some of them, while by the time the National Convention started its deliberations in Durban on 12 October 1908 Smuts had prepared a programme which he had good reason to believe would be acceptable to the majority of the delegates. In this chapter we shall examine these basic problems and the attitude of Merriman and Smuts and the South African public to them.

At the outset it is desirable to review the general political and constitutional ideas of the two politicians whose influence was most far-reaching. Merriman once described himself as a Whig, and the word gives a clue to his political philosophy. He had an almost romantic veneration for the British Constitution as he imagined it to have been in the Gladstonian era of his youth. The functions of a Government should be limited; taxation and public expenditure should be kept to a minimum; an unbalanced budget was a major evil; and Parliament should be the sovereign element in a Constitution—the real forum of a nation, where decisions should be made by free votes after full public debates. He was opposed to many of the trends of the early twentieth century— to the increase in the range of government action, to manhood suffrage, to equal constituencies, and to party discipline and the rise of the caucus. South Africa he regarded as an essentially aristocratic country, particularly unsuited to 'democratic shibboleths'. The landowner should have the decisive say in politics and not 'the shifting population of the towns'. Events had also led Merriman to become a passionate anti-imperialist, a fervent believer in colonial autonomy. In all this Merriman's outlook was consistent. Perhaps, indeed, with his increasing years, it was becoming somewhat inelastic.

If Merriman was a Whig, Smuts, who was his junior by twenty-nine years, appeared to have become a Radical after the South African War. Looking to the British Liberal Party for favours in 1906 he had accepted, or been prepared to flirt with, the whole gamut of egalitarian doctrines which Merriman despised so heartily. To what extent his radicalism was based on conviction it is difficult to say. One cannot be sure that he had any fixed constitutional principles at this time. His mental range was exceptionally broad. The natural sanguineness of his temperament had been reinforced by his wide reading in nineteenth-century philosophy and science, and he had acquired an optimistic, Darwinian bias which he never lost. The concept of a dominant natural principle of accretion, which he later formulated in *Holism and Evolution*, was already present in his mind. Such a man could never identify himself exclusively with the somewhat narrow purposes of a sectional nationalist movement. Already, before the Jameson raid, he had been attracted by Rhodes's doctrine of South Africanism, and although he had then thrown himself heartily into the republican cause, when the war was over he discarded republicanism as impracticable and concentrated on the objective of fusing Boer and Briton in South Africa.

Between Smuts and Merriman the differences were therefore immense. Merriman looked backwards: Smuts looked forward. Merriman's political conduct flowed from fixed premisses: Smuts's lacked any such basis. Merriman's success as a politician was often compromised by the fact that he was swimming against the tide of public opinion: Smuts could adapt himself to new situations. There were, in particular, two aspects of South African affairs on which they disagreed. Merriman's whiggism and long experience of political life in the Cape Colony caused him to boggle at the idea of a hard and fast political colour-bar, while Smuts, since he had settled in the Transvaal, had come to accept the northern point of view and to recoil from the prospect of allowing the African any part in the government of the country. On the other hand, Smuts accepted the principle of equal rights for all white men, which had been embodied in the Transvaal Constitution, as part of the political environment of the twentieth century, while Merriman continued to loathe it. The result was that Merriman's opponents regarded him as stubborn and bigoted, while Smuts's opponents—and even some of his colleagues—doubted his sincerity, though nobody doubted that he possessed quite exceptional talents.

2. THE FORM OF THE CONSTITUTION

Two main questions of form have to be decided by the creators of a Constitution. Firstly, is it to be flexible, like the British Constitution, under which there is no distinction between the requirements for the making of an ordinary law and the requirements for the making of a law to amend the Constitution itself, or is it to be rigid, like most other constitutions, which lay down special and stiffer requirements for the enactment of constitutional amendments, so that a bare majority in the legislature is not competent to change the fundamental structure of the State? Secondly, is it to be unitary, like the British Constitution, under which the Central Government is supreme over all regional authorities, or federal, like the constitutions of the United States of America, Canada, and Australia, under which the central and regional governments are each limited to their own spheres and within those spheres are independent of one another?[1] These two questions are intimately connected, because a federal Constitution is necessarily rigid,[2] whereas a unitary Constitution may be rigid, like the Irish, or flexible, like the British.

In South Africa the issue between flexibility and rigidity was not given the independent consideration that its importance merits, and even in the National Convention, as we shall see, it was not handled very skilfully. It was the issue between federalism and unification that was zealously canvassed in the press and on public platforms and which assumed priority in the minds of all the delegates in the National Convention, including Merriman and Smuts. Nevertheless, it is logical to examine South African attitudes to the question of flexibility or rigidity first.

Notwithstanding their differences of age, temperament, and political outlook, Merriman and Smuts approached this question with a similar bias. Smuts's views were conditioned by his legal training in the British milieu of Cambridge University, where he had come under the influence of men such as F. W. Maitland, who expounded the historical, evolutionary interpretation of the British Constitution, and Merriman, too, was steeped in British constitutional history, so that both of them were disposed to desire to create in South Africa a legislature which, like the British Parliament, would be an uncontrolled legislature, rather than

[1] Here I follow K. C. Wheare's lucid exposition of the essential attributes of a federation in *Federal Government* (London, 1946), pp. 11–15.

[2] Nevertheless, Wheare points out (op. cit., p. 55) that a federal constitution could be flexible in those respects which do not concern the relations between the central and the regional governments. This is now the case in Canada.

one which, like the American Congress, would be subject to legal limitations; and both of them were averse to the process of judicial interpretation which is the natural corollary of a rigid Constitution. They, like
most British politicians and constitutional lawyers to this day, did not
raise the question whether a Parliament might abuse its powers. Nor did
they consider whether there might be special reasons for preferring the
American system in South Africa, as a means of mitigating the consequences if a racist party acquired a majority of the seats in Parliament,
because both of them were thinking primarily of the white section of the
population and assuming that its Boer and British elements would soon
merge into a single nation with a uniform culture and that political
divisions would not follow racial lines. Merriman, certainly, did not
view violations of personal liberty with indifference: far from it. In 1906
he was deeply concerned by the reports of the misconduct of the Natal
Militia against the Native rebels, and he threw out the suggestion that
there should be a Bill of Rights for South Africa;[3] but he was thinking
of a Bill of Rights on the British model rather than the American—a Bill
which would be no more difficult to amend than any other law.

South African experience was not, however, solely on the side of
flexibility.[4] The drafters of the Orange Free State Constitution of 1854
had taken over several of the basic features of the American Constitution.
The rights of peaceful assembly and petition, equality before the law,
and the right to property were guaranteed in the Constitution without
qualification, and the entire Constitution was very rigid, requiring a
three-quarters majority in the Volksraad in two (originally three) successive annual sessions for any amendment. Moreover, these limitations had
been generally respected and no less a person than J. B. M. Hertzog,
as a judge of the Orange Free State High Court, had declared in his *ratio
decidendi* in the case of *The State* v. *Gibson*, 1898, that[5]

> The Volksraad of this State is not in possession of the exercise of a single
> one of these six attributes of the sovereign power [as enunciated by Van
> Alphen], but is everywhere controlled and limited by the Constitution. . . .

Thus in law and in practice the Free State Volksraad had been subject
to definite limitations. The experience of the South African Republic
had been very different. Although the Constitution as introduced in 1858

---

[3] Merriman to Smuts, 1 May 1906, Smuts Papers.

[4] I have dealt more fully with the constitutional history of the two Boer republics in
'Constitutionalism in the South African Republics', *Butterworths South African Law
Review, 1954*, pp. 49–72.

[5] The *Cape Law Journal*, xv. 1–10, sets out the judgment in an anonymous article
entitled 'Liability for Defamation of Legislative Body'.

had included a number of limitations upon the Volksraad, including the requirement that any law was to be passed by a three-quarters majority, the limitations had been ignored from the very beginning; and when in the famous case of *Brown* v. *Leyds*, 1897, Chief Justice Kotzé ruled that laws passed contrary to the provisions of the Constitution were invalid, a crisis arose which culminated in the dismissal of the Chief Justice by President Kruger, in terms of a 'law' hastily enacted by the Volksraad. In practice, therefore, the Constitution of the South African Republic had always been fully flexible and the Volksraad had always managed to pass laws on any topic, including constitutional amendments, by a bare majority. Moreover, the conduct of the Volksraad had not been effectively moderated by conventions of the sort that impose real, if extra-legal, restraints upon the British Parliament. The Transvaal Boers had in fact found their flexible Constitution a useful instrument for maintaining their virtually exclusive control of a multi-racial State. They had regarded Kotzé's stand, taking place as it did between the Jameson raid and the South African War, as a conspiracy against the integrity of their Republic, and they had agreed with Kruger's forthright statement that judicial interpretation was 'the principle of the Devil'. There were therefore two distinct Boer traditions. According to the one a Constitution is a fundamental document which grants limited powers to the various organs of government and makes the judiciary responsible, in the last resort, for declaring legislation invalid if it is in conflict with the Constitution; and, according to the other, a Constitution merely sets the necessary organs of government in motion and leaves it to the legislature to change them in any way at any time in response to 'the will of the people'.

The constitutions of the four self-governing British South African colonies[6] were not rigid in the normal way, for Bills to amend them could be approved by both Houses of the colonial parliaments by simple majorities in the same manner as other Bills.[7] But there was still the question whether a Bill thus passed by both Houses of a colonial Parliament would obtain the assent of the Governor or the King and become a valid law. Like other British colonies at the time, the South African colonies could not change their status; nor (it was generally believed)

---

[6] 1640 (1852–3), Cape of Good Hope Constitution Ordinance; C. 7013 (1893–4), Natal Constitution Act; Cd. 3250 (1906), Transvaal Constitution; Cd. 3526 (1907), Orange River Colony Constitution.

[7] That is to say, there were no special provisions as to the 'Manner and Form' of legislation by the South African Parliaments (unless the deadlock provisions in the Transvaal and Orange River Colony Constitutions and the quorum provisions in all the Constitutions can be considered such). Cf. Colonial Laws Validity Act, 1865, s. 5.

could they legislate with extra-territorial effect; and their legislation was invalid, under section 2 of the Colonial Laws Validity Act, 1865, if it was repugnant to imperial legislation specifically extending to them.[8] Their governors were legally bound by their Royal Instructions (as distinct from other instructions issued by the Secretary of State) to reserve for the King's pleasure various classes of Bills—Bills providing for divorce, Bills conferring favours on the governor, Bills affecting the colonial currency, Bills imposing differential duties, Bills running counter to imperial treaties, Bills interfering with the discipline of imperial forces, and Bills seriously affecting the royal prerogative, the rights of non-resident British subjects, or British trade and shipping.[9] The governors of Natal, the Transvaal, and the Orange River Colony were also specifically obliged to reserve Bills imposing special disabilities on non-Europeans, and the two latter governors were specifically obliged to reserve Bills amending the Constitution or providing for the importation of indentured labour.[10] Furthermore, the King was empowered to disallow Acts of the South African parliaments within two years after they had been assented to by the Governor.[11] It will be observed that all these rigid elements in the British South African Constitutions consisted of imperial controls. This fact had two important consequences. Firstly, it meant that if all the imperial controls were eliminated, the constitutions would become fully flexible, so that the British South African colonies were embryonic Britains. Secondly, it caused anti-imperialist South Africans to assume that any type of rigidity was a mark of subordination, and that full flexibility was a mark of national autonomy, so that a flexible Constitution seemed to be the proper national ideal—a confusion of thought which has persisted in South Africa to the present day.

On balance, therefore, South African experience led to a general preference for a flexible Constitution. During the year 1908 only one

[8] The question of imperial control over the Parliaments of self-governing British colonies and dominions is dealt with in A. B. Keith, *Responsible Government in the Dominions* (2nd ed., Oxford, 1928, 2 vols.), ii. 745–1064.

[9] e.g. Cd. 3250, p. 36, Transvaal Royal Instructions, s. 7.

[10] In Natal this obligation was imposed on the Governor in the Royal Instructions, s. 8; in the Transvaal and Orange River Colony it was imposed in the constitutions themselves (Transvaal Constitution, s. 39, Orange River Colony Constitution, s. 41).

In practice by the twentieth century the royal assent was almost always given to reserved Bills, e.g. it was given to Bills imposing special disabilities on Transvaal Indians (Transvaal Acts Nos. 2 and 15 of 1907).

[11] Cape of Good Hope Constitution Ordinance, s. 83; Natal Constitution Act, s. 7; Transvaal Constitution, s. 41; Orange River Colony Constitution, s. 43.

In practice by the twentieth century the power of disallowance had become obsolescent. Indeed, it never was applied to the legislation of a self-governing South African colony.

man put the case for a rigid Constitution cogently before the public, and that was J. G. Kotzé, who had found a quieter billet in the Eastern Districts Court of the Cape Colony since his departure from the Transvaal. Addressing the Grahamstown Closer Union Society late in October 1908, he said:[12]

When once we have a written Constitution, with a clause indicating how alone amendments of it can take place, we shall have a fundamental law, higher in standing and authority than the ordinary laws passed by the Federal Parliament and the local Legislatures. To it all other Acts, whether legislative or executive, will be subordinate, and it will then become the duty, whenever the occasion arises, of the Superior Courts of Justice to test the validity of the ordinary laws by reference to the Constitution.

He went on to explain that the alternative system, under which Parliament decides on the constitutionality of its own Acts, creates the danger that the Government of the day, supported by a subservient parliamentary majority, might place itself above the Constitution, so that the Constitution might be 'frittered away ... and the whole machinery of Government subverted and changed from what the framers of the Constitution intended'. But he was speaking a different constitutional language from the majority of the South Africans of the day who, like Smuts and Merriman, were unwilling to recast their thinking in the alien mould of rigidity and judicial restraint, so that his advice fell on deaf ears.

Down to the middle of 1908 nearly everyone assumed that when the South African colonies joined together they would form a federation. This was largely because the obvious precedents—those of Australia, Canada, and the United States of America—were federal ones, and also because all previous proposals for the combination of the South African states and colonies, including Sir George Grey's proposal of 1858, the abortive South Africa Act of 1877, and P. A. Molteno's book, *A Federal South Africa*, of 1896, had envisaged a federation, so that the term 'Federation' had become generally accepted for any such combination. Furthermore, it was widely believed in Boer, British South African, and Kindergarten circles alike that South Africa was too large and the colonial vested interests were too strong to make a unitary Constitution desirable or possible. The paper which Richard Feetham wrote in October 1906 reflected contemporary South African thought on the subject.[13] In it he said that he regarded 'the enormous area' of South Africa as

---

[12] *Cape Times*, 3 Nov. 1908.

[13] 'Some Problems of South African Federation and Reasons for Facing them.'

'a fatal obstacle to a unification system' and that unification seemed in any case to be impossible because the colonies would not be prepared 'to merge themselves entirely and lose their identity in one South African State'. Nevertheless, he went on to propose that the South African federation should be as 'tight' as possible, with residual powers vested in the Federal Parliament on the Canadian rather than the Australian model, so as to create a strong Central Government and to minimize friction between the central and the provincial authorities and the costs of provincial establishments. Thereafter Lord Selborne and the Kindergarten gradually moved towards the opinion that unification was the ideal, for the reasons which Feetham had given in favour of a tight as opposed to a loose federation; but until the Intercolonial Conference of May 1908 they still considered that a unitary Constitution would not be possible.[14] G. R. Hofmeyr, the Clerk of the Transvaal Legislative Assembly, expressed similar views in a pamphlet published in March 1908: unification, he wrote, was the ideal, because 'in the union of the hearts of the two great white peoples alone will the permanent peace and prosperity of South Africa lie'; but it was not practical politics, so federation must be accepted as a second best.[15] But outside of Natal, where the British electorate almost unanimously preferred federation, because they wished to preserve the identity of their colony and retain for their own Parliament exclusive powers over a wide field, only a few regarded federation as the best solution.[16] Among those who did were J. H. Hofmeyr, the veteran of the Afrikaner Bond, and F. S. Malan. On 4 September 1906 Malan published an article in *Ons Land* in which he defended federalism on its merits, arguing that the vast area of South Africa made it necessary to retain provincial parliaments and expressing the opinion that unification would lead to inefficient administration and neglect of the farmers.[17]

Merriman's mind had long since been set in favour of a unitary Constitution. As early as the 1870's he had formed the opinion that federalism was an extravagant and unnecessarily complicated form of government and that had been one of his reasons for condemning Carnarvon's federation project. Consequently, as soon as a union of some sort became a practicable proposition, Merriman began to declaim to his friends on the vices of federalism. Thus in June 1904, answering Smuts's first mention of the desirability of making 'a move in the direction of federa-

---

[14] Selborne to Sir Henry de Villiers, 2 May 1908, de Villiers Papers.

[15] Gijs R. Hofmeyr, *Closer Union of South African Colonies* (Pretoria, 1908).

[16] The case of Natal is dealt with separately in Chapter IV (3) below.

[17] Malan's article is reprinted in Johann F. Preller (ed.), *Die Konvensie-Dagboek van F. S. Malan* (Cape Town, 1951), pp. 257-60.

tion', Merriman wrote: 'I have always been of the opinion that one Parliament and one Ministry would be enough for South Africa. . . .' He went on to say, however, that he supposed that 'local jealousy' would prevent this; and to suggest, as Feetham was to suggest two years later, that in that event 'The next best thing will be the Canadian model rather than the Australian.'[18] But it was not long before Merriman became more optimistic and more determined, and when Steyn had told him that he was inclined to agree with him he assured him, early in 1906, that 'Everything points to "unification" rather than the more complicated scheme.'[19] Smuts, however, took longer to make up his mind. In May 1904 he had written of 'Federation' as the goal; in August 1906 he used the phrase 'a Unified or Federal South Africa', and in December 1906 'Federation or rather (if possible) Unification'; but by September 1907 his mind was finally set on a unitary Constitution and he was writing that 'The trouble will be about Federation, in which I don't have any particular faith as distinguished from Unification.'[20] Eight months before the Intercolonial Conference of May 1908, therefore, Merriman, Smuts, and Steyn were in agreement on this important question.

What were their reasons? Merriman's preference for a unitary Constitution flowed logically from his political premisses. Since, in his view, economy was of paramount importance in public affairs and a unitary system, with only one Parliament and Cabinet, seemed to be considerably more economical than a federal system, with several parliaments and cabinets, it followed that the former was superior; and that was the reasoning that was dominant in his letters and speeches on the subject. Secondly, since he believed that a Parliament should be the supreme power in a State and a federal system necessarily imposed limitations upon the power of the Central Parliament, it followed that federalism was also defective on those grounds. Under a federal system, moreover, if the American, Canadian, and Australian precedents are followed, the courts acquire the power to interpret the Constitution and Merriman was averse to giving them that power. He also considered that history was against federalism. He was greatly impressed by F. S. Oliver's biography of Alexander Hamilton, which was sympathetic to Hamilton's desire for a unitary Constitution in America, and by John A. Macdonald's arguments for a unitary Constitution for Canada in the Quebec Conference of 1864; and he had reached the conclusion that federalism had been

18 4 June 1904, Smuts Papers.

19 Steyn to Merriman, 10 Nov. 1905, Merriman Papers; Merriman to Steyn, 9 Feb. 1906, Steyn Papers.

20 Smuts to Merriman, 30 May 1904, 30 Aug. 1906, and 23 Dec. 1906, Merriman Papers; Smuts to Duncan, 28 Sept. 1907, Duncan Papers.

largely responsible for the American Civil War and that it was causing extravagance and incessant disputes in Canada and Australia. He distinguished between the white racial problems of Canada and South Africa, believing that Boer and Briton would easily fuse into a single homogeneous nation, since both were of Teutonic descent and members of Protestant churches, whereas French and British Canadians were kept apart by ethnic and religious differences. Furthermore, he realized that although federalism provided some security for the French Canadians, since most of them still lived in the single province of Quebec, it would not provide any significant security for either of the white groups in South Africa, since both Boer and Briton were to be found in nearly every part of the country and they were approximately equal in numbers in each of the two largest colonies. Merriman used several of these arguments in his speech in the Cape Parliament in support of the Closer Union Resolutions on 22 June 1908:[21]

They in this country [i.e. the whites in South Africa] were a mere handful; they counted last year 1,151,000 people. They had four separate Parliaments, 325 members of Parliament, and four separate Ministries, and he thought they would agree with him that this country was over-governed. . . . He . . . believed that the future union of South Africa should be, as far as possible, to make this one people, with one Parliament, with strong local powers devolving upon the different parts of South Africa. . . . He did not shut his eyes to the fact that in other Federations people were also strongly in favour of a united form of government. In the United States the great Washington and the great Hamilton were strongly in favour of a united and a strong form of government. The parochialists, however, carried the day. In Canada, in the same way, Sir John Macdonald—perhaps the keenest intellect in Canada—was also strongly in favour of Parliamentary Government. The fates were against him, because they had there an alien church and an alien people, unlike the people in this colony, that practically formed one homogeneous population. In this country they had no alien church and no alien race, for the two races in this country sprang from a common stock, and there was nothing to prevent them from intermingling in every possible way. They had only to turn to their sister colony of Australia, where they began upon the very principle which was advocated here. In Australia they had succeeded in making a bundle of jangling and wrangling States, whose only salvation was to unite, or they would probably break up. If they wanted a warning, let them take it from Australia and not follow in their footsteps. . . .

Smuts was susceptible to all these arguments, but with him the argument for economy was less weighty than the argument for concentration of

21 *Cape Hansard, 1908,* pp. 39–40.

power at the centre, as may be seen from his speech in the Transvaal Parliament on 23 June 1908:[22]

The federal system is not only undesirable because it involves even more expense and means more machinery superimposed on the people of South Africa, which is already groaning under all this administration, but to my mind the great difficulty with federation is this, that it assumes that a number of independent parties come together and enter into a compact, into an agreement, which is binding for the future. The federal system is one of checks and balances. . . . The natural result of that system is that it becomes a hide-bound system—a contract between a number of parties which the future cannot attempt to change, and the result is a rigid, inflexible Constitution which cannot develop as times go forward. Is that the sort of Constitution we want for South Africa, for a country in its infancy? Do we want a Constitution which will lead to civil wars as the American Constitution led to? No; we prefer to follow a different type—that of the British Constitution. . . . We must not be prevented in far-off years, from going forward because we have an agreement which cannot be altered. That is the great drawback about a Federal Constitution. What we want is a supreme national authority to give expression to the national will of South Africa, and the rest is really subordinate. . . .

After the Intercolonial Conference public opinion outside of Natal gradually swung round to the unitary point of view. One reason for this was the constant advocacy of Smuts and Merriman, which had the effect of converting those of their colleagues, like Malan, who had originally had federal leanings. Another lay in the attitude of the Kindergarten. Since the publication of the Selborne Memorandum in July 1907 Curtis had been preparing a book in which he sought to reiterate the lessons of the dangers of continued disunion and to provide the factual background which would help South Africans to draft an efficient Constitution. After collecting information from the government records in the four colonial capitals, he wrote *The Government of South Africa*, with help from Duncan and others. It was first published anonymously in five instalments between May and October 1908, and from the second instalment onwards it came down heavily on the unitary side. 'The authors began this work', they wrote in the introduction to the revised edition which appeared on the eve of the first meeting of the National Convention, 'in the belief that federation was the only form of union possible in South Africa. As, however, their enquiries into the actual facts of South African government advanced, they found themselves carried in the opposite

[22] *Transvaal Leg. Ass. Deb., 1908*, cols. 180–1. For comments on some of these arguments, see below, pp. 482–3.

direction.' They had reached the conclusion that under a federal Constitution the national interest would be certain to suffer from the legal disputes which would result from the division of powers between the central and the provincial authorities; that the process of transition would be easier to a unitary State than to a federal one; and that the 'Native question', with its ramifications in 'every department of life in South Africa', needed uniform treatment as could only be achieved under a unitary Constitution. On this question there was therefore a complete identity of purpose between the Kindergarten and the governments of the Cape Colony and the Transvaal.

Meanwhile Curtis had launched the Closer Union Societies movement. The first societies were founded in Cape Town and Johannesburg during May 1908, with the support of members of all political parties, and by the end of the year there were twenty-two societies in South Africa— fourteen in the Cape Colony, three in the Transvaal, three in Natal, and two in the Orange River Colony. Their main activity was the holding of public meetings, which were addressed by men with some claims to special knowledge of constitutional problems. The meetings were fully reported in the press and many of the addresses were subsequently republished in pamphlet form. Nearly all the speakers devoted their attention to the question of the form of the Constitution and most of them announced their preference for unification. For example, Sir Perceval Laurence, a judge of the Cape Supreme Court, informed the Cape Town Society that he believed that South Africa did not possess enough men of calibre to run provincial parliaments and governments as well as a Central Parliament and Government, and that federalism was extravagant, and would lead to excessive litigation and the undermining of public confidence in the courts.[23] These were weighty words to come from an experienced judge. Laurence was followed by a professor of history, John Edgar, who asserted that history shows that 'Federations are in general short-lived'; and by an advocate, A. J. McGregor, who said that federalism leads to weak government.[24]

The unitary trend of public opinion was also promoted by a number of exaggerated criticisms of federal institutions in Canada and Australia which appeared in the South African press. The story is a curious one. Sir Henry de Villiers spent slightly over a week in Canada in July 1908 as the representative of the South African colonies at the Quebec tercentenary celebrations, and to the delight of Merriman he returned a 'convinced and ardent unificationist' and informed the press that the Canadian Constitution had erred in giving wide powers to the provincial

[23] *Cape Times*, 10 July 1908.   [24] Ibid., 13 Aug. and 2 Oct. 1908.

legislatures, because it had prevented the merging of the French and British Canadians into a single nation.[25] This was, of course, a somewhat superficial judgement of the Canadian Constitution, and no less a person than Sir Wilfrid Laurier, the French Canadian Prime Minister of Canada, advised Smuts that South Africa would be wise to adopt federalism:[26]

My opinion is very strong [he wrote] that with the duality of races, such as they have it in South Africa and such as we have it in Canada, the form of union should be federative. Even if there were homogeneity of races I would still favour the federative system. . . . To me the point does not admit of discussion. . . . I may add [he concluded] . . . that our Constitution has worked remarkably well. We have had some troubles but, on the whole, we have got through them to the satisfaction of all classes.

But whereas publicity was given to de Villiers's strictures of Canadian federalism, the South African press was not informed of the views of the Canadian Prime Minister. As regards Australia, a series of articles appeared in the South African press making much of the judicial and financial difficulties which the Commonwealth was experiencing in its early years and implying that most Australians considered that their Constitution was a failure.[27] But leading Australian authorities, when approached by Smuts's staff for their views, denied that the position was nearly as black as it had been painted. Professor W. H. Moore of Melbourne remarked that 'A few extremists on both sides talk of unification and the abolition of State Legislatures. . . . But no radical alteration of that kind is likely'; and R. H. Garran, the co-author of the standard work on the making of the Australian Constitution, asserted bluntly that 'The views expressed in the articles by a special correspondent of the

[25] Merriman to Botha, 27 Aug. 1908, Merriman Papers (copy of telegram); *Cape Times*, 20 Aug. 1908.

[26] On 20 June 1908 R. H. Brand, acting on behalf of Smuts, wrote to E. W. Thomson, a Canadian journalist, asking for his opinion of the working of the Canadian Constitution. Thomson replied on 26 July, warmly defending the Canadian system, which worked 'excellently well, in my opinion'. Thomson also referred Brand's letter to Sir Wilfrid Laurier, whose reply of 28 July he forwarded to Brand two days later. This is the letter which is quoted in the text. Later, when he had been informed that South Africa was likely to adopt a unitary Constitution, Thomson told Brand (24 Oct. 1908): 'May I be permitted to say that it seems to me very possible that you gentlemen in South Africa, so long accustomed to War and huge troubles, may possibly set too much store on the advantage of Centralization, or Unification, as a system giving to or fortifying the Principal Power in authority and in ability for quick strokes. . . . May I suggest that you are all apt to, or may be apt to think *like soldiers* in S.A., and so, like Generals, value centralization of authority far too much. . . . To think of S.A. going to Unification . . . fills me with a kind of regret or dismay.' Brand Papers.

[27] e.g. *Cape Times*, 5 May, 25 May, 15 June, and 9 Oct. 1908.

Transvaal Leader . . . are, in my opinion, both prejudiced and misleading. I have no hesitation in saying that there is, in Australia, no general
dissatisfaction with federation as a system and no popular demand for
unification. Our Constitution has, as a whole, worked well.'[28] But these
comments, too, were not published, and South Africans continued to
gain the impression that federalism had proved a failure in Australia and
Canada.

The cumulative effect of these forces was that by the time of the
National Convention the majority of the South African politicians and
voters favoured unification. Federalism continued to be preferred by
most of the people of Natal; but elsewhere it was a declining force, though
the *Cape Argus* and a few individuals in the Cape Colony remained
federalists. Among them was J. H. Hofmeyr;[29] but on this question at
least his views were no longer sacrosanct to the younger and more active
leaders of the Afrikaner Bond. A Cape Progressive, Sir Bisset Berry,
who was a former Speaker of the House of Assembly, also remained a
staunch federalist, and in addressing the Queenstown Closer Union
Society early in October he denied most of the allegations that had been
made against federalism and contended that it was the right form of
government for South Africa on the ground that it was the only way of
safeguarding the interests of the Cape Colony and her colour-blind
franchise.[30] W. P. Schreiner also continued to lean towards federalism
for the same reason, and he would probably have argued for it tena-
ciously in the National Convention if he had not withdrawn from the
Cape delegation to defend Dinizulu on the charges of treason brought
against him by the Natal Government. Perhaps the most original and
penetrating statement of the case for federalism was the one made by
his sister, Olive Schreiner. She had already attracted attention in South
Africa and overseas as the authoress of *The Story of an African Farm*
and as a feminist and anti-imperialist, and towards the end of 1908 she
brought her sensitive mind and keen moral sense to bear upon the
question of closer union. Invited by the editor of the *Transvaal Leader*
to answer a number of questions on the subject, she wrote an extensive
essay on South African affairs, breaking through many of the popular
assumptions of the day.[31] South Africa, she wrote, should become a loose

[28] Brand Papers.

[29] On 19 June 1908 Hofmeyr informed C. P. Crewe, a Unionist member of the Cape
Parliament, that he had always regarded unification as impracticable and that 'if the
choice of a capital proved an insuperable stumbling-block, I would almost content
myself with some form of capital-less League'. Hofmeyr Papers (draft).

[30] *Cape Times*, 6 Oct. 1908.

[31] *Transvaal Leader*, 22 Dec. 1908. Subsequently republished as a booklet, *Closer*

federation, with most powers retained by the local parliaments. The colonies should retain their personalities because 'in small States there tends ... to be more personal freedom, more individuality, and a higher social vitality than in large', and because a federal Constitution 'will present a far greater obstacle to the undue dominance of any interest, class or individual than the same territory under a unified and centralised government'. She also deplored the popular expectation that union would be 'a kind of Father Christmas who will drop a pound into every empty pocket', and she regretted the indications that the politicians were trying to sweep South Africa into a hasty union. Above all she pleaded for wisdom and justice in the handling of the Natives, 'the root question in South Africa'. But the problems which she raised, like the problems which were raised by J. G. Kotzé, did not strike a chord in the minds of the politicians or the people of South Africa, and the *Cape Times* complacently remarked that she was 'out of touch with the trend of recent events'.[32] Indeed, by the time of the National Convention the federalists outside of Natal were lone voices crying in the wilderness.

Thus the stage was set for the drafting of a Constitution which would be unitary and comparatively free of legal limitations upon the powers of the Central Parliament other than those imperial limitations which still applied to any self-governing British colony or dominion—a Constitution like the British Constitution and unlike that of the United States of America.

3. POLITICAL RIGHTS

Of several obstacles to the achievement of a legislative union of the four self-governing British South African colonies, one of the most formidable was their wide differences in law, practice, and sentiment on the question of political rights.

In the Cape Colony political rights were dependent upon the possession of simple educational and economic qualifications regardless of race, colour, or creed, but they were confined to the male sex. The right to be registered on the common roll to vote in the elections for the members of both Houses of Parliament was open to any male British subject of mature age who could sign his name and write his address and occupation and who either earned £50 wages a year or occupied a house and land together worth £75—but land occupied under tribal African tenure (i.e. most of the land which was reserved for the exclusive use of the

Union: a letter on the South African Union and the Principles of Government (London, 1909).   [32] *Cape Times*, 24 Dec. 1908.

Africans) did not count towards the property qualification. Any voter was eligible for election to the House of Assembly; and any voter who owned immovable property worth £2,000 clear of mortgage was eligible for election to the Legislative Council. In practice no Coloured man or African ever became a member of the Cape Parliament, and in 1909 there were 142,367 registered voters in the colony of whom 121,346 (85·2 per cent.) were white men, 14,388 (10·1 per cent.) were Coloured men (including Malays, Indians, Chinese, and Hottentots), and 6,633 (4·7 per cent.) were Africans.[33] This meant that roughly two-thirds of the white men were registered, one-eighth of the Coloured men, and one-sixtieth of the Africans. The Cape Colony whites therefore still had an effective control of the political machinery although they only numbered a quarter of the total population of the colony. Nevertheless, the Coloured and African voters were numerous enough in several constituencies for their votes to be solicited by candidates of both the main parties, and the Parliament of the Cape Colony paid considerably more attention to the opinions and interests of the non-Europeans than any other legislature in South Africa.

The laws governing political rights in Natal created economic qualifications and they were framed and administered so as to debar not only women but also practically every non-European. Any white man of mature age could become registered as a voter or nominated for election to the Legislative Assembly if he was a British subject and if he either owned immovable property worth £50, or paid £10 rent a year, or received £8 wages a month, and in practice about two-thirds of the white men were registered. Law No. 11 of 1865 disqualified all those who were subject to Native Law. An African man could, however, apply for exemption from Native Law on the ground that he was civilized and then, after seven years as an 'exempted Native', he could apply for the franchise provided that he possessed one of the economic qualifications. The Governor, acting on the advice of his ministers, had complete discretion in dealing with both types of applications, and in practice both types of certificates were granted very sparingly.[34] Until 1896 it had been possible for Natal Indians who were not serving labour indentures to

[33] *Statistical Register for the Colony of the Cape of Good Hope, 1909*, p. 15.

[34] By the end of 1908 about 1,800 Africans had been exempted from Native Law. In Dec. 1906 S. O. Samuelson, Under-Secretary for Native Affairs, stated that only three Africans had been granted the franchise, and that three other African applicants had been refused it, to his knowledge. In 1908 there were believed to be six African voters on the rolls. *Natal Native Affairs Commission, 1906–7, Report and Evidence* (Pietermaritzburg, 1907, 2 vols.), ii, evidence of S. O. Samuelson; Anon., *The Government of South Africa* (Cape Town, 1908, 2 vols.), ii. 410; U. 17 (1911), *Blue Book on Native Affairs, 1910*, p. 16.

acquire the vote if they possessed one of the economic qualifications, and some had done so; but then in Act No. 8 of that year the Natal Parliament devised an ingenious formula to stop further Indian registrations. No more persons were to be enrolled as voters 'who (not being of European origin) are Natives or descendants in the male line of Natives of countries which have not hitherto possessed elective representative institutions founded on the parliamentary Franchise unless they shall first obtain an order from the Governor in Council exempting them from the operation of this Act'.[35] The members of the small Coloured community in Natal were legally entitled to the franchise on the same qualifications as white men, but some magistrates tended to treat them as though they were subject to Native Law and only a few managed to become registered as voters. The result was that in 1907 there were 23,686 registered voters in Natal of whom it was estimated that 23,480 (99·1 per cent.) were white men, 150 were Indians, 50 were Coloured men, and 6 were native Africans.[36] Political power in Natal was therefore, in practice if not in theory, an effective monopoly of the whites, who formed less than one-eleventh of the total population of the colony; and the Natal Parliament normally paid scant attention to the opinions and the interests of the non-Europeans, as was revealed by the Native Affairs Commission which was appointed after the 1906 rebellion.

The two Boer republics had been founded on the principle of racial discrimination, and had always debarred all non-Europeans from political rights. The conquest of the republics by Great Britain was not followed by the slightest relaxation of the political colour-bar. Article 8 of the Treaty of Vereeniging stated that 'The question of granting the franchise to natives will not be decided until after the introduction of self-government', and the British Liberal Government gave it the widest application in the Letters Patent providing for self-government.[37] In both the Transvaal and the Orange River Colony any white man of mature age could be registered as a parliamentary voter and was eligible for election to the Legislative Assembly provided that he was a British subject and had resided in the colony for six months; but all non-Europeans—Coloured men and Asiatics as well as native Africans—were excluded from political rights. Thus there was the somewhat remarkable combination between manhood suffrage for whites and no votes at all for non-whites in the Transvaal where the whites formed a quarter of

[35] G. W. Eybers (ed.), *Select Constitutional Documents illustrating South African History, 1795–1910* (London, 1918), p. 215.

[36] *The Government of South Africa*, ii. 410.

[37] See above, pp. 11, 26–27.

the total population and in the Orange River Colony where the whites formed a third of the total population.

Like most European countries at that time, all the South African colonies excluded women from political rights. Nevertheless, the British suffragette movement was beginning to have repercussions in South Africa. Botha was open-minded on the question and so were Moor and other Natal politicians; but although zealous women prepared a petition to the National Convention in favour of women's suffrage they could only muster 1,415 signatures, whereas a counter-petition, describing women's suffrage as a violation of the 'natural distinction between men and women', was signed by over 7,000 women.[38] The time was not yet ripe for admitting women to the franchise in South Africa. As regards the age and residential qualifications, there were no overt differences of opinion among white South Africans in 1908. The laws of the South African Republic, which had patently been designed to maintain the dominance of the Boers over the Uitlanders, were discredited for the time being and everyone was prepared to accept a minimum age of 21 and a comparatively brief residential qualification.

The other three qualifications were closely interrelated. In the Cape Colony, where there were economic and educational qualifications but no racial ones, the effect in a rough and ready way was to grant political rights to the 'civilized' members of the population and to withhold them from the 'uncivilized' members of all races; and there was the logical implication that in the course of time more and more Coloured men and Africans would become registered as voters, until eventually they would be in a political majority. On the other hand, the laws of the Transvaal and the Orange River Colony, where there was a colour-bar but no economic or educational qualification, were based on the Voortrekker concept of a privileged white community, 'democratic' within itself, but permanently distinct from and dominant over the rest of the inhabitants —a convenient adaptation of the Calvinist doctrine of the elect.

To what extent did public opinion correspond with these differences? It was certainly not nearly so sharply differentiated as the laws. To read the evidence taken by the South African Native Affairs Commission of 1903–5[39] is to gain the impression that nearly every white South African, in the Cape Colony as well as in the northern colonies, treated all non-Europeans as his social inferiors, relied on non-Europeans to provide

---

[38] House of Assembly, National Convention Minutes, ii, iv. The quotation is from the counter-petition in iv.

[39] *South African Native Affairs Commission, 1903–5, Report and Appendices* (Cape Town, 1905, 5 vols.), ii–v.

domestic and industrial labour at low wages, and believed that non-Europeans should never be allowed to control the political machinery. To that extent nearly all white South Africans were imbued with the spirit of a dominant caste. Nevertheless, to read the evidence is also to gain the impression that there were significant differences of opinion and that the dividing line ran not so much between Boer and Briton as between the Cape Colony and the northern colonies: environment was the decisive factor. In the Cape Colony, especially in its south-western districts in and near the Cape peninsula, there was a greater willingness to deal with racial problems empirically and humanely and to accept a gradual softening of the caste lines; whereas in the Transvaal and Natal and to a slightly lesser extent in the Orange River Colony, the prevalent attitude was more exclusive, more dogmatic, and less humane.

The attitudes of the whites in the south-western Cape were comparatively mild because there were very few Africans there, and the cultural traits of the Coloured people, with whom they had been in peaceful daily contact for generations, were essentially western in type. The attitudes of the whites in the eastern districts of the Cape Colony were less mild because those districts had been the scene of a century of frontier warfare against native Africans, whose culture was quite different and who were greatly superior in numbers. The result was that no voice was heard to suggest that the Coloured people should be treated on a different basis in politics; but there was an undercurrent of apprehension about the African vote. Moreover, if one was apprehensive one could easily find grounds to criticize the actual operation of the African vote in the Cape Colony. For example, the only Africans who were legally entitled to purchase liquor were those who were registered voters, and many Africans seem to have been more interested in the liquor than the vote. Thus Major Musgrave, an Inspector of Native Locations in the Glen Grey district, told the South African Native Affairs Commission that 'The harder the drinker, the harder does the fellow struggle to get the vote. I have no hesitation in saying that out of a register of Christian voters, you can parade as fine a squad of wholesale drunkards as you will find in any part of the world.'[40] The commission also discovered that some of the registration officers were licensed purveyors of liquor, who therefore had a financial interest in enrolling Africans as voters![41] Some of the critics would have been content to see the existing qualifications more strictly observed; others considered that the qualifications should

[40] Ibid. ii, ans. 12,471.
[41] Ibid. ii, ans. 10,258–353, evidence of R. J. Crowe, farmer, hotel-keeper, and field-cornet of Debe Nek.

be raised to include a more effective educational test; and others again would have liked the African voters to be removed from the common roll and given a fixed number of representatives in the Cape Parliament; but very few went so far as to wish to deny the Africans any form of parliamentary representation. The leading politicians of both parties were unwilling to abandon the principle of a colour-blind common roll, and they did not regard the irregularities as serious enough to warrant fresh legislation in matters of detail. The Cape's half-century of experience of the system had convinced them that they were on the right lines, and they saw no reason for fearing an early threat to white leadership since the non-European voters were not inclined to vote as a block —indeed, their votes were divided fairly evenly between the two parties. Thus the Cape politicians believed that their franchise policy was right, not only as a matter of expediency but also in principle. The most outspoken of them was J. W. Sauer, who told the commission that he thought that the Cape system should be extended throughout South Africa because 'a policy of justice is more likely to avert trouble and danger than any other' and 'it is not justice that one section of the community paying taxes should be deprived of political rights'. He added:

I do not believe that where representative institutions exist . . . a class that is not represented will ever receive political justice, because after all it is material interests that will eventually prevail and, therefore, the class or classes having no political power will suffer.[42]

The evidence given to the South African Native Affairs Commission makes it quite clear that harsher attitudes prevailed among the whites in the northern colonies. Physical violence was recommended by some as the one sure method of handling Africans. Thus E. A. O. Schwikkard, a witness representing the Natal Farmers' Congress, testified as follows:[43]

My great idea is this, that with regard to the Natives, we must put sentiment aside. . . . The Native is the most tractable man going, as long as he knows you have your foot on his neck. . . . I think the thing that should be used very freely is the lash, for it is bodily pain that the Native fears. He fears nothing else. We have got to get him into such a state that we want something drastic before we are able to get him back to what he used to be.

With others cupidity was the uppermost thought: G. G. Munnik, a leading Transvaal farmer, recommended that the Africans should be compelled to vacate land which was suitable for white settlement and argued that they required less water than white men; while W. K. Tucker,

[42] *South African Native Affairs Commission, 1903–5, Report and Appendices*, iv, ans. 45,075–7.   [43] Ibid. iii, ans. 22,085.

a spokesman of the Rand Pioneers, said that the basic tendency of Native policy should be 'to make them work continuously to earn a living'.[44] In such an atmosphere a northern politician would have compromised his career if he had publicly espoused any form of effective political representation for non-Europeans, even for the Coloured people. In fact, however, most of the northern politicians held views which were not very dissimilar from those of their constituents. For example, F. R. Moor told the commission:[45]

At this stage in our history we can tolerate no terms whatsoever of political or social equality, and it is something deeper than any doctrines or dogmas that implants that feeling in every white man's brain. It is a racial instinct which, in its tendency, is wiser than any laws which we might make to bring about terms of equality between the races.

The farthest that any of the Natal witnesses was prepared to go was to allow a few white men to be nominated by the Government to express the views of Africans in the Natal Parliament; but others, like H. D. Winter, a former Minister of Agriculture, thought that even this was unnecessary, and he produced the transparent argument that 'every Member of Parliament at the present time represents the Natives, both directly and indirectly' in Natal.[46] The Transvaal politicians held similar views for the most part, though there were some, like Sir Percy Fitzpatrick, who had broader vision. In the Orange River Colony, with its smaller African population and its simpler social and economic structure, leading men were more open-minded. C. H. Wessels, a former Chairman of the Free State Volksraad, was drawn by the commission to admit that the Cape Native franchise was justified and to accept the idea that even in his own colony intelligent Coloured men and intelligent African landowners should have a vote; while J. G. Fraser, another former Chairman of the Volksraad, was willing to allow the Africans to elect a few white men to represent them in Parliament.[47]

After the Natal Native Rebellion and when the inland colonies had been granted responsible government and closer union had become a matter of practical politics, white opinion hardened perceptibly along colonial lines. In the Cape Colony, before and during the general election of 1907–8, the leaders of both the political parties gave the strongest

[44] Ibid. iv, ans. 40,355–6, 43,811.
[45] Ibid. iii, ans. 20,790.
[46] Ibid. iii, ans. 25,171. This is the old argument of 'virtual representation', which had been used by Britain against her North American colonies in the eighteenth century and by opponents of parliamentary reform in Britain in the nineteenth century.
[47] Ibid. iv, ans. 37,852–4, 38,932–39,008.

public assurances that they stood by the principle of 'equal rights for all civilized men' and would not sacrifice it for union. On the Unionist side E. H. Walton, Treasurer in Jameson's Cabinet, said that he was not prepared to depart from it 'for any consideration', and Jameson himself said:

> There is, I find, an insuperable obstacle in the way of unification, and that is the question of the Native franchise, and that is why we must go for Federation, so that we may hold to our Native policy until the neighbouring colonies are sufficiently educated to agree to allow equal facilities for blacks and whites to rise in the scale of humanity.

For the South African Party F. S. Malan announced:

> The South African Party is against drawing a colour line for political purposes. . . . I do not wish the colour line drawn in the Cape Colony, and I would not like to see the colour line in a Federated South Africa; if it is necessary to wait for five or ten years it will be better to do so.

Merriman echoed him with the assurance that he would not 'under any circumstances retreat from' the Cape system.[48] These were very clear pledges. In the northern colonies, on the other hand, the feeling against any relaxation of the colour-bar was stronger than ever; there was a widespread determination to reject any Constitution providing for the extension of political rights to non-Europeans beyond the Orange River; and during the 1907 general election in the Orange River Colony men like C. H. Wessels and J. G. Fraser were no longer heard expressing open-minded views in public. South Africa seemed to be divided into two irreconcilable camps: and on the surface it appeared likely that the question of non-European representation in the South African Parliament would be the rock on which closer union of any sort, let alone a unitary Constitution, would founder.

This difficulty had been foreseen and several efforts had already been made to narrow the gap between the different systems and to lay down general principles of Native policy for all British South Africa. In 1892, when Rhodes introduced the legislation which raised the occupational qualification for the franchise from £25 to £75 and created the elementary educational test in the Cape Colony, he expressed the hope that it would make the Cape system less of a stumbling-block to federation. Then in 1903, at the Intercolonial Conference held in Bloemfontein,

---

[48] These statements are printed in U.G. 54 (1937), *Report of Commission of Inquiry regarding the Cape Coloured Population of the Union*, p. 224.

Moor tried to persuade the delegates of all the South African colonies to accept the principle that 'the political status of the Native should conform to conditions which will ensure the constant dominance of the White Race', and Lord Milner gave him strong support from the chair; but the proposal was dropped in the face of opposition from the Cape delegates.[49] Nevertheless, the conference passed a unanimous resolution which led to the appointment of the South African Native Affairs Commission, with the instruction to try and devise a basis for a uniform Native policy throughout British South Africa. Reporting in 1905, the commission reviewed the evidence which has been analysed above and unanimously recommended that there should be no Native voters on the common electoral rolls, but that Natives should elect a fixed number of representatives to each colonial Parliament, 'the number not to be more than sufficient to provide an adequate means for the expression of Native views and the ventilation of their grievances, if any, and not to be regulated by the numerical strength of the Native vote'. This method was to be adopted by each colony as it became self-governing, which implied that it should be done at once in the Cape Colony and Natal and subsequently in the Transvaal, the Orange River Colony, and Rhodesia, and elsewhere, so that there would be 'a uniform and permanent political status for the Natives throughout South Africa'.[50] The recommendation was still-born. Neither party in the Cape Colony was prepared to take the initiative in removing the Cape Native voters from the common roll; no group in the Natal Parliament wished to grant the Natal Natives representation of even so limited a type; and all the white political organizations in the Transvaal and the Orange River Colony insisted that article 8 of the Treaty of Vereeniging should be applied with the widest possible interpretation.

While a constitution for the Transvaal was being considered in 1906 the issues were discussed in private correspondence by Merriman, Smuts, and Steyn. Merriman took the initiative in raising the subject from the standpoint of one who had regarded Milner's post-war policy as an attempt 'to reconcile the whites over the body of the blacks',[51] and who believed that 'no sympathy for the Boer cause can ever excuse any sort of departure from a liberal native policy'.[52] Replying in June 1904

[49] The printed records of the South African Intercolonial Conference, 1903, consist of: (a) brief *Minutes*, being a record of resolutions carried; and (b) longer *Minutes* (103 pp.), which include a summary of the speeches and were given a restricted circulation. Brand Papers.

[50] *S.A. Native Affairs Commission, 1903–5*, i, paras. 443–6.

[51] Merriman to Mrs. A. Merriman, 4 Oct. 1903, Merriman Papers.

[52] Merriman to F. Mackarness, 22 Nov. 1903, ibid. (copy).

to Smuts's first letter suggesting that the time for closer union was approaching, Merriman had said that 'the crux of any union in South Africa will be native policy', that it was important to avoid a north–south division inside South Africa like that which had led to civil war in the United States of America, and that the best way out of the difficulty would be to have a high, uniform, colour-blind franchise for the Union Parliament.[53] Smuts had not answered him on this point; but early in 1906 he sent Merriman a copy of his memorandum for the Colonial Office in London, pleading, on the one hand, for 'the unreserved application of Liberal principles to the government of the new colonies, by showing a statesmanlike trust in the people of the land, of whatever race', and, on the other hand, for white manhood suffrage.[54] This gave Merriman his cue. He pointed out that[55]

What struck me at once on reading your admirable remarks on liberal principles was, that they were open to the same objection in kind to the American declaration of Independence—viz. that you ignore $\frac{3}{4}$ of the population because they are coloured.

And he went on to present the argument of expediency for a high, uniform, colour-blind franchise:

I do not like the natives at all and I wish we had no black man in S. Africa [he admitted]. But there they are, our lot is cast with them by an over ruling providence and the only question is how to shape our course so as to maintain the supremacy of our race and at the same time do our duty.

He then contended that the Cape system, with a more effective educational test, would not mean that the Natives would exercise any great weight in elections but that it would provide a necessary 'safety-valve'. To allow no Native vote at all would be 'building on a volcano'. Finally, to combine manhood suffrage for whites with a colour-bar would be to 'cut your own throat' because 'the poor whites will be as venal as any native'. In his reply, Smuts probably came as close to revealing his innermost convictions on the subject as he ever did:[56]

I sympathize profoundly with the native races of South Africa whose land it was long before we came here to force a policy of dispossession on them. And it ought to be the policy of all parties to do justice to the natives and to take all wise and prudent measures for their civilisation and improvement. But I don't believe in politics for them. Perhaps at bottom I do not believe

---

[53] Merriman to Smuts, 4 June 1904, Smuts Papers.
[54] Merriman Papers, No. 240/1906. See above, p. 25.
[55] Merriman to Smuts, 4 Mar. 1906, Smuts Papers.
[56] Smuts to Merriman, 13 Mar. 1906, Merriman Papers.

in politics at all as a means for the attainment of the highest ends; but
certainly so far as the natives are concerned politics will to my mind only
have an unsettling influence. I would therefore not give them the franchise,
which in any case would not affect more than a negligeable [*sic*] number of
them at present. When I consider the political future of the natives in S.A.
I must say that I look into shadows and darkness; and then I feel inclined to
shift the intolerable burden of solving that sphinx problem to the ampler
shoulders and stronger brains of the future. Sufficient unto the day etc. My
feeling is that strong forces are at work which will transform the Africander
attitude to the natives. . . .

On manhood suffrage I frankly disagree with your old-world Toryism.
The poor white is corruptible, but my experience is that the rich white is
even more so. And the way to raise up the poor white is not to ostracise him
politically. So let us agree to differ.

They continued to correspond on the subject until June 1906, without
approaching agreement. Merriman warned Smuts that 'a benevolent
paternal policy will never take the place of political status'. For one
thing, he said, such a policy was sheer Milnerism, with the Natives taking
the place of the Boers. For another, children grow up, and where then is
the justification for paternalism? No, he reiterated, a colour-blind franchise was essential as a safety-valve. Moreover, it would enable the
South African Governments to snap their fingers at Exeter Hall and
Downing Street.[57] As a parting shot Merriman told him on 26 June:[58]

I confess the prospect as far as you are concerned is pretty hopeless. You
accept a faulty basis and then proceed to build illogical conclusions thereon.
How can you without blushing talk of manhood suffrage and exclude of
design ⅔ of the population?

To defend himself against these attacks, Smuts was driven to take refuge
in the argument of political necessity:

We have had to go in for manhood suffrage [he wrote in April], not only
because it existed among the burghers before the war, and seems a democratic principle to which it shows high principles to appeal, but also because
the even low franchise of Milner's constitution resulted in the disfranchisement of some 10,000 bywoners and grown up sons on farms, the loss of
whom we cannot afford.[59]

Meanwhile, Steyn had informed Merriman that he was not opposed in
principle to giving the vote to civilized Natives, but that no such vote

[57] Merriman to Smuts, 18 and 30 Mar. 1906, Smuts Papers.
[58] Merriman to Smuts, 26 June 1906, ibid.
[59] Smuts to Merriman, 3 Apr. 1906, Merriman Papers.

should be provided for in the constitutions of the inland colonies, because the Treaty of Vereeniging should not be altered without the permission of 'the people', and because 'if the Natives have to get the franchise they must get it from our parliament, so that the natives be not brought under the delusion that only the Englishman is their friend, and whenever there is an election go with the party who claims the flag as belonging solely to them'.[60] Later, after discussing the subject in the Transvaal with Botha, Smuts, and some of their colleagues, Steyn assured Merriman that 'no injustice will be done to the natives from our side'.[61] And there the matter rested. The Transvaal and Orange River Colony constitutions provided for white manhood suffrage and a complete political colour-bar, the combination which Merriman had deplored. Merriman had lost an important preliminary round.

Soon afterwards Merriman asked Smuts to consider the problem of Native representation in a United South African Parliament, but Smuts gave no reply.[62] Merriman continued to ponder the question in his own mind, and in October 1907 he invited advice from the historian, Goldwin Smith, with whom he had been corresponding for some years.[63] There were, he explained, three possibilities. The best solution would be to have a uniform high franchise 'with a real educational test', but it appeared to be impracticable because of 'the tendency of the democratic age' and because of 'the existing franchises here and the colour prejudice'. Secondly, there was the possibility of having separate representation for Natives on the New Zealand model, as had been recommended by the South African Native Affairs Commission, but he saw overwhelming objections to that solution:

They have 45,000 Maories and 800,000 Europeans and they give the Maories 4 members in a House of 70. We have 2,000,000 Natives and 500,000 Europeans (in the Cape) and a suggestion was made that the Natives should have 4 members in a House of 104. Obviously this would not be a settlement and the 4 members would be up for sale to the party who promises to redress their grievances.

There was, too, a third possibility, that of preserving the existing differences in the franchise laws:

Then there is an alternative of keeping the Cape franchise for the Cape —and having a differential franchise for other parts of S. Africa. Is this

---

[60] Steyn to Merriman, 7 Mar. 1906, Merriman Papers.
[61] Steyn to Merriman, 21 Mar. 1906, ibid.
[62] Merriman to Smuts, 30 Dec. 1906, Smuts Papers.
[63] Merriman to Goldwin Smith, 26 Oct. 1907, Merriman Papers.

possible—Are there any precedents in England or elsewhere? I fancy in my ignorance that in the pre-levelling days there must be many such.

Goldwin Smith does not appear to have replied to this inquiry; but Merriman continued to think along these lines, and as he did so he came to believe that it would be essential to provide some security for the Cape franchise laws against their amendment by a bare majority of the Union Parliament. On 24 February 1908 he informed Smuts that the difficulty might be overcome by 'leaving the question of the franchise to the Provinces themselves and providing that the local franchise should not be altered, except on a $\frac{2}{3}$ majority, to be ascertained by a plebiscite of registered voters in the Province'.[64]

Smuts did not get to grips with the problem until after the meeting of the Intercolonial Conference. When he did so it soon became clear to him that the existing colonial franchise qualifications would have to be left as they were until they were altered by the South African Parliament. To attempt to achieve uniformity in the Constitution at the expense of the established rights of the Cape non-Europeans would be to invite its rejection by the Cape Colony; and to attempt to do so by any relaxation of the colour-bar in the Transvaal, the Orange River Colony, and Natal would be to invite its rejection by those colonies. But there was also another aspect of the matter to consider. Was there not a danger that the British Parliament might insist upon some representation for the non-Europeans of the northern provinces of a South African Union? The House of Commons had only approved the franchise qualifications in the Letters Patent establishing the constitutions of the Transvaal and the Orange River Colony with reluctance and because it considered that its hands had been tied by the Treaty of Vereeniging; and it would certainly give careful and critical attention to the franchise provisions of a South African Constitution. Indeed, on 13 May 1908 Colonel Seely, the Colonial Under-Secretary, referring to the Closer Union Resolutions of the Intercolonial Conference, gave the House of Commons the following assurance:[65]

What His Majesty's Government are committed to is that in any solution of the South African question some special representation must be found for the natives in order to safeguard their rights, and with that, I am glad to think, all people in South Africa are now practically agreed.

A month later J. A. Hobson, the English economist and anti-imperialist

---

[64] Merriman to Smuts, 24 Feb. 1908, Smuts Papers.
[65] *Parl. Deb.*, 4th Ser., clxxxviii. 1248.

whose pen had been wielded in the pro-Boer cause during the war, wrote to tell Smuts that a committee had been set up in London to consider the effects of South African union on the Natives. What, asked Hobson, would be the South African reaction to an attempt by British Liberals to secure 'some real representation for native interests' in the South African Parliament?[66] In reply Smuts explained that the existing franchise qualifications would have to be left as they were until they had been changed by the Union Parliament:[67]

My impression [he wrote] is that the only sound policy at this stage is to avoid any attempt at a comprehensive solution of the various questions surrounding the political status and rights of the natives. With the chaotic state in which public opinion on this subject is at present, any solution at present would be a poor compromise which might probably prejudice a fairer and more statesmanlike settlement later on. Public opinion in the majority of the South African States is against a native franchise in any shape or form, and while it cannot be denied that on this delicate subject responsible men are probably in advance of the rather crude attitude of the people at large and would be prepared to consider the subject on its merits, still the fear of the people will be with them and they will probably shrink from any far-reaching innovation. The danger then is that a poor makeshift arrangement will be framed; and there is the further and graver danger that the people, who will have ultimately to ratify any Constitution, may veto it on the ground that it confers the franchise on natives. This latter danger is a very real one, and will be a strong inducement to all who seriously desire to bring about a United South Africa to shelve this question at this stage in order to attack it under more favourable conditions after Union has been brought about. My view is that the different franchise laws of the several Colonies ought to be left undisturbed and that the first Union Elections ought to take place thereunder, and that the question of a uniform franchise law be gone into only after the Union has been brought about. You will then avoid the dangers I have referred to; and you will in the Union Parliament, representing as it will all that is best in the whole of South Africa, have a far more powerful and efficient instrument for the solution of the question along broad and statesmanlike lines than you will have in the Union Convention which is going to meet next October or November. The political status of the natives is no doubt a very important matter, but vastly more important to me is the Union of South Africa, which if not carried now will probably remain in abeyance until another deluge has swept over South Africa.

Merriman, consulted by Smuts, reiterated his views on the franchise question and said that he agreed with the tenor of Smuts's answer to

[66] 14 June 1908, Smuts Papers.
[67] 13 July 1908, Merriman Papers (copy).

Hobson; but he also reminded him that he considered there should be adequate security in the Constitution for the Cape franchise:[68]

I entirely agree with you that it would be quite impossible to dream of any general native franchise at the present time. If it were adopted at the Convention it would unquestionably lead to the rejection of the Constitution in the majority of the States. I ought also to add that in the Cape we are pledged as far as the most solemn assurances can go to maintain the rights conferred by our franchise.

I have always looked to effecting a compromise on the basis of a separate franchise for the provinces with material safeguards in the Constitution as regards alteration. At the same time we should base the distribution of representation purely on the European population. This as it seems to me would while fulfilling our obligations not offend the susceptibilities of any community.

I have tried to find a better solution in vain.

If such a solution were adopted in South Africa, would it be approved by the British Parliament? Smuts and Merriman calculated that, whatever interpretation might be placed on Colonel Seely's statement, the British Government and Parliament would not incur the risk of precipitating a crisis in their relations with the South African colonies—and very likely with Canada, Australia, and New Zealand also—by trying to alter a settlement drawn up by a South African National Convention and endorsed by the colonial parliaments or electorates, provided that it safeguarded established non-European rights, even though it did not extend them. Merriman put this calculation to the test by expounding his views to P. A. Molteno, a Liberal Member of Parliament and a son of Sir John Molteno, the first Prime Minister of the Cape Colony. In his reply Molteno argued at length for the extension of the Cape franchise throughout South Africa as the only guarantee for 'an orderly and peaceful development', but he also admitted that 'until some franchise is agreed upon—however high the qualification may be, provided that there is no distinction between black and white—it would almost seem that the *status quo* will have to be observed . . .'.[69] This was reassuring, because Molteno's views were known to be distinctly liberal on the franchise question, and if he would not oppose the compromise it was unlikely that many of his colleagues would do so. As for Smuts, in the constitutional schemes which he prepared for the Convention he dealt with the question along the lines suggested by Merriman; and ten days before the Convention met he reiterated his decision to Merriman:[70] 'Let us

[68] n.d. [July 1908], Merriman Papers (draft).
[69] 19 Aug. 1908, ibid.   [70] 2 Oct. 1908, ibid.

therefore adhere to the comfortable doctrine of *laisser faire*. To us Union means more than the Native question and it will be the only means of properly handling that vexed problem.' At the same time, although he had tried to assure Hobson that the Union Parliament would in due course make some provision for the representation of Natives in the northern provinces, he confessed to Merriman that his mind was 'full of Cimmerian darkness' as to the ultimate place of the Natives in South African society.

The question of the future of Basutoland, Bechuanaland Protectorate, and Swaziland was linked with the franchise question. At the Inter-colonial Conference the delegates of the South African governments had reached the conclusion that it would impose too great a burden on the first Government of the Union if it were given the additional task of taking over the protectorates, and that it would be best for the Constitution to ignore them, so that they could be absorbed 'as a matter of course' later on.[71] But Curtis, foreseeing difficulties if they remained under British administration, favoured their immediate inclusion in the Union and soon after the Conference Smuts, possibly under Curtis's influence, came to the same conclusion.[72] Replying to J. A. Hobson, who had pointed out that the British attitude to the question would depend upon the franchise provisions of the Constitution, Smuts made a strong bid for their immediate transfer:[73]

If I were a British statesman [he informed Hobson on 13 July] I would trust the people of South Africa in this matter and commit the Government of the whole of British South Africa unreservedly to their charge. Such trust is not likely to be misplaced and will most impressively bring home to South Africans their solemn duties in the matter.

But men like Hobson were not convinced by such protestations. Britain recognized that she had special obligations to the Native inhabitants of those territories, and she was averse to allowing them to be included in the projected Union unless the Constitution provided some form of effective parliamentary representation for the non-Europeans throughout the country. This had become evident on 13 May 1908, when the House of Commons adopted a resolution moved by P. Alden and seconded by Sir Charles Dilke, declaring:[74]

---

[71] 'Debate on "Closer Union" Resolutions', Merriman Papers, No. 60/1908.
[72] Curtis to the author, 18 Jan. 1952.
[73] Merriman Papers (copy).
[74] *Parl. Deb.*, 4th Ser., clxxxviii. 1215. The words of this motion are, perhaps,

That this House, recognising signs of a growing opinion on the part of the self-governing Colonies of South Africa in favour of safeguarding the rights and future of the natives in any scheme of political unification or federation, expresses its confidence that His Majesty's Government will welcome the adoption of provisions calculated to render possible the ultimate inclusion of the whole of British South Africa in federal union.

Moreover, Lord Selborne did not agree with Curtis on this question. He regarded Natal's administration of Zululand as an inauspicious precedent for the incorporation of 'native territories' in self-governing colonies where there was a colour-bar; he considered that the protectorates should not be incorporated in the Union if their native inhabitants were palpably opposed to it; and he was beginning to receive evidence that that was the case.[75] Consequently, Sir Richard Solomon, the Transvaal Agent-General in London, found that the Colonial Office was distinctly chilly towards any suggestion of immediate transfer, and in the light of that knowledge he drew up a memorandum, which he sent to Smuts on 3 September, making definite proposals for the handling of the protectorates question by the convention.[76] Solomon had formed the same opinion as Merriman about the franchise and he recommended that the existing colonial franchise laws should be left as they were and entrenched against amendment by a bare parliamentary majority. Britain, he said, would not agree to the immediate transfer of the protectorates, but he felt certain that they could be incorporated in the Union 'at some time or other . . . on terms agreed upon between the Imperial Government and the South African Government'. If the Constitution ignored the protectorates, however, a special Act of Parliament would be needed for their admission into the Union and 'such an Act dealing only with such admission might have considerable opposition in the House of Commons'. It would therefore be better if the Constitution provided for their subsequent transfer by an Order-in-Council (which would not have to be submitted to Parliament for approval); but since Parliament would not be prepared to give the Government a blank cheque in the matter, it would be necessary to include in the Constitution a statement of the conditions under which the South African

ambiguous; but the debate showed that its intention was as indicated in the text. The motion was carried without a division after a short debate, during which Seely made the statement quoted on p. 121 above.

[75] Curtis to the author, 18 Jan. 1952.

[76] There is a copy of this memorandum in the de Villiers Papers. I have not found the memorandum in the Smuts Papers, but they include Solomon's covering letter, dated 3 Sept. 1908, and another letter dated 10 Sept. 1908, in which Solomon reiterates his recommendations.

Government would take them over, so as to 'make future negotiations for the admission of these territories easy' at some later stage.

An awkward compromise on the franchise question therefore seemed to be inevitable. Smuts and Merriman had reached the conclusion that the differences between the colonies were too deep to make a uniform franchise possible, and that the existing laws would have to remain in force until they were amended by the Union Parliament. But if this were done two consequences would follow: Merriman himself would insist that his ideal of a flexible Constitution should be departed from in this one respect, to provide some security for the established rights of the non-Europeans of the Cape Colony; and the British Government would retain the responsibility for administering the protectorates for an indefinite period, because of the failure of the Constitution to provide parliamentary representation for the non-Europeans of the northern colonies.

4. THE ELECTORAL SYSTEM

The problem of devising an electoral system for South Africa was also very difficult. Notwithstanding the optimism of men like Botha and Smuts that Boer and Briton would soon fuse into a single nation and that party divisions would cease to follow racial lines, Boer and Briton were in fact more sharply differentiated from one another than ever in consequence of the war, and the vast majority of the Afrikaners supported the South African Party in the Cape Colony, Het Volk in the Transvaal, and the Orangia Unie in the Orange River Colony, while the vast majority of the British South Africans supported the Unionists, the Progressives, and the Constitutionalists. Moreover, in South Africa as a whole, as in the Cape Colony, Afrikaners were distinctly more numerous than people of British descent, though it seemed possible that the balance might eventually be changed by British immigration and by the anglicization of the urban fringe of the Afrikaner community. In these circumstances much would depend on the manner in which the parliamentary seats were divided between the rural areas (where the electorate was predominantly Afrikaner) and the urban areas (where the electorate was predominantly British). Any system which gave even a slight advantage to the rural voters might tilt the balance decisively in favour of the Afrikaners: and vice versa.

Several different methods of dealing with this problem had been used by the South African colonies and republics.[77] In the Cape Colony the Constitution Ordinance of 1853 did not lay down any mathematical rule —it merely divided the Colony into twenty-two constituencies, corresponding with the existing administrative divisions, gave them forty-six members in the House of Assembly, and left the colonial Parliament to make further provision as and when it thought fit. Nine Additional Representation Acts were subsequently passed by the Cape Parliament, the last of them in 1904, after which the House of Assembly consisted of 107 members elected in forty-six constituencies. In 1907 there were 151,314 registered voters in the colony, giving a norm of 1,414 voters to a member, but only twenty-one constituencies were within 20 per cent. of the norm, while eighteen constituencies were over-represented and seven were under-represented by more than 20 per cent. The under-represented constituencies were the urban ones of the Cape peninsula, Port Elizabeth, East London, and Kimberley, whose voters formed 43 per cent. of the total electorate of the colony and only returned 24 per cent. of the members of the Assembly. The extremes were Victoria East, a rural constituency, with 445 voters to a member, and Woodstock, an urban constituency in the Cape peninsula, with 2,691 voters to a member. Thus there were considerable variations from the norm, and they were almost entirely to the advantage of the rural voters—that is to say, the South African Party. In Natal, unlike the other colonies, the majority of the white farmers as well as townsmen were of British descent, so that the electoral system did not have racial implications. The Natal Charter of 1856 allotted the parliamentary seats empirically and subsequent Natal laws continued the process, with the result that after 1903 the Legislative Assembly consisted of forty-three members elected in seventeen constituencies.[78] In 1907 there were 23,686 registered voters in Natal, giving a norm of 551 voters to a member, but none of the constituencies was within 20 per cent. of the norm. Twelve were over-represented and five were under-represented by more than 20 per cent. The only real urban constituencies in the colony—Durban Borough and Pietermaritzburg City—were both badly under-represented: their voters formed 38 per cent. of the total electorate and only returned 19 per cent. of the members of the Legislative Assembly; and while Durban Borough had 1,500 voters to a member, the 389 voters of Alfred County returned two

[77] The electoral systems in the South African colonies on the eve of Union are analysed in *The Government of South Africa*, ii, Statements 33, 34.

[78] Act. No. 40 of 1908 made provision for three more seats in the Legislative Assembly, and if it had been applied it would have reduced the inequalities; but it was never applied as no further general election was held in Natal. Consequently the last Natal Legislative Assembly contained forty-three members, as mentioned in the text.

members. The result was that the farming element always had the decisive say in Natal politics. In the South African Republic everything possible had been done to keep political power in the hands of the Afrikaner farmers, mainly by imposing stiff residential qualifications for the franchise, and in 1899 Johannesburg, with 76,500 white inhabitants, returned only one member to the First Volksraad—which was the sovereign legislature—while the district of Lydenburg, with 3,500 white inhabitants, returned two members. In the Orange Free State, on the other hand, the preponderance of the Boer element in the white population had been so great that there had been no demand for artificial aids, and each district had received a reasonable proportion of the seats in the Volksraad.

Many arguments had been used in the Cape Colony, Natal, and the South African Republic for giving advantages to the rural voters. It was contended that the farmers, as 'the old-established section of the white population', were entitled to a greater say in politics than 'the shifting population of the towns', who were accused of having no intention of living permanently in South Africa and no concern for the lasting interests of the country. It was contended, too, that some allowance should be made for area as well as for people, since a representative could not maintain proper contact with his constituents if his constituency was too large. And precedents were found in other countries, including Great Britain and New Zealand. These arguments were not without some substance in the circumstances. It was true that many of the white inhabitants of the towns had left their families behind them in England or elsewhere and did not remain in South Africa for very long. There was, for example, a frequent coming and going of young Cornish miners to and from the Witwatersrand. It is not possible to assess the relative strength of this temporary element in the urban population with any precision; but the fact that according to the 1904 census there were 169,623 white men and only 118,966 white women in the Transvaal suggests that the proportion was fairly large in that colony. It was also true that away from the railway lines horses and ox-wagons were still the only means of transport, so that it was difficult for many rural representatives to keep in touch with their constituents.[79] Furthermore, similar empirical methods had caused somewhat similar discrepancies between the weight of the urban vote and the rural vote in Great Britain; while in New Zealand, where the constituencies were delimited on a mathematical basis, there was a statutory provision for adding 28 per cent. to the actual rural

[79] The first motor-car journey from Johannesburg to Cape Town was made in Aug. 1905 and took eleven days. *Cape Times*, 26 Aug. 1905.

population, so that 1,000 rural voters had the same representation as 1,280 urban voters.[80] Thus when the Jameson Ministry introduced the 1904 Additional Representation Bill, which went some way towards redressing the inequalities in the Cape Colony (but not very far, as the figures given in the last paragraph indicate), the South African Party attacked the Bill as a gerrymander, designed to 'crush the Dutch'.[81]

This issue, it will be recalled,[82] was at the centre of the struggle between the Progressives and Het Volk over a Constitution for the Transvaal in 1905–6. In the Transvaal there was a particularly close coincidence between racial and geographical divisions. Afrikaners— men, women, and children—formed about half of the white population of the colony,[83] but the Afrikaner men were already outnumbered by other white men, most of whom lived in the Witwatersrand district, and it was expected that when the depression passed there would be a fresh influx of immigrants from Britain.[84] In these circumstances the Progressives wished every constituency to contain as nearly as possible the same number of voters, and fresh delimitations to be made at frequent intervals; while Het Volk wished the white population to be taken as the basis of delimitation (if there had to be a mathematical basis) and fresh delimitations to be infrequent (if there had to be any). The Lyttelton Constitution, laying down economic qualifications for the franchise and providing for equal constituencies on the voters' basis with no more than a 5 per cent. latitude either way, suited the Progressives well. When the electoral rolls were completed in April 1906 there were 46,203 registered voters in the Witwatersrand district and 42,120 in the rest of the colony,[85]

[80] In 1881, when this loading device was introduced in New Zealand, 31½ per cent. was added to the actual rural population; in 1887 it was changed to 18 per cent.; and in 1889 it was changed to 28 per cent., where it stood until 1946 when loading was abolished. Rt. Hon. Walter Nash, 'Parliamentary Government in New Zealand', *Parliamentary Government in the Commonwealth* (London, 1951), p. 50.

[81] A. S. du Plessis, speaking in the debate on the second reading. *Cape Hansard, 1904*, p. 64. [82] See above, pp. 22–23, 25–27.

[83] The best indication of the Afrikaner proportion of the white population of the Transvaal is to be found in the religious sections of the census reports: in 1904 49·32 per cent. were shown as belonging to the Dutch Reformed Churches; in 1911, 48·52 per cent.

[84] In 1906 it was estimated (*Cape Times*, 10 Mar. 1906) that the white population of the Transvaal was distributed as follows:

	Witwatersrand District	Other Districts
Men	53,017	53,106
Women . .	24,827	32,686
Children . .	36,513	89,865
	114,357	175,657

[85] *Cape Times*, 25 Apr. 1906.

so that if the Lyttelton Constitution had come into force well over half the seats in the assembly would have gone to the Witwatersrand. The Constitution which did come into force, however, was less satisfactory to the Progressives, since it provided for white manhood suffrage, it gave the Witwatersrand only thirty-four out of sixty-nine seats in the first assembly, and it allowed a latitude of up to 15 per cent. either way from the norm on the voters' basis in the division of the three regions—the Witwatersrand district, Pretoria town and suburbs, and the rest of the colony—into single-member constituencies. On the other hand, there was to be a fresh delimitation every four years, when each of the three regions was to obtain as many seats as it was entitled to on the strict voters' basis; moreover, the criteria for dividing the three regions into single-member constituencies were existing boundaries, community or diversity of interest, means of communication, and physical features, and no mention was made of sparsity or density of population. The same principles were embodied in the electoral sections of the Constitution of the Orange River Colony, where there was a primary division of the seats between the rural areas and the towns and villages, and the latter were given eleven seats out of thirty-eight in the first assembly; but each region was to receive its due proportion of the seats on the strict voters' basis in all subsequent delimitations.[86]

When the general election was held in the Transvaal early in 1907 there were 105,368 voters on the rolls—54,967 in the Witwatersrand district, 8,441 in Pretoria town and suburbs, and 41,960 in the rest of the colony, giving an average of 1,617 voters in the Witwatersrand constituencies, 1,407 in the Pretoria constituencies, and 1,447 in the other constituencies. Thus there was a variation from the current voters' basis to the disadvantage of the Witwatersrand and the Progressive Party, but the variation was not as great as it was in the Cape Colony and Natal. In the general election which was held in the Orange River Colony later in 1907 the average number of voters registered in an urban constituency was 608 and the average number of voters registered in a rural constituency was 1,095, so that there was a larger variation from the current voters' basis than there was in the Transvaal and it was to the disadvantage of the rural districts and the Orangia Unie.[87] On the other hand, if the Letters Patent had remained in force, the variations in both the inland colonies would have been reduced to a minimum in all subsequent general elections: the urban complex of the Witwatersrand would have

[86] See above, p. 29.
[87] The numbers of registered voters in the electoral divisions of the Transvaal and the Orange River Colony are given in *The Government of South Africa*, ii. 411–13.

received its exact share of the seats in the Transvaal Legislative Assembly, calculated arithmetically on the voters' basis from up-to-date electoral rolls; and likewise with the rural areas of the Orange River Colony; and the latitude of up to 15 per cent. either way within the urban and the rural groups of constituencies would not have had any marked effect on the strengths of the parties in the parliaments.

There was therefore a striking contrast between the electoral systems of the coastal colonies and those of the inland colonies. The former gave great advantages to the rural voters: the latter contained the principles of equal constituencies and frequent re-delimitations.

As the politicians looked ahead towards a Constitution for a united South Africa, they naturally tended to view this question from the party point of view. It was obviously in the interests of the parties which derived most of their support from rural areas to apply the coastal system throughout South Africa; or, if any mathematical rule was to be adopted, to select the white population basis rather than the voters' basis, or to apply a loading factor as in New Zealand. And it was obviously in the interests of the parties which derived most of their support from towns that the provisions of the Transvaal and Orange River Colony constitutions should be applied throughout South Africa.

Merriman was always a firm believer in the rural point of view. 'Of all ways of settling the representation of a country', he wrote in June 1906, 'the mechanical one of basing it on the numerical population of registered voters seems to me the most unfair.'[88] When he read the Transvaal Letters Patent he commented: 'What an age this is for the worship of democratic shibboleths!'[89] And his views did not change thereafter. Smuts, on the other hand, gradually modified his opinion. Negotiating with the British Government early in 1906, as we have seen, he virtually accepted the proposition that the Transvaal constituencies should be allotted on some sort of mathematical basis, but argued for the white population basis and plenty of latitude. Then in July 1906, defending himself against Merriman's gibes, he wrote:[90]

I could not help smiling at your sharp criticism of our false position. We are so absolutely in accord with you and made strong representations against any numerical principle. But we saw that the day was going against us, and what could one do but study discretion? I sometimes think you have not fought sufficiently with these beasts of Ephesus with whom our hard lot has been cast. You *cannot* expect any British government to put in the wrong

---

[88] Merriman to Smuts, 26 June 1906, Smuts Papers.
[89] Merriman to Smuts, 18 Dec. 1906, ibid.
[90] Smuts to Merriman, 11 July 1906, Merriman Papers.

their own compatriots in the Transvaal, even in the year 1906; and when those compatriots are such as you and I know them to be, the position of a poor devil of a 'Dutchman' becomes very difficult indeed. No wonder that you sometimes surprise us in a little supper with the devil, but we do our best to use long spoons. Let us never be in too great a hurry, knowing that 'the good can well afford to wait' and will yet assuredly arrive. Our English friends have to be conciliated and their suspicions have to make way for whole-hearted confidence and loyalty of spirit before we shall succeed.

Before the National Convention met, however, two further factors had made deep impressions on Smuts's mind. One was the sweeping victory of Het Volk at the polls under the provisions of the new Transvaal Constitution. If that could be done in the Transvaal, could it not be repeated in a South African Union, even if an electoral system similar to the Transvaal one were adopted? The other was that he was extremely anxious that the South African Constitution should carry the support of both the white racial groups, and it became clear to him that the Progressives would not support it unless it established 'equal rights' in the political field, which they regarded as the one vital issue. Consequently, Smuts moved towards complete acceptance of the idea that the electoral system of the Transvaal, or something like it, should be embodied in the South African Constitution.

Smuts's colleagues were anxious about the political effects of such provisions in a united South Africa. In August 1908 Botha explained to Merriman that if the constituencies were to contain an equal number of voters most of the Natal constituencies would become urban ones, which would be detrimental to the prospects of a party formed from Het Volk and its allies, and he asked Merriman what the effects would be in the Cape Colony.[91] Merriman replied with a forthright attack on the very idea of equal political rights:[92]

The question that you put to me about the 'one vote one value,' and I suppose this includes 'one man one vote' with an automatic redistribution, is a highly important one. I may say at once that I regard both as democratic shibboleths utterly unsuited to this country where we must, in the nature of things, always be an aristocracy or rather society must be on an aristocratic basis. . . . If we are to keep this country in a sane and sober state we must see to it that the balance of power is in the hands of the landed interest, and, with the 'one man one vote' principle, this is impossible. . . . Just see how Australia is ridden by its large cities, and be warned in time. I can conceive no greater misfortune for South Africa with its overwhelming native population than a reproduction of Australian conditions, in which a

[91] 6 Aug. 1908, Merriman Papers.   [92] 17 Aug. 1908, ibid. (draft).

white democracy without any of the responsibilities that land holding confers, should dominate our policy. . . . You are quite right in drawing attention to the forces behind all this pretended love for democratic principles. They are really a wish to see the Capitalist from oversea the master instead of the man on the land; and the notion that we shall be drawn into the current of modern Imperialism with all the negation of right that it stands for.

Facing pressure from Botha, Smuts included the population and not the voters' basis in his early constitutional projects, but on the eve of the National Convention, as will be explained, Fitzpatrick made a firm stand for the voters' basis and Smuts included it in his final proposals. Merriman tried his best to dissuade him from doing any such thing, but he replied:[93]

I am interested in your protest against the new-fangled notions of equal voters' areas and automatic redistribution. Our Progressive friends however decline to consider Union except on such terms of 'equal rights' and it may be that you will have to move with the times, however distasteful the process may seem to such an old-fashioned Tory. No doubt there is much in all this to justify your fears, but remember that we achieved victory in our last elections notwithstanding these doctrinaire aids to the manhood of the Rand.

Indeed, Smuts had become a convert to yet a further device for securing political justice. This was a period when proportional representation was making considerable headway in democratic countries. It had been adopted for the elections of the central legislatures in Denmark in 1855, in Belgium in 1899, in Japan in 1900, and in Sweden in 1907, and during 1908 it was under serious consideration in France and the Netherlands. It was also used for the elections of the local legislatures in eight of the Swiss cantons, in the American states of Illinois and Oregon, and in Tasmania; and even in Britain the House of Lords had recently passed a Bill to introduce it in municipal elections. The advocates of proportional representation argued—as they still argue—that it is the only way of ensuring the due representation of minorities and of making it unlikely or impossible for a minority of the voters to elect a majority of the Members of Parliament, and thus to determine the Government. They believed that proportional representation was the consummation of the mechanics of political democracy. Moreover, some observers contended that Belgian experience showed that it mitigated racial cleavages in bi-racial countries. R. H. Brand, who was impressed by these facts and

[93] 2 Oct. 1908, ibid.

arguments, reached the conclusion that it would be desirable to apply proportional representation in South Africa, in the form of the single transferable vote, which was the form advocated in England, and before the end of August 1908 he had convinced Smuts, who included it in his projects of a South African Constitution. Propaganda was obtained from the English Proportional Representation Society and worked up for South African consumption by Brand, who made the most of the Belgian precedent. Addressing the Johannesburg Closer Union Society in September 1908 he said:[94]

South Africa is unfortunately somewhat in the position of Belgium. There are in this country two races fairly equal in numbers and influence. The one is collected mainly in the towns and the other in the country. Under the present system of representation it follows as a general rule that the minority of the one party in the country and of the other in the towns is entirely unrepresented. Thus racial difficulties are exaggerated, and the racial cleavage intensified by the division between town and country. . . . With proportional representation both these classes will obtain such representation as is their due, and since the system is absolutely fair to all parties, no recrimination will be possible. It cannot be doubted that the result would be, as in Belgium, not only the softening of the sharp line between town and country, but also the mitigation of the asperity of racial conflicts.

It was not easy, however, to make this proposal popular. Nothing nearly as complicated as the single transferable vote had ever been used in South Africa.[95] Even the Progressives found it difficult to understand and were lukewarm in their support, while most of the politicians of the rural parties agreed with Merriman that it was yet another 'democratic shibboleth'. But Smuts was not deterred; and by adopting proportional representation as well as equal constituencies and automatic redistribution he was meeting the demands of the Progressives for equal political rights in a most generous manner.

[94] Two pamphlets advocating proportional representation were written by Brand and distributed to the members of the National Convention: (a) R. H. Brand, *Proportional Representation*, being a paper read to the Johannesburg Closer Union Society in September and published about 1 Oct. 1908; and (b) Anon., *Proportional Representation*, a larger pamphlet, including twelve annexures describing the working of proportional representation in several countries, &c., published about 26 Oct. 1908. The quotation in the text is from (a), at p. 17.

[95] The cumulative vote, a rudimentary type of proportional representation, had always been used for the election of the members of the Cape Legislative Council, and until 1893 it had also been used for the election of the Cape Town members of the House of Assembly (Cape of Good Hope Constitution Ordinance, ss. 40, 46; Cape Act No. 16 of 1893); but South Africa had had no experience of any of the more advanced and complicated types of proportional representation which were being applied or advocated in other countries.

5. LANGUAGE

While the support of the Transvaal Progressives for a South African Constitution would depend largely on the extent to which its electoral provisions satisfied them, the support of the Orangia Unie would depend upon its language provisions. By 1908, it will be recalled, the young poets and prose-writers of the Afrikaans language movement were beginning to provide Afrikaners with a substantial basis for cultural pride, the protagonists of Dutch and the protagonists of Afrikaans as the vehicle for the expression of their national culture were forming a common front against anglicization, and the Government of the Orange River Colony was introducing legislation to make both English and Dutch compulsory media of instruction in the government schools of that colony.[96] Hertzog's Education Bill was published on 21 April 1908, introduced into Parliament on 19 June, and passed by both Houses on 24 August. The violent opposition which it evoked, not only from the Constitutionalists in the Orange River Colony Parliament but also from the English-medium press throughout South Africa, made Hertzog extremely suspicious of all British South African politicians and single-minded to the point of obsession in his approach to the problem of a Constitution for South Africa. The Constitution would be acceptable to him if it provided that the Dutch and the English languages would receive 'equal treatment' throughout the Union in the schools, the civil service, Parliament, and the courts, because then, and then only, would he be satisfied that the white South African nation would become truly bilingual and bi-cultural. Otherwise he would prefer that the Orange River Colony should remain a separate citadel for the preservation and nourishment of Afrikaner culture. Previously Steyn had corresponded agreeably with Merriman about other aspects of a Constitution for South Africa and had concurred with his views on most of them, including his preference for a unitary Constitution. By the middle of 1908, however, Hertzog had conveyed his apprehensions to Steyn and he, too, became guarded and anxious.

From their point of view their fears were justified. The politicians of the Opposition parties in the Cape Colony, the Transvaal, and the Orange River Colony, and most of the leading Natal politicians, certainly hoped that English would be the dominant language throughout South Africa and that Dutch and Afrikaans (which most of them despised and few of them could speak) would gradually fall into disuse. Most of the leaders of the South African Party and Het Volk, moreover, were much less far-reaching than Hertzog and Steyn in their demands. Malan, indeed, would

[96] On the Afrikaner cultural movement, see above, pp. 19–20, 36.

support them to the full, but Merriman spoke and wrote Dutch with difficulty, and although he believed that it was wise to grant concessions when they were generally desired by Afrikaners, he thought that it only needed conditions of freedom for English ultimately to prevail as the language of all South Africans. In his opinion it would be quite sufficient to include in the Constitution a section making the use of Dutch permissive in Parliament and the courts, similar to section 133 of the Canadian Constitution, according to which

Either the English or the French language may be used by any person in the debates of the Houses of the Parliament of Canada and of the Houses of the Legislature of Quebec; and both those languages shall be used in the respective Records and Journals of those Houses; and either of those languages may be used by any person or in any pleading or process in or issuing from any Court of Canada established under this Act, and in or from all or any of the Courts of Quebec.

The Acts of the Parliament of Canada and of the Legislature of Quebec shall be printed and published in both those languages.

Somewhat similarly, Botha and Smuts, whose educational legislation for the Transvaal had fallen far short of Hertzog's Orange River Colony Bill, thought that the South African Constitution should contain a simple declaration that both English and Dutch were to be official languages in the Union. To Hertzog and Steyn, however, it was not enough to create the equality of free competition, under which the weaker party goes to the wall, because as things were it would probably be Dutch that would go to the wall in South Africa. It was vital to them to ensure permanent equality by protecting the weaker party, which meant making it obligatory for civil servants and teachers to be bilingual and for all children in government schools to become thoroughly fluent in Dutch as well as English.

During June 1908 Steyn was able to gain an important tactical advantage. Botha and Smuts regarded it as essential that he should accept nomination to the National Convention, because they feared that if he did not do so he might use his great prestige to rally Afrikaner opinion against its recommendations. They therefore pressed him to accept:[97]

I ask you now [wrote Botha], come with us and help us—if you come on

[97] 'Ik vraag U nu, kom met ons saam en hulp ons—als U op de conventie als afgevaardigde van de O.R.K. komt dan zal dit onze positie hier versterken en verbeteren. Uw persoon hebben wy noodig en Uwe raad en daad. Zonder U kunnen wij mogelijk de zaak geheel en al verkeerd aanpakken en U weet de oogen van Zuid Afrika zijn op U en wij zullen zeer dankbaar zijn als U het U zal laten welgevallen om op die conventie benoemd te worden.' 19 June 1908, Steyn Papers.

the Convention as representative of the O.R.C. then it will strengthen and improve our position here. We need you yourself and your counsel and action. Without you we might possibly tackle the thing entirely wrongly and you know that the eyes of South Africa are on you and we shall be very grateful if you will allow yourself to be nominated on the Convention.

Merriman also regarded Steyn's presence as of crucial importance:[98]

You probably carry more weight than any one in South Africa with the 'Platteland' folk who will have to be reckoned with and your voice will be final. Therefore at any personal inconvenience do try and make this sacrifice for South Africa.

But Steyn acted with great circumspection. He consulted J. H. Hofmeyr and explained to him why he would not be satisfied with a section like the Canadian one.[99] He expounded his doubts to Merriman:[1]

As you know I am heart and soul for this Closer Union. My sole reason is that I see in it the only way of uniting the two races and so forming them into one strong Nation. To do this however the new Constitution must put the two races on absolute equality. For as long as the one race considers itself in ever so slight a way placed in an inferior position to the other, there will never be that harmonious co-operation which is so necessary and so desired by us all. I could therefore only be a consenting party to a Constitution in which that equality is not only laid down but in which it is safeguarded against any future racial feeling that may arise. I of course know that the Constitution will not be a law of the Medes and Persians, but I feel that a view strongly expressed in the first Constitution will not be easily altered in the future.

Why I put this matter before you is that I feel so strongly on this point and I know that as regards the language etc. we will have to fight those members of the opposition who will be appointed as delegates by the various Parliaments, and I am quite prepared to fight them, but I do not feel that I could go to a Convention if I had to fight men in our own ranks on such Cardinal points.

Steyn parried the advances of Botha and Merriman until late in June, when Botha travelled to his farm 'Onzerust', near Bloemfontein, and pleaded with him. Then he only gave his consent after receiving very strong assurances.

His great difficulty is with reference to the Dutch Language [reported Botha to Merriman[2]], and he has objection to going on the Convention unless we are in earnest as regards the absolute equality of both languages.

---

[98] 31 May 1908, ibid.
[1] 8 June 1908, Merriman Papers.

[99] 11 June 1908, Hofmeyr Papers.
[2] 29 June 1908, ibid.

I gave him my assurance on this point telling him that it would be impossible for me to carry my party with me unless this principle were adopted; I also said that I felt convinced that the Cape would take the same line. I am glad to be able to tell you that I have persuaded him and that he will now consent to be appointed on the Convention.

Thus Steyn had won an important preliminary round for the Unie point of view. Although there remained underlying differences of opinion as to the full implications of the phrase 'the absolute equality of both languages', Botha could hardly fail to support any proposal for a section providing for language equality emanating from Hertzog and Steyn.

It is now possible to review the factors which would determine the principal ingredients of the South African Constitution. Outside of Natal a unitary and flexible Constitution was generally favoured. There were, however, three contentious issues which it would be difficult to resolve in such a Constitution. The first was the Cape non-European franchise, the second the Progressive demand for equal political rights for all white men, and the third the Orangia Unie demand for language equality. The first might be settled within a unitary Constitution by an agreement to differ, and the second and the third might be balanced against one another. In that event, however, departures would probably have to be made from the principle of flexibility to provide special safeguards for the provisions concerning one or more of these three issues.

CHAPTER IV

PREPARATIONS FOR THE NATIONAL CONVENTION

1. CONVENING THE CONVENTION

AFTER the Intercolonial Conference the leaders of the South African Party, Het Volk, and the Orangia Unie were agreed in regarding the consummation of union as an urgent objective. The sense of urgency was particularly marked in Botha and Smuts because of the continued growth of isolationist sentiment in the Transvaal, where more and more Afrikaners were becoming disappointed by their Government's conciliatory policy towards Great Britain and the Transvaal British, and where several Johannesburg and Pretoria businessmen, contrasting the economic revival of the Transvaal with the continued depression of the coastal colonies and noting the refusal of the coastal colonies at the Intercolonial Conference to modify the customs tariff and railway rates as they desired, were inclined to prefer that the Transvaal should withdraw from the Customs Union and assert her economic independence. Fortunately for Botha and Smuts these groups—the conservative Afrikaners and the practical men of business—had little in common with one another and could not easily be combined into a single isolationist movement. Moreover, neither group produced a leader competent to organize opposition rapidly and effectively. Nevertheless, Botha and Smuts were seriously alarmed. They therefore hurried the session of the Transvaal Parliament to a rapid conclusion—with the use of the 'Steam Roller', Botha boasted to Merriman[1]—and Smuts then had six weeks in which to perfect his constitutional plans for the convention. They also tried to keep Merriman up to the mark. In June Smuts was finding fresh arguments for this purpose:[2]

we who have taken up this issue have practically burnt our boats and may therefore not look back. If we fail, we shall be ruined politically, so that there is this additional inducement to do our best to achieve success within a reasonable time.

And in September Botha was advising him:[3]

[1] 24 July 1908, Merriman Papers.
[2] 10 June 1908, ibid.   [3] 23 Sept. 1908, ibid.

If we are not successful in obtaining Closer Union now I very much fear that it will be infinitely more difficult to get the Transvaal to join later on. Our finantial [*sic*] position is steadily improving and I would not be surprised if under the new Gold Law the Gold Industry brings us in an extra million, so that our surplus at the end of the present finantial [*sic*] year may be larger than ever. I think that we should all do our utmost now to inspire the people of South Africa with a South African Spirit.

Merriman's perspectives were rather different. Having been a bitter critic of the 'extravagance' of Jameson's Administration, he was anxious to restore the Cape Colony's financial credit and stability, and he plunged into the fray with enthusiasm. In answer to Smuts, who had cautioned him not to stir up ill-feeling against his Government by drastic taxation, he protested that with an accumulated deficit of £3 millions and a public debt of £52 millions he could not carry on for another year on the existing revenue basis, which would produce another deficit of over £1½ millions. To do so would be to ruin the credit of all South Africa and to play into the hands of the Transvaal isolationists.[4] He also feared that it would weaken the influence of the Cape Colony in the National Convention. So his budget, presented in June, was designed to balance the accounts for the ensuing year by raising new taxes (an income tax affecting everyone who earned more than £50, succession duties, a tax on patent medicines, and increased licence fees), by suspending the Sinking Fund, and by reducing civil service salaries. These proposals aroused vehement opposition, prolonged the Cape parliamentary session until 11 September—three weeks after the end of the Transvaal session—and left Merriman with little time or energy for calm consideration of the problems which the convention would have to deal with. The Orange River Colony Parliament also had a stormy session in which Hertzog piloted his Education Bill through both Houses. Nevertheless, distracting though these parliamentary struggles were, union remained 'the great question' to Merriman, and he and Fischer were almost as anxious as the Transvaal leaders to bring it to an early conclusion for fear of an imperialist reaction in England:[5]

every possible effort will be made to prevent any form of Union being adopted until our 'Progressive' friends out here and the Jingos [on the] other side are again in power [wrote Fischer]. This again means an attempt to dictate Union 'Imperially' and from without: what we have to fight for is one Colonially and from within.

4 13 June 1908, Smuts Papers.
5 Fischer to Merriman, 16 July 1908, Merriman Papers.

When the 'closer union resolutions' of the Intercolonial Conference were published on 11 May the first reaction of the English South African press was adverse.[6] The *Cape Times* contrasted them with the Australian resolutions of 1890 and 1893, which had provided that the members of the Australian Federal Convention should be elected by the people, that each self-governing colony should have the same number of representatives, and that the draft Constitution should be submitted to referenda in each colony. It also reminded its readers that the Opposition parties had not been represented at Pretoria and suggested that the motives of the leaders of the South African Party, Het Volk, and the Unie were 'more slim than wise'. The Natal press was almost unanimous in its disapproval. Editors vied with one another in abusing them. A National Convention formed in accordance with the resolutions would be a 'monstrosity', said the *Times of Natal*. 'Pre-nuptial coercion', complained the *Natal Advertiser*. 'Wholly unacceptable', pronounced the *Natal Mercury*; 'our delegates would be helpless against the solid phalanx of the other twenty-five'. Natal should stay out of any union conceived in such a spirit, and 'if forced, we must simply gird our loins and prepare to work out our salvation as an independent British State'. A similar point of view was expressed by Major P. A. Silburn in a pamphlet written at this time.[7] In the Transvaal, while the *Transvaal Leader* echoed the Natal press, the *Star* and the *Rand Daily Mail*, though critical, were prepared to support the resolutions, and Sir George Farrar, the Leader of the Opposition, urged the public to suspend judgement until the Government declared its intentions about the selection of the delegates to the convention. Farrar was in fact satisfied because he had come to an agreement with Botha that three of the eight Transvaal delegates would be Progressives.[8] Smuts did what he could to allay the suspicions. He persuaded Duncan to see the editor of the *Transvaal Leader* and ask him to moderate its tone;[9] and on 16 May he made a tactful after-dinner speech in Johannesburg, appealing to Natal to 'Go in on a basis of trust', denying that there was any Afrikaner plot, and giving the assurance that the Transvaal Government would seek the co-operation of the Opposition in selecting the delegates to the convention.[10] The *Transvaal Leader* and the *Cape Times* then softened their criticisms. But Natal was still anxious: the Pietermaritzburg Chamber of Commerce repudiated the resolutions, and

[6] The statements which follow were published or republished in the *Cape Times*, 12 and 13 May 1908.

[7] *The Constitutional Crisis in South Africa* (Durban, n.d. [1908]).

[8] Farrar to Botha, 21 May 1908, Transvaal Archives, Prime Minister, LX (iii).

[9] Smuts to Duncan, 11 May 1908, Duncan Papers.

[10] *Cape Times*, 18 May 1908.

a public meeting held in Durban demanded equal representation for Natal as well as the popular election of Natal's delegates and a referendum on the draft Constitution.[11] Nevertheless, the Natal press was somewhat mollified when the decision of the conference that the National Convention should open its sessions in Durban was published on 30 May. Even the *Natal Mercury* agreed that Natal could hardly stay out of a convention that was to meet in Durban.[12]

Public attention then became focused on the four colonial capitals, where the parliaments met to deal with the closer union resolutions in the middle of June. The resolutions had an easy enough passage through the Transvaal Parliament,[13] where the only serious opposition to them came from the Afrikaner side. A. D. W. Wolmarans, a legislative councillor and a member of the Head Committee of Het Volk, had for many years been a confidant of Paul Kruger and a member of the republican Volksraad, and during the war he had served on the Executive Council and represented the Republic in Europe. On account of ill-health he did not attend the caucus of Het Volk when it met on 18 June to consider the closer union resolutions, but he had already made his position clear in a private letter to Botha. 'First the Transvaal and the interests of This People! and afterwards the interests of others',[14] was his plea. It would be 'moral and Financial Murder'[15] for the Transvaal to unite with the other colonies before it had put its own house in order—especially before it had solved its poor white problem. Would not union mean the swamping of the Transvaal by 'coolies' from Natal? Was it not the declared policy of the Cape Ministry to extend the non-European vote throughout South Africa? Why should the Transvaal have fewer representatives than the Cape Colony in the convention? And what authority had the Government to deal with closer union without consulting the people? Botha had tried to have the matter thrashed out in the privacy of the Head Committee of the party, but Wolmarans had said that he was not well enough to attend, and in his continued absence the caucus decided unanimously to support the resolutions.[16] The Progressive caucus came to the same decision. Consequently, when Botha moved the resolutions in the Legislative Assembly on 22 June Farrar seconded them and they

[11] *Cape Times*, 21, 23, 27 May 1908.

[12] Ibid., 30 May 1908.

[13] *Transvaal Leg. Ass. Deb., 1908*, cols. 95–186; *Transvaal Leg. Co. Deb., 1908*, cols. 17–61.

[14] 'Eerst Transvaal en de belangen van Dit Volk! en daarna de belangen van anderen.'

[15] 'moreele en Finantieele Moord'.

[16] Wolmarans to Botha, 16 and 25 June 1908; Botha to Wolmarans, 23 June 1908 (copy). Transvaal Archives, Prime Minister, LX (v). Botha to Steyn, 19 June 1908, Steyn Papers.

were carried without a division on the following day. In the Legislative Council, on the other hand, Wolmarans expounded his objections and accused the Government of acting autocratically, but he was constrained to admit that he had been a member of the Head Committee which had drafted his party's manifesto, the first article of which favoured closer union, and when the vote was called for his voice was the only 'not content'.

If the outbursts of Wolmarans revealed that 'Little Transvaaler' views were not dead, the other speeches in the Transvaal Parliament showed that the willingness of the leaders of Het Volk and the members of the Kindergarten to co-operate for the purpose of uniting South Africa was already penetrating downwards through the rank and file of all the Transvaal parties. Most of the speakers trod common ground in contending that union would put an end to the Anglo-Boer racial feud and pave the way for the creation of a single white South African nation. Here, then, was the genesis of the mood of optimism and the idealism which was increasingly to pervade white South Africa during the following years. Nevertheless, there were significant variations of emphasis. While all agreed that it would be a good thing if union resulted in a curtailment of British interference in South African affairs, it was evident that men like F. W. Beyers (Het Volk) were hoping that South Africa would become a completely independent nation State, while others like Drummond Chaplin (Progressive) talked of 'the common desire to consolidate the British Empire'.[17] Many Progressives, again, laid much stress on the principle of equal political rights for all white men, and one of them, H. L. Lindsay, went so far as to voice his fears of the growth of a sectional, Afrikaner nationalism; but such points were studiously ignored by Het Volk spokesmen. On the question of non-European rights members of all parties showed their abhorrence of the Cape system. Here, too, the emphasis varied. At the one extreme there were men like J. A. Joubert (Het Volk) who said that his main reason for supporting the resolutions was his hope that union would enable them to 'keep the natives in their place',[18] while at the other extreme J. W. Quinn (Labour) wanted the Transvaal delegates to deal with the question 'in as broad a spirit as they possibly could'[19] in the convention. There was, however, no detailed or informed discussion of the principles that should be written into a South African Constitution. Beyond general expressions of fear of a non-European vote and the Progressives' insistence on equal political rights for all white men, the only point touched on was the form

[17] *Transvaal Leg. Ass. Deb., 1908*, col. 165.
[18] Ibid., col. 107.   [19] Ibid., col. 136.

of the Constitution, and while several speakers said they preferred a unitary Constitution, none advocated federalism. Replying to the debate in the Lower House, Smuts came out strongly in favour of a unitary Constitution and said that he was confident that it would enable them to solve South Africa's many problems, including the Native problem, which should on no account be allowed to continue to 'drift' towards 'chaos and ruin'.[20] Botha, replying to the debate in the Upper House, concentrated on the theme of Anglo-Boer harmony. 'There is to be no question of the one white race lording it over the other', he said. 'True equality in all respects should be our goal. . . . "Unity is strength" should be the motto of us all.'[21]

The Prime Minister and the Leader of the Opposition then gave effect to their agreement in terms of which five of the Transvaal delegates to the convention were to be chosen by the Government and three by the Opposition. The Government selected Botha, Smuts, General S. W. Burger, and General J. H. de la Rey (Het Volk), and H. C. Hull (Nationalist), and the Opposition selected Farrar, Fitzpatrick, and H. L. Lindsay (Progressives). Botha and Smuts had not included Burger and de la Rey because they expected them to make any important contribution to the constitutional work of the convention, but because they hoped that their influence would be valuable later, when the convention's recommendations would have to be defended among the rank and file of the rural Afrikaners.[22] When these names were submitted to the Legislative Assembly, Labour members complained that they would not be represented, but the names were agreed to without a division.[23]

In contrast with the definite and enthusiastic lead given by Botha and Smuts in the Transvaal Parliament, Fischer, who steered the resolutions through both Houses in the Orange River Colony, spoke vaguely and uninspiringly.[24] Political union of some sort he regarded as necessary, if only for economic reasons; but he was not prepared to express a preference for any particular form of union and he believed that the colony's delegates should enter the convention with a completely free hand. Hertzog, preoccupied as he was with his educational legislation, did not participate in the debates. Orangia Unie back-benchers were cautious— regretful that the colony was to have only five members in the convention, reluctant to see the identity of the old Free State merged in a larger

[20] *Transvaal Leg. Ass. Deb., 1908*, col. 178.
[21] *Transvaal Leg. Co. Deb., 1908*, col. 61.
[22] Botha to Merriman, 29 June 1908, Merriman Papers.
[23] *Transvaal Leg. Ass. Deb., 1908*, cols. 505–8.
[24] *O.R.C. Leg. Ass. Deb., 1907–1908*, cols. 631–82; *O.R.C. Leg. Co. Deb., 1907–1908*, cols. 83–100, 140–66.

whole, and very suspicious of the Cape native franchise. On this point, said W. Ehrlich, 'they could not compromise'. Since both parties in the Cape seemed to be committed to a Native vote, union seemed 'almost impossible to achieve' and the Orange River Colony should be prepared to stand alone.[25] On the other hand, H. Potgieter felt sure that they would overcome all difficulties because 'the people of the country were bound together by three great cords, blood, language and race'.[26] Sir John Fraser and other members of the Opposition supported the resolutions, which were carried unanimously in both Houses. In the selection of the Orange River Colony delegates to the convention, the same procedure was adopted as in the Transvaal and on 3 July the Leader of the Opposition seconded the Prime Minister's motion that the colony should be represented by Steyn, Fischer, de Wet, and Hertzog (Orangia Unie), and Fraser (Constitutionalist). During August, however, Fraser withdrew owing to ill-health and A. Browne, a Constitutionalist member of the Upper House, was appointed in his stead.[27]

In the Cape Parliament the resolutions were cordially supported by men of all parties, and there was evidence of the same spirit of Anglo-Boer *rapprochement* that existed in the Transvaal.[28] Introducing the resolutions in the House of Assembly, Merriman gave two main reasons for closer union—the need for economy in government and the need 'to get rid of a great deal of that mischievous interference which has been . . . the bane of the different States in this country'.[29] He also announced that he hoped for a completely unitary Constitution. T. W. Smartt, acting as Leader of the Opposition in the absence of Jameson, who was overseas, agreed with Merriman in preferring a unitary Constitution and raised the question of Native rights. This question was taken further by Colonel C. P. Crewe (Unionist), who said he hoped that it would be dealt with fully by the convention and not left as a skeleton in the cupboard to be handled by a South African Parliament. From the government side of the House S. C. Cronwright Schreiner (South African Party), the husband of Olive Schreiner, sounded a note of warning against excessive haste and centralization and said that it was most important to preserve freedom at all costs. Then, Bond spokesmen having reminded the House that union under the British flag had always been one of the first principles of the Bond, Merriman dealt with Crewe's remarks by saying that the convention 'was mainly intended to unite the European communities'[30] and that

---

[25] *O.R.C. Leg. Ass. Deb., 1907–1908*, col. 658.
[26] Ibid., col. 678.   [27] Ibid., cols. 827, 1291.
[28] *Cape Hansard, 1908*, pp. 38–48; *Cape Leg. Co. Deb., 1908*, cols. 35–49.
[29] *Cape Hansard, 1908*, pp. 38–39.
[30] Ibid., p. 47.

he was sure that the presence of J. W. Sauer in the convention would be a sufficient guarantee that the interests of the Natives would be safeguarded. Moving the resolutions in the Legislative Council, Sauer showed how he proposed to approach that task. Union, he said, was an essential step towards the solution of the Native problem. It would create confidence among the Europeans and justice would be the natural product of that confidence. The resolutions were carried without a division in both Houses. The appointment of the Cape delegates to the convention did not follow quite the same smooth path of inter-party co-operation as in the Transvaal and the Orange River Colony, because Merriman insisted on pressing the claims of J. W. Jagger against those of one of the other Unionists proposed by Smartt, and the South African Party caucus supported Merriman, who had his way.[31] Nevertheless, when the list was moved in the House of Assembly it was accepted without discussion after an adjournment. It formed, indeed, a well-balanced cross-section of the Cape Parliament: Sir Henry de Villiers (Chief Justice and Chairman of the Legislative Council) (Independent), Merriman, Malan, Sauer, J. H. M. Beck, H. C. van Heerden, and G. H. Maasdorp (South African Party), Jameson, Smartt, E. H. Walton, and J. W. Jagger (Unionist), and W. P. Schreiner (Independent). In September, however, Schreiner announced in Parliament that before accepting nomination he had undertaken to defend Dinizulu on the charges brought against him by the Natal Government, that it had now become clear that the trial would coincide with the sessions of the convention, and that he had therefore decided to resign from the convention. This quixotic decision had significant results. Schreiner was a federalist, a staunch supporter of African rights, and an experienced politician; and he was the type of man who would have stood to his guns in the convention. In his place Parliament appointed Colonel W. E. M. Stanford (Independent), a retired Native administrator, who was a man of the highest integrity but lacked political experience.[32]

The resolutions met with a more critical reception in the Natal Parliament.[33] The four Labour members in the Lower House attacked them vigorously. Natal, they maintained, should not take part in any conven-

[31] Smartt to Merriman, 12 June 1908, Merriman Papers; Merriman to Smuts, 19 June 1908, Smuts Papers; Merriman to Botha, 26 June 1908, Transvaal Archives, Prime Minister, LX (iii).

[32] *Cape Hansard, 1908*, pp. 48, 62–63, 714–15, 733; *Cape Leg. Co. Deb., 1908*, 35–49.

[33] The Natal Parliament still observed the custom of holding long debates on the Reply to the Address, so that the closer union resolutions were, in effect, debated twice over—during the debates on the Reply to the Address, and on the motions for their approval. *Natal Leg. Ass. Deb.* xliv. 3–129, 186–235; *Natal Leg. Co. Deb.* xviii. 5–11, 16–32.

tion where she was under-represented or where it was obvious that the majority of the delegates were determined to obtain a unitary Constitution. At Pretoria, said N. P. Palmer, the Natal ministers had found themselves confronted with a cut and dried plan, and they had yielded: the same thing would happen in the convention. J. Connolly predicted that it would be a case of the lady and the tiger, with Natal as the lady. But none of these Labour members was able to show how Natal could make her way as a separate colony alongside a union of the Transvaal, the Cape Colony, and the Orange River Colony; and only one other member, J. Schofield, voted against the resolutions, which were carried by thirty-five votes to five. In the Legislative Council, where there were no Labour members, the resolutions were adopted without a division. Nevertheless, most of the members of both Houses expressed regret at the terms of the resolutions and stated emphatically that they did not want a unitary Constitution, while some, including W. B. Morcom, went so far as to say that the Natal delegates should leave the convention if unification was carried. On the other hand, the Afrikaner members from northern Natal, who had been in contact with Louis Botha,[34] expressed satisfaction with the resolutions. They considered that the delegates should be given a completely free hand, and they scoffed at the idea that Natal was competent to stand alone. The leaders on both sides were more guarded than the back-benchers. T. Hyslop said that, in his opinion, a satisfactory compromise could be found between a unitary Constitution and a federal one: 'Unification, if accompanied by a large measure of local government, may not be very far removed from Federation, with large powers centred in the Federal Parliament.'[35] Smythe took the idea farther in saying that he believed in leaving large powers to the local legislatures, but it was 'merely a matter of terms' whether it was called unification or federation.[36] Winding up the debate in the Legislative Assembly, Moor assured the House that the politicians in the other colonies were deeply divided between federalists and unificationists, and that there would certainly be strong federalists in their delegations, so that if the Natal delegates stood firm they could hope to carry federation. Nevertheless, he went on to agree with Hyslop and Smythe: 'I care not what they call it', he said, 'as long as they give us the local control over our local interests.'[37]

During the debate on the closer union resolutions in the Lower House a motion that the Natal delegates to the convention should be chosen by

---

[34] Botha to M. Myburgh, &c., 14 May 1908 (copy); Myburgh to Botha, 18 May. Transvaal Archives, Prime Minister, LX (i).   [35] *Natal Leg. Ass. Deb.* xliv. 57.
[36] Ibid., p. 190.   [37] Ibid., p. 235.

popular election was defeated by twenty-nine votes to ten. Moor and
Smythe, however, were unable to agree upon a list of delegates, so
instead of following the Transvaal procedure they held an informal
ballot among the members of the Legislative Assembly and the names
of the men thus elected were then formally approved by the assembly.
The result was that Natal's delegates to the National Convention were
F. R. Moor (Prime Minister), E. M. Greene (Minister of Railways and
Harbours), C. J. Smythe (the previous Prime Minister), T. Hyslop (the
previous Treasurer), and W. B. Morcom (a former Minister of Justice);
while T. Watt (another former Minister of Justice) was to succeed to any
vacancy.[38] Finally, Smythe tried to persuade Moor to give an undertaking
that the draft Constitution would be submitted to a referendum in Natal
before it became binding upon her. Moor at first refused; and when
Smythe tried to introduce a Bill to provide for a referendum, the motion
for leave to introduce it was opposed and defeated. However, Smythe
gained his point. During the debate on the motion Moor gave a definite
assurance that a referendum would be held in Natal before she joined in
any form of union with the other colonies.[39]

These parliamentary proceedings showed up Natal's weaknesses. The
closer union resolutions, which had been sprung upon the Natal delegates
at Pretoria and strongly opposed by the Natal press, were approved by
Parliament, though with reluctance and many misgivings. Moreover,
three of the men who were chosen to represent Natal in the National
Convention had exposed themselves on a crucial point. Moor, Smythe,
and Hyslop had showed that they did not appreciate that in a unitary
Constitution the local authorities exercise their powers subject to the
supremacy of the Central Parliament, and that if the Constitution is also
flexible those powers can easily be reduced or even obliterated. Consequently, although the British people in Natal were extremely anxious to
preserve the identity of their colony and wished merely to grant a few
essential powers to a federal parliament and government, as the price of
economic and military security, their political leaders had virtually made
it known that they were prepared to yield. Merriman and Smuts must
have read their remarks with relish!

The colonial parliaments having approved the closer union resolutions
and appointed their delegates to the National Convention, there remained
a number of questions which were not covered by the resolutions and on
which it was necessary or desirable that agreement should be reached
before the convention met. Merriman was determined that the High

[38] *Natal Leg. Ass. Deb.* xliv. 548–9.   [39] Ibid. xlvi. 79–93.

Commissioner should have no hand in these preliminaries, lest he should force the intrusion of the imperial factor. Consequently, on 22 July 1908 he took the initiative in suggesting to the other three prime ministers that the convention should start work early in October, that E. F. Kilpin (the Clerk of the Cape House of Assembly) and G. R. Hofmeyr (the Clerk of the Transvaal Legislative Assembly) should be appointed joint secretaries, that the delegations should be permitted to bring official advisers to Durban and to consult them on specific points, that the meetings of the convention should be strictly private, and that Rhodesia should be invited to send an official observer.[40] Fischer promptly thanked Merriman for taking the initiative and suggested that, as 'the oldest Parliamentarian amongst us', he should act as convener of the first meeting of the convention.[41] Botha agreed;[42] but Moor, harassed by his Parliament and press and mindful of Merriman's unpopularity in Natal, replied tardily and did not expressly accept his leadership, with the result that no convener was officially recognized, though Merriman continued to initiate and co-ordinate the necessary correspondence.[43]

Merriman was anxious that the convention should open as soon as possible after the end of the sessions of the colonial parliaments, because he regarded it as 'all important' that the British Parliament should deal with the South African Constitution during its 1909 session, when there could be no doubt that the Liberals would still be in power.[44] Moor, on the other hand, wished to delay the opening of the convention until November, to give the Natal delegates time to recuperate from their session (which did not end until 28 September) and to prepare for the convention, and Botha at first took a similar line.[45] Fischer, however, agreeing with Merriman that the matter was urgent, brought the question of Steyn's health forward as a decisive argument, intimating that if the convention was to meet after 12 October he would propose that the venue should be changed to a cooler place than Durban for the sake of Steyn, whereupon Moor accepted 12 October as the opening date under the combined pressure of the other three prime ministers.[46]

In May Smuts had privately proposed to Merriman that R. H. Brand, the secretary of the Intercolonial Conference, should be invited to be

[40] Merriman Papers (copy).   [41] 27 July, ibid.
[42] Botha to Merriman, 5 Aug., ibid.
[43] Moor to Merriman, 15 Aug. (telegram), ibid.
[44] Merriman to Smuts, 20 July, Smuts Papers.
[45] Moor to Merriman, 18 Aug. (telegram); Botha to Merriman, 5 Aug. Merriman Papers.
[46] Fischer to Merriman, 19 Aug. (telegram); Botha to Merriman, 19 Aug. (telegram); Merriman to Moor, 19 and 20 Aug. (copies of telegrams); Moor to Merriman, 20 Aug. (telegram). Ibid.

secretary to the convention.[47] Merriman had reacted adversely. He wanted no Kindergarten official to hold such an appointment. However, his suggestion that there should be two secretaries, one from the Cape Colony and one from the Transvaal, was not to the liking of the smaller colonies, and after some wrangling it was decided that each of the four colonies should nominate a secretary and that the four secretaries should be on an equal footing until the convention had appointed one of them to be Chief Secretary—it being generally understood that the choice would fall on E. F. Kilpin, who was far the most experienced parliamentary official in South Africa.[48]

Botha had wanted Sir Richard Solomon, the Transvaal Agent-General in London, to be invited to be draftsman to the convention, but he had dropped the proposal in the face of opposition from Merriman, who cast doubts on Solomon's abilities, and from Fischer, who feared that Solomon would be unsympathetic to the Afrikaner point of view on the language question and to the northern point of view on the franchise question.[49] The prime ministers then agreed that the delegations could bring expert advisers to Durban and consult them there, and that none of them would be admitted to the conference chamber except the interpreter who would accompany the Transvaal delegation.[50]

Merriman was 'most strongly' in favour of secrecy in the convention, following the American and Canadian precedents but not the Australian one. He feared that publicity would result in 'long orations to the gallery' and 'ill-informed comments of the London press', which would impede union.[51] Fischer and Botha agreed and it was therefore tolerably certain that the convention would resolve to keep its proceedings secret, although Moor hoped that there would be at least a full official record of all speeches.[52]

The idea of giving Rhodesia some footing in the convention seems to have originated with Sir Lewis Michell, Chairman of De Beers and a director of the British South Africa Company.[53] In his letter of 22 July Merriman proposed that 'as a matter of grace' one Rhodesian representative should be invited to attend the convention as an observer, without

[47] R. H. Brand's manuscript, Brand Papers.

[48] Moor to Merriman, 17 Sept. (telegram); Fischer to Merriman, 18 Sept. (telegram). Merriman Papers.

[49] Botha to Merriman, 30 June; Merriman to Botha, 10 July (copy). Merriman Papers. Fischer to Botha, 1 July, Transvaal Archives, Prime Minister, LX (iv).

[50] Fischer to Merriman, 27 July; Botha to Merriman, 5 Aug. Merriman Papers.

[51] Merriman to Botha, 11 July, Transvaal Archives, Prime Minister, LX (iv).

[52] Fischer to Merriman, 16 July; Botha to Merriman, 5 Aug.; E. F. Kilpin to Merriman, 7 Oct. Merriman Papers.

[53] Merriman Papers, Nos. 307–8/1908.

the right to speak or vote. Fischer agreed. Botha, less suspicious of the Chartered Company and more anxious to ease the way for the later inclusion of Rhodesia in the South African union, replied that he considered that Rhodesia should be invited to send 'one or two' representatives and that they should be given the right to speak in the convention but not the right to vote.[54] Merriman accepted the recommendation and invited the British South Africa Company to nominate two Rhodesian representatives on those terms.[55] The company nominated Sir Lewis Michell and W. H. Milton, the Administrator of Southern Rhodesia, whereupon the elected members of the Southern Rhodesian Legislative Council protested that their interests were being overlooked. Their leader, Charles Coghlan, informed Botha that unless one of them was added the settlers would not be represented in the convention. Botha then proposed that the company should be invited to send a third Rhodesian delegate, provided that he was not an official. The other prime ministers agreed and so did the company, and on 26 September the elected members of the Legislative Council met and chose Coghlan to be the third Rhodesian delegate.[56]

The prime ministers also agreed upon the choice of a president and a vice-president of the convention well before it opened its sessions. The presidency was discussed informally by the delegates at the Intercolonial Conference, and Merriman was able to tell de Villiers that there was 'a general consensus of opinion that you should occupy the position'.[57] This choice was far the best that could be made, for as Chief Justice of the Cape Colony de Villiers was the only delegate who stood completely outside party politics, and yet as the *ex officio* President of the Legislative Council he had had ample experience of presiding over a political body. Then in September Merriman was able to inform Steyn that the other prime ministers had approved of his being nominated for the vice-presidency and to assure him that the office would be purely honorary, as de Villiers would preside at all the meetings of the convention.[58]

---

[54] Fischer to Merriman, 27 July 1908; Botha to Merriman, 5 Aug. 1908. Ibid.

[55] Merriman to W. H. Milton, 4 Sept. 1908 (copy of telegram), ibid.

[56] Botha to Merriman, 16 Sept. (telegram); Merriman to Milton, 19 and 24 Sept. (copies of telegrams). Merriman Papers. See J. P. R. Wallis, *One Man's Hand: the story of Sir Charles Coghlan and the liberation of Southern Rhodesia* (London, 1950), pp. 100–1.

[57] Merriman to de Villiers, 31 May (copy), Merriman Papers.

[58] Merriman to Steyn, 12 Sept. (copy of telegram), ibid.

2. THE PREPARATIONS OF J. ʻC. SMUTS

While the responsibility for convening the National Convention fell on the shoulders of Merriman and his fellow prime ministers, it was Smuts who did most of the effective planning for the real work of the convention—the drafting of a Constitution for South Africa. This task was congenial to him. He was always more at home with the written word than the spoken word, in the realm of thought than in the realm of personal relations; and with his legal training, his wide reading, his acute sense of political realities, and his exceptional powers of concentration, he was admirably equipped for the task.

Until it was prorogued on 22 August much of his time was necessarily spent in the Transvaal Parliament, where he was the principal government spokesman. Nevertheless, by the end of August he had drawn up a 'Suggested Scheme for South African Union' and sent copies of it to Merriman, de Villiers, and Steyn,[59] explaining that

The paper represents merely my personal opinions. . . . If the main ideas are approved, I propose to prepare a draft constitution which might largely expedite the work of the Convention; and time is of enormous importance in this matter.

At the outset of his 'Suggested Scheme' Smuts defined the central problem as follows:

The question of South African political union presents many difficulties but the most fundamental of all centres round the question whether any and what form of local government should be permitted and provided for

[59] Smuts's letters of 29 Aug. 1908, sending copies of his 'Suggested Scheme' to Merriman and de Villiers, are in the Merriman and de Villiers Papers. The quotation is from the letter to de Villiers. Copies of the 'Suggested Scheme' are in the Merriman, de Villiers, Smuts, and Brand Papers. I have found no trace of the 'Suggested Scheme' or the covering letter in the Steyn Papers.

In spite of the wording of his reference to a draft Constitution in his covering letter to de Villiers, Smuts had prepared at least two draft constitutions by the end of August. Among the Smuts Papers there are:

(a) An undated, incomplete draft, in Smuts's hand, heavily amended and scored, consisting of a preamble and several sections under each of the following heads: 'I The Union', 'II The Parliament', 'III The Executive Government', 'IV The Provincial Constitutions', 'V Legislative Power', 'VI The Judicature', 'VII Finance and Trade', and 'VIII Natives'.

(b) A neatly typed complete draft (on p. 1 of which Smuts has written 'August 1908 JCS'), consisting of 133 sections, consecutively numbered, grouped under the same eight heads as (a) and also 'IX New Provinces and Territories', and 'X Miscellaneous'.

(a) would seem to be Smuts's earliest extant draft Constitution; and (b) is the draft which corresponds with his 'Suggested Scheme for South African Union'.

inside the Union. It is felt that to sweep away the present Colonial administrations and legislatures and to erect in their stead one common Parliament
and Government for South Africa would not only meet with the most determined opposition from the people of the various Colonies but may also
prove in the end an unworkable scheme, as it would overload the Central
Parliament and Government with work with which, for many years to
come, at any rate, they would not be able to cope, thus resulting in an
administrative and legislative deadlock which might seriously retard the
peaceful progress of South Africa. On the other hand it is felt equally
strongly that any form of political union must provide for a Central
authority which is supreme and whose supremacy is undisputed. The problem therefore is to devise a form of political union which will, as far as possible, leave in existence a substantial form of local administration and
legislation to carry on the work with which a Central authority could not
usefully cope, and to erect, over and beside these local administrations, an
undoubtedly supreme authority for all common concerns of South Africa
as a whole.

The paper then went on to propose that the union should consist of five
provinces—an Eastern and a Western Cape Province, an Orange Province (comprising the Orange River Colony plus Griqualand West), a
Transvaal Province (comprising the Transvaal Colony plus British
Bechuanaland), and Natal. Legislative power would be vested in the
King, a Senate, and a House of Representatives. There would be forty-
eight senators—twelve each from the Transvaal, the Orange Province,
and Natal, and six each from the Eastern and the Western Cape Provinces. The House of Representatives would contain 120 members—
thirty-two from the Transvaal, twenty each from the Orange Province
and Natal, and twenty-four each from the Eastern and the Western Cape
Provinces. In this way there would be an equal number of senators from
each of the founder colonies, while the representatives would be allotted
to the founder colonies in the proportions in which they were represented
in the National Convention. Both Houses would be directly elected by
the same electorate, the Senate for six years (with half the members
retiring every three years) and the House of Representatives for five
years. Until the Union Parliament changed them, the qualifications of
voters in each province would remain as they were before union in the
corresponding colony. The electoral divisions would be delimited by a
commission every five or ten years, after a census had been taken, and
the basis of delimitation would be the white population. Senate constituencies would return six senators, House of Representative constituencies would return four representatives, and both Houses would
be elected by proportional representation. The Union Executive would

consist of a Cabinet responsible to Parliament. Each province would have a Cabinet responsible to a uni-cameral legislature—a House of Assembly, containing as many members as represented the province in the House of Representatives, elected by the same voters in the same manner. The Union Parliament would be the supreme legislative authority in South Africa and its legislation would prevail over provincial legislation; but existing colonial laws would remain in force in the several provinces, except in so far as they were nullified by the Constitution, until they were superseded by legislation of the Union or provincial legislatures. On the inauguration of the Union the Central Government and Parliament would immediately assume exclusive powers in the fields of railways and harbours, customs and excise, posts and telegraphs, defence, Native affairs, external relations, and immigration, and would possess the power to assume control in other fields at their discretion, leaving the provinces ultimately with powers only in 'matters of a merely local or private nature'. The judiciary would consist of a High Court in each province and a Supreme Court, which would have appellate jurisdiction and original jurisdiction 'in a large number of questions arising under the Constitution or between the Provinces or residents of different Provinces, or under any special laws of the Central Parliament'. On the inauguration of the Union the Central Government would take over all the debts of the colonies and their principal assets—the railways and harbours; and customs and other large sources of revenue would accrue at once to the Union treasury. The railways and harbours would be administered by a Board as a non-profit-making business undertaking and railway rates would be non-discriminatory. The Governor-General would be the Paramount Chief over all the Natives and, on the advice of the Executive Council, would possess legislative as well as administrative powers over Zululand and the Transkei. The English and Dutch languages would be treated equally in the Union Parliament and in the Union courts of law. And, finally, the Constitution would only be amendable 'by a law of the Central Parliament which has been passed by an absolute majority of both Houses of Parliament, and which has also been approved by the legislatures of any Provinces directly affected by the alteration'.[60]

---

[60] Smuts's first draft Constitution—labelled (a) in the previous footnote—differs from the 'Suggested Scheme' in the following main respects: the Union would consist of six, not five, provinces, the Cape Colony being divided into three provinces; the House of Representatives would be elected in single-member constituencies and not by proportional representation; and the capital of the Union would be Pretoria, whereas the 'Suggested Scheme' merely said that the capital 'would probably have to be settled in the constitution'. Smuts's draft Constitution labelled (b) in the previous footnote does

The Cape parliamentary session was a particularly arduous one for Merriman and did not end until 11 September, three weeks later than the end of the Transvaal session, so that he was not able to give Smuts's memorandum the careful consideration he would have wished. But he recorded some 'fragmentary' impressions while his Parliament was still sitting and dispatched them to Smuts.[61] In the light of the ground which had been covered in their earlier correspondence, Merriman had reason to be disappointed with Smuts's proposals. 'The crying need of South Africa at the present moment is economy of administration', he wrote. Therefore this scheme, with its six parliaments and six cabinets, was far too cumbersome and costly, besides introducing the evil of judicial interpretation of the Constitution. Provincial councils of a sort were, of course, necessary, but they should only be entitled to pass ordinances in a few defined fields and the Central Government should have the power to veto them. There was no need for cabinet government in the provinces: a single executive officer would suffice in each of them. The Central Parliament should be the one supreme legislature in South Africa:

it should be supreme both over the Courts of law and the local bodies. . . . I mean that the Legislature and not the Courts should lay down the law of the Constitution, and that the Courts should be bound to administer the law so laid down without cavil or dispute. This is the Swiss system, as opposed to that of the United States, Canada and Australia where endless friction is caused by the power given to the Courts to override the Legislature in the interpretation of a written document.

Furthermore, there should be no *imperium in imperio* in Native affairs, of the sort proposed by Smuts, for Parliament should be supreme in every field. Merriman's other serious objection was to the electoral system proposed by Smuts. The parliamentary constituencies should not be delimited on any mathematical basis. Such a 'doctrinaire contrivance' would merely place power in the hands of the urban communities, which were 'largely non South African'. It would be better to fall back on 'the old fashioned rule of thumb in one shape or other'. For the rest he suggested that rather than being directly elected the Senate might consist of some members elected by the provincial councils and others, such as

not conflict with the 'Suggested Scheme', but amplifies it: among other less important details it allows for appeals from the Supreme Court to the Privy Council, it provides for free trade throughout South Africa, and it states that railway rates should be arranged so as 'to reduce the burden of transportation and the cost of living to the people of the inland Provinces'. Its 'routine' sections were for the most part taken over from the Canadian, the Australian, and the Transvaal constitutions.

[61] I have found no trace of Merriman's memorandum in the Smuts Papers, but it was probably dispatched early in September. A draft, n.d., is in the Merriman Papers, No. 159/1908.

retired judges, former cabinet ministers, and the provincial executive officers, appointed *ex officio*; he agreed that the existing franchise laws would have to be left as they were, but added that 'certain guarantees will have to be inserted in the Constitution to this effect';[62] and he proposed that the Constitution should state that judicial appeals would not be allowed to go to the Privy Council.

Although Sir Henry de Villiers, as the President of the Legislative Council, was also engaged in the Cape parliamentary session, he had more time at his disposal than the harassed Prime Minister, and his reply to Smuts, dated 5 September, was more systematic.[63] Like Merriman he objected to the establishment of cabinet governments in the provinces, both on the grounds of expense and because his visit to Canada had left him with a strong preference for a clear-cut unitary Constitution. Ideally, he told Smuts, local affairs should come under an Administrator appointed by the Central Government and a Provincial Council, whose powers should be as limited as those of municipalities. He hoped that there would be no need to schedule a list of colonial laws which would become unalterable without the concurrence of the provincial councils, and no need to give the Supreme Court jurisdiction in constitutional cases. On economic grounds he also objected to the idea of creating a fifth province and he proposed, instead, that the Cape should be reduced to a reasonable size by making cessions of territory to the Transvaal and the Orange River Colony. On the other hand, he took the opposite view from Merriman on electoral questions. Far from disliking a mathematical basis for the distribution of the seats in the Lower House, he believed that it should be applied without qualification. Accordingly, he approved of proportional representation and the regular delimitation of constituencies on a population basis; but why, he asked, should the seats be divided between the provinces in an arbitrary manner? Would it not be possible to apply an intelligible principle at the outset and divide the seats between the provinces, as well as within the provinces, on the white population basis (with some allowance for the Native population, if necessary, to meet the claims of Natal)? He also suggested that the senators should be elected by the provincial councils and that the Lower

---

[62] The logical implication of this statement is that the South African Constitution should state that the colonial franchise laws could only be amended by some special procedure. But what would be the value of such a provision if, according to Merriman, the Legislature and not the courts was to 'lay down the law of the Constitution'? Or did Merriman mean that in this one field the courts should have the power to declare legislation invalid if it was not passed in accordance with the prescribed procedure? I think that the answer is that Merriman, who was no lawyer, had not thought the problem through.   [63] Smuts Papers.

House should be called the House of Commons or the House of Assembly, rather than the House of Representatives; and he agreed that the colonial franchise laws should be left unchanged.

Ex-President Steyn, the third recipient of Smuts's 'Suggested Scheme for South African Union', confined his reply to the language question.[64] He was distressed to find that Smuts proposed to do no more than to provide for equal treatment for the Dutch and English languages in Parliament and the courts. It was essential, he wrote, that there should also be equality in the schools and the public service. Indeed, it must be made quite clear that the two languages would be on an equal footing as the official languages of the entire country. Otherwise there could be no true union.

By the time Smuts had received these replies he had acquired the full-time services of R. H. Brand, the Kindergarten official who had been secretary of the Intercolonial Conference, and F. Lucas, a young Johannesburg barrister, both of whom worked with him in Pretoria during the last six weeks before the Transvaal delegation left for Durban on 9 October.[65] Brand had been devoting all his spare time since May to reading up the constitutional authorities and he was well prepared to give Smuts expert advice. On considering Smuts's 'Suggested Scheme' he quickly reached the conclusion that it was technically inadequate— that it provided no solution to the problem of the relations between the Central Government and the provinces, because the phrase used to describe the fields in which the provincial legislatures would be competent to legislate—'matters of a purely local or private nature'—was far too vague. His criticisms, added to those of Merriman and de Villiers, convinced Smuts that the problem had to be thought out afresh. Accordingly, they devoted much attention to it, and to the related question of the provincial constitutions; and as they proceeded they moved closer to the outright unitary ideas of Merriman and de Villiers.

By the end of September they had completed two alternative plans on these questions.[66] The first plan (which was subsequently abandoned)

[64] 3 Sept. 1908, ibid.

[65] The Brand Papers are an important source for the rest of this section and for Chapter V. R. H. Brand kept copies of most of the documents which were drafted by the Transvaal advisers from Sept. 1908 until the end of the Cape Town session of the National Convention on 3 Feb. 1909; and soon afterwards he wrote a connecting account (referred to in the footnotes as Brand's manuscript), in which, *inter alia*, he indicated the approximate date, the authorship, and the function of each document. There are also many relevant documents in the Smuts Papers, but without a connecting account, and since most of these documents are typed, undated, and unsigned, their precise significance is not always clear.

[66] The relevant documents appear as annexures to Brand's manuscript, which is

was a modification of Smuts's August scheme. Each of the four colonies would become a province of the Union, with a Cabinet responsible to a uni-cameral legislature. On the inauguration of the Union the fields specified in the August scheme would pass exclusively to the Union Parliament and the provincial legislatures would be able to pass laws in other fields; but such provincial laws would require the approval of the Governor-General-in-Council (i.e. the Union Government) and would be valid only so long as and in so far as they were not repealed by legislation of the Union Parliament; and when such a repeal took place the exclusive power of legislation in that field would pass permanently to the Union Parliament. In this way the Union Parliament would be indubitably supreme in all fields: it would exercise its supremacy at the outset in specified fields and it would have the power to exercise it in any other field at any time. Under the second plan (which contained the kernel of the arrangement which was eventually adopted) the Union .would consist of seven provinces—three from the Cape Colony, two from the Transvaal, the Orange Province, and Natal. Each province would have a uni-cameral legislature which would not be subject to dissolution during its three-year term, so that the executive would not be responsible to it. The Executive Council of a province would consist of three ordinary members and a President, all of whom would be elected by the provincial legislature. In these proposals Smuts had in mind the Swiss model of a non-party executive, which he favoured because of its resemblance to the executive councils of the South African Republic and the Orange Free State. The Union Parliament would have the power to make laws for the peace, order, and good government of South Africa, notwithstanding anything to the contrary in the Constitution; and the provincial legislatures would have the power to make laws on specified topics—direct taxation, the raising of loans, provincial officers, hospitals, asylums and charities, municipal institutions, local public works, fines and penalties for breach of provincial laws, game preservation, and 'generally all matters which are in the opinion of the Governor-General-in-Council of a merely private or local nature'; but such laws would be subject to the 'active' veto of the Governor-General-in-Council and they would be invalid in so far as they were inconsistent with Union laws. This plan also contained the ingenious suggestion that the Union Parliament might delegate to the provincial executives the execution of any Union law, or the administration of any Union department or ser-

referred to in the previous note: Annexure C, two drafts of Chapter V, Legislative Power; Annexure D, draft of Chapter IV, The Provincial Constitutions; and Annexure E, two draft plans of Union.

vice, more particularly in the fields of primary and secondary education, public health, agriculture, public works, Natives and Asiatics, mines, and lands. It will be seen that both these plans assured the supremacy of the Union Parliament. The difference was that the first plan was designed to ease the burden falling on Parliament in the early years, by making it unnecessary for it to exercise its responsibilities outside a few essential fields, whereas under the second plan Parliament would assume its full responsibilities at the outset. In the former case it was considered that the provinces would require cabinet governments to enable them to fulfil their wide initial responsibilities, while in the latter case cabinet governments were not deemed necessary for the provinces.

Smuts and his collaborators did not embody these two plans in complete draft constitutions, but by the end of September they had drafted documents which show what their intentions were on most other questions.[67] For the most part they were similar to Smuts's August plans, but changes were made in the financial, judicial, and amending sections to give further effect to the preference of Merriman and de Villiers for a more unitary and a more flexible Constitution. According to these documents the Union Treasury would receive all revenue paid under the existing colonial laws during the first three years of the Union, and the provinces would be financed by the Union Government, pending investigation and legislation; the Supreme Court would not be expressly granted jurisdiction in constitutional cases; and a constitutional amendment would only require an absolute majority of both Houses of Parliament, and not the concurrence of any provincial legislature. Furthermore, Merriman's demand for special safeguards for the existing colonial franchise laws was met by the proposal that no Union law should prevent anyone who had, or who acquired, the right to vote under the existing laws of any colony from voting in Union elections.[68] Smuts also seems to have intended to give effect to Steyn's plea for language equality, though this was only recorded in the brief phrase—'English and Dutch languages to be equal'. On the question of electoral divisions, Smuts and his collaborators moved in the direction of de Villiers's recommendations and away from those of Merriman, proposing that the seats in the House of Representatives should be divided between the provinces 'in proportion to the respective numbers of the white population'. The only other significant departure from Smuts's August scheme was the provision that

[67] The relevant documents appear as annexures to Brand's manuscript—Annexure E, two draft plans of Union; Annexure F, Draft Constitution of South Africa (incomplete); Annexure G, draft sections on finance and trade.

[68] The proposal took this form in Annexure E. In Annexure F, however, the safeguard was only to apply to those who already had the right to vote in colonial elections.

the House of Representatives should contain three times as many seats as the Senate—if there were seven provinces, the Senate would contain forty-two seats, six for each province, and the House of Representatives 126 seats; and each Senate constituency would return six members and each House of Representatives constituency would return three or more.

Smuts was in a position to know that these plans were likely to be supported in general by de Villiers, whose opinions would influence many middle-of-the-road delegates in the convention; by Steyn, and through him by the other three Orangia Unie delegates, provided that they were allowed to have their way in the phrasing of the language section; and by Merriman, and through him by many of the South African Party delegates from the Cape Colony, except that Merriman could be expected to continue to press his objections to the mathematical principle in the electoral system. Smuts, however, was anxious to go farther and have his plans accepted in broad outline by the entire Transvaal delegation, Progressives as well as government supporters, before the convention met. If this could be done he could feel reasonably certain of obtaining a majority in the convention on most of the basic issues.

Accordingly, at the end of September Smuts and his collaborators summarized their proposals for submission to the Transvaal delegates. In making this summary[69] they introduced further changes. In particular they devised a synthesis between the two alternative September plans concerning the provincial constitutions and the division of legislative power. Each of the four self-governing colonies, according to the main proposal now prepared, would become a province of the Union. The provincial executive councils, including their presidents, would be elected by the provincial legislatures from among their own members, but they would not be responsible to the legislatures and the legislatures would not be subject to dissolution during their three-year terms. On the inauguration of the Union, Parliament would acquire 'full power to pass all laws for the peace, order and good government of South Africa' and the exclusive power to pass laws in twenty-five specified fields, while the provincial legislatures would acquire the power to pass laws in the nine fields specified in the second of the September plans, but provincial laws would be subject to the 'active' veto of the Governor-General-in-Council and would be invalid if inconsistent with the Union laws. For the rest the summary followed the September plans, except that it included a reversion from the principle of equal provincial representation in the Senate and a delay in the application of the principle that the provinces should be represented in the Lower House in proportion to their white

69 Brand's manuscript, Annexure H, outline of proposed plans.

population: the Senate would contain forty seats—fourteen for the Cape Province, twelve for the Transvaal, eight for the Orange Province, and six for Natal; and the House of Commons (as it was now called) would contain 120 seats—fifty-four for the Cape Province, thirty-two for the Transvaal, eighteen for the Orange Province, and sixteen for Natal— during the first ten years, after which the division would be made on the white population basis.[70] The existing colonial franchise laws would remain in force, the members of both Houses would be directly elected by proportional representation, the English and Dutch languages would be 'equal', and the Constitution would be amendable 'by an absolute majority of both Houses of Parliament subject to possible reservation on certain points'. The summary also included as an alternative the suggestion that the Cape Colony should be divided into two or three provinces and the Transvaal into two.

None of the Transvaal Progressives or Cape Unionists had made any systematic plans for the National Convention. Farrar had left for Rhodesia soon after the end of the Transvaal parliamentary session and he did not return to the Transvaal until 22 September. The Cape Unionists were equally rudderless, since Jameson did not arrive back in Cape Town after a six months' absence from South Africa until 6 October. It was Fitzpatrick alone who tried to instil some semblance of unity into the Opposition delegates. During the first half of September he visited Natal, the Orange River Colony, and the Cape Colony, preaching the gospel of Equal Rights—new delimitations of the constituencies at frequent intervals and, above all, the voters' basis. Back in the Transvaal, he asked Smuts for an interview, with the result that on 19 September he had a discussion with Botha, Smuts, and Hull. He suggested that the Transvaal delegation should go to the National Convention with a common programme and he undertook to serve loyally under Botha's leadership if they would rise above race and party. Smuts asked, what were his terms? 'Equal Rights', he replied. 'And what will you do if we cannot meet you on this point?' inquired Smuts. 'Stump the Transvaal and whip up every prejudice that exists against Union with the impoverished coastal Colonies', replied Fitzpatrick.[71]

---

[70] The numbers 54, 32, 18, and 16 were adopted as a compromise between the white population basis (which, using the 1904 census, would have given 62, 32, 15, and 11) and the proportions accorded to the colonies in their representation in the National Convention (which would have given 48, 32, 20, and 20).

[71] The above paragraph is based on the following documents in the Fitzpatrick Papers: Fitzpatrick to J. Wernher, 21 Sept. 1908 (copy); Fitzpatrick to Sir Matthew Nathan, 21 Sept. 1908 (copy); Fitzpatrick to Drummond Chaplin, 7 Oct. 1908 (copy); Fitzpatrick, 'Equal Rights' (unpublished manuscript, c. 1929).

The meetings of the eight Transvaal delegates and their advisers—including Brand, who had been appointed their secretary—took place in Pretoria between 30 September and 6 October.[72] All the points in Smuts's summarized programme were discussed at length. Fitzpatrick had been disturbed to find that when Farrar returned from Rhodesia he was hesitant on the question of Equal Rights, but he managed to cajole him and Lindsay into adopting an unequivocal attitude at the delegates' meetings and eventually Smuts and his colleagues undertook to support the voters' basis. In return, Fitzpatrick, Farrar, and Lindsay accepted the principle of language equality, but with 'no compulsion'. Fitzpatrick also disputed Smuts's proposal that the colonial franchise laws should be left as they were. He considered that it was essential that a uniform franchise should be established in the Constitution and in a written memorandum he argued that, whatever the difficulties, the occasion was 'not one for compromising or postponing vital questions', and proposed that men of three-quarters or more European descent should be entitled to vote if they earned £120 a year and passed a dictation test in English or Dutch, and that non-Europeans should in addition have to satisfy a special tribunal that they had lived continuously for ten years since reaching the age of twenty-one 'in every respect in accordance with the recognised standard of European civilisation' or were the descendants of 'two generations who have continuously so lived'.[73] Duncan also considered that there should be a uniform franchise, but the other delegates agreed with Smuts that it was impossible. On all the other points in Smuts's summarized plans there was general agreement. The delegates preferred his alternative proposal that the Cape Colony should be divided into two or more provinces and that the Transvaal should be divided into two, rather than that each colony should become a province of the Union. And they were unanimous in the view that the provinces should have as little legislative power as possible, Hull adding that it would be unwise to specify the fields in which the Union Parliament should assume exclusive legislative powers at the outset, since each item might then become a subject for debate in the convention. The discussions also showed that the Transvaal delegates were fully aware of the fact that their colony's financial strength could be used as a powerful lever. Calculations were made by Fitzpatrick and others of the effect of adopting wealth as the criterion for the division of the parliamentary seats between the provinces. Whereas the white population basis would give the Transvaal

[72] The meetings of the Transvaal delegates are described in the last two documents mentioned in the previous footnote and in Brand's manuscript.

[73] Brand's manuscript, Annexure M.

only thirty-two seats, the revenue basis (1907–8 estimates of ordinary revenue) would give the Transvaal forty-eight seats in a Lower House of 120.[74] Nevertheless, the delegates considered that it was far more important to obtain the capital of the Union for Pretoria than it was to obtain more than thirty-two seats in Parliament.

In the light of these discussions Brand prepared three final alternative drafts on the subject of legislative power before he left Pretoria for Durban with the Transvaal delegates.[75] All three drafts started with strong assertions of the supremacy of the Union Parliament. The first draft, in response to Hull's observations, simply went on to 'delegate' to the provincial legislatures the power to make laws under eight specified heads, and those alone—direct taxation, the borrowing of money, hospitals, asylums and charities, municipalities, local public works, fines and penalties, and 'any further matter on which legislative powers may be delegated by the Parliament'. The second draft contained the same provisions, with the addition that on the inauguration of the Union exclusive *administrative* powers in only twenty-five specified fields would pass to the Union Government, the rest remaining with the provincial governments until Parliament decided otherwise. And the third draft provided that on the inauguration of the Union exclusive *legislative and administrative* powers in those twenty-five fields would pass to the Union Government and Parliament, the rest remaining with the provincial authorities until Parliament decided otherwise. On this key subject, therefore, the Transvaal plans were flexible, though all were within the framework of the supremacy of the Union Parliament. Which version would be pressed would depend upon the reaction of the National Convention to the resolutions which were going to be moved at the outset, with the object of committing the convention to the principle of unification.

During September Smuts and Brand had reached the conclusion that it would be wise tactics to put this principle squarely before the convention at its first business sitting. They prepared a draft resolution which asserted the supremacy of the Union Parliament 'within the limits imposed by the Constitution of Great Britain', left it an open question whether the Cape Colony should be divided into two or more provinces, recognized the need for creating subordinate provincial legislatures and executives, and stated that 'the Constitution and all laws passed by the Parliament of the Union shall be binding on the Courts, judges and people of the Union'.[76] Merriman independently reached the same

---

[74] Ibid.

[75] Brand to Smuts, 7 Oct. 1908, Smuts Papers; Brand's manuscript, Annexure J.

[76] Brand's manuscript, Annexure L (1).

conclusion as to the advisability of starting with some such resolution, and he sent Smuts a simpler draft which stated that it was desirable to create a legislative union of the four self-governing colonies with provision for 'extended powers of local administration' and for the later admission of Rhodesia.[77] Brand and Smuts regarded Merriman's resolution as inadequate, but on 7 October they amended their own draft, deleting the references to the British Constitution and to the binding character of the South African Constitution and laws, and adding a provision for the later admission of both Rhodesia and the protectorates.[78]

Two days later, as he listened impassively to Botha's descriptions of the fighting that had taken place eight years earlier over the ground they were traversing on their way by train to Durban,[79] Smuts had reason to look back with satisfaction on the work accomplished and to look forward with confidence to the work that lay ahead. During August, in the midst of an active parliamentary and ministerial life, he had devised a comprehensive constitutional scheme, which was for the most part technically sound and which took cognizance of the major political forces that had to be reckoned with; during September, with the help of well-selected assistants, he had polished that scheme and modified it to make it acceptable to the Orangia Unie and South African Party delegates and to Sir Henry de Villiers; and in the last few days he had made sure that, with one further amendment, it would be supported by the Progressives as well as by the government members of the Transvaal delegation. Rarely, if ever, had the ground been so carefully prepared for the success of a constitutional convention. Perhaps the only serious doubt in Smuts's mind was the reaction of the Natal delegates, none of whom was in his confidence. Would they reject his plans outright and thus make the Union incomplete? Or would they succeed in having them watered down so that they would become unrecognizable? Or would they, perhaps, be prevailed upon to accept them more or less as they stood? To a consideration of this problem we must now turn.

[77] Merriman to Smuts, 27 Sept. 1908, Smuts Papers; Brand's manuscript, Annexure L (2).

[78] Brand's manuscript, Annexure L (3).

[79] There is an interesting and discursive account of the railway journey of the Transvaal delegates to Durban in Sir Percy Fitzpatrick, *South African Memories* (London, 1932), chap. ix.

3. NATAL APPROACHES THE CONVENTION

Nearly everyone outside Natal who was interested in the closer union movement was anxious that Natal should join the Union at the outset. To the British Government, as we have seen, Natal had been a frequent source of embarrassment as a separate colony; and it seemed that the occasions for embarrassment might increase if a union were formed without her, because she would then be inclined to claim British support in the disputes that might arise with her more powerful neighbour. And so, although Britain was prepared to retain direct responsibility for the three protectorates, she was not willing to encourage Natal separatism. Secondly, the British officials in South Africa, the Transvaal Progressives, and the Cape Unionists, who had decided to co-operate in the creation of the Union, were alarmed at the thought that the British people would become a hopeless minority in the Union if Natal was excluded; whereas with Natal included, they hoped they might eventually become a majority. Consequently, every effort was made from such quarters to persuade Natal to enter the Union. Lord Selborne was in Natal during June to 'do his best to disarm opposition to union'.[80] Patrick Duncan was there in August, proclaiming the advantages of union at public meetings and trying to win over the politicians and businessmen in private talks.[81] A leading Progressive (probably Sir Percy Fitzpatrick) was writing to Natal in September, arguing that it was the Afrikaner extremists—men like Fischer and J. H. Hofmeyr—who were trying to thwart union, and that for Natal to do likewise would be to play into their hands.[82] And Sir Walter Hely-Hutchinson, who had been Governor of Natal from 1893 to 1901, when he was transferred to the Cape Colony, was there at the beginning of October, shortly before the convention opened, reasoning with the leading men and writing back to advise Merriman how to handle the Natal delegates in the convention.[83] Thirdly, many of the leaders of the government parties in the other three colonies were anxious for Natal to join the Union because they feared that a separate Natal would become a bridgehead for imperialism and would impede the evolution of a white South African nation. Louis Botha also had a sentimental regard for the colony of his birth and he made special efforts to bring Natal in. In May he wrote to the Afrikaner members of the Natal Parliament, urging them to support the closer

[80] Smuts to Merriman, 10 June 1908, Merriman Papers.
[81] Duncan to Lady Selborne, 15 Aug. 1908, Duncan Papers.
[82] Natal Archives, Prime Minister, CIX. The names of the author and the addressee of this letter, which is dated 21 Sept. 1908, have been carefully deleted.
[83] 7 Oct. 1908, Merriman Papers.

union resolutions.[84] He also tried to win the support of Moor. 'I am very anxious', he wrote to him in August, 'to see my native colony heartily joining with the rest and I should be very sorry if Natal were to find out her mistake too late if she were not to go in for closer union.'[85]

The British people of Natal were not eager to respond to these pressures. Many of them were suspicious of the governments of the other colonies and believed that they intended to impose Afrikaner domination on all South Africa. Their suspicions were evident in many of the speeches made in the Natal Parliament during the debates on the closer union resolutions. To take but one example: 'Unification', said C. A. S. Yonge, 'means Dutch control of South Africa.'[86] They were also evident in the tone of the press. It was Major Silburn who gave them the most striking expression. Addressing ex-servicemen on 1 August, he described the members of the governments of the other three colonies as 'quasi-republicans' who were using closer union as a cloak to conceal their real objective, 'the total extinction of the imperial factor in South Africa', and he advised his audience not to forget that 'the sword is only laid aside temporarily'.[87] Then, as the time for the meeting of the National Convention approached, it was rumoured that the governments of the other colonies were preparing a cut-and-dried plan of unification and that Natal would be told to accept it as it stood or to stay out in the cold and starve. Unification, it was said, would be followed by the compulsory introduction of the Dutch language in the Natal schools on the Orange River Colony model, and by the replacement of British civil servants by Afrikaners.[88] Smuts tried to dispel such fears by publicly denying that the Transvaal was preparing a draft Constitution: 'No draft constitution was being prepared by the Transvaal delegates', he said. 'All their efforts were being confined merely to a study of the complex problems connected with a possible future Constitution . . . they would leave it to the Convention to evolve a Constitution for South Africa.'[89] This, however, did little to reassure Natal and her delegates were not consulted by Smuts at any stage before the National Convention met.

Among the rumours that were current in Natal there was another strong and persistent one which created grave suspicion. Natal had always been touchy on the question of Transvaal relations with the

[84] Botha to M. Myburgh, &c., 14 May 1908, Transvaal Archives, Prime Minister, LX (i) (copy).

[85] Botha to Moor, 6 Aug. 1908, Natal Archives, Prime Minister, CVI.

[86] *Natal Leg. Ass. Deb.* xliv. 21.

[87] *Natal Mercury*, 3 Aug. 1908.

[88] Sir Walter Hely-Hutchinson, Governor of the Cape Colony, to Merriman, 7 Oct. 1908, Merriman Papers.   [89] *Cape Times*, 26 Sept. 1908.

Portuguese administration of Mozambique, and unwilling to regard the *modus vivendi* as an equitable agreement; and during June and the following months she was swept by a rumour that the Transvaal Government was negotiating with the Portuguese with the object of replacing the *modus vivendi* with an agreement which would be still more injurious to Natal trade. In its most alarming form the story was that the Transvaal was going to take over the control of Delagoa Bay and of the railway from there to the Transvaal—a step which, it was believed, would cripple the port of Durban and the Natal railways. Selborne and Botha tried to allay this rumour. They admitted that negotiations were taking place with the Portuguese, but they reminded Moor that he had been told in May that the Transvaal intended to enter into negotiations, they assured him that the Transvaal's objective was to replace the *modus vivendi* with an agreement which would be more to the advantage of the Cape Colony and Natal, and they undertook not to conclude any formal agreement before Natal and the other colonies had been given ample opportunity to make any representations they wished. Moor and his colleagues were not satisfied, however, because they were not told the details of the proposals which the Transvaal was placing before the Portuguese.[90]

The cumulative effect of these rumours was a widespread and profound distrust of the Transvaal. 'When I got to Natal [early in October]', wrote Sir Walter Hely-Hutchinson, 'I found that all the people to whom I spoke in Durban, and Nathan [the Governor] himself, were under the impression that Natal would be presented with an ultimatum involving the surrender of everything to the will and pleasure of the central government, and with an agreement between Transvaal and Delagoa which would seriously compromise, if not ruin, the commercial interests of Durban.'[91]

These were the main reasons why Natal approached the National Convention with profound misgivings. There were, too, various secondary reasons. Most of the Natal whites detested the Cape non-European franchise and were concerned lest union might sooner or later involve its extension to Natal. The sugar producers were anxious lest a Union Government should cut off the regular supplies of indentured labour from India which they relied on. And there were some who could not easily reconcile themselves to the prospect of losing a niche in the existing political system or in the social life which was focused on Government House. Natal had always tended to dissociate herself from the rest

---

[90] The above paragraph is based on documents in the Natal Archives, Prime Minister, cv.

[91] Hely-Hutchinson to Merriman, 16 Oct. 1908, Merriman Papers.

of South Africa and she could not easily bring herself to be moved by the ideal of white South African nationhood which had become the inspiration of the political leaders, both Afrikaner and British, of the Transvaal. On the contrary, the ideal of most of the Natal whites was that Natal might remain a separate colony—British to the core.

It was their misfortune that this ideal was unrealizable. Natal could not remain a separate colony because she could not stand on her own feet. This was the conclusion reached by the politicians as they realized that railway receipts, which were largely derived from the Transvaal trade, still formed more than half of the total revenue, and they recalled that there had been a deficit in each of the last four financial years. It was also the conclusion reached by many of the leading commercial men, especially the Durban import merchants. If the other three colonies formed a union without Natal, it would obviously become their interest to divert Durban's share of the Transvaal trade to the Cape ports and Delagoa Bay; and it was obvious, too, that this could easily be done by manipulating their railway rates and customs tariff, so that Natal, it seemed, would face bankruptcy, and ultimately be forced to make such terms as she could with a triumphant Union. That was the logic that dominated the political thinking of her responsible men, whatever their ideals and prejudices may have been.[92]

Natal's National Convention delegates were therefore placed in an extremely difficult position—ignorant of the plans which were being prepared in the Transvaal, emotionally averse to joining a union which might sooner or later fall under exclusively Afrikaner control, and yet unable to find the economic means to keep out of any union that was created. There were, however, some political compensations as well as material ones to be sought in union. British though they were in their outlook, they had been deeply hurt by what they regarded as the unsympathetic attitude of the British Liberal Government towards their conduct of Native affairs, and it seemed logical for them to suppose that a united South Africa, being a much stronger State than Natal, would be comparatively immune from 'British interference'.[93] In these circumstances the delegates gave the impression of vacillation and weakness. 'Gallant little Natal is still sitting on the fence and I only hope that common sense will prevail and prevent them from freezing into the fence', wrote Botha at the end of June, referring to the debates on the

[92] Lady Selborne to Duncan, 27 June 1908, Duncan Papers; Hely-Hutchinson to Merriman, 7 Oct. 1908, Merriman Papers; *The Times*, 10 Oct. 1908 (special article).

[93] On 28 July 1908 T. F. Carter, the Minister of Justice, speaking in the Natal Parliament, indulged in a long denunciation of the Zululand policy of the British Government from 1879 onwards and his speech was well received. *Natal Leg. Ass. Deb.* xliv. 555–75.

closer union resolutions in the Natal Parliament.[94] Early in August, however, Moor assured Botha that he would do everything he could to bring Natal into union: 'I cordially agree with you in the sentiment that all who have the interests of South Africa at heart should co-operate in the effort to bring about some satisfactory form of closer union, and you may rely on it that I shall do my utmost to bring the movement to a successful issue.'[95] And yet a week later Moor was giving Patrick Duncan a very different impression, and Duncan was finding that he could turn the unpopularity of the leading Natal politicians into a useful argument for union: 'What is the use of talking to Moor?' asked Duncan. 'It makes me feel like trying to stop a leak with a piece of blotting paper. One really cannot have much respect for a colony which lets itself be governed by such men. I found them useful as an argument against people in Durban who drew fearful pictures of what their condition would be under Unification. I could always in the last resort ask whether they thought their affairs would be more inefficiently managed than they are now and none of them could truthfully say that their worst apprehension went as far as that.'[96] Finally, on the very eve of the convention, Sir Walter Hely-Hutchinson reported that Moor was 'so weak that he may turn round again'.[97]

If Natal had been able to have her own way she would have got the best of both worlds by joining in a loose federation, thereby preserving her legal identity, retaining a considerable measure of control over her own affairs, and yet acquiring financial relief and military security. Before the National Convention met this idea was embodied in a draft Constitution, prepared by or on behalf of the Natal delegates for submission to the convention.[98] According to this draft the four self-governing colonies would become the states of a 'Federal Dominion'. The Federal Senate would contain eight senators from each state, elected by the state legislatures. The seats in the first Federal House of Representatives would be divided among the states in a manner which was not specified (the numbers were left blank). An additional seat would accrue to a state whenever its total population increased by 54,000 people, irrespective of colour, so that Natal would thus obtain recognition for her large Native

[94] Botha to Merriman, 29 June 1908, Merriman Papers.

[95] Moor to Botha, 8 Aug. 1908, Natal Archives, Prime Minister, CXXII (copy).

[96] Duncan to Lady Selborne, 15 Aug. 1908, Duncan Papers.

[97] Hely-Hutchinson to Merriman, 7 Oct. 1908, Merriman Papers.

[98] House of Assembly, National Convention Minutes, II, Annexure 32. I have not been able to discover who drafted this document, printed copies of which were tabled in the convention. It was perhaps W. B. Morcom, the Natal delegate who held the most distinctively federal views, or C. H. Lepper, who served as secretary to the Natal delegates between August and November.

population. Nevertheless, the federal franchise would be limited to Europeans. The states would be governed by ministries responsible to uni-cameral legislatures, which would possess the exclusive power to pass laws in twenty-one specified fields, including Native tribal affairs and primary education. The Federal Parliament would be able to pass laws in all other fields, 'subject to the constitution', and the Federal High Court would have jurisdiction in constitutional cases and the Constitution would be binding upon it. As in Australia, a constitutional amendment would require an absolute majority of each House of the Federal Parliament and, in a referendum, a majority of the electors voting in a majority of the states (including a majority of all the electors voting); while for amendments changing a state's representation in either House of Parliament, or changing the boundaries of a state, a majority of the electors voting in that state would also be required.[99]

In preparing such a document for submission to the National Convention the Natal delegates cannot have seriously supposed that it would meet with the approval of the other delegates. They probably had their eyes fixed on the record. The most that they seem actually to have hoped for was that the convention would accept a solution of the sort that had been suggested by Hyslop, Moor, and Smythe during the debates on the closer union resolutions in the Natal Parliament, when they had said that they would agree to the principle of unification provided that it was accompanied by a large measure of local self-government.[1] It does not appear, however, that they made any systematic study of the problems involved in this line of thought, though under the guidance of Sir Matthew Nathan and Sir Walter Hely-Hutchinson it was eventually developed into a concrete proposal. On 7 October Sir Walter was writing to Merriman to advise him that Natal, if treated tactfully, would accept the principle of unification provided that three safeguards were included: firstly, the Constitution should state that certain specified powers were 'delegated' to the local legislatures and could not be taken away from them without an amendment of the Constitution; secondly, any constitutional amendment should be difficult to effect; and thirdly, the Constitution should make it impossible for the interests of Durban to be sacrificed to those of Delagoa Bay. He added that he felt sure that Natal would not willingly join the Union without such safeguards.[2] In two further letters, written to Merriman after the convention had opened, Sir Walter returned to the theme: 'I am wondering what is happening in the Convention, and whether you are taking the line of "unification with

---

[99] This section was identical with s. 128 of the Australian Constitution.
[1] See above, pp. 147–8.   [2] Merriman Papers.

safeguards" or not. I believe unification without safeguards to be impossible. "Safeguards" is a "blessed word"—and will provide a bridge, golden or otherwise, for the federationists who have been condemning unification—as well as for the unificationists who have been preaching too much centralization.'[3] And again: 'Nathan is strong for decentralization: but he told me he had no objection to the principle of delegation from the central government (which is the main principle of unification) provided that sufficient delegation be guaranteed, and that the central government be deprived of the power of resuming powers agreed to be delegated, without an alteration of the constitution.'[4]

It was certainly in Natal's interest, as Hely-Hutchinson advised, that the powers of the provinces should be as wide as possible and that they should be effectively entrenched; but it is doubtful whether the sort of Constitution that was being proposed, for all the use of the word 'delegation', would have been a unitary Constitution in any orthodox sense.[5] Merriman must certainly have regarded the proposal with abhorrence as being perniciously rigid, if not federal, in character; and the practical question that would arise in the first few days of the Convention was: how would the Natal delegates react to the carefully prepared resolution which was going to be moved at the very outset for the acceptance of a unitary Constitution without reference to any entrenchment of provincial powers? In all the circumstances they would be likely to place their federal project on the record, to be out-voted, to protest—and to yield by remaining in the convention and subscribing to recommendations which would leave the future of Natal in the hands of a bare majority of the Parliament of the Union of South Africa.

[3] 13 Oct. 1908, ibid.
[4] 16 Oct. 1908, ibid.
[5] The question whether Hely-Hutchinson's proposals adumbrated a federal or a unitary Constitution would seem to be unanswerable, since they did not define the amending procedure. If the amending procedure enabled the Central Parliament, with or without some special majority, to deprive the local legislatures of all their powers, then the Constitution would still, in the last resort, have been unitary. But if, on the other hand, a local legislature could only be deprived of its powers with its own consent, or with the consent of the electorate to which it was responsible, then such a Constitution would have had a genuinely federal character.

CHAPTER V

THE NATIONAL CONVENTION

1. PRELUDE

At 11 o'clock on the morning of 12 October the delegates attended a mayoral reception in the Durban Town Hall. Botha was given a cordial welcome by the crowd and even Merriman was loudly applauded when, as senior Prime Minister, he replied to the mayor's speech. At 11.45 the delegates went upstairs to the council chamber which had been equipped for their use and there, beneath the portraits of Lord Milner and Joseph Chamberlain, they turned to business.[1]

As had been agreed by the colonial governments, Moor started proceedings by nominating Sir Henry de Villiers for the office of President of the Convention. His election having been unanimously approved, this dignified and austere man, who had left the bench for the market-place at several crises in South African affairs, took the Chair of the Conference which had been convened to fulfil his old dream of a South African Union. He was not the man to interpret his office in any narrow sense. He would preside with firmness, he would be active in debate, he would vote in divisions, he would mediate between the convention and the High Commissioner on matters of mutual concern, and he would play a leading part in the drafting of the Constitution. In the main he would be supported by all the delegates in the ways he did these things; but when they were baulked by the chair, delegates of British descent would recall that he had fanned the pro-Boer cause in England during the war and Afrikaner delegates would not forget his strictures of the Kruger régime; while the legal advisers, when they were asked to assist

---

[1] Some days before the convention met the portrait of Milner was covered with 'a red and baize curtain', so as not to offend the Afrikaner delegates; but someone had second thoughts and the curtain was removed. *Cape Times*, 7 and 13 Oct. 1908.

For the convention's proceedings of 12 Oct., see G. R. Hofmeyr (ed.), *Minutes of Proceedings with Annexures (selected) of the South African National Convention held at Durban, Cape Town and Bloemfontein, 12th October, 1908, to 11th May, 1909* (Cape Town, 1911), pp. 1–8; Johann F. Preller (ed.), *Die Konvensie Dagboek van sy edelagbare François Stephanus Malan, 1908–1909* (with an English translation by A. J. de Villiers) (Cape Town, 1951), pp. 18–23; Sir Edgar Walton, *The Inner History of the National Convention of South Africa* (Cape Town, 1912), pp. 38–41. These three books are cited as *Minutes*, Malan, and Walton, respectively. Page references to Malan are to both the Dutch original (even numbers) and the English translation (odd numbers).

in the work of embodying the convention's resolutions in a Constitution Bill, would be dismayed at the tenacity with which he would adhere to his own form of words.

After taking the chair de Villiers delivered a carefully prepared homily to his fellow delegates, first in English and then in Dutch. He reminded them that they had a mandate 'to enquire, not whether an early union is desirable, for that has already been decided upon by our principals, but what form that union should take and what should be the machinery for bringing it into being'. He appealed to them to enter upon their work in a spirit of mutual trust and not to seek to secure advantages for their respective parties or colonies. He assured them that the people of South Africa were enthusiastic for the cause which had brought them together and that they had the best wishes of Great Britain and the rest of the Empire. And he exhorted them to proceed 'with the full determination not to dissolve until we have succeeded in framing a scheme of union which shall be durable and destined to create a strong and united, prosperous and contented South African nation within the folds of the British Empire'. He then read telegrams conveying the good wishes of King Edward VII and the British Government.

M. T. Steyn was then unanimously elected Vice-President of the Convention and he accepted in a brief speech in both languages.

After the credentials of the delegates had been put in and some procedural questions had been dealt with, Sir Matthew Nathan, the Governor of Natal, was admitted to the Council Chamber to address them:

. . . The whole people of South Africa are looking at you [he said] to devise a scheme which will unite them in a great nation, a nation of white people, maintaining their virility and increasing in numbers, ruling themselves and a contented native population in the common interests of all, a nation governed in such a way that the vast resources of the land may be developed and its productiveness may be constantly increased, in such a way that a world commerce may be established commensurate with the favourable position of the country between western and eastern oceans and with the commercial instincts of its people descended from the two historic trading nations of Europe, in such a way that peace and good order may be continuously maintained within and security provided against attack from without, so that the new commonwealth may add to and not draw on the strength of the Empire of which it will form part, in such a way that education and the arts and sciences may advance so that in culture as in strength South Africa may be among the foremost nations of the world, and in such a way as to carry on through the coming centuries the ideals of honesty and justice, of courage and purity which have made great the nations from which British and Dutch in South Africa have sprung. . . .

Nathan then withdrew; and as the door closed behind him it excluded the imperial factor from all further direct participation in the National Convention. The conduct of its proceedings was entirely in the hands of the delegates of the South African colonies.

Nevertheless, Lord Selborne was in residence in Durban (and later, in Cape Town) while the convention was in session. He and his fellow governors of the South African colonies were supplied with copies of the minutes of the convention's proceedings, and from time to time he had discussions with de Villiers and his Transvaal ministers on two questions in which his Government was specially interested—the franchise question, and the question of the future of Basutoland, Bechuanaland Protectorate, and Swaziland. The Imperial Government had also sent a cruiser squadron to Durban on a courtesy visit as a tangible reminder of South Africa's dependence on the Royal Navy for protection from foreign invasion.

2. THE DELEGATES[2]

Most of the delegates to the National Convention were in the prime of life. Their average age was 52, ranging from Merriman (67) and de Villiers and Michell (66) to Smuts (38) and Malan (37). Only one of them would die before the Union was inaugurated and that was Morcom, who resigned from the convention on account of ill-health during the Christmas recess to be succeeded by Watt, the alternate Natal delegate.[3]

They included the completely unschooled and the university graduate, the unsophisticated Boer and the Witwatersrand director of mines, the Bondsman turned Progressive and the Progressive turned Bondsman, the Raider himself and the Boer guerrilla leader. All of them who were of British descent had had a formal school education, whereas Botha, Burger, and de la Rey had probably never been to school in their lives. On the other hand, only two of the British delegates were university graduates, whereas six of the Afrikaners had graduated at British or continental universities.[4]

The dominant economic interest represented in the convention was,

---

[2] See Appendix B below for biographical notes on the delegates.

[3] Morcom died in Apr. 1910. The next to die were Sauer and Fischer (1913) and de la Rey and de Villiers (1914); and the last to die were Watt and Lindsay (1947) and Smuts (1950).

[4] Jameson and Smartt, Beck, Malan, and Smuts were at British universities; Hertzog was at Amsterdam University; and de Villiers and Steyn became members of the English bar after studying on the Continent. Browne and Maasdorp were also undergraduates in England, but they did not graduate; and Watt, who succeeded Morcom, qualified in law at Glasgow University.

of course, farming. Eleven of the delegates had practised as lawyers and
three as medical doctors, two were primarily journalists, three civil
servants, two directors of gold-mining companies, one a banker, one the
head of a commercial house, and ten of them may be regarded as
farmers pure and simple apart from their political activities;[5] but in
addition to these ten, four of the lawyers had abandoned their profes-
sions for farming and politics[6] and there were at least another six who
owned farms,[7] so that not less than twenty delegates were in some sense
farmers. Mining, banking, and commerce were comparatively poorly
represented, and the manufacturing industries and white labour were not
represented at all—nor were the non-Europeans. However significant
the interracial and intercolonial rivalries may have been, therefore, the
convention could be counted on not to neglect the interests or to ignore
the prejudices of the white farmers of South Africa.[8]

The governing parties of the Cape Colony, the Transvaal, and the
Orange River Colony had fifteen votes in the convention—exactly half
the total—the parties in opposition to them had eight votes, Natal had
five, and there were two Cape Colony independents.[9] These party

[5] *Lawyers*: Coghlan (who, as a Rhodesian delegate, had no vote in the convention),
de Villiers, Fischer, Greene, Hertzog, Hull, Lindsay, Morcom, Sauer, Smuts, and Steyn.
   Doctors: Beck, Jameson, and Smartt.
   Journalists: Malan and Walton.
   Civil Servants: Browne and Stanford (both of whom had retired) and Milton (who, as
a Rhodesian delegate, had no vote in the convention).
   Directors of gold-mining companies: Farrar and Fitzpatrick (of whom the latter had
recently retired).
   Banker: Michell (who, as a Rhodesian delegate, had no vote in the convention).
   Commerce: Jagger.
   Farmers: Botha, Burger, de la Rey, de Wet, Hyslop, Maasdorp, Merriman, Moor,
Smythe, and van Heerden.
[6] Hertzog, Sauer, Smuts, and Steyn.
[7] Beck, de Villiers, Farrar, Fitzpatrick, Greene, and Smartt.
[8] Any classification like the one made in the above paragraph is necessarily inexact,
because several of the delegates could be placed in more than one category. Malan has
been classified as a journalist because he had scarcely begun to practise law before he
became editor of *Ons Land*; Jameson has been classified as a doctor because he practised for several years, but by 1908 he was primarily a director of companies; and Merriman has been classified as a farmer, although in his time he had tried his hand as a land
surveyor, a diamond dealer, and a wine merchant, before he became a politician and
a farmer. Watt, like Morcom whom he succeeded, was a lawyer.
[9] *Governing parties*: Merriman, Beck, Maasdorp, Malan, Sauer, and van Heerden
(South African Party); Botha, Burger, de la Rey, Smuts (Het Volk), and Hull
(Nationalist); and Fischer, Steyn, de Wet, and Hertzog (Orangia Unie).
   Opposition parties: Jameson, Jagger, Smartt, and Walton (Unionists); Farrar, Fitz-
patrick, and Lindsay (Progressives); and Browne (Constitutionalist).
   Natal: Moor, Greene, Hyslop, Morcom, and Smythe.
   Cape Colony Independents: De Villiers and Stanford.

alignments corresponded closely with the racial division in white South Africa. Thirteen of the delegates who were members of the governing parties were Afrikaners and the eight opposition delegates and the five Natal delegates were of British descent.[10] With the war so fresh in their memories, many of the Afrikaner delegates were anxious lest a united South Africa should result in the loss of identity of their people, while many of the British delegates were sensitive to the possibility that a united South Africa might eventually become a larger and stronger South African Republic, based upon the Krugerist principle that all real power should be kept in Afrikaner hands. If both sides had frankly put their cards on the table, they might have found it wise to agree upon a Constitution which divided political power between a number of different authorities, so that, even if a party became organized on a racial basis and acquired a majority of the seats in the central legislature, it would not be able to dominate all the instruments of government. As we have seen, however, the only delegates who favoured such a solution were the Natal delegates, and they had little influence outside their own colony. The other delegates of British descent and the Afrikaner delegates were each optimistic enough to believe that in the long run their own racial group would form the political majority in South Africa and would thereby be immune from domination by the other group, even if the Constitution concentrated all real power in the party which had a majority in the central legislature. Fitzpatrick, for example, followed Lord Selborne and the Kindergarten in reasoning that a united South Africa would attract a large stream of British immigrants, so that there was nothing to fear provided only that the electoral system was a fair one.

If we get the fundamental conditions of the Transvaal constitution regarding the basis of representation, viz., the voters' basis, equal constituencies and automatic redistribution, the future will work out all right [he explained in a letter to Balfour]. . . . The future, as I see it, lies this way: both races hope for prosperity, prosperity means expansion, expansion means immigration,

[10] Of the nineteen delegates (including the three Rhodesian delegates, who had no vote) who were of British descent, seven were born in South Africa (Coghlan, Fitzpatrick, Greene, Hull, Lindsay, Moor, and Stanford), seven in England (Browne, Farrar, Jagger, Merriman, Michell, Milton, and Morcom), three in Scotland (Hyslop, Jameson, and Smythe), one in Ireland (Smartt), and one in Ceylon (Walton). Considering that the white population of South Africa had increased nearly fivefold in the previous forty years, the proportion of the delegates who were born abroad was not very high. Moreover, all of them had lived in South Africa for at least twenty-five years, except Browne, who arrived in 1891, and all of them had come to regard South Africa as their home and would in due course be buried there, except Jameson, who kept a footing in both countries and would spend the last five years of his life in England.

immigration means British! So there is one great essential, and that is, to provide the machinery by which, when they come, they will be represented.[11]

The most race-conscious of the Afrikaner delegates, on the other hand, saw that under union their people would be brought together in the same state for the first time since the Great Trek and that, as things stood, they would form a majority of the white population of that state, so that they could hope to control it provided only that they stood together. Consequently they focused their attention on the language question in the belief that if the Constitution gave the fullest possible protection to their language, Afrikaner solidarity would be preserved. Thus delegates drawn from the two races which had so recently been at each other's throats were able to enter the convention to create a legislative union on the British model. It was the mark of the statesmanship of Botha and Smuts that they had adopted a policy which was acceptable to both extremes. They were able to do so because their own outlook had become non-racial and because they believed that it was only a matter of time and fair government before all white South Africans would think like-wise and would naturally fuse into a homogeneous nation. With such a philosophy before the public it would have been impolitic for others to admit that they were moved by racial ambitions, or even racial fears. So all the delegates paid at least lip-service to the Botha–Smuts ideal and each side was prepared to grant the other its principal demand, and the granting of it would remove suspicions and promote the growth of mutual confidence.

It is relevant to add that the governing parties of the Cape Colony, the Transvaal, and the Orange River Colony were much more efficiently represented in the convention than their opponents. In Smuts, Merriman, Steyn, and Malan they had delegates who were well read in constitutional history and law and who had made a serious study of the problem of devising a Constitution for South Africa, whereas no Opposition or Natal delegate was so well informed or so well prepared. Then again, the governing parties were led by men who had made politics their main concern and had become extremely able practitioners of the art, whereas the ablest of the Opposition leaders were part-time politicians who had been thrust into their responsibilities in default of others. Contrast, for example, the political concentration and acumen of Merriman, Botha, Smuts, and Hertzog with the amateurism of Farrar, who was essentially a man of business, of Fitzpatrick, who in spite of occasional bursts of intense political activity was too much of a romantic to be a politician of

[11] Quoted by J. P. R. Wallis in *Fitz, The Story of Sir Percy Fitzpatrick* (London, 1955), p. 137.

the first order, or of Jameson, who was bored to distraction by the work of the convention and longed, day after day, for the end of the sitting and the chance to relax on the golf course or at the bridge table. The government delegates included men of tough political fibre who could never be carried away by the camaraderie of the convention into accepting decisions which might be inimical to the interests or prejudices of their constituents, whereas Jameson and Fitzpatrick were prone to mistake personal friendliness for enduring political realities.

Furthermore, there was more unity among the delegates of the governing parties of the Cape Colony, the Transvaal, and the Orange River Colony than among their opponents. Nearly all of them represented the single economic interest of farming, and six years after the war most of them still had the consciousness of a need for solidarity that a defeated group always shows. It is true that the gulf between the Transvaal and the Orange River Colony leaders, which had originated at Vereeniging, had become wider since they came into power in 1907, and Hertzog and his colleagues suspected that Botha and Smuts had become corrupted by the anglicizing influence of the Witwatersrand. Nevertheless, in the last resort most of the Afrikaner delegates were primarily concerned to safeguard the interests of their own people, and once Hertzog and Steyn gave them a lead they rallied behind them in support of their demands for the protection of the Dutch language. The Opposition and Natal delegates, on the other hand, had no semblance of cohesion. They, far more than the government delegates, had been embroiled in the inter-colonial railway and customs disputes, they represented different and conflicting economic interests, there was no accord between the Natal delegates and the rest and, as Milner had found, they were comparatively indifferent to any plea for racial solidarity. Even on the electoral question, which was so vital to Fitzpatrick's calculations, they did not pull together, because the Natal delegates, three of whom were farmer-politicians, were accustomed to defending the grossly unequal electoral system that prevailed in their own colony. In fact the Opposition and Natal delegates did not vote *en bloc* in a single division in the convention, whereas the delegates of the governing parties of the Cape Colony, the Transvaal, and the Orange River Colony did so thirteen times.[12] Duncan's comment was as follows:[13] 'The Boers whatever their differences may be are in the last resort solidly fenced round by national and racial feelings.

[12] Here, as throughout this section, no account has been taken of the session of the National Convention which was held in May 1909 in Bloemfontein, though there, too, the Opposition and Natal delegates did not once vote *en bloc*.
[13] Duncan to Lady Selborne, 28 Jan. 1909, Duncan Papers.

The others have about as much cohesive principle as chaff on a windy day.'

With the unfolding of the tactical position in the convention, therefore, the delegates of the governing parties were more successful in protecting the interests of their constituents than the Opposition and Natal delegates, because they included abler politicians and because they were more nearly united.

The racial factor rarely broke surface in the convention. The delegates were representatives of colonies and not of races, they held frequent caucus meetings on a colonial basis in rooms set aside for each delegation, and for the most part they acted colonially. Thus in the sixty-six divisions that took place both the Natal and the Orange River Colony delegations voted *en bloc* forty-two times, the Transvaal delegation thirty-six times, and the Cape delegation eighteen times.[14]

The Transvaal delegation was far the most efficient. It came to Durban as a united team with an agreed programme, and all its members loyally sunk their party differences throughout the convention. They were 'united in aim and policy, co-operating heartily and working eagerly for the same end', as Fitzpatrick later recalled, 'led and inspired by the brain and immense working capacity of Smuts'.[15] It was, too, far the best served of the delegations, being accompanied by a staff of nineteen men, including P. Duncan and R. H. Brand of the Kindergarten, as well as a number of competent young South Africans such as N. J. de Wet and F. Lucas, whereas the staffs of the other delegations were far smaller. These advantages were impressively reinforced by economic strength, since the Transvaal alone among the South African colonies had a thriving and expanding economy. The gold production of the Witwatersrand was soaring, her white population was increasing, and her treasury was accumulating large annual surpluses without the aid of an income tax, whereas in the other colonies, and more particularly the coastal colonies, trade was still stagnant, the white population was still decreasing, and deficits were still the order of the day.[16] The Transvaal delegates were therefore the only ones who could face the failure of the convention and the consequent disintegration of the Customs Union with complete equanimity from the material point of view. For the most part, however, they did not use their economic power for selfish ends; but there were three questions on which they felt very strongly indeed. One was that the

[14] I have allowed for one or (rarely) two absentees from a colonial delegation in a division.

[15] 'The Language Question' (unpublished manuscript, c. 1930), Fitzpatrick Papers.

[16] The reader is referred to the statistics in Appendix A.

Constitution should be unitary. Another was that the state railways should be operated on 'business principles' and not used as a source of taxation, so that imported food, clothing, and machinery would be as cheap as possible for Transvaal consumers. The third was that the capital of the Union should be at Pretoria. All sections of the Transvaal electorate were behind them on these questions and they were in a position to insist that their demands should be met as the price of the Transvaal's accession to the Union.

The Cape Colony delegation, with twelve votes, and with members like de Villiers, Merriman, Sauer, and Malan, was strong in numbers and in talents, but it was a delegation of individualists and not a team. It was typical of Merriman that he had continued to indulge in party strife with his usual ferocity until he left for Durban, that he had made no attempt to convene a meeting of the Cape delegates, nor even of the delegates of his own party, to work out a common line of action, and that he gloried in this approach, publicly affirming in Cape Town on the eve of his departure that each Cape delegate would go to Durban 'free and unfettered to speak his own mind'.[17] The result was that the Cape delegates seldom acted in concert except when they stood firm for the maintenance and entrenchment of the Cape non-European franchise and for a share of the Union capital.

The Natal delegation was the weakest. Its federal proposals merited serious consideration, but it was unable to do justice to them,[18] and when they had been rejected it tended to move towards the Transvaal, because Natal's material interests lay with the Transvaal rather than the Cape and because the Natal delegates had more confidence in Botha and Smuts than in Merriman and Malan. The Orange River Colony delegation included abler men in Steyn and Hertzog, but Steyn's influence, like Botha's and Jameson's, was exerted rather in the field of personal relations outside the convention chamber than in the day-to-day work of the convention, and Hertzog was concerned almost to the point of obsession with the language question and made few major contributions on other issues.

Consequently Transvaal preparations, Transvaal brains, Transvaal teamwork, and Transvaal economic strength prevailed on most issues in the convention.

[17] *Cape Times*, 3 Oct. 1908.
[18] It is somewhat ironical that the one non-Natalian who held federal views and had been selected as a delegate was W. P. Schreiner, and that he had withdrawn from the Cape Colony delegation because the Natal Government was unwilling to arrange that the trial of Dinizulu should not coincide with the meetings of the convention.

3. PROCEDURE

The convention normally sat for three hours in the morning and two in the afternoon from Monday to Friday inclusive.[19] Most of the delegates were regular in their attendance and there was never any difficulty in raising the quorum of twelve. Malan missed one day, Morcom two,[20] Steyn three, and de la Rey and de Wet both missed six days; and the other twenty-five delegates from the self-governing colonies were present every day that the convention sat and de Villiers presided throughout. Two of the Rhodesian delegates, on the other hand, were frequently absent. Milton did not attend any of the Cape Town sittings and Coghlan missed thirteen days. Michell, however, was present every day except the last three.

So far as practicable the convention did its business in plenary session, but when a question appeared to be particularly intractable or technical it was referred to a committee of delegates, with instructions to draft resolutions for the consideration of the convention. Sixteen such committees were appointed.[21] They normally met out of convention hours in the late afternoons and evenings, but sometimes the convention was adjourned to enable a committee to continue its work.

Motions did not require to be seconded and delegates were able to speak more than once to the same question. Questions were decided by a majority, the thirty delegates of the four self-governing colonies having the right to vote, and if the president's announcement of the result of a vote was challenged a count was made, with the Ayes standing and the Noes remaining seated. Sixty-six divisions were taken in all and the President had cause to use his casting vote on only one occasion.[22] When a resolution had been adopted the question could not be re-opened before the drafting stage was reached without the consent of all the

[19] Except where otherwise stated or implied, the information in this section is derived from the *Minutes*, which are well indexed and have a useful explanatory note by the editor, G. R. Hofmeyr. The procedure of the convention was determined mainly by: (a) the resolutions of the Intercolonial Conference of May 1908, which laid down that voting should be *per capita* and that the chairman should have a deliberative as well as a casting vote ; and (b) resolutions passed by the convention at its first sitting on 12 Oct.

[20] Morcom missed the last two days before the Christmas recess. During the recess he resigned and when the convention resumed on 11 Jan. 1909 his place was taken by T. Watt, whom the Natal Parliament had appointed to succeed to any vacancy in the Natal delegation. Morcom died on 24 Apr. 1910.

[21] Here, and throughout this section, no account is taken of the session of the convention held in Bloemfontein in May 1909.

[22] This was on 29 Jan., when there was a tie, fifteen–fifteen, on a Smuts motion to amend what became section 129 of the South Africa Act. The President gave his casting vote with the Noes to preserve the section as already agreed to. *Minutes*, p. 234.

delegates present, but the drafting committee which was appointed on 18 December was empowered to recommend amendments of substance, and when the convention began to consider the committee's report on 12 January it decided by a sixteen to fourteen majority to allow amendments of its earlier resolutions to be moved in the ordinary way.[23]

Besides the delegates, five officials were admitted to the convention chamber—four secretaries and an interpreter. The secretaries, who had been nominated by the governments of the self-governing colonies, were E. F. Kilpin, the Clerk of the Cape Colony House of Assembly, G. R. Hofmeyr, the Clerk of the Transvaal Legislative Assembly, A. M. N. de Villiers, the Clerk of the Orange River Colony Legislative Assembly, and G. T. Plowman, the secretary to the Prime Minister of Natal. Of these, Kilpin, the doyen of South African parliamentary officers, was appointed chief secretary. The interpreter was Dr. W. E. Bok, the secretary to the Prime Minister of the Transvaal. The delegates were entitled to speak in English or in Dutch, and English was normally used in the convention by all of them except Burger, de la Rey, and de Wet, who could scarcely speak it, and Botha, who spoke English fluently in private conversation but was still too self-conscious to attempt to do so in public.[24] Hertzog and Steyn sometimes spoke in English and sometimes in Dutch and the rest of the delegates invariably used English. Since all the delegates could understand English, Bok's services were not called on when speeches were made in it, but he translated speeches which were made in Dutch for the benefit of several of the British delegates, who would not otherwise have understood them.[25] The advisers of the delegations were not admitted to the chamber, but they were given office accommodation in rooms near by.

A number of petitions and letters were received by the convention. Many were messages of congratulation and encouragement, but some were intended to influence the convention in its decisions. There were communications for and against women's suffrage, for effective representation for non-Europeans in the South African Parliament, for 'equal rights' for the Dutch language, and in favour of the claims of several towns to that coveted trophy, the South African capital.[26]

The outcome of any such assembly is largely determined by the relations between the delegates outside the formal conference room. The South African National Convention was no exception. At first many of

[23] *Minutes*, pp. 143, 153.
[24] It was not until 1910 that Botha made his first public speech in English. Previously he had always addressed English-speaking audiences through an interpreter.
[25] Walton, pp. 37–38; Fitzpatrick, 'The Language Question'.
[26] House of Assembly, National Convention Minutes, II, IV.

the delegates were unknown to one another and suspicious of one another and contacts outside the chamber tended to be restricted to delegates from the same colony or delegates of the same race; but in the course of time the barriers were gradually broken down and eventually all of them were affected by an excellent *esprit de corps*. Contentious questions were often hammered out in advance over dinner and bridge tables, so that when they came to be dealt with formally in the convention they were settled comparatively easily and without long debates. Botha and Jameson, ardent bridge players both of them, were largely responsible for the development of this convention spirit. 'There is an excellent spirit among the delegates', de Villiers informed Rose Innes, the Chief Justice of the Transvaal, on 22 October.[27] 'All crooning like doves', wrote Jameson to his brother on the 25th. 'Botha is the great factor and plays a capital game of Bridge. He dined with me the other night and went away minus 70s. He, Steyn, and I are great pals—so the world wags.'[28] Even the more serious-minded Malan, summing up the Durban session on 5 November, wrote that 'Generally speaking the delegates were well-disposed.'[29]

It was Smuts, above all, who steadily kept his eye on the main task. As soon as he reached Durban he asked Brand, Duncan, de Wet, and Lucas to draft resolutions to give effect to the Transvaal programme, and within a day or two they handed him a nearly complete set of resolutions. Thereafter they prepared amended and additional resolutions as he required them, so that he was always in a position to take the initiative in the convention with well-considered proposals. When the other delegates left Durban on 5 November Smuts stayed behind with Farrar, Hull, and some of the Transvaal staff to do another fortnight's hard work, co-ordinating the resolutions which the convention had passed, detecting a number of errors and inconsistencies, and drafting further resolutions on topics which the convention had not yet dealt with.[30] But Smuts was not the only delegate with resolutions to move. Soon after they reached Durban both Merriman and de Villiers wrote out draft resolutions, dealing mainly with the composition and powers of the Central Executive and Legislature; Hertzog was ready with a resolution on the language question which he was determined to bring before the convention at the earliest possible moment; and the Natal delegates had their own draft Constitution and never ceased to cast nostalgic eyes at it. Moreover, the

[27] Innes Papers.
[28] Ian Colvin, *The Life of Jameson* (London, 1922, 2 vols.), ii. 279–80.
[29] Malan, pp. 76–77.
[30] Brand's manuscript. (See above, p. 157, n. 65.)

convention decided on 12 October that any delegate could give notice
of a motion at any time and that motions would be dealt with in the
sequence in which notice had been given.[31] Confusion and inefficiency
might have resulted if there had not been give and take between the
delegates, especially between de Villiers, Smuts, and Merriman. Most of
the motions in the convention were moved by Smuts himself, or by Hull
or Farrar at his request, but sometimes he incorporated Merriman's
phraseology and at others he stood aside for Merriman to move his own
motions. De Villiers rarely took the initiative, except when they were
dealing with the judicial sections of the Constitution, though he would
often come in with amendments to reconcile differences of opinion which
had emerged during debate. After the convention moved to Cape Town,
however, it organized its business more methodically by appointing de
Villiers and the four prime ministers as a standing committee to arrange
the order paper in such a way that questions would be dealt with in a
logical sequence, irrespective of precedence.[32]

On the first day the convention adopted Merriman's proposal that its
proceedings should be 'absolutely secret' and that 'no record of any
speeches' should be made, with the result that the minutes recorded no
more than the times of the sittings, the names of the absent delegates,
the terms of the motions, and the results of the divisions (except for the
minutes of the opening sitting, which included verbatim reports of the
inaugural speeches by de Villiers and Nathan). Each day the delegates
were supplied with copies of the minutes of the previous day's proceedings and of the agenda for the day, but these documents were marked
'Confidential' and they were not to be removed from the chamber.[33] No
records were kept of the proceedings of the committees. These precautions were reasonably effective in preventing leakages. Although newspaper correspondents made every effort to obtain information, the
delegates became experts at parrying their questions and most of the
reports which appeared in the press were as uninformative as the following contemporary burlesque suggests:

Everything is going on well [announced the *Cape*, a lively weekly journal,
on 23 October]. It is semi-officially stated that everything is going on well.

[31] This resolution was not very clearly phrased : 'That notices of motion may be given
at any time for discussion when so given ; but that notices of which previous notice has
been given shall have precedence.' *Minutes*, p. 8.

[32] Ibid., p. 73 (23 Nov. 1908).

[33] On 18 Dec., however, the convention resolved that the delegates should be allowed
to remove the resolutions which had been agreed to, and that the members of the drafting committee should also be allowed to remove their copies of the minutes.

I learn on what may be considered unimpeachable authority that everything is going on as well as can be expected.

Indeed, some of the delegates were so scrupulous in observing the secrecy resolution that they refrained from committing anything to paper touching on their work. Thus Stanford recorded in his diary on 14 October that 'it would be contrary to the agreement entered into by the delegates that strict secrecy should be observed in regard to the proceedings to say anything about them even in a diary', and the private letters written by the delegates were for the most part innocent of explicit statements about the proceedings.[34]

If Merriman had had his way again on 2 February, all the copies of the minutes would have been destroyed when the convention had completed its labours, but the convention preferred Smuts's proposal that in the interests of future historians each delegate should be allowed to keep his copy of the minutes, provided that he treated them as private and confidential.[35] In 1911 they were published by resolution of the South African House of Assembly, under the competent editorship of G. R. Hofmeyr, the Transvaal secretary to the convention. The historian must also be grateful that the professional instincts of the two journalist members of the convention made them less strict than their fellow delegates in interpreting the secrecy resolution. Walton, aspiring to the role of a Madison, made notes of some of the speeches as they were delivered, and Malan kept a diary in which he summarized each day's proceedings, recorded some of his own speeches at length, and added his personal reflections from time to time. In 1912 Walton published *The Inner History of the National Convention of South Africa* after the manuscript had been read by de Villiers and G. R. Hofmeyr; and *Die Konvensie Dagboek van sy edelagbare François Stephanus Malan, 1908–1909* was published by the Van Riebeeck Society in 1951, with an English translation opposite the original Dutch text. These two accounts are complementary to one another. Although both of them were members of the Cape Colony delegation, Walton was a Port Elizabeth Unionist and Malan a Cape Town Bondsman, so their special interests and prejudices were poles apart. The most reliable parts of Walton's book are those in which he gives summaries of speeches which were made in the convention—summaries which Hofmeyr was able to certify as being generally

---

[34] The reports which appeared in *The Times* were more specific and more accurate than the reports which appeared in the South African press; and according to an account written by Fitzpatrick many years later it was no less a person than de Villiers, the President of the convention, who gave *The Times* correspondent valuable hints on at least one occasion. 'The Language Question', Fitzpatrick Papers.

[35] *Minutes*, p. 248; Malan, pp. 220–1.

accurate, with only a few reservations.[36] The other passages need to be treated with caution, because he was not in the confidence of any of the Afrikaner delegates and was therefore unable to produce the complete 'inner history' at which he aimed. Malan's diary, a sincere personal record written without a view to early publication, is less pretentious and less misleading, and in many respects the more valuable source of information.[37]

The convention sat in Durban from 12 October to 5 November 1908 and passed resolutions on the form of the Constitution, the language question, and the powers and composition of the Central Executive and Legislature. By that time Durban's hot and humid summer climate was imposing a strain on many of the delegates, especially de Villiers and Steyn, and the Orange River Colony delegates were anxious to return to Bloemfontein, where a disastrous fire had gutted the government buildings. Consequently, the convention adjourned on the afternoon of 5 November and reassembled in the somewhat milder climate of Cape Town on 23 November. By 18 December it had passed further resolutions on the provincial governments, the judiciary, the civil service, the amendment of the Constitution, and the future of Rhodesia and the High Commission Territories. After a Christmas recess it met again in Cape Town on 11 January and dealt with finance and railways, devised a draft Constitution based on its resolutions, and settled the question of the capital of the Union. On 3 February the convention adjourned after unanimously adopting a report comprising the draft Constitution and recommendations to the colonial parliaments for further action.

4. FEDERATION OR UNION?

When procedural matters had been settled, Merriman and Smuts were eager to launch their motion on the form of the Constitution. It will be recalled that both of them had independently reached the conclusion that this question should be dealt with at the outset.[38] Smuts and Brand had polished up their draft on the subject before they left Pretoria; Merriman had amended his on board ship in consultation with de Villiers, Sauer, and Malan; and when they met in Durban Merriman, Botha, and Smuts worked out a synthesis of the two versions. They drew the Unie leaders

[36] G. R. Hofmeyr, 'Report on Sir Edgar Walton's proposed Convention Publication', Walton, pp. 329–46, especially p. 331.

[37] Where precision is required, the English translation of Malan's diary should be treated with caution.

[38] See above, pp. 163–4.

into their discussions, but found that Hertzog would not undertake to support any such motion unless it included a section on the language question.[39]

During the morning of 13 October Merriman rose and moved the following motion:[40]

(*a*) That it is desirable for the welfare and future progress of South Africa that the several British Colonies be united under one Government in a legislative union under the British Crown.

(*b*) That provision be made for the constitution of Provinces, with powers of local legislation and administration; the present self-governing Colonies being taken as Provinces.

(*c*) That provision be made for the admission into the Union, as Provinces or Territories, of all such parts of South Africa as are not included from its establishment.

(*d*) That the Union shall be styled 'South Africa.'

His speech was devoted exclusively to arguing the case for a unitary Constitution. He sought to discredit federalism by painting a black picture of its effects in America and Australia. Had not the American Constitution caused one of the greatest civil wars in history? And were not Australians already regretting that their Constitution was federal? South Africans should profit from the errors of other people and create a supreme central authority—which would, of course, delegate ample powers to the local authorities! Smuts followed with a second broadside at the same target. They would never get out of the rut of friction in South Africa, he said, except on a basis of complete trust: they should trust one another in the convention; they should trust the people of South Africa outside the convention; and they should trust the future people of South Africa. Federalism would involve a rigid Constitution, which would be a denial of trust and would shackle their successors. Under a federal Constitution the last word would be given by judges and not by the representatives of the people, and governments would therefore be tempted to make judicial appointments on political grounds, so that the bench would become corrupted. Under a unitary Constitution, on the other hand, there would be a single sovereign Parliament in South Africa, as in the United Kingdom; the evils of rigidity and judicial interpretation could be avoided; the country would prosper as a single economic unit; the Native question could be dealt with on uniform lines;

---

[39] Merriman's diary, 8–12 Oct. 1908; Brand's manuscript.

[40] The motion and amendments are in the *Minutes*, pp. 10–13; the debate is described in Malan, pp. 22–39, and Walton, iii; and there are comments by Hofmeyr in Walton, pp. 333–5.

and true patriotism would develop without the break of local loyalties. But Smuts was careful to explain that he was not proposing that the South African Constitution should be a unitary one without qualification. The motion, he said, pointed to a 'middle course'. Local interests would be protected by local legislatures, which would be granted definite powers in the Constitution.

Moor was evidently quite unprepared for this powerful opening attack. He asked to be given time to consider the motion. He disputed Merriman's interpretation of American history—surely, he said, the United States had prospered greatly under their federal Constitution—and he concluded by asking that Natal should be allowed to retain her name as 'the Colony of Natal' and that the powers of her 'parliament' should be clearly defined in the Constitution. Fischer then made an ambiguous speech and moved an ambiguous amendment. He started by admitting that a unitary Constitution was theoretically preferable, but he doubted whether it would be acceptable to the people of South Africa without more effective qualifications than those included in the motion. Nor did he agree with Smuts that Parliament should have the last word in constitutional disputes, because Parliament might not always be impartial. It would be better, said Fischer, to give that power to the courts. He then proposed that the second section of Merriman's motion should be amended to read:

(b) That provision shall be made for the constitution of Provinces, with powers of legislation and administration in local matters and in such others as may be specially reserved to be exclusively dealt with by each Province separately; the present self-governing Colonies being taken as Provinces.

Having heard a delegate from each of the four self-governing colonies, the convention adjourned for the day at 12.15, to give members time to consider the motion and the amendment and to discuss them informally. Most of the delegates were uncertain in their own minds as to the precise implications of the words. Malan thought that the amendment did 'not affect the principle of *legislative unity*, at least not to any great extent', while Merriman regarded it as 'not hostile but embarrassing in direction of assigning definite functions to the local councils'.[41]

Any prospect that the two smaller colonies might make a joint stand for state or provincial rights was destroyed the following morning when Steyn, the first speaker, came out strongly in support of Merriman's motion. The internal boundaries of South Africa, he said, were artificial and had been the cause of most of their troubles in the past. A federal

41 Malan, pp. 24–25 ; Merriman's Diary, 13 Oct. 1908.

Constitution would perpetuate them and he was afraid of it. Nevertheless, he went on to say, the Constitution should give some protection to local interests, and it should, like the Constitution of the Orange Free State Republic, only be amendable by a three-quarters majority. Steyn was followed by Morcom of Natal, who assured the convention that the people of his colony would insist on the powers of the Central Government being limited and defined, and residual powers being vested in the 'States'. He therefore moved that the motion should be amended to read:

(a) That it is desirable for the welfare and future progress of South Africa that the several British Colonies be united under one Government under the British Crown.

(b) That provision be made whereby the present self-governing Colonies shall as such become States of the Union so created.

(c) That provision shall be made for the admission into the Union, as States, of the Territories of all such parts of South Africa as are not included from its establishment.

(d) That the Union shall be styled 'The Dominion of South Africa.'

The debate continued until the afternoon of 15 October and most of the delegates took part in it. Five Transvaalers spoke—Botha, Burger, de la Rey, Farrar, and Fitzpatrick—and all of them supported Merriman's motion. The Het Volk delegates concentrated on the point that the Transvaal would be making a material sacrifice in entering into any form of union with the other colonies. She was, they said, prepared to join them in a legislative union; but she would have no truck with federalism. The Progressives warmly endorsed Smuts's plea for mutual trust. In the Transvaal, said Farrar, the wise and tolerant policy of Botha and Smuts had brought Boer and Briton together and put an end to racialism; and if South Africa was to be made immune from civil war they must have one sovereign authority—which was as much as to say that the Botha-Smuts régime should be extended over all South Africa.

Cape Colony delegates also supported Merriman's motion. Sauer said that to perpetuate a plurality of parliaments in South Africa would be to perpetuate friction. Malan (who has left us a complete record of his speech) explained why he had changed his views since he had advocated federalism in *Ons Land* in 1906. He had come to believe that Native policy should be determined by the Central Government and Parliament and that the only logical way of doing this was under a unitary Constitution. Furthermore, a federal Constitution would cause wrangling between the Central Government and the states, would lead to political interference in judicial appointments, because the courts would inevitably possess the 'testing right', and would have undesirable financial effects, as in Australia. The South African Constitution should therefore be unitary. It should also be fully flexible for the most part, but some sections, such as those dealing with the electoral system, should only be amendable by a more difficult process than that required for ordinary legislation. Of the Unionists, Jagger produced figures to show that federalism had cost the Australian taxpayers an extra million pounds in 1907, Jameson, who went out of his way to pay compliments to the Boer generals, claimed that he had always regarded a unitary Constitution as the better type and that the debate had opened his eyes to the fact that it was now practicable in South Africa, and Walton expressed the opinion that a federal Constitution would not have any significant effect in removing the causes of intercolonial friction. Both Malan and Walton made a point, however, of assuring the Natal delegates that if they accepted Merriman's motion they would find the convention sympathetic to them when they came to the allocation of powers to the provincial councils.

The later Orange River Colony speakers also supported unification. De Wet said that the war had shown that unification was the only safeguard against further trouble and Browne moved that the word 'exclusively' should be removed from Fischer's amendment, which would make it no more than an innocuous amplification of the second section of Merriman's motion. To the relief of Merriman and Smuts, Fischer accepted this suggestion.

The Natal delegates therefore found themselves being swept away by a strong current. Greene admitted that federalism had defects and said he would approve of the creation of a sovereign Parliament, provided that the powers of the local 'parliaments' were reasonable in scope and were clearly defined and fully protected in a rigid Constitution. Smythe supported him. So did Hyslop, who contended that unqualified unification would lead to more friction than a federal Constitution, because of the wide differences between the colonies in their qualifications for the franchise, their attitudes towards Indian immigration, and their treatment of the Dutch language. But nobody moved an amendment to give effect to these ideas.

The outcome was that Merriman rephrased the second section of his motion to incorporate the sense of Fischer's amendment, as amended, and to include a change of little significance proposed by Greene.[42] He also dropped his fourth section on the name of the South African Union.

---

[42] Greene's amendment was that section (b) of the motion should start: 'That provision shall be made in the Constitution for the establishment of Provinces . . .', instead of 'That provision be made for the constitution of Provinces. . . .'

The President put Morcom's amendment to the convention and the only Ayes came from the Natal delegates, who did not call for a division. Merriman's motion was then carried *nem. con.* in the following form:[43]

(*a*) That it is desirable for the welfare and future progress of South Africa that the several British Colonies be united under one Government in a legislative union under the British Crown.

(*b*) That provision shall be made in the Constitution for the establishment of Provinces with powers of legislation and administration in local matters and in such others as may be specially reserved to be dealt with by each Province separately, the present self-governing Colonies being taken to be the Provinces of the Union.

(*c*) That provision be made for the admission into the Union as Provinces or Territories of all such parts of South Africa as are not included from its establishment.

When the convention's drafting committee prepared a draft Constitution in January 1909, this resolution became the basis of the preamble. It was de Villiers, as chairman of the drafting committee, who cast it into an appropriate form, inserted a new clause stating that it was expedient to provide for the union of those colonies which might assent thereto and to define the powers to be exercised in the government of the Union, and amended the final clause so that it declared that it was expedient to provide for the 'eventual' admission into the Union as provinces or territories of such parts of South Africa as were not originally included. This version of the preamble was adopted by the convention, with no more than verbal amendments, on 28 January.[44]

It will have been noted that although Natal had a weak hand she failed to make the best use of the cards she held. The majority of the delegates were much more strongly in favour of a unitary Constitution than a fully flexible one, and if Natal had come in, after Steyn's impressive speech on the morning of the 14th, with a proposal to add a section to Merriman's motion, making the entire Constitution moderately rigid, it is possible that she would have succeeded. Such an addition, in conjunction with the second part of Merriman's motion, would have made the Constitution quasi-federal in practice and would have created

[43] The English translation of Malan's diary is inaccurate here. The original Dutch reads, 'zonder enige tegenstem' (i.e. *nem. con.*), which is translated as 'unanimously'. The *Minutes* merely state that the motion was 'put and agreed to'. Malan, pp. 38–39; *Minutes*, p. 13.

[44] *Minutes*, pp. 224, 237, 282; Walton, p. 308; 'Remarks on Draft Constitution' (unsigned, undated; written by E. M. Greene, the Natal member of the convention's drafting committee), Natal Archives, Prime Minister, cx. The preamble was subsequently amended in England (see below, p. 409).

definite legal barriers against arbitrary government in South Africa. But she did not take the opportunity; and when the convention came to the vote it had to choose between Morcom's out-and-out federal motion and Merriman's. Nevertheless, Natal's hopes were not necessarily completely destroyed by the adoption of the resolution. There was still room for wide powers to be allotted to the provincial governments and there was still room for rigidity; and the Natal delegates seem to have thought that they would gain successes in both respects.

Merriman thought quite differently. He believed that his out-and-out unitary ideas had been completely triumphant and that all that was left for Natal was to press for minor concessions within the framework of a unitary Constitution. He entered up his diary on the evening of 15 October in a mood of unwonted satisfaction: '. . . In the afternoon we came to the vote. Morcom's amendment for Federation was negatived without a division and my resolution with some unimportant amendments was adopted. . . .'

5. THE LANGUAGE SECTION

It will be recalled that during June Steyn had inquired anxiously of Merriman and Botha whether they intended to meet him on the language question and that he had only consented to serve in the convention after he had received strong assurances from Botha that the Constitution would provide for 'the absolute equality of both languages'.[45] Thereafter Smuts had included a brief section on the subject in all his draft plans, the Progressives had accepted the principle of official bilingualism at the meeting of the Transvaal delegates in Pretoria,[46] and the draft motions which Brand prepared for Smuts in Durban (drafts which certainly embodied Smuts's view of the matter) included the following:[47]

Both the English and Dutch languages shall be official languages of the Union and may be employed in the Parliament and in its proceedings and also in the Courts of Law.

Merriman's draft did not go so far:[48]

Either the English or the Dutch language may be used by any person in the debates of the Houses of Parliament of the Union, and both these languages shall as far as Parliament may deem fit be used in the respective records and journals of these Houses, and either language may be used by any person in any pleading or process in any court of the Union.

Both of them, that is to say, were prepared to make the use of Dutch, as

45 See above, pp. 137-8.   46 See above, p. 162.
47 Brand's manuscript, Annexure N.   48 Ibid., Annexure P.

well as English, permissive in Parliament and the law courts, while Smuts was also willing to add the general statement that they would both be 'official languages', and in so doing they seem to have thought that they would be satisfying the Orangia Unie delegates.

They were wrong. To Hertzog and Steyn it was not enough for the Constitution to declare the two languages to be official languages, for that phrase had no precise legal connotation. Nor was it enough to make their use permissive in Parliament and the courts, because that would merely produce the equality of free competition, under which the weaker goes to the wall. The problem, as they saw it, was to ensure the survival of the Dutch language in South Africa, where it had been threatened by a century of British rule, culminating in Milner's effort to obliterate it. That could only be done by a measure of protection, of the sort that was being applied in the Orange River Colony. Competence in Dutch, as well as English, should be necessary attainments for all people in the service of the State—civil servants, railwaymen, and government school-teachers —and then, and then only, was the future of the Dutch language in South Africa reasonably secure, and with it the future cohesion of the Afrikaner people. And so, in the train on the way from Bloemfontein to Durban, Hertzog busied himself with the drafting of his own motion, which read as follows:[49]

In order to effect a Closer Union of the Colonies represented at this Convention, and in order fully to attain the object of its establishment, it is essential that both English and Dutch be recognised as the National and Official languages of the Union; to be treated on a footing of equality and to possess and enjoy equal freedom, rights and privileges in all the various offices, functions and services of whatsoever kind or nature administered by or under the Union; and that every appointment under the Union shall be made with a due regard to the equality of the two languages and to the right of every citizen of the Union to avail himself and to claim either language as the medium of communication between himself and any officer or servant of the Union; and that all the records, journals and proceedings of the Union Legislatures, as likewise all Bills and Laws of the Union, and all official notifications of general public importance or interest published in the *Gazette*, or otherwise, shall be issued and published in both the English and Dutch languages.

Steyn and Fischer agreed with Hertzog's draft, and soon after they reached Durban the three of them began to canvass some of the other delegates and to circulate the draft among them.

Most of the Afrikaner delegates were delighted with Hertzog's draft.

[49] Ibid., Annexure P (1).

But most of the English-speaking delegates who saw it were appalled by it. As they saw the problem, they would be making a great concession if they supported a resolution like Smuts's. Hertzog's seemed quite impossible, because its spirit of compulsion reminded them of everything they disliked in the Orange River Colony Education Act. Hull, the Transvaal Nationalist, described it in private as 'a notarial deed drawn up by a pettifogging attorney'.[50] Wherever delegates met one another outside the chamber during the first week of the convention, the language question was one of the main themes of conversation. It was discussed at caucus meetings of each colonial delegation, it was discussed at caucus meetings of the Boer delegates and caucus meetings of the British delegates, and it was discussed over dinner tables and bridge tables.[51]

Hertzog took no part in the debate on the form of union because he was not prepared to collaborate in the drafting of a South African Constitution before the language section had been settled to his satisfaction. Then on the afternoon of 15 October Sauer informed Jameson and Fitzpatrick that Hertzog and Steyn would 'walk out of the Convention' if their resolution was not accepted, to which Jameson and Fitzpatrick replied that they would not accept an ultimatum from anyone. An hour or so later the motion for legislative union was carried and de Villiers, not realizing how dangerous the undercurrents were, read out the next order on the agenda, which was for Hertzog to raise the language question. There was an ominous silence. Fitzpatrick, after a hurried consultation with Jameson, walked to Hertzog's chair and asked him to move the adjournment, assuring him that an immediate debate would cause trouble, but that if they could discuss it informally they would be able to reach an acceptable settlement. Then, says Fitzpatrick, Hertzog 'turned round in his chair and looked at me—hard—then he took off his spectacles and turned further round and had another look at me: then he said, "I will do it."'[52]

That evening it appears that the two of them met in private, for the first time in their lives, and that Fitzpatrick explained to Hertzog that he and his colleagues had come to Durban to obtain 'Equal Rights', by which they meant language equality as well as equal constituencies, and

[50] Brand's manuscript.

[51] Walton, pp. 97–100; Malan, pp. 24–25; Merriman's Diary, 12 Oct. 1908; C. M. van den Heever, *Generaal J. B. M. Hertzog* (Johannesburg, 1943), p. 267.

[52] The above paragraph is based on a typed document in the Fitzpatrick Papers, which is in the form of a letter, dated 12 Apr. 1911, with the name of the addressee left blank. The incidents described are not confirmed from other sources, but they are inherently probable, and there is some circumstantial support for them in Malan's diary entry for 15 Oct. (pp. 38–39): 'After the vote [on the form of Union] General Hertzog moved the adjournment until to-morrow.'

that although they stood by this principle they could not accept every word of Hertzog's draft resolution, more particularly the words which would debar from the civil service all people who could not speak Dutch. Hertzog seems to have been astonished by Fitzpatrick's readiness to meet him. 'He was puzzled,' Fitzpatrick recalled a few years later, 'taken aback, dumbfounded as a man may well be who expects and is prepared to make a desperate fight for a position and finds that he has only to occupy it. . . . He said that he wished to consult his friends; that we must not think him suspicious; but "in fact [and he laughed nervously] I am taken by surprise—I am so surprised by the manner in which this question has been approached and the fairness of those who have differed from me that I cannot quite realise things all at once".' [53]

The following day in the convention Hertzog gave notice of a motion which followed his original draft, but omitted some of the words which the British delegates objected to, namely, that 'every appointment under the Union shall be made with a due regard to the equality of the two languages and to the right of every citizen of the Union to avail himself and to claim either language as the medium of communication between himself and any officer or servant of the Union'. [54]

Over the weekend the subject continued to form the main topic of conversation among the delegates and by the morning of Monday 19 October it was ripe for debate in the convention. Among the communications read from the chair at the start of the day's business was a well-timed telegram from the Zuid Afrikaanse Taalbond, drawn up by J. H. Hofmeyr, requesting 'mutual concessions between our two great European races (the English and the Dutch), in regard to their respective languages, so that they may obtain equal rights in the Legislatures, the Courts of law, the Civil Service and the educational establishment of a Federated or Unified South Africa'. [55] Then Hertzog rose to make one of the most important speeches of his life. [56] Speaking with great earnestness he said he wanted 'a real and lasting settlement of the language

[53] The above paragraph also is based on the document in the Fitzpatrick Papers mentioned in the previous footnote. But Fitzpatrick writes as though his private discussion with Hertzog on the evening of 15 Oct. resulted in their agreeing on the final form of the language resolution, whereas in fact a final formula was not found until the evening of 19 Oct. Fitzpatrick has therefore confused the details: but the general tenor of the above paragraph is probably correct.

[54] Malan, pp. 38–39; *Minutes*, p. 18.

[55] House of Assembly, National Convention Minutes, II; *Minutes*, p. 18; J. H. Hofmeyr, in collaboration with Senator F. W. Reitz, *The Life of Jan Hendrik Hofmeyr (Onze Jan)* (Cape Town, 1913), p. 622. The next day similar petitions were read from the Afrikaansche Christelijke Vrouwen Vereeniging and the Oranje Vrouwen Vereeniging. *Minutes*, pp. 21–22.

[56] Walton, pp. 101–3; Malan, pp. 38–41. The quotations are from Walton.

question'. A simple expression of equality would not be enough; it was necessary 'to make equality effective and to make it compulsory throughout the public service of the country'. Only then could the Union become 'a union of hearts, a union in which no section of the people felt themselves to be unjustly treated'. He could not advise the people of the Orange River Colony, where 'they had already taken the necessary steps to protect the language rights of the people', to join the Union unless this was done. 'The Dutch people of South Africa would never accept a settlement which left the absolute equality of their language in doubt.' Steyn followed, speaking in English so that he could address himself directly to all the British delegates.[57] Boer and Briton, he declared, had been kept apart from one another by a series of errors and misunderstandings, culminating in the tragedy of the war. Now they had a splendid opportunity to 'drive the devil of race hatred, which is to-day the curse of social and political life, out of the country once and for all', by placing the two languages on a footing of 'absolute equality in Parliament, in the Courts, in the schools and public services—everywhere'. He demanded equality, not as a favour, but as a right, since Dutch had only lost its official status by force. He also pleaded for it as wise statesmanship, because it would put the language question 'above and outside politics'. 'Once the races are assured that whoever gains control of affairs, there will be no danger of either race as such being menaced, Parties will be formed on more sensible and useful bases than those of racial divisions.' By the time Steyn had finished the emotional atmosphere in the convention had become highly charged, for the significance of his words was enhanced by his impressive bearing in physical adversity. Malan tells us that he and other Afrikaner delegates were moved to tears and the impact upon many of the British delegates was also profound. Jameson was considerably affected and, rising to speak, he gave his blessing to a principle which he had consistently opposed in Cape politics.[58] But although he was now 'quite prepared to agree to equality', he was 'not prepared to agree to compulsion', and he hoped that Hertzog would consent to remove every trace of it from his motion. Hertzog, gratified by this response, promptly undertook to amend his motion in that direction. Greene said that they would have to be 'extremely careful of the wording of the resolution'. Merriman, explaining that he regarded the matter as 'entirely a question of sentiment', supported the motion as it stood and

[57] Walton, pp. 103–4; Malan, pp. 40–41. I have followed Steyn's own notes, which are published in Afrikaans in N. J. van der Merwe, *Marthinus Theunis Steyn: 'n Lewensbeskrywing* (Cape Town, 1921, 2 vols.), ii. 227–9.

[58] Walton, p. 105; Malan, pp. 40–41. The quotations are from Walton.

so did Fischer.[59] The debate was then adjourned until the next day. Jagger had proposed that the question should be referred to a committee, but he did not press his suggestion, and when the afternoon session was over Hertzog, Malan, Farrar, Fitzpatrick, Browne, and Coghlan met informally to try and work out a formula which all could accept. Taking the motion which Hertzog had moved that morning as a basis, they made a number of deletions, and eventually they agreed upon the following:[60]

Both the English and Dutch languages shall be official languages of the Union, and shall be treated on a footing of equality, and possess and enjoy equal freedom, rights and privileges; all records, journals and proceedings of the Union Parliament shall be kept in both languages, and all Bills, Acts and notices of general public importance or interest issued by the Union Government shall be in both languages.

The next morning it was Farrar who moved this version in the convention. Although Greene and Browne said that they regarded it as still being unnecessarily long, Hertzog, Malan, de Wet, Fischer, and Botha, as well as Farrar, gave it their cordial blessing and it was adopted unanimously 'amid loud cheers'.[61] This resolution, with a few immaterial changes, became section 138 of the draft Constitution recommended by the convention in its report of 3 February 1909, and section 137 of the South Africa Act as enacted.

The Afrikaner delegates were delighted with it. Malan, as he listened to the Leader of the Transvaal Progressive Party moving it, momentarily wondered whether they were not, perhaps, giving up too much, but he dismissed the thought from his mind, and that evening he wrote in his diary, 'Truly this is a good sign. One of the biggest obstacles in the way of unification has been removed. May God bless the work.'[62] As for Hertzog, he was overjoyed. '*Great victory*', ran his diary entry. '10.27 this morning—20 October 1908—resolution unanimously adopted whereby it is declared that both Dutch and English as the official languages of the Union shall be treated equally and enjoy equal freedom, rights and privileges, etc.'[63] Then he repeated the time and the date, and signed his name. From then onwards he and all the other Afrikaner

[59] Walton, pp. 106–7; Malan, pp. 40–41. The quotations are from Walton.
[60] Malan, pp. 42–43; *Minutes*, pp. 18, 22.
[61] Ibid., p. 22; Walton, p. 107; Malan, pp. 42–47. The quotation is from Malan.
[62] Malan, pp. 46–47.
[63] Van den Heever, p. 269: '*Groot oorwinning*; 10.27 vanmore—20 Oktober 1908— besluit algemeen aangeneem waardeur verklaar word dat beide die Hollandse en Engelse taal as die offisiële tale van die Unie behandel sal word op gelyke voet, en gelyke vryheid, regte en voorregte, ens., te geniet.'

delegates co-operated fully in the work of the convention and were determined to see it through to a successful conclusion.

The British delegates, on the other hand, believed that they had been saved from something a great deal worse by the watering down of Hertzog's original draft. What, after all, did the resolution mean when it said that the English and Dutch languages would be 'official languages' and would be 'treated on a footing of equality, and possess and enjoy equal freedom, rights and privileges'? They had obviously conceded the principle of 'equality'. But had they conceded the principle of 'compulsion'? Fitzpatrick and Walton were both firmly of the opinion that they had not and that the Afrikaner delegates had committed themselves to that view during the debates. 'The idea was equality of numbers [whatever that may mean], and no compulsion or coercion in any circumstances whatever', was Fitzpatrick's later recollection of the debates.[64] But Hertzog and Steyn, who had gone to Durban with the conviction that equality without compulsion was not enough, do not seem to have believed that they had committed themselves. Consequently, the struggle for the interpretation of the resolution in fields such as education remained to be fought out in the future between the advocates of free competition and the advocates of compulsory protection for Dutch.

6. EXECUTIVE GOVERNMENT

The convention adopted five resolutions on the subject of the Executive Government of the Union on 16 October. When Smuts, Hull, Farrar, and some of the Transvaal advisers made a draft of the executive chapter of the Constitution during the November recess, they included six more sections. The convention's drafting committee incorporated those sections in its report, which the convention dealt with on 14 January. These were the main steps in the production of the executive chapter of the draft Constitution.[65]

[64] 'The Language Question.' Similarly Walton, p. 108.

[65] For the convention's proceedings of 16 Oct. concerning the Executive Government, see the *Minutes*, pp. 14–17, Malan, pp. 38–39, and Walton, pp. 113–15. The drafting work done by Smuts, Hull, and Farrar and their advisers is described in Brand's manuscript and Annexures T and BB thereto. There are comments on the work done by the convention's drafting committee in January 1909 in 'Remarks on Draft Constitution', Natal Archives, Prime Minister, cx (written by Greene, the Natal member of the committee). The report of the drafting committee, as presented to the convention on 12 Jan. 1909, is in the *Minutes*, Appendix E. For the convention's proceedings dealing with the executive sections of that report see the *Minutes*, pp. 159–60, and Malan, pp. 166–7. For the draft Constitution recommended by the convention in its report of 3 Feb. 1909, see the *Minutes*, Appendix F. For the South Africa Act as enacted, see the *Minutes*,

It was common ground among the delegates that the South African Executive should be based on 'the principles of the British Constitution' —that is to say, that the Government should be exercised by the British sovereign or his representative, on the advice of ministers responsible to an elected legislative body. Nobody seems to have suggested that the Constitution should include any of the distinctive features of the executives of the United States of America, or of the Boer republics (where the President was directly elected and the other members of the Executive Council included permanent officials as well as persons chosen by the Volksraad), although at one time Merriman had been critical of the cabinet system[66] and several of the Afrikaner delegates from the northern colonies would no doubt have liked to have modified it if they had thought it was practicable to do so.

The motions of 16 October were moved by Smuts. The first was taken over from Merriman's draft[67] and stated that the Executive Government of the Union would be vested in the British sovereign and exercised by him personally or by a Governor-General as his representative 'according to the well-understood principles of the British Constitution'. This was carried, with the omission of the word 'well-understood', but on 14 January the convention decided to accept the advice of its drafting committee and delete the reference to the British Constitution, which was regarded as being too vague. The resolution, thus amended, became section 7 of the draft Constitution recommended by the convention. Its only novel feature was that, unlike the corresponding sections of the Canadian and Australian constitutions, it authorized the British sovereign to administer the government of the Union in person.[68]

Smuts's second motion of 16 October provided for the appointment and summons by the Governor-General of an Executive Council to advise him or the sovereign in the government of the Union. It was adopted by the convention without question, but on 28 January, in one of its final revisions of the Constitution, the convention deleted the words 'the sovereign', so that the Executive Council was only authorized to advise the Governor-General;[69] and in that form, which was almost identical with the wording of the corresponding section of the Australian Constitution, it became section 11 of the draft Constitution recommended

Appendix L. The convention's decision concerning the capital of the Union was not made until 2 Feb. and it is dealt with separately in s. 14 of this chapter.

[66] Merriman to W. Ayliff, 17 May 1902, Merriman Papers (draft).

[67] Brand's manuscript, Annexure P.

[68] S. 8 of the S.A. Act is virtually identical. Cf. s. 9 of the B.N.A. Act, 1867, and s. 61 of the Australian Constitution, 1900.

[69] *Minutes*, p. 224.

by the convention.[70] Smuts's third and fourth motions of 16 October were also modelled rather closely on the Australian provisions. They empowered the Governor-General to appoint ministers, not exceeding ten in number, to administer departments of state during his pleasure; such ministers were to be members of the Executive Council and, after the first general election, they were not to hold office longer than three months without becoming members of one of the Houses of Parliament. The convention accepted these motions with the addition of a sentence proposed by Walton, to enable a minister to speak, but not to vote, in the House of which he was not a member—as was permitted in the South African colonial parliaments. There was some discussion of the number of ministers. Merriman, on grounds of economy, wanted seven to be the maximum, but when he called for a division—the first to take place in the convention—his amendment was defeated by twenty-five votes to four. These two resolutions were subsequently combined in section 13 of the draft Constitution, except for the sentence empowering a minister to speak in the House of which he was not a member, which was transferred to the chapter on the Union Parliament.[71] The last of the motions moved by Smuts on 16 October was for the transfer to the Governor-General, or to the Governor-General-in-Council, or to 'the authority exercising similar powers under the Union', as the case might be, of the powers and functions previously vested in the Governor, or the Governor-in-Council, or any other authority of a colony, saving such powers as might be delegated to another authority by the Constitution, or by an Act of the Union Parliament, or by the Governor-General-in-Council. This was carried with the omission of the phrase empowering the Governor-General-in-Council to delegate powers, and with verbal amendments it became section 15 of the convention's draft Constitution.[72]

In drafting their six supplementary sections, Smuts, Hull, Farrar, and the Transvaal advisers used the Australian Constitution as a model, and when these sections, having been incorporated in the drafting committee's report, came before the convention on 14 January, four of them were approved without amendment. Section 8 of the convention's draft Constitution provided for the appointment by the King of a Governor-General, who would exercise the royal powers and functions assigned to him by the King during the King's pleasure, but 'subject to this Act';[73] section 12 stated that the provisions of the Constitution referring to the

[70] S. 12 of the S.A. Act is identical. Cf. s. 62 of the Australian Constitution.
[71] S. 14 of the S.A. Act is identical. See also s. 52 of the S.A. Act. Cf. ss. 43, 64, 65 of the Australian Constitution.
[72] S. 16 of the S.A. Act is identical. Cf. s. 70 of the Australian Constitution.
[73] S. 9 of the S.A. Act is identical. Cf. s. 2 of the Australian Constitution.

Governor-General-in-Council 'should be construed as referring to the Governor-General acting with the advice of the Executive Council';[74] section 14 stated that the appointment and removal of all public servants of the Union would be vested in the Governor-General-in-Council, saving appointments delegated to another authority by the Governor-General-in-Council, or by the Constitution, or by an Act of Parliament;[75] and section 16 vested the command-in-chief of the Naval and Military forces within the Union in the King or in the Governor-General as his representative.[76] In the drafting committee Merriman had argued that the last of these sections was unnecessary and undesirable, but he had yielded to the opinions of de Villiers and Smuts that the Imperial Government would insist upon some such provision since the forces in question were British, and it was not questioned when it came before the convention. The other two new sections proposed by the drafting committee were amended by the convention. One of them dealt with the salary of the Governor-General. This question had already been referred to the convention's finance committee, which had recommended that the salary should be £10,000 per annum, but the report was referred back to the finance committee.[77] In the drafting committee's report the figure was left blank; but on 14 January the convention inserted the figure of £10,000, and section 9 of the draft Constitution provided accordingly, and stated that the salary should not be altered during a Governor-General's term of office.[78] The other new section applied the provisions relating to the Governor-General to his deputy. The drafting committee's report included a proviso that no such officer should receive any other salary from the Union during his administration of the Government, but the convention decided to omit the proviso, and the section, as thus amended, became section 10 of the convention's draft Constitution.[79]

Meanwhile, on 7 December Stanford had moved a long resolution to vest the control and administration of Native affairs throughout the Union in the Governor-General-in-Council. Two principles were involved in this proposal. One was the unitary principle, which Stanford and several other delegates were especially anxious to apply in this connexion, because they believed that a Union Government would show

---

[74] S. 13 of the S.A. Act is identical. Cf. s. 63 of the Australian Constitution.
[75] S. 15 of the S.A. Act is identical. Cf. s. 67 of the Australian Constitution.
[76] S. 17 of the S.A. Act is identical. Cf. s. 68 of the Australian Constitution.
[77] *Minutes*, pp. 125, 142, 152 ; Malan, pp. 158-9.
[78] S. 10 of the S.A. Act is identical. Cf. s. 3 of the Australian Constitution.
[79] S. 11 of the S.A. Act commences with the words of s. 10 of the convention's draft Constitution ; but it also includes a second sentence, inserted in England, providing for the appointment of a deputy Governor-General. Cf. s. 4 of the Australian Constitution.

a greater sense of responsibility in handling Native questions than the Natal Government had shown. The other was the principle that powers hitherto reserved to be exercised by the colonial governors independently of their cabinets [80] should now be exercised by the Governor-General-in-Council—that is to say, the last vestiges of independent imperial authority were to be eliminated from the internal administration of the Union. The discussion of this resolution in the convention on 7 December was brief. Stanford did not deal directly with either of the principles, but he explained that it was desirable that the Constitution should 'make it clear to the Native Peoples that their well-being had been cared for and provision made for their protection and good government under the law', and he said that although a uniform Native policy would not be possible for some time, full responsibility should rest with the Union Government so that uniformity could gradually be attained.[81] On 10 December the convention referred this resolution and the question of the future of the protectorates to a committee consisting of de Villiers, the four prime ministers, Stanford, and Michell. The committee reported a week later and recommended that a brief section based on Stanford's resolution should be included in the Constitution. The convention agreed.[82] Consequently, section 148 of the convention's draft Constitution provided that

The control and administration of native affairs throughout the Union shall vest in the Governor-General-in-Council, who shall exercise all special powers in regard to native administration hitherto vested in the Governors of the Colonies or exercised by them as supreme chiefs.[83]

Thus the convention had little difficulty in agreeing upon the sections of its draft Constitution which dealt with the Executive Government; but the drafting of the sections on the Parliament of the Union raised several most controversial questions and took up a great deal of the convention's time.

[80] Stanford's resolution expressly mentioned the powers of the Governor of Natal as supreme chief, the powers of the Governor of the Transvaal as paramount chief, and the powers of the Governor of the Cape Colony in regard to the proclamation of laws in the Transkeian Territories and over the Glen Grey District Council and the Transkeian General and District Councils.

[81] *Minutes*, p. 117; Malan, pp. 116–17; Walton, pp. 296–8. The quotation is from Walton.

[82] *Minutes*, pp. 125, 137–8, 150, 193, 307.

[83] The corresponding section of the S.A. Act, s. 147, includes insertions made in England.

7. PARLIAMENT

A. *Form and Powers*

Two important resolutions concerning the form and powers of the South African Parliament were passed by the convention on Monday, 19 October.[84] The first involved the acceptance of the bicameral principle. It cannot be said, however, that there was much enthusiasm for it. There had been no Second Chamber in the Boer republics; those in the South African colonies had done little to justify their existence; scarcely any of the delegates were impressed by the standard arguments that a Second Chamber would be valuable as a House of revision or as a check upon hasty legislation; and the only ardent advocates of bicameralism were the Natal delegates, who hoped that the Second Chamber would protect the interests of the smaller colonies by being composed on the basis of provincial equality. Nevertheless, all the delegates seem to have gone to Durban reconciled to bicameralism, Merriman moved the motion to give effect to it, and the convention accepted it without question. The only differences of opinion that were expressed concerned the names of the two Houses. Merriman proposed the names Legislative Council and House of Assembly, as in the Cape Colony, but Fischer's amendment to call the Upper House the Senate was accepted without a division, whereas Smuts's amendment to call the Lower House the House of Commons was defeated by eighteen votes to ten and Fischer's amendment to call it the House of Representatives was defeated by sixteen votes to thirteen. Thus the convention resolved that 'The legislative power of the Union shall be vested in a Parliament, to be styled the Parliament of South Africa, and to be composed of the King, a Senate, and a House of Assembly.' Four days later, when the convention began to deal with the composition of the Senate, the President allowed a general discussion of the bicameral principle, and it was then that the lack of enthusiasm became apparent;[85] and in January, finding it difficult to draft the Senate sections of the Constitution, de Villiers, Merriman, and Hertzog all urged the drafting committee to eliminate the Senate, but Greene insisted that its retention was vital to Natal and so the Senate remained.[86] On the other hand, the drafting committee proposed that the name of the Lower House should be changed to the Legislative Assembly, as in the three northern colonies, but the convention reaffirmed its earlier decision by seventeen votes to thirteen.[87] Thus the first of the

---

[84] *Minutes*, pp. 18–21; Walton, pp. 115–16; Malan, pp. 40–41.
[85] Malan, pp. 58–61; Walton, pp. 161–2.
[86] Greene's 'Remarks on Draft Constitution'.   [87] *Minutes*, p. 160.

resolutions of 19 October, with no more than verbal changes, became section 18 of the Constitution recommended by the convention.[88]

The second was also the outcome of a motion moved by Merriman. Smuts had intended that the convention should adopt a brief resolution giving full legislative powers to the Union Parliament, but Merriman's motion went on to say that Parliament would not be competent 'to alter, repeal, or amend . . . any laws dealing with the franchise or qualifications of electors, existing at the date of such Union in any Colony forming part thereof . . . except in the manner prescribed for altering the Constitution of the Union'. Before the debate could turn into a general one on the questions of the franchise and constitutional amendment, however, Lindsay, probably acting at Smuts's behest, came in with an amendment to reduce the motion to the crisp, strong statement that 'The Parliament of South Africa shall have full power to make laws for the peace, order and good government of South Africa', and this was accepted by the convention without a division and with hardly any discussion. Hyslop realized that the convention was strongly reaffirming the unitary principle in granting Parliament such sweeping powers, but his motion for the addition of words excepting 'laws dealing with local matters, and such others as may under the Constitution be specially reserved to be dealt with by each Province separately' was defeated by twenty-seven votes to three, with only Morcom and Smythe supporting him. Subsequently, the convention accepted the drafting committee's recommendation that the resolution should read, 'Parliament shall have full power to make laws for the peace, order, and good government of South Africa'. In that form it became section 59 of the convention's draft Constitution.[89]

B. *The Senate*

The composition of the Senate proved to be a particularly difficult problem for the convention to deal with and it was not finally settled until the January session. There was general agreement on only one basic point, and that was that most of the senators should be elected in such a way that the political parties would be represented in the Senate approximately in proportion to their strengths among the electorate. When the convention started even Smuts, Merriman, and de Villiers, who saw eye to eye with one another on so many constitutional ques-

[88] S. 19 of the S.A. Act is identical.

[89] S. 59 of the S.A. Act is identical, except that 'the Union' was substituted for 'South Africa'. See below, p. 409. Contrast s. 91 of the B.N.A. Act and ss. 51, 52 of the Australian Constitution.

tions, disagreed on three matters relating to the composition of the Senate:[90] Smuts and Merriman favoured an unequal division of the seats between the provinces, so that the two larger ones would have more seats than the two smaller ones,[91] while de Villiers considered that each province should have the same number of seats; Smuts and de Villiers thought that the senators should be elected directly by the same voters who elected the members of the Lower House, while Merriman considered that they should be elected indirectly by the provincial councils; and whereas Smuts thought that all the senators should be elected in that fashion, Merriman provided for eight nominated senators in a House of forty and de Villiers provided for twelve nominated senators in a House of sixty. On this last point Merriman and de Villiers were not aiming at increasing the parliamentary strength of the Government of the day, but rather at improving the quality of the Senate by introducing men with special experience and special talents, so that half of Merriman's nominated senators were to be the heads of the provincial executives, *ex officio*, and the other half were to be former cabinet ministers and republican presidents, while all of de Villiers's were to be retired judges and former presiding officers of South African legislative bodies.

After the convention passed the resolutions for a unitary Constitution on 15 October, Smuts decided to modify his scheme so as to placate the Natal delegates and to incorporate some of the ideas of Merriman and de Villiers; and he tabled a number of motions according to which, for ten years after the establishment of the Union and thereafter until Parliament decided otherwise, there would be nine senators for each province —three elected by the Provincial Council, three elected by the members of the House of Assembly for the province, and three nominated by the Governor-General-in-Council. When the first of these motions was moved in the convention on 23 October the President allowed a general discussion, as has already been noted, on the desirability of creating a Second Chamber. In the course of the discussion it was suggested that a Second Chamber should serve two special purposes in South Africa. The Natal delegates explained that they regarded it as the House which should protect the interests of the smaller provinces, by being composed on the basis of provincial equality, and the President said that it should

[90] As indicated by the proposals which Smuts put before the Transvaal delegates before they left Pretoria, and by the resolutions which de Villiers and Merriman drafted soon after they reached Durban. Brand's manuscript, Annexures H and P.

[91] Smuts favoured fourteen seats for the Cape Province, twelve for the Transvaal, eight for the Orange River Colony, and six for Natal; and Merriman favoured fifteen for the Cape Province, nine for the Transvaal, six for the Orange River Colony, and six for Natal, as well as eight nominated senators.

be used as a means for the expression of the views of the non-Europeans.[92] These suggestions made some impression on the convention and influenced it in its subsequent decisions.

After long debates the convention passed two principal resolutions on the composition of the Senate on 26 and 27 October.[93] The first dealt with the size of the Senate, the number of the nominated senators, and the grounds for their nomination. There was general agreement that there should be about a third as many senators as members of the House of Assembly and the proposals for the number of senators ranged from thirty-five to forty-five. Ten of the twelve motions which were moved on the subject provided for some nominated senators, but it was generally felt that they should not be numerous enough to give the Government of the day a large say in the composition of the Senate. Eventually, Farrar's motion for twelve nominated senators in a House of forty was rejected by eighteen votes to twelve, as being too high a proportion, and Malan's motion for eight nominated senators in a House of forty was adopted by the convention without a division. As for the grounds for nomination, de Villiers proposed that half of them should be selected mainly for 'their thorough acquaintance, by reason of their past or present official position, or otherwise, with the reasonable wishes and wants of the coloured races in South Africa'. Malan sought to have the phrase altered in a liberal direction by making it read, more simply, that they should be selected mainly for 'their thorough acquaintance, by reason of their past or present official position, or otherwise, with the coloured races in South Africa', but his amendment was rejected without a division, while a slight alteration, pointing if anything in the opposite direction, was moved by Fischer and carried. De Villiers also proposed that the other half of the nominated senators should be drawn from retired judges and former cabinet ministers and chairmen of South African legislative bodies, but Sauer's amendment for the deletion of these conditions was carried by the narrow margin of sixteen votes to fourteen, so that the Governor-General-in-Council would be unrestricted in its selection of four of the eight nominated senators. The resolution incorporating these decisions was eventually carried without a division on 26 October. It stated that 'For ten years after the establishment of the Union, and thereafter until Parliament otherwise provides', the Senate was to consist of forty members, of whom eight were to be nominated by the Governor-General-in-Council, and that in nominating four of them the Governor-General-in-Council was to 'be guided mainly by their thorough acquaintance, by

92 Malan, pp. 58–61 ; Walton, pp. 161–2.
93 *Minutes*, pp. 27–38, 41 ; Malan, pp. 58–63 ; Walton, pp. 158–65.

reason of their official experience, or otherwise, with the reasonable wishes and wants of the coloured races in South Africa'. The next day the convention amplified this resolution by deciding that the first eight senators to be nominated would hold office for ten years.

The second main resolution was based on a motion moved by Smuts to the effect that the thirty-two elected senators should be divided equally between the four provinces and that in each province four should be elected by proportional representation by the members of the House of Assembly for the province, and the other four should be elected by proportional representation by the members of the Provincial Council (except in the case of the first Union Senate, when the second group should be elected by both Houses of the Colonial Parliament sitting together). By the time this motion was discussed all the delegates were agreeable that the elected senators should be equally divided between the provinces at the outset; but whereas the Natal delegates hoped that provincial equality would be assured for all time, some of the others, notably the Cape Unionists, hoped that in due course the elected senators would be allotted in proportion to the number of white people or voters in each province, and Smartt moved an amendment to that effect. As regards the mode of election, many proposals were made, ranging from that of Fitzpatrick, who wanted them all to be directly elected by proportional representation, with each province forming a single constituency, to those of Jagger and Fischer, who wanted them all to be indirectly elected by proportional representation by the provincial councils (and by the colonial parliaments in the case of the first Senate). The argument of Merriman and others against direct election was that it might encourage the Senate to claim equal authority with the House of Assembly, contrary to established British practice; and the argument against indirect election by the provincial councils was that it might lead to corruption and to the introduction of party politics into those bodies, which the convention hoped to prevent. After some discussion on 26 October these questions were referred to a committee consisting of the President as chairman and two delegates from each colony—Merriman and Jameson, Moor and Hyslop, Botha and Fitzpatrick, and Fischer and Browne. The next morning the President submitted a motion which had been drafted by the committee. It proposed that there should be eight elected senators for each province; that for the first Senate each Colonial Parliament, with both Houses sitting together, should elect 'not fewer than eight and not more than sixteen candidates' by proportional representation and the Governor-General-in-Council should choose the successful eight from among these candidates; that these senators should hold office for six years; and that Parliament should decide what system should be adopted thereafter and how vacancies should be filled in the meantime. Hyslop moved an amendment to ensure that the election of senators should not be taken out of the hands of the provinces after the first six years, and it was carried by seventeen votes to thirteen, whereupon Smuts proposed that the system introduced after the first six years should only last for another four years, and this was carried by twenty-three votes to seven, with Fischer, Hertzog, and the Natal delegates forming the minority. The committee's motion, as amended, was carried without a division. Hyslop then tried to have a sentence added declaring that Parliament should never depart from the principle of equal provincial representation in the Senate, but his motion was defeated, the twenty-five delegates from the other colonies voting solidly against Natal.

When Smuts, Hull, Farrar, and their principal advisers reviewed these resolutions during the November recess, they realized that they were seriously defective in making provision neither for the reconstitution of the Senate in the event of a dissolution during the first ten years nor for the survival of the Senate at the end of ten years, unless Parliament passed legislation on the subject within that period. In preparing their draft sections on the subject they remedied these deficiencies by making the Senate indissoluble for the first ten years and providing for its continuation thereafter on the original basis, but with the electoral colleges of the provinces consisting of their retiring senators and their members of the House of Assembly, until Parliament made some other provision.[94] In January the convention's drafting committee devoted a great deal of attention to these sections. It decided to recommend, firstly, a section which dealt with the composition of the Senate for the first ten years and which differed from the October resolutions in giving the colonial parliaments the final say in choosing the original elected senators (instead of authorizing the Governor-General-in-Council to make a choice if the parliaments elected more than eight candidates), and making the Senate indissoluble for ten years and providing for the replacement of senators who vacated their seats during that period; and, secondly, a section under which the Senate would continue along the same lines at the end of ten years, with the provincial councils as the electoral colleges, unless Parliament had provided otherwise. Smuts objected to the second of these sections in the committee, contending that provincial equality should not be perpetuated and that the senators should not be elected by

[94] Brand's manuscript and Annexures T and BB thereto.

the provincial councils, but Greene reacted strongly and was supported by Hertzog and de Villiers.[95] These two sections of the drafting committee's report were dealt with by the convention on 25 and 26 January, when there was a long discussion and several amendments were moved.[96] The first section was eventually carried with only minor changes; and the second with one substantial change. Among the amendments which were rejected was one moved by Fitzpatrick for half of the nominated senators to be defined simply as 'persons who are thoroughly acquainted with the conditions and requirements of the coloured races in South Africa'. Most attention was given to the composition of the electoral colleges. The Natal delegates pleaded for the adoption of the committee's recommendation that all elections of senators should be in the hands of the provincial councils alone; but Smuts, Malan, and others contended that to give the provincial councils a say in the election of senators would be to vitiate the hope that they would be free from party politics. Eventually the convention left the power of filling vacancies during the first ten years with the provincial councils alone, but adopted an amendment moved by Smuts for subsequent elections to be conducted by electoral colleges consisting of the members of the House of Assembly for the province as well as the provincial councillors. Smuts was not content with these decisions and at his request both sections were referred back to the drafting committee. When it reported three days later, however, the drafting committee had rephrased parts of both sections but had made no substantial changes, and the convention adopted its report with minor amendments.[97]

Thus at last the convention had settled the composition of the Senate. Section 23 of its draft Constitution provided that for the first ten years the Senate would consist of eight senators nominated by the Governor-General-in-Council and eight senators elected for each of the original provinces; that all of them would hold their seats for ten years; that half of the nominated senators would be 'selected on the ground mainly of their thorough acquaintance, by reason of their official experience or otherwise, with the reasonable wants and wishes of the coloured races in South Africa'; that the elected senators would be elected at specially convened sittings of the colonial parliaments, with both Houses sitting together; that any vacancy among the nominated senators would be filled by the Governor-General-in-Council, the new senator holding his seat for ten years; and that any vacancy among the elected senators

---

[95] *Minutes*, pp. 284–5 ; 'Remarks on Draft Constitution'.
[96] *Minutes*, pp. 161, 212–17 ; Malan, pp. 194–7.
[97] *Minutes*, pp. 230–2.

would be filled by the Provincial Council, the new senator holding his seat only for the completion of the original ten year period.[98] Section 24 of the convention's draft Constitution stated that Parliament might provide for the constitution of the Senate after the first ten years; and that 'unless and until such provision shall have been made' eight nominated senators would continue to be appointed by the Governor-General-in-Council as previously for ten year terms, eight senators would be elected for each province by its provincial councillors and members of the House of Assembly to hold their seats for ten years unless the Senate was dissolved earlier, and any vacancy among the elected senators would be filled by the same electoral college, the new senator holding his seat only as long as his predecessor would have done.[99] Furthermore, both these sections were governed by section 136 of the convention's draft Constitution, which stated, *inter alia*, that the elections of senators would be 'according to the principle of proportional representation, each voter having one transferable vote', and that for the first elections the Governor-in-Council of each of the colonies, and for later elections the Governor-General-in-Council, was to frame and promulgate the necessary regulations.[1]

In concluding our survey of these proceedings certain statements may be made about the attitude of the convention towards the Senate. One is that the differences of opinion as to whether each province should continue to have equal representation in the Senate after the first ten years were never reconciled: the Natal delegates hoped that equality would be maintained indefinitely, but others like Walton hoped that in due course the elected senators would be allotted to the provinces in proportion to the numbers of their voters or their white inhabitants. On another question, however, there was never any serious difference of opinion: in all the debates on the subject there was scarcely a single suggestion that less than about four-fifths of the senators should be elected, and that they should be elected in such a way that they would fairly represent the relative strengths of the political parties in the provinces.[2] Finally, the convention seems to have believed that half of the nominated senators would be persons who were genuinely sympathetic with the non-

[98] S. 24 of the S.A. Act is identical, except that the words 'in respect of the original provinces' were added to the first sentence.

[99] S. 25 of the S.A. Act is identical.

[1] S. 134 of the S.A. Act is the same in this respect.

[2] On 26 Jan. Smuts seems to have thrown out the suggestion that they might have to fall back on a wholly nominated Senate, but Merriman and de Villiers promptly objected and so did Malan, who 'thought too that the nominee system would be unacceptable as it was foreign to the spirit of the population of South Africa'. Malan, pp. 194–7.

European peoples of South Africa and that they would be chosen primarily for that reason, rather than for their party loyalties.[3]

The convention passed its basic resolution on the qualifications of senators on 27 October. In contrast to the democratic provision in the Australian Constitution, it included a high minimum age and a fixed property qualification.[4] Smuts proposed that a senator should be at least thirty years of age, should possess the qualifications for the franchise, should have resided in the Union for five years, should be a British subject, and should be the owner of immovable property in the Union to the value of £500 over and above his debts and liabilities. The first three of these qualifications were adopted without question. The fourth was not questioned either; but a motion to limit membership of both Houses of Parliament to persons 'of European descent' had already been moved by Greene and referred to the franchise committee,[5] which had not yet reported, and Greene now proposed that the phrase should be added to the fourth qualification, so that a senator would have to be 'a British subject of European descent', and the convention accepted it without a division and, it appears, without any particular comment, although the non-Europeans in the Cape Colony had always been entitled to become members of both Houses of Parliament on the same conditions as white men. After some discussion, the convention decided to fix the property qualification at £1,000, 'over and above any conventional or special mortgages', but to exempt the nominated senators from it. Subsequently, the convention made only one substantial change in the qualifications and that was to the property qualification, which was altered to £500 'over and above any special mortgages'.[6] The resolutions thus amended became section 25 of the convention's draft Constitution.[7]

The last five sections of the Senate sub-chapter of the convention's draft Constitution were easily settled. Two were derived from resolutions which the convention adopted on 27 October. One of these resolutions was to the effect that the Senate should elect a President from among its members and that he should hold office until the end of his senatorial term, subject to removal by a vote of the Senate; but in

[3] An interesting essay in the history of the Union of South Africa could be written around the application of the phrase, 'selected on the ground mainly of their thorough acquaintance . . . with the reasonable wants and wishes of the coloured races in South Africa'.   [4] *Minutes*, pp. 38–40; Walton, pp. 162–4.

[5] *Minutes*, pp. 24, 26–27, 38–39. On this point see also pp. 218–21, 225 below.

[6] Ibid., pp. 161, 218, 233, 285.

[7] S. 26 of the S.A. Act is identical, except that an explanatory final sentence was added in England. See below, p. 410. Cf. s. 23 of the B.N.A. Act and ss. 16, 34 of the Australian Constitution.

January the convention accepted its drafting committee's recommendation that the clearer and fuller wording of the corresponding section of the Australian Constitution should be adopted, and it became section 26 of the convention's draft Constitution.[8] The other resolution of 27 October was taken over from the Transvaal Constitution and provided that questions in the Senate should be decided by a bare majority and that the President should have a casting vote, but no deliberative vote, and this became section 30 of the convention's draft Constitution.[9] The remaining three sections were derived from proposals passed on by Smuts, Farrar, Hull, and their advisers to the drafting committee and thence to the convention in January.[10] Section 27, providing for the appointment of an Acting President in the absence of the President, was taken over from the Australian Constitution;[11] section 28, providing for the resignation of senators, was slightly amended by the convention;[12] and section 29 fixed the Senate quorum at twelve.[13]

C. *The House of Assembly*

(i) *The Franchise*

The thorny problem of the parliamentary franchise was first raised in the convention on 19 October. On 3 and 4 November the convention passed its basic resolutions on the subject and these resolutions were amplified during the drafting stage in January.

It will be recalled that some time before the convention started Merriman and Smuts had somewhat reluctantly reached the conclusion that if Union was to be achieved at all the existing franchise laws would have to remain in force in the corresponding provinces of the Union at the outset, and that Merriman had gone on to warn Smuts that he would insist on the inclusion in the Constitution of 'material safeguards' for the future preservation of the established political rights of the non-Europeans of the Cape Colony.[14] Merriman intended that the safeguards should be strong and effective, but Smuts intended to resist the inclusion of any safeguards for such a purpose.[15] Several of the other delegates, on the

[8] *Minutes*, pp. 40, 285. S. 27 of the S.A. Act is identical, except for a minor addition made in Bloemfontein. Cf. s. 17 of the Australian Constitution.

[9] Ibid., p. 41. S. 31 of the S.A. Act is identical. Cf. s. 29 of the Transvaal Constitution, 1906.

[10] Brand's manuscript and Annexures T and BB thereto.

[11] S. 28 of the S.A. Act is identical. Cf. s. 18 of the Australian Constitution.

[12] *Minutes*, pp. 161, 217–18, 233. S. 29 of the S.A. Act is identical.

[13] S. 30 of the S.A. Act is identical.   [14] See above, p. 123.

[15] There may seem to be some doubt as to whether Merriman was constant in his hope for stiff and effective safeguards, since one of the motions which he drafted soon after

other hand, went to Durban believing that it was vital that the franchise qualifications should be the same in all the provinces of the Union from the start, but they differed among themselves as to what those qualifications should be. There were Cape Colony delegates who believed that they should be the same for men of all races; there was Fitzpatrick who believed in qualifications which differentiated between Europeans and non-Europeans but which made it possible for non-Europeans to acquire the franchise if they could pass a searching 'civilization test';[16] and there were northern delegates who hoped to create an absolute political colour-bar. In these circumstances the problem was bound to evoke a wide variety of suggestions in the convention and it would be some time before the advocates of the colour-bar and the opponents of the colour-bar, and the advocates of uniformity and the opponents of uniformity, would be able to agree upon a compromise.

On 20 October, after the convention had passed the language resolution which gave him such satisfaction, Malan noted in his diary: 'The European race problem had been proved soluble after a war—what about the coloured—Native—race issue? A great difference was noticeable: the Natives were not directly represented at the Conference.'[17] He was, of course, correct in observing that the absence of non-European representatives from the convention was bound to have profound effects upon its decisions. Nevertheless, anyone who was interested in the subject was able to bring his views to the notice of the convention by way of

his arrival in Durban (Brand's manuscript, Annexure P) and the motion which he moved in the convention on 19 Oct. (*Minutes*, p. 20) stated that the existing franchise laws would be amendable 'in the manner prescribed for altering the Constitution of the Union.' It is probable, however, that Merriman, who was not a precise draftsman, intended that this motion should be coupled with an amending section prescribing a specially stiff process for the alteration of the colonial franchise laws. This interpretation is borne out by circumstantial evidence : as early as Feb. 1908, he had suggested to Smuts that the colonial franchise laws should only be amendable with the consent of two-thirds of the voters of the province concerned (above, p. 121) ; on 19 Oct., the very day on which he moved the ambiguous motion mentioned above, he gave notice of a motion under which the colonial franchise laws should only be amendable with the consent of three-quarters of the members of both Houses of Parliament, in joint sitting (Malan, pp. 40–43, Walton, pp. 118–19) ; and on 20 Oct. and thereafter he steadily and unambiguously strove in the convention for stiff safeguards.

As for Smuts, his written pre-convention plans were vague on the point. In the plans he submitted to the Transvaal delegates before they left Pretoria he suggested that certain (but unspecified) sections of the Constitution should require a stiffer (but unspecified) amending process than the rest, which should be amendable by absolute majorities in both Houses of Parliament ; and the motions which his staff drafted for him in Durban included a similar provision (Brand's manuscript, Annexures H and N). His conduct in the convention was all in the direction of opposing any safeguards for the Cape non-European franchise.

[16] Brand's manuscript, Annexure M.   [17] Malan, pp. 46–47.

letter and petition, and some did so. J. M. Orpen, a man of Irish birth who had spent over half a century in South Africa and was living in retirement in Durban, sent the President a long letter on the subject and copies of it were distributed to all the delegates.[18] 'There never has been,' he wrote, 'there is not and cannot be any section of any community which, if alone represented in the Government of any country, would not, consciously or unconsciously, prefer its own interests to those of the unrepresented section and do it injustice.' He contended that the British Parliament would not and should not enact any Bill for the unification of South Africa, unless it included 'some really fair provision . . . for Native representation'. There were also non-Europeans who petitioned the convention on their own behalf. The Coloured people (as distinct from the Bantu-speaking Africans) had a well-established body, with branches in three of the self-governing colonies, known as the African Political Organization, and during October its Cape Town leaders drew up a document in which they expressed confidence that 'the rights of the Coloured men in the Cape Colony will most assuredly be confirmed to them' by the convention and requested that they should be extended throughout the country. They asked, not for universal suffrage, but for a vote for everyone in South Africa who was 'fully civilized'. Three copies of this document, with minor variations, were dispatched to the convention as petitions from the executive committees of the African Political Organization in the Cape Colony, the Transvaal, and the Orange River Colony. They were presented to the convention by the prime ministers and the convention referred them to its franchise committee.[19] The Bantu-speaking Africans had no such established organization to act on their behalf. The suggestion had been mooted in the Bantu press that an African Convention should be held at the same time as the National Convention, to demand the extension of the Cape franchise laws to the northern colonies; but no such meeting took place, mainly because most of the literate Africans in the Cape Colony considered that it would be impolitic for them to take any steps to bring their opinions to the notice of the convention. Their line of thought is illustrated by the following extract from *Imvo Zabantsundu Bomzantsi Afrika*, a leading Bantu newspaper published in King William's Town:[20]

It is reasonable for the Africans of the Northern Colonies to be restless;

[18] House of Assembly, National Convention Minutes, II.

[19] Ibid. The A.P.O. petitions were presented to the convention on 28 and 29 Oct. and 2 Nov. *Minutes*, pp. 42, 43–44, 48–49.

[20] Quoted in E. Mamkile, 'African public opinion and the unification of South Africa' (unpublished essay). The passage cited is from the *Imvo* issue of 6 Oct. 1908, and has been translated from the Xhosa.

they have always been excluded from the enjoyment of civil rights because of the antagonism of the Europeans in those Colonies, there being also no doubt that the delegates of those Colonies will enter the Convention still imbued with their old and bad spirit of antipathy towards Africans. There would be nothing wrong in the holding of meetings by the Africans of the Northern Colonies. The Cape Africans are in a different position altogether. Their civil rights are not doubted by anyone. There is no fear that the Cape delegates will speak for anything other than the retention of civil rights by the Cape Africans, of whom they have wide experience. Any agitation by Cape Africans at this stage would have the effect of discouraging our delegates and also make them appear as though they are ignorant of their obligation; even their defence of our rights would appear to have been prompted only by their fear of our agitation. Our enemies, the representatives of the Northern Colonies, would then throw it in the teeth of our delegates that they were influenced by fear of African agitation. That would also entrench the opposition of the enemy towards the granting of rights to Africans in their Colonies by giving them reason to believe that the grant of civil rights to Africans in those Colonies might put them in the position of also having to fear African agitation. For this and other reasons which, given space, we could advance, we think that an African agitation while the National Convention is in session at Durban on 12th October would be a wrong step and one that might impair African rights.

Consequently no action was taken by the Africans in the Cape Colony. On the other hand, during October an African organization on the Witwatersrand, the Transvaal National Natives Union, drew up a petition asking that Africans throughout the Union should be able to qualify for the franchise on the same conditions as white men and that those who were unable to qualify should have their interests protected by some form of separate representation. The petition, with 1,994 signatures, did not, however, reach the convention until 23 November, over a fortnight after it had passed its basic resolutions on the subject.[21]

When the convention was considering the motion on the powers of Parliament on 19 October, Stanford proposed that a sentence should be added, stating that 'All subjects of His Majesty resident in South Africa shall be entitled to franchise rights, irrespective of race or colour, upon such qualifications as may be determined by this Convention.' Before the end of the sitting, however, Stanford withdrew his amendment and gave notice that he would move it as a substantive motion the following day, and Merriman said that he would propose that the colonial franchise

[21] The T.N.N.U. petition was read to the convention by the President on 23 Nov. A further 1,770 signatures were received by the convention on 11 Jan. 1909. House of Assembly, National Convention Minutes, II; *Minutes*, pp. 73, 151.

laws should 'remain in force until repealed or altered by the Parliament of South Africa' and that any such repeal or alteration should require 'a majority of not less than three-fourths of the members of both Houses sitting and voting together'.[22]

These two motions came before the convention the next morning after it had passed the language resolution.[23] Speaking first, Merriman explained that although he disapproved of a political colour-bar he had come to believe that the only basis on which they could reach agreement was by leaving the existing franchise laws as they were and creating safeguards against their alteration. Stanford then spoke simply and sincerely in defence of a colour-blind system, as a 'safety-valve' which provided 'a free outlet for the expression of opinion' and as a means of promoting the cultural advancement of the Natives. Next Fitzpatrick suggested that the convention should devise a test of civilization, to be applied by a permanent tribunal to Native applicants for the franchise, so that the door would be open to the truly civilized and closed to those who had nothing but 'a surface education'. Moor followed and argued that there should be an absolute colour-bar throughout the Union. 'The history of the world proved', he asserted, 'that the black man was incapable of civilisation. . . . He would protect the native interests, he would secure them justice and freedom, but he was absolutely opposed to placing them in a position to legislate for white men.' Thus the first four speakers recommended four radically different solutions. By the end of the day's sitting four more delegates had expressed their views. Sauer, speaking as 'one of those who believed that a great principle never yet shown to have failed in the history of the world would be a safe principle in South Africa to adopt at this great moment of her life', supported Stanford. 'The great principle of justice was at stake in this discussion', he said, 'and there must be a just native policy or the white man would go under in South Africa. . . . It was impossible to govern fairly unless the people themselves were represented in the government.' The other three speakers agreed with Merriman that it was impossible for the convention to agree upon a uniform system and that they should therefore leave the existing franchise laws as they were; but they differed on the question of safeguards. Smuts recommended that the Union Parliament should be able to change the franchise laws by simple majorities in both Houses; Jagger thought that they should only be alterable 'with the consent of a majority

[22] *Minutes*, pp. 20–21; Malan, pp. 40–43; Walton, pp. 118–19.

[23] For the franchise debates from 20 to 22 Oct. see the *Minutes*, pp. 23–27; Walton, pp. 119–44; Malan, pp. 46–59. Except where otherwise indicated, the quotations from speeches are from Walton.

in both Houses of Parliament of the representatives' of the province in question and he moved an amendment to that effect; and Fischer, who explained that he personally believed in keeping the races in separate kraals as a matter of 'self-preservation', does not appear to have indicated what safeguards, if any, he wished to include. By the end of the sitting of 20 October, therefore, it appeared likely that a compromise would develop on the basis of the maintenance of the *status quo*, but there was still no agreement in sight as to whether there should be any safeguards and, if so, what they should be.[24]

On the morning of 21 October Sir Henry de Villiers made an important statement from the chair about the attitude of His Majesty's Government. He said that when he was in England in June he had had discussions with the Colonial Secretary, Lord Crewe, and other members of the British Cabinet, who had told him that the convention would have a free hand except in regard to the non-European franchise and the protectorates. De Villiers went on to explain that at his request Lord Selborne had sent him a letter setting out the views of the British Government and he proceeded to read the letter to the convention.[25] In it Selborne suggested that there should be one franchise system throughout South Africa. It was justifiable, he wrote, to distinguish between European and non-European applicants for the franchise, because Europeans could be presumed to be civilized and the South African non-Europeans could not. Therefore, in addition to any general qualifications which a South African would have to possess before he could be enrolled as a voter, a non-European applicant should have to possess a certificate of civilization. The issue of these certificates should be at the discretion of a judge, or some other person nominated by the Supreme Court, who would only grant a certificate if he was satisfied that the applicant had a fair education, that he was industrious, that he lived in a civilized home, and that he was not a polygamist. A Native applicant should be at least thirty years of age, but a Coloured applicant might be younger. Selborne went on to say that His Majesty's Government would be distressed if there was 'the slightest appearance of want of harmony between them and the South African National Convention', but that they would undoubtedly be appealed to if the Constitution left no door open to civilized Natives or Coloured men. Furthermore, His Majesty's Government construed

[24] The substantive motion before the convention on 20 Oct. was Stanford's. Merriman's and Jagger's were amendments. Nevertheless, Walton and Malan both state that Merriman was the first to speak. Walton and Malan differ, however, as to the sequence of the other speeches and neither of them clearly distinguishes between the speeches of 20 and 21 Oct. The position stated in the text appears to be the most probable.

[25] House of Assembly, National Convention Minutes, V.

article 8 of the Treaty of Vereeniging as implying that some provision for a non-European franchise would be made in the Transvaal and the Orange River Colony soon after they received responsible government and they considered that the time was now appropriate to make such a provision. As to Merriman's motion of 20 October, which de Villiers had asked him to comment on, Selborne pointed out that it would cut both ways—against the extension of the franchise to the non-Europeans in the northern colonies as well as against the curtailment of the existing rights of the non-Europeans in the Cape Colony. Finally, Selborne explained that His Majesty's Government's views on the nature of the conditions for the transfer of the protectorates would be affected by the convention's decision on the franchise.[26]

Other delegates then explained their points of view.[27] Four Cape delegates—Malan, Smartt, Jagger, and Walton—spoke in favour of a uniform and colour-blind franchise throughout the Union. Malan placed great stress on the need for uniformity. Otherwise, he feared that Union politics would be vitiated by differences between the whites on the question and that the Natives would consider that they were being treated unfairly. He could not support any suggestion that the Cape Natives should be deprived of the rights they already possessed. He admitted, however, that the system had been applied too laxly in the Cape Colony and he suggested, somewhat like Selborne, that a Native should obtain a 'certificate of citizenship' before he could become a voter. Only if a committee found it quite impossible to agree upon a uniform franchise could he support a solution like Merriman's.[28] Most of the northerners remained adamant. Greene and Hyslop favoured an absolute colour-bar throughout South Africa and Greene moved an amendment to exclude non-Europeans from membership of both Houses of Parliament. Hertzog said that he 'could not shake himself free of the anxiety he felt in regard to this question and he saw great danger ahead if once the principle were adopted of giving votes to the natives. There would be constant pressure to lower the qualification standard and in the near future the native voter would swamp the European.' Farrar said that he shared Hertzog's apprehensions, but he thought that Selborne's proposal should be carefully examined and he was willing to give the Natives a limited number of separate parliamentary representatives, in accordance with the recom-

[26] The protectorates question is dealt with in section 11 of this chapter.

[27] De Villiers made his statement fairly early in the sitting of 21 Oct., but no mention of it appears in the *Minutes*, and it is not clear from the accounts by Walton and Malan which of the delegates (other than Malan) spoke before him and which spoke after him.

[28] Malan states that he spoke immediately after de Villiers and he set out his arguments at some length in his diary, pp. 48–53.

mendations of the South African Native Affairs Commission of 1903–5.

Early the next morning Botha spoke out strongly against any provision for a Native franchise in the northern provinces. 'Their first duty', he said, 'was to bring about the union of the white races in South Africa and after that it would be possible to deal with the native population. . . . He was convinced that the people of the country were not ready to adopt the principle of a civilisation test. . . . In his opinion if vested interests were safeguarded that was as far as they could go but on one point there must be no manner of doubt,—they could only have Europeans in Parliament.' That speech by Botha was decisive. Burger and de la Rey confirmed that he had spoken correctly for the Transvaal. De Wet said that 'if the Native Franchise were embodied in the Constitution not five per cent of the electors of the Orange River Colony would support Union. . . . Providence had drawn the line between black and white and we must make that clear to the Natives not instil into their minds false ideas of equality.' And Maasdorp claimed that 'The views expressed by the delegates from the Cape so far were not the views held by all the electors there and it was open to question whether they were the views of the majority. Among farmers in the Cape there was a strong feeling against the Franchise for Native and Coloured men. . . .' In these circumstances Jameson observed that they would have to abandon the search for uniformity. So did Michell. But Fitzpatrick continued to strive for qualifications which could be attained by civilized Natives and would be the same in all the provinces. He moved for the appointment of a committee with instructions to devise such a scheme, or, if that proved impossible, to recommend some other means by which the Union Government could 'ascertain the wishes and consult the interests of the Native and Coloured population'. Malan, too, tried hard to stem the tide. 'By not facing squarely the disagreement over the Natives', he said, 'they were once again heading for a struggle and tears and suffering. People spoke about the necessity to unite the white races first and then to tackle the Native franchise question but a union of this kind would not be a genuine union. The germs of discord would continue to exist.'[29] But Botha rose to his feet again and said that Malan seemed to be trying 'to force the rest of South Africa to accept the principle of the Native franchise of the Cape Colony. If this were done he might just as well go home.'[30] Nevertheless, Walton spoke in favour of safeguarding the rights of the Cape non-European voters and devising some access to the franchise for the non-Europeans in the northern colonies and Merriman, replying to the debate, said that he would support Greene's motion for the exclusion of

non-Europeans from Parliament, but made a final plea for the acceptance
of 'a broad and liberal principle' as regards the franchise. The convention then adopted, without a division, Botha's motion for the appointment of a committee, comprising two delegates nominated by each Prime
Minister and one nominated by Milton, to consider the various proposals
that had been made and to submit a draft resolution to the convention.[31]

The committee consisted of Sauer and Walton, Smythe and Greene,
Fitzpatrick and Smuts, Hertzog and Fischer, and Coghlan, and it met
during the following evenings, after the convention rose. It had before it
the various proposals that had been made in the convention. There was
Stanford's motion for a colour-blind franchise throughout the Union.
There was Merriman's proposal that the existing franchise laws should
remain in force, coupled with three different methods of entrenchment:
Merriman's, that none of them should be altered except by three-quarters
of the members of both Houses of Parliament, in a joint sitting; Jagger's,
that none of them should be altered except 'with the consent of a majority
in both Houses of Parliament of the representatives of such Colony'; and
Beck's, that 'in so far as these laws apply to Native electors in the Cape
Colony, there shall be no such alteration, except in the manner prescribed
for altering the Constitution of the Union'. There was also a proposal by
Smuts that the existing franchise laws should remain in force without any
safeguards. Finally, there was Greene's proposal that 'only persons of
European descent shall be eligible as members of either House of Parlia-
ment'.[32]

De Villiers kept in close touch with the committee and he was able to
give reassuring information about the attitude of the Imperial Government. On the evening of 21 October he had written to Selborne explaining the trend of opinion in the convention and asking four questions, to
which Selborne replied the next day.[33] To the question whether, if a
civilization test was adopted, he thought that it should be applied
throughout the Union, even if that meant removing the names of some
Native voters from the Cape rolls, Selborne replied that he did not think
it would be reasonable to remove the names of voters already on the

[31] Fitzpatrick's motion fell away when Botha's was carried. An amendment moved
by Fischer, to instruct the committee that 'save in so far as may be necessary to safeguard interests where natives have acquired the franchise, or other rights and privileges,
it is undesirable and unnecessary that the Committee should frame resolutions in regard
to the future native policy of South Africa', was negatived by the convention without a
division. Walton's and Malan's accounts are again not in agreement concerning the
sequence of the speeches on 22 Oct.

[32] *Minutes*, p. 26.

[33] De Villiers to Selborne, 21 Oct. 1908 (copy); Selborne to de Villiers, 22 Oct. 1908.
De Villiers Papers.

rolls, but that it would be reasonable to disappoint the expectations of men who were not yet registered as voters, especially if this would apply to whites as well as to non-whites. Secondly, to the question whether His Majesty's Government would agree to the application of the civilization test to non-whites and not to whites, Selborne replied that he believed they would, 'as part of a general settlement of the franchise question in South Africa which gave an adequate permanent access to the franchise to the Coloured people and Natives in all the British South African Colonies'. De Villiers's third question was whether His Majesty's Government would agree to the maintenance of the *status quo* 'until altered by the Union Parliament, either with or without the proviso that such alteration shall not be allowed in regard to the qualification of coloured persons in the Cape Colony unless carried by a majority of not less than three-fourths of the members of both Houses, sitting together'. Selborne's reply was:

This question is of a more general character and it is not so easy to give a definite reply to it. I think His Majesty's Government would feel that they could not satisfactorily answer the question until they were aware of all the main details of the general scheme of Closer Union, and how each part reflected upon another, and also until they knew how far the general scheme agreed upon represented the unanimous or practically unanimous opinion of the members of the National Convention, or whether the opinion of the delegates was divided in nearly equal proportions on any of the more important parts of the scheme. *I am confident however that in default of a general settlement of the native franchise question they would warmly sympathise with any provision securing to the Cape Colony Coloured persons and Natives that access to the franchise which they at present enjoy.*[34]

And fourthly, to the question whether His Majesty's Government would agree to a provision making non-Europeans ineligible for membership of either House of Parliament, Selborne replied:

I do not think that His Majesty's Government would object to such a provision as part of an otherwise satisfactory settlement of the Native franchise question.

Selborne also expressed the hope that if the convention was unwilling to extend the franchise to civilized Natives in the northern colonies it might at least respond to the stronger claims of the Coloured men.[35] This letter was crucial. It enabled de Villiers to inform the committee that it was probable that the British Government would co-operate in the enactment

---

[34] The italics here and in the following quotation are mine.
[35] Selborne also wrote privately to Fitzpatrick on 23 Oct. urging him to make a move on behalf of the Coloured people. Fitzpatrick Papers.

of a Constitution for South Africa, even if it maintained the absolute political colour-bar in the inland provinces and the nearly absolute political colour-bar in Natal, and even if it also excluded non-Europeans from the South African Parliament.

The committee also had before it another proposal emanating from Selborne and representing his last effort to obtain some voting rights for civilized non-Europeans in the northern provinces. According to this proposal a non-European whose father was not a registered voter would be unable to qualify before the age of 31 when, if he passed a civilization test, he would be given a vote worth one-tenth of a European's vote. His son would be able to qualify, if he passed the test, at the age of 30, when he would be given a vote worth two-tenths of a European's vote. And so on, until in the tenth generation of unbroken 'civilization' a non-European would acquire a full vote at the age of 21.[36]

The committee's report came before the convention on 2 November. Its recommendation on the main issue was extraordinarily badly drafted. On the one hand, it provided that Parliament would not be competent to 'withhold the franchise from any persons by reason of their colour or race in any province wherein franchise laws at the time the Union Constitution takes effect admit of their inclusion'; and, on the other hand, it also provided that 'Nothing herein stated shall prevent the Parliament of the Union by a general law from altering the qualifications of voters throughout the Union.'[37] Walton believed that this resolution would secure the franchise rights of the Natives and Coloured men of the Cape Colony 'for all time',[38] in which case it might also have been construed as introducing a completely colour-blind franchise in Natal! When it was shown to Duncan and Brand they immediately pointed out to Smuts that it was at least ambiguous and possibly made far more sweeping concessions to the Cape than had ever been contemplated by the Transvaal delegation. To illustrate his point Duncan wrote out an alternative draft, empowering the Union Parliament to pass any franchise law applying throughout the Union by a bare majority, save only that no such law should disqualify any person who was already actually registered as a voter. Smuts said that that was exactly what the committee had intended (which can hardly have been true) and he arranged that Hull should move it in the convention as an amendment.[39] When Hull did so on 3 November there was considerable consternation, and after a brief, confused debate the resolution was referred back to the committee.[40]

---

[36] Walton, pp. 147–8.
[37] *Minutes*, pp. 56–57.
[38] Walton, p. 152.
[39] Brand's manuscript.
[40] *Minutes*, pp. 59, 62; Walton, pp. 152–4; Malan, pp. 70–71.

The next morning the committee brought up a second and more efficient report. It recommended that the colonial franchise laws should remain in force until altered by parliament; that any law to disqualify any persons in the Cape Province 'by reason of their race or colour only' would require to be passed 'by a majority of two-thirds of the members of each House of Parliament'; and that no law should disfranchise persons actually registered as voters in any province solely on the grounds of race or colour. Malan proposed that the two-thirds majority safeguard should apply to the Natal non-Europeans as well as to those in the Cape, but the convention reacted adversely and he withdrew his amendment. Whereupon Smythe made a last stand for a nation-wide colour-bar by moving the omission of everything except the statement that parliament could pass laws determining the franchise, but when he called for a division his amendment was rejected by twenty-four votes to six, the five Natal delegates and de la Rey forming the minority. One amendment, which seriously weakened the safeguard for the Cape franchise, was moved by Botha and adopted, however, and that was to provide that the two-thirds majority should be obtained in a joint sitting of both Houses of Parliament, rather than in each House sitting separately. Then at last the resolution, as amended, was carried by the convention without a division.[41]

During the drafting stage in January the convention rearranged this resolution and amplified it by providing, *inter alia*, that the two-thirds majority required for disqualifying Cape Province voters on the grounds of race or colour should be obtained 'at the third reading', that 'A bill so passed at such joint sitting shall be taken to have been duly passed by both Houses of Parliament', and that members of His Majesty's regular forces on full pay would not be eligible for the franchise.[42] These changes were non-controversial and they were adopted by the convention without a division and with hardly any discussion.

The question of a female suffrage, on the other hand, was contentious both in itself and in its special South African implications.[43] 3,733 South African men and women had signed petitions to the convention in favour of women's suffrage; and 7,256 South African women had signed

[41] *Minutes*, pp. 64–66; Walton, 154–6; Malan, pp. 72–73.

[42] *Minutes*, pp. 162, 287. Most of the amendments were made on the recommendation of the drafting committee. It was Malan who moved the insertion of the sentence: 'A bill so passed at such joint sitting shall be taken to have been duly passed by both Houses of Parliament', and no information has survived as to his reasons for doing so.

[43] On the women's suffrage question in the convention, see the *Minutes*, pp. 13, 22, 24, 25, 98, 133–4, 142–3, 151–2, 220, 222–3; Malan, pp. 144–7, 156–9, 196–7, 200–1; Walton, pp. 304–6.

counter-petitions. On 16 December Moor had introduced a motion that there should be a provision in the Constitution to enable Parliament to extend the franchise to women of European descent by a simple majority.[44] De Wet and Merriman had roundly denounced the principle of women's suffrage, but Fitzpatrick and Botha had supported Moor and so had Smuts, who had moved an amendment that the drafting committee should be instructed to provide accordingly, whereupon Stanford had moved a further amendment opposing a motion which pointed to the creation of a political colour-bar in the Cape Province. No decision had then been made, but the convention returned to the subject after the drafting committee reported in January. Then there was a difference of opinion as to whether the relevant sections empowered Parliament, by a bare majority, to extend the franchise to white women only. De Villiers considered that they did. Sauer thought not. Malan believed that de Villiers had given the sounder interpretation of the meaning of the sections and he moved that they should be amended in such a way as to eliminate the possibility of such action. Then Greene, eager as always to be in the van of a movement to strengthen or extend the colour-bar, objected to Malan's proposal and Malan eventually withdrew it. By that time the convention was weary of the subject. No change was made and the convention's draft Constitution included the following two sections:

35. (i) Parliament may by law prescribe the qualifications which shall be necessary to entitle persons to vote at the election of members of the House of Assembly, but no such law shall disqualify any person in the Province of the Cape of Good Hope who, under the laws existing in the Colony of the Cape of Good Hope at the establishment of the Union, is or may become capable of being registered as a voter from being so registered by reason of his race or colour only, unless the Bill be passed by both Houses of Parliament sitting together, and at the third reading be agreed to by not less than two-thirds of the total number of members of both Houses. A Bill so passed at such joint sitting shall be taken to have been duly passed by both Houses of Parliament.

(ii) No person who at the passing of any such law is registered as a voter in any Province shall be removed from the register by reason only of any disqualification based on race or colour.[45]

36. Subject to the provisions of the last preceding section, the qualifica-

---

[44] Moor's motion read : 'That provision be made in the Constitution for extending the franchise to women of European descent.' In his speech he made it clear that his intention was as stated in the text.

[45] S. 35 of the S.A. Act is identical, except that the words 'in the Province of the Cape of Good Hope' were inserted after 'from being so registered' in sub-section (i) at the Bloemfontein session of the convention in May 1909.

tions of parliamentary voters, as existing in the several Colonies at the establishment of the Union, shall be the qualifications necessary to entitle persons in the corresponding Provinces to vote for the election of members of the House of Assembly: Provided that no member of His Majesty's regular forces on full pay shall be entitled to be registered as a voter.[46]

The franchise committee's report of 2 November also endorsed Greene's proposal that only persons of European descent should be eligible for membership of either House of Parliament and the convention resolved accordingly on 4 November without a division and, apparently, with scarcely any discussion. Stanford, indeed, had given notice of a motion of opposition, but he withdrew it.[47] Meanwhile, on 30 October, Smuts had introduced a motion to prescribe two qualifications for members of the House of Assembly: eligibility for the franchise and three years' residence in the Union. The convention settled the question on the last day of its Durban session. It adopted Smuts's first qualification, it increased the period of residence from three to five years, and it added a third qualification, requiring members of the House of Assembly, like senators, to be British subjects of European descent.[48] During the drafting stage in January, Stanford protested against the exclusion of non-Europeans from the House of Assembly, but section 44 of the convention's draft Constitution was virtually identical with its resolution of 5 November.[49] Two non-controversial sections of the convention's draft Constitution also emanated from the report of the franchise committee: section 37, providing for the application of the relevant colonial laws to the conduct of the elections for the Union House of Assembly,[50] and section 139, providing that the naturalization of persons of European descent in any of the colonies should count as naturalization throughout the Union.[51]

These results were a compromise. The northerners conceded the maintenance and entrenchment[52] of the established franchise rights of the non-Europeans in the Cape Colony, and the southerners conceded

[46] S. 36 of the S.A. Act is identical.

[47] *Minutes*, pp. 57, 59, 66 ; Malan, pp. 72–73.

[48] *Minutes*, pp. 49, 60, 69–70.

[49] Ibid., pp. 175, 290 ; Malan, pp. 174–5. S. 44 of the S.A. Act is identical, except that a final sentence, explaining that 'For the purpose of this section, residence in a Colony before its incorporation in the Union shall be treated as residence in the Union', was added in England.

[50] *Minutes*, pp. 57, 59, 162, 224, 287. This section, as slightly amended in Bloemfontein, became s. 37 of the S.A. Act.

[51] Ibid., pp. 57, 59, 191, 306. The words 'of European descent' were deleted at Bloemfontein (below, p. 382) and, as thus amended, it became s. 138 of the S.A. Act.

[52] On the question of entrenchment, see also section 12 of this chapter.

the maintenance of the established colour-bar in the northern colonies and the principle that only Europeans should sit in Parliament. Considering the state of public opinion among the colonial electorates, it seems reasonably certain that no very different type of decision could have been successfully defended by all the delegates in their parliaments. But whether the decision was in the best interests of South Africa is a different matter.

Lord Selborne's letters, it may be remarked, did not make the convention's decision any more liberal than it would otherwise have been. What Selborne wanted was 'a permanent adequate access to the franchise' for any 'civilized' man in South Africa, and that was not granted. What was granted—the maintenance and entrenchment of the Cape non-European franchise—was secured by the insistence of the Cape delegates rather than by Selborne. Indeed, his intervention probably acted in the opposite direction, since it embarrassed those Cape liberals, like Merriman, Sauer, and Malan, who were also anti-imperialists, and since his second letter to de Villiers went a long way towards removing any doubts as to the willingness of the British Government to co-operate in giving effect to the convention's wishes. De Villiers, on the other hand, played his cards skilfully. Looking ahead, he had wisely sought to extract an assurance that the convention's decisions would be supported by the British Government, and he had achieved a considerable measure of success.

(ii) *The Constituencies*

The convention dealt with the division of the Union into constituencies for the election of the members of the House of Assembly concurrently with the franchise. It passed its basic resolutions on the subject at the end of the Durban session and amplified and amended them during January.

The first question dealt with was the division of the seats between the provinces. If the division was to be made on some population basis, Natal, with far the highest ratio of non-Europeans to Europeans, would do best on the basis of the total population of all races, the Cape Colony and the Orange River Colony would do best on the white population basis, and the Transvaal, with the highest ratio of white men to white women and children, would do best on the white male adult basis. The position is illustrated by the following table, which is derived from the 1904 census reports:[53]

[53] A census was taken in each colony on 17 Apr. 1904. The reports are similar but not identical in form. All of them give exact numbers for the total population and the white population; but the age tables in three of them do not distinguish between majors and minors, so that the numbers of white adults can only be estimated by interpolation

Division of the seats between the provinces in a House of Assembly of 120 members

	Cape	Trans-vaal	O.R.C.	Natal
Total population	55·9	29·4	9·0	25·7
White population	62·3	32·0	15·3	10·4
White male adult population . . .	56·8	36·9	14·3	12·0
Ditto, excluding British troops . . .	58·0	36·8	13·2	12·0

The Transvaalers were not content to use the 1904 census results, because it was generally believed that since 1904 the white population of the Transvaal had increased considerably and the white population of the coastal colonies had decreased considerably; but since the colonies did not keep records of population movements across their land frontiers the convention had no means of assessing such changes.[54] More recent information was available, however, concerning the numbers of registered voters, as the voters' lists had been brought up to date in all four

(e.g. from the 20–24 age group). The absolute numbers obtained in this way and used for calculating the relative numbers given in the text are:

	Cape	Transvaal	O.R.C.	Natal	Total
Total population . .	2,409,804	1,269,951	387,315	1,108,754	5,175,824
White population . .	579,741	297,277	142,679	97,109	1,116,806
White Male adult population	174,820	113,493	43,968	36,787	369,068
Ditto, less British troops .	167,889	106,493	38,274	34,784	347,440

Results of the census of 17 Apr. 1904: Cape Colony, G. 19 (1905); Natal (Pietermaritzburg, 1905); Transvaal and Swaziland (London, 1906); Orange River Colony (Bloemfontein, n.d.).

[54] *The Statistical Register for the Colony of the Cape of Good Hope for the Year 1907* (Cape Town, 1908) contains estimates of the white populations of the four colonies in 1907, 'compiled from information courteously supplied by the respective administrations' (p. xxxii). According to these estimates (p. 182) the changes in the white populations of the four colonies since the 1904 census were: Cape Colony, an increase of 30,939; Transvaal, an increase of 27,973; Orange River Colony, an increase of 14,521; Natal, a decrease of 1,669. The Cape Colony estimate cannot be taken seriously. In 1907 the white population of the Cape Colony was certainly less than in 1904, because many white people had migrated to the Transvaal. Indeed, the next census was to show that even on 7 May 1911, when conditions had improved, the white population of the Cape Province was only 2,636 more than in 1904, and the second delimitation commission calculated that the white male adult population of the Cape Province decreased by 15,911 between 1904 and 1911 (U.G. 15 (1913), para. 6).

The compiler of T.G. 25 (1908), *Statistics of the Transvaal Colony for the Years 1902–1907*, refrained from making any estimate of the change in the Transvaal population since the 1904 census, because 'no reliable information is available as regards ordinary immigration and emigration' (p. 3, n. 1).

colonies in 1907. The following table shows the effect of adopting a 1907 voters' basis:[55]

Division of the seats between the provinces in a House of Assembly of 120 members

	Cape	Trans-vaal	O.R.C.	Natal
Total voters	57·3	40·1	13·7	8·9
White voters	52·5	43·3	14·7	9·5

A voters' basis was patently inequitable, however, because of the wide differences between the qualifications for the franchise in the four colonies. The white voters' basis was the most favourable of all to the Transvaal, with its white manhood suffrage, and the least favourable to the Cape Colony, with its economic qualifications for the franchise. The total voters' basis was less unjust to the Cape Colony, with its non-European voters, but its adoption was politically impracticable owing to the general feeling in the northern colonies against political rights for non-Europeans. In all the circumstances, indeed, there was no basis for dividing the seats between the provinces which was patently fair to all of them, so that the situation provided ample scope for special pleading and mathematical manœuvring by an astute delegate.

Before the convention met Smuts, Merriman, and de Villiers were agreed that the first House of Assembly should contain about 120 members, and that the two smaller colonies should be given specially favourable treatment in the early years. Beyond that their views differed. According to the plans which they drafted soon after they arrived in Durban, Smuts intended that the seats should be divided between the provinces on the white voters' basis, but that for the first ten years Natal and the Orange River Colony should be allowed more seats than they would be entitled to; de Villiers favoured an arbitrary division of fifty-one, thirty-three, eighteen, and eighteen; and Merriman considered that

[55] The numbers of voters registered in the Cape Colony, Natal, and the Orange River Colony in 1907 are given in *The Government of South Africa*, ii. 401, 410, 411. The number of voters registered in the Transvaal in 1906 is given in ibid., p. 413, as 105,368. The 1907 Transvaal number was published in T.G. 28 (1909), *Statistics of the Transvaal Colony for the Years 1903–1908*, p. 33, and was presumably available to the convention. The 1907 numbers are:

	Cape	Transvaal	O.R.C.	Natal	Total
Total voters . . .	152,121	106,536	36,261	23,686	318,604
White voters . . .	129,337	106,536	36,261	23,480	295,614

the initial division should be arbitrary—fifty, thirty, twenty, and twenty —and that from 1921 onwards a province should acquire an extra seat for every increase of 10,000 in its white population above the 1904 census figure.[56]

In the convention on 27 October Smuts moved a resolution that the seats should be divided between the provinces on the white voters' basis (which was the most favourable to the Transvaal), whereupon Merriman moved as an amendment the white population basis (which was the most favourable to the Cape Colony).[57] The debate which followed ranged over the whole field of the delimitation of constituencies, and most of the speakers concentrated their attention on the question of the division of the provinces. Sauer and Walton pointed out, however, that the white voters' basis would be unfair to the coastal colonies and de Villiers spoke strongly in support of Merriman's amendment, saying that 'the Cape Colony was not prepared to relinquish her numerical superiority' and that in the last resort 'the Cape was quite capable of standing alone'. On 28 October the whole problem of the composition of the House of Assembly was referred to a committee consisting of de Villiers as chairman, Merriman, Sauer, and Jameson, Moor, Greene, and Hyslop, Botha, Smuts, and Farrar, and Fischer, Hertzog, and Browne.

The following afternoon the committee reached agreement on the question of the division of the seats between the provinces. It recommended that the House of Assembly should be composed of members elected directly by the voters and that in the first Parliament there should be 121 members (resolution 1); that fifty-one of them should be elected in the Cape Colony, thirty-six in the Transvaal, seventeen in the Orange River Colony, and seventeen in Natal (resolution 2); and that no original province should have less than its original number of members before the four original provinces returned a total of 150 members (resolution 3). It also recommended a complicated method for enlarging the House (resolution 4). A census of the white population would be held in 1911 and every five years thereafter. After each census there would be a readjustment of provincial representation in the House of Assembly. The total number of white male adults in the Union at the latest census would be divided by the total number of members in the existing House of Assembly to give the 'quota'. The resolution continued:

Every Province whose total number of white male adults has increased

---

[56] Brand's manuscript, Annexures N and P.

[57] For the debate described in this paragraph, see the *Minutes*, pp. 42–43 ; Walton, pp. 165–75 ; Malan, pp. 62–65. The quotation is from Malan, pp. 64–65.

since the last census, so that, after deducting therefrom the quota multiplied by the number of members representing it in the House of Assembly, it has a surplus above the number of white male adults at the last preceding census equal to at least the quota or any multiple thereof, shall be entitled to an additional member, or additional number of members equal to such multiple in respect of any such increase.

The change would come into effect at the next general election. This would continue until the House contained 150 members, when there would be no further change unless Parliament provided otherwise.[58]

How did the committee arrive at its decision for the division of the seats between the provinces in the first Parliament? According to Malan it took the white male adult basis as a starting-point and then made arbitrary changes to meet the claims of Natal and the Orange River Colony for special treatment in the early years. He wrote in his diary that the white male adult basis gave the ratios: Cape Colony 55·46, Transvaal 39·45, Orange River Colony 13·58, and Natal 11·51; that four and a half seats were then taken from the Cape Colony and given to Natal, and three and a half were taken from the Transvaal and given to the Orange River Colony, producing fifty-one, thirty-six, seventeen, and sixteen; and that finally Natal's demand for parity with the Orange River Colony was met by creating an additional seat for her. He added, however, that 'What was not quite clear to me was how the number of "European male adults" was arrived at.'[59] Walton understood, on the other hand, that the white male adult basis was used for the Cape Colony, the Orange River Colony, and Natal and that 'the Transvaal had been met by accepting its Voters' Basis . . .'.[60] It is virtually certain that what actually happened was that Smuts had already extracted from the 1904 census reports the estimates of the white male adult populations of the four colonies (excluding British troops) which he subsequently used in the convention, namely, Cape Colony 167,546, Transvaal 106,493, Orange River Colony 41,014, and Natal 34,784;[61] that he persuaded the committee to increase the Transvaal number to 119,179 as an allowance for the increase that had taken place since 1904; and that the ratios 55·46, 39·45, 13·58, and 11·51 were calculated from these numbers.[62] Three comments may be made. Firstly, the numbers were more or less

[58] *Minutes*, pp. 44–45.

[59] Malan, pp. 64–67.

[60] Walton, p. 177.

[61] These were the numbers which Smuts subsequently proposed for insertion in section 33 (vii) of the convention's draft Constitution.

[62] This statement is justified by the fact that the ratios given by Malan are exactly those which are derived from the numbers 167,546, 119,179, 41,014, and 34,784.

correctly taken out of the 1904 census reports, except in the case of
the Orange River Colony number, which was nearly 3,000 too high.[63]
Secondly, although it is not clear what justification could have been given
for raising the Transvaal number by over 12,000, the Transvaal white
male adult population had probably increased by at least that amount
by 1908.[64] And, thirdly, since the number of seats given to the Transvaal
in the first Parliament was based on a white male adult population of
119,179, the Transvaal should only have become entitled to additional
seats under resolution 4 in respect of white male adults in excess of
119,179, and *not* 106,493.

The first three of the committee's resolutions were adopted by the
convention on the afternoon of the 29th without a division and without
much discussion.[65] The Natal delegates were pleased with the concession
that was being made to Natal and Moor and Greene expressed their gratitude, but there was some bickering between the other three delegations.
De la Rey and Hull contended that the Transvaal was being unfairly
treated, 'especially in view of the mines', whereupon Fischer retorted that
'This is the first time that we have heard anything about the purse', while
Malan said that the Cape was making a heavy sacrifice for the smaller
colonies. The fourth resolution evoked a keener debate. Malan moved an
amendment to exclude from the formula for the increase in the members
of the House of Assembly men who were not British subjects. This was
defeated by twenty-one votes to nine, the Transvaal delegates voting
solidly against it. Malan then moved another amendment, to exclude the
members of the imperial naval and military forces on active service, and
it carried by sixteen votes to fourteen. When the debate was resumed the
next day, Smuts moved an amendment with a different formula for the
readjustment of provincial representation in the House of Assembly:[66]

Every Province, whose total number of white male adults, divided by the
number of members representing such Province in the House of Assembly,

[63] By interpolation from the tables on pp. 47 and 154 of the Orange River Colony
census report it may be estimated that the white male adult population, excluding British
troops, was 38,274 in 1904.

[64] The Union census of 7 May 1911 was to show the following changes in the
white male adult populations of the four provinces, excluding British troops, since
the 1904 census: Cape Colony, a decrease of 15,911; Transvaal, an increase of 27,278;
Orange Free State, an increase of 4,347; and Natal a decrease of 4,350. U.G. 15 (1913),
para. 6.

[65] For the convention debate on this first report of the Constitution of the House of
Assembly Committee see the *Minutes*, pp. 45–48; Walton, pp. 176–7; Malan, pp. 66–69.
The quotations are from Malan.

[66] *Minutes*, pp. 46–47. This amendment was to replace that part of the committee's
resolution 4 which is quoted in the text above.

produces a quotient greater than the quota, shall be entitled to additional representation if the total number of its white male adults exceeds that of the last preceding census by a number equal to, or greater than, the quota, such additional representation shall be given by adding to the members allotted to such Province a number equal to whatever multiple its excess of white male adults over the last preceding census may be of the quota.

After a long discussion, in which 'Malan and others asserted that the meaning and the words did not agree',[67] Smuts withdrew his amendment and the resolution was adopted without a division in the form recommended by the committee, with the addition of Malan's amendment excluding members of British forces from the formula.[68]

Reviewing the convention's work during the November recess, Smuts, Hull, Farrar, and the Transvaal advisers reached the conclusion that the resolution dealing with the increase in the number of members of the House of Assembly was unsatisfactory, because its formula might produce unintended results (for example, if the white male adult population of Natal decreased by 3,000 between 1904 and 1911 and increased back to the 1904 number thereafter, Natal would become entitled to an additional seat), and because the automatic redistribution of seats between the provinces was to come to an end when the number of members in the House reached 150, so that the provincial distribution would then become stereotyped without relation to the white male adult or any other population basis.[69] The Transvaalers therefore prepared an alternative draft which eliminated these defects.[70] In January Smuts persuaded the convention's drafting committee to adopt the Transvaal draft,[71] and the

---

[67] Malan, pp. 68–69.

[68] A fortnight later Fitzpatrick wrote as follows in a private letter: 'Smuts has been twice caught and exposed in deliberate trickery, phrasing his resolutions with amazing cleverness so that they can mean the very opposite of what he appears to concede. But he has no feeling of shame or resentment, and resumes at once his too perfect air of camaraderie and overdone boyish frankness. By two totally wanton and short-sighted acts of duplicity he has managed to give every man in the Convention the same feeling of profound mistrust that dogs him in all he does. It is wonderful that so clever a man should not be clever enough to be reasonably straight. It almost convulsed me with laughter to see Sauer's look of speechless incredulity, and almost horror, when Smuts's little game was exposed—whether it was because of the audacity of the attempt and the cool-bloodedness of the deception, or the fact that he himself had been caught trusting, I don't know.' Fitzpatrick to J. Wernher, 15 Nov. 1908, Fitzpatrick Papers (copy). Allowance must be made for Fitzpatrick's tendency to exaggerate. Nevertheless, it is probable that there was some substance in the charges made in this letter and that the two episodes referred to were: (1) Smuts's conduct when the first report of the franchise committee was before the convention on 2 and 3 Nov. (above, p. 222); and (2) Smuts's amendment mentioned in the text above.

[69] Brand's manuscript.

[70] Ibid., Annexure T.

[71] Greene's 'Remarks on Draft Constitution'.

committee's report dealt with the question as follows: The Union quota was to be a constant, obtained by dividing the total number of white male adults (other than British troops) enumerated in the four colonies at the 1904 census by the original number of members of the House of Assembly. A census of the white population of the Union would be held in 1911 and every five years thereafter and the division of the seats between the provinces would be readjusted after every census. In each readjustment until the total number of members reached 150 a province whose number of white male adults had increased by a quota since 1904 would receive one more than its original number of members, and a province whose white male adult population had increased by a multiple of a quota would receive that number of additional members, except that no addition would be made before the number of the province's white male adults exceeded the Union quota multiplied by its existing number of seats, and then only in respect of such excess. After the total number of members had reached 150 the total would remain stable at that number, but at each readjustment the members would be divided between the provinces on the white male adult basis.[72]

When these recommendations came before the convention, Natal vigorously opposed the provision that the seats should be divided on the unqualified white male adult basis after the House had reached 150, but Watt's amendment to secure a minimum of seventeen seats for Natal for all time was rejected by eighteen votes to twelve and the committee's proposal was adopted with only a minor concession to Natal, to the effect that no province should have fewer than its original number of seats for the first ten years.[73] The other recommendations were approved by the convention with only verbal amendments.[74] No delegate seems to have challenged the new formula for the allocation of additional seats, although it was similar to the formula which Smuts had proposed and withdrawn on 30 October. The convention, however, added two new sub-sections. One defined adults as persons over 21 years of age.[75] The other stated that for the purpose of the Act the number of white male adults (other than British troops) enumerated in the 1904 census was to be 'taken to be': Cape Province 167,546, Transvaal 106,493, Orange Free State 41,014, and Natal 34,784. This last addition was proposed by Smuts on 30 January and it does not appear to have evoked any discussion in the convention.[76]

[72] *Minutes*, pp. 286–7.   [73] Ibid., pp. 207–8.
[74] Ibid., pp. 162, 200–1, 207–9.
[75] Ibid., pp. 162, 201, 234, 237.
[76] Ibid., p. 237.

Thus section 31 of the Convention's draft Constitution provided that the House of Assembly should be composed of members elected directly by the voters of the Union;[77] section 32 provided that the first House of Assembly should consist of fifty-one members elected in the Cape Province, thirty-six in the Transvaal, seventeen in the Orange Free State, and seventeen in Natal, and that no province should have fewer than its original number of members before the total membership reached 150 or until ten years had elapsed since Union, whichever was the longer period;[78] and section 33 provided that the number of members elected in a province should be readjusted every five years in the manner set out above.[79]

The most striking aspect of the initial division was that it made concessions to the Orange Free State and Natal which it was illogical to make in the composition of the Lower House of the Parliament of a legislative union. It was hoped that they would help in reconciling the people of Natal to the unitary principle. The initial division was reasonably fair, however, as between the two larger colonies. So great were the demographic changes that had taken place since the 1904 census that the convention was justified in taking cognizance of them, although they were not accurately recorded in the colonial statistics.

The formula for increase during the interim period, on the other hand, not only provided for the continuation of the concessions to the Orange Free State and Natal but was also distinctly unfair to the Cape Province. It meant that the Cape Province would obtain an additional seat for every 2,891 white male adults more than 167,546, the Transvaal would obtain an additional seat for every 2,891 white male adults more than 106,493, and the Orange Free State and Natal would obtain an additional seat for every 2,891 white male adults more than 49,147.[80] This was unfair to the Cape Province because the Transvaal's original number of seats had been based on a white male adult population of 119,179,[81] which is 12,686 more than 106,493, so that the Transvaal would obtain several seats more than she was entitled to on the white male adult basis in the second Parliament and in all subsequent parliaments until the total

[77] S. 32 of the S.A. Act is identical.
[78] S. 33 of the S.A. Act is identical.
[79] S. 34 of the S.A. Act is virtually identical.
[80] The Union quota was fixed at 2,891, being the sum of the numbers specified in sub-section (vii) divided by 121. For the Cape Province and the Transvaal sub-section (iii) gave the larger and operative numbers; and for the Orange Free State and Natal sub-section (iv) gave the larger and operative numbers (2,891 × 17 = 49,147). The delimitation commissions acted accordingly. U.G. 15 (1913), paras. 5–9.
[81] See above, pp. 230–1.

membership of the House of Assembly reached 150.[82] Since Smuts had paid particular attention to all stages of the drafting of this part of the Constitution, and since it was he who moved the sub-section that was inserted on 30 January, it can scarcely be doubted that he had intentionally outwitted the Cape delegates. Moreover, in ignoring all the non-Europeans, including the non-European voters of the Cape Province, the formula diminished the political weight of a vote in the Cape Province still further.[83] It is astonishing that no Cape delegate seems to have contested either of these decisions.

Sooner or later, however, if the white population of South Africa continued to increase, the interim provisions would cease to operate and the 150 seats in the House of Assembly would be divided between the provinces on the strict white male adult basis. There would then be no more concessions to the Orange Free State or Natal. Nevertheless, a Cape Province vote would continue to carry less weight than a vote in a northern province, unless the section was amended by an Act of the Union Parliament.

Of much greater political significance than the division of the seats in the House of Assembly between the provinces was the electoral system within the provinces. The background to this question has been examined in earlier chapters.[84] It will be recalled that the interests of

[82] The following table shows how the interim provisions were in fact applied by the first five delimitation commissions:

Census	White male adults				D.C.	Parliament	Seats			
	Cape	Transvaal	O.F.S.	Natal			C.	T.	O.	N.
1904	167,546	106,493	41,014	34,784	1	1910–15	51	36	17	17
1911	151,635	133,771	45,361	30,434	2	1915–19	51	45	17	17
1918	163,292	145,998	48,642	39,061	3	1920–4	51	49	17	17
1921	169,478	149,489	49,277	41,893	4	1924–9	51	50	17	17
1926	188,120	162,641	52,291	48,527	5	1929–33	58	55	18	17

Reports of delimitation commissions: first, *Gov.Gaz.Extraordinary*, 1 June 1910; second, U.G. 15 (1913); third, U.G. 58 (1919); fourth, U.G. 27 (1923); fifth, U.G. 21 (1928).

[83] The following table shows the average number of registered voters to a constituency in each of the provinces during the interim period:

D.C.	Registered voters to the constituency			
	Cape	Transvaal	O.F.S.	Natal
1	2,791	2,715	2,131	1,647
2	2,913	2,557	2,342	1,729
3	3,655	2,869	2,793	1,939
4	3,863	2,824	2,884	2,035
5	3,381	2,506	2,641	2,259

[84] See above, pp. 25–29, 126–34, 161–2.

the South African Party, Het Volk, and the Orangia Unie—the predominant rural and Afrikaner parties—lay in giving some advantage to the rural voters, either by adopting the white population basis for the division of the provinces into constituencies, or by applying some arbitrary loading factor to make the rural constituencies contain fewer voters apiece than the urban constituencies; while the interests of the Unionists, the Progressives, and the Constitutionalists—the predominantly urban and British parties—lay in adopting the voters' basis without qualification and providing that the constituencies should be redelimited by impartial commissions at regular intervals. To Fitzpatrick, the principles 'one vote, one value' and 'automatic redistribution' were the crux of the entire Constitution. With them, imperial interests and the interests of British South Africans would be reasonably secure: without them, the Union might fall under the domination of a racialistic Afrikaner party. But whereas Hertzog had had the unflinching support of most of the Afrikaner delegates for his language proposals, Fitzpatrick would only receive half-hearted support from many of the British delegates in his fight for 'equal rights' in politics. He knew that his own leader, Farrar, was liable to succumb to pressure, that Jameson would be satisfied with almost any settlement which was closer to equality than the existing arrangements in the Cape Colony, and that the Natal delegates were so accustomed to defending the gross inequalities in their own colony that they were not convinced that 'equal rights' were necessary as a safeguard for the entire British South African community.[85] On the other hand, he had obtained a signal triumph in persuading Smuts and Botha to undertake to support the voters' basis, as well as regular redelimitations and proportional representation. In the last resort the issue would depend on the extent to which Smuts and Botha were loyal to this undertaking when they were confronted with the inevitable pressures from the Orangia Unie and South African party delegates—not least from Merriman, whose abhorrence of equal constituencies was undiminished.

The question was first debated in the convention on 27 October when Merriman, moving his amendment to Smuts's proposal that the seats should be divided between the provinces on the white voters' basis, spoke for the white population basis in general and did so with his customary platform vigour.[86] He described the voters' basis as 'unsound and not in

[85] Fitzpatrick to Jameson, 9 Oct. 1908 (copy); Fitzpatrick to J. Wernher, 15 Nov. 1908 (copy); 'The Language Question'. Fitzpatrick Papers.

[86] For the convention debate dealt with in this paragraph see the *Minutes*, pp. 42–43; Walton, pp. 168–75; Malan, pp. 62–65. The Merriman quotation is from Walton and the de Villiers quotation is from Malan.

accordance with the practice followed elsewhere. It opened the door to fraud and to the influence of wealth. . . . The people of the towns did not take the same interest in the affairs of the country as the more stable population on the land. They were a shifting population, people who were here to-day and gone to-morrow. . . . On the other hand the people on the land must stay and must pay. . . . There was no chance there', he added, with a thrust at the Transvaal Progressives for their alleged iniquities, 'of swindling by a political party, no chance for the swindling politician with money to swell a register by putting on bogus names as it had been done in the past.' Thus, as Malan noted in his diary that evening, the convention descended for the first time to the level of party polemics. Steyn, Sauer, Malan, and de la Rey supported Merriman and Fitzpatrick, Farrar, Jagger, and Walton opposed him, arguing that the voters' basis was the only fair one because the townsmen paid the bulk of the taxes. Next morning de Villiers rebuked Merriman for his partisan speech and appealed to the convention to discuss the problem dispassionately. He also suggested that the provinces should be divided into constituencies on the voters' basis, but with a loading factor so that the rural constituencies would contain fewer voters than the urban constituencies, 'to give the country population the benefit of property and area' as was done 'in all other countries'. The whole question of the composition of the House of Assembly was then referred to a committee consisting of de Villiers and three delegates from each of the self-governing colonies, as has been mentioned above.

The committee brought up its second report, dealing with the division of the provinces into constituencies, on 3 November.[87] It was based on the relevant provisions of the Transvaal and Orange River Colony constitutions of 1906 and 1907.[88] Following those precedents it proposed that a commission should divide the provinces into constituencies soon after the enactment of the Constitution and that further commissions should make periodic re-delimitations thereafter (resolutions 1 and 4). But whereas the Transvaal and Orange River Colony constitutions provided for single-member constituencies, the committee was persuaded by Smuts to recommend a system of proportional representation. Each electoral division was to return three or more members, 'unless the Commissions decide in favour of a smaller number in special cases of sparsely populated areas', and the members were to be elected 'according to the principles of proportional representation, with the single transferable vote' (resolutions 3 and 5). Furthermore, there were significant

---

[87] *Minutes*, pp. 57–58.
[88] Cd. 3250, Schedules I and III; Cd. 3526, Schedules I and III. See above, pp. 26–29.

departures from the Transvaal and Orange River Colony constitutions in the principles laid down to guide the delimitation commissions (resolution 2). Whereas the Transvaal and Orange River Colony constitutions provided that the second and all subsequent commissions should assign to the principal urban areas their exact share of the seats according to the voters' basis, no such provision was recommended by the committee. And whereas the commissions under the Transvaal and Orange River Colony constitutions, in dividing the urban areas and the rural areas into constituencies, were authorized to depart from the voters' basis to up to 15 per cent. either way and in so doing to give 'due consideration' to only four factors—existing boundaries, community or diversity of interests, means of communication, and physical features—the committee proposed that the Union commissions, in dividing the provinces into constituencies, should also be authorized to depart from the voters' basis to up to 15 per cent. either way and in so doing to give 'due consideration' not only to the same four factors, but also to a fifth—'sparsity or density of population'. In adding this phrase the committee intended, although its report did not expressly say so, that sparsely populated areas should have fewer voters to a member than densely populated areas. The cumulative effect of these differences in the principles laid down for the guidance of commissions was considerable. Under the Transvaal and Orange River Colony constitutions the urban complex of the Witwatersrand, Pretoria town and suburbs, and the towns of the Orange River Colony would have received the exact numbers of seats to which they were entitled on the voters' basis in the second and all subsequent general elections, but under the committee's proposals the towns throughout the Union would receive fewer seats than they were entitled to on the voters' basis, because the 15 per cent. variation either way would tell against them under two of the five sub-sections—'means of communication' and 'sparsity or density of population'. The extent of the inequality would depend upon the manner in which the commissions exercised their discretion.

Fitzpatrick had been somewhat anxious because he was not a member of the committee, but he had kept in touch with Botha, Smuts, and Farrar, the three Transvaal members, and when Farrar had asked his opinion whether he should stand out against the rest of the committee for a reduction of the maximum loading from 15 to 5 per cent. either way he advised him not to do so. He regarded the 15 per cent. as nothing 'to grumble at' in view of the much greater inequalities that had always existed in the coastal colonies and he considered that Botha and Smuts were being completely loyal to their compact. He hoped, however, that the composition of the delimitation commissions would be amended when the report came before the convention. According to the report the first delimitation would be made by four colonial commissions, each consisting of a judge and 'two other members' appointed by the colonial Government, and subsequent commissions would be appointed by the Governor-General-in-Council and 'presided over by a judge'. Fitzpatrick wanted all the members of all the delimitation commissions to be judges, as a guarantee of their impartiality, and if this were done he would be completely satisfied with the settlement.[89] The Afrikaner delegates also seem to have been satisfied with the essential features of the report, men like Hertzog realizing that an approach to equal constituencies was a *quid pro quo* for the language section.

The result was that the report was disposed of rather quickly when it was dealt with by the convention on the afternoon of 4 November.[90] Resolutions 1 and 4 were amended to meet Fitzpatrick's wishes, so that all the members of all delimitation commissions were to be judges, and the other resolutions were carried as moved. Merriman was the only delegate who criticized proportional representation and he drew a blank when he ironically invited one of the least sophisticated of the Boer generals to explain how it worked. But the pamphlets which Brand had prepared and distributed had had their effect and proportional representation was adopted without a destructive amendment having been moved, if also without enthusiasm.

These decisions were not substantially altered by the convention during the drafting stage. The drafting committee cast them into six sections of its draft Constitution and added two new sections, taken over from the Transvaal Constitution of 1906, concerning the reports of the delimitation commissions and the date on which changes in electoral divisions were to come into force.[91] When the report was before the convention in January the two sections concerning proportional representation were combined into one section and transferred to the penultimate chapter of the Constitution.[92] The key section concerning the principles on which the provinces were to be divided into constituencies was accepted without further debate, but the sections concerning the appointments and the powers of the commissions were considerably expanded.[93] There was also some discussion of the frequency of delimitations. Resolution 4 of

[89] Fitzpatrick to J. Wernher, 15 Nov. 1908 (copy); 'The Language Question'. Fitzpatrick Papers.
[90] *Minutes*, pp. 66–68; Walton, pp. 180–7; Malan, pp. 72–75.
[91] 'Remarks on Draft Constitution'; Brand's manuscript, Annexures BB and CC; *Minutes*, pp. 288–9.   [92] *Minutes*, pp. 224, 227, 233.
[93] Ibid., pp. 163, 174, 201–2, 209, 225, 248.

4 November had provided for delimitations every five years. On 18 January Malan spoke in favour of ten-year intervals, arguing that more frequent delimitations would cause 'much inconvenience and unnecessary trouble', but Fitzpatrick replied that he was not prepared to accept such an alteration and Malan refrained from moving an amendment.[94]

The convention's draft Constitution accordingly dealt with the division of the constituencies within the provinces in the following manner. Section 38 provided that after the enactment of the South Africa Act the Governor-in-Council of each of the colonies should nominate a judge to a joint commission to make the first delimitation.[95] Section 39 provided that the commission should divide each province into electoral divisions each returning 'three or more members', but 'in special cases of sparsely populated areas the commission may delimit divisions in which less than three members shall be returned'.[96] Section 40 laid down the following principles:

40. (i) For the purpose of such division as is in the last preceding section mentioned, the quota of each Province shall be obtained by dividing the total number of voters in the Province, as ascertained at the last registration of voters, by the number of members of the House of Assembly to be elected therein.

(ii) Each Province shall be divided into electoral divisions, so that the number of voters in each division shall subject to the provisions of subsection (iii) be a multiple of the quota and the number of members to be elected therein shall be equal to such multiple.

(iii) The commissioners shall give due consideration to
    (a) community or diversity of interests;
    (b) means of communication;
    (c) physical features;
    (d) existing electoral boundaries;
    (e) sparsity or density of population;
in such manner that while taking the quota of voters as the basis of division, the commissioners may, whenever they deem it necessary, depart therefrom, but in no case to any greater extent than fifteen *per centum* more or fifteen *per centum* less than the quota.[97]

Section 41 provided that after every quinquennial census the Governor-

[94] Malan, pp. 172–5.
[95] S. 38 of the S.A. Act contains minor amendments made in Bloemfontein and in England.
[96] Contrast s. 39 of the S.A. Act, which provides for single-member constituencies. This important change was made at Bloemfontein. See below, pp. 367–72.
[97] Ss. 40 (i) and 40 (iii) of the S.A. Act are identical. S. 40 (ii) was amended at Bloemfontein in consequence of the dropping of proportional representation. See below, p. 372.

General-in-Council should appoint a commission consisting of three judges 'to carry out any re-division which may have become necessary' and in so doing to 'proceed upon the same principles' as the first commission.[98] Section 42 dealt with the form of the reports of the commissions and allied topics.[99] Section 43 provided that any changes prescribed by a commission should come into operation at the next general election.[1] And section 136 provided that the election of the members of the House of Assembly, *inter alia*, should be 'according to the principle of proportional representation, each voter having one transferable vote' and that the Governor-General-in-Council should frame and promulgate regulations for voting and for the duties of the returning officers.[2]

These sections represented a compromise between the two main interests represented in the convention. In providing a definite system for the regular re-delimitation of the constituencies, under the control of judges, who were likely to be the most impartial persons available, they were a great advance on the methods which had prevailed in the Boer republics and which still prevailed in the coastal colonies, where any change in representation required special legislation, and disputes on the subject were continual. Moreover, the principles laid down for the guidance of the delimitation commissions would produce a closer approach to equity than had been achieved in the South African Republic and the coastal colonies. On the other hand, section 40 (iii) had serious defects. As Brand realized, the new phrase 'sparsity or density of population' was 'open to quite different interpretations according to the temperament and opinion of the judge who is carrying it out and its vagueness invites the judges into the dangerous path of party politics. . . . It will be a great temptation to any Government to persuade by any means open to them the judges to read it in the light the Government may at the moment desire.'[3] Moreover, the range of discretion of 15 per cent. either way which was granted to the commissions was by no means negligible. Under South African conditions, if it was applied rigorously to the advantage of the rural voters, a minority of the voters might frequently obtain a majority of the seats in Parliament. But the Progressive delegates in the convention do not seem to have discerned this possibility, or, discerning it, they do not

[98] S. 41 of the S.A. Act is identical.

[99] S. 42 of the S.A. Act was amended in Bloemfontein in consequence of the dropping of proportional representation. Cf. s. 16 of the Transvaal Constitution.

[1] S. 43 of the S.A. Act is identical. Cf. s. 17 of the Transvaal Constitution.

[2] The corresponding section of the S.A. Act, s. 134, was amended in Bloemfontein in consequence of the dropping of proportional representation for the election of members of the House of Assembly. See below, p. 372.

[3] Brand to Smuts, 28 Dec. 1908, Smuts Papers.

seem to have been alarmed. Thus Fitzpatrick, always the most ardent advocate of 'one vote, one value', was as pleased with the electoral resolutions as Hertzog had been with the language resolution. 'Here is the great question settled!' he wrote. 'Yesterday, 4th November, should be a great day, and a turning point in South African history. *I am satisfied.*'[4]

(iii) *General*

Section 45 of the draft Constitution, determining the duration of the House of Assembly, also originated in the full convention. The Lower Houses of Parliament in the Cape Colony, the Transvaal, and the Orange River Colony were elected for five years, and the Natal Legislative Assembly for four years, subject to earlier dissolution by the Governor. On 30 October Smuts proposed that every Union House of Assembly should continue for five years, subject to earlier dissolution by the Governor-General, and the convention agreed.[5] The remaining five sections of the House of Assembly sub-chapter were modelled on the provisions of the Australian and Transvaal constitutions. Smuts, Hull, Farrar, and their advisers included them in the draft they made during the November recess, the drafting committee adopted them, and the convention agreed in January. Section 46 provided that the House of Assembly should elect a Speaker from among its members and that he would be removable by a vote of the House, section 47 provided for the election of a Deputy Speaker, section 48 provided for the resignation of members, section 49 fixed the quorum at thirty members, and section 50 provided that all questions in the House should be determined by a bare majority and that the Speaker or his deputy should have a casting vote but no deliberative vote.[6]

D. *Miscellaneous*

Most of the remaining sections of the parliamentary chapter of the Constitution fall into three groups: those concerning Money Bills and the relations between the two Houses, those concerning disqualifications for membership of Parliament and allied topics, and those concerning the royal assent to Bills and their enrolment.

On 2 November the convention passed a resolution, based upon a motion by Smuts, to provide that subject to the provisions of the Con-

---

[4] Wallis, *Fitzpatrick*, p. 139.

[5] *Minutes*, pp. 48, 175, 290. S. 45 of the S.A. Act is identical.

[6] *Minutes*, pp. 175, 225, 232, 290; Brand's manuscript, Annexures T, BB, and CC; 'Remarks on Draft Constitution'. Ss. 46–50 of the S.A. Act are identical, except for a minor amendment to s. 46. Cf. ss. 35, 36, 37, 39 of the Australian Constitution and s. 29 of the Transvaal Constitution.

stitution all laws in force in a colony at the establishment of the Union should remain in force in the respective province until repealed or amended by Parliament, or by the Provincial Council in matters in which it was competent to make ordinances. With verbal amendments, this resolution became section 137 of the convention's draft Constitution.[7]

The convention then turned to Money Bills and the relations between the two Houses, and it became apparent that the majority of the delegates were anxious to clip the wings of the Second Chamber as short as possible. In spite of the fact that he had recently become Prime Minister of the Cape Colony as a result of a general election following a dissolution of Parliament caused by the rejection of the annual Appropriation Bill by the Legislative Council, Merriman stood for a weak Senate. This was because he feared lest the Senate, with its quasi-federal composition, might become a supporter of provincial rights and also because his sympathies lay with the British House of Commons in its conflict with the House of Lords, which had already rejected the 1906 Education Bill and the 1908 Licensing Bill. The Unie delegates and several of the Cape delegates of both parties agreed with Merriman. On the other hand, the Natal delegates wished the Senate to be as strong as possible.

According to resolutions which the convention passed on 2 November all Money Bills (i.e. Bills appropriating revenue or imposing taxation) were to originate in the House of Assembly and were to be immune from amendment (but not from rejection) by the Senate. Furthermore, the annual Appropriation Bills were not to include extraneous material and all Appropriation Bills were to emanate from recommendations to the House of Assembly by the Governor-General. So far as they went these resolutions were similar to the provisions of the Australian Constitution, but unlike the Australian Constitution they did not prevent Taxation Bills from dealing with more than one subject of taxation, nor did they grant the Senate the power to suggest amendments when actual amendments were not permitted. During the debate Merriman called for a division on his motion to withhold from the Senate the power to reject Money Bills, but it was defeated by eighteen votes to twelve—the four Unie delegates, seven Cape Colony delegates, and de la Rey forming the minority. In the drafting committee in January Merriman returned to the attack with a proposal that the Senate should not be competent to reject annual Appropriation Bills. The majority of the members of the committee considered that if there was to be a Second Chamber at all it should not be so emasculated, but Merriman, Hertzog, and de Villiers said they were willing that the Senate should be abolished altogether, and

[7] *Minutes*, pp. 49, 238, 308. S. 135 of the S.A. Act is identical.

the committee would probably have made a recommendation to that effect if Greene had not declared that Natal would regard the Senate as 'a vital principle of the whole Constitution'. The result was that sections 60–62 of the convention's draft Constitution were substantially the same as the resolutions of 2 November.[8]

Another resolution passed by the convention on 2 November arose from a proposal by Smuts to adopt the procedure laid down in the Transvaal and Orange River Colony constitutions for overcoming disagreements between the two Houses. If in two successive sessions the Upper House failed to pass a Bill which had been passed by the Lower House, or passed it with amendments to which the Lower House would not agree, the Governor-General would be able to convene a joint sitting of both Houses, when the Bill would be passed if it received an absolute majority of the votes of the total number of members of both Houses; or, alternatively, the Governor-General would be able to dissolve the Lower House, or both Houses, and after a general election to convene a joint sitting if the Lower House again passed the Bill and the Upper House again failed to pass it. This was carried by the convention with two amendments. The majority required in the joint sitting was changed to a bare majority of the members present and the dissolution alternative was deleted. Subsequently, the convention made a third amendment to the effect that if the Senate rejected an Appropriation Bill a joint sitting could be convened forthwith. Merriman had proposed that it should be possible to convene a joint sitting forthwith if the Senate rejected any class of Bill, and he persuaded the drafting committee to include the proposal in its first report, but the convention referred the section back to the committee and the earlier position was then restored. Consequently, section 63 of the convention's draft Constitution provided that the Senate would be able to delay legislation, other than Appropriation Bills, for one session, after which a joint sitting could be convened and the Bill would pass if it received the votes of a majority of the members present. Since the Senate would be outnumbered by more than three to one in a joint sitting, this provision would enable the House of Assembly to prevail in most cases.[9]

[8] Walton, pp. 193–5; Malan, pp. 70–73; 'Remarks on Draft Constitution'; *Minutes*, pp. 49–52, 177, 209, 292. Ss. 60–62 of the S.A. Act are identical. Cf. ss. 53–56 of the Australian Constitution.

[9] Walton, p. 194; Malan, pp. 70–71; 'Remarks on Draft Constitution'; *Minutes*, pp. 52–54, 177–8, 202, 209–10, 292–3. S. 63 of the S.A. Act is identical. Cf. s. 37 of the Transvaal Constitution and s. 57 of the Australian Constitution. The Australian provision only allows for a joint sitting after a dissolution of both houses and a general election.

When the procedure for overcoming disagreements between the two
Houses had been dealt with on 2 November, Malan proposed that the
Governor-General should be able to dissolve both Houses simultaneously
(with the proviso that a dissolution should not affect the nominated
senators), or the House of Assembly alone, and this was carried by
twenty-three votes to seven, the Natal delegates voting in the minority.
Walton's suggestion that the Governor-General should also be able to
dissolve the Senate alone was negatived without a division and so was
Merriman's suggestion that he should be able to dissolve the Senate alone
if it rejected an annual Appropriation or Taxation Bill. There followed
a considerable debate on the mode of replacing the elected senators in
the event of the dissolution of both Houses within the first ten years of
Union and on 3 November the convention decided that in that event the
elected senators would 'be chosen by the provinces in such manner as the
Parliament shall provide'. But this decision did not meet the case of a
dissolution taking place without Parliament having made the necessary
provision for the election of senators, and the drafting committee altered
it to an outright prohibition on the dissolution of the Senate within the
first ten years, which was accepted by the convention on 26 January.
Accordingly, section 19 of the convention's draft Constitution empowered
the Governor-General to convene and prorogue Parliament and to
dissolve both Houses or the House of Assembly alone, provided that
the Senate should not be dissolved within the first ten years, and that a
subsequent dissolution of the Senate should not affect the nominated
senators.[10] Section 20, providing that the first Parliament should meet
within six months of the establishment of the Union, was inserted by the
drafting committee, and section 21, providing for annual sessions of
Parliament, originated in a resolution passed by the convention on
23 November.[11]

The convention began to consider the disqualifications for membership
of either House of Parliament and allied topics on the first day of the
Cape Town session, when, after debate, they were referred to a committee consisting of Sauer, Hull, Hertzog, and Morcom. Hull was ready
with proposals which had been drafted during the recess and were
derived from the Australian and Transvaal constitutions. The committee adopted most of them and the convention passed its report on

---

[10] Walton, pp. 194–5; Malan, pp. 70–73, 194–5; *Minutes*, pp. 54–56, 60–61, 152, 215,
284. S. 20 of the S.A. Act is identical. Cf. s. 74 of the Cape of Good Hope Constitution
Ordinance, 1853.
[11] *Minutes*, pp. 77, 284. Ss. 21, 22 of the S.A. Act are identical.

30 November with a few amendments. Some further changes were subsequently made by the drafting committee and the convention. The
treason disqualification for membership of Parliament was the most contentious point, because 'armed protest' was deep-rooted in the Boer tradition and the disfranchisement of several thousand Cape Colony Boers for
participating in the war was fresh in the minds of the delegates. Jagger
and others wished persons convicted of treason to be permanently disqualified, but Sauer, Steyn, and Malan pressed for a less stringent penalty,
Sauer remarking that 'high treason was sometimes only another name for
"unsuccessful rebellion" and without rebellion there would perhaps have
been no freedom'.[12] The outcome was that section 53 of the convention's
draft Constitution disqualified a person convicted of treason, murder, or
any other offence for which he had been sentenced to a year's imprisonment without the option of a fine, unless he had received a free pardon,
or unless the period of imprisonment had expired five years before the
date of his election. It also disqualified unrehabilitated insolvents, persons of unsound mind, and holders of offices of profit under the Crown,
except ministers of State, pensioners, retired or half-pay members of the
British forces, and part-time members of the South African forces. Section 54 provided that a member of either House should vacate his seat if
he became subject to any of these disabilities, or if he ceased to possess
the necessary qualifications, or if he failed to attend the House for a
whole ordinary session without special leave. Section 55 prescribed a
penalty of £100 a day for any person sitting or voting as a member of
either House while disqualified and having reasonable grounds for knowing that he was disqualified. Section 56 provided allowances of £300 a
year for members of both Houses, with deductions of £2 a day for every
day's absence. Section 57 provided that Parliament should declare the
powers, immunities, and privileges of the Senate and the House of
Assembly and that until declared they were to be those of the House of
Assembly of the Cape Colony. And section 58 empowered each House
to make rules and orders for the conduct of its proceedings (with those
of the Legislative Council and House of Assembly of the Cape Colony
applying meanwhile) and provided that at joint sittings of both Houses
the Speaker of the House of Assembly should preside and the rules of the
House of Assembly should apply as far as practicable.[13] On 16 December the convention adopted a resolution prescribing the oath of affirma-

[12] Malan, pp. 80–81.
[13] Walton, pp. 195–8; Malan, pp. 80–81, 98–101; *Minutes*, pp. 73–77, 81–82, 94–98,
175–7, 225, 291–2. Ss. 54, 55, 57, and 58 of the S.A. Act are identical. Ss. 53 and 56 were
amended in Bloemfontein (see below, pp. 381–2). Cf. Australian Constitution, ss. 44–46,
48–50; Transvaal Constitution, ss. 18, 30.

tion to be taken by senators and members of the House of Assembly in the same form as required by the Australian Constitution, and this became section 51 of the convention's draft Constitution.[14] The drafting committee also inserted what became section 52, prohibiting a member of one House from taking part in the proceedings of the other House, except that a minister would be able to sit and speak (but not to vote) in the House of which he was not a member.[15] This exception had also been made in the constitutions of the four South African colonies.[16]

On 18 December, the last day's sitting before the Christmas recess, three resolutions concerning the royal assent were moved by de Villiers from the chair and carried without debate or amendment. The first provided that when a Bill was presented to the Governor-General for the royal assent he was to declare 'according to his discretion, but subject to the provisions of this Act', that he assented in the King's name, or that he withheld assent, or that he reserved the Bill for the signification of His Majesty's pleasure; and it empowered him to return the Bill to the House of Parliament in which it had originated with recommendations for its amendment. The second authorized the King to disallow any law within a year after it had been assented to by the Governor-General. The third provided that a Bill which had been reserved should not have any force unless it received the King's assent within two years. Provisions like these were to be found in all the British dominion and colonial constitutions of the day, although the power of disallowance, for example, was no longer actually exercised. The convention's resolutions, in fact, were taken almost word for word from the Australian Constitution and their most notable features were that, unlike the Transvaal and the Orange River Colony constitutions, they did not expressly oblige the Governor-General to exercise his discretion subject to his royal instructions, nor did they expressly oblige him to reserve Bills on particular topics. The drafting committee made a substantial change in the third resolution, reducing from two years to one the period within which the King's assent was to be given if reserved Bills were to become law. Otherwise, with a few verbal amendments, sections 64–66 of the convention's draft Constitution followed the resolutions of 18 December.[17]

[14] *Minutes*, pp. 133, 290. S. 51 of the S.A. Act is virtually identical. Cf. Australian Constitution, s. 42.

[15] *Minutes*, pp. 290–1. S. 52 of the S.A. Act is identical.

[16] Cape of Good Hope Constitution Ordinance Amendment Act, 1872, s. 4; Natal Constitution Act, 1893, s. 10; Transvaal Constitution, s. 47 (4); Orange River Colony Constitution, s. 49 (4).

[17] *Minutes*, pp. 143–4, 178, 293; 'Remarks on Draft Constitution'; Brand's manuscript,

Section 67, the last section of the parliamentary chapter of the convention's draft Constitution, was inserted by the drafting committee in January. It provided for the enrolment of copies of laws in the office of the Registrar of the Appellate Division of the Supreme Court of South Africa, as conclusive evidence as to their provisions. The Transvaal Constitution had included a section on the subject, according to which the enrolled copy was to be in the English language and signed by the Governor. The version proposed in the drafting committee by the Transvaalers was in similar terms, but Hertzog persuaded the committee to agree to a different formula. Two copies of every law, one in English and one in Dutch, were to be enrolled, but only one of them would have been signed by the Governor-General, and in case of conflict between them the signed copy would prevail. When this recommendation came before the convention on 18 January, Farrar and Fitzpatrick wished it to be stated that the Governor-General should always sign the English copy. Jagger, Stanford, and Steyn expressed the opinion that the Governor-General would in practice sign the English copy and so did de Villiers, who added that this would be advisable since the final interpretation of some of the laws might rest with the judicial committee of the Privy Council, whose members would for the most part be ignorant of Dutch; but Hertzog and Steyn appealed to the convention to accept the committee's recommendation and it was adopted without substantial amendment. They had succeeded in preserving the principle of language equality throughout the Constitution.[18]

8. THE PROVINCES

When the convention adopted its resolution on the form of the Constitution on 15 October, the Natal delegates did not consider that they had entirely lost their fight for provincial autonomy. They had grounds for optimism in the wording of section (b) of that resolution, according to which the provinces were to have 'powers of legislation and administration in local matters and in such others as may be specially reserved to be dealt with by each Province separately'; in Smuts's declaration during the debate that the sort of Constitution he had in mind was 'a middle course' between the purely unitary and the purely federal; and in Malan's

Annexures T, BB, and CC. Ss. 65 and 66 of the S.A. Act are identical. Important amendments were made to s. 64 in Bloemfontein (see below, pp. 372, 377). Cf. ss. 58–60 of the Australian Constitution and ss. 38–42 of the Transvaal Constitution.

[18] *Minutes*, pp. 178, 225, 293; 'Remarks on Draft Constitution'; Malan, pp. 174–5; Walton, pp. 108–10, 336–7; 'The Language Question'. S. 67 of the S.A. Act is identical. Cf. s. 45 of the Transvaal Constitution.

assurance that when they came to drafting the details of the Constitution they would 'find friends in unexpected quarters'.[19] Their first reaction was a curious one. On 16 October Moor laid the Natal draft British South Africa Act on the table of the convention and announced that he proposed to move it section by section.[20] Nothing further was heard of that proposal, but on 22 October Moor gave notice of a motion consisting of section 57 of the Natal draft Act, which provided that the provincial legislatures would be able to make laws on twenty specified subjects, including subjects as important as public lands, mining, property, and civil rights, the administration of justice, and the amendment of the provincial constitutions.[21]

The Natal delegates' hopes of gaining adequate support from other members of the convention were doomed to disappointment. Smuts and Merriman and their colleagues were satisfied that they had already achieved a decisive victory on the main issue by virtue of section (a) of the resolution of 15 October, which committed the convention to a legislative union, and by virtue of the resolution of 19 October, which gave the Union Parliament 'full power to make laws for the peace, order and good government of South Africa'. By the end of the Durban session they also considered that more than enough concessions had already been made to Natal in the composition of the Senate and the House of Assembly. Consequently, the plan of provincial government which Smuts drew up with Hull, Farrar, and the Transvaal advisers during the November recess embodied the most unitary of the three schemes which the Transvaalers had devised in Pretoria at the beginning of October. When Smuts discussed this plan with Merriman and de Villiers a day or two before the convention resumed in Cape Town, they persuaded him to accept modifications which made it still more decisively unitary, and the three of them agreed that Merriman should move the modified plan in the convention.[22] The main features of this plan (which will be referred to as the Smuts–Merriman plan) were as follows:[23] In each province there would be a Provincial Council, containing as many members as represented the province in the House of Assembly, elected by the same voters, voting in the same constituencies and by the same method of proportional representation. The provincial councils would be elected for three years and would be immune from earlier dissolution. The heads of the provincial executives would be administrators appointed by the Governor-General-in-Council (it was Merriman and de Villiers who had

---

[19] See above, pp. 188–91.   [20] *Minutes*, p. 13.
[21] Walton, pp. 209–10.   [22] Brand's manuscript, Annexure U.
[23] Walton, pp. 211–14; *Minutes*, pp. 90–92.

insisted on this). The administrators would preside over executive committees, comprising between three and five other members elected by the provincial councils by proportional representation, and would have both a deliberative and a casting vote in committee. Subject to the consent of the Governor-General-in-Council and unless and until Parliament decided otherwise, the provincial councils would be able to make ordinances on ten subjects, all of them somewhat trivial. Unless and until Parliament decided otherwise, the provincial governments would have powers of administration in the same ten fields and also in certain others, including 'education other than higher and technical education'. At first, and until Parliament provided otherwise, the provinces would be paid annual subsidies from the general revenue of the Union to the extent of their expenditure, as colonies, in the financial year 1908–9 on the services that were to be administered by them.

When Moor and his colleagues tried to press their views upon the convention after the November recess, therefore, they were confronted with a concerted plan which left no loophole for provincial autonomy. According to the governing sentence of Moor's motion a Provincial Legislature would be able to 'make laws in relation to matters coming within the classes of subjects hereinafter enumerated . . .'. Directly the debate was resumed on 24 November Merriman moved as an amendment the relevant section of the Smuts–Merriman plan, providing that an Administrator, with the advice and consent of the Provincial Council, would be able 'to exercise such powers of legislation or administration as shall be delegated or entrusted to him by the Parliament, and unless and until Parliament otherwise provides, such Provincial Council may make laws or ordinances in relation to matters coming within the following classes . . .'. The debate which followed was confused and heated. The Natal delegates were shocked that Merriman's amendment gave the provinces no protection against interference by Parliament, and they struggled desperately to prevent its adoption. Hyslop moved the deletion of the words 'unless and until Parliament otherwise provides', Morcom and others seized on the differences between the word 'reserved' in section (b) of the resolution of 15 October and the word 'delegated' in Merriman's amendment, and Greene protested that the amendment amounted to 'a breach of faith', but later he withdrew those words and apologized. Asked to explain the difference between 'reserved' and 'delegated', de Villiers said that any powers granted to the provincial councils in the Constitution would be 'reserved' powers, but that they would not be immune from parliamentary control unless the Constitution provided that they were only to be amended or repealed in a specified manner. Eventually Hull moved a new governing sentence, which stated that: 'Subject to the provisions of this Act the Administrator, with the advice and consent of the Provincial Council, may make ordinances in relation to matters coming within the following classes of subjects. . . .' This amendment, which left the main question open, was adopted without a division.[24]

The convention then proceeded to deal with the list of twenty subjects which Natal proposed to place within the legislative competence of the provinces, and it did so ruthlessly. Five were rejected in divisions in which the Natal delegates stood alone—the management and sale of public lands, trading and other licences, the supply and sale of intoxicating liquor, local police, and the affairs of Native tribes. Six were rejected without divisions being called—the amendment of the provincial constitutions, the incorporation of companies, property and civil rights, the administration of justice, the registration of titles to lands, and mining and forestry. One was withdrawn—land reserved for Natives. Four were adopted with amendments which severely limited their scope. The proposal that the provincial councils should be able to legislate for 'the borrowing of money on the sole credit of the Province' was qualified by the addition of the words, 'with the consent of the Governor-General-in-Council, and in accordance with regulations to be framed by Parliament'. The proposal that they should be able to legislate for the establishment of provincial offices and the appointment of provincial officers was qualified by the addition of the words, 'subject to the provisions of any law passed by Parliament regulating the conditions of appointment, tenure of office and superannuation of provincial officers'. The proposal that they should be able to legislate for 'local works and undertakings' was qualified by the addition of the words, 'within the Province, other than railways, harbours and such works as extend beyond the borders of the Province, and subject to the power of Parliament to declare any work a national work, and to provide for its construction by arrangement with Provincial Councils or otherwise'. And the proposal that they should be able to legislate 'generally [on] all matters of a merely local or private nature in the Province' was amended to read, 'generally [on] all matters which, in the opinion of the Governor-General-in-Council, are of a merely local or private nature in the Province'. Only four subjects were adopted by the convention substantially as moved by Natal—direct taxation, hospitals and charitable institutions, municipal and other local institutions, and fines and penalties for the enforcement of provincial ordinances. The convention also added two subjects to the list—markets

[24] *Minutes*, pp. 77–78; Malan, pp. 80–85; Walton, p. 215.

and pounds, and roads, ponts, and bridges, other than bridges connecting two provinces. Indeed, the legislative powers which the convention granted to the provincial councils on 24 and 25 November were closely similar to those in the Smuts–Merriman plan.[25]

As they watched the mutilation of their proposals the Natal delegates became disheartened. During the 24th Greene appealed to the convention to be considerate, explaining that otherwise it would be difficult to get the Constitution approved in Natal, and late on the 25th he handed in a written protest in which he said that the powers of the provincial councils had been limited to an extent that was contrary to the spirit of section (b) of the resolution of 15 October. That evening Malan recorded in his diary that 'there was a rumour that the Natal delegates were thinking of leaving the Conference'.[26]

Smuts was anxious to placate Natal and the next morning he proposed that the whole question of the powers of the provincial councils, including the resolutions already passed, should be referred to a committee, but Steyn opposed the re-opening of a decided question and Hertzog and Malan wished the subject to be fully debated in the convention before it was handled by a committee. The chairman ruled that Smuts's motion was unacceptable if any delegate objected and, Hertzog objecting, Smuts withdrew it. Merriman then proceeded to move the first section of the Smuts–Merriman plan of provincial government and in doing so he spoke of the plan as a whole. In particular he emphasized that the administrators should be appointed by the Union Government to be the active heads of the provincial executives; that the executive committees should resemble the executives of the Boer republics, by being elected by the provincial councils for definite periods, rather than cabinets of the British type; and that the financial relations between the Union Government and the provinces should be settled by the Union Government, with the provinces receiving subsidies from the Union Treasury in the interim. Every delegate who spoke in the ensuing debate was sympathetic to the general character of the plan. Smuts, giving his full support, repeated his earlier assertion that the Constitution would be original in principle, neither federal nor unitary—but it is doubtful whether he carried much conviction to the Natal delegates, who remained silent throughout the debate. Most of the discussion concerned the mode of appointment of the administrators. Fischer and Steyn were for as close an approximation to the republican model as possible and they reminded the convention that the republican presidents had been elected by popular vote. Stanford thought that the choice should be vested in the provincial councils. De Villiers suggested that they should be nominated by the provincial councils and appointed by the Union Government, but Hertzog pointed out that this would give rise to serious difficulties in the event of disagreement between the Union Government and a Provincial Council, and so did Malan, who was inclined to agree with Jagger that the Administrator should be a figurehead without real executive authority. Towards the end of the debate, however, Merriman reiterated his wish that the Administrator should be appointed by the Governor-General-in-Council to be the effective executive head of the province. This discussion cleared the air and on the 27th, when Smuts again moved that the whole matter should be referred to a committee, the convention agreed.[27]

The committee, consisting of de Villiers, Merriman, Jameson, Smuts, Farrar, Fischer, Hertzog, Greene, Hyslop, and Coghlan, had before it the Smuts–Merriman plan, the convention's resolution on the legislative powers of the provincial councils, and a notice of motion by Morcom comprising sections 104–9 of the Natal draft British South Africa Act, which set out a Constitution for the Natal Provincial Legislature. On 1 December the committee succeeded in producing a unanimous report, which was almost identical with the Smuts–Merriman plan as amended by the convention's resolution on the legislative powers of the councils, with the following exceptions. The legislative powers of the councils were to be increased by the omission of the qualification from the subsection on matters 'of a merely local or private nature', and by the addition of four new sub-sections—trade and entertainment licences, agriculture (subject to conditions to be defined by Parliament), fish and game preservation, and, much more significantly, education other than higher education. Moreover, in appointing an administrator the Governor-General-in-Council was as far as possible to give preference to residents of the province. New sections were inserted for the appointment of provincial auditors by the Governor-General-in-Council and empowering the Union Parliament to divide a province into two or more provinces on the petition of the provincial council. Pending the report of the finance committee and the selection of a Capital for the Union, no recommendations were made on the financing of the provinces or the sites of the provincial capitals.[28]

When the Transvaal advisers saw the report they urged Botha and Smuts to oppose the unqualified grant to the provinces of the power to

[27] *Minutes*, pp. 87–90; Malan, pp. 98–99; Walton, pp. 218–19.
[28] *Minutes*, pp. 90–93, 99–104.

legislate on matters 'of a merely local or private nature', because they feared that it would undermine the unitary principle, and Botha himself seems to have taken objection to the unqualified grant of power in the field of school education. Consequently, when the report was tabled on the morning of 2 December, Botha moved the adjournment and most of the day was spent in unofficial negotiations.[29]

The discussion of the report in the convention started on the afternoon of the 2nd and continued until 8 December.[30] Most of the committee's recommendations concerning the legislative powers of the provinces were adopted, but the sub-sections on licences and provincial officers were deleted, a new sub-section empowering Parliament to delegate additional legislative powers was inserted, the qualification empowering the Governor-General-in-Council to decide what matters were 'of a merely local or private nature' was reintroduced, and the educational sub-section was amended. This sub-section produced a long debate. All the other powers which were granted to the provinces were comparatively unimportant, but educational policy is liable to become the stuff of high politics in any country—the United Kingdom had been ridden with controversy on the subject in 1902—and especially in a country where the electorate is divided in language, race, and religion, as current events were showing very clearly in the Orange River Colony. The Orangia Unie delegates and the Natal delegates supported the committee's recommendation—the former because they wanted their own Education Act to remain in force and the latter because they feared that otherwise something like that Act would be imposed upon Natal. The Transvaal Progressives and the Cape Unionists, on the other hand, were loath to grant the power to the provinces, for they had looked to Union to lead to educational uniformity along the lines of Smuts's Transvaal Act. Botha said that he considered that education should come entirely under the Union, but that he was willing to leave it to the provinces for a limited period, and eventually the convention unanimously adopted his amendment, giving the provinces the power to legislate on 'Education, other than higher education, for a period of five years, and thereafter until Parliament otherwise provides.' The debate left Walton with the impression that there was an 'understanding between delegates both English and Dutch that Education should not be allowed to become contentious, that it should be regarded rather as a sacred duty and a thing apart from political passion'.[31] Malan, it is true, subscribed to that ideal and had

[29] *Minutes*, p. 104; Malan, pp. 100–3; Walton, p. 220; Brand's manuscript.
[30] *Minutes*, pp. 104–13, 115–16, 121; Malan, pp. 102–19; Walton, pp. 220–8.
[31] Ibid., p. 224.

reasoned that education should be left to the provinces as a means of keeping it outside party politics, but Smartt had shown greater insight in saying that to grant the power to the provinces would be to introduce party politics into the provincial councils. It could not reasonably be expected that education would be divorced from politics in such a country as South Africa.

The convention endorsed the rest of the committee's report with only five substantial amendments, three of which were concessions to Natal. Firstly, in response to the plea that the Natal Provincial Council would be too small to do its work efficiently if it contained no more members than represented Natal in the House of Assembly, the convention agreed that no Provincial Council should contain fewer than twenty-five members. This decision necessitated the second substantial amendment, making the Union Delimitation Commissions responsible for carrying out separate provincial council delimitations in the Orange River Colony and Natal—a considerable addition to their duties. Thirdly, the Administrator was deprived of his deliberative vote and left with only a casting vote in the Executive Committee. Fourthly, the section granting the provinces powers of administration in specified subjects over which they had no powers of legislation was deleted, since it had become attenuated by the transfer of school education to the legislative list. Finally, a new section was adopted, empowering the councils to appoint provincial officers and to make regulations for their organization and discipline, subject to parliamentary legislation.

There was a long discussion of the committee's recommendation that Parliament should be able to divide a province on the petition of the Provincial Council. It will be recalled that in several of his early constitutional plans Smuts had intended that the Cape Colony—and possibly the Transvaal also—should be divided into two or more provinces and that early in October the Transvaal delegates had favoured such a division. The terms of section (b) of the resolution of 15 October, however, had made that impossible.[32] The only delegate who regarded the question as important was Walton, who now proposed that Parliament should be able to divide a province if it received a petition from fifteen members of the Provincial Council—that is to say, from less than a third of the members in the case of the Cape Provincial Council. He was opposed by Sauer, who somewhat acidly remarked that Walton was 'the last representative of the political school which fifty years ago had wished to divide the Eastern and Western Provinces', and by Maasdorp and van Heerden, members of the Afrikaner community of the eastern Cape,

[32] See above, pp. 153, 158, 161, 162, 191.

which had never supported the separation movement.[33] The section was eventually carried in the form recommended by the committee.

There the question of the provincial constitutions rested until after the Christmas recess. Most of the amendments and insertions made on the recommendation of the drafting committee in January were merely verbal, but three were of some consequence. Insertions providing for the enrolment of provincial ordinances in precisely the same way as Acts of Parliament and stating that a provincial ordinance would be invalid in so far as it was repugnant to any Act of Parliament were approved by the convention without opposition. An amendment restoring to the Administrator a deliberative as well as a casting vote in the Executive Committee —it was Smuts who had insisted on this in the drafting committee notwithstanding the convention's decision to the contrary—was vigorously resisted by the Natal delegates and some of the Cape Colony delegates. On 19 January Hyslop pressed the issue to a division, to be defeated by seventeen votes to thirteen, with the Transvaal and Orange River Colony delegations voting solidly against him, and a week later van Heerden did so, to be defeated by nineteen votes to eleven. Meanwhile, on 20 January, Watt had tried to persuade the convention to include a statement that the Administrator would be bound to act with the advice and consent of the executive committee in exercising his powers in the fields in which a Provincial Council was competent to make ordinances. His proposal had then been defeated by twenty-two votes to seven, but on 28 January the convention yielded on this point.[34] On the same day the convention adopted, with minor amendments, a proposal of the finance committee that on the inauguration of the Union all the colonial revenues should accrue to the Central Government and that, pending the report of a commission of inquiry and a decision by Parliament, the provinces should receive annual subsidies from the Treasury to the extent of the sums voted in the colonial estimates for the financial year 1908–9 for education, other than higher education, with any additional sums that the Governor-General-in-Council might deem necessary.[35] There remained two more relevant decisions. On 29 January Jameson proposed that the sentiment of the Afrikaners of the Orange River Colony should be respected by restoring the name Orange Free State, Fitzpatrick supported him, and the proposal was unanimously adopted. Then on 2 February, when the convention had at last settled the question of the Capital of the

[33] Malan, pp. 114–19; Walton, pp. 226–8.
[34] Brand's manuscript, Annexures BB and CC; 'Remarks on Draft Constitution'; Minutes, pp. 178–83, 192–3, 218–19, 225–8, 234–5, 237, 293–8; Malan, pp. 176–9.
[35] Minutes, pp. 155–6, 163–5, 228; Walton, pp. 225–6.

Union, it decided that Cape Town, Pretoria, Bloemfontein, and Pieter-maritzburg, the four colonial capitals, should be the seats of the provincial governments.[36]

Accordingly, sections 68 and 69 of the convention's draft Constitution provided that the Governor-General-in-Council should appoint administrators in each province, giving preference to residents of the province, and that the administrators would hold office for five years, subject to dismissal by the Governor-General-in-Council for cause assigned. Sections 70–77 concerned the provincial councils. They would be elected by the parliamentary voters of the province. In a province with twenty-five or more members in the House of Assembly the council would contain the same number of members, elected in the same constituencies, while in a province with fewer representatives in the House of Assembly the council would contain twenty-five members, elected in constituencies specially delimited by the parliamentary delimitation commissions according to the same principles. The councils would have annual sessions and would continue for three years without earlier dissolution. They would elect their own chairmen, and they would make their own rules for the conduct of their proceedings subject to the veto of the Governor-General-in-Council. The disqualifications for membership of Parliament would apply to councillors, and if a councillor became a member of either House of Parliament his membership of the council would cease. Councillors would receive allowances fixed by the Governor-General-in- Council and they would enjoy freedom of speech in council and be immune from legal actions arising out of such speech. Sections 78–84 dealt with the provincial executive committees. They would consist of the Administrator, as chairman, and from three to five other members, 'as the Governor-General-in-Council may prescribe', who would be elected by the council, from among its own members or otherwise, at its first meeting after a general election. They would hold office for three years and would receive remuneration as determined by the council with the approval of the Governor-General-in-Council. The Administrator and any other member of the committee who was not a member of the council would have the right to speak but not to vote in the council. The committee would administer provincial affairs on behalf of the council and would be able to make rules for the conduct of its proceedings subject to the approval of the Governor-General-in-Council and to appoint public officers subject to the provisions of any Act of Parliament regulating their conditions of service, but the Administrator would have both a deliberative and a casting vote in the committee and

[36] *Minutes*, pp. 234, 245; Malan, pp. 208–9; Walton, pp. 224–5.

he would be able to act without reference to the committee when required to do so by the Governor-General-in-Council in fields in which no powers were vested in the council. The legislative powers of the provincial councils were set out in section 85:

Subject to the provisions of this Act and the assent of the Governor-General-in-Council as hereinafter provided, the Provincial Council may make ordinances in relation to matters coming within the following classes of subjects, that is to say:—

(i) Direct taxation within the Province in order to raise a revenue for provincial purposes.

(ii) The borrowing of money on the sole credit of the Province with the consent of the Governor-General-in-Council and in accordance with regulations to be framed by Parliament.

(iii) Education, other than higher education, for a period of five years and thereafter until Parliament otherwise provides.

(iv) Agriculture to the extent and subject to the conditions to be defined by Parliament.

(v) The establishment, maintenance and management of hospitals and charitable institutions.

(vi) Municipal institutions, divisional councils and other local institutions of a similar nature.

(vii) Local works and undertakings within the Province, other than railways, harbours and such works as extend beyond the borders of the Province and subject to the power of Parliament to declare any work a national work and to provide for its construction by arrangement with the Provincial Council or otherwise.

(viii) Roads, outspans, ponts and bridges, other than bridges connecting two Provinces.

(ix) Markets and pounds.

(x) Fish and game preservation.

(xi) The imposition of punishment by fine, penalty or imprisonment for enforcing any law or any ordinance of the Province made in relation to any matter coming within any of the classes of subjects enumerated in this section.

(xii) Generally all matters which in the opinion of the Governor-General-in-Council are of a merely local or private nature in the Province.

(xiii) All other subjects in respect of which Parliament shall delegate the power of making ordinances to the Provincial Council.

Section 90 provided that when a draft ordinance had been passed by a Provincial Council it was to be presented to the Governor-General-in-Council for his assent and that within a month he should declare that he gave his assent, or withheld his assent, or reserved it for further consideration, in which case it would have no effect unless the Governor-

General-in-Council gave his assent within a year. Section 91 provided that an ordinance assented to by the Governor-General-in-Council and promulgated by the Administrator would have the force of law within the province 'subject to the provisions of this Act', but under section 86 it would have no effect in so far as it was repugnant to any Act of Parliament. Sections 87 and 88 empowered a Provincial Council to recommend legislation to Parliament on subjects on which it was not competent to legislate and to take evidence and submit reports for private Acts of Parliament. Under section 89 no money was to be issued from the provincial fund except under an appropriation ordinance passed by the council on the recommendation of the Administrator and under a warrant signed by him, and under section 92 the warrant was to be counter-signed by a provincial auditor, appointed and removable by the Governor-General-in-Council. The last two sections of the provincial chapter of the draft Constitution provided for the continuation of powers vested in municipal and divisional councils and declared the seats of the provincial governments.[37] Sections 117 and 118 of the draft Constitution contained the financial arrangements which have been mentioned above, section 136 provided that the provincial councillors and the members of the executive committees of the provinces should be elected by proportional representation, and section 150 empowered parliament to alter the boundaries of a province or divide a province into two or more provinces on the petition of the provincial council of every province affected.[38]

These decisions accorded closely with the wishes of Merriman and de Villiers, who had persistently striven for a Constitution that would be unitary without qualification, had regarded Smuts's 'Suggested Scheme for South African Union', with its provincial cabinets, as perniciously federal, and had persuaded Smuts that the provincial executives should

[37] The numbers of the sections in the provincial chapter of the S.A. Act are the same as those in the convention's draft Constitution. The contents are virtually identical, except that an addition was made to s. 70 in Bloemfontein creating qualifications for members of provincial councils, s. 78 (1) was amended in Bloemfontein to fix the number of members of an executive committee at four besides the administrator, and verbal amendments were made to ss. 71 (3), 75, and 85 (vii) and (xiii). Note, too, that in Bloemfontein an addition was made to s. 64, providing that 'all Bills abolishing provincial councils or abridging the powers conferred on provincial councils under section eighty-five, otherwise than in accordance with the provisions of that section', were to be reserved for the King's pleasure. See below, p. 377.

[38] The numbers of the corresponding sections of the S.A. Act are 117, 118, 134, and 149. Ss. 117–18 of the S.A. Act are identical. S. 134 [136] was amended in Bloemfontein, where proportional representation was abandoned for the election of the members of the House of Assembly and provincial councils, but retained for the election of senators and members of the provincial executive committees (see below, p. 372). S. 149 [150] was verbally amended in England.

be headed by administrators appointed by the Governor-General-in-Council. The provinces were to be more strictly subordinated to the Union than Smuts had proposed in any of his pre-convention plans, and his concept of a middle course between federalism and unification had disappeared. Natal's hopes for 'unification with safeguards' had also been utterly defeated. The convention had not restrained Parliament from reducing the powers of the provinces nor, indeed, from overthrowing the entire provincial system by a bare majority.[39] The only significant concession was the grant of the power to legislate on primary and secondary education: but that power, like the other powers of the provincial councils, was limited by the veto of the Governor-General-in-Council, by the overriding power of Parliament, and by the extent of the financial resources which Parliament was to provide; while the qualification amounted to an invitation to Parliament to review the concession after five years.

Ideally, de Villiers had written in September 1908, local affairs should come under an Administrator appointed by the Central Government and a Provincial Council whose powers should be as limited as those of municipalities.[40] His ideal had been satisfied. There were to be no federal checks upon the supremacy of Parliament.

9. THE SUPREME COURT

In the judicial chapter of the Constitution the convention could either have left the existing courts as they were in composition and functions and created a new Appeal Court as a sort of coping-stone, or have scrapped the existing courts and created an entirely new, more logical, and more economical judicial structure for South Africa, or have devised some synthesis between the two extremes. It was a question of federalism *versus* unification in the judicial field.

The existing superior courts consisted of a Supreme Court in each of the self-governing colonies, exercising original jurisdiction in civil and criminal cases which were beyond the competence of the magistrates' courts as well as appellate jurisdiction from the magistrates' courts. From these colonial supreme courts appeals lay to the Judicial Committee of the Privy Council in England in civil cases where the sum in dispute exceeded £500 (or £2,000 in the case of the Transvaal) and in other cases only with special leave. The Supreme Court proper of the Cape Colony sat in Cape Town and there were also two local superior courts, the

[39] See also s. 12 of this chapter, dealing with constitutional amendment.
[40] See above, p. 156.

Eastern Districts Court at Grahamstown and the High Court of Griqualand West at Kimberley, which exercised concurrent jurisdiction in their
areas, but appeals from which, as from the High Court of Southern
Rhodesia, went to Cape Town. The Supreme Court of the Transvaal sat
in Pretoria and one of its judges presided over a high court on the Witwatersrand, from which appeals went to Pretoria. The supreme courts of
Natal and the Orange River Colony[41] sat in Pietermaritzburg and Bloemfontein respectively. There were strong Bars in Cape Town and Pretoria
and somewhat weaker Bars in Pietermaritzburg, Bloemfontein, Grahamstown, Kimberley, and Johannesburg; and whereas no division existed
between advocates and attorneys in Natal there was a clear-cut division
between the two branches in the other three colonies.

In these circumstances what may be called the 'federal' solution had
obvious attractions. If the existing courts were left with their constitutions and functions untouched and a South African Appeal Court was
created to replace the Judicial Committee of the Privy Council as the
normal ultimate court of appeal, national sentiment would be satisfied
and the vested interests of judges, advocates, and attorneys would not be
dislocated. On the other hand, a solution of that sort would be uneco-
mical and the new Appeal Court might become a white elephant, since
very few cases were being sent to the Privy Council from South Africa.

The President of the convention, as the doyen of the South African
bench, naturally took the lead in this matter and he proved to be a
federalist in this field, notwithstanding his otherwise strongly unitary
views. The scheme he placed before the convention on 4 November was
essentially 'federal'.[42] Its principal features were as follows: The existing
superior courts would remain unchanged in composition and functions,
though their judges would become officers of the Union. In addition,
a new Supreme Court of South Africa would be created, consisting of a
Chief Justice, two ordinary judges, the chief justices of the four provinces, and the Judge President of the Eastern Districts Court. It would
have original jurisdiction in eight matters (including matters 'arising
under this Act') and appellate jurisdiction from the provincial courts in
all cases in which appeals were previously allowed to the Privy Council
(with the lowest limit for such appeals reduced to £250) and in other
cases by special leave. There would be no appeals from the Supreme
Court of South Africa to the Privy Council except by special leave of the

---

[41] The correct designation of the Orange River Colony Court was the High Court of
the Orange River Colony, but since it corresponded in status with the supreme courts of
the other three colonies it has been described in the text as a supreme court, to avoid
confusion with the high courts at Kimberley and Johannesburg.

[42] *Minutes*, pp. 62–63.

council and the Union Parliament would be able to make laws limiting the matters in which special leave might be asked, Bills containing any such limitations being reserved for His Majesty's pleasure.

When these proposals were debated the next day, Malan propounded the 'unitary' solution—the abolition of the existing superior courts and their replacement by a single South African Supreme Court, comprising provincial divisions of one or more judges and an Appellate Division, with appeals going direct to the appellate division from any superior court. Merriman, as was to be expected, supported Malan on grounds of economy, but Morcom and Hertzog said that Natal and the Orange River Colony preferred de Villiers's proposals. The question was then referred to a committee, consisting of de Villiers, Merriman, Sauer, Greene, Morcom, Smuts, Lindsay, Fischer, Hertzog, and Coghlan.[43]

Before the committee prepared its report, the Transvaal delegation's legal advisers scrutinized de Villiers's plan and de Villiers consulted several other judges. Lucas, de Wet, and Duncan advised the Transvaal delegates that de Villiers's plan should be modified in two respects: the new Supreme Court should have scarcely any original jurisdiction, and it should consist exclusively of full-time members, rather than include men who would be almost fully occupied as the chief justices of the provincial courts.[44] On 30 November Rose Innes, the Chief Justice of the Transvaal, and W. H. Solomon, his ablest colleague, handed de Villiers a memorandum in which they strongly advocated the 'unitary' solution. They recommended the abolition of all the existing superior courts and their replacement by a single Supreme Court of South Africa, with divisions in each of the provinces and a distinct and separate appellate division, composed of from four to six full-time appeal judges, to hear appeals direct from every other superior court.[45] On the other hand, J. W. Wessels, another member of the Transvaal bench, advised Smuts to leave the existing courts as they were and not to create a full-time appeal court if there would not be enough work to justify its existence, but rather to appoint a Chief Justice of South Africa and empower him to call on the services of provincial judges when cases came on appeal.[46]

The committee succeeded in working out a practicable synthesis between de Villiers's original plan and the ideas of Innes and Solomon and the Transvaal legal advisers, and its report became the basis of the judicial chapter of the convention's draft Constitution, though it was amended and amplified by the convention on 8 December and again, on

[43] *Minutes*, p. 70; Malan, pp. 74–77; Walton, p. 202.
[44] Brand's manuscript, Annexure W.
[45] De Villiers Papers.   [46] 7 Dec. 1908, Smuts Papers.

the advice of the drafting committee, on 20 January, while several verbal amendments were made at the suggestion of the legal advisers on 28, 29, and 30 January.[47] The result was that the judicial chapter of the convention's draft Constitution provided for the creation of a single Supreme Court of South Africa, comprising an Appellate Division, provincial divisions, and local divisions. The Appellate Division was to consist of a Chief Justice of South Africa, two ordinary judges of appeal, and two additional judges of appeal temporarily assigned from the provincial divisions as required. The colonial supreme courts were to become the provincial divisions of the Supreme Court of South Africa and the other superior courts were to become local divisions. The provincial and local divisions would continue to exercise their established original jurisdictions and in addition they would have jurisdiction in matters in which the Union Government was a party, matters in which the validity of a provincial ordinance was questioned, and electoral matters. The established rights of all existing judges were protected. The Chief Justice of South Africa, the two ordinary judges of appeal, and all other judges appointed to any division of the Supreme Court after Union would be appointed by the Governor-General-in-Council. Their salaries would be fixed by Parliament and they were not to be diminished during their continuance in office. No judge was to be removed from office 'except by the Governor-General-in-Council, on an address from both Houses of Parliament in the same session praying for such removal on the ground of misbehaviour or incapacity'. When vacancies occurred in any division of the Supreme Court other than the Appellate Division, if the Governor-General-in-Council considered that the number of judges might be reduced with advantage to the public interest, he would be able to postpone filling the vacancy until Parliament decided whether the reduction should take place. All appeals which would previously have gone to the Supreme Court of any of the colonies from a superior court, including the High Court of Southern Rhodesia, would go direct to the Appellate Division; and so would all appeals which would previously have gone to the Privy Council from the Supreme Court of any of the colonies, but the right to appeal from the provincial divisions in civil suits would no longer be limited by the amount of money in dispute. Appeals which would previously have gone to a superior court from an inferior court in any of the colonies would go to the corresponding division of the Supreme Court and in such cases there would be no further appeal except to the Appellate Division, and then only with its special leave. No appeals would be

47 *Minutes*, pp. 117–23, 184–6, 226–7, 233–7, 298–302; Malan, pp. 118–21, 178–83, 204–5; Walton, pp. 202–5; 'Remarks on Draft Constitution'; Brand's manuscript.

allowed from South Africa to the Privy Council except by special leave of the council and Parliament would be able to make new laws limiting the matters in which special leave might be asked, such Bills being reserved for His Majesty's pleasure. The three permanent members of the Appellate Division would be able to make rules for the conduct of its proceedings and prescribing the time and manner of making appeals, subject to the approval of the Governor-General-in-Council; and the judges of the provincial divisions would be able to make rules for the conduct of their proceedings, subject to the approval of the Governor-General-in-Council in consultation with the Chief Justice of South Africa. The Appellate Division quorum was fixed at five judges for the hearing of appeals from courts of two or more judges and three judges for the hearing of appeals from a single judge. Provision was made for the execution of the processes of the Appellate Division and the provincial divisions throughout South Africa, for the transfer of suits from one provincial division to another, for the appointment by the Governor-General-in-Council of a registrar and other officers of the Appellate Division, and for the removal of suits pending at the establishment of the Union to the corresponding divisions of the Supreme Court. The established rights of advocates and attorneys were recognized and all advocates and attorneys entitled to practise before any provincial division were to be entitled to practise before the Appellate Division.[48] Furthermore, section 140 in the general chapter of the convention's draft Constitution provided that the administration of justice throughout the Union should be under the control of a Cabinet Minister and that in each province an Attorney-General, appointed by the Governor-General-in-Council, would be responsible for criminal prosecutions.[49]

In general the scheme was sound. Some delegates had hoped for more radical changes for the sake of economy, but when Maasdoorp gave expression to their point of view on 20 January Smuts was able to show that the scheme provided a sure means of gradually reducing the number of judges in South Africa, if that was thought necessary, without affecting the established rights of existing judges.[50] The important section on the tenure of office by judges—section 101—was similar to the corresponding sections of the Australian and Transvaal constitutions.[51] The

[48] The sections in the judicial chapter of the convention's draft Constitution were numbered 95–116. The corresponding sections of the S.A. Act have the same numbers, but include a considerable number of amendments, made in Bloemfontein and in England. See below, pp. 379–80, 410–11.

[49] S. 139 of the S.A. Act, which also includes a proviso inserted in Bloemfontein.

[50] Malan, pp. 178–83.

[51] Nevertheless, while s. 72 (ii) of the Australian Constitution and s. 48 (ii) of the

only section which was seriously contested was that restricting appeals to the Privy Council. Merriman warmly approved of it but, mindful of the attempt which had been made by the Unionist Government to upset the corresponding section of the draft Australian Constitution, he warned the convention that it might arouse opposition in the British Parliament. Nevertheless, the convention was satisfied when Malan pointed out that the British Government had eventually yielded in the case of Australia and that the draft section was modelled on the relevant part of the corresponding section of the Australian Constitution as enacted. Consequently, Smartt's motion for the deletion of the words empowering the Union Parliament to limit the matters in which special leave to appeal might be asked met with little support and was negatived without a division.[52] There were, however, a number of defective details in the judicial chapter which were to give rise to criticisms when the draft Constitution was published.

10. THE CIVIL SERVICE

A number of questions were involved in the preparation of the civil service sections of the Constitution. To what extent should the provincial services be distinct and separate from the Union service? How should the initial reorganization be effected on the establishment of the Union? Should the Constitution give public servants some protection against arbitrary action by the Government of the day, and if so, what protection?

These questions were controversial. There were wide differences between the salaries and conditions of service which prevailed in the civil services of the four colonies, those in the Transvaal being the most attractive.[53] There were, too, differences of outlook on racial and party lines. Whereas the services of the Cape Colony and Natal were generally regarded, at least by the Europeans, as being non-partisan, Milner had started new services in the Transvaal and the Orange River Colony from scratch after the conquest of the republics and manned them largely with

Transvaal Constitution provided that a judge should only be removed by the Governor-General- (or Governor-) in-Council on an address from both Houses 'praying for such removal on the ground of proved misbehaviour or incapacity', the word 'proved' does not occur in the South African section.

[52] *Minutes*, p. 123 ; Malan, pp. 120–1 ; Walton, p. 204. Compare s. 106 of the S.A. Act with s. 74 of the Australian Constitution. For the attempt by the Unionist Government to amend the Australian section, see below, p. 388, n. 88.

[53] The Transvaal public service had recently been placed on an improved footing by Act 19 of 1908, while the Cape Colony and Natal services were still regulated by earlier and less adequate legislation—Cape Act 32 of 1895 and Natal Act 21 of 1894.

youngish, imported men, who were still regarded by many Afrikaners as agents of British imperialism. The Botha and Fischer governments had moved cautiously in the matter since they came into power, but there had been a number of retirements and appointments which had led the Oppositions to accuse them of partiality. In these circumstances most of the Afrikaner delegates wished to give the Union Government a free hand in the matter, subject to its responsibility to Parliament, while most of the British delegates wanted the Constitution to include guarantees for the established rights of the members of the existing colonial services and strong precautions against partisan appointments and dismissals— precautions which are not normally included in Constitutions.[54]

The way to a radical solution of the problem was paved on 3 and 4 December, when, dealing with the report of the committee on the provincial constitutions, the convention refrained from giving the provincial councils any powers of legislation on the subject of provincial services, and only empowered the councils to appoint provincial officers and to make and enforce regulations for their organization and discipline 'subject to the provisions of any law passed by Parliament regulating the conditions of appointment, tenure of office, retirement and superannuation of public officers'.[55] The next step was taken on the 10th, when the convention appointed a committee, consisting of Merriman, Jameson, Morcom, Smythe, Smuts, Fitzpatrick, Steyn, Hertzog, and Michell, to draft resolutions on the civil service and other matters.[56] Resolutions drafted by Duncan and Brand[57] formed the basis of the committee's report, which recommended as follows:[58] On the establishment of the Union all the civil servants of the four colonies should become officers of the Union and as soon as possible after the passing of the Act of Union the Governor-General-in-Council should appoint a public service commission to make recommendations for the reorganization of the service and for the transfer to the provinces of the officers necessary for the fulfilment of their responsibilities. Later, a permanent public service commission should be appointed by the Governor-General-in-Council to make recommendations for appointments and retirements, subject to parliamentary legislation. All the existing civil servants of the four colonies should remain entitled to the pensions, gratuities, and other benefits provided for under colonial laws, whether they were retained in the public service or not, and no existing officer's services should be dispensed

[54] B. Beinart, 'The Legal Relationship between the Government and its Employees', *Butterworths S.A. Law Review, 1955*, pp. 21–72.
[55] *Minutes*, pp. 101, 110, 113.
[56] Ibid., p. 125.
[57] Brand's manuscript, Annexure Z.   [58] *Minutes*, p. 127.

with 'by reason solely of his want of knowledge of either the English or Dutch language'.

It had possibly been the intention of Duncan, who had drafted the relevant proposal for Smuts, that the first public service commission should complete its work before the day appointed for the inauguration of the Union, so that when the first government took office it would have the commission's report to guide it in the reorganization of the departments. His proposal had started with the injunction that 'As soon as possible after the passing of the Act of Union the Governor-General-in-Council' should appoint a public service commission to make recommendations for the initial reorganization, and similar words appeared in the report of the civil service committee in December and the first report of the drafting committee in January.[59] But the words were ambiguous because there would be an interval between the enactment of the Constitution and the inauguration of the Union—and with it the coming into being of a Governor-General-in-Council. Some amendment was therefore desirable, if only in the interests of clarity. Either the colonial Governors-in-Council could have been authorized to appoint the first public service commission, like the first delimitation commission, any time after the British Parliament passed the South Africa Act, or the Governor-General-in-Council could have been authorized to appoint it 'as soon as possible after the establishment of the Union'. Eventually, the convention decided on the latter course and it also empowered the Governor-General-in-Council to 'place at the disposal of the provinces the services of such officers of the Union as may be necessary' pending the completion of the commission's report. Consequently, sections 141 and 142 of the convention's draft Constitution provided that on Union Day all the servants of the four colonies were to become Union civil servants, and that the Governor-General-in-Council would be able to place the services of the necessary officers at the disposal of the provinces. As soon as possible thereafter, the Governor-General-in-Council was to appoint a public service commission to make recommendations for the reorganization of the departments and the assignment of officers to the provinces, and when it had reported he would be able to make such assignments, and such officers would become 'officers of the province'.[60] Since the reorganization of the departments could not possibly be delayed once the Union was inaugurated, this was a clumsy scheme, conducive to administrative confusion on Union Day. It would have been

[59] Brand's manuscript, Annexure Z; *Minutes*, pp. 127, 306–7.
[60] Ibid., pp. 191–3, 227, 230–3; Malan, pp. 184–5; Walton, pp. 284–92. The corresponding sections of the S.A. Act are numbered 140 and 141 and are otherwise identical.

better to have provided that the first public service commission, like the first delimitation commission, should be appointed well in advance of the inauguration of the Union.

In discussing the report of the committee on 15 and 16 December, the convention concerned itself mainly with the question of the powers to be granted to the permanent civil service commission. A similar question had been debated at length in the Transvaal Parliament as recently as July 1908, when Smuts, as minister in charge of the Public Service and Pensions Bill, had resisted the strenuous efforts of the Opposition to give independent powers to the civil service board which the Bill was to establish.[61] Duncan's draft resolutions on the subject included the proposal that the Union Government should normally act on the advice of the commission in making appointments and causing retirements and that it should be obliged to give Parliament its reasons in writing for any failure to do so.[62] That proposal was not included in the committee's report, but on 15 December Walton moved it as an amendment in the convention, which rejected it by twenty votes to nine, the minority consisting entirely of British delegates. Sauer, Smuts, de Villiers, and Merriman all explained that they were anxious not to derogate from the powers and responsibilities of the Union Government and Parliament, and de la Rey bluntly said that the Government should be given a completely free hand in the matter. The outcome was that the convention watered down the committee's recommendation and section 143 of the draft Constitution merely stated that after the establishment of the Union the Governor-General-in-Council was to appoint a permanent civil service commission, 'with such powers and duties relating to the appointment, discipline, retirement, and superannuation of public officers as Parliament shall determine'.[63] So the South African Constitution, like other constitutions, set no legal checks on the authority of the Government over the public service. The permanent commission might develop into an impartial and effective body, or the spoils system might take root: everything would depend upon the conduct of South African governments.

Sections 144–6 of the convention's draft Constitution followed the recommendations of the committee and provided for the continued validity of the retirement benefits due to the civil servants of the four colonies under the existing laws and regulations, and assured them that they would not be dismissed for any ignorance of English or Dutch, now

[61] *Transvaal Leg. Ass. Deb., 1908*, cols. 905–6, 1093.

[62] Brand's manuscript, Annexure Z.

[63] *Minutes*, pp. 129–32, 307; Malan, pp. 134–9; Walton, pp. 284–92. The corresponding section of the S.A. Act is numbered 142 and is otherwise identical.

that they were to serve a State which was officially bilingual. Section 147 was added on the suggestion of Greene to ensure that the Union Parliament should make some provision for the parliamentary officers of the colonies where necessary.[64]

11. RHODESIA AND THE HIGH COMMISSION TERRITORIES

Among white South Africans there was a general expectation that the Union would in due course expand and incorporate many of the less developed territories in southern and central Africa. Rhodes had dreamed of a self-governing British dominion stretching from the Cape to the Zambesi and beyond; Kruger had desired a greatly enlarged South African Republic; and now Botha and Smuts believed that the Union would become the heir to both traditions. The convention could do nothing about South-west Africa, which was a German protectorate, or Mozambique, which was a Portuguese colony, but since the Constitution would be enacted by the British Parliament it could include provisions to ease the way for the subsequent incorporation of African territories under British influence or control, in much the same way as the British North America Act had included provisions for the admission of other British colonies to the Dominion of Canada. Such territories fell into two main groups—Southern Rhodesia, North-western Rhodesia, and North-eastern Rhodesia, which were administered by the British South Africa Company under its royal charter of 1889; and Basutoland, Bechuanaland Protectorate, and Swaziland, which were administered by the British High Commissioner for South Africa.[65]

The attitude of the Southern Rhodesian settlers towards the closer union movement was similar to the attitude of the British colonists in Natal, for they, too, were a British community vastly outnumbered by Bantu-speaking Africans, they, too, had recently experienced an African rebellion, and they, too, were witnessing the Afrikaner revival with some misgivings. Unlike the British people of Natal, however, they were able for the present to remain aloof from the Union and they proposed to watch the evolution of its policy before they committed themselves to joining it. If it became British in orientation, they would probably be willing to join when they were strong enough to do so without merely becoming absorbed, but if not they might decide to remain on their own, or to associate themselves with the territories to their north. The directors

---

[64] *Minutes*, pp. 132, 193, 227, 307. The corresponding sections of the S.A. Act are numbered 143–6 and are otherwise identical, except for a verbal change in section 144 [145].   [65] See above, pp. 49–51.

of the British South Africa Company would perhaps have liked to have freed themselves from the Southern Rhodesian imbroglio with profit to their shareholders by selling most of their rights there to the self-governing colonies, and if Rhodes had been alive it is possible that he would have negotiated with the convention to that end. But the settlers would have opposed it, for it would have been tantamount to selling the country which they regarded as theirs above their heads, and so would many of the delegates. At one time Merriman had suspected that such a deal was contemplated. In fact, however, the company's policy towards the union movement was much the same as the policy of the settlers. Milton, the Administrator, in his speech opening the 1908 session of the Legisative Council on 15 June, had defined Southern Rhodesia's attitude towards the National Convention as one of 'detachment' and 'sympathy' and expressed the hope that 'when the development of Southern Rhodesia is sufficiently advanced, it will take its rightful place as a member of the Union'.[66] That statement was satisfactory to the settlers and also to the colonial premiers who, it will be recalled, had invited Southern Rhodesia to send delegates to the convention, with the right to speak but without the right to vote.[67]

The result was that the Rhodesian question was not a contentious one in the convention and, since the delegates had many more pressing questions to engross their attention, it led to scarcely any discussion. Malan did not refer to it in his diary, nor did Walton in his book, and even Michell, Rhodesian delegate though he was, said nothing of it in his unpublished Reminiscences.[68] The *Minutes* show, however, that the committee which was appointed on 10 December to draft resolutions concerning the civil service was also instructed to deal with 'New Provinces', and that in reporting on 14 December it recommended under this head that the Union Parliament should be empowered to admit 'new Provinces or Territories' into the Union and to 'make or agree to such terms and conditions, including the extent of representation in either House of Parliament, as it thinks fit'. Two days later the convention referred the question to its Native affairs committee, comprising de Villiers, the four prime ministers, Stanford, and Michell, who drafted a resolution based on section 146 of the British North America Act. The convention agreed on 17 December, and in January it inserted additional words to make it quite clear that the section applied to the Rhodesias.

[66] *S.R. Leg. Co. Deb.*, 1st Sess., 4th Co., p. 1. Throughout the ensuing session, which ended on 3 July 1908, there was no further reference to the forthcoming National Convention.   [67] See above, pp. 150–1.

[68] Michell Papers, No. 28.

Thus section 151 of the convention's draft Constitution provided that, on receipt of addresses from both Houses of the Union Parliament, the King-in-Council would be able to admit into the Union any additional colonies and territories, 'including the Territories administered by the British South Africa Company', on conditions set out in the addresses and approved by the King, and that the provisions of an Order-in-Council giving effect to such a decision would have the force of law, as if they had been enacted by the British Parliament.[69]

This section was not intended, however, to apply to the three non-self-governing territories which were administered by the British High Commissioner for South Africa—Basutoland, Bechuanaland Protectorate, and Swaziland. They were dealt with in a separate section and a schedule, which were the product of negotiations of a diplomatic character between the High Commissioner and the convention.

It will be recalled that the future of these territories had already been the subject of considerable thought and discussion in England and in South Africa before the convention met. During September Smuts had been informed by Sir Richard Solomon, the Transvaal Agent-General in London, that the British Government was unwilling for them to be transferred at once, particularly if there was to be a political colour-bar in the South African Constitution. Solomon had therefore advised him to make provision in the Constitution for their subsequent transfer by order-in-council and to include a statement of the conditions under which the Union Government would administer them, so that transfer could take place at any time by agreement between the two governments without further reference to the British Parliament.[70]

During September and October Lord Selborne and the other South African governors had been giving attention to the question of the conditions of transfer in consultation with men like Stanford,[71] who were experienced Native administrators, and on 20 October, in writing to de Villiers mainly on the franchise question, Selborne added a statement concerning the protectorates. The British Government, he said, had 'obligations of the greatest possible weight' to the Native tribes of Basutoland and the Bechuanaland Protectorate, who had voluntarily come under the domain of Queen Victoria and been the loyal subjects of the British Crown ever since, and although the history of the British connexion with

[69] *Minutes*, pp. 125, 127–8, 132, 150, 238, 308, 340; Greene's 'Remarks on Draft Constitution'. Cf. s. 146 of the B.N.A. Act. S. 150 of the S.A. Act is identical, except that in England the scope of the section was limited to 'the territories administered by the British South Africa Company'.

[70] See above, pp. 124–6.   [71] Stanford's Diary, 23–26 Sept. 1908.

Swaziland was different, the British obligations to the Native tribes of Swaziland were different only in degree. It was certain, he continued, that those tribes would be unwilling to be transferred to the Union and that their transfer would be opposed both in England and in South Africa. Nevertheless, he considered that 'there is no doubt that it is to the permanent interest of those tribes and of the Imperial Government, no less than the South African Government, that that transfer should take place'. He therefore proposed a solution along the lines which Solomon had sketched out for Smuts. The Constitution should empower the British Government to transfer the protectorates to the Union on conditions to be embodied in the Constitution and consistent with the obligations of the British Government.[72]

Replying on 21 October, de Villiers dealt exclusively with the franchise, but four days later he and Selborne met for a long discussion on the protectorates and on the 26th Selborne sent de Villiers a memorandum indicating the line of action which he proposed the convention should take. Basutoland, Bechuanaland Protectorate, and Swaziland could not be included in the Union at the outset, but their transfer might take place later at the discretion of the Secretary of State. The Constitution should include a section empowering the Governor-General-in-Council to take them over, singly or jointly, and it should also include a list of the conditions under which they would be administered after their transfer. The most important of these conditions would be that Native land would be inalienable, the sale of intoxicating liquor would be prohibited, the territories would receive their due share of the Union custom duties, the Basutoland National Council would be maintained, the territories would be administered by commissioners appointed by the Governor-General-in-Council and removable only by resolutions of both Houses of the Union Parliament, and legislation for the territories would take the form of proclamations issued by the Governor-General-in-Council on the advice of the same commissioners.[73]

Soon afterwards Selborne and Nathan put these proposals to the prime ministers and Smuts. Their reactions were adverse. They seem to have expected that the Union would be given *carte blanche* to deal with the territories as it wished after transfer had taken place. Merriman, Fischer, Botha, and Smuts, who were sounded out by Selborne, all told him that they would prefer that the protectorates should be included in the Union at once. Merriman went on to inquire what the reasons were for the delay. Fischer said that at least the date of transfer should be agreed

[72] House of Assembly, National Convention Minutes, V.
[73] Selborne to de Villiers, 26 Oct. 1908, de Villiers Papers.

upon. Otherwise he considered that conditions should not be included in the Constitution, because their publication would lead to bargaining by the Natives and their friends for better conditions. But Botha and Smuts, while reserving their right to try and persuade His Majesty's Government to allow immediate transfer, agreed that in any event the conditions of transfer should be settled at once and embodied in the Constitution. Moor, on the other hand, when interviewed by Nathan, did not argue for immediate transfer. He said that the Constitution should make no reference to the protectorates, on the grounds that any attempt to deal with the subject would increase the difficulties of the convention and that the publication of the conditions would cause anxiety among the Native inhabitants of the protectorates. As regards the actual conditions which Selborne had mentioned, Merriman, Fischer, Botha, and Smuts all strongly objected to the implication that the proposed commission should have powers independent of the South African Government and they insisted that this could not be tolerated. They accepted the principles in the other proposed conditions, with reservations in detail on particular points. For example, Fischer thought that there should be some qualification added to the land section to empower the South African Government to transfer tribes from one area to another with their consent, and both Fischer and Merriman thought that the territories' shares of the customs revenue should be calculated by some rule to avoid complex book-keeping. Moor told Nathan that he regarded the conditions as fair and proper in themselves, except that he thought there should be some provision for using parts of Bechuanaland Protectorate to relieve the congestion in the Native reserves in other parts of South Africa.[74]

There the matter rested until 29 November, when de Villiers discussed it with the four prime ministers, and the next day he was able to report to the High Commissioner that Merriman, Fischer, and Botha were now willing to accept all the principles embodied in his memorandum, save as to the composition and powers of the proposed commission, which they still thought should be merely an advisory body, analogous to the Council for India, and consisting of members appointed for ten-year terms. They also thought that 'the transfer of the Protectorates, if made at all, should be made as soon as possible after Union'. Moor, on the other hand, was still of the opinion that the convention had no mandate

---

[74] Nathan to Moor, 3 Nov. 1908 (informing him of the substance of his report to Selborne of Moor's views) (copy); Selborne to de Villiers, 17 Nov. 1908 (enclosing typed memoranda, being Selborne's notes of his interviews with Fischer (1 Nov.) and Merriman (3 Nov.), and explaining the views of Botha and Smuts). De Villiers Papers.

to deal with the subject, but if some decision had to be come to he would agree with the other three prime ministers.[75] Replying on 5 December, Selborne went some way to meet the views of the prime ministers. He suggested that after their transfer the protectorates should be administered by the Prime Minister of the Union with the assistance of three commissioners, whom he should be obliged to consult and to supply with all relevant papers, but that in the event of a disagreement, while the commissioners should be entitled to have their views made known to Parliament, the Governor-General-in-Council should have the last word. Selborne said, however, that he considered that the commissioners should hold office for longer than the ten years proposed by the prime ministers.[76]

On the morning of 10 December Selborne conferred with de Villiers and the prime ministers and that afternoon the question came before the convention for the first time, when de Villiers, the four prime ministers, Stanford, and Michell were appointed as a committee to prepare resolutions on the subject.[77] The committee met the next day and drew up a number of draft resolutions which de Villiers forwarded to Selborne, who replied suggesting a number of amendments and additions, most of which the committee then adopted. The revised report was then sent back to Selborne, who accepted it as satisfactory, on the understanding that the Secretary of State would still have the opportunity to propose modifications on matters of detail.[78]

The committee's report was submitted to the convention on 17 December. It recommended as follows: A section should be included in the Constitution to empower the King, with the advice of the Privy Council, on addresses from both Houses of the Union Parliament, to transfer to the Union 'any territory under the protectorate of His Majesty, inhabited wholly or in part by natives', whereupon the Governor-General-in-Council would be able to govern the territory on the terms and conditions embodied in the schedule to the Constitution. The draft schedule provided that after a territory had been transferred the Governor-General-in-Council would have the power to legislate for it by proclamation, subject to the right of the Union Parliament to pass a resolution repealing any such proclamation. The Prime Minister would be responsible for the administration of the territory and he would be assisted by a commission of not less than three members and a secretary. It would be the duty of the secretary to carry out the recommendations of the com-

[75] De Villiers to Selborne, 30 Nov. 1908, de Villiers Papers (copy).
[76] Ibid.   [77] *Minutes*, p. 125.
[78] De Villiers to Selborne, 12 and 15 Dec. 1908 (copies); Selborne to de Villiers, n.d. and 15 Dec. 1908. De Villiers Papers.

mission when they had been approved by the Prime Minister. The commissioners would be appointed by the Governor-General-in-Council for ten years and they would be eligible for reappointment for further periods of five years. They would be paid fixed salaries and would only be removable by the Governor-General-in-Council on addresses from both Houses of Parliament. The Prime Minister would preside at meetings of the commission, but he would only have a casting vote. The commissioners would have access to all relevant papers and the Prime Minister would be obliged to consult them before taking any administrative or legislative decision concerning the territory, other than a routine decision, except that in cases of urgency he would be able to act independently. In the event of a disagreement between the Prime Minister and the commission, the commission would be entitled to record its views and have them laid before the Governor-General-in-Council, whose decision would be final, but if the Governor-General-in-Council did not accept the commission's advice its views would be brought to the notice of Parliament, unless the Governor-General-in-Council was of the opinion that publication would be gravely detrimental to the public interest. A Resident Commissioner would be appointed by the Governor-General-in-Council and his duties would include the preparation of the annual estimates for the territory, which would continue to receive its due share of the Union customs revenue, calculated on the basis of its proportion of the total in the three years preceding the establishment of the Union. All the revenues of the territory were to be expended within it and special duties were not to be levied on its produce, while the Union Government was to make good any annual deficit. No land in Basutoland, nor in the Native reserves of Bechuanaland Protectorate and Swaziland, was to be alienated from the Native tribes and no liquor was to be sold to the Natives in the territories. The custom of holding Native assemblies was to be maintained where it existed. There was to be free intercourse for all the inhabitants of the territory with the rest of the Union, 'subject to the ordinary laws, including the pass laws of the Union'. The King would be able to disallow any proclamation for a territory. The commissioners' salaries and pensions would be chargeable to the territories and the rights of civil servants employed in the protectorates, as existing on 16 December 1908, would remain in force. Appeals from the courts of the territory would go to the Appellate Division of the Supreme Court of South Africa. And, finally, annual reports on the territory would be laid before the Union Parliament.[79]

The convention debated the principle of this report at considerable

[79] *Minutes*, pp. 134–8.

length. The two delegates who were members of the Natal Government, embroiled as they were with the Imperial Government on the question of the payment of Dinizulu's salary, were highly critical. Moor said that he was still wholly opposed to laying down conditions and that the delegates had no authority to deal with the question, and Greene indulged in polemics against 'British interference'. Hyslop, too, contended that it was unnecessary to lay down conditions at that stage and so did Fitzpatrick and Smartt. Underlying these objections there was a sense of humiliation at Britain's unwillingness to trust white South Africa to do justice to the Natives of the territories. Hertzog also opposed the principle of the report, but for different reasons. He said that it was undesirable to make any provision for the transfer of the protectorates. They were white elephants and if the Union took them over Britain would recall her troops, leaving South Africa with higher defence costs and the possibility of Native risings which she might be unable to quell. He also denied that the transfer of the protectorates would eliminate the imperial factor from South Africa, because, he said, the British Government would see to it that the conditions were enforced after transfer had been effected. But only a minority of the delegates attacked the principle of the report. It was defended by de Villiers, Merriman, Fischer, Botha, Smuts, Steyn, Stanford, Malan, Farrar, Jameson, and Beck. Fischer, for example, said that the Imperial Government was not to be blamed for raising the matter and that the terms proposed were reasonable and better than would be obtained later. Steyn admitted that the Native policies of South African states and colonies had not always been sound and that British suspicions were therefore justifiable. He thought that by settling the matter they would remove a source of friction between South Africa and Great Britain, but he disapproved of some of the conditions which were proposed. Malan considered that it was wise to persuade the House of Commons to give the British Government the power to hand the protectorates over to the Union without further reference to it. Eventually, Greene's amendment, that the operative clause should merely empower the King to transfer the protectorates to the Union 'upon terms and conditions to be mutually agreed upon', was defeated by twenty-one votes to seven, with Burger, de la Rey, Smartt, and the four Natal delegates who were present forming the minority; and the clause was adopted with only a verbal alteration.[80]

The schedule was then dealt with clause by clause and carried with a few minor changes and one addition. Divisions were taken on two motions to amend the financial clauses, but the amendments were

[80] *Minutes*, pp. 143–5; Malan, pp. 146–55; Walton, pp. 300–1.

defeated by twenty-one votes to five and twenty votes to seven, the four Natal delegates who were present voting with the minority on each occasion. The addition was moved by the President and empowered the Union Parliament to amend the schedule, such Bills being reserved for His Majesty's pleasure.[81]

Forwarding a copy of these resolutions to the High Commissioner, de Villiers reported that there had been considerable difficulty in getting them through the convention. He said that he feared the colonial parliaments would be loath to ratify them and he hoped the Secretary of State might meet some of the objections.[82] At about the same time Merriman wrote a strongly worded letter to his Governor, Sir Walter Hely-Hutchinson. Although he had supported the resolutions in the convention, he told Hely-Hutchinson that he and Sauer considered that the High Commissioner's insistence on conditions had been unwarranted, that the colonial parliaments would resent them, and that opponents of Union would use them as a weapon against the entire Constitution. He therefore asked Hely-Hutchinson to do what he could 'to modify a course which will I am sure be prejudicial to Union'.[83]

Selborne and Hely-Hutchinson informed the Secretary of State of these criticisms, with the result that on 11 January, when the convention reassembled after the Christmas recess, Selborne wrote to tell de Villiers that the Secretary of State had proposed an alternative line of action: The resolutions passed by the convention concerning the protectorates might be regarded as merely provisional; the convention could now proceed to pass six brief resolutions outlining the main principles of a settlement; only these six resolutions need be published on the subject with the report of the convention; and the full agreement could be worked out in London between the Secretary of State and the South African delegates who would go there to arrange for the enactment of the Constitution.[84] De Villiers did not regard the suggestion as a profitable one. He had no wish to reopen the question in the convention and he considered the six principles proposed by the Secretary of State to be somewhat vague. It is doubtful, indeed, whether de Villiers seriously believed that any Colonial Parliament would regard the schedule as a major obstacle to the ratification of the Constitution. Accordingly, he made no attempt to bring the suggestion before the convention, and when the schedule came up for review on 21 January it was confirmed without difficulty, although Moor

---

[81] *Minutes*, pp. 145–50; Malan, pp. 154–5.
[82] De Villiers to Selborne, 19 Dec. 1908, de Villiers Papers (copy).
[83] Merriman to Hely-Hutchinson, Dec. 1908, Merriman Papers, No. 277/1908 (draft).
[84] De Villiers Papers.

reiterated his disapproval and Jagger called for a division on a financial amendment which was defeated by twenty-one votes to seven.[85] During its last few sittings the convention made a number of further minor changes in the schedule and one amendment of some substance, moved by Malan, which empowered the Governor-General-in-Council to appropriate part of a territory's revenue as a contribution to the cost of the defence of the Union.[86] Thus the convention's draft Constitution contained a schedule of twenty-five clauses, related to section 152, which read as follows:

The King, with the advice of the Privy Council, may, on addresses from the Houses of Parliament of the Union, transfer to the Union the government of any territories, other than the territories administered by the British South Africa Company, belonging to or under the protectorate of His Majesty, and inhabited wholly or in part by natives, and upon such transfer the Governor-General-in-Council may undertake the government of such territory upon the terms and conditions embodied in the Schedule to this Act.[87]

Lord Selborne had succeeded in carrying out his instructions by obtaining the consent of the convention to nearly all his conditions. The result would be that if the protectorates were transferred to the Union soon after its establishment, as was expected to happen, the schedule would provide real safeguards for their Native inhabitants for a considerable period, though ultimately, should the Union become a sovereign State, they would only have a moral effect and their Native inhabitants, like the rest of the population of the Union, would be subject to the pleasure of the South African Government and Parliament. On the other hand, if the protectorates were not transferred at an early date, there was the possibility that Native policies based upon completely different principles might be pursued by the Union and by Britain, in which case they might become an apple of discord between the two countries.

Finally—and with reference to the Rhodesias as well as to the high commission territories—it may be observed that whereas a territory might be willing to become a province of a federation, in which there are enduring safeguards for provincial autonomy in specified fields, it might be unwilling to run the risk of being completely absorbed by a union. Federalism had facilitated the expansion of the United States of America

[85] *Minutes*, pp. 193–5; Malan, pp. 182–5.
[86] *Minutes*, pp. 222, 228, 238, 248; Malan, pp. 198–201.
[87] S. 151 of the S.A. Act is identical, except that the word 'protection' was substituted for the word 'protectorate'. Several amendments were made to the schedule in England: see below, pp. 412–14.

and the Dominion of Canada: its unitary Constitution might prove to be an obstacle to the expansion of the Union of South Africa.

12. THE AMENDING SECTION

Throughout its Durban session and the first fortnight of its Cape Town session the National Convention did not focus its attention on the vital question of the requirements for constitutional amendment (except when it decided to lay down a special procedure for the amendment of the franchise section). There were two reasons for the postponement of this topic. Firstly, when the convention started none of the delegates had regarded the question as being of exceptional importance; and, secondly, after its first week the convention had been dealing with topics approximately in the sequence in which they normally appear in a written Constitution—and the amending section normally comes at the end. The postponement had important effects upon the decision which was eventually made. Although Smuts and Merriman preferred a flexible Constitution, both of them went to Durban expecting to allow for at least some distinction between the requirements for an ordinary Act and the requirements for an Act to amend the Constitution. Smuts's August scheme had required absolute majorities in both Houses of Parliament and the approval of the legislatures of any provinces affected by the amendment; and the plan which he persuaded the Transvaal delegation to accept early in October had required absolute majorities in both Houses of Parliament for most amendments and some stiffer procedure for the amendment of a few sections;[88] while the resolutions which Merriman had drafted in Durban before the convention opened drew an unspecified distinction between the two types of legislation.[89] Furthermore, on 14 October Steyn told the convention that he favoured making any constitutional amendment require a three-quarters majority, as in the Orange Free State Republic,[90] and it is likely that his Orangia Unie colleagues would have supported such a proposal. A high degree of rigidity was certainly desired by the Natal delegation. The convention would probably have agreed, therefore, if, during the debates of 13–15 October, a delegate had moved an addendum to Merriman's motion on the form of the Constitution, to make the entire Constitution moderately rigid; but no such addendum was moved.[91]

[88] Brand's manuscript, Annexures A and H.
[89] Ibid., Annexure P. [90] See above, p. 189.
[91] See above, pp. 191–2, where it is pointed out that the Natal delegates were foolish to have missed this opportunity, because a rigid Constitution which created regional governments and defined their powers would have gone a long way towards satisfying their primary demand, which was federalism.

The convention took its first steps in the matter on 10 December, when it accepted Smuts's proposal that a committee should be appointed to deal with various outstanding topics, including 'Alterations of the Constitution'. The committee consisted of Steyn, as chairman, Merriman, Jameson, Morcom, Smythe, Smuts, Fitzpatrick, Hertzog, and Michell.[92] By that time Smuts and Merriman saw their way clear to making most of the Constitution completely flexible, since the convention had only insisted on protecting one of its decisions and it had done so by laying down requirements which every delegate regarded as exceptional, and not as applying to the entire Constitution. They succeeded in persuading the other members of the committee, except Morcom, to agree with them, but Steyn and Hertzog insisted that if any section was to be protected the language section should be, while Fitzpatrick insisted that in that event the electoral system should also be protected. Consequently, the committee recommended that the sections dealing with the 'Basis of representation' and 'The Language Question' should be subject to the special amending requirement which had already been laid down for the 'Native Franchise in the Cape Colony' (i.e. a two-thirds majority of the total members of both Houses of Parliament, sitting together), and that the rest of the Constitution should be amendable by laws passed in the ordinary manner.[93]

When the convention debated this report on 16 December, no delegate questioned the desirability of giving special protection to the sections which it specified, but it became apparent that there were three schools of thought as to how the rest of the Constitution should be treated. Morcom moved, as he had moved in the committee, that any constitutional amendment should require absolute majorities in both Houses of Parliament. He was given partial support by Jagger, Farrar, and Fischer and full support by Greene, who said that 'If the Constitution was not put on a higher footing than an ordinary act it was unnecessary to go into such detail'. De Villiers and Steyn said that they did not desire to subject all the sections of the Constitution to a special amending procedure, but that they were willing to add further sections to the protected list. Smuts, Malan, Smartt, and Jameson supported the committee's recommendations as they stood and in doing so Smuts reasoned that 'many of the resolutions already adopted presupposed that Parliament could amend them in the usual way'. Eventually the matter was referred back to the committee for further consideration.[94]

[92] *Minutes*, p. 125.   [93] Ibid., p. 128.
[94] Ibid., p. 133; Malan, pp. 138–43; Walton, p. 311. Greene and Smuts are quoted as reported by Malan.

On the following day the committee brought up a revised amending section, which included two changes. Firstly, it now started with the words 'Subject to the terms and restrictions of this Act . . .'—words which were probably inserted with the purpose of ensuring that Parliament should not tamper with any of the provisions which were to operate for a limited period only. Secondly, it added the amending section itself to the sections protected by the two-thirds majority requirement, and in so doing the committee clearly sought to prevent Parliament from circumventing the intentions of the convention by altering the amending section by a bare majority and then proceeding to alter the sections which it had protected.[95]

This report had not been dealt with by the convention by the time it adjourned for its Christmas recess on 18 December and during the next few days, while Smuts and Hull, with Duncan, de Wet, and Brand, of the Transvaal staff, and Plowman, of the Natal staff, were casting the convention's resolutions into the form of an incomplete draft South Africa Act, they included an amending section which differed from the committee's revised report in the following respects. Instead of the introductory phrase, 'Subject to the terms and restrictions of this Act . . .', which the Transvaalers regarded as dangerously vague, it stated that no section which prescribed a definite period of time for its operation should be amended or repealed during that period. Instead of protecting the entire 'Basis of representation', it only protected the two sections dealing with the division of the seats in the House of Assembly between the provinces —and it protected them only until the number of members in the House of Assembly reached 150. And instead of stating vaguely that for the amendment of the specified sections a two-thirds majority was to be obtained at a joint sitting of both Houses of Parliament, it stated that it was to be obtained for a special resolution after the Bill had passed through all the normal stages at a joint sitting of both Houses.[96]

When the convention's drafting committee, consisting of de Villiers, Merriman, Greene, Smuts, Hertzog, and Michell, prepared a draft Constitution early in the new year, it adopted this Transvaal version of the amending section with only one alteration, which required the two-thirds majority for the amendment of the protected sections to be obtained at the third reading of the Bill in the joint sitting.[97] On 21 January the amending section of the drafting committee's report came before the convention and, although it was then referred back to the drafting committee, it was agreed to by the convention without alteration five days

[95] *Minutes*, p. 142.   [96] Brand's manuscript, Annexure BB.
[97] *Minutes*, p. 308; 'Remarks on Draft Constitution'.

later. The only opposition came from the Natal delegates, who pressed two amendments to divisions. One, moved by Watt, was for the inclusion of section 85, which set out the legislative powers of the provincial councils, among the sections to be protected, and the other, moved by Hyslop, was that no section should be amended without absolute majorities in both Houses of Parliament. Both amendments were defeated by twenty-five votes to five, the Natal delegation standing alone in the minority.[98] Subsequently the convention made two final changes in the amending section. The division of the seats between the provinces was to be protected by the two-thirds majority procedure for at least ten years, even if the membership of the House of Assembly reached 150 earlier, and a sentence was added at the end, stating that a Bill passed by the special procedure was to 'be taken to have been duly passed by both Houses of Parliament'.[99]

Consequently, section 153 of the convention's draft Constitution[1] started with the words, 'Parliament may by law repeal or alter any of the provisions of this Act' and it proceeded to set out two provisos. The first proviso stated that no provisions of the Act which prescribed a definite period of time for their operation were to be repealed or altered during that period. This would apply—although it was not expressly stated—to the composition of the Senate for the first ten years[2] and the competence of the provincial councils to pass ordinances dealing with education, other than higher education, for the first five years.[3] The second proviso stated that the amending section itself, the franchise section,[4] the language section,[5] and the sections determining the allocation of the seats in the House of Assembly between the provinces (until the number of members of the House reached 150, or for ten years after the establishment of the Union, whichever was the longer period)[6] were only to be amended by Bills 'passed by both Houses of Parliament sitting together, and at the third reading . . . agreed to by no less than two-thirds of the total number of members of both Houses'. It also stated that Bills so passed were to 'be taken to have been duly passed by both Houses of Parliament'.

The intention of this somewhat complex section was clear enough.

[98] *Minutes*, pp. 151–2, 193, 219–21 ; Malan, pp. 198–9.
[99] *Minutes*, pp. 235, 238.
[1] S. 152 of the S.A. Act is identical, with the necessary adjustments of the numbers of the sections mentioned in it.
[2] S. 23 of the convention's draft Constitution : s. 24 of the S.A. Act.
[3] S. 85 (iii) of the convention's draft Constitution and of the S.A. Act.
[4] S. 35 of the convention's draft Constitution and of the S.A. Act.
[5] S. 138 of the convention's draft Constitution : s. 137 of the S.A. Act.
[6] Ss. 32, 33 of the convention's draft Constitution : ss. 33, 34 of the S.A. Act.

The entire Constitution was to be fully flexible, with the exception of the sections covered by the first proviso, which were unalterable during the brief periods for which they were to operate, and the sections covered by the second proviso, which were only to be altered by Parliament acting in the particular manner laid down.

On the question of sanctions, however, the draft Constitution was silent. It said nothing as to whether the Supreme Court should, or should not, recognize a 'law' as a valid law if it purported to amend the Constitution, even though it had been enacted contrary to the terms of one of the provisos of the amending section. During the convention a few of the delegates expressed a marked aversion to the 'testing right'.[7] But did they consider that the testing right—the power of judicial review—would exist under the Constitution which they had created? There is no evidence as to what most of the delegates thought on this question at the time, and the probability is that very few of them faced up to it. Perhaps the Transvaalers assumed that the testing right would not exist, for Brand had produced a memorandum asserting that 'If in the South African Constitution the Union Parliament is to be supreme, any provision that it can be altered only in a peculiar manner will presumably only be morally and not legally binding on future South African Parliaments.'[8] Furthermore, on 24 February 1909 Smuts publicly declared that the safeguard for the Cape Native franchise 'was not a powerful check, perhaps it was not a check at all';[9] and de Villiers, in pencil jottings on his copy of the convention's report, included the words, 'Interference of Courts prevented.'[10] On the other hand, it is certain that Malan believed that the Supreme Court would possess the power of judicial review over legislation amending any of the sections protected by the provisos. This follows logically from the fact that on 15 October he noted in his diary: 'If we have a Constitution which can only be altered in a special way then "testing right" of the Supreme Court is essential, whether under Unification or Federation'.[11] Of these opinions, Malan's was the sounder. The powers of the Supreme Court over legislation in the fields covered by the provisos of the amending section would be like those of the American and Australian courts over legislation amending any section of the American and Australian constitutions—and for the same reasons. The

[7] Malan, pp. 34–35, 140–3 ; Walton, pp. 60–61.
[8] Brand to Hull, 4 Nov. 1908, Brand Papers (copy).
[9] *Cape Times*, 3 Mar. 1909.   [10] De Villiers Papers.
[11] Malan, pp. 30–31. Likewise, ibid., pp. 140–1, where Malan gives as one of his reasons for opposing Morcom's proposal that no section of the Constitution should be altered without absolute majorities in both Houses: 'By the adoption of the Morcom motion the testing right would be introduced with regard to all the laws'.

American and Australian courts automatically apply any valid law, including the Constitution itself, and they therefore declare a subsequent 'law' to be invalid if it has not been passed in accordance with conditions laid down in the Constitution. Thus in the United States the Supreme Court came to exercise the power of judicial review over any 'law' amending any section of the Constitution, since the American Constitution states that no section of it may be amended except in a special manner, and it did this notwithstanding the fact that the Constitution does not expressly provide for judicial review. Likewise in Australia. Under the Constitution which the convention had drafted for South Africa it would be equally natural for the Supreme Court to declare to be invalid a 'law' which purported to amend the Constitution, if it had been enacted contrary to the terms of one of the provisos of the amending section. Furthermore, so long as the Colonial Laws Validity Act remained applicable, any South African law which was repugnant to an act of the British Parliament extending to South Africa (e.g. the South Africa Act) would be 'absolutely void and inoperative' to the extent of its repugnancy,[12] and the courts would be bound to declare it so.[13]

13. FINANCE AND RAILWAYS

Botha and Smuts had great faith in the future of the Union's economy. They, like the Transvaal Progressives, had accepted the thesis of the Selborne Memorandum that once South Africa threw off the shackles of

[12] Colonial Laws Validity Act, 1865, s. 2.

[13] The legal efficacy of the provisos would also be *reinforced* by s. 5 of the Colonial Laws Validity Act (see above, p. 99). It was subsequently assumed in some quarters that their legal efficacy *depended solely on* the Colonial Laws Validity Act and, after it had been enacted in the Statute of Westminster, 1931, s. 2, that 'The Colonial Laws Validity Act, 1865, shall not apply to any law made after the commencement of this Act by the Parliament of a Dominion', the assumption was that the Union Parliament could enact valid legislation without complying with the conditions laid down in the second proviso. This assumption, however, was rejected by the Appellate Division of the Supreme Court in 1952.

Much literature has recently been produced on this question, notably D. V. Cowen, *Parliamentary Sovereignty and the Entrenched Sections of the South Africa Act* (Cape Town, 1951); D. V. Cowen, 'Legislature and Judiciary: Reflections on the Constitutional Issues in South Africa', *Modern Law Review*, xv. 283–96, xvi. 273–98; B. Beinart, 'Parliament and the Courts', *Butterworths S.A. Law Review, 1954*, pp. 134–81; B. Beinart, 'The South African Appeal Court and Judicial Review', *Modern Law Review*, xxi. 587–608; Geoffrey Marshall, *Parliamentary Sovereignty and the Commonwealth* (Oxford, 1957), xi. See also the judgments of the Appellate Division of the Supreme Court in the two important cases of 1952: *Harris* v. *Minister of the Interior* [1952 (2)] S.A. 428, *Minister of the Interior* v. *Harris* [1952 (4)] S.A. 769.

disunity she would enter into a phase of rapid agricultural and industrial development. Indeed, it was confidence in the economic consequences of unification that formed one of the chief bonds between the Government and Opposition members of the Transvaal delegation, who went to Durban with an elaborate programme for the financial chapter of the Constitution.[14]

This Transvaal programme may be considered in two parts. The main points of its general proposals were as follows: At the outset the Union was to assume full responsibility for all the colonial debts and full control of all the colonial assets, including all the existing sources of revenue, and the provinces would be dependent on subsidies from the Union until a permanent system of provincial finance had been laid down by Parliament, following investigation and report by a commission. The debts in question totalled some £113 millions, on which interest and sinking fund charges were being paid at an average annual rate of 3·86 per cent., but it was hoped that investors would be sufficiently confident in the financial stability of the Union to enable the Union Government to consolidate them at a lower rate of interest, with considerable benefit to the taxpayer. The principal capital assets in question were the colonial railways and harbours, to the approximate value of £84 millions. In the financial year ending on 30 June 1908 the four colonies had a net deficit of about £2 millions on their ordinary accounts (excluding railways) and a net surplus of about £3½ millions on their railways. It was hoped that the Union accounts (excluding railways) would produce a surplus without additional taxation, through savings in the cost of government and from the increase in economic activity and, consequently, in revenue that were expected to follow the establishment of the Union.

The Transvaal railway proposals were based in part on the supplement to the Selborne Memorandum, entitled 'South African Railway Unification and its effect on Railway Rates', in which Philip Kerr, as the assistant secretary of the Intercolonial Council of the Transvaal and the Orange River Colony which was responsible for administering the Central South African Railways, had drawn attention to the fact that State railways tend to be inefficient and uneconomic unless they are managed and controlled by an independent commission, and thus sheltered from political influences.[15] South African history provided ample evidence of the evils which Brand had discussed. In the Cape Colony, in particular, members had frequently been returned to Parliament pledged to obtain funds for new railway lines in their constituencies and a number of

---

[14] Brand's manuscript, Annexures E, G, H, and K.
[15] Cd. 3564, pp. 65–108.

uneconomic 'political' lines had been constructed. According to the Transvaal programme the railway and harbour accounts would be separated from the other public accounts and the railways and harbours would be administered by a permanent board, presided over by a cabinet minister and subject to the ultimate authority of the Governor-General-in-Council. The programme went on to enunciate the principles on which the railways and harbours were to be administered—principles which were derived from Kerr's memorandum and from the case which the Transvaal representatives had presented to the intercolonial railway conferences of the previous years. They were to be administered as 'commercial undertakings' and not used as 'instruments of taxation', rates were to be kept as low as possible, and there were to be no 'unreasonable' preferences. These principles were vigorously endorsed by the chambers of commerce of Johannesburg and Pretoria in statements they submitted to the Transvaal Government on the eve of the convention. They believed that secondary industries in the Transvaal had been seriously hampered by the exorbitant railway rates which the Cape Colony and Natal had insisted on levying for revenue purposes, and they predicted rapid development if the railways were operated at cost.[16] Fitzpatrick went still further. In a memorandum written for the Transvaal delegates at the end of September he argued that the rates should be made to bear only the working and maintenance costs of the railways and not the interest on capital borrowed for railway construction.[17] Smuts and his colleagues were not prepared to go as far as that, but the Transvaal programme provided that if Parliament decided to construct a line which the Board could not recommend as a 'commercial undertaking' and which failed to produce sufficient revenue to cover the interest on its cost of construction as well as its working and maintenance costs, the difference should be made good from the general revenue.

On balance this programme was bound to be most attractive to the delegates of the coastal colonies, to whom the pooling of resources with the gold-producing Transvaal appeared as the best, if not the only, means by which their own areas might recover from the prolonged depression. In the last financial year, which ended in June 1908, the inland colonies had produced a net surplus of £564,112 and the Central South African Railways had made a profit of over £2 millions, while the Cape Colony accounts, including railways, had showed a deficit of £991,854 and the Natal accounts, including railways, had showed a deficit of £179,402. The current year seemed likely to yield still larger surpluses for the inland

16 Transvaal Archives, Prime Minister, LX (x).
17 Brand's manuscript, Annexure M.

colonies and, notwithstanding Merriman's stringent economies, a further deficit seemed likely in the Cape Colony if not in Natal. Furthermore, the public debts of the inland colonies amounted to only about £39 millions, while some £52 millions were owed by the Cape Colony and £22 millions by Natal. The Transvaal programme would therefore enable the depressed coastal colonies to spread their debts more widely and to benefit to the fullest possible extent from the prosperity of the Transvaal. Although some of the other features of the Transvaal programme were in themselves unattractive, they did not offset these vital advantages. Moreover, even though the railway proposals involved the surrender of the position which the coastal colonies had taken up at the intercolonial conferences and seemed likely to promote development inland at the expense of the ports, not all the interests in the Cape Colony and Natal would be prejudiced. Kimberley and Ladysmith, for example, stood to gain as much as the Transvaal and the Orange River Colony.[18]

On 16 October the convention appointed a committee under the chairmanship of Browne, who had been Treasurer in the crown colony administration of the Orange River Colony, to prepare financial statistics for the guidance of the convention. Its report, including a volume of useful data collected by R. H. Brand and by S. E. Court, the Transvaal statistician, was tabled on 30 November.[19] A week later the convention appointed a committee, comprising Merriman (who was subsequently relieved by Sauer), Jagger, Hyslop, Greene, Hull, Farrar, Fischer, Browne, and Michell, to make recommendations on finance and trade.[20] By that time the Transvaalers had given a final polish to their financial programme and while the committee was working Duncan and Brand kept Hull and Farrar supplied with additional statistics and with fresh drafts of resolutions.[21] The committee produced a report on 17 December, but the convention had not begun to deal with the report when it adjourned for the Christmas recess.[22] After the resumption the Transvaal delegates tried to delay further action until the capital question had been settled, as they wished to use their financial programme as a lever for obtaining the capital for Pretoria.[23] On 12 January the report was referred back to the committee.[24] Then between the 15th and the 18th the

[18] For the economic background see above, Chapter I (5), and for statistics see below, Appendix A, vi–xi.

[19] *Minutes*, pp. 13–14, 93. The statistics are not reprinted in the published *Minutes*; they are in the House of Assembly, National Convention Minutes, II.

[20] *Minutes*, pp. 114, 125, 131.

[21] Brand's manuscript and Annexure V thereto.

[22] *Minutes*, pp. 139–42. [23] Malan, pp. 158–61.

[24] *Minutes*, p. 152.

convention considered a revised report and referred some of its clauses back again and it was not until the 22nd that they had been adopted after further revision.[25] Finally, in considering the report of the drafting committee, the convention made several further verbal amendments in the financial chapter between 25 and 30 January.[26]

In spite of these delays and revisions, the result was that the first ten sections of the financial chapter of the convention's draft Constitution were very similar to the general proposals in the Transvaal financial programme and virtually identical with the corresponding sections in the first report of the finance committee. Section 117[27] established the principle of the separation of the railway and harbour accounts from the other public accounts, by providing that all revenues derived from the administration of the railways and harbours were to be paid into a railway and harbour fund, which was to be appropriated by Parliament for railway and harbour purposes, and that all other revenues were to be paid into a consolidated revenue fund, to be appropriated by Parliament for other Union purposes. Section 118[28] dealt with the financing of the provincial administrations. As soon as possible after the establishment of the Union the Governor-General-in-Council was to appoint a commission, consisting of one representative of each province and a British official as chairman, to inquire into the question. Meanwhile, pending the report of the commission and provision by Parliament, a province would receive an annual subsidy from the consolidated revenue fund equal to the amount which the corresponding Colonial Parliament had appropriated for education, other than higher education, for the financial year 1908/9, and any additional amount which the Governor-General-in-Council might consider necessary; and no expenditure was to be incurred by a province which was not provided for in annual estimates submitted to and approved by the Governor-General-in-Council. Section 119,[29] which was a modification of section 103 of the British North America Act, provided that the costs of collection, management, and receipt of the consolidated revenue fund were to be the first charge on the fund; and section 120,[30] a modification of section 104 of the British North America Act, provided that the annual interest and sinking fund charges

[25] *Minutes*, pp. 155–9, 163–74, 186–91, 195–8; Malan, pp. 166–89.

[26] *Minutes*, pp. 202–6, 210–12, 219, 228–9, 233–4, 237–8; Malan, pp. 208–9. The section providing compensation for the colonial capitals was not completed until 2 Feb. and is dealt with in s. 14 of this chapter.

[27] S. 117 of the S.A. Act is identical.   [28] S. 118 of the S.A. Act is identical.

[29] At Bloemfontein this section was omitted from the draft Constitution.

[30] At Bloemfontein this section, which became s. 119 of the S.A. Act, was amended to make these items a first charge on the fund.

on the public debts of the colonies were to be the second charge on the fund. Section 121,[31] which was virtually identical with section 106 of the British North America Act, provided that, subject to the payments charged on the consolidated revenue fund in the preceding sections, all payments from the consolidated revenue fund were to be appropriated by Parliament; and section 122[32] provided that no money was to be withdrawn from the fund, or from the railway and harbour fund, without appropriation by law, but it empowered the Governor-General-in-Council to draw and spend money from the fund until two months after the first meeting of the first Parliament. Sections 123, 124, and 125[33] provided that all stocks, cash, bankers' balances, and securities, all crown lands, public works, and other properties, and all mineral rights belonging to the colonies were to become the property of the Union on its establishment. Section 126[34] provided that the Union should assume all the debts and liabilities of the colonies, subject to the conditions imposed by the laws under which they were incurred, and empowered the Union to convert, renew, or consolidate them.

When these sections were before the convention, their principles were not challenged. It was recognized that the financial subordination of the provinces to the Union was the inevitable counterpart to the pooling of the colonial assets and liabilities, but several of the Cape delegates questioned the interim arrangements for the financing of the provinces, because the public schools in the Cape Colony were financed from local rates as well as by Parliament. However, when van Heerden proposed that the local rates should be taken into account in assessing the extent of the temporary subsidy, Merriman said that he was satisfied with the committee's proposal and van Heerden withdrew his amendment.[35] On 15 January Fischer raised the question of safeguards for the completion of public works for which funds were voted by the colonial parliaments before Union, and to meet his point an addendum was included in section 123, providing that any balances of such funds were to be deemed to have been appropriated by the Union Parliament for the purposes in question. To prevent this decision from being abused the four prime ministers prepared a list of works which they intended to proceed with and they agreed not to exceed the amounts which they set down against them.[36] Section 126 also necessitated an agreement between the four

[31] At Bloemfontein this section was omitted from the draft Constitution.
[32] S. 120 of the S.A. Act is identical.
[33] Ss. 121–3 of the S.A. Act are identical except for one verbal amendment.
[34] This section, with amendments, became s. 124 of the S.A. Act.
[35] *Minutes*, pp. 163–4; Malan, pp. 168–9; Walton, pp. 243–4.
[36] *Minutes*, pp. 168, 186–8; Walton, pp. 246–7.

prime ministers, who informed the convention on 27 January that with one exception they would not contract fresh debts before the inauguration of the Union. The exception was that the Transvaal undertook to lend Natal and the Orange River Colony half a million pounds each for their immediate needs—an arrangement which in the circumstances amounted to a bribe to the two smaller colonies to join the Union.[37]

The next seven sections embodied practically all the important points in the Transvaal proposals concerning railways and harbours. Section 127[38] provided that all railways and harbours belonging to the four colonies were to become the property of the Union and that no railway for the conveyance of public traffic and no port or harbour was to be constructed without the sanction of Parliament. Section 128[39] established a Board for railway and harbour administration. 'Subject to the authority of the Governor-General-in-Council, the control and management of the railways, ports, and harbours of the Union' were to be 'exercised through a Board', consisting of a cabinet minister as chairman and not more than three commissioners, who were to be appointed by the Governor-General-in-Council for five-year terms, during which they were to have the same security of tenure as judges. Section 129[40] stated the principles on which the railways and harbours were to be administered. They were to 'be administered on business principles, due regard being had to agricultural and industrial development within the Union and the promotion, by means of cheap transport, of the settlement of an agricultural and industrial population in the inland portions of the Union'. Railway and harbour earnings were 'so far as may be' to be 'not more than are sufficient to meet the necessary outlays for working, maintenance, betterment, depreciation, and the payment of interest due on capital'. The Governor-General-in-Council was to give effect to these provisions within four years after the establishment of the Union. Section 130[41] empowered the Board to establish a fund from railway and harbour revenue 'to be used for maintaining, as far as may be, uniformity of rates notwithstanding fluctuations in traffic'. Section 131[42] placed the balances in the existing colonial railway and harbour funds under the control of the Board, to be used for the purposes for which they had been

[37] Walton, p. 247; Malan, pp. 200–1.
[38] S. 125 of the S.A. Act is identical.
[39] S. 126 of the S.A. Act is identical.
[40] S. 127 of the S.A. Act contains amendments made in Bloemfontein. See below, pp. 377–8.
[41] S. 128 of the S.A. Act contains amendments made in Bloemfontein.
[42] S. 129 of the S.A. Act is identical.

provided. According to section 132[43] the Board was to examine all proposals for new construction before they were submitted to Parliament and if Parliament authorized a work contrary to the advice of the Board, the annual loss (i.e. the difference between the revenue received from the work and the costs of its working and maintenance and the interest on the capital invested in it) was to be made good by the consolidated revenue fund to the railway and harbour fund, to the extent that it had been anticipated by the Board in estimates submitted to and approved by the Auditor-General. Finally, section 133[44] provided that the consolidated revenue fund should also make good to the railway and harbour fund any losses incurred in consequence of concessions granted by Parliament or the Governor-General-in-Council.

The principle that the railways and harbours should be administered by a Board, subject to the overriding authority of the Governor-General-in-Council, was not contested in the convention, though it was a novelty for the Cape Colony and Natal, and there were several discussions of the wording of the section.[45] The enunciation of the principles on which the railway rates were to be based was a different matter. Jagger in the finance committee and Beck and other Cape delegates in the convention fought hard against the Transvaal demand for low rates. They attacked the Transvaal proposal that the railways and harbours should be administered as 'a commercial undertaking', they tried to eliminate the reference to the development of 'the inland portions of the Union', they sought to include sinking fund charges among those to be borne by the railway and harbour revenues, and they insisted on a proviso setting out a period of time before the principles were to be bound to be applied. The Transvaalers were adamant on the first three points, except that they humoured Jagger in the committee by allowing the substitution of the phrase 'on business principles' for the phrase 'as a commercial undertaking', which they regarded as being a change without a difference. On the last point they yielded in the committee and consented to a four year interim period, at the end of which the principles were to be applied without qualification.[46] There was, however, a curious episode in the convention on 29 January, when Smuts moved the omission of the phrase 'on business principles'. He appears to have reached the conclusion that the case for low rates would not have been weakened by its omission and to have been anxious to placate the Cape delegates on this point because

[43] S. 130 of the S.A. Act is virtually identical.
[44] S. 131 of the S.A. Act is identical.
[45] *Minutes*, pp. 141, 157, 165, 204, 210; Walton, p. 248; Malan, pp. 166–9.
[46] *Minutes*, pp. 141, 157, 166–7, 204, 210–11, 219; Walton, pp. 248–9; Malan, pp. 166–7; Brand's manuscript.

the Capital crisis was still unresolved. The division on his amendment resulted in a tie and de Villiers gave his casting vote with the Noes to preserve the section in the form in which it had already been adopted.[47] The provisions that the consolidated revenue fund should be responsible for losses sustained from the granting of concessions and from the construction of uneconomic lines against the advice of the Board also met with a certain amount of opposition, but once again the Transvaal proposals were adopted without significant amendment.[48]

Section 134 of the draft Constitution emanated, not from the Transvaal, but from Merriman, who regarded it as essential that the Constitution should provide for the appointment of an Auditor-General of the public accounts and for the definition of his powers and duties, while the Transvaalers considered that this was a question which should be left entirely to Parliament. The result was a compromise, under which such an officer was to be appointed by the Governor-General-in-Council, with reasonable security of tenure, but the definition of his powers and duties was left to the Governor-General-in-Council, pending parliamentary legislation.[49]

One other section of the draft Constitution was intimately connected with the financial chapter. It concerned the highly contentious questions of the supply of Mozambique labour for the Transvaal gold-mines and the Lourenço Marques share of the Witwatersrand traffic.[50] Before the convention started the Transvaal Government had opened negotiations with the Portuguese authorities for a convention to replace the *modus vivendi* of 1901. The Transvaal was anxious to meet Natal criticisms of the *modus vivendi* and to check the decline in the volume of trade coming through Durban, but at the same time she feared that, if Union was accomplished without agreements binding all parties, the Union Government might break the railway clauses of the *modus vivendi* and the Portuguese might retaliate by prohibiting the recruitment of Mozambique Native labour for the Transvaal mines. She therefore wished to conclude a new convention, providing for the continuation of recruitment in Mozambique and placing a ceiling on the Lourenço Marques share of the Witwatersrand traffic, and to have its contents approved by the other colonies and made binding on the Union. While the convention was sitting the negotiations continued in Cape Town between Transvaal

[47] *Minutes*, pp. 233–4; Malan, pp. 208–9.
[48] *Minutes*, pp. 141–2, 158, 167, 170, 186–8, 205, 211, 237; Walton, pp. 251–3; Malan, pp. 180–1.
[49] *Minutes*, pp. 158, 168–9, 206, 212, 229, 233, 237; Walton, p. 254; Malan, pp. 168–9. S. 132 of the S.A. Act is identical.
[50] See above, pp. 13, 54–60, 166–7.

and Portuguese representatives, and Botha informed the convention that it was vital to the gold-mining industry and to all South Africa that a new treaty should be concluded and honoured by the Union, especially since the Chinese labourers were being repatriated and the industry would soon be wholly dependent on African supplies of unskilled labour. 'He regarded the treaty with Portugal as essential', Walton reported, 'and he put it to the Convention to assent to it.'[51] The committee which had been appointed to deal with the civil service and miscellaneous topics included in its report of 14 December a recommendation that all the treaty rights and obligations of the colonies should become binding on the Union.[52] The convention referred this recommendation to its finance committee, to which Hull submitted a draft of the proposed convention, under which Lourenço Marques would be assured of at least 50 per cent. of the gross tonnage of commercial seaborne goods destined for the Witwatersrand. This amounted to a concession by the Portuguese, because during 1908 under the existing *modus vivendi* no less than 63 per cent. of the Witwatersrand traffic was imported through Lourenço Marques, against only 24 per cent. through Durban, and 13 per cent. through the Cape ports. Nevertheless, the Cape and Natal members of the finance committee were most disappointed, since there was a widespread impression that one of the fruits of Union would be the diversion of nearly all the Witwatersrand traffic to Durban and the Cape ports, and they declined to take the responsibility of recommending approval of the draft convention.[53] Eventually, however, the colonial prime ministers consented to it, on the understanding that the Transvaal would insist on the inclusion of a clause allowing the Union to revise the railway rates if the Lourenço Marques share of the Witwatersrand traffic rose above 55 per cent., and on 23 January Botha was able to inform the other three prime ministers that the negotiations with the Portuguese had reached 'a definite conclusion' on that basis and that the new convention would come into force on the day of Union.[54] But that was not all. Moor and Greene had for some time been insisting that Durban should be assured of at least 30 per cent. of the Witwatersrand traffic and, although Merriman and Sauer disliked the idea intensely, negotiations proceeded between the Transvaal, Natal, and the Cape Colony, and eventually on 2 February Hull, Greene, and Sauer, as the responsible ministers, signed an agreement under which Natal would receive 30 per cent. of the Wit-

---

[51] Walton, p. 258.　　　　　　　　　　　　　　　[52] *Minutes*, p. 128.
[53] Ibid., p. 232.

[54] Transvaal Archives, Prime Minister, LX (xiv) (copy). The convention was signed on 1 Apr. 1909 and published in Cd. 4587 (1909).

watersrand traffic and the Cape ports would receive the remaining 15–20 per cent., and the railway rates would be subject to revision if the Natal share rose above or fell below 30 per cent. or if the Cape share rose above 20 per cent.[55] Accordingly, it was understood that section 149 of the draft Constitution,[56] which stated that 'All rights and obligations under any conventions or agreements which are binding on any of the Colonies shall devolve upon the Union at its establishment', referred in particular to the new convention between Mozambique and the Transvaal and the railway agreement between the Transvaal, the Cape Colony, and Natal.

The Transvaal–Mozambique Convention and the intercolonial railway agreement would provide the Railway and Harbour Board with the insoluble problem of attempting to make a rigid division of the Witwatersrand traffic between the ports and at the same time administering the railways and harbours 'on business principles' and fixing the railway rates at cost. In all other respects the financial provisions of the draft Constitution applied the unitary principle without qualification. For the first time since the Voortrekkers had migrated from the Cape Colony and established independent republics the ineluctable economic interdependence of the several parts of South Africa was fully recognized, and the way was opened for the development of the country as a single unit without artificial restraints. Furthermore, by refraining from any attempt at a division of the colonial assets and liabilities between the provinces and the Union they obviated the necessity for interregional bargaining of the sort that had caused tensions and complications in Canada and Australia before and after federation; and in creating a Railway and Harbour Board they made a valiant effort to check political jobbery in the administration of the railways and harbours—though its efficiency would depend upon the quality of the men selected as commissioners and the manner in which the Government exercised its overriding powers.[57]

14. THE CAPITAL

After steering a successful course through many formidable dangers, the convention very nearly came to grief over the comparatively minor issue of the selection of a capital for the Union. Both material and sentimental factors lay behind this struggle. Merchants and estate agents

[55] Natal Archives, Prime Minister, cvii; Merriman's Diary, 3 and 19 Jan. 1909.

[56] S. 148 of the S.A. Act includes an addition made in Bloemfontein, explicitly referring to the railway agreement. See below, p. 378.

[57] The financial sections are discussed by R. H. Brand in *The Union of South Africa* (Oxford, 1909), ix, and by Jean van der Poel in *Railway and Customs Policies in South Africa, 1885–1910* (London, 1933), pp. 142–5.

believed that their future depended upon the result, and the newspapers, which were local in circulation and outlook, conveyed the impression that the average man outside the convention, however ill-informed and apathetic he might be about the more fundamental issues, had become emotionally aroused to regard the decision on the capital as the one easily comprehensible gauge of the success of his representatives.

Among the Cape delegates were men like Jagger and Sauer who regarded Cape Town as the only legitimate choice, and with the local press, both English and Dutch, behind them they were able to infuse something like unity into their colleagues. Moreover, they had a strong case, for Cape Town was to a unique extent a mother city. Whereas the American and Australian continents had been settled and developed through several ports of entry, Cape Town, from the days of van Riebeeck until well into the nineteenth century, had been the single funnel for immigration, the sole seat of government, and the only real town in all South Africa, and it was still the capital of the most populous colony and the headquarters of the only South African university. The Transvaal delegates were equally determined to stand firm for Pretoria. The Pretoria and Johannesburg press, both English and Dutch, gave them to understand that to yield would be to give the isolationists a powerful, perhaps a decisive weapon against the entire Constitution; and they could argue that Cape Town was too remote from the other main centres of population—a railway terminus and not a junction—while Pretoria was more exclusively South African, would be centrally placed when the Union fulfilled its destiny and absorbed the Rhodesias, and, above all, deserved the prize as the capital of the colony which was making financial sacrifices for Union. The Natal delegates realized that they could not hope to win the trophy for themselves, but they had no difficulty in choosing between the two main claimants. Their sympathies were entirely with Pretoria, which lay within the field of Natal's trade connexions, rather than with the more distant Cape Town, one of Durban's traditional competitors. Consequently, the Orange River Colony delegates held the balance. Their five votes, added to the Cape Colony's twelve, or to the thirteen votes of the Transvaal and Natal, would be decisive in any straight fight between Cape Town and Pretoria. However, they found it extremely difficult to choose. Cape Town was twice as distant and its atmosphere was in many respects the more alien to them. On the other hand, Pretoria was alarmingly close to the still more alien influences of the city of gold, which, they suspected, were already corrupting the Het Volk leaders. They were also loath to commit themselves to either side for the further reason that, as Fischer put it, the longer the big dogs fought, the greater

the chance that the small dog would get the bone.[58] Indeed, if the issue
had been decided on its merits and geographical position and efficient
communications had been regarded as the most important criteria, the
capital of the Orange River Colony would have had a very good chance,
for Bloemfontein was the most central of the four colonial capitals, with
railway communications radiating out to the other colonies, though its
opponents pointed out that it was a dusty, undeveloped town with only
about 25,000 inhabitants of all races. Thus the capital issue was explosive. It led to some of the sharpest exchanges in the convention. It
revealed and intensified the rift between the Afrikaner leaders of the
Transvaal and those of the Orange River Colony. It caused long delays
and almost a complete breakdown. And it was only settled by following
an inauspicious precedent—the judgement of Solomon.

From the very beginning of the convention the delegates who felt most
keenly about it began to manœuvre for position. Something of what was
going on may be seen through the eyes of Sauer, who reported to the
veteran J. H. Hofmeyr on 23 October that [59]

the competition seems to me . . . as I thought before leaving Cape Town to
be between the mother of all South African towns and cities and Pretoria.
Bloemfontein will advance her claims no doubt but with I think no chance
of getting what she wants. My impression is that if Bloemfontein is out of the
running . . . the Free State men will be with us. Steyn, Herzog [sic], Fischer
and old de Wet are I believe sufficiently good Africanders not to want the
capital near a centre like the Rand. It would mean corruption, extravagance,
an alien and cosmopolitan spirit . . . I am doing all I can . . . to bring the
position of the case before such men as I have named above. The key of the
position lies with the Free State delegates. . . . In discussing this matter with
the Free State I avoid the question of *whose* the capital should be, but enter
into the matter of whose it should *not* be for National reasons. That prevents
the discussing the merits or otherwise of Bloemfontein and deals with the
undesirableness of Pretoria, Cape Town's real competitor. . . . I wish you
would write to Steyn on the subject.

Nevertheless, the manœuvring produced no clear results and, except for
noting letters setting forth the claims of two rank outsiders, Queenstown
and Rosmead Junction (which were followed later by similar pleas for
Mafeking, Parys, Potchefstroom, and Kroonstad),[60] the convention took
no formal cognizance of the question until nearly two months after the
commencement of its labours.

[58] Walton, p. 269.
[59] Hofmeyr Papers.
[60] House of Assembly, National Convention Minutes, II and III, Annexures 36, 69,
99, 117, 118, 120, 138.

Then on 9 December Botha moved 'That it is desirable for the Convention to settle the capital of the Union.'[61] He and his colleagues wished to deal with the capital before they had committed themselves in the field of finance, so that they could use the Transvaal's financial strength as a lever. Speaking to his motion Botha argued that grave difficulties would be created if the convention did not settle the matter, saying, according to Malan, 'that he was in favour of the Union and that he was prepared on behalf of the Transvaal to pool everything and to keep back nothing specifically for the Transvaal. But if this important matter was left undecided he would have to take into serious consideration whether it was desirable to go on with this matter of bringing about the Union.' Hyslop, Greene, and Moor showed their hand by supporting Botha and going on to suggest that the colonial capitals which were not selected to be the capital of the Union should be given financial compensation. Hertzog, on the other hand, opposed Botha's motion. He said that all the delegates except those from the Orange River Colony were known to be committed to support one of the existing colonial capitals, that the question was outside the convention's terms of reference, and that to proceed to deal with it would be to run the risk of having the Constitution rejected by the people. He therefore considered that the choice should be left to the Union Parliament. A third suggestion came from the President, who said that while he agreed with Botha that the convention should settle the matter, no delegate would be justified in making it a 'breaking' question because it had not been raised earlier. As things were, he thought that it would be best to complete the rest of the Constitution and then, at the very end, to choose a capital. Botha's motion was then adopted without a division being called; whereupon Fischer moved a supplementary motion along the lines which de Villiers had suggested, to the effect that the convention should appoint a committee to recommend a procedure for the selection of a capital, and that its report should not be dealt with until resolutions had been passed covering all other aspects of the Constitution. The Cape supported Fischer's motion, but the Transvaal and Natal opposed it, and in the course of the debate there were sharp exchanges between Fitzpatrick and the President. Fitzpatrick referred to 'manoeuvring' by the other side, de Villiers took umbrage at the very suggestion of such a thing, and Fitzpatrick retorted that 'The Transvaal would have to pay for the Union and he did not want the question of the capital put off until all the work of the Convention had been

[61] For the convention's proceedings concerning the capital on 9 and 10 Dec. 1908, see the *Minutes*, pp. 124–6; Malan, pp. 122–33; and Walton, pp. 270–2. The terms of Botha's motion are in the *Minutes*. The other quotations are from Malan.

disposed of.' At the end of the sitting of 9 December a Transvaal amendment for the deletion from Fischer's motion of the sentence for the postponement of the consideration of the committee's report was defeated
by eighteen votes to twelve, the Orange River Colony, the Cape Colony,
and Smuts defeating the rest of the Transvaal delegates and Natal.

Although Smuts had shown by his vote that he did not regard this
decision as a bad one, Botha and most of his colleagues feared that once
the financial sections were passed by the convention the Transvaal's
chances of obtaining the capital would be seriously weakened, and that
evening they tried to persuade the Cape Colony and Orange River
Colony delegates to change their minds. Jameson responded to a personal
appeal from Botha and the next day in the convention, when Botha
asked that the decision should be reversed, Jameson supported him.
Malan and de Villiers agreed, but Sauer and the Unie delegates were
loath to do so. There was an ominous clash between Steyn and Botha,
Steyn objecting to the Transvaal flinging its riches in the teeth of the
other delegates and Botha bristling in his denials that any such thing was
being done. Eventually, Fischer withdrew the words which had given
offence to the Transvaal and his motion, as amended, was adopted without a division. The convention then proceeded to give effect to it by
appointing de Villiers, Botha, Hertzog, Sauer (with Maasdorp as his
alternate), and Hyslop (with Greene as his alternate) to be a committee
to devise a procedure for selecting the capital of the Union.[62]

The committee met frequently during the following week and considered several schemes, but before the Christmas recess it could do no
better than present an interim report, in which it confessed that it had
been unable to come to a decision and proposed that during the recess
the prime ministers should try to solve the whole question by agreeing
upon a capital. In a brief debate on this report de Villiers threw out the
suggestion that if no other solution proved possible the King should be
asked to appoint an impartial commission of non-South Africans to
select a capital, but de la Rey stifled discussion by objecting to the re-
opening of the question which had been decided by the passing of Botha's
motion.[63]

No headway was made during the recess and when the convention
reassembled in January there was a general feeling that it had reached
a deadlock, with the finance and the capital sections of the Constitution
still undecided. On the 12th, when the prime ministers met, Botha tried
shock tactics, proposing that the convention should be adjourned *sine*

[62] The alternate members of the committee were appointed on 14 Dec. *Minutes*, p. 128.
[63] Ibid., pp. 138–9; Malan, pp. 142–5; Walton, pp. 272–4.

die,[64] and the next day he told the convention that he feared they might not be able to proceed, whereupon Hertzog observed that 'If General Botha wished to make a breaking-point of the capital question, then it would be much better to say so clearly'.[65] It was Steyn who poured oil on the troubled waters, appealing to the delegates' sense of responsibility. At that stage Malan calculated that a straight vote for a capital between Cape Town and Pretoria would result in a tie, with Fischer, Hertzog, and Browne supporting Cape Town and de Wet and Steyn preferring Pretoria.[66] On the 15th the atmosphere became more hopeful when the Transvaal permitted the convention to proceed with the financial resolutions. Then on the 18th the capital committee produced another report. Again it admitted its failure to make a unanimous recommendation but this time it included the terms of two proposals, one by Hertzog and the other by Botha.[67] This report was before the convention repeatedly between 22 and 29 January, without any advance being made towards a solution.[68] At the outset Steyn repeated Hertzog's earlier proposal that the selection of the capital should be left to the first Union Parliament, but Botha insisted that they were bound by their decision to settle the matter in the convention. Malan proceeded to move that the question should stand over until the rest of the draft Constitution had been completed, but his motion was defeated without a division. Then Hertzog moved the proposal which appeared under his name in the committee's report, according to which the convention would decide in which colony the capital should be situated by eliminating colonies one by one until, after the third vote, only one colony remained, when any delegate could 'challenge' that colony and propose another one, in which case there would be a fourth and final vote between the two. No doubt this method was estimated by Hertzog to result in a victory for the Orange River Colony, on the fourth vote if not the third. Botha followed and moved the proposal which appeared under his name in the committee's report—a proposal which was similar to Hertzog's, but which allowed no 'challenge' after the third vote had been taken. As the debate continued the tensions increased. Fitzpatrick baldly announced that the Transvaal 'demanded'[69] the capital in return for her financial sacrifices and Farrar supported him, whereupon Hertzog made a forthright attack on Pretoria for its proximity to the city of gold, evoking from Burger an indignant denial that Pretoria was influenced by Johannesburg. On 26 January Botha

---

[64] Merriman's Diary, 12 Jan. 1909.   [65] Malan, pp. 162–3.
[66] Ibid., pp. 164–5.   [67] *Minutes*, pp. 172–3.
[68] Ibid., pp. 198–200, 206–7, 221, 223, 235; Malan, pp. 184–95, 198–207; Walton, pp. 276–9.
[69] Malan, pp. 188–9.

skilfully shifted his ground. He withdrew his motion and suggested instead that they should first take a straight vote on the question whether the capital should be located in a coastal colony or an inland one (in the hope that both Natal and the Orange River Colony would support an inland colony). The next day Smuts, who had previously played little part in these edifying proceedings, made a carefully prepared speech, in which he reasoned that it was vital to come to a decision which would be acceptable to the people of the Transvaal who were making the largest sacrifice. He informed the convention that at last he had discovered a principle at the root of the problem, and that was that it would be wrong to have the capital at the coast. 'Cape Town', his notes ran, 'is too exposed and it is too far from the heart of the Union. Union will go up to [the] Congo soon and perhaps embrace [the] whole continent south of that. Is it wise to fix on [the] most extreme point in [the] South almost on an island away from [the] Continent for [the] capital?'[70] Merriman was unmoved by Smuts's special pleading—'very poor', he noted in his diary[71] —nor did the Orange River Colony rise to the bait. Hertzog, who was still out of humour with the Transvaal, withdrew his own motion, but made it clear that he could not support the latest Transvaal proposal. Late on the 27th, however, Steyn brought them back to realities by suggesting that Botha and Merriman should meet to find a solution and that, if they were unsuccessful, de Villiers's plan of an impartial commission should be adopted.

By this time the convention was near to collapse. The newspapers had got wind of what was causing the delay. Their correspondence columns were filled with the subject, and editorials were in one and the same breath berating the delegates for their lack of statesmanship and admonishing them to come to the decision they desired, those in the Transvaal insisting on the capital, the whole capital, and nothing but the capital for Pretoria, and those in the Cape extolling the amenities of the mother city and the democratic virtues of a referendum.[72] The delegates were stale and quarrelsome and had had enough of revising a draft Constitution which might never come into operation. 'It looks like breaking', were the last words Merriman wrote in his diary on the evening of the 26th[73]—and it seems probable that if Jagger and Sauer, Fitzpatrick and de la Rey had had their way the dispute would have wrecked the convention and with it the Union.

[70] Smuts Papers.   [71] Merriman's Diary, 27 Jan. 1909.
[72] *Cape Times*, 16 Jan.–3 Feb. 1909. It frequently printed extracts from other newspapers.
[73] Merriman made brief entries in his diary every evening between 11 Jan. and 3 Feb. 1909, and nearly all of them referred to the capital dispute.

However, several of the most influential delegates were determined to prevent a breakdown. One was Merriman, to whom the capital had always been a question of minor importance and who was prepared to attempt to negotiate a compromise, distasteful though the whole affair had become to him. Another was Jameson, who remained indifferent to details and confident in the basic integrity of Botha, so that it was to him, rather than to the members of the Cape Government, that Botha turned when he felt most exasperated. 'These Cape ministers are hopeless', said Botha to Duncan after a fruitless session with Merriman and Sauer. 'I am going across to Groot Schuur to see Dr. Jameson. He is the only man I can talk to.'[74] Another was Steyn, who had been a powerful influence for moderation ever since the language question had been settled to his satisfaction. During the critical period he asked Fitzpatrick and Jameson to meet him privately and he told them that he was convinced that an Anglo-German conflict was imminent. It was essential, he continued, that South Africa should be united before that day, so that they could defend her as one man if it became necessary. Therefore they should on no account allow the capital crisis to wreck union. This plea, coming from the man who had been the most determined of the Boer bitter-enders only seven years earlier, made a profound impression upon Fitzpatrick.[75] Then, too, there was Smuts, who, unlike Botha, never allowed his feelings to become involved in the capital dispute. He used his forensic skill to the utmost on behalf of Pretoria, but he also exercised his fertile mind in exploring all sorts of ingenious compromises, for it was his one object to get the Constitution through, and it was probably he who first suggested that they should apply the judgement of Solomon to their problem.[76]

Already on 12 January Malan had noted that the possibility of dividing the capital was being mooted[77] and by the 25th Smuts was seeking advice as to whether, if a division was to be made, Pretoria would do

[74] Sir Patrick Duncan, 'South African Reminiscences' (unpublished manuscript), Duncan Papers.

[75] N. J. van der Merwe, *Marthinus Theunis Steyn: 'n Lewensbeskrywing* (Cape Town, 1921, 2 vols.), ii. 341; Fitzpatrick, 'The Capital Question' (unpublished manuscript), Fitzpatrick Papers. These two accounts of the discussion agree to the extent indicated in the text above. In his manuscript, and in a public speech, Fitzpatrick went further, asserting that Steyn had also said that the German people were determined on war against England and that when the war broke out the Germans would invade South Africa. Steyn, however, denied that he had said these things and dismissed them as the embellishment of Fitzpatrick's poetic imagination. Van der Merwe, loc. cit.

[76] Duncan to Lady Selborne, 28 Jan. 1909: 'The fertile mind of Smuts busies itself in producing compromises on this and other contentious questions. His one object is to get the thing through.' Duncan Papers.

[77] Malan, pp. 160–1.

better as the seat of the Executive or the seat of Parliament.[78] Then, in conclave on the morning of the 28th, Merriman and Botha tentatively broached the possibility of a division. They found it easy to agree upon the line of a division, because Merriman, as a parliamentarian through and through, regarded Parliament as the larger share of the cake, while to Botha the Executive was much more important. But Botha was bound by the Transvaal caucus to go no further than to suggest that Pretoria should be the capital and that Parliament should meet in Cape Town until it decided otherwise. The following day, however, Botha was able to allow that Parliament should be regarded as being permanently located in Cape Town, but he still insisted that Pretoria should have the higher status, with the designation of capital. When Merriman reported this to his caucus, the Cape delegates refused to consent that Cape Town should have anything less than complete equality with Pretoria, but in the last resort they were willing to accept Bloemfontein as the sole capital.[79] Jagger was so distressed by this decision that he went to G. H. Wilson, of the *Cape Times*, and told him that unless immediate action was taken the convention would split the capital, giving Pretoria the seat of the Executive Government, with the result that the *Cape Times* of 30 January carried a leading article by Wilson, stating that 'It has been proposed . . . that the administrative capital shall be in Pretoria, and the political capital in Cape Town', denouncing the proposal as impossibly extravagant and impracticable, and reiterating the demand for a referendum. When the convention met that morning de Villiers drew attention to the article—the first and only leakage of information designed to influence the convention in an important decision—and said that it showed a breach of faith by a delegate. Jagger rose and confessed his responsibility, saying that he considered that the threat to Cape Town was so serious that it was his greater duty to make the communication rather than to maintain the pledge of secrecy.[80] The convention then turned to business. At the beginning of the afternoon sitting Merriman moved that 'The Seat of the Executive Government of the Union shall be at Pretoria and the seat of the Legislature shall be at Cape Town', and Botha moved as an amendment that 'Pretoria shall be the capital and the seat of the Government of the Union; the sessions of Parliament shall, however, be held at Cape Town.' The convention did not react favourably to the principle of division. Greene said that it would be imprac-

---

[78] Selborne to Smuts, 26 Jan. 1909, Smuts Papers.

[79] Merriman's Diary, 28–29 Jan. 1909; Malan, pp. 206–7; Walton, pp. 279–80.

[80] G. H. Wilson, *Gone Down the Years* (Cape Town, n.d. [1947]), pp. 203–4. Wilson describes Jagger's disclosure without assigning a precise date to it, but he almost certainly refers to the leading article in the *Cape Times* on 30 Jan. 1909.

ticable, de la Rey announced that 'if Pretoria did not become the full capital, he would not support Union', Jagger moved that there should be a referendum, and the Orange River Colony delegates became hopeful that they might carry off the prize.[81]

The debate continued in a stormy fashion throughout Monday, 1 February. Botha was now willing to delete the word 'capital' from his motion, but the Cape delegates were still dissatisfied. Hull sent up another *ballon d'essai* from the Transvaal lines, proposing that the Union Parliament should be empowered to locate the capital 'at some place on the Vaal river', whereupon Sauer moved an amendment to give Parliament full freedom to place the capital where it wished. Before the day was over both these motions had been withdrawn, but a perky Natal motion, for the capital to be at Pietermaritzburg, remained on the agenda, with those of Merriman, Botha, and Jagger.[82]

Moving the adjournment of the debate at 4.35 p.m., Smuts suggested that the prime ministers should make a final effort to come to some agreement. Meeting that evening, the prime ministers started to talk on the basis of a single capital, but Botha would not budge south of the Vaal river and Merriman would not go north of Bloemfontein. They then called in de Villiers and at his suggestion they reverted to the idea of a division and eventually—somewhat in desperation—they patched up a compromise on that basis.[83] Section 17 of the draft Constitution would declare that 'Save as in section twenty-two excepted, Pretoria shall be the seat of Government of the Union.'[84] Section 22 would state that 'Cape Town shall be the seat of the Legislature of the Union.'[85] And section 109 would read, 'The Appellate Division of the Supreme Court of South Africa shall sit in Bloemfontein, but may from time to time for the convenience of suitors hold its sittings at other places within the Union.'[86] Merriman and Botha also agreed that they would try to make a success of the compromise and 'not agitate without reason'[87] for a change, though it was understood that they would not attempt to bind Parliament

[81] The convention's proceedings concerning the capital on 30 Jan. are dealt with in the *Minutes*, pp. 238–9; Malan, pp. 208–13; Walton, p. 281. De la Rey is quoted as reported by Malan.

[82] The convention's proceedings concerning the capital on 1 Feb. are dealt with in the *Minutes*, pp. 239, 243–4; Malan, pp. 212–17; Walton, pp. 281–2.

[83] The only contemporary accounts of the discussions of the evening of 1 Feb. are a very brief entry in Merriman's diary and the summary by Malan, pp. 216–19, of the statements made to the convention by de Villiers and Merriman the next day.

[84] S. 18 of the S.A. Act is virtually identical.

[85] S. 23 of the S.A. Act is identical.

[86] S. 109 of the S.A. Act is virtually identical.

[87] Malan, pp. 218–19.

in the matter. In the convention the next day Merriman and de Villiers explained what had happened. Fischer made no attempt to conceal his disappointment that the prize had so narrowly eluded Bloemfontein, and Greene reiterated his opinion that the scheme was impracticable. Nevertheless, the insertions in the draft Constitution were approved *nem. con.* and it was also decided that the existing colonial capitals should become the seats of their respective provincial governments.[88]

There remained the question of compensation. After considerable discussion the convention had already agreed that the colonial capitals which did not become the capital of the Union should be compensated for their 'diminution of prosperity or decreased rateable value' with annual payments from the revenue fund of 2 per cent. of their municipal debts, as existing in January 1909, for up to twenty-five years, provided that at any time after ten years the Governor-General-in-Council with the approval of Parliament would be able to reduce or withdraw the payments 'after due enquiry'.[89] The question now arose: What further action should be taken, if any, in view of the fact that the capital was to be divided? Neither the Transvaal nor the Cape delegation was prepared to admit that it had been worsted in the capital decision, but while Pretoria municipality was prosperous and only had a debt of about £1 million, Cape Town municipality was in financial straits and had a debt of £4½ millions. Consequently, the Transvaal proposed that Cape Town should receive compensation and Pretoria should not, while the Cape maintained that both towns should be compensated. Eventually, the 'undignified wrangle'[90] ended in an agreement that the commission which was to report on the financial relations between the Union and the provinces should also recommend what compensation, if any, Cape Town and Pretoria should receive, up to a maximum of 1 per cent. of their existing municipal debts for twenty-five years, and subject to the same proviso which applied to compensation for Bloemfontein and Pietermaritzburg.[91] These decisions were embodied in section 135 of the draft Constitution.[92]

The division of the capital was undoubtedly a clumsy expedient—clumsier in the long run than the Australian decision to build a new town on a virgin site—for cabinet ministers and civil servants would be put to

[88] Merriman's Diary, 2 Feb. 1909; *Minutes*, pp. 244–5; Malan, pp. 216–19; Walton, pp. 282–3.

[89] *Minutes*, pp. 159, 170–2, 186, 189–91, 195–8, 206, 212, 237; Walton, pp. 254–5; Malan, pp. 160–1, 168–73, 184–5.

[90] Merriman's Diary, 2 Feb. 1909.

[91] *Minutes*, pp. 246–8; Malan, pp. 218–21; Walton, pp. 255–6.

[92] S. 133 of the S.A. Act is virtually identical.

the inconvenience of biannual migrations of a thousand miles, costs would be increased, and efficiency would be reduced. On the other hand, inconvenience, additional expense, and a measure of inefficiency were perhaps not too great a price to pay for the achievement of harmony on an issue which, rightly or wrongly, was generally regarded as vitally important, while it is not altogether a bad thing in so large a country that ministers and civil servants should be obliged to experience the atmospheres of two centres which differ as widely as Cape Town and Pretoria.

15. THE REPORT OF THE CONVENTION

By the time 'that damned capital question'[93] had been settled the convention had decided on the steps which should be taken to gain the approval of the colonial parliaments to the draft Constitution and to inaugurate the Union. Sections 4–6 of the draft Constitution covered much of the ground. They were based on resolutions which the convention passed on 15 December, following recommendations by the committee on the civil service and miscellaneous matters, and they provided that the sequence of events leading to Union should be as follows: firstly, the parliaments of the Cape Colony, Natal, the Transvaal, and the Orange River Colony would be invited to agree to the Constitution; secondly, if two or more of them did so, the South Africa Act would be enacted by the Imperial Parliament; thirdly, the King, on the advice of the Privy Council, would issue a proclamation to bring the Union into being on a specified day; fourthly, the King would be able to appoint a Governor-General for the Union at any time after the proclamation had been issued; and, lastly, on the day specified the South Africa Act would come into force, with the four colonies as the original provinces of the Union, unless one or two of them had failed to pass the required resolutions before the date of the proclamation, in which case they would only be able to enter the Union in the manner prescribed for the admission of new provinces.[94]

Before the convention met, it may be recalled, Merriman had hoped that it would be possible to ignore the Imperial Parliament by having the Constitution enacted by the colonial parliaments with the approval of the Crown, but de Villiers had always considered that the Constitution would have to be enacted by the Imperial Parliament, as 'the only Legis-

[93] Jameson, in a private letter dated 7 Jan. 1909. Colvin, *Jameson*, ii. 281.

[94] *Minutes*, pp. 126, 129, 154, 159, 224, 282–3. Ss. 4–6 of the S.A. Act were amended in England by the omission of the reference to the possibility that one or more of the colonies might refrain from passing the necessary resolutions, since all four colonies had by that time done so.

lature which in theory has the power of legislating for South Africa as a whole . . . a power which would not be exercised except at the request of the Colonies of S. Africa'.[95] When this question came before the convention on 15 December, neither Merriman nor any other delegate questioned the committee's recommendation that the Canadian and Australian precedents should be followed. There was, however, some discussion as to whether the first Union Parliament should be elected before or after the inauguration of the Union. Fitzpatrick and Moor wanted the Parliament to be elected first, so that the Governor-General could be guided by the election results in deciding whom to invite to form a Government, but de Villiers, Smartt, and Malan contended that it would not be practicable to hold an election before the Union was inaugurated and their view prevailed. The report of the committee had not allowed for the contingency that one or two of the self-governing colonies might refrain from passing the necessary resolutions for the Union, and it was at Smuts's suggestion that provision was made for the creation of the Union even though only two of the colonies consented—a significant insertion, which would be a warning to critics of the draft Constitution that if a colony rejected it she would probably have to make her own way in the world in competition with a union of the other three colonies.[96]

Sections 4–6 of the draft Constitution did not determine what steps were to be taken to gain the consent of the colonial parliaments. Accordingly, on 29 January the convention appointed a committee, consisting of de Villiers and the four prime ministers, to draft the necessary recommendations to form part of the report of the convention, and the next day it was agreed to recommend that the colonial parliaments should meet on 30 March to consider the draft Constitution, that if necessary the convention should reassemble in Bloemfontein during May, and that during June the revised document should be submitted to the four parliaments to pass the necessary resolutions and to appoint delegates to proceed to England to facilitate the passing of the South Africa Act. The report of the convention,[97] comprising these recommendations and the draft Constitution, would be released for publication at 8 p.m. on 9 February, with a précis of the Constitution prepared by a committee under Walton's chairmanship and a Dutch version prepared by a committee under the chairmanship of Hertzog.[98]

[95] See above, pp. 85–88.
[96] Malan, pp. 132–5.
[97] Minutes, pp. 312–45 ; Cd. 4525 (1909), Report to the Respective Parliaments of the Delegates to the South African Convention, 1908–1909; with copy of the Draft South Africa Constitution Bill.
[98] Minutes, pp. 235–6, 239–44, 248 ; Malan, pp. 208–9, 220–1 ; Walton, pp. 314–20.

The convention completed its work on 3 February, when votes of thanks were passed to the President, to the secretaries and legal advisers, and to the Government of the Cape Colony and the Mayor and Town Council of Cape Town, and every delegate who was present signed the report, the five absentees doing so later.[99]

Considering the strife and tension which had marred the relations between white South Africans during the previous generation, it is remarkable that thirty-three such men should unanimously have appended their signatures to an instrument for the creation of a union of the four self-governing colonies. None of them was wholly satisfied with the report, for compromise had been the price of unanimity and the prolonged deadlock over the capital had caused irritation and exhaustion, but every delegate had been through an experience which would profoundly affect his attitude towards his fellow white South Africans for the rest of his life and every delegate had become inspired to some extent by the Botha–Smuts ideal of a united white South African nation. On 12 December de Wet, the guerrilla general of 1901, publicly affirmed that 'today it does not matter what race we belong to . . . as long as we are South Africans', and Fitzpatrick, the political prisoner of 1896, echoed him with the assurance that they were making 'a final peace' between Boer and Briton.[1] On 2 February Botha explained the capital compromise to the editor of the *Volksstem* and concluded with the appeal, 'Let us honestly support the covenant; it is an honourable understanding';[2] and soon afterwards Smuts, the principal architect of the covenant, penned the following words:[3]

The greatest and most pressing need of South Africa today is the welding of the various sections of its white people into one compact nationality inspired by one common pervading national spirit. That has been the ideal of all true South African Statesmen and now—with one common flag over South Africa, with the sobering effect which the dreadful experiences of the last decade have had on its people and the spirit of mutual respect and

[99] *Minutes*, pp. 248–9. The absentees on 3 Feb. were de Wet (who had gone home during the weekend, exasperated at the failure of the Cape Colony and the Transvaal to agree upon a capital), Steyn (who had left, somewhat exhausted, the previous day), Malan (who went to Bredasdorp to open an agricultural show), and two Rhodesians, Milton and Coghlan.

[1] *Cape Times*, 14 Dec. 1908. Many public speeches by the delegates touched the same note during the period of the convention.

[2] Botha to F. V. Engelenburg, quoted by Engelenburg in *General Louis Botha* (London, 1929), p. 178.

[3] In the Smuts Papers there is a folder marked 'Pamphlet', containing these and other notes in Smuts's hand, written soon after the convention rose. He appears to have intended to publish a pamphlet appealing to South Africans to support the draft Constitution, but the work was not completed.

reconciliation which is noticeable everywhere in the land—the ideal has become practicable and attainable.

And again:

In the creative Spirit of History the blunders of men are often more valuable than their profoundest wisdom. . . . From the blood and tears of nations which human passions have caused she proceeds calmly and dispassionately to build up new nations and to lead them along new undiscovered paths of progress. And when the darkness of the night has passed at last and the light of a new national consciousness forms, the scales fall from men's eyes, they perceive that they have been led, that they have been borne forward in the darkness by deeper power than they ever apprehended to a larger goal than they ever conceived, and they stand silent in the presence of that greatest mystery in the world, the birth of the soul of a new nation.

But when the convention rose the delegates went their separate ways and within a week their design was exposed to the scrutiny of journalists and politicians who had not gone through the tempering experience of labour in its creation—including some whose ideal of a South African nation was narrower and others whose ideal was more comprehensive than that of Louis Botha and Jan Christiaan Smuts.

CHAPTER VI

SOUTH AFRICA APPROVES OF THE CONSTITUTION

1. INITIAL REACTIONS TO THE REPORT OF THE CONVENTION

WHILE the National Convention was sitting, Lionel Curtis had been building up the closer union societies as a means of preparing the white people of South Africa to give a favourable reception to the convention's report. Until October 1908 the societies had no central organization, but then representatives of eleven societies met in Durban and formed an association, with a central executive as a co-ordinating body. Curtis then toured South Africa addressing public meetings and encouraging prominent local men to found new societies. The association also launched a monthly journal, the *State*, which was edited by Philip Kerr. Each number contained over a hundred pages of text and several illustrations and it had a wide circulation because a donation of £6,000 by Abe Bailey made it possible to fix the price at 6*d*. a copy. The first two numbers were published before the convention's report. They contained information about the growth and the activities of the societies; they reiterated the arguments for union and rebutted Olive Schreiner's contention that the politicians were rushing the question; and they explained the complications of several of the major problems confronting the convention, including the problems of the franchise, the protectorates, and the capital, so that readers might be willing to endorse compromise solutions. On 12 February a special Constitution number appeared, with an analysis of the draft Constitution by Patrick Duncan and an explanation of proportional representation by R. H. Brand, and during the rest of February the societies held numerous meetings to discuss the draft Constitution. Although the societies had been initiated by Lionel Curtis and he and other members of the kindergarten continued to be their main driving force, every effort was made to obtain bi-partisan support in each colony and to concentrate on the single issue of the successful completion of a South African union. The Durban conference elected W. P. Schreiner as President of the association, and he was succeeded in March 1909 by M. T. Steyn; F. S. Malan, J. A. Neser, and E. Rooth were among the vice-presidents; J. G. van der Horst and H. S. van Zijl were members of the organizing sub-committee; and Afrikaners predominated in several of the societies—e.g., C. J. Langenhoven, a leading light of the Afrikaans language movement, was secretary of the Oudtshoorn society. Furthermore, the *State* appeared in both English and Dutch editions and the first number included messages of encouragement from Merriman, Malan, Botha, Smuts, and Fischer as well as from Jameson, Farrar, and Moor. Nevertheless, the main impact of the closer union societies and the *State* was upon the English-speaking white South Africans in the towns and villages of the Transvaal, the Cape Colony, and the Orange River Colony—and there their influence was considerable.[1]

The news of the capital compromise was released to the press on 3 February and it caused a considerable flutter, but when the full report of the convention was published on the 9th the English-medium newspapers outside Natal gave it a favourable reception, though they criticized many of the details from a colonial standpoint. On 10 February the *Cape Times* declared that 'taken as a whole, the Constitution is at once bold and ingenious and statesmanlike' and the next day the Johannesburg *Star* pronounced it to be 'a notable achievement'. During the following weeks the Progressive, Unionist, and Constitutionalist delegates expounded and defended it at public meetings in their colonies. Each admitted that it contained details which he disliked, but all of them recommended that it should be accepted as a fair compromise between the two white races and the four colonies.[2] The result was that opinion among the English-speaking whites in the Transvaal, the Cape Colony, and the Orange River Colony gradually crystallized in favour of the adoption of the draft Constitution without amendment. The language section evoked very little criticism and there was general confidence in the principle of Anglo-Afrikaner unity. This trend reached its climax when the closer union societies held a conference in Johannesburg between 3 and 5 March to debate the draft Constitution.[3] It was attended by eleven members of the executive of the association and by 111 representatives of fifty-three societies, of whom about three-quarters were of British descent and most of the others were Afrikaners. The proceedings started with addresses by Smuts and Farrar, who appealed to the conference to endorse the work of the convention. Duncan then moved 'That

[1] *State*, i, especially 1–29, 104–16 (Jan. 1909), 117–35, 233–4 (Feb. 1909), and the special Constitution number, 12 Feb. 1909.

[2] e.g. Jagger in Cape Town on 13 Feb., Jameson in Grahamstown on 15 Feb., Fitzpatrick in Pretoria on 18 Feb., and Farrar in Boksburg on 22 Feb.

[3] *Proceedings of the Annual Meeting of the Association of Closer Union Societies at Johannesburg, March 3rd, 4th and 5th, 1909* (Johannesburg, n.d. [1909]), being a full **verbatim** report.

the Association of Closer Union Societies approves of the draft South Africa Act, and recommends its adoption by the Colonies of South Africa', and F. Burger, the secretary of Het Volk, seconded. In a three-day debate several amendments to the draft Constitution were moved and considered, but none were carried. Most of the representatives were convinced by the argument that to tinker with the unanimous report of the convention would be to endanger Union, and Duncan's resolution was adopted unanimously, though some who were members of colonial parliaments reserved the right to support amendments on particular points. Finally, the conference was addressed by Fitzpatrick, who was present as an observer, and his peroration struck the note which had been dominant throughout the proceedings. 'For the first time', he said, 'it has been possible for the two white peoples to come together and make a peace that, as I think, has come to last for all time. Everything else is small in comparison. Go out as missionaries of union to bring about the settlement for ever of the differences between the white races of South Africa.'

The reaction of the Natal press to the draft Constitution was extremely adverse. The *Advertiser* described it as 'a sentence of death', the *Natal Witness* said it would result in the 'obliteration' of Natal 'as an independent factor in South African politics', the *Mercury* regarded it as 'impossible' in its present form, and only the *Times of Natal* counselled acceptance—and then only if the amending section was changed to make any constitutional amendment require at least absolute majorities in both Houses of Parliament.[4] On 16 February, however, Moor convened a private meeting of the members of the Natal Parliament, and when he had explained that he and his fellow delegates had been unable to obtain better terms for Natal and had advised them to accept the draft Constitution, if only for economic reasons, most of them were inclined to agree with him.[5] But then on 22 February Moor ran into organized opposition when he addressed a public meeting in Pietermaritzburg, where a resolution was passed condemning the draft Constitution unless it was substantially amended to increase and safeguard the powers of the provinces, and soon afterwards local citizens formed a Constitution Amendment Association, which was supported by the *Natal Witness* and the town council of Pietermaritzburg.[6] Elsewhere in Natal there were other critics, of whom Major Silburn was the most outspoken. In Durban,

---

[4] Quoted by the *Cape Times*, 11 and 13 Feb. 1909.
[5] Sir Walter Hely-Hutchinson to Merriman, 18 Feb. 1909, retailing information probably received from Sir Matthew Nathan, Governor of Natal, Merriman Papers.
[6] *Natal Witness*, 23, 25, and 26 Feb. 1909.

at the end of February, at a dinner held to commemorate the relief of Ladysmith, he said that 'the patriotism which held Ladysmith for Natal, and Natal for the Empire, against the assaults of a gallant enemy, would, he trusted, be proof against the more serious assault now being made upon the independence of themselves and their descendants' and he reminded them of Cromwell's motto: 'Put your trust in God and keep your powder dry.'[7] The closer union societies had never made great headway in Natal, and differences of outlook had developed between the Natal representatives and the others at the Durban Conference in October. Silburn attended the Johannesburg Conference in March, and when Duncan's resolution in favour of the draft Constitution had been adopted he publicly repudiated it and declared that unless the Constitution was amended to her satisfaction Natal would remain independent.[8] Meanwhile Moor, Watt, Greene, and Hyslop were doggedly applying themselves to the task of trying to make the draft Constitution seem palatable to the white people of Natal. Watt found that the northern districts, with their large Afrikaner population, were satisfied; and Moor found that Durban was less critical than the capital because her people were more aware of the economic implications of isolation and they were pleased with the electoral provisions, which redressed their longstanding grievance of under-representation in the Natal Parliament.[9] But Moor and his fellow delegates were embarrassed by the endemic suspicions of the Transvaal, which had been reinforced by a remark by Smuts who, trying to counter the allegation that the Transvaal was making all the sacrifices for union, had publicly described the railway sections of the draft Constitution as 'the Magna Carta of the inland colonies'—a phrase which was taken up by the Natal press as proof of Smuts's intention to throttle the coastal industries.[10] Furthermore, the negotiations between the Transvaal Government and the Portuguese were still dragging out, with the Portuguese raising fresh points which had not been accepted by the colonial prime ministers in Cape Town, and the Transvaal could not allow the publication of all the terms of the intercolonial railway agreement so long as the new Transvaal–Mozambique Convention was unsigned, so that an atmosphere of mystery surrounded the question of Natal's future share of the Witwatersrand traffic.[11] Nevertheless, during March the Natal press was calmer and more people were becoming reconciled to the idea that Natal should join the Union, though it was generally hoped that the

[7] *Natal Advertiser*, 1 Mar. 1909.   [8] *Rand Daily Mail*, 8 Mar. 1909.
[9] *The Times*, 23 and 27 Feb. 1909.
[10] *Natal Witness*, 26 Feb. 1909.
[11] Documents relating to this question are in the Natal Archives, Prime Minister, CVII, CIX.

draft Constitution would be amended to increase the powers of the provinces and to protect them from alteration by a bare majority in the Union Parliament.

Among the Europeans in the Orange River Colony there was no serious opposition to the draft Constitution. Some regarded the capital compromise as unfair to Bloemfontein and feared that Bloemfontein would suffer from union, and others found it difficult to accept the existence of non-European voters in the parliamentary constituencies of the Cape Province, but the language section and the restoration of the name Orange Free State gave great satisfaction to the Afrikaners. After his return from Cape Town, Fischer convened a private meeting of the members of the Colonial Parliament and explained the document to them,[12] and thereafter he and his fellow delegates addressed meetings up and down the colony, obtaining support for the draft Constitution. After speaking at Senekal and Winburg, Steyn wrote to Merriman on 26 February to tell him that 'the spirit of our people is all that can be desired. The Draft Act was unanimously approved of in both places. It was most encouraging and makes one hopeful for the future.'[13] The campaign came to a head on 4 March when the Orangia Unie held a special congress in Bloemfontein, attended by Fischer, Steyn, and Hertzog and about fifty delegates from the branches. Fischer said that the convention 'had endeavoured to eliminate racial feeling, and the great principle of equal rights for all white people had been laid down once and for all',[14] Steyn spoke in similar vein, and the following resolution was unanimously adopted: 'The Congress having carefully considered the contents of the Draft Constitution for United South Africa, and having heard the explanation of the members of the National Convention, approves the principle of union, as laid down therein, and resolves to recommend its adoption to the people.'[15] The same evening Sir John Fraser, the Leader of the Opposition, addressed his constituents in the Bloemfontein city hall. Fischer appeared with him on the platform and seconded his motion, which was carried amid cheers, giving Fraser a free hand in Parliament 'to vote for the adoption of the draft, and to secure any amendments thereto he considers necessary'.[16] Thus both parties in the Orange River

[12] *Cape Times*, 13 Feb. 1909.   [13] Merriman Papers.

[14] *Cape Times*, 5 Mar. 1909.

[15] 'Het Congres nauwkerig gelet hebbende op den inhoud van de Ontwerp Constitutie voor Verenigd Zuid Afrika, en na die toelichting der leden van de Nationale Conventie te hebben gehoord, keurt het principe van vereeniging, zooals daarin neergelegd, goed, en besluit de aanname daarvan aan het volk aan te bevelen.' *Verrichtingen van het Buitengewoon Congres der Orangia Unie ... en van het Vierde Jaarlijksch Congres ...* (Bloemfontein, 1909), p. 6.

[16] *Cape Times*, 5 Mar. 1909.

Colony were solidly behind the draft Constitution and Steyn had no compunction in accepting the office of President of the association of closer union societies, to which he was elected by the Johannesburg Conference on 5 March, in succession to W. P. Schreiner.

In the Transvaal, also, the Dutch as well as the English press was favourable to the draft Constitution, but a group of young Afrikaner lawyers tried to foment opposition. Making much of a statement by Sauer that the arrangement about the capital was only binding for five years and that thereafter Cape Town need have no fears, and arguing that the Constitution would make the Transvaal 'the milch cow' of the coastal colonies and that 'the Kaffir vote' would soon be extended to the northern provinces, they obtained support from diverse quarters—from A. D. W. Wolmarans and a number of predikants, who looked back nostalgically to Kruger's republic, from traders and industrialists, including J. B. Robinson, a director of gold-mining companies, who feared that running the railways at cost would mean increased taxation of the mines, and from British as well as Afrikaner negrophobes, including Sir Aubrey Woolls Sampson, who could not stomach the Cape non-European franchise.[17] There was, however, no real danger of a landslide of Afrikaner opinion in the Transvaal, and when the Het Volk parliamentary caucus met on 23 February Wolmarans was the only member who opposed the decision to support the draft Constitution without amendment.[18] The next evening Botha and Smuts addressed a mammoth public meeting in Pretoria.[19] Botha said that the only alternative to the adoption of the draft Constitution was continued division and further bloodshed, and he invited the people of the Transvaal to be not 'Little Transvaalers' but 'great South Africans'—'to grasp the hand of brotherhood over the graves of the fallen, and to make one happy, united country'. He made a special appeal to Afrikaners to respond to the advances of their British fellow countrymen who, he said, had been extremely generous over the language question. Botha and Smuts then toured the Transvaal, addressing public meetings and obtaining approval of the draft Constitution. On 17 March Botha was able to inform Merriman, 'We have now toured nearly the whole country and have carried practically unanimous resolutions everywhere, accepting the Draft Constitution and leaving it to Parliament to approve of it with such amendments as may seem desirable to that body.' He added, however, that he had found widespread criticism

---

[17] Botha to Steyn, 16 Feb. 1909, Steyn Papers. Botha to Merriman and Smuts to Merriman, 19 Feb. 1909, Merriman Papers.
[18] Wolmarans to Botha, 19 Mar. 1909, Transvaal Archives, Prime Minister, LX (v).
[19] Star, 25 Feb. 1909; Volksstem, 26 Feb. 1909.

of the Cape Native franchise and that he had had great difficulty in preventing resolutions from being passed for its removal: 'I can assure you that a very great number of people in the Transvaal, English as well as Dutch, are quite prepared to wreck Union on this question.' He also said that he had been worried by a cry for a referendum, which was being raised by the Labour Party and taken up by some of the farmers, but that he did not propose to yield to it.[20] By that time a Progressive congress in Johannesburg had unanimously resolved to support the draft Constitution,[21] so that in the Transvaal, as in the Orange River Colony, the Government and the official Opposition were in complete agreement.

In the Cape Colony, on the other hand, there was a formidable movement for substantial amendments to the draft Constitution. One of the organizers was J. G. van der Horst, the editor of the *Cape*, an English-medium weekly published in Cape Town. Van der Horst, like many thoughtful Afrikaners in the Cape Colony, had drunk deeply of the writings of the British Liberal economists and political philosophers. He had viewed the racial policy of the Government of the South African Republic with considerable misgivings, but the events of the years 1895 to 1905 had made him intensely suspicious of British imperialism and of the gold-mining industry of the Witwatersrand which, he feared, were using Botha and Smuts for their own nefarious purposes. It is not surprising, therefore, that he found the draft Constitution wanting and that he atacked it in the *Cape*. The first page of the number of 12 February predicted that under the draft Constitution the Cape Province would never have its fair share of power in the Union because it would always be under-represented in Parliament, that the liberal Native policy of the Cape Colony would be undermined and sooner or later all the non-Europeans would be disfranchised, that the Union Parliament would be moved to Pretoria and Cape Town would be impoverished, and that the entire country would be dominated by the gold-mining corporations, that is to say, by cosmopolitan capitalism. 'It means, in a word', the article concluded, 'that the Cape will be ANNEXED by the Transvaal.' These criticisms were vividly illustrated by D. C. Boonzaier, among whose most telling cartoons were drawings of Hoggenheimer, a mythical gold-mining magnate—opulent, crafty, and semitic. The *Cape* of 12 February carried a full-page drawing of a statue of Hoggenheimer 'The Nation-Maker', with the caption that it was 'proposed to be erected in the Capital of the United South Africa'. The next issue showed Merriman as the 'young lady of Riga, who went for a ride on a Tiger'.

Another forthright critic of the draft Constitution was W. P. Schreiner,

[20] Merriman Papers.   [21] *Rand Daily Mail*, 13 Mar. 1909.

the former Prime Minister. An independent member of the House of Assembly, he had withdrawn from the Cape delegation to the National Convention to fulfil his undertaking to defend Dinizulu from the charges brought against him by the Natal Government. Like his sister, Olive, he held federal views and he believed that 'the fundamental unalterable principle of the Constitution' should be a firmly entrenched provision against 'discrimination or distinction upon such grounds as colour or race'.[22] When the draft Constitution was published he was at Greytown, Natal, where the Dinizulu trial was still dragging on, and he promptly sent a long telegram to the *Cape Times*, describing it as 'narrow, illiberal and short-sighted in its conception of the people of South Africa' because 'The great majority are not of European race or descent, and their rights and future are not adequately safeguarded.'[23] This attitude was anathema to most white South Africans, but it was shared by a number of ecclesiastics and others, most of whom lived in Cape Town. A long argument developed in the correspondence columns of the *Cape Times* on the question whether the Cape delegates to the National Convention had fulfilled their promises to protect the established rights of the non-Europeans. The argument turned on two main points: firstly, whether the two-thirds majority requirement was an adequate safeguard for the non-European franchise, and, secondly, whether the limitation of membership of the Union Parliament to men of European descent amounted to a deprivation of an established right. At their public meetings the Cape delegates were hard pressed to justify their conduct, and their confident assurances that the necessary two-thirds majority would never be found to curtail the non-European franchise were offset by reports of speeches made in the Transvaal. At the Pretoria meeting on 24 February Botha said that 'The only possible course for us to follow was followed in the Draft Constitution, and that was to create machinery which would enable the people of South Africa to settle the matter', and Smuts said that 'There was a vast majority of people in South Africa opposed to the Native Franchise. . . . On the first occasion the Parliament met it could be swept away. It was found necessary that there should be some check on such arbitrary action. It was not a powerful check, perhaps it was not a check at all. It had been put in there, but he did not think it meant much.'[24] Still more disturbing was a report that F. E. T. Krause, a member of the Transvaal Parliament, speaking at Newton on 9 March, said that 'as long as they did not turn traitor to their own skin, they would

---

[22] From a letter written to Basil Williams, *The Times* special correspondent, while the convention was sitting; quoted in Walker, *Schreiner*, p. 311.
[23] *Cape Times*, 12 Feb. 1909. [24] Ibid., 3 Mar. 1909.

never allow the coloured man to have a vote in this country. The Constitution would give them power to deal with the question'. He added, 'when once we can diddle the British Government to give us that power, by Jove! we will use it.'[25]

The first pronouncements of J. H. Hofmeyr on the draft Constitution were guarded, but his reactions were similar to those of van der Horst, and he was enough of a Liberal to have some sympathy with Schreiner's criticisms, and within a few days he decided to use his influence to try to secure radical amendments. When the Cape Town branch of the Afrikaner Bond met on 18 February to define its attitude, Hofmeyr's views prevailed by a small majority, and a statement was issued to the press roundly condemning the draft Constitution.[26] It deplored the under-representation of the Cape Province in Parliament and the 'total subjection' of the provinces to the Central Government. It stated that 'a parliamentary experience of about fifty years has not proved the necessity for the introduction of colour restrictions in respect of the membership of the Parliament of the Cape Colony', and that the two-thirds majority to be required for the withdrawal of the Cape non-European franchise should include a majority of the representatives of the Cape Province. It declared that it was 'imperatively necessary' that the electoral divisions in thinly populated areas should be single-member divisions and that it was 'rash' to introduce proportional representation without previous experiment or experience. It recommended that the principle of official bilingualism should be explicitly extended to the provincial governments. It criticized the Constitution as being too flexible —constitutional amendments should require some special majority in Parliament and 'in order to give stability or security to the Constitution, the principle of a majority of two-thirds, as set forth in Article 153 of the Draft Act, ought to be extended further than is done in that article'. It also declared that a referendum should be held in the Cape Colony before the Constitution was enacted.

The publication of this resolution precipitated intense discussions throughout the Bond, culminating at its annual congress which was held at Dordrecht from 4 to 8 March.[27] J. H. Hofmeyr did not attend, but van der Horst was there as the delegate of the Cape Town branch. After debating the draft Constitution in private sessions the congress unanimously adopted a somewhat ambiguous resolution, which was a compromise between the views of those who were loath to endanger union

[25] Ibid., 10 Mar. 1909.   [26] Ibid., 19 Feb. 1909.

[27] *Vijf en twintigste Centrale Vergadering van de Afrikaander Bond en Boeren Vereeniging* . . . (Cape Town, 1909).

and those who were determined to have the draft Constitution amended. It stated 'First of all . . ., that under no circumstances should differences of opinion concerning items of minor importance be allowed to wreck the great object of Union.' 'Secondly', it continued, 'the Union will be the firmer according as the following principles are recognised in her Constitution'—and it then proceeded to set out eleven principles, which included most of the points which had been made by the Cape Town branch of the Bond. 'And, thirdly', the resolution concluded, 'the Central Committee considers the subject of Closer Union of such overwhelming importance that no one's conscience should be stifled by party influence. Therefore, although the Central Committee earnestly hopes that our Parliament will accept its opinion, it wishes clearly to lay down that it does not desire to dictate to members of Parliament in this matter, where they may have a difference of opinion on these points.'[28]

By that time judgment had at last been delivered in the *Dinizulu* case and Schreiner had returned to Cape Town, where he had discussions with J. H. Hofmeyr. Then he went to Queenstown where, addressing his constituents on 18 March, he used several of Hofmeyr's criticisms of the draft Constitution, and a few days later he was back in Cape Town to do the same at a crowded meeting in the city hall, with Hofmeyr alongside him on the platform.[29]

Merriman was grievously embarrassed by this opposition. If he had not been a member of the National Convention it is possible that he would have associated himself with the Bond's criticisms, for nobody was more suspicious of the Transvaal or more averse to the principle of equal constituencies than he. As it was, he privately admitted that the Cape had lost 'everything' in the draft Constitution 'except in mere finance',[30] but he was anxious to avoid another session of the convention, because he was convinced that it would be unable to agree upon any substantial concessions to the Cape. Consequently, to Merriman the critics were 'wreckers'. Speaking in the Cape Town city hall on 22 Feb-

[28] 'Allereerst . . ., dat onder geen omstandigheden verschillen over ondergeschikte punten het grote doel van vereniging mogen doen schipbreuk lijden ; Ten tweede, dat de Unie te hechter zal zijn naarmate de volgende beginsels worden erkend in haar Konstitutie . . . ; Ten derde : Beschouwt het Centraal Bestuur het ontwerp van nauwere vereniging van zulk overweldigend belang, dat niemands geweten behoort gesmoord te worden door partij invloed. Dienshalve, alhoewel het Centraal Bestuur ernstig hoopt, dat ons Parlement zijn opinie zal aannemen, wenst het duidelik neer te leggen, dat het niet verlangt parlementaire leden in deze zaak voor te schrijven, waar zij op deze punten mogen verschillen.' *Vijf en twintigste Centrale Vergadering van de Afrikaander Bond en Boeren Vereeniging*, pp. 33–38.

[29] *Cape Times*, 20 and 26 Mar. 1909.

[30] Merriman to Sir Somerset French, Agent-General for the Cape Colony in London, 10 Feb. 1909, Merriman Papers (copy).

ruary he explained that every amendment which was being canvassed had been thrashed out in the convention and he appealed to everyone 'to participate in the overwhelming general benefits of Union'.[31] Botha, Smuts, and Steyn sympathized with him in his difficulties and encouraged him to stand firm.[32] 'Schreiner, Hofmeyr, van der Horst and that section', wrote Botha on 19 February, 'will of course make a great noise but I expect that before it actually comes to a fight they will seek cover.... I do not think that their opposition need be taken too seriously.' Smuts wrote on the same day: 'I cannot understand a man of Hofmeyr's position now cutting himself practically adrift from the noblest aspirations of the people of South Africa and apparently on mere paltry grounds— for the reasons given in his document [i.e. the resolution of the Cape Town branch of the Bond] . . . are purely paltry.' And Steyn, a week later: 'It will indeed grieve me if Onze Jan [Hofmeyr] should do anything which may appear as if he wished to wreck the Draft Constitution.'

The resolution of the Bond Congress was a serious blow to Merriman. He complained about it to Botha and Smuts,[33] and to Steyn he confided that it 'will strengthen the hands of all wreckers in the Country' and expressed his surprise and disappointment that it should come from the Afrikaner side:[34]

It does seem to me inconceivable that men who have been talking about 'nationale gevoel' for years should deliberately set themselves to wreck the only chance they get of union. . . . We shall have a rough time in the Parliament with our Bond malcontents and the Schreiner group and even if we carry union their action will give a backing to the people in England who will take up the question of Native rights. Another detestable outcome will be the recrudescence of racial feeling for oddly enough the English are solid for Union and it is the Dutch who are jibbing or rather a section of them.

One final effort was made to rally white opinion behind the draft Constitution before the Cape Parliament met and that was by Sir Henry de Villiers who, like Merriman, had viewed the development of opposition with profound misgivings. Hitherto he had refrained from speaking in public on the draft Constitution, but on 19 March he spoke at Paarl, admitting that he disliked proportional representation and the compromises concerning the capital and the Cape Native franchise, but ardently supporting the Constitution as a whole:[35]

[31] *Cape Times*, 23 Feb. 1909.   [32] Merriman Papers.
[33] Merriman to Botha, 9 Mar. 1909, Transvaal Archives, Prime Minister, LX (ii); Merriman to Smuts, 12 Mar. 1909, Smuts Papers.
[34] Merriman to Steyn, 8 Mar. 1909, Steyn Papers.
[35] *Cape Argus*, 20 Mar. 1909; quoted in Walker, *de Villiers*, pp. 470–2.

The sacrifice we are asked to make is a great one, but remember that every other Colony is making great sacrifices. . . . I am firmly convinced that the draft Act of Union, with all its defects, is worthy of acceptance. . . . If we do not succeed in now uniting when circumstances are so propitious we shall never unite, at all events, not in the lifetime of the present generation. There will be a repetition, in an aggravated form, of all the dissensions of the past. . . . Even if Union be not indefinitely postponed, rest assured that delay will not improve the position of this Colony. From what I know of the inner workings of the Convention . . . the same terms will not be offered again. . . . It is my fervent hope . . . that before the year has come to an end the Act of Union may have passed to serve as a treaty of perpetual peace and amity between peoples and races which have hitherto been kept asunder by artificial boundaries, local jealousies, constant misunderstandings, and want of a common South African patriotism.

Between the adjournment of the convention and the middle of March, Botha and Smuts, Fischer and Steyn, and Merriman and Sauer had been in broad agreement with one another on policy, but then developments took place which threatened to disturb their harmony. On 13 March Lord Selborne explained to Botha that the British Government was anxious to avoid an autumn session of Parliament and would like to take the South Africa Bill 'at the end of July or the beginning of August'. In his reply Botha said that the delegates of the South African colonies would be unable to reach England until later in the year, and he asked that the Imperial Parliament should hold a special session for the South Africa Bill. Botha sent copies of this correspondence to Merriman, Fischer, and Moor and asked them to support him.[36] Before Merriman received it, he had written to Botha, saying that delay would unnecessarily prolong the state of uncertainty in South Africa and strengthen the 'wreckers'. Merriman therefore recommended that during their sessions starting on 30 March the parliaments of the Cape Colony, the Transvaal, and the Orange River Colony should be persuaded to pass the draft Constitution without amendment and also to pass addresses for union, leaving Natal with the choice of either accepting or rejecting the draft Constitution as it stood. Then there would be no need for another session of the convention and the South Africa Bill could easily be dealt with by the Imperial Parliament during its present session.[37]

By this time there was also another complicating factor. J. G. van der Horst had made estimates of the political effects of sections 39 and 40 of the draft Constitution and had reached the conclusion that the Unionists

[36] Botha to Merriman, 16 Mar. 1909, enclosing copies of Selborne to Botha, 13 Mar., and the reply, 16 Mar., Merriman Papers.

[37] Merriman to Botha, 18 Mar. 1909, Transvaal Archives, Prime Minister, LX (ii).

would win twenty-seven or twenty-eight of the fifty-one Cape Province seats in the first House of Assembly.[38] These estimates had been brought to the notice of the Bond congress at Dordrecht in the report of the *Kommissie van Toezicht*, which had been signed by J. H. Hofmeyr,[39] and no doubt van der Horst had explained them to his fellow delegates. Van der Horst had also shown them to D. P. de Villiers Graaff, minister without portfolio in the Cape Cabinet, who became so alarmed that he went to Bloemfontein and Pretoria in the middle of March to report to Fischer and Botha. Botha was shaken. On 17 March he wrote to Merriman: 'If this is correct I do not see what reply we shall be able to give to our people when they ask us why we altered their majority into a minority. At the convention Smuts and I went through the figures with you and Sauer and we arrived at a very different conclusion. . . . We are also getting all your figures in order to work it out for ourselves. I still hope that Graaff is not right and in that case we should I think pass the Draft Constitution without any amendments.'[40] The question was distasteful to Merriman. He instructed Graaff to tell Botha that, while he had always been opposed to proportional representation and remained so, 'the horrid thing is logically fair', and he was convinced that 'any attempt to upset that provision in [the] Constitution would lead to serious disruption and undo much of the good which I sincerely believe has been effected'. 'To rip the whole framework up now', he said, 'would be very risky.'[41] Then when he received Botha's letter of the 17th he telegraphed back that in any case he had 'never given much thought' to the 'party aspect', that he was 'confident that the most united and most competent party is sure to dominate Parliament', and that he did not anticipate that Parties would be formed 'either on racial or territorial lines' in the Union.[42] He also wrote to Steyn expounding these views at length.[43] De Villiers, too, was dismayed by the agitation against sections 39 and 40 and in his Paarl speech on 19 March he included the following statement: 'I regret to see that there is a tendency in some quarters to enter into minute enquiries as to how many seats this party will lose and that party gain by adopting the proposals of the Convention. Ladies and gentlemen, if these pro-

---

[38] Botha's letter of 17 Mar. to Merriman mentioned twenty-seven seats; but according to a detailed calculation sent from the Cape to E. Rooth of Pretoria, and forwarded by him to Botha, the Unionists would win twenty-eight seats and the South African Party twenty-three. Rooth to Botha, 19 Mar. 1909, ibid.

[39] *Vijf en twintigste Centrale Vergadering van de Afrikaander Bond en Boeren Vereeniging*, p. 24.

[40] Merriman Papers.

[41] Merriman to Graaff, Merriman Papers, No. 72/1909 (draft telegram).

[42] Merriman to Botha, 20 Mar. 1909, Merriman Papers, No. 84/1909 (draft telegram).

[43] Merriman to Steyn, 18 Mar. 1909, Steyn Papers.

posals are fair and just they should be accepted without regard to their effect on the fortunes of any party. The party whose cause is just will in the end prevail.'[44] By that time, however, Botha and Smuts had worked through the Cape figures themselves and had reached the conclusion that Graaff's alarm was groundless, and on the 19th Botha wrote to tell Merriman that 'We calculate that the S.A.P. will have 31 members and the Progressives 20 [for the Cape Colony]. I have pointed out to Graaff where he went wrong in his calculations. . . . I am quite convinced that van der Horst's figures are misleading . . . [and] . . . that it is best not to try to amend the Draft Constitution, because that would be very dangerous, and I think that the Transvaal delegates will certainly not support amendments.'[45]

When Merriman received his copy of Botha's correspondence with Lord Selborne he consulted Sauer and invited the other colonial prime ministers to meet him at Bloemfontein to straighten out their time-table differences.[46] The meeting took place on 24 March. Sauer, Hull, Greene, and Hertzog attended, as well as the four prime ministers, and they came to the following agreement: In the special sessions of the colonial parliaments which were due to start on 30 March the procedure would be to pass the draft Constitution 'without amendment', but the parliaments would not be deterred from making 'recommendations' to the National Convention for amendments. The National Convention would reassemble in Bloemfontein on 3 May to consider any such recommendations. The colonial parliaments would meet again on 1 June to approve the draft Constitution as finally reported by the National Convention, to pass addresses to the King, and to appoint delegates to go to England, and the delegates would leave South Africa on 9 June.[47] Thus Merriman's hope that a further session of the convention might be avoided was not fulfilled: but nor was Botha's hope that the South Africa Bill would not come before the Imperial Parliament until towards the end of the year.

The prime ministers and their colleagues also discussed sections 39 and 40 of the draft Constitution at Bloemfontein.[48] Although he was not a member of the ministerial conference, Graaff was in Bloemfontein on 24 March,[49] not fully satisfied with the Transvaal predictions of the

---

[44] *Cape Argus*, 20 Mar. 1909; quoted in Walker, *de Villiers*, p. 472.

[45] Merriman Papers.

[46] Draft telegrams in the Merriman Papers, Nos. 55, 60, 61, and 63/1909; Merriman's Diary, 19 Mar. 1909.

[47] Minutes of the 'Informal Meeting of Ministers held at Bloemfontein on 24th March 1909', enclosed in Hull to Merriman, 26 Mar. 1909, Merriman Papers.

[48] For ss. 39 and 40 of the draft Constitution, see above, p. 240.

[49] Merriman's Diary, 24 Mar. 1909.

effects of the sections, and he succeeded in persuading Sauer—and probably Fischer also—that it was vital to have the sections amended to make
it obligatory for the delimitation commissions to divide all the rural
areas into single-member constituencies and to give them the greatest
possible benefit of the permitted variation from the provincial quotas, so
that, as nearly as possible, for every eighty-five voters to a member in
a rural constituency there would be 115 voters to a member in an urban
constituency.[50] No detailed record has survived of what transpired, but
the conference apparently agreed that it would be reasonable to make
'recommendations' to the National Convention that the two sections
should be phrased more clearly. Three days later Fischer informed
Merriman by telegram that two recommendations were 'likely to be
moved' in the Orange River Colony Parliament 'for the consideration of
the Convention at its next session'—one for 'the definition of the terms
"sparsely populated area" and "sparsity or density of population"' and
the other 'for more clearly expressing the meaning and intent of the
Draft Act in regard to the cases in which the quota of voters should be
departed from (to the extent of not exceeding 15 per cent one way or the
other) in the delimitation of electoral divisions'.[51] Merriman replied that
he concurred,[52] but he was probably unaware that what Sauer, at least,
had in mind was a radical departure from the principle of equal rights
in the interests of the rural, that is to say, the Afrikaner parties. Sauer's
intentions were set out clearly enough in a letter he wrote to Smuts on
29 March:[53]

Dear Smuts,

I was sorry that you too had not come to Bloemfontein as I was particularly anxious to discuss the 'one vote one value' principle with you. That I
may say is the only amendment to the Draft Act I would like to see. One
man never was and never will be of the same value as another. But allowing
that for theoretical purposes there is equality under the provisions of the
draft Act there will be serious practical inequality: centres of population can
quickly and effectively exercise influence which sparse populations cannot.
Therefore in England, Australia and New Zealand the large centres of
population have on the basis of numbers less representation than the Country
people. And in New Zealand as you know it is fixed by law that fewer votes
in the Country are required to get a member than in the Towns. In this
Colony the Country people to-day have an advantage of 42% over the
Centres of population. And I can assure you that unless we get the full

[50] Sauer to Smuts, 29 Mar. 1909, Smuts Papers.
[51] Merriman Papers, No. 108/1909.
[52] Ibid., No. 109/1909 (draft telegram).   [53] Smuts Papers.

advantage of the '15% above or below' and a liberal application of the principle of one or two member Constituencies our majority would vanish. I have heard of the result you have worked out, but take it from me, to quote a great man, I am right. And I know the difficulty and danger of rushing in with an amendment, but this is a vital question and we should do what we can in the matter. Botha and Hull will tell you that it came up for discussion in Bloemfontein last week, and that it was understood that Fischer should take the lead in the matter. Natal is entirely with the view herein expressed. Now you will have seen that the clause of the '15% above or 15% below' including density and sparseness of population has given rise to differences of opinion as to its meaning. Some read it to mean something considerable, others as mere pious opinion. And in Bloemfontein Hull, Hertzog, Green[e] and I did not agree as to the meaning of the Clause or clauses in question. It occurred to me that we might say it is necessary to *define* or *make clear* what was intended by the Convention. That would not be like coming with an amendment. Hull will tell you how it was suggested to make clear what was intended, and he will also tell you what interpretation a Judge of the Free State gave to the Clauses. I beg of you to give this matter your most earnest consideration as the consequences to the future of the Country and the cause will be serious if we have anything like a mathematical application of the principle of 'one vote one value.' It is really the only matter criticised in this Draft that I wish or care much to see altered or correctly defined, and if we are not careful it may yet stop union for the present at least.

With kindest regards,
Yours very truly,
J. W. Sauer.

Thus of all the objections to the draft Constitution which had emanated from the Afrikaner Bond it was the objection to the principle of equal political rights which was to be pressed home most vigorously. Botha and Smuts were perplexed by this development, for they well knew that 'one vote, one value' had been the essential basis of the co-operation of the Progressives in the convention. Nor was Botha reconciled to the Bloemfontein decision that the delegates should leave for England on 9 June. He wrote to Merriman and Moor pleading for their support 'in asking the Imperial Government to either pass the draft Constitution in an Autumn Session or else to take it early in the Session next year so that our general election could take place some time between November 1910 and February 1911'.[54] He did not give Merriman or Moor his reasons, but he set them out in a letter to Fischer: 'You know the position of our Boer population in the Transvaal as well as I', he wrote, 'and if we now carry through the Union too hastily we shall have an election in South

---

[54] 1 Apr. 1909, Transvaal Archives, Prime Minister, LX (ii) (copy).

Africa more or less during the Winter. That would be fatal for us here because at least 30% of our best men go to the Bushveld during the Winter and we should then have to lose all their votes. I shall therefore be very grateful if you will support me so that the elections only take place between November and February.'[55]

Nearly all the politically conscious non-Europeans in South Africa were bitterly disappointed in the draft Constitution. When Stanford toured the Transkei early in March he found that even tribal Africans were concerned about the provision to exclude non-Europeans from Parliament.[56] The urban Africans were deeply resentful. From the first the Bantu newspapers criticized the sections maintaining the colour-bar in the northern provinces, excluding non-Europeans from Parliament, and providing a method for the amendment or removal of the Cape non-European franchise. 'The Draft Constitution issued by the National Convention, whatever its advantages to other people, does not seem to have been conceived in a liberal spirit towards the Africans', commented *Imvo*[57] on 16 February. 'This is greatly to be regretted, because it was hoped that it would have been found possible in the arrangements for Union to provide an opening for the reasonable aspirations of the African man, instead of leaving him out in the cold so that he remains nothing in the body politic of this land. It would appear that the unreasoning and unreasonable prejudices of the Transvaal, Free State, Natal, and perhaps the Rhodesian delegates have been effective.' And again, in the same issue: 'To alienate the Africans at the very outset of Union is dangerous and bad indeed. May our beloved country be spared from it.'[58] *Izwi Labantu* went further and contended that the Cape delegates to the National Convention had been party to a diabolical plot to pave the way for the complete obliteration of the Cape Native vote.[59] During March,

---

[55] 'U kent de positie van onze Boeren Bevolking in Transvaal even goed als ik en als wy nu de Vereeniging te haastig doorzetten dan zullen wy eenie electie in Zuid Afrika krygen min or meer gedurende den Winter. Dat zou voor ons hier fataal zyn want minstens 30% van onze beste menschen gaan gedurende den Winter naar het Boschveld en wy zouden dan al hunne stemmen moeten verliezen. Ik zal daarom zeer verblijd zyn als U my zult ondersteunen dat de electies niet plaats vinden dan tusschen November en Februari.' 1 Apr. 1909, Transvaal Archives, Prime Minister, LX (ii) (copy). Botha meant that many of the Transvaal Boers were still seasonally migrant pastoral farmers who were away from the constituencies in which they were registered, and thus unable to cast their votes in the absence of machinery for postal voting, during the winter months.

[56] Stanford's Diary, 3–9 Mar. 1909.

[57] The full name is *Imvo Zabantsundu Bomzantsi Afrika*.

[58] *Imvo*, 16 Feb. 1909 (original in Xhosa). This (and the rest of the information in this paragraph) is derived from E. Mamkile, 'African Public Opinion and the Unification of South Africa' (unpublished essay).   [59] *Izwi*, 23 Feb. 1909.

meetings were held in many of the urban Native locations and resolutions of protest were passed. 'This meeting', read a resolution passed at Ndabeni location, Cape Town, 'notes with regret that the contemplated Union is to be a Union of two races, namely the British and the Afrikaners—the African is to be excluded.'[60] Under the leadership of the Rev. W. Rubusana, the editor of *Izwi Labantu*, J. T. Jabavu, the editor of *Imvo*, and Dr. J. L. Dube, the editor of *Ilanga Lase Natal*, it was decided that an appeal should be made to the Imperial Government, but that a Native Convention should first meet and draw up resolutions for submission to the colonial governors and prime ministers. Accordingly, delegates were elected from all the four colonies to a 'South African Native Convention' which opened at Bloemfontein on 24 March, the same day that the prime ministers' conference was taking place there. The convention elected an executive 'to promote organisation and to defend the interests of the Natives' and passed resolutions approving of the principle of union, but declaring that the Imperial Government was 'bound by both fundamental and specific obligations towards the Native and Coloured races of South Africa to extend to them the same measure of equitable justice and consideration as is extended to those of European descent', recording 'a strong and emphatic protest against the . . . "colour bar"', requesting that 'all persons within the Union shall be entitled to full and equal rights subject only to the conditions and limitations established by law and applicable alike to all citizens without distinction of class, colour or creed', and claiming that under article 8 of the Treaty of Vereeniging the Imperial Government had incurred an obligation to see that the franchise was extended to non-Europeans in the inland colonies, now that they had obtained responsible government.[61]

The Coloured people's African Political Organization proceeded in a similar way. On 5 March it organized a crowded meeting of Coloured people in the Cape Town city hall. The mayor of Cape Town presided and there were other Europeans on the platform, but the main speaker was Dr. Abdurahman, the President of the A.P.O., who described the draft Constitution as 'wicked', 'unjust', and 'un-British'.[62] Similar meetings were held in sixty other centres and at all of them resolutions criticizing the draft Constitution were unanimously adopted.[63] Eventually, a conference of sixty A.P.O. delegates was held in Cape Town between 13 and 17 April. The conference passed resolutions favouring 'a lasting Union of British South Africa . . . founded upon the eternal rule of order

[60] *Izwi*, 12 Mar. 1909 (original in Xhosa).
[61] Ibid., 1 Apr. 1909.
[62] *Cape Times*, 6 Mar. 1909.   [63] Ibid., 19 Apr. 1909.

and justice', but deploring the exclusion of men of colour from the Union Parliament and asking for permanent protection for the Cape non-European franchise and for the extension of the franchise to 'all qualified coloured persons in the contemplated union'. These resolutions were duly forwarded to the National Convention.[64] The conference also resolved that a fund should be opened 'to protect the interests of the coloured people as affected under the draft South Africa Act, including the sending of a delegation to England if necessary';[65] it recorded its appreciation of the work of the African congress at Bloemfontein; and finally it declared

That the time has arrived for the co-operation of coloured races in British South Africa, and that the executive of the A.P.O. is hereby instructed and empowered to communicate with the executives of all the various organisations to act unitedly to protect the rights of all coloured races and secure an extension of civil and political liberty to all qualified men irrespective of race, colour or creed throughout the contemplated Union.[66]

2. THE REACTIONS OF THE COLONIAL PARLIAMENTS

A. *The Transvaal*[67]

The extraordinary session of the Transvaal Parliament was opened by the Governor on 30 March and in the Legislative Assembly the next day Botha moved that the House should go into committee to approve of the draft South Africa Act. Farrar seconded, and the debate which followed was analogous to a second reading debate on a Bill. P. Whiteside (Labour) proposed that Parliament should be dissolved and a general election should be held before the Constitution was approved, but his motion fell away for want of a seconder. H. W. Sampson (Labour) then proposed that there should be a referendum on the Constitution and J. Reid (Labour) seconded. Their contention that Parliament had no clear mandate to approve of the draft Constitution was rebutted from both sides of the House. Het Volk members rose one after the other to announce that they had held meetings in their constituencies and that the overwhelming majority of the people who had attended them had approved. Indeed, it was only at a few urban meetings that resolutions

---

[64] House of Assembly, National Convention Minutes, III.
[65] *Cape Times*, 17 Apr. 1909. [66] Ibid., 21 Apr. 1909.
[67] *Transvaal Debates of Both Houses of Parliament, Extraordinary Session, 1909* (in one vol.); *Transvaal Leg. Co. Min., Extraordinary Session, 1909*; *Transvaal Leg. Ass. Votes and Proceedings, Extraordinary Session 1909*. The quotations are from the *Debates*.

had been passed for a referendum. Consequently the amendment was defeated by fifty-one votes to three, the minority consisting of the mover and seconder and W. J. Wybergh (Nationalist), all of whom held urban seats.

During this debate many members said that the white racial question was being settled for all time. Botha declared that they would never be happy so long as one called himself a Boer, another a Briton. Jacob de Villiers, the Attorney-General, was sure that the language section of the Constitution would solve the racial question and predicted that South Africans would 'stand as one man with the British Empire'[68] in any future war; G. G. Munnik and F. W. Beyers (Het Volk) paid tributes to Botha as the creator of racial harmony; and F. J. Bezuidenhout (Het Volk) thought that 'the thousand years of peace'[69] had come. Fitzpatrick cordially endorsed these sentiments. If there were any members who did not share them, but stored up bitterness and exclusive ambitions in their hearts, they did not declare it.

The Progressives were already alarmed, however, at the Bond agitation against the principle of equal constituencies, and they asked the House to refrain from insisting on a single amendment to the draft Constitution, so that the Transvaal delegates would be able to oppose amendments brought to Bloemfontein by the other delegations. To their great relief Botha himself advised against amendments, saying, in reply to the debate, that he had seen that amendments were being proposed elsewhere, but that they must not be allowed to pass.

In the committee stage there was a debate on the composition of the Senate. Botha and Farrar had already expressed regret that each province was to have the same number of elected senators, and they had implied that they hoped that Parliament would use its powers to reconstitute the Senate after ten years in such a way that the provinces would be represented in proportion to their white populations. Now Wybergh moved that the committee should recommend that the nominated senators should be eliminated and that the senate should initially consist of thirty-two men, eight elected directly by proportional representation by the voters of each province, a province forming a single constituency for the purpose. He said that he hoped members would vote freely on the merits of the case, so that the delegates would know their feelings. J. W. Quinn (Independent) at once rose and said that he regarded the motion as an amendment in disguise and that he would therefore vote against it, as he would vote against every such motion. Smuts opposed the motion on its merits, but he also asked the House not to tie the hands of the dele-

[68] Col. 173.   [69] Col. 275.

gates by passing it, Farrar and other Progressives spoke to the same effect, and it was negatived without a division.

Soon afterwards Whiteside moved that the committee should recommend the omission of the property qualification laid down for senators. Several members agreed with him in disliking the property qualification, but Smuts implored them not to bind the delegates, Fitzpatrick said the draft Constitution was to be accepted or rejected as a whole, like a treaty, and Farrar confessed that he saw no way in which members could safely test the feeling of the House. The motion was defeated by fifty-one votes to eight, the minority consisting of the three Labour members, two Nationalists, and three members of Het Volk. Wybergh then declared that since the House seemed determined to regard recommendations as binding and embarrassing to the delegates, he would not move the other motions which stood in his name on the order paper.

One more attempt was made to carry a recommendation for amendment of the draft Constitution. It arose from the feeling, which was widespread in the Transvaal, against the maintenance and entrenchment of the Cape non-European franchise. During the debate on the motion to go into committee several of the delegates had taken pains to explain that they had been unable to obtain terms which would have been more to the liking of the Transvaal, and Botha and Farrar had also pointed out that the time might come when they would be able to eliminate the non-European franchise by the necessary two-thirds majority. Wybergh (Nationalist) and Dr. F. E. T. Krause (Het Volk) had then suggested that the British Government should be warned not to veto a Bill disfranchising the Cape Native voters, when the two-thirds majority had been obtained. On the other hand, F. W. Beyers had defended the franchise section on the grounds that the draft Constitution deprived the Cape Natives of far more than it granted them, because it made them ineligible to sit in Parliament, it did not count them in the allocation of parliamentary seats to the Cape province, and it incorporated them in a union with three colonies which were hostile to the Native vote. W. Hosken (Progressive) had gone further, defending the Cape system and rebuking Smuts for laughing while he did so. In committee Sir Aubrey Woolls Sampson (Progressive) moved a recommendation for the deletion of the safeguard for the Cape non-European franchise, but Botha appealed to him not to press it, though he made it clear that he agreed with Sampson's intention, and it was then negatived without a division.

After that, members did no more than draw the attention of the delegates to points in the draft Constitution which they considered should be improved. It was suggested that Members of Parliament should be paid more than the £300 per annum laid down. Attention was drawn to the fact that there were no qualifications laid down for provincial councillors. J. A. Neser (Independent) expressed the opinion that the Constitution should prescribe the highest possible legal qualifications for judges, but the Attorney-General disagreed, on the grounds that the South African courts had an incorruptible tradition and that they could trust the Union Government to appoint the right people.

The resolution approving of the draft Constitution was then adopted without amendment by the committee, the Speaker resumed the chair, and the draft South Africa Act was approved by the Legislative Assembly without a division and without further debate.

The next day the same procedure was followed in the Legislative Council. Smuts was in charge of the resolution and, moving that the House should go into committee, he made his most elaborate speech on the work of the convention. He started by drawing attention to the 'wonderful unanimity' of white South Africans on the question of union, which was 'convincing proof that this . . . is a truly national movement . . . and is carrying along with it the vast bulk of the white population of South Africa'.[70] Its effects, he said, were 'already being felt in the direction of the subsidence of party spirit' and he was certain that it would ultimately 'be the remaking of South Africa and start it on a higher plane of political and national life'.[71] He eulogized the unitary principle. The Canadians had been unable to obtain a unitary Constitution because of the opposition of the French Canadians, 'a minority with a different language, nationality and religion from the majority'. In South Africa, on the other hand, Boer and Briton lived side by side in every colony and were 'already fusing and being fused under the existing form of colonial constitutions', so that it was unnecessary and would, indeed, be futile to try to 'keep up racial distinctions'.[72] Being generally flexible, the Constitution would 'be moulded by the wants and the experiences of the people', and the law courts—'a power quite apart from the desires or will of the authority elected by the people'—would not be able to decide upon the validity of legislation.[73] He was sorry, however, that a few sections would not be fully flexible. Above all he was anxious about the differential franchise, because 'dualism on the most fundamental matter in South African politics' might cause a serious division between white South Africans. 'If there is one thing in the Constitution which I regret it is that there should be this apple of discord placed before South Africa—an apple of discord which, unless Providence is kind to us, may afterwards

[70] Col. 19. [71] Cols. 19–20.
[72] Col. 23. [73] Col. 24.

lead to very grave consequences in the history of South Africa.'[74] But the convention was not to be blamed for this. 'It is embedded in the structure of South Africa to-day. All we could do was to admit our inability to remove it.'[75] Smuts also regretted that each province was to have the same number of elected senators, fearing lest a senate thus composed might become a stronghold for provincial rights, contrary to the spirit of union. He thought it had been a mistake to give the provinces powers over education but he expected that after the prescribed five-year period the central Parliament would exercise its right to assume control of education. And he regretted the capital compromise, adding, however, that he hoped that South Africans would make it work as well as possible. He concluded with a warning to those who thought that the millennium was at hand:[76]

Union itself will not in the immediate future create any wonderful change at all. It is an instrument, the great effects of which will only be felt as time goes on. . . . We . . . have honestly endeavoured to put the people of South Africa on the right journey for their future development.

Amid the general chorus of approval for the draft Constitution, three councillors made speeches of some moment. A. D. W. Wolmarans (Het Volk) reiterated his opposition to union, announcing, however, that he would neither vote nor move amendments. W. A. Martin (Progressive) said that nearly every one of the recommendations of the Johannesburg Chamber of Commerce had been incorporated in the Constitution and that he was confident that it would promote prosperity in the Transvaal. And Richard Feetham (Progressive), one of the kindergarten councillors, declared that the Progressive members of the convention had already made the utmost concession in the electoral sections of the draft Constitution, and that any attempt to achieve a further departure from the principle of equal constituencies would endanger union.

When the council had approved of the draft Constitution without an amendment having been moved, Smuts thanked the Transvaal Parliament for having set a good example to the other colonies, and expressed the hope that no fundamental changes would be made at Bloemfontein. The Transvaal Parliament was then prorogued, having approved of the draft Constitution without any qualification.

B. *The Orange River Colony*[77]

Initiating the equivalent of a second reading debate on the draft Con-

[74] Col. 28.   [75] Col. 29.   [76] Col. 32.
[77] O.R.C. Leg. Co. Deb., 1909, cols. 1–48; O.R.C. Leg. Ass. Deb., 1909, cols. 1–81.

stitution in the Orange River Colony Legislative Assembly on 30 March, Fischer made a bow to the convention spirit and expressed approval of many of the features of the draft Constitution, but said he regretted that Bloemfontein 'had not received her full rights'[78] and that he would have preferred to have left over the settlement of the terms under which the protectorates were to be administered by the Union until the time came for their incorporation. He advised the House that 'There should be amendments, but not amendments which might wreck the Constitution.'[79] The next morning Sir John Fraser, Leader of the Opposition, seconded the motion, declaring himself completely satisfied with the convention's work. During the course of a brief debate, Hertzog expressed his delight at the convention's unanimous acceptance of the language section. The House then resolved to go into committee to consider 'whether any and if so what amendments are deemed desirable to recommend through the delegates of this Colony to the consideration of the Convention at its next session'.[80]

In committee three proposals were made for amendment to the senate sections—proposals for the definition of the phrase 'of European descent' as a qualification for senators, for the deletion of the property qualification, and for Parliament to be empowered to reconstruct the senate after five years, instead of ten. Fischer spoke against all three motions and they were rejected without divisions.

The opposition to the Cape non-European franchise was strong and determined. On 30 March Fischer had said that the Orange River Colony did not approve of a Native vote but that, since one already existed in the Cape Colony, there was no reason to take it away, and he had gone on to attack the 'faddists' who were alleging that the Constitution was unfair to the non-Europeans. He had questioned 'whether the people of South Africa had done any act of injustice to the natives' and declared that the overriding law was 'the law of self-preservation'. 'The black man's rights were not the rights of the white man, but they were of another kind. They were not the equals of the white man, who had no intention of acknowledging that they were such now.'[81] Fraser, too, had deplored the allegation that the Constitution was unfair to the Natives, but considered that the Prime Minister had spoken too sharply on the subject and that the time might come when Coloured and Native men should have the vote—for 'Who could say what would take place in fifty

The numbers of sections are those in the draft S.A. Act in the convention's first report (Feb. 1909); and unless stated to the contrary the numbers of the corresponding sections of the S.A. Act as enacted are the same.

[78] *O.R.C. Leg. Ass. Deb., 1909*, col. 11.   [79] Ibid., col. 21.
[80] Ibid., col. 34.   [81] Ibid., col. 15.

years' time?'[82] In the committee stage G. L. Steytler (Orangia Unie) moved that the convention should be asked to amend section 35, so that it would provide the same protection against the creation of a non-European franchise in the northern provinces as it provided for the maintenance of the non-European franchise in the Cape Province. This proposal gave rise to a long and uninhibited debate. Many Unie back-benchers supported it, expressing anxiety lest the Cape Members of Parliament, dependent on the non-European vote, should otherwise succeed in extending it to the northern provinces. C. A. van Niekerk said 'he had a mandate from his constituents against the provision regarding the coloured franchise. . . . There were white persons with black hearts who were willing to agitate on behalf of the natives.'[83] Fischer, Hertzog, and Fraser opposed the amendment. Fischer took his stand on the proposition that 'it was dangerous to meddle with cardinal points'[84] in the Constitution, but Hertzog went further, groping, perhaps for the first time but certainly not for the last time, towards a philosophical view of the Native question. The Native, he asserted, was undeniably a human being, but he was not yet entitled to political rights because he was still a child, 'in matters of civilisation . . . thousands of years behind the whites'. They had, however, to take account of the fact that the Cape Colony Natives had already been given political rights; it was reasonable that those rights should be protected, because it was easy 'to arouse public feeling against the natives'; and there was no danger of an extension of the Native vote under the section as it stood, because nearly all white South Africans of both stocks were opposed to it.[85] 'The giving of the vote to the Native was so far off that they could safely leave it in the hands of the legislature of that day.'[86] This analysis was too advanced for J. P. G. Steyl (Orangia Unie), who, speaking as a voortrekker would have spoken, bluntly announced that he could not accept Hertzog's basic proposition that the Native was a human being. 'The Hon. the Attorney-General said that the native was a man and that he was entitled to rights. He did not agree with that. If he were, then he would grow long hair. Providence had provided that he should remain a drawer of water and a hewer of wood.'[87] C. L. Botha (Constitutionalist), a Bloemfontein lawyer, supported the amendment and declared that 'He did not care how much dissension he created between the white man and the coloured. . . . He was tired of the talk of justice to the native. He wished the black man to have all his rights in his own country and the white man in his.'[88] Fischer, Hertzog,

---

[82] Ibid., col. 27.

[84] Ibid., col. 42.

[86] Ibid., col. 47.

[87] Ibid., col. 48.

[83] Ibid., cols. 44–45.

[85] Ibid., col. 46.

[88] Ibid., col. 51.

and Fraser deprecated the tone of these speeches. Fumbling for fresh arguments, Fischer said that the Cape franchise 'was only entrenched for a certain time',[89] and Fraser warned the House that the debate might prejudice the acceptance of the draft Act in Britain. In his reply to the debate Steytler seized on Fraser's statement. 'The great bogey held before them', he said, 'was that of the Imperial Government. But the British Government had acknowledged the feeling of the people in the constitutions of the Transvaal and the Orange River Colony, which contained no provision for a native vote.'[90] He would therefore press his amendment so long as there was a chance of getting it adopted, but if that were impossible he would support the Constitution as it stood. A division was then taken and it resulted in a tie, the eighteen Ayes comprising sixteen members of the Unie and two Constitutionalists (Botha and Ehrlich) and the eighteen Noes comprised eleven members of the Unie (including the five cabinet ministers), the four Independents, and three Constitutionalists. The Speaker gave his casting vote with the Noes and the amendment was thus defeated.

Fischer, in his speech on 30 March, had said no more about the electoral system than that he and a majority of the members of the convention had preferred the population to the voters' basis, but that they had yielded to the minority and arrived at 'a reasonable compromise'.[91] In committee the electoral sections were dealt with at almost precipitate speed. J. G. Keyter, a Unie backbencher, moved the first of the two resolutions which Fischer had reported to Merriman after the prime ministers had conferred on 24 March: 'This Committee recommends that it be recommended, through the delegates of this Colony, to the consideration of the Convention, the necessity for the definition of the terms "sparsely populated areas" and "sparsity and density of population", occurring respectively in sections 39 and 40 of the draft South Africa Act.'[92] Three Constitutionalists opposed the motion and so did Fischer, who said that he thought that the provision should be left as it stood. Nevertheless, when it came to a division Fischer voted for the motion, which was carried by eighteen votes to fourteen. The majority consisted exclusively of Unie members and included, besides Fischer, two other cabinet ministers, Dr. A. E. W. Ramsbottom and C. H. Wessels, but Hertzog and de Wet did not participate in the division. The minority comprised the five Constitutionalists, the four Independents, and five members of the Unie. G. A. Kolbe, another Unie backbencher, moved the second of the resolutions which Fischer had reported to

---

[89] *O.R.C. Leg. Ass. Deb., 1909*, col. 50.
[91] Ibid., col. 13.

[90] Ibid., col. 58.
[92] Ibid., cols. 36–37.

Merriman: 'This Committee recommends: That through the delegates of this Colony be recommended for consideration of the Convention at its next session the necessity for more clearly expressing the meaning and intent of the draft Act in regard to the cases in which the quota of voters should be departed from to the extent of not exceeding 15 per cent. (one way or the other) in the delimitation of electoral divisions referred to in sub-section (e) of section 3 of clause 40 of the draft Act.'[93] On this motion there was no debate at all. The mover merely remarked that 'to his mind the 15 per cent. was not sufficiently defined and therefore he asked how the adjustment was to be made';[94] and then a vote was taken and the motion was carried by twenty-two votes to twelve. Again the majority consisted exclusively of members of the Unie and this time it included all the five cabinet ministers; while the minority consisted of the five Constitutionalists, the four Independents, and three members of the Unie.

Fraser then suggested that the duration of the provincial councils should be extended from three to four years, but he withdrew his motion when Fischer had defended the provision in the draft Act. Fraser also suggested that education should be removed from the list of subjects to be dealt with by the provincial councils, but Hertzog made it clear that it was Natal which had insisted on provincial control of education for at least five years and that Parliament would be competent to take it over at the end of that period, and again Fraser withdrew. On the other hand, two non-contentious recommendations were carried without divisions —one for the inclusion of a section prescribing qualifications for provincial councillors and the other for the addition of words to section 96 to make judges of the local divisions as well as judges of the provincial divisions of the Supreme Court eligible for appointment to the Appellate Division.

The report of the committee having been adopted without a division by the Legislative Assembly, it came before the council on 2 April. By that time the council, following the assembly's procedure, had reached the committee stage. The assembly's recommendations for amendments to the electoral sections were opposed by Browne, the Constitutionalist delegate to the convention; and after short debates the recommendation for definitions of 'sparsely populated areas' and 'sparsity and density of population' was defeated by five votes to four, while the recommendation concerning section 40 (iii) was carried by five votes to four. The council concurred in the other recommendations of the assembly without a division.

<hr>

[93] Ibid., col. 61.   [94] Ibid.

The assembly debated the council's message reporting these decisions on the evening of 2 April. Keyter proposed that the assembly should persist in the recommendation which the council had rejected, challenging the right of a nominated house to reject a motion passed by 'the chosen of the people'.[95] But Fischer said that the council had acted within its rights and undertook to inform the convention of the content of the motion it had rejected. 'As to how much weight was to be attached to the opinions of the two Houses would be decided by the Convention.'[96] Keyter then withdrew his proposal and the House regained its equanimity.

Then, both Houses having approved of the draft Constitution with recommendations for amendments to sections 40 and 96 and for the insertion of qualifications for provincial councillors, and the Lower House having recommended a further amendment to sections 39 and 40, the Orange River Colony Parliament was prorogued.[97]

C. *The Cape Colony*[98]

How Merriman must have envied Botha and Fischer their short and easy sessions! The special session of the Cape Colony Parliament, also, was opened on 30 March, but it did not end until 17 April.

At the outset of the equivalent of a second reading debate on the draft Constitution, Merriman warned the House against amendments 'that might tear the whole framework to pieces',[99] and asked the House, if it must, to pass recommendations, but not outright amendments; but while he carefully defended the convention's decisions regarding the political rights of non-whites, he made no attempt to expound or defend the delimitation provisions.

W. P. Schreiner then made a long speech, contending that amendments were necessary and that a referendum or general election should be held before the Cape became committed to joining the Union. Though he still considered that a federal system would have been better for South Africa, he was now prepared to accept a unitary Constitution, but in the document before them the Cape was not receiving sufficient representation in

---

[95] *O.R.C. Leg. Ass. Deb., 1909*, col. 76.   [96] Ibid., col. 77.

[97] The resolutions which were adopted by both houses of the Orange River Colony Parliament are in Hofmeyr, *Minutes*, pp. 348–9.

[98] *Cape Hansard, 1909*, pp. 1–156; *Cape Leg. Co. Deb., 1909*, cols. 1–12; *Cape H. of A. V. & P., 1909*, pp. 1–49; *Cape Leg. Co. Min., 1909*, pp. 1–19. Where there are discrepancies between the division lists in *Hansard* and those in the *Votes and Proceedings*, the latter have been followed. The numbers of sections are those in the draft S.A. Act in the convention's first report (Feb. 1909); and except where stated to the contrary the numbers of the corresponding sections of the S.A. Act as enacted are the same.

[99] *Cape Hansard, 1909*, p. 6.

Parliament and the delimitation sections were very vague. These, however, were only questions of detail compared with the colour question. It would be dishonourable not to insist that the Cape Province should be able to send non-Europeans to Parliament. They should also insist on more effective safeguards for the Cape franchise.

General Smuts talked of the white nation; but did that not leave a bad taste in the mouth? Was fairness and equality only to be shown to the white races? . . . If a small number of Cape representatives in the Union Parliament were not true to that trust, and with others voted for the coloured franchise being removed, would not the rights of the native and coloured peoples vanish into thin air, under Parliamentary sanction? . . . It was no use them saying that they were satisfied with a certain amount of protection; they must go further, and have absolute protection. . . . Union without honour . . . was the greatest danger any nation could incur.[1]

The next four speakers were members of the South African Party, and all of them said that amendments were essential. S. C. Cronwright Schreiner objected to the European descent qualification, denounced 'one vote one value', and demanded a referendum. A. S. du Plessis said that a referendum was unnecessary, for he had met his constituents and knew their wishes, but he considered that amendments should be made to the electoral sections. So did J. A. Vosloo: 'the poor man would have no means of contesting such large constituencies. They would need a motor-car to visit their constituents.' This sally caused laughter and a voice interjected, 'Airships'.[2] Vosloo also said that the franchise section should be amended to ensure that Cape province non-whites should not be disqualified without the consent of two-thirds of the Cape Members of Parliament, while J. A. Greer criticized many aspects of the draft Constitution and made a personal attack on the Prime Minister and leader of his party for attempting to stifle amendments.

Assistance came to Merriman from the other side of the House. On 1 April the Cape delegates to the convention dined together and the next morning Jameson declared that 'The position of the Opposition for this session of Parliament has absolutely disappeared. . . . I look upon myself as the lieutenant of the Prime Minister in this matter.'[3] He said that Schreiner's speech would have been useful if it had been made at the beginning of the convention, but that at this stage it might endanger union. He defended the actions of the Cape delegates on the colour question, saying that the Cape franchise was completely safe and predicting that the Cape doctrine of equal rights for all civilized men was sure to

[1] Ibid., pp. 18–19.
[2] Ibid., p. 21.   [3] Ibid., pp. 26–27.

prevail throughout the Union in the long run. He also made a decisive statement on the electoral question:

. . . it was surely a good thing to establish a principle on the question of representation, not like the Prime Minister, who says, 'Oh, bother these principles; I like a good old rule of thumb.' I agree with him if it is my thumb. But if it is the Prime Minister's thumb I confess I prefer to have a principle.[4]

Nevertheless, continued Jameson,

I do not believe in a very congested district that the value of the vote should be the same as in an extremely sparsely-populated part of the country. . . . I know there are extremists who do, but that is driving principle to an idiotic point.[5]

The problem, he said, had been fully discussed in the convention and 'the idea of every member was that the judges should go up to the full 30 per cent' in extreme cases.

We tried to define it. We discussed it over and over again . . . by all means let this House . . . recommend that there shall be a definite meaning laid down. Don't leave it to chance, or God Almighty or anyone else—try and get it defined, and we will support it.[6]

After that member after member got up from the government side of the House to insist on amendments to sections 39 and 40. Nothing less than the full 30 per cent. would satisfy D. H. W. Wessels. The farmers would otherwise be ruined, said C. E. Tod. Sauer seized on Jameson's statement and said that all that was needed was a definition of what the convention really intended, namely, that the country districts should get the full benefit of the 30 per cent., and Malan, also, declared that the sections should be rephrased to express the convention's intention. The Opposition seems to have been somewhat bewildered by Jameson's compromising speech. Walton and Smartt did not speak at all in the debate and Jagger confined his remarks to the economic aspect of union. Several backbenchers, however, defended 'one vote one value'. G. A. L. Green explained that townsmen felt as strongly about it as Bondsmen felt about language equality, and W. D. Baxter pointed out that single-member constituencies in the country districts combined with proportional representation in the towns would give the rural parties an unfair advantage. On the other hand, a small group of Unionist backbenchers supported the demand for amendment, B. Upington saying that equal constituencies would lead to plutocratic rule, and G. Blaine announcing

---

[4] *Cape Hansard*, 1909, p. 28.   [5] Ibid., pp. 28–29   [6] Ibid., p. 29.

that he would move an amendment in the committee stage. Sauer and the Bondsmen therefore had good reason to be satisfied with the debate.

The sections dealing with the political rights of non-whites were also criticized from both sides of the House. Upington pointed out that Cape non-whites were indubitably being deprived of an existing right in being made ineligible for membership of Parliament; and T. Searle (S.A.P.) and M. Alexander (Unionist) doubted whether the two-thirds majority requirement would prove to be a sufficient safeguard for the maintenance of the Cape franchise. The sections were defended by Sauer, who, like Jameson, predicted a liberal trend in the Union Parliament; by Stanford, who was sure that union on the conditions recommended by the convention would be better than no union at all; and by Malan, who resorted to the specious argument that since non-whites had never been able to vote for the election of a united South African Parliament, they were not being deprived of an existing right. Several backbenchers of both parties expressed satisfaction with the sections, notably C. J. Levey, a South African Party member for Tembuland (a constituency with a large number of Native voters), who asserted that the vote should never have been given to Natives, that the influence of missionaries was unwholesome, that the Natives should trust the Union Government, and that 'It was absurd for a native to imagine that he could become a European; if he became a useful agriculturalist he would do well.' South Africa, he predicted, would build up a Native policy that 'would astonish the world'.[7]

By the time the motion to go into committee was carried without a division on the afternoon of 7 April, Merriman had serious doubts whether it would be possible to bring the Cape Colony into the Union. His policy of no outright amendments had been challenged at every meeting of his party caucus and even in Cabinet he found his colleagues 'rather unsympathetic'.[8] On 1 April he wrote to Botha and Smuts to explain that Schreiner and Hofmeyr might persuade a majority of the members of the assembly that mere recommendations were not enough.[9] Two days later he told Steyn that the opposition was 'a thoroughly organised effort . . . to destroy . . . the work of the Convention' and admitted that there was 'an entire rupture in the ranks of our party'.[10] However, at a meeting of the party caucus on the evening of the 5th Merriman was persuaded to support amendments to the electoral sections, and the next day he telegraphed Botha, saying that if those

---

[7] Ibid., p. 57.   [8] Merriman's Diary, 3 Apr. 1909.
[9] Transvaal Archives, Prime Minister, LX (ii); Smuts Papers.
[10] Steyn Papers.

sections were not amended the Cape might not join the Union.[11] He explained himself more fully in a letter:

There is a knot of people with headquarters in Cape Town who for one reason or another do not like Union. I should say that Hofmeyr was the head centre. He has an able lieutenant in Van der Horst and they have the entire control of *Ons Land*. . . . This section has put forward a good many trivial objections that have not caught on—but undoubtedly in the provision for one vote one value &c they have the entire farming community Dutch and English behind them. . . . In this direction we shall certainly have amendments put forward and unless some relief is gained I can see that we shall have the greatest difficulty in forcing the constitution through in time.[12]

Botha replied to the telegram promptly, warning Merriman that the Transvaal Progressives would never accept amendments to the electoral sections,[13] while Steyn wrote to advise him to 'Allow them to blow off their steam' and to let amendments be proposed, provided they did not bind him. Steyn hoped that the convention would meet the Cape's wishes on the electoral question, but he was confident that in any case the Cape would accept the draft Constitution, observing shrewdly that 'Het is maar een beetje politiek' (it is only a little politics). If, however, the Cape were by any chance to stand out, the Free State would certainly join the other two colonies, because 'the Free State and Transvaal are Siamese twins'.[14]

Directly the House went into committee Merriman was worsted on a procedural question. He wished to speed up the work of the committee by taking the draft Constitution chapter by chapter, but B. Upington (Unionist) and H. E. S. Fremantle (S.A.P.) objected, and the House adopted Schreiner's proposal to take it section by section. Then under section 4 Schreiner moved a recommendation for an amendment to make a referendum or a general election necessary before a colony could join the Union. In 1908 Merriman himself had spoken in favour of submitting the Constitution to a referendum and Sauer had said that it would be wrong to do otherwise.[15] Now, however, Merriman, Sauer, and other delegates said that a referendum was unnecessary and Schreiner's motion was rejected without a division.

Soon afterwards the committee came to section 25,[16] prescribing qualifications for senators. Petitions had been received from the A.P.O., the Bloemfontein Native Convention, a Wynberg Coloured organization, and the Evangelical Church Council, asking for the removal of the par-

---

[11] Transvaal Archives, Prime Minister, LX (ii).
[13] 6 Apr., Merriman Papers (telegram).
[15] *Cape Hansard, 1908*, p. 12 ; *Cape Leg. Co. Deb., 1908*, col. 40.
[16] S. 26 of the S.A. Act.

[12] Ibid.
[14] 6 Apr., ibid.

liamentary colour-bar and for more effective safeguards for the Cape franchise;[17] and from 12 April until the end of the session a motion stood on the order paper, but was never debated, praying that Dr. Abdurahman, the President of the A.P.O., should be heard at the bar of the House. Schreiner moved a recommendation that the convention should amend section 25 to allow non-Europeans to become senators for the Cape Province. All that he was asking, he said, was that the Cape non-whites should retain their existing right to sit in Parliament. Merriman opposed the motion, saying it would endanger Union and provoke an agitation against the Cape franchise in the northern colonies, but Schreiner gained support from both sides of the House. It was pointed out that both parties had stood for 'equal rights for all civilized men' in the last general election, that the Cape delegates had undertaken to maintain existing rights, and that the European descent clause was in direct conflict with these pledges. Sauer, Beck, and Walton justified their conduct, however, by saying that they had been unable to get anything better in the convention, that union was in the best interests of the Natives themselves, and that the liberal attitude of the Cape Colony would gradually permeate the entire Union; but Stanford, who was clearly embarrassed, said that although he felt bound by his signature to the convention's report to support its recommendations, his Native constituents felt strongly about the disqualification, and he confessed that it would please him if the motion was passed. Furthermore, most members who participated in the debate, including those who spoke against the motion, said that they regretted the decision of the convention, and only a very small minority, including F. Ginsberg (Unionist) and C. J. Levey and W. J. van Zijl (S.A.P.), criticized the principle of equal rights for all civilized men. The motion was rejected by seventy-seven votes (54 S.A.P., 21 Unionists, and 2 Independents) to twenty (7 S.A.P., 11 Unionists, and 2 Independents). Under section 35, five recommendations to strengthen the safeguards for the Cape franchise were moved and three of them were pressed to divisions. Merriman spoke strongly against even the mildest of them, urging the committee not to tie the hands of the delegates, and appealing for confidence in the liberalizing effects which education would have on the people of the other colonies. Cronwright Schreiner drew attention to what had been said in the other colonial parliaments, to show that northerners were only too anxious to disfranchise the Cape Natives, and T. Searle remarked that it was doubtful whether white opinion would move in a liberal direction after Union.

[17] All these petitions were presented on or before 7 Apr., except the petition from the Native Convention, which was presented on 12 Apr.

The first division was on W. P. Schreiner's motion for a recommendation that the section should be amended to make Parliament absolutely incompetent to disqualify anyone in the Cape Province by reason of his race or colour only, and it was rejected by seventy-nine votes to sixteen (7 S.A.P., 7 Unionists, and 2 Independents). The second was on another W. P. Schreiner motion for a recommendation that for such disqualification the agreement of two-thirds of the parliamentary representatives of the Cape Province should be required, as well as two-thirds of the total members of Parliament, and it was rejected by eighty-six votes to fourteen (7 S.A.P., 5 Unionists, and 2 Independents). The third was on a recommendation that the agreement of a majority of the parliamentary representatives of the Cape Province should be required, as well as two-thirds of the total members of Parliament. This proposal had been endorsed by the Bond congress at Dordrecht. It was moved by Vosloo and rejected by the narrow margin of fifty-three votes (33 S.A.P., 18 Unionists, and 2 Independents) to forty-seven (32 S.A.P., 13 Unionists, and 2 Independents). Later, when they came to section 44, Schreiner moved a recommendation that non-Europeans should be eligible for election as members of the House of Assembly for the Cape Province, remarking that the argument that amendments would wreck union had been exploded by the fact that the committee had already passed amendments to sections 39 and 40. Nevertheless, Merriman opposed the motion, saying testily that 'little tinkering amendments'[18] would only create hostility in the convention and the Union Parliament against the Native vote, and it was defeated by seventy-four votes to twenty-three (8 S.A.P., 13 Unionists, and 2 Independents). In all these divisions against the colour-bar and for more effective safeguards for the Cape franchise the convention delegates voted with the Noes.[19]

The committee dealt with the electoral sections on 12 April. Under section 39 J. C. Molteno (S.A.P.) proposed that they should only approve of the draft Constitution subject to the proviso that the delimitation commissions should be obliged to create electoral divisions returning less than three members 'in all cases of sparsely populated areas' and the words 'sparsely populated areas' were clearly defined.[20] Molteno said that if this amendment was not made the permanent population would be deprived of its legitimate interest in the affairs of the country. Sauer

---

[18] *Cape Hansard, 1909*, p. 122.

[19] Except that Beck abstained from voting on Schreiner's first amendment to s. 35. Two of the twelve Cape delegates were not in a position to vote—de Villiers (who was not a member of the House of Assembly) and van Heerden (who was in the chair as chairman of committees).

[20] *Cape Hansard, 1909*, p. 111.

agreed. The rural constituencies, he said, would be so large that the farmer would disappear from public life. He only wanted what they had intended in the convention, and nothing more. Merriman said he deplored the fact that the convention had ignored his advice and adopted 'ridiculous, democratic ideas . . . which would never suit the country',[21] and he announced that, although he now accepted the principles of 'one vote one value' and proportional representation, he wanted them to be more accurately defined. Other members of the South African Party spoke in similar vein. Jagger opposed the amendment which, he declared, was being moved for party political purposes and no other. British South Africans wanted to enter the Union on a footing of perfect political equality, just as Afrikaners wanted language equality. But Jameson supported this amendment, saying that if possible the convention should define what was meant. When the amendment was put to the vote the chairman declared that the Ayes had it and nobody called for a division. Then under section 40 (iii) G. Blaine, a Unionist member for the farming constituency of Cathcart, moved his promised amendment. It was to the effect that the delimitation commissions should be obliged as nearly as possible to give sparsely populated areas one member for every 15 per cent. fewer voters than the quota, and densely populated areas one member for every 15 per cent. more voters than the quota, with a sliding scale for intermediate areas. That is to say, what the convention had recommended as a maximum permissive departure from the quota was to become obligatory, and what the convention had recommended as one of five equal factors was to become the operative factor. Otherwise, said Blaine, the Constitution would be a death-trap for the farming community. Jagger and other Unionists said that they had opposed other amendments in consequence of the Prime Minister's appeal, and now they were being asked to support amendments which were blatantly partisan; but Merriman declared that the motion was an elucidation rather than an amendment of a principle in the draft Act, and Jameson said he would stretch a point and treat it as an elucidation—though it was 'a very powerful elucidation . . . an elucidation of one side only'.[22] On the other hand, W. P. Schreiner admitted that it was a substantial amendment and said he supported it because he believed 'one vote one value' was not suited to South Africa. After a phrase asking the convention to define 'sparsity or density of population' had been added without a division, Blaine's motion was carried by seventy-four votes (65 S.A.P., 6 Unionists, and 3 Independents) to twenty-six (25 Unionists and

---

[21] Ibid., p. 115.
[22] Ibid., p. 120.

1 Independent).[23] In this division the convention delegates were divided on party lines: Merriman, Malan, Sauer, Beck, and Maasdorp (S.A.P.) supported the amendment, and Jameson, Jagger, Smartt, and Walton (Unionist), and Stanford (Independent) opposed it. Later on, under section 71, C. E. Tod (S.A.P.) moved a further amendment to the effect that all the members of the provincial councils should be elected in single-member constituencies, and that the duration of the provincial councils should be increased from three to five years, and it was adopted without a division. Thus, while the committee rejected all proposals which were in the interests of the non-whites, it insisted on the systematic loading of the parliamentary constituencies to the advantage of the rural voters and on the abandonment of proportional representation for provincial council elections.

Twenty other amendments or recommendations for amendment were moved, many of them by Schreiner, but they were opposed by Merriman and other delegates and they were all either withdrawn, or rejected without a division, or defeated by a majority of at least two-thirds of those who voted. Two were intended to improve or safeguard the status of Cape Town after union. Two were attempts by Afrikaner members to amplify the language section, by making it obligatory for the Governor-General to sign both an English and a Dutch copy of every Act of Parliament, and by making express provision that the records of provincial councils should be kept in both languages. One was for the elimination of the nominated senators, another for an increase in the property qualification for senators. A recommendation to admit women to the franchise for provincial council elections was rejected by sixty-nine votes to nineteen, after Merriman had made a characteristic assertion that women were quite unfit to exercise the vote. A recommendation for the dropping of proportional representation from parliamentary as well as provincial council elections was rejected without a division after Merriman had undertaken to raise the question again in the convention. Among several

[23] The resolution read as follows: 'To add to the original motion the words: "subject to the following: that the meaning and intent of the Draft Act in regard to the cases in which the quota of voters may be departed from in the delimitation of electoral divisions referred to in paragraph (c) of sub-section (iii) of section forty be more clearly expressed so as to ensure that the departure from the quota shall not be in the discretion of the Commissioners, but shall be made in accordance with the considerations set forth in section forty, sub-section (iii) (a), (b), (c), (d) and (e), so that in sparsely populated areas as nearly as possible fifteen per cent. less voters than the quota and in densely populated areas as nearly as possible fifteen per cent. more voters than the quota shall be entitled to a member, and that areas not falling within either of the above descriptions be dealt with on a sliding scale of departure from the quota made in accordance with the above consideration and within the limit of percentage referred to, and that the terms 'sparsity or density of population' be clearly defined".'

recommendations on the financial sections, two gave expression to the fears which had been aroused by Smuts's description of section 129[24] as the Magna Charta of the inland colonies and by the publication of the convention between the Transvaal and Mozambique. Another sought to make it clear that a colony would have the right to alter the incidence of taxation before union.[25] It was a product of the agitation of the wine-farmers against the brandy excise—an agitation which reached a climax on 14 April, when special trains brought a horde of wine-farmers to Cape Town. There were also motions that British Bechuanaland should be transferred from the Cape Colony to the Transvaal and that Parliament should be able to divide a province into two or more provinces without petitions from the provincial councils.

Thus at last, on the afternoon of 15 April—'After Schreiner had expressed his opinion 64 times and Fremantle 46 times', Merriman noted in his diary—the Speaker resumed the chair and the House of Assembly adopted the committee's resolutions approving of the draft Act, subject to amendments to sections 39, 40, and 71.

The next day, introducing this resolution into the Legislative Council,[26] Merriman referred briefly to the assembly's 'amendments, or he would rather call them elucidations'.[27] The council agreed to them without a division, while a recommendation that European descent should be unnecessary for Cape Province senators was rejected by fifteen votes to seven, and a recommendation that European descent should be unnecessary for Cape members of the House of Assembly was rejected without a division, and so was a recommendation to strengthen the safeguard for the Cape franchise.

On the other hand, the council adopted several recommendations for further amendments. One was that section 23[28] should be amended, so that a senator nominated to replace a retired or deceased nominated senator should only hold his seat for the unexpired part of the term instead of for a further period of ten years. Another, which was moved by J. A. C. Graaff, the brother of the minister, was that 'the meaning and intent of section 138[29] should be more clearly expressed, so as to ensure

[24] S. 127 of the S.A. Act.

[25] Merriman said it would be dishonourable to remit taxes before Union, but it would be possible to change one tax for another, provided that the total revenue was not thereby diminished.

[26] The Legislative Council Debates are very meagre for this session, filling only twelve columns, because for reasons of economy the council did not renew its contract for reporting, printing, and publishing its debates.

[27] *Cape Leg. Co. Deb., 1909*, col. 8.

[28] S. 24 of the S.A. Act.

[29] S. 137 of the S.A. Act.

the application of the principle of equality of the English and Dutch languages to the Provincial Councils, and Courts of Justice and Public Service generally'.

The remaining recommendations were moved by Sir Henry de Villiers, who was President of the council. On 8 March Lord Selborne had written to inform him that the Colonial Secretary had drawn his attention to section 64 of the draft Constitution. Section 55 of the British North America Act, Selborne pointed out, provided that the Governor-General of Canada should assent to a Bill in the Queen's name, or withhold the Queen's assent, or reserve the Bill for the signification of the Queen's pleasure, 'according to his discretion, but subject to the provisions of this Act and to Her Majesty's instructions', whereas section 58 of the Australian Constitution omitted the underlined words, and a controversy had arisen between the Australian and the Imperial Government. The Australian Government contended that the question whether a Bill should be reserved should be left to the personal discretion of the Governor-General, and the Imperial Government contended that it was competent for the Crown to give any instructions to the Governor-General with regard to the reservation of a Bill and that the Governor-General was to exercise his discretion subject to such instructions. Section 64 of the draft South Africa Act followed the Australian section. Selborne therefore suggested that the convention might

think it better to prevent in advance any such controversy as has arisen between His Majesty's Government and the Commonwealth Government by the introduction into section 64 of the draft South Africa Act of some such words as are used in section 55 of the British North America Act, to make it clear that the Governor-General must use the discretion entrusted to him subject to any instructions which he may receive from His Majesty.[30]

De Villiers had replied on 16 March, saying that he would lay Selborne's letter before the convention and that he thought the suggestion would be acceptable:

I am not aware that the Convention had any special reason for following the 58th section of the Australia Constitution Act instead of the 55th section of the British North America Act. I myself prefer the latter and as it is quite in accordance with the practice which has hitherto prevailed in the South African Colonies I am inclined to think that the Convention . . . will adopt the same view.[31]

Accordingly, de Villiers took the opportunity of asking the Legislative

---

[30] House of Assembly, National Convention Minutes, III.
[31] Ibid.

Council to recommend that the convention should amend section 64 by inserting words obliging the Governor-General, when a Bill was presented to him for the King's assent, to exercise his discretion subject to the provisions of the South Africa Act 'and to such instructions as may from time to time be given in that behalf by His Majesty, his heirs or successors'. The council adopted this recommendation without a division.

De Villiers's other proposals concerned the judicial chapter of the draft Constitution. J. G. Kotzé, the President of the Eastern Districts Court at Grahamstown, was offended because the Constitution appeared to make the judges of the Eastern Districts Court and the High Court of Griqualand West ineligible for appointment to the Appellate Division. He also objected to the provision in chapter 96 under which two additional judges of appeal would 'from time to time be temporarily assigned by the Governor-General-in-Council to the Appellate Division'. In a letter to Innes, the Chief Justice of the Transvaal, he had written:

> Suppose now a case of a constitutional or political character came before the Court of Appeal, whose decision is final, the Ministry can influence the Court by placing its friends thereon. Such a thing may not happen in our time, but we are framing a Constitution under which the young State is to grow and prosper and we should be careful not to lay down a wrong principle.[32]

Innes agreed with Kotzé and had informed de Villiers that he regarded it as 'a most undesirable arrangement', and he had also suggested other amendments.[33] Consequently de Villiers moved five recommendations in the Legislative Council: Section 96 should be amended so that the two additional judges of appeal would be 'assigned by the Governor-General-in-Council to the Appellate Division from any of the Provincial or Local Divisions of the Supreme Court', though they would still, as in the draft Act, 'continue to perform their duties as judges of their respective Divisions when their attendance is not required in the Appellate Division'. Section 97 should provide for the appointment of a temporary additional judge of appeal in the event of a temporary vacancy occurring through illness or other cause. Section 103 should allow 'appeals against

---

[32] Kotzé to Innes, 12 Feb., Innes Papers. Kotzé and his fellow judges of the Eastern Districts Court also recorded their opinions in a memorandum sent to de Villiers on 12 Mar., de Villiers Papers.

[33] 22 Mar., de Villiers Papers. Hertzog came to the same conclusion after a discussion with the Orange River Colony judges, and wrote to Smuts on 12 Feb. to point out that a Government might make temporary appointments of appeal judges 'specially with a view to having a judgement according to their desires—and so as it were pack the Bench'; but Smuts wrote across the top of Hertzog's letter, 'Answered negativing his contentions'. Smuts Papers.

judgments on interlocutory applications or on matters of procedure in civil cases or . . . questions of law reserved by a Judge presiding at Criminal Sessions' to be heard by the provincial divisions. Section 108 should empower the Chief Justice and the other judges to frame rules for the conduct of the proceedings of all the provincial and local divisions of the Supreme Court, subject to the approval of the Governor-General-in-Council. Finally, section 113 should empower the local as well as the provincial divisions to order the transfer of civil suits to other divisions.[34] The council adopted these recommendations, also, without a division.

On the afternoon of 16 April the council approved of the assembly's resolution, with its own additional recommendations. The next morning the assembly sat for only ten minutes to endorse the additional recommendations, and when the assembly's message of concurrence was reported to the council, J. A. C. Graaff declared that the amendments to sections 39 and 40 were vital, and that if the convention failed to give effect to them, the prospects of union would be imperilled.

The Cape Colony Parliament was then prorogued. Whereas the Transvaal Parliament had approved of the draft Constitution without qualification, and the Orange River Colony Parliament had approved with nothing more than recommendations for amendments, the approval of the Cape Colony Parliament was 'subject to' far-reaching amendments to the electoral system.[35]

D. *Natal*[36]

Moor and his fellow delegates—Greene, Hyslop, Smythe, and Watt—were convinced that Natal's best interests lay in joining the Union, even though it was not to be the federal type of union which they would have preferred. They knew that amendments in conflict with the basic principles of the draft Constitution would never be accepted by the convention and they feared that the Natal electorate, when it came to the referendum which they had undertaken to hold, would reject union if

---

[34] Sir Richard Solomon and Innes had also informed de Villiers that they disapproved of the selection of Bloemfontein as the seat of the Appellate Division, but de Villiers realized it was impracticable to reopen the question, and with it the entire capital question, in the convention. He expected that much use would be made of the provision in s. 109 empowering the Appellate Division to sit elsewhere 'from time to time for the convenience of suitors'. Solomon to de Villiers, 6 Feb., Innes to de Villiers, 22 Mar., 15 Apr., de Villiers Papers; de Villiers to Innes, 25 Mar., Innes Papers.

[35] The resolutions of the Cape Parliament are in Hofmeyr, *Minutes*, pp. 345–6.

[36] *Natal Leg. Ass. Deb.* xlvii; *Natal Leg. Co. Deb.* xix; *Natal Leg. Ass. V. & P.* lxviii; *Natal Leg. Co. V. & P.* xx. The numbers of sections are those in the draft S.A. Act in the convention's first report (Feb. 1909); and except where stated to the contrary the numbers of the corresponding sections of the S.A. Act as enacted are the same.

the Natal Parliament recommended fundamental amendments and the convention rejected them. They therefore did all they could to persuade their Parliament to approve of the draft Constitution, with no more than a few amendments on points of detail.

On 31 March Moor moved that the Legislative Assembly should go into committee on the draft South Africa Act. Urging the House to endorse the work of the convention, he defended the principle of parliamentary sovereignty and sought to show that the interests of Natal were sufficiently safeguarded:

We have equal representation in the Senate. . . . We have within the Constitution certain powers reserved for the local bodies . . . and our central Parliament would not dare to interfere with those provincial rights unless it was the will of the people that that should come about; and instead of the powers of these Provincial Councils being limited in the future, I honestly believe that these powers will be increased by the central Parliament.[37]

Moor then expressed the hope that members would only press for a few vital but moderate amendments, explaining that the Natal delegates would not be able to obtain the sympathy of the convention if they came with a mass of indiscriminate criticisms, and predicted that continued disunion would be a calamity for Natal, while union in terms of the draft Constitution would promote immigration, capital investment, industrial expansion, and general prosperity. He concluded:

In our own interests, in the interests of the white people of South Africa, both Dutch and English, in the interests of the Natives of South Africa, . . . in the interests of England . . . and in the interests of that grand Empire that we are all so proud of . . . I move the resolution that is standing in my name.[38]

In the ensuing debate three Labour members were highly critical of the draft Constitution and insisted on radical amendments. N. P. Palmer said that the Natal delegates 'went to the Convention professed Federationists; they have come back absolute Unificationists, with some illusory, dissolving views of Provincial Councils'.[39] While agreeing with the Prime Minister that union would probably lead to material prosperity, he contended that the Constitution should provide greater stability and he expressed the hope that members would not be deterred from bringing forward amendments and that the delegates would try their best to have their amendments accepted by the convention. C. H. Haggar said that it was essential that no part of the Constitution should be alterable except

[37] *Natal Leg. Ass. Deb.* xlvii. 12.
[38] Ibid., p. 15.
[39] Ibid., p. 20.

by a referendum, while D. Taylor wanted constitutional amendments to require the consent of the provincial councils and said that if Natal joined the Union she should possess the right to secede. Three other members were equally critical from the British imperialist point of view and declared that Natal should remain outside the Union if their amendments were not accepted by the convention. C. A. S. Yonge gave expression to their deep-seated fears that unification would lead to Afrikaner domination of the entire country. 'I say that Unification does, and can only, mean not the advancement equally of British and Dutch in South Africa, but the dominance of one to the disability of the other.'[40] And again: 'I say that legislative union . . . can mean nothing else but the absolute absorption by Parliament of every institution and every power now possessed by the people of South Africa.'[41] He indulged in tirades against the Witwatersrand magnates, whom he suspected of combining with the Afrikaners to force the Constitution through for their own nefarious purposes, and against the British Liberal Government, whom he accused of deserting the South African loyalists. 'It is treachery to the right, treachery to the left, treachery without, and treachery within. And that is unhappy little Natal's reward for all she struggled to do to maintain the imperial interest.'[42] P. A. Silburn spoke in similar terms and promised to do all he could to defeat the draft Constitution, while J. Schofield said that he was sure that Natal could and should preserve her identity.

Watt and Hyslop tried to refute these criticisms. Watt, like Moor, made much of the sections providing for provincial equality in the senate and for the creation of provincial councils. He said that Natal could not afford to remain outside the Union and he announced that he would oppose all amendments, because 'I gave my pledge as a delegate to do my best to get the people of Natal to accept the Constitution as it stands'.[43] Hyslop stressed the advantages of having 'the whole of the forces of South Africa at our back' in the event of another rebellion.[44] He said there was no possibility of Afrikaner domination, because parties would be formed on non-racial lines and the two white races would fuse into one.

We have in South Africa two strong, virile races. They are of common origin, and of the same religion. There is nothing whatever to hinder these two races amalgamating. With this question of Union before us, it is for us to accept the hand of fellowship which is held out to us by the Dutch-speaking people of South Africa, and to assist in building up a great nation which will be one of the brightest jewels in the British Crown.[45]

---

[40] *Natal Leg. Ass. Deb.* xlvii. 43.   [41] Ibid., p. 44.   [42] Ibid., p. 45.
[43] Ibid., p. 25.   [44] Ibid., p. 84.   [45] Ibid., p. 85.

The Afrikaner members gave unequivocal support to the draft Constitution and repudiated the contentions of the imperialists. Dr. E. G. A. Niemeyer said:

There is not going to be Dutch dominance. There is going to be British dominance. We are all Britishers alike now. We have all accepted the British flag, and the majority of us—we have a few extremists, too, but the majority of us wish to form one nation with you, to the glory of the British Empire.[46]

M. W. Myburgh said that it was the duty of every South African to support the moderate party which had sprung up since the war between the two racial extremes and appealed for trust in the governments of the other three colonies; and T. Nel junior and F. Fergg spoke in similar terms.

From the tone of their speeches it is evident that most of the British members were torn between fear of Afrikaner domination and a reluctant realization that Natal would not be able to survive apart from the Union. Some were so delighted with the delimitation sections of the draft Constitution that they discounted other features of which they disapproved—notably W. McLarty and M. S. Evans, Durban members who had for years been striving for equal constituencies in Natal, and J. Connolly, the fourth Labour member of the House, who had previously been as adamant as anyone in demanding a strictly federal Constitution. Nevertheless, nearly everyone who participated in the debate, other than the delegates and the Afrikaner members, spoke of the need for amendments to give greater security for the provincial institutions, though they did so with many different shades of emphasis.

Replying to the debate on 7 April, Moor reiterated his warning that the alternative to union was strife:

I never uttered more earnest words in my political life than when I warned my Colony that South Africa to-day has come to the parting of the ways. . . . We are going to have that strife, as surely as the sun is going to rise to-morrow, if we don't get this Union commenced. It will come about by jealousies of trade, and will be accentuated by the dissociation of our interests, and we shall be eventually driven into two hostile camps.[47]

The vote was then taken and the motion to go into committee was carried by thirty-one votes to three. The three imperialists—Schofield, Silburn, and Yonge—formed the minority, while the Labour members voted with the majority, except for Taylor who, with five others, abstained from the division.[48]

---

[46] Ibid., p. 64. [47] Ibid., p. 122.

[48] The names of the five other members who did not participate in this division were E. M. Greene, the Minister of Railways and Harbours, G. S. Armstrong, C. Hitchins,

The committee stage may be divided into two phases. In the first phase, which ended on the morning of the 15th, the committee dealt with the draft Constitution section by section and passed twelve outright amendments out of fifty-one which were moved. In the second phase, on the 15th, the committee dealt with several sections which had been standing over and others which were reverted to, passed one more outright amendment out of twenty-three which were moved, and also adopted two resolutions of instructions to the Natal delegates.[49]

The most prolific movers of amendments were the Labour group—Haggar, Palmer, and Taylor—who moved nineteen during the first phase, and the imperialists—Schofield, Silburn, and Yonge—who moved twelve. First of all Schofield moved an amendment to section 1, for the short title of the Act to be the British South Africa Act instead of the South Africa Act. The Prime Minister and Morcom opposed the amendment and when it came to the vote five Afrikaner members supported it, to demonstrate their loyalty, but it was defeated by twenty-one votes to nine, the delegates voting solidly against it. Several of the other amendments moved by the imperialists received no support from other members—they included proposals that the colonies should become known as states and not provinces, and that provincial ordinances need not be enrolled in both languages; and several of the Labour amendments received no support from other members, including proposals that there should be no second chamber in the Union Parliament, that the elected senators should be elected directly by the voters, and that the duration of the House of Assembly should be three, not five years. In some cases Labour amendments were supported by the imperialists, and vice versa, but all those which were pressed to divisions were defeated by large majorities. That was the fate of proposals that Parliament should not be competent to legislate on topics allotted to the provincial councils, that the provincial executive committees should hold office during the pleasure of the provincial councils, and that provincial ordinances should not require the assent of the Governor-General-in-Council, nor be invalid if repugnant to Acts of Parliament.

As it became apparent that the delegates were opposing all their amendments[50] and gaining the support of a large majority of the House,

---

T. P. O'Meara, and J. W. Moor, the brother of the Prime Minister. Furthermore, Sir J. L. Hulett and J. A. Polkinghorne had leave of absence for the entire session. No significance is attached to the absence of Greene from the division, because he supported the draft Constitution as ardently as any of the other delegates.

[49] The committee stage was not as long as it might appear, since the House only sat on 7, 8, 13, 14, and 15 Apr.

[50] No delegate voted for any amendment moved by the Labour group or the Imperial-

the Labour and imperialist members became exasperated, and on 8 April Silburn moved that the chairman should leave the chair (i.e. that the committee should refuse to approve of the draft Act), but this was defeated by twenty-nine votes to three (Schofield, Silburn, and Taylor), whereupon Taylor tried unsuccessfully to persuade the committee that the Speaker should be asked to give a ruling as to whether the delegates, being committed to the draft Act, were entitled to record their votes against amendments.

Eleven of the amendments which were carried were moved by middle-of-the-road members—E. A. Brunner, W. F. Clayton, M. S. Evans, and J. S. Wylie—and the twelfth was moved by Yonge. Half of these amendments were intended as safeguards for the material interests of Natal: There was to be a new section providing that 'There shall at all times be absolute Free Trade throughout the Union', which Greene and Hyslop declared was quite unnecessary but which was not opposed by anyone; section 128[51] was amended to make the railway and harbour board contain not less than three members, instead of not more than three members, besides the minister; in section 129,[52] which laid down the principles on which the railways were to be administered, the reference to the development of the inland, as distinct from the other parts of the Union, was deleted and a proviso was inserted empowering Parliament to use railway revenues for general union purposes during the first four years; in section 135[53] the sentence empowering the Governor-General-in-Council in certain circumstances to reduce or withdraw the annual payments of compensation to the former colonial capitals ten years after the establishment of the Union was deleted; and in section 149,[54] which made the existing treaty obligations of the colonies binding on the Union, a specific mention of the intercolonial railway agreement of 2 February 1909 was inserted. The committee also inserted a new section to make the existing colonial laws prohibiting the sale of liquor to Natives unalterable except by a two-thirds majority in a joint sitting of both Houses of Parliament, and made a verbal change in clause 18 of the schedule.[55] All these amendments were carried without divisions, except the amendment to section 135, which was carried by twenty-seven votes to three,

---

ist group, except that Morcom supported Palmer's amendment to s. 153 [152]. At least four delegates voted against every Labour and Imperialist amendment which was pressed to a division.

[51] S. 126 of the S.A. Act.   [52] S. 127 of the S.A. Act.
[53] S. 133 of the S.A. Act.   [54] S. 148 of the S.A. Act.
[55] The words 'black and white' were deleted from the provision that 'There shall be free intercourse for the black and white inhabitants of the Territories with the rest of South Africa subject to the laws, including the pass laws, of the Union.'

and the amendment to section 149, which was carried by twenty-seven votes to six.[56]

The other amendments which were carried were intended as political safeguards for Natal. Section 32[57] was amended to make Parliament incompetent to reduce the number of seats of any of the original provinces in the House of Assembly (i.e. to ensure that Natal should always have at least seventeen seats). Smythe, the Leader of the Opposition, who spoke but rarely during the session, supported this as a vital amendment. Greene spoke against it on the ground that Parliament would certainly never reduce Natal's representation below seventeen (thereby showing that he was ignorant of the plain meaning of the section, which provided that the seats should be divided between the provinces in proportion to their total white populations after the total number of seats had reached 150), and so did Watt, on the grounds that Natal had been very generously treated by the convention and that it was inexpedient to reopen the question, and Evans, who wanted the principle of equal constituencies to be applied without qualification. Nevertheless, the amendment was carried without a division. So was an amendment to section 82, depriving the provincial administrators of their deliberative votes in the executive committees.[58]

All the above amendments were on comparatively minor points. None of them cut at the principle of parliamentary supremacy, which was the crux of the problem if Natal was to have real security for her provincial institutions. When the committee came to the amending section, however, a determined effort was made to limit the competence of a bare parliamentary majority. At the outset Palmer, on behalf of Haggar, proposed that all the important sections of the Constitution should be extremely difficult to amend: the Constitution should not be amended 'in any matter dealing with the Franchise, the rights, status, or powers of any Provincial Council or House of Parliament, or in any material respect', except with the consent of, firstly, a majority of the members of any Provincial Council 'immediately concerned', and, secondly, a majority of the members of both Houses of Parliament, and, thirdly, a two-thirds majority of the South African electorate.[59] He claimed that

---

[56] The minority in the division on the amendment to s. 135 [133] comprised Watt, the convention delegate, J. J. C. Emmett, and J. Farquhar; and the minority in the division on the amendment to s. 149 [148] comprised the four Labour members, Connolly, Haggar, Palmer, and Taylor, and F. A. R. Johnstone and M. W. Myburgh.

[57] S. 33 of the S.A. Act.

[58] It may be recalled that the Natal delegates had fought persistently for this in the convention.

[59] *Natal Leg. Ass. Deb.* xlvii. 227.

the delegates should support his proposal, because it was similar to the amending section in the draft Constitution they had submitted to the convention, but, Hyslop having announced that he opposed it because, and only because, there was not the slightest chance of carrying it in the convention, it was rejected by twenty-five votes to seven (Palmer, Haggar, and Taylor, Schofield and Silburn, and Wylie and Morcom). Taylor then moved a milder proposal, to make any amendment which was 'regarded by any particular State [i.e. Province] as being vital to its existence or prosperity' require 'the majority support of the representatives of the State so affected'.[60] He contended that it was vital for Natal that his motion should be adopted, because he did not trust, and did not feel justified in trusting, the other colonies:

> Sir, this Clause 153 puts the power into the hands of the Union to annihilate this little Colony. It is no use for any member . . . of the Transvaal Parliament, Cape Parliament, or Orange Free State Parliament, to come to me and tell me that they are not going to do it, and ask me to accept that as being a sufficient guarantee. Because my reply to them is this: . . . If I make an agreement with anybody, I am quite prepared to put it in black and white; and if I were not prepared to put it in black and white, I would be quite prepared to accept the charge of intending to be dishonourable in my actions.[61]

Taylor also reminded the House that the other colonies had refused Natal equal representation in the convention, that the delegates of the other colonies had done practically nothing to meet the wishes of Natal in the convention, and that the Transvaal had taken care to protect her own interest by concluding the Mozambique agreement as a prior condition of union; and he referred to recent speeches and actions by Afrikaners in the other colonies to vindicate his thesis that Natal would be annihilated under a flexible and unitary Constitution. Palmer then spoke for over an hour in support of the amendment, quoting at length from the Hansard reports of the speeches which had been made by Moor, Greene, Morcom, Hyslop, and Watt, when the closer union resolutions had been before Parliament in 1908, to show how completely they had committed themselves to a federal Constitution. These telling points were answered by F. Fergg, J. Connolly, and A. T. Oliff. Fergg, an Afrikaner member for Vryheid, rebutted the suggestion that the Afrikaners could not be trusted to remain loyal to the Crown:

> I declare most emphatically that I have never heard from one single Dutchman that he wants to get rid of the Union Jack. I do think the Dutch

[60] Ibid., p. 229.   [61] Ibid.

may be given credit for possessing common-sense as well as patriotism. They know perfectly well that, having lost their independence, there is nothing that could protect them better from any outsider than the Union Jack. I know quite well that the Dutch will stick to their principle, and they will depend upon this protecting flag for ever. We want to be a South African people; but we don't want to be Little Englanders or Little Dutchmen.[62]

Connolly said that he supported the Constitution as it stood because, so he contended, it contained the principle of federation and because there was no need to tie their children's hands by making it rigid. And Oliff, the treasurer, said that it was essential that Natal should accept the work of the convention, because if she remained separate from the Union it would 'be utterly impossible for us to pay our way in this Colony unless we can do a trade with our neighbours, or unless we are in a position to stand three times the amount of personal taxation that we are having to stand to-day'.[63] Nevertheless, Palmer stood his ground and so did Taylor, who predicted that 'if this Colony does not protect itself in that Constitution, it will live to regret it'.[64] Meanwhile, however, Morcom had declared that, while he was unable to support Taylor's amendment, he considered that it was essential to make some distinction between constitutional amendments and ordinary legislation. 'An Act of Union is, I take it, a treaty, more or less, between the several self-governing Colonies in South Africa, and, as such, the conditions of that treaty should be made as far as possible impossible of hasty alteration.'[65] He therefore moved, as an 'irreducible minimum', that no amendment should be valid unless it was passed by absolute majorities in both Houses of Parliament.[66] W. F. Clayton moved another amendment to include additional sections of the Constitution among those which were to be protected by the two-thirds majority, joint sitting requirement. When they came to a decision on the evening of the 14th, Taylor's amendment was rejected by twenty-seven votes to five (Schofield and Silburn, and Haggar, Palmer, and Taylor), but the proposals of Morcom and Clayton were adopted without divisions. Thus section 153[67] was to provide that 'Parliament may by law

---

[62] *Natal Leg. Ass. Deb.* xlvii. 245.   [63] Ibid., p. 249.

[64] Ibid., p. 248.   [65] Ibid., p. 244.

[66] Ibid., p. 245. The conduct of W. B. Morcom is of some interest. He had resigned from the convention during the Christmas recess on account of ill health, but there were rumours that the real reason was that he strongly disagreed with the decisions of the convention. These rumours appear to have been groundless: in parliament he voted steadily against the Labour and Imperialist amendments, except when they came to section 153 [152], when he voted in favour of the Palmer–Haggar amendment, which was the most drastic, opposed the Taylor amendment, which was milder, and moved the amendment to which this note refers.

[67] S. 152 of the S.A. Act.

which must be passed by an absolute majority of each House of Parliament repeal or alter any of the provisions of this Act', except that, firstly, provisions which were to operate for a definite period of time were not to be altered or repealed during that period, and, secondly, the joint sitting, two-thirds majority requirement was to apply permanently not only to sections 32, 35, 138, and 153[68] (as in the convention's draft Act) but also to sections 33 (concerning the division of the seats in the House of Assembly between the provinces), 70 (concerning the constitution of the provincial councils), and 71 (concerning the election of provincial councillors).[69] In one sense this did not constitute a drastic revision. The requirement of absolute majorities in both Houses would rarely be likely to inconvenience a Government, and the additional sections to be protected by the two-thirds majority requirement were perhaps more remarkable for what they did not include (e.g. the powers of the provincial councils) than for what they did include. On the other hand, by distinguishing, to however slight an extent, between the requirements for ordinary legislation and the requirements for constitutional amendments, the Natal version of the amending section contained a new principle, which was important in itself and which carried with it, as a natural corollary, the equally important principle that the validity of an amendment to any section of the Constitution might be tested in the courts.

After these proceedings had been completed during the morning of 15 April, the Labour and Imperialist groups persisted in their endeavour to obtain further and more fundamental amendments. For the second time Silburn moved the destructive proposal that the chairman should leave the chair, but this was defeated by twenty-four votes to six (Schofield, Silburn, and Yonge, and Haggar, Palmer, and Taylor). Then, dealing with several sections which had been standing over and others on which notice to revert had been given, the committee considered twenty-three more amendments—nine moved by Schofield and Silburn, eleven by Haggar, Palmer, and Taylor, and three others—and rejected all but one of them without divisions or by large majorities. Most of them were designed to increase the political safeguards for Natal. They included proposals that the administrators of the provinces should be appointed by the King instead of by the Governor-General-in-Council; that no more than four of the members of the Cabinet should have been subjects of a foreign state; and, most striking of all, that a province should be expressly entitled to secede from the Union. The one additional amendment which was carried—it was moved by Palmer and carried without

[68] Ss. 33, 35, 137, 152 of the S.A. Act.
[69] Ss. 34, 70, 71 of the S.A. Act.

a division—was for the deletion of the provincial executive committees from the bodies which were to be elected by proportional representation, so that all the members of such a committee, other than the Administrator, would be chosen by the party which had a majority in the Provincial Council.

Two resolutions of instructions to the Natal delegates were then adopted. The first concerned the franchise and delimitation sections of the Constitution, which had already been debated from various angles. Several members had ventilated their dislike of the Cape non-European franchise, and Farquhar had moved an amendment to prevent its extension to the northern provinces, except by a two-thirds majority in a joint sitting of both Houses. On the other hand, Schofield had moved an amendment to give Natal non-Europeans the same protection as Cape non-Europeans in section 35 (i), and Haggar had proposed the deletion of the European descent qualification for members of the House of Assembly. Moor and Hyslop had opposed all these motions and they had been rejected by large majorities. Amendments had also been moved to sections 35 and 36 with the object of preventing Parliament from tampering with the franchise qualifications, for example, by fixing a long residential qualification, as had been done in the South African Republic, but they had been opposed by delegates on the ground that they were quite unnecessary and defeated by large majorities. Sections 39 and 40 had been passed rather rapidly on 8 April. Evans, speaking as one who had always fought for equal rights for all white men in Natal, had expressed complete satisfaction with them, since they would be bound to effect a great improvement over the existing position for the Natal townsmen. By 15 April, however, Evans was alarmed by the press reports of the proceedings in the Cape Parliament. He therefore moved a resolution to instruct the Natal delegates, when the convention reassembled, 'to do all in their power to preserve intact the liberal provisions regarding the franchise contained in the Draft Act of Union, and to strenuously oppose any attempt to limit or alter those clauses which provide for equal political rights'.[70] There was no opposition to the resolution and it was adopted without a division.

The other resolution was the result of the publication on 2 April of the new Transvaal–Mozambique Convention, which had caused a revulsion of feeling in Natal against the Transvaal and against union. Previously many Natal people seem to have believed that the Union's railway rates and customs tariff would be used to divert the Witwatersrand trade from Delagoa Bay and to exclude Mozambique produce from the Transvaal.

[70] *Natal Leg. Ass. Deb.* xlvii. 293.

They were shocked to discover that, for ten years after the establishment of the Union, Delagoa Bay was to be assured of at least half the gross tonnage of seaborne goods traffic to the competitive zone in the Transvaal and Mozambique produce was to be admitted to the Transvaal free of duty. They saw visions of vast agricultural and industrial expansion in Mozambique: in particular, they feared that Mozambique sugar, assisted by bounties, would capture the Transvaal market and reduce the Natal sugar planters to penury. Such fears were not justified, since free trade had existed between the Transvaal and Mozambique ever since 1875 without producing the results envisaged. Moreover, whatever might happen to Natal if she joined the Union, her prospects if she remained outside would be infinitely gloomier, since the railway agreement assuring her 30 per cent. of the traffic to the competitive zone would not come into force, her share of that traffic might dwindle away to nothing, and her produce might be excluded from the Transvaal.[71] Nevertheless, J. G. Maydon, who was one of the most influential men on the Natal coast and who had presided over the Johannesburg Conference of the closer union societies and been satisfied with its resolution approving of the draft Constitution, expressed the general reaction when he wrote a curt note to Patrick Duncan on 3 April, saying: 'I have not had the time to read the Mozambique Treaty more than once, but that once is enough. I am against the Union in consequence.'[72] In these circumstances the Legislative Assembly had already devoted a great deal of attention to section 149[73] of the draft Constitution (which provided that the existing treaty obligations of the colonies should devolve upon the Union) and, as has been mentioned, an amendment was carried on 14 April for the insertion of a specific mention of the railway agreement, guaranteeing Natal 30 per cent. of the Witwatersrand traffic. J. Kirkman had moved a further amendment to nullify any obligations which might be 'injurious to the agricultural and industrial progress of any part of the Union'.[74] He had described the Mozambique convention as the *modus moriendi* as far as Natal was concerned, but this proposal, like others with a similar purpose, was opposed by Greene and rejected by a large majority. Now,

[71] *The Times* carried reports of the Natal reaction to the Transvaal–Mozambique Convention on 3, 12, and 19 Apr. The views of the Natal Government and Parliament are in statements by Greene in the Legislative Assembly on 2 and 20 Apr. and the discussion which followed the latter statement, *Natal Leg. Ass. Deb.* xlvii. 65–71, 317–41, 343–78; and in statements by Moor in the Legislative Council on 6 and 20 Apr., *Natal Leg. Co. Deb.* xix. 8–11, 15–18.

[72] Duncan Papers.

[73] S. 148 of the S.A. Act.

[74] *Natal Leg. Ass. Deb.* xlvii. 224.

however, after the adoption of Evans's resolution, W. F. Clayton moved that the delegates should be instructed, when the convention reassembled, to try to arrange for an intercolonial treaty, providing, firstly, 'That, any Treaty notwithstanding, no part of the Union shall, in regard to commerce, industry, or agriculture, be placed in a worse position than an outside State or Power', and, secondly, 'That the products of any State or Power outside the Union, the manufacture or exploitation of which may be assisted by any bounty or equivalent thereto, shall not be admitted at a lower duty than shall be equal to the amount of such bounty.'[75] J. Kirkman seconded the resolution, nobody opposed it, and it was adopted without a division.

Before the House went out of committee, F. O. F. Churchill moved a resolution criticizing the Natal delegates for having failed to assist the committee to improve the draft Act. Hyslop then said that he had discouraged all amendments in the belief that if he had not done so his hands would have been weakened when he came to propose them in the convention, and he undertook to do his best to have the amendments carried. Watt, too, undertook to support the Natal amendments in the convention, but he asked Members of Parliament to urge the electorate to vote in favour of union when the referendum took place, even if not all the Natal amendments had been accepted. Having extracted these statements, Churchill withdrew his resolution. A final gesture then came from Silburn: 'I cannot let this Act go out', he said, 'without uttering my protest against what I consider to be the most iniquitous Act ever passed by a British Legislature, and to register that protest, I move that you do leave the Chair.'[76] Nobody supported him, however, and, the Prime Minister's motion that the chairman should leave the chair and report the decisions of the committee having been adopted without a division, the Speaker took the chair and the House approved of the committee's report without further opposition.

Greene then moved the second reading of the Referendum Bill. In debate it was suggested that some special majority should be required in the referendum, such as an absolute majority of the electorate, or two-thirds of the votes cast, but no such suggestion was adopted. The Bill received its third reading on 20 April. It provided that a referendum should be held on the question whether Natal should enter the Union in terms of the draft Act as finally recommended by the National Convention. Persons qualified to vote for the election of members of the Legislative Assembly would be entitled to vote in the referendum; each

[75] *Natal Leg. Ass. Deb.* xlvii. 293.
[76] Ibid., p. 299.

voter would have no more than one vote;[77] and the question would be decided by a majority of the votes cast.[78]

On the evening of the 20th the Legislative Council endorsed the draft South Africa Act, and the assembly's amendments and resolutions, without a single division being called or a single fresh amendment being suggested. Moving the motion to go into committee, the Prime Minister declared in general terms that he would do his best to have the Natal amendments accepted by the convention, but it was only under pressure that he referred directly to the amendments to section 153, and then most guardedly, so that it was evident that he did not expect that they would be adopted. On the other hand, he said that he whole-heartedly believed in the principles embodied in the two resolutions and that he expected to be able to give effect to them. The only fundamental criticism of the draft Constitution came from T. Kirkman, who described it as 'an elastic constitution that is simply a farce', 'a constitution of . . . easy virtue'.[79] Moor replied that he remained a staunch federalist and was satisfied that the draft Constitution contained 'the federal principle of government' in that 'local interests' were to be 'managed by local bodies'[80] (a criterion by which, it need hardly be said, the United Kingdom or any other unitary state in the modern world would rank as a federation). C. G. Smith, who had recently visited the Transvaal with J. G. Maydon and discussed the Mozambique convention with Farrar, Hull, and Smuts, declared that he still considered that the Government had made an egregious error in consenting to the convention. He recognized, however, that the condition of Natal would be infinitely worse outside than inside the Union. Consequently, he would fight for union while continuing to denounce the convention. This reasoning must have brought some wry relief to the Prime Minister. The Referendum Bill was read in the council a first time at about 4.15 on the afternoon of 21 April and three-quarters of an hour later it had passed through all its stages without amendment (standing rules and orders having been suspended) and received the Governor's assent.

Thus the Natal Parliament endorsed the draft South Africa Act with somewhat surprising docility and with only a few, and for the most part

[77] In Natal parliamentary elections many people were able to poll two or more votes. There were 25,463 registered voters in Natal in 1908: but in the 1906 general election 15,152 voters actually went to the polls and they polled 38,908 votes. Cd. 5099 (1909), *Correspondence respecting an Act for a Referendum in Natal on the Draft South Africa Union Act*, p. 10.

[78] *Natal Leg. Ass. Deb.* xlvii. 299–317, 341–3; Natal Act No. 2 of 1909; Cd. 5099 (1909).

[79] *Natal Leg. Co. Deb.* xix. 23. [80] Ibid., p. 28.

minor, amendments;[81] and left the final responsibility for determining the fate of the colony to the electorate.[82]

3. THE BLOEMFONTEIN SESSION OF THE NATIONAL CONVENTION

The Cape Parliament's amendments to the electoral sections of the draft Constitution caused widespread consternation. They were denounced by nearly every English-medium newspaper in South Africa and many leading articles were devoted to exposing the fallacies in the Bond arguments. The *State*, also, made strong comments in its May number, which was published shortly before the convention reassembled:

As Mr. Schreiner said in the Cape House, there is no use pretending that the amendments were simply intended to ensure the 'elucidation' of obscure clauses in the Constitution. . . . The amendments were moved because a majority in the Cape Parliament believed that equal voting rights between town and country were not to the best interests of South Africa, and that rural voters should be placed in a privileged position.[83]

After rehearsing the arguments for and against giving the rural voters an advantage, the *State* continued:

The clauses as they stand in the Constitution represent, with the clause giving equality to the two languages, the fundamental basis of the settlement between the two races. They are a compromise which can only be tampered with at the risk of wrecking Union itself. Any alteration of the manifest intention of the clauses means that one or other of the two races is to give up the rights which the first Convention unanimously agreed ought fairly and justly to be theirs.[84]

Fitzpatrick was deeply distressed, for he had always regarded 'one vote one value' as the essential feature of a South African Constitution—a necessary and sufficient safeguard against the domination of the Union by an exclusively Afrikaner party. He had telegraphed Jameson on 8 April, urging him to oppose the amendments: 'It is quite impossible for us to depart from the compromise agreed to and embodied in the draft. You will remember that the appointment of four judges to interpret the meaning of that whole clause was the final consideration which induced us to agree to the mention of sparsity and density at all. I believe an alteration will simply burst things up here.'[85] On the 12th he stated his

---

[81] The resolutions and amendments of the Natal Parliament are in Hofmeyr, *Minutes*, pp. 346–8.

[82] The Referendum Act, Natal Act No. 2 of 1909.

[83] *State*, i. 482.   [84] Ibid., p. 484.   [85] Fitzpatrick Papers (copy).

case in a letter to the *Transvaal Leader*. Sections 39 and 40, he said, embodied a compromise which had been unanimously accepted by the convention after full discussion. If the agitation in the Cape was meant to wreck union, 'the most devilish ingenuity could not have devised a better way'. His colleagues agreed with him. Lionel Phillips obtained an interview with Merriman, who had more confidence in him than in any of the other Progressives, and tried to convince him that the amendments were impossible.[86] Phillips also wrote a letter which was published in the *Cape Times* on 21 April:

> The proposed amendments to clauses 39 and 40 strike at the fundamental principle of equality, and if persisted in, may wreck the Union. . . . To allot a 30 per cent. preferential treatment to country districts (for that is what the amendments in the Cape Parliament practically amount to) is not only to deal a fatal blow to equality, but to open the door to no end of intrigue for further concessions, possibly accentuating the proposed inequality in the future. . . . I do not believe that a Parliament in which the majority might represent rural interests would be unjust to urban interests, or vice versa, but I do believe that a majority secured through preferential treatment, arbitrarily settled in the Constitution, would cause strife in the first place, and that it would seek to further entrench its privileged position in the second place. This must not be permitted. It cannot make for peace, contentment, and those settled conditions so greatly needed in South Africa.

Five days later Farrar, speaking as the leader of the Progressive Party, publicly reaffirmed that 'under no conditions would the Transvaal compromise on equal rights'.[87]

Of the Cape Unionists, Jagger was in complete accord with the Progressives. Jameson's attitude was not so clear. Writing to Fitzpatrick to explain his attitude in the Cape Parliament, he said that he had found it necessary to support Merriman lest he should be ousted from the premiership by the Bond extremists. 'What we must hang on to', continued Jameson, 'is their own words "Elucidation, no amendment". Of course it is all humbug: but you have sometimes to hold the spoon to the devil so long as you give nothing away. We must have consultations before we get into Convention; and of course the position must be maintained.'[88] The consultations took place in Johannesburg towards the end of April, but complete identity of purpose was not achieved. The Progressives went to Bloemfontein anxious, above all, to preserve the electoral sections of the draft Constitution without any amendment, and rather than

---

[86] Merriman's Diary, 19 Apr. 1909.
[87] *Cape Times*, 27 Apr. 1909.
[88] Jameson to Fitzpatrick 'Sunday' [18? Apr. 1909], Fitzpatrick Papers.

yield they were prepared to risk the collapse of the union movement; whereas Jameson went to Bloemfontein determined to achieve union, even at the cost of accepting some 'elucidations' of the electoral sections.

Pressure was also brought to bear upon de Villiers, Botha, Smuts, and Hull to maintain the electoral sections without amendment. Curtis sent de Villiers a long exposition of the Progressive attitude,[89] and James Rose Innes, the Chief Justice of the Transvaal, assured de Villiers that the allegation that it was only the Witwatersrand capitalists who were demanding equal political rights was 'really very uninformed', because 'it is not the mining magnates but the *people*—the urban population—who are determined upon the one vote one value principle'.[90] Brand sent Botha, Smuts, and Hull a memorandum criticizing Blaine's amendment. 'It is unnecessary', he wrote, 'to dwell upon the point that this amendment is not a "definition" or "elucidation" of Clause 40. It involves a fundamental alteration in the principle underlying it. Clause 40 prescribes equality, but leaves the Commissioners with discretion; the amendment prescribes inequality and divests the Commissioners of discretion. Clause 40 treats all the five considerations as of equal value; the amendment treats the first four as entirely subordinate to the last.' Brand also showed that the amendment, with its sliding scale between the densely populated and the sparsely populated extremes, was a mathematical absurdity. What, for example, was to be done in the Orange Free State, where nearly all the constituencies would be sparsely populated?[91]

Even Lord Selborne, who had previously acted with a scrupulous sense of constitutional propriety, was so shocked by the agitation against equal constituencies that he too addressed Botha on the subject. On 8 April he warned him that the proceedings in the Cape Parliament would have a bad effect on public opinion in England. 'It will be said that the Bond will take everything and give nothing, that it is ready to take equal rights for the Dutch language with both hands but refuses to give equal political rights to the British who live in the towns.'[92] On 29 April Selborne went so far as to threaten to work against union if the Cape amendments were carried by the convention:

I am absolutely convinced that Union can only be accomplished by an unwavering adherence to the 'equal rights' compromise as embodied in clauses 39 and 40 of the draft South Africa Act. . . . Is it probable or even possible that the Liberal Party and H.M.G. would be parties in 1909 to depriving the people of the Transvaal or Orange River Colony of those equal rights, which they deliberately advised the King to confer upon them

---

[89] 2 May 1909, de Villiers Papers.   [90] 2 May 1909, ibid.
[91] 28 Apr. 1909, Transvaal Archives, Prime Minister, LX (ii).   [92] Ibid.

in 1906 and 1907, and which have worked with so great a measure of success in the intervening years?

My own position is quite clear in the matter. I never wavered in my support of the electoral provisions of the Transvaal Constitution, because I knew that those provisions were fair. I have done all that I could to promote the Union of South Africa, because I knew that Union on the basis of equal rights is for the true advantage of all the people of South Africa and of the whole Empire; but the only form of Union, which I have ever contemplated, is one framed in the spirit of the Transvaal and Orange River Colony Constitutions and granting equal political rights to the dwellers in town and country alike. The compromise in clauses 39 and 40 falls short of my ideal, but nevertheless I unreservedly accept it. I firmly believe that Union, based on that compromise, will produce immense benefits to South Africa, and there is no sacrifice or effort on my part which I would spare to promote it. But I equally firmly believe that union based on any mutilation of that compromise will produce disaster to South Africa, and that it will be much better for the Transvaal and the other Colonies to continue in disunion than to unite on such a false basis. If, therefore, Mr. Hofmeyr succeeded in his opposition to your declared policy in this matter, there is no sacrifice or effort which I would not equally make to prevent the consummation of an Union, which I know would bring disaster and not happiness to South Africa.[93]

The advocates of the Cape amendments were no less active in preparing for the Bloemfontein session. *Ons Land*, the *South African News*, and the *Cape* supported them vehemently. 'The issue before the Convention is clear enough', said the *Cape*. 'The delegates have to choose between the Cape Parliament and the mining industry of the Rand. In other words, it is the people of the largest and oldest and most populous State of South Africa against the associated mining companies of Johannesburg.'[94] The case was presented more rationally by J. A. C. Graaff, W. J. van Zijl, and L. A. W. Beck in letters to the editor of the *Cape Times* in reply to Phillips. They contended that sections 39 and 40 were so vaguely worded as they stood that if they were not amended the delimitation commissioners would in effect be obliged to formulate policy, which was not their proper function; that the Transvaalers were not justified in demanding equality within the provinces, since they had refused to apply that principle between the provinces; and that the voters' basis was not an equitable basis for the delimitation of constituencies, so that it was only fair to provide for a compulsory variation from mathematical equality.[95]

[93] Ibid.   [94] *Cape*, 30 Apr. 1909.
[95] *Cape Times*, 22 and 24 Apr. 1909.

Besides the press campaign, every effort was made to obtain the support of the Het Volk and Orangia Unie delegates. On 20 April Merriman wrote to Steyn and to Botha. The Cape amendments, he claimed, adhered to the principles of the draft Act and did no more than 'define them and make them absolute', as had been agreed by all four prime ministers at their meeting on 24 March, and if they were not adopted by the convention he doubted whether the Cape Colony would come into the Union.[96] Malan asked Botha not to commit himself in public against the Cape amendments and told Steyn that some concession to the Cape was essential for the sake of union.[97] And J. H. Hofmeyr got to the root of the matter when he informed Steyn that 'If one gives the magnates their way in *their* conception of "One vote one value" and if one then adds Rhodesia as well, with a nice representation and a pretty debt, our Union population will acquire an entirely one-sided complexion.'[98] In other words the Cape amendments were necessary to ensure that the Afrikaners should be the dominant political force in the Union.

Thus the stage was set for a dangerous conflict on racial lines at Bloemfontein. The key to the position was held by Botha and Smuts. If they opposed all amendments to the electoral sections, they would almost certainly succeed in carrying a large majority of the delegates with them, but they would thereby imperil their own political prospects and the Cape Colony might refuse to enter the Union. If, on the other hand, they supported the Cape amendments and managed to persuade the convention to adopt them, Natal might stay outside the Union, the other colonies would only join it against the wishes of their British inhabitants, and there would be a general resurgence of racialism. Could they therefore find a compromise which would satisfy the Hofmeyrs without alienating the Fitzpatricks? The strain on them must have been immense; and while it made no apparent impression on Smuts it was taking its toll of the more sensitive Botha, who had been in poor health since February and spent most of April on his farm, away from public affairs.

Lunching together in Bloemfontein on 2 May, Merriman, Sauer, Steyn, and Fischer sought to co-ordinate their plans. They reached the conclusion that Smuts had thrown in his lot with the Rand and that no support would be forthcoming from the Transvaal delegation, that the Natal delegates would be bound by their Parliament's instruction, and that the

[96] Steyn Papers; Transvaal Archives, Prime Minister, LX (ii).

[97] 10 and 19 Apr., ibid.

[98] 21 Apr. 1909, Steyn Papers. The original reads: 'Geeft men den Magnaten hun sin in *hun* opvatting van "One vote one value" en hecht men dan nog Rhodesia aan, met 'n mooie vertegenwordiging en schuld, dan krygt ons Unie-volk 'n heel eenzydige kleur.'

Unionists and Browne had been rallied by the Progressives, so that the Cape amendments would only be supported by the six South African Party delegates and the four Unie delegates. That evening Merriman summed up the prospects for the session in a gloomy letter to his wife: 'I gather that the general opinion is that it will end in a fiasco. . . . I can see that when it comes to a vote I shall be the only Englishman voting for our amendments. . . . I do not feel very cheerful at the prospect of the last year's work being wrecked in port but so is the world!'[99]

The convention[1] reopened on the morning of 3 May in the old Raad-zaal—the debating chamber of the Orange Free State Volksraad where, just ten years earlier, Milner and Kruger had met and, failing to agree upon a formula for the franchise in the South African Republic, had lost an opportunity of averting the South African War. All the delegates were present except Michell, who was absent from the entire session. After dealing with formal business the convention adjourned and the delegates held caucus meetings. In the afternoon the convention re-assembled and began to deal with the Constitution, section by section; and when they came to section 32[2] Hyslop moved the Natal amendment to the effect that no original province should ever have fewer than its original number of members in the House of Assembly, even after the total membership had reached 150. This amendment was carried without opposition. Soon afterwards they came to sections 39 and 40 and Sauer moved that they should stand over, but Fitzpatrick objected, saying that 'as this was a vital question . . . he did not want to leave until this was decided'. However, the Unie and South African Party delegates had not yet agreed upon the wording of their concerted amendment, so Sauer moved the adjournment. This was agreed and the convention rose for the day at four o'clock.[3]

[99] Merriman Papers. Likewise Merriman's diary entry for 2 May 1909: 'Very gloomy feeling as to prospects of Conference   Natal hostile and venal   Tvaal overbearing.'

[1] The principal published sources for the Bloemfontein session are G. R. Hofmeyr (ed.), *Minutes of Proceedings with Annexures (selected) of the South African National Convention* (Cape Town, 1911), pp. 250–74, 349–54, and Johann F. Preller (ed.), *Die Konvensie-Dagboek van sy edelagbare François Stephanus Malan* (with an English translation by A. J. de Villiers) (Cape Town, 1951), pp. 222–51. Walton does not devote a separate chapter of his book, *The Inner History of the National Convention of South Africa* (Cape Town, 1912), to the Bloemfontein session, but he touches upon it in several chapters. Two unpublished collections are of great value: the Brand Papers, which contain a general account of the session (Brand's manuscript) and a number of relevant annexures, notably Annexure XX, an account of the Equal Rights dispute written within a few days of the events it describes; and the Merriman Papers, which contain letters written almost every day during the Bloemfontein session by Merriman to his wife.

[2] This became s. 33 of the S.A. Act.

[3] *Minutes*, pp. 250–4; Malan, pp. 222–5; Brand's manuscript, Annexure XX; and

When the Transvaal advisers were shown the amendments which had been adopted, they pointed out that the amendment to section 32 would perpetuate a departure from the principle of equal rights in the composition of the House of Assembly. Farrar and Fitzpatrick then realized that in allowing it to pass they had compromised their own position in regard to sections 39 and 40 and they persuaded Smuts to ask the convention to reverse its decision.[4]

Smuts did so when the convention met the next morning, but his motion was rejected by sixteen votes to fourteen. Tempers were roused by this division, because the majority comprised not only the Natal and the Orange River Colony delegates (as was to be expected), but also six of the Cape delegates, including Merriman and Sauer, who had opposed a motion similar to the Natal amendment in Cape Town. The Transvaal delegates believed that Merriman and Sauer had voted against them 'simply from a cynical desire to put the Transvaal people in a hole about equal rights' and they refused to return to the conference chamber after the tea interval. After a while Farrar, Lindsay, and Burger returned, but the other five remained away for the rest of the morning sitting and the convention began to discuss sections 39 and 40 in their absence. When the convention resumed after lunch, however, all the Transvaal delegates were present and the debate on these sections continued after Botha had declared that he still hoped to obtain a reversal of the decision on section 32.[5]

It was Fischer who moved the amendment which had been worked out by the Unie and South African Party delegates to give expression to the intentions of the Orange River Colony and Cape parliaments: 'extremely sparsely populated areas' were defined as areas containing one registered voter or less to a square mile, and the delimitation commissioners were to be obliged to give them one seat for every 15 per cent. fewer voters than the provincial quota; 'extremely densely populated areas' were defined as areas containing ten registered voters or more to a square mile, and the delimitation commissioners were to be obliged to give them one seat for every 15 per cent. more voters than the provincial quota; and 'intermediate areas' were to be dealt with 'as far as practicable on a sliding scale of departure from the quota within the limit of percentage as above fixed'. Fischer, Hertzog, Merriman, and Sauer spoke for the amendment. They argued that it was no more than the convention had

Merriman to Mrs. Merriman, 3 May 1909, Merriman Papers. The quotation is from Malan.

[4] Brand's manuscript, Annexure XX.

[5] *Minutes*, pp. 254–5; Malan, pp. 224–9; Brand's manuscript, Annexure XX; Merriman to Mrs. Merriman, 4 May 1909, Merriman Papers. The quotation is from Brand.

originally intended. Merriman and Sauer also said that if section 40 meant that all the constituencies in a province were to contain the same number of voters it would cause a political revolution in the Cape Colony, and that they were not prepared to endorse it without holding a referendum, which would very likely result in the rejection of the Constitution; and Hertzog said that he would not be able to recommend the ratification of the Constitution to his Parliament unless the amendment was carried. Nevertheless, as Merriman had feared, the amendment was not supported by any delegate who was not a member of the Unie or the South African Party. Jagger opposed it vigorously; Browne opposed it; Farrar and Fitzpatrick said that the Transvaal would reject the Constitution if section 40 was amended; even de la Rey briefly opposed it; and so did Watt of Natal. The result was that at the end of the day's sitting the convention was near to breaking point.[6]

The idea that an acceptable compromise might be achieved by dropping proportional representation and leaving the other electoral provisions as they were seems to have originated in the mind of Sir Henry de Villiers. He had thrown it out to Merriman and discussed it with him in the train on the way to Bloemfontein;[7] writing to Curtis on 3 May he had mentioned it as a possibility;[8] during the lunch period on the 4th he had told Brand that it seemed to be 'the only possible thing to do';[9] and now on the evening of the 4th he broached it to Smuts and other Transvaalers, telling them that he had reason to believe that the Cape would accept it.[10] Before the convention met the next morning the proposal was discussed in the Transvaal caucus. Smuts was for accepting it on the ground that union should not be wrecked for the sake of proportional representation, and Botha and the other Het Volkers appeared to agree with him, but the Progressives did not commit themselves.[11] Then when the convention met on the morning of the 5th, after Steyn had added his support to the Fischer amendment, de Villiers, 'looking as if butter would not melt in his mouth', moved his proposal and appealed to all the delegates to accept it as a fair compromise. Soon afterwards the convention adjourned.[12] The Cape delegates then discussed the proposal in caucus and

---

[6] *Minutes*, pp. 255–6; Malan, pp. 226–31.

[7] Merriman to Mrs. Merriman, 2 May 1909, Merriman Papers. Some of Merriman's subsequent letters convey the impression that the idea of eliminating proportional representation was his as much as de Villiers's; but his letter of 2 May is reasonably clear on the point: 'The Chief was quite genial full of the work I think has hit upon a reasonable compromise if only other people will accept of which I am not sanguine.'

[8] Brand's manuscript, Annexure JJJ (copy).   [9] Ibid., Annexure XX.

[10] Ibid.   [11] Ibid.

[12] *Minutes*, p. 256; Malan, pp. 230–3; Merriman to Mrs. Merriman, 5 May 1909, Merriman Papers. The quotation is from Merriman's letter.

accepted it unanimously. Merriman was delighted. 'If this goes through', he informed his wife, 'we shall in my opinion have done *Splendidly* far better than we could have dared to hope for. All our men are solid. Jameson has behaved *very* well. We are quite the same nest of sucking doves.'[13] In the Transvaal caucus, on the other hand, there was a division of opinion. According to an account written a few days later by Brand, who was present, Farrar said that he was not inclined to accept the compromise as it stood, because he and his party attached great importance to proportional representation and because 'the events of the last two days had been a great shock to him' and 'his faith and trust had been entirely shattered by the bad faith of the Cape delegates and the devious manœuvres of Sauer and Fischer'. He therefore asked that section 40 should be entrenched: if that was done he and his colleagues would consider what line they would take. Smuts replied that he could not agree to the entrenchment of section 40 by a two-thirds majority. Farrar then said that he hoped that Smuts's reply was not final. 'Meanwhile as he was not prepared to break his party on it he had sent for two of his party . . . and after consulting them he would give his final answer.' Later in the day Farrar, Fitzpatrick, and Brand discussed the situation with Lord Selborne and his private secretary, Dougal Malcolm, at Government House. They came to the conclusion that the Progressives should not support the de Villiers proposal unless the electoral sections of the Constitution were placed on the same footing as the language section, so that both the political and the linguistic provisions for equal rights should be subject to the same amending procedure; but whereas Brand preferred that this should be done by unentrenching the language section, the others wished to entrench the electoral sections.[14]

On the morning of the 6th the convention sat for only twenty minutes.[15] Drummond Chaplin and Abe Bailey had arrived from Johannesburg and after the convention adjourned they conferred at Government House with Farrar, Fitzpatrick, Lindsay, Duncan, Curtis, and Lord Selborne. Duncan was strongly of the opinion that the Progressive delegates should make it a breaking question and at one stage the others were on the point of agreeing with him, but eventually Curtis persuaded them to adopt a more supple policy. Firstly, the Progressive delegates should press for the entrenchment of the electoral sections; secondly, if that could not be got, they should press for the unentrenchment of the lan-

[13] Merriman to Mrs. Merriman, 5 May 1909, Merriman Papers. According to Brand, who of course was not present, Malan stood out for some time. Brand's manuscript, Annexure XX.

[14] Brand's manuscript, Annexure XX

[15] *Minutes*, pp. 256-8.

guage section; and in the last resort they should insist on the reservation of all Bills amending any of the electoral sections. After lunch the Transvaal delegates met in caucus. Farrar and Fitzpatrick demanded the entrenchment, but Smuts, discerning from the expression on Farrar's face that he was not intending to break on it, said that he could never consent, and the caucus broke up without any agreement having been reached.[16]

When the convention resumed at 2.30 it was the only occasion in all its meetings that the Transvaal delegates were openly divided. Farrar and Fitzpatrick were still seething with suspicion and Botha and Smuts were indignant that their Governor should have participated in an opposition caucus.[17] At the outset Smuts asked Fischer whether he would withdraw his amendment and inquired what Merriman's attitude was. Merriman replied that he was prepared to drop the Cape amendments and support the President's proposal; Fischer said that he too would yield if the convention would unanimously adopt the alternative; but Farrar then rose and declared that he could not agree unless section 40 was entrenched for ten years or until the number of members of the House of Assembly reached 150, whichever was the longer period. After Fitzpatrick and Greene had spoken in support of Farrar, Malan said that he could not accept the President's proposal if conditions were to be attached to it. Botha then appealed to the Progressives to support it unconditionally. 'This was the first occasion', he said, 'on which he differed from them during the Conference but it was not on the principle of equal rights. He insisted on carrying through with Union and that the population should be trusted. South Africa had already suffered enough through distrust. After this Conference he could not but associate with men like Sir George, Sir Percy and Dr. Jameson on a friendly footing. By not seeing it through we should be doing a bad turn to the British Empire and it could happen that South Africa would then stone us and the Empire curse us.'[18] Despite this appeal no agreement was in sight at the end of the day's sitting and that evening Merriman informed his wife: 'We may really break at any moment. We are just like spiders. When we have got our web almost complete something comes to break it away and we have to begin all over again.'[19]

[16] Brand's manuscript, Annexure XX.

[17] Merriman's Diary, 6 May 1909: 'We adjourned Convention for purpose of Farrar and Fitzpatrick holding a meeting with their political friends and Lord Selborne. The conduct of the latter is causing much comment as he is the centre of opposition to his own ministry collecting round him all the rump of Milnerism. Botha has taken him to task.'

[18] *Minutes*, p. 260; Malan, pp. 234–7. The quotation is from Malan.

[19] Merriman Papers.

During the evening Botha, Smuts, Steyn, and others held further discussions. Smuts was still unwilling that the convention should entrench section 40 even for a limited period, because he feared that if it did so it would not be able to resist the Natal demands for further entrenchments and the Constitution would move down a slippery slope towards general rigidity. He was prepared, however, to meet the second request of the Progressives—the unentrenchment of the language section, but this Steyn would not permit on the ground that he would have great difficulty in explaining it to his people. The next morning, the 7th, Farrar made this proposal to the Transvaal caucus, which was sympathetic, and Steyn was then approached again, but he was adamant.[20] When the convention met Botha moved that the whole question should be referred to a committee. The convention agreed and the committee consisted of de Villiers, Sauer, Jameson, Smuts, Farrar, Moor, Greene, Steyn, Fischer, and Coghlan. After lunch it brought forward a unanimous report, based on the President's proposal and the last of the proposals of the Transvaal Progressives, and without more ado the convention unanimously adopted the necessary amendments to sections 39, 40, and 64. Section 39 was amended to provide for single-member constituencies; section 40 remained as before, except for a consequential amendment in sub-section (ii); and section 64 was amended to provide that any Bill for the alteration of any section in the sub-chapter dealing with the House of Assembly was to be reserved for His Majesty's pleasure.[21] The next day when they came to section 136 Smuts made an effort to retain a vestige of proportional representation, suggesting that when there were more than two candidates for a seat in the House of Assembly or a Provincial Council the alternative vote system should be used, so that every member would be elected by a clear majority of votes; but Merriman, van Heerden, and Malan opposed the suggestion and it was dropped. Accordingly, section 136 was amended to provide that only senators and members of the provincial executive committees were to be elected by proportional representation.[22]

The Unionist and Progressive delegates were content with the outcome of this struggle. They were delighted that there had been no tampering with section 40; they regarded reservation as an adequate safeguard; and they were pleased that it had been extended to cover Bills amending the franchise qualifications. Jameson, indeed, believed that he had won

[20] Brand's manuscript, Annexure XX.

[21] *Minutes*, pp. 260–2; Malan, pp. 238–9. These sections have the same numbers in the South Africa Act.

[22] *Minutes*, p. 267; Malan, pp. 242–3; Brand's manuscript, including Annexures XX and GGG. This became s. 134 of the S.A. Act.

a great victory. He wrote to tell his brother that 'we have given up nothing that mattered. Proportional representation was an experiment—one might almost say a fad, and for the present certainly not suited to this scattered community. . . . The result is that Hofmeyr for one has been outmanœuvred.'[23] Farrar and Fitzpatrick were almost as jubilant. The essential plank in the Progressive platform had always been 'one vote one value'. Originally they had been content to strive for it within the framework of a single-member constituency system and it was only on the eve of the first meeting of the convention that they had been converted—by Smuts—to proportional representation. Although since the publication of the first report of the convention they had publicly declared that proportional representation was an essential feature of the Constitution, it is doubtful whether they fully understood its political implications for South Africa. They certainly had no profound regrets at its elimination; and they were completely satisfied that Botha and Smuts had been true to their compact.[24]

Brand, on the other hand, was most disappointed. He wrote a long letter to R. H. Humphreys, the secretary of the English Proportional Representation Society, describing what had happened. His letter concluded as follows:

I feel therefore that it is not unfair to state that the loss of proportional representation has been due partly to ignorance and partly to prejudice. It is most regrettable that the leaders of the Dutch in Cape Colony were not animated by the same broad and statesmanlike spirit as those in the Transvaal. . . . The danger to proportional representation in this country has always been that it is a reform too far ahead of the opinions of the people. There was some chance of securing its adoption and that was that it should be carried into effect on the top of the same wave of enthusiasm which created the Constitution. We have now failed to secure this and I fear that it will be years before another chance of bringing about this reform offers itself. It will be a thousand times more difficult to persuade any Parliament to adopt it.[25]

Smuts also was genuinely sorry. He had seen no other way out of the impasse and he knew that Botha and the other members of his party had never shared his enthusiasm for proportional representation. Writing to

---

[23] Colvin, *Jameson*, ii. 284.

[24] In 'Equal Rights', an unpublished manuscript written in about 1929, Fitzpatrick summed up his recollections of the conduct of Botha and Smuts as follows: 'All I need add is that throughout the Convention no one ever had more loyal or capable comrade or leader than these men proved themselves to be. They held to the letter and to the spirit of their undertaking, and it was a real happiness to work with them.' Fitzpatrick Papers.   [25] 10 May 1909, Brand Papers (copy).

Lord Courtney, the President of the English Proportional Representation Society, he said that he was 'very much disappointed', because he 'had hoped that its adoption would mean the best insurance possible against the revival of racial politics in South Africa'; but he added, with his usual optimism, that he intended to introduce proportional representation for the municipal elections in Johannesburg and Pretoria 'as an object lesson to the rest of South Africa', in the hope that this would pave the way for its adoption for parliamentary elections.[26]

The South African Party and Unie delegates were as satisfied as the Progressives and the Unionists. It is doubtful whether they had ever seriously believed that they would be able to carry their amendment to section 40, or anything like it; and they were not unaware that the elimination of proportional representation was to their political advantage. Merriman, of course, was overjoyed. 'We have not got the Cape amendments', he told his wife, 'but we have got something which in my opinion is much better—single member constituencies and no proportional voting thus disposing of two "newfangled jim-jams".'[27] 'I only wonder what the dear old Mole will do', he added. 'Some of us think that he will adopt our amendment and claim the parentage.'[28] Malan and Steyn also were anxious about Hofmeyr's reaction and they wrote to inform him what had happened and to urge him to accept and support the decision.[29]

In these letters Malan and Steyn referred also to the language question. It will be recalled that Hofmeyr had been dissatisfied because the language section had not included an explicit provision that the two languages were to be treated equally in the provincial councils, and that the Cape Parliament had recommended that it should be amended. When Malan reached Bloemfontein he discussed the question with Steyn and Hertzog and found that they were averse to any change. They considered that the phrase 'official languages of the Union' was sufficiently clear and all-embracing and that any addition might weaken rather than strengthen the section; and they feared that any amendment might have an adverse effect upon the Natal referendum. Nevertheless, as late as 7 May Malan intended to move the insertion of the words 'and the provincial councils' after 'Parliament';[30] but when they came to the section on the following day Malan refrained from moving any amendment.[31] In their letters to Hofmeyr, Malan and Steyn invited his approval of their conduct.

26 14 May 1909, Brand Papers (copy).
28 8 May 1909, ibid.
30 Malan to Hofmeyr, 7 May 1909, ibid.

27 7 May 1909, Merriman Papers.
29 7 and 10 May 1909, Hofmeyr Papers.
31 Malan, pp. 242–5.

Although no colonial parliament had recommended an amendment to the sections dealing with the political rights of non-whites, a number of requests for such amendments came before the convention. A letter from the general secretary of the African Political Organization set out nine resolutions which had been adopted by its Cape Town Conference in April. These resolutions protested against the exclusion of non-whites from Parliament (sections 25 and 44), the insecurity of the Cape franchise (section 35), and the selection of the white male adult population as the basis for the division of the seats in the House of Assembly between the provinces (section 33).[32] They also asked that provision should be made in the Constitution for the extension of the franchise to all qualified persons in the northern provinces of the Union, and that the High Commission Territories should not be transferred to the Union, except on conditions satisfactory to their chiefs and councillors.[33] Another letter, dated 30 April, was signed by clergy of all the leading Protestant churches in South Africa other than the Dutch Reformed Church—by William M. Carter, the Anglican archbishop of Cape Town, J. J. McClure, a former moderator of the Presbyterian Church of South Africa, E. Barker, the president elect of the Baptist Union of South Africa, A. Pitt, the acting president of the Evangelical Church Council of Cape Town, R. Balmforth, a minister of the Free Protestant Unitarian Church, and G. Robson, a Wesleyan minister. This letter was a classical statement of the case for basing political rights upon other grounds than race or colour, and it dealt with all the arguments which had been used by advocates of the colour-bar. The other communications of a similar nature were from organizations of Coloured people in Wellington and Wynberg, Cape Colony, from the headmen and leading Africans of the Baralong tribe at Thaba 'Nchu, Orange River Colony, from J. A. Sishuba, a Cape Colony African, and from E. O. Barrett, a Wesleyan minister.[34] All these documents were laid on the table and the letter from the clergy was also read to the convention by order of the President. But no discussion ensued, no amendment was moved; and the sections dealing with non-white political rights were left as they were.[35]

It was not until 11 May that the convention completed its work, although it had made its decision on sections 39 and 40 on the 7th. The main cause for the delay was the Natal amendments. Looking ahead to

[32] In the S.A. Act s. 25 of the draft Act became s. 26, s. 33 became s. 34, and ss. 35, 44 retained the numbers they had in the draft Act.

[33] House of Assembly, National Convention Minutes, III.

[34] Ibid.

[35] *Minutes*, pp. 250, 256–7, 262–3.

the Natal referendum, most of the delegates were anxious to humour Natal with a few concessions in matters of detail, but they were not prepared to accept any fundamental change or any change which, in their opinion, would weaken the document. The Natal delegates, on the other hand, strove persistently for nearly every amendment which had been adopted by their Parliament, with the result that tempers became frayed on both sides. From time to time the Natalians, especially Greene, resorted to the threat that they would keep Natal out of the Union, but the other delegates regarded the threat as sheer bluff, and they were certainly right, for when all the Natal amendments had been disposed of the Natal delegates regained their equanimity, although they had achieved no more than a few somewhat trivial concessions.[36]

It will be recalled that the Natal amendment to section 32, providing that no original province should ever have fewer than its original number of members in the House of Assembly, was accepted by the convention on 3 May and survived the Transvaal challenge on the 4th. Eventually, however, the Transvaal had her way. The section was reverted to on the 10th and Smuts's motion for the restoration of the words which had been omitted was adopted without opposition—probably as a *quid pro quo* for a concession to Natal in the commercial field. It may be noted in passing that at this stage Malan wished to go farther and reopen the question of the number of seats to be allotted to the Cape Province in the House of Assembly. He argued that since the Cape had yielded to the Transvaal on section 40, the Transvaalers, as 'the great champions of "equal rights"', should grant the Cape her proper share of the seats in the House of Assembly. But Farrar and Smuts objected and Malan dropped the subject without moving an amendment.[37]

The convention made only one minor concession to Natal in the chapter dealing with the provinces. It rejected the proposal that the provincial executives should be constituted like the British Cabinet—the Natal amendment to section 136, which would have enabled a party with a majority in the Provincial Council to elect all the members of the Executive Committee (instead of the election taking place by proportional representation), was defeated by twenty-five votes to five, the Natal delegates standing alone.[38] Smuts also opposed the Natal amendment to section 82, under which an administrator would not have had a deliberative vote in the Executive Committee; and Natal withdrew it

---

[36] Merriman to Mrs. Merriman, 8 May 1909, Merriman Papers.

[37] *Minutes*, p. 271; Malan, pp. 244–7. S. 32 of the draft Act became s. 33 of the S.A. Act.

[38] *Minutes*, p. 267; Malan, pp. 242–3. S. 136 of the draft Act became s. 134 of the S.A. Act.

when the convention had agreed to amend section 78, by fixing the composition of the committee at four members besides the administrator.[39] This amendment meant that it would be impossible for an Administrator and one other member to determine the policy of a provincial Executive Committee.

The Natal amendment for the entrenchment of colonial laws which prohibited the sale of intoxicating liquor to Natives was rejected without a division.[40] On the other hand, the verbal amendment to clause 18 of the schedule was adopted.[41]

Far the most fundamental of the amendments which had been passed by the Natal Parliament was that which required an absolute majority in both Houses of Parliament for any amendment of the Constitution and entrenched additional sections under the two-thirds majority, joint sitting procedure. Since feeling in Natal was strong on the subject, it might have been expected that the Natal delegates would have made a supreme effort to have this amendment accepted by the convention. They did no such thing. They did not even move the amendment in the convention. The failure of the Transvaal Progressives to obtain the entrenchment of the electoral sections seems to have convinced them that there was no hope of introducing any such additional elements of internal rigidity into the Constitution; and when they found that Smuts was agreeable to a further extension of the reservation safeguard, they jumped at it as an adequate solution to their problem. Accordingly, on 10 May Smuts moved that another insertion should be made in section 64, for the reservation of 'all Bills abolishing Provincial Councils, or abridging the powers conferred on Provincial Councils under section Eighty-five otherwise than in accordance with the provisions of that section'; and this insertion was adopted by the convention without opposition.[42]

The Natal delegates fought hard for their Parliament's amendments to the economic sections. Nevertheless, the convention rejected its amendments to sections 128 and 135.[43] There was a long struggle over the phrase in section 129 which declared that the railways and harbours were to be administered on business principles with due regard, *inter alia*, to the promotion by means of cheap transport of an agricultural and industrial population 'in the inland portions of the Union'. The Natal

---

[39] *Minutes*, pp. 262–3; Malan, pp. 240–1. Ss. 78 and 82 of the draft Act have the same numbers in the S.A. Act.

[40] *Minutes*, p. 269.　　　　　　　　　　　　　　　　　[41] Ibid., p. 271.

[42] Ibid.; Malan, pp. 246–7; Brand's manuscript. S. 64 of the draft Act has the same number in the S.A. Act.

[43] *Minutes*, p. 266. Ss. 128 and 135 of the draft Act became ss. 126 and 133 of the S.A. Act.

delegates were most anxious to eliminate this phrase, for Smuts's description of it as the Magna Charta of the inland colonies had aroused grave suspicions. Eventually, however, Smuts suggested that it should be replaced by the phrase, 'in the inland portions of all provinces of the Union', and the Natal delegates promptly accepted this suggestion, although it is difficult to see that it amounted to a substantial change in the meaning. The other Natal amendment to this section, which concerned the arrangements during the first four years after the establishment of the Union, was adopted in a modified version, drafted by the Transvaal staff.[44] There was also a keen debate on the Natal proposal for the insertion in section 149 (under which the rights and obligations of the colonies were to devolve upon the Union) of an explicit mention of the intercolonial railway agreement securing 30 per cent. of the Witwatersrand traffic to the Natal ports. Hull tried to persuade his Transvaal colleagues to reject it. Eventually, however, Botha and Smuts decided to yield and, despite opposition from several Cape Colony and Orange River Colony delegates, the convention added a new sub-section 149 (ii), providing that 'The provisions of the Railway Agreement between the Governments of the Transvaal, the Cape of Good Hope and Natal, dated the 2nd February, 1909, shall as far as practicable be given effect to by the Government of the Union.'[45] The Natal request for the insertion of a section providing that 'There shall at all times be absolute Free Trade throughout the Union' was criticized on two grounds. Firstly, to apply it without qualification immediately after the establishment of the Union would be to dislocate the fiscal system, because the excise taxes differed in the four colonies; secondly, it was considered unnecessary to enunciate the principle of free internal trade in the Constitution of a unitary State. On 10 May, however, the convention yielded to the importunities of the Natal delegates and adopted a modified version of the Natal amendment, reading as follows: 'There shall be Free Trade throughout the Union, but until Parliament otherwise provides the duties of customs and excise leviable under the laws existing in any of the Colonies at the establishment of the Union shall remain in force.'[46]

The last request of the Natal delegates arose from their Parliament's instruction that, to dissipate the fears which had been created by the

[44] *Minutes*, p. 266; Malan, pp. 240–3; Brand's manuscript. S. 129 of the draft Act became s. 127 of the S.A. Act.

[45] *Minutes*, pp. 269–70; Malan, pp. 244–5; Brand's manuscript. S. 149 of the draft Act became s. 148 of the S.A. Act.

[46] *Minutes*, pp. 257, 268; Malan, pp. 244–5; Brand's manuscript. This became s. 137A of the revised draft Act and s. 136 of the S.A. Act, with a verbal amendment made in England.

Transvaal–Mozambique Convention, they were to negotiate an inter-colonial treaty. This request the Transvaal would not grant. Natal then proposed that the Constitution should include a section dealing with bounties, but after considering a draft section on the subject the finance committee recommended that it should not be included in the Constitution and the convention agreed.[47] It was eventually arranged, however, that Botha would address a letter to Moor setting out the Transvaal's interpretation of the controversial clauses of the Mozambique Convention. The letter was drafted by Brand and released for publication on 13 May. It dealt specifically with clauses 25 and 32 of the convention, which had evoked the fear that Mozambique industries would be fostered by bounties and would compete unfairly with Natal industries, especially the Natal sugar industry. It explained that the possibilities of industrial expansion in Mozambique had been greatly exaggerated; that Portugal had not hitherto granted any bounties to Mozambique produce; and that the Union would be able to retaliate if Portugal did grant bounties, by imposing countervailing duties or by altering the railway rates—indeed the customs union tariff expressly provided for the imposition of counter-vailing duties on bounty-fed sugar. The letter concluded:

I feel sure that the above statements with regard to the points raised by you will assist you to remove the suspicions which have arisen in Natal. May I add that although it is obviously just as impossible for my Government as it is for the Natal Government to determine what will be the policy of the future Government of the Union, it is our firm desire to foster by every legitimate means industries no matter in what part of British South Africa they are situated.[48]

Several changes were made in the judicial chapter of the Constitution on 8 and 10 May. The convention had left this chapter in an unsatisfactory form in several respects in its first report, and it will be recalled that the Cape Parliament had recommended a number of amendments.[49] Since then Rose Innes, the Chief Justice of the Transvaal, had sent de Villiers a suggestion for a further improvement in section 103[50] and Smuts and the Transvaal staff had drafted other amendments. The main Transvaal proposal was that the judges presiding over the provincial divisions should be called judge presidents and not chief justices (except in the case of the former chief justices of the colonies, who would retain the title Chief Justice if and so long as they presided over provincial

[47] *Minutes*, pp. 258, 268 ; Brand's manuscript.
[48] Brand's manuscript, Annexure ZZ.   [49] See above, pp. 347–8.
[50] 23 Apr. 1909, de Villiers Papers.

divisions).[51] Eventually, therefore, there would only be one Chief Justice in the Union. This was approved by the convention and sections 95, 98 (i), and 99 were amended accordingly. The Cape Parliament's recommendations concerning sections 96, 97, 108, and 113 were also adopted without opposition.[52] There was a considerable discussion on section 103. In the first report of the convention it had simply provided that in all cases in which appeals had previously been made from a superior court to a colonial Supreme Court the appeal should in future go direct to the Appellate Division. The Cape Parliament had recommended that in certain types of cases such appeals should be heard by the provincial divisions; but Innes had not been satisfied with the wording of this recommendation and he had drafted another version. Smuts now moved an amendment which was based on Innes's draft. It provided that in all cases in which appeals had previously been made to a colonial Supreme Court the appeal should in future go direct to the Appellate Division, except, firstly, in civil cases 'of orders or judgments given upon application by way of motion or petition or on summons for provisional sentence or judgments as to costs only which by law are left to the discretion of the Court', and, secondly, in all criminal cases. In these excepted cases appeals would be heard by the relevant provincial division and there would be no further appeal unless the Appellate Division gave special leave. Hull moved that the special leave for appeal to the Appellate Division in the excepted cases should be required to be given by the provincial division, but his motion was defeated by seventeen votes to twelve and Smuts's motion was then adopted.[53] Subsequently a minor change was made in section 114 and a redundant phrase was deleted from that section and from sections 103, 104, 105, 107, and 109.[54] Section 140, concerning the administration of justice, also came under review. Smuts wished it to be omitted, but it was passed with the addition of a clause providing for the continuation of the offices of Solicitor-General for the eastern districts and Crown Prosecutor for Griqualand West.[55] The result of these amendments was that the judicial provisions of the Constitution were considerably improved.

The convention also had before it two requests emanating from His Majesty's Government. Firstly, there was the request which Lord Sel-

[51] Brand's manuscript.

[52] *Minutes*, pp. 263–5 ; Malan, pp. 240–1 ; Brand's manuscript. All the sections in the judicial chapter of the draft Act have the same numbers in the S.A. Act.

[53] *Minutes*, pp. 264–5, 272 ; Malan, pp. 240–1 ; Brand's manuscript.

[54] *Minutes*, pp. 265, 272.

[55] Ibid., pp. 267–8 ; Malan, pp. 244–5. S. 140 of the draft Act became s. 139 of the S.A. Act.

borne had expounded to Sir Henry de Villiers and which had led the Cape Parliament to recommend an amendment to section 64, to provide that the Governor-General, in exercising his discretion in respect of Bills submitted to him for the King's assent, should act subject not only to the provisions of the South Africa Act but also to 'such instructions as may from time to time be given in that behalf by His Majesty, his heirs or successors'.[56] The convention adopted this proposal without opposition, thereby reversing its earlier decision.[57] Secondly, the convention had before it a report from the Secretary of State that the British Treasury considered that the draft Constitution did not provide adequate security for the Transvaal loans which had been guaranteed by the Imperial Government.[58] To meet this criticism the convention adopted a number of amendments to the financial sections without opposition on 6 May. Section 119, which provided that the costs of collection, management, and receipt of the consolidated revenue fund should be the first charge on the fund, was omitted. Section 120 was amended to make the annual interest on the public debts and sinking funds of the colonies the first, instead of the second, charge on the consolidated revenue fund. Section 121, which provided that the consolidated revenue fund should be appropriated by Parliament for the public service, subject to the payments charged by the Constitution, was omitted. And section 126 was amended, so that the Union's power to convert, renew, or consolidate the colonial debts and liabilities would be exercised 'without prejudice to any rights of security or priority in respect of the payment of principal, interest, sinking fund and other charges conferred on the creditors of any of the Colonies'.[59]

Three other amendments of some substance were adopted by the convention. Section 56 was amended to increase the allowances of Members of Parliament from £300 to £400 a year and to increase the penalty for a day's absence from £2 to £3. This was a Transvaal proposal and it was carried by nineteen votes to eleven, nine of the Cape delegates voting with the minority.[60] Section 70 was amended by an insertion providing that any person qualified to vote for the election of members of a Provincial Council would be qualified to become a member of that council.

[56] See above, pp. 346–7.

[57] *Minutes*, p. 262; Malan, pp. 238–9; see above, p. 247. S. 64 of the draft Act has the same number in the S.A. Act.

[58] Hely-Hutchinson to de Villiers, 18 Apr. 1909, enclosing copy of telegram, Selborne to Hely-Hutchinson, 17 Apr. 1909. De Villiers Papers.

[59] *Minutes*, pp. 251, 258–9. Ss. 120 and 126 of the draft Act became ss. 119 and 124 of the S.A. Act.

[60] Ibid., p. 261; Malan, pp. 238–9. S. 56 of the draft Act has the same number in the S.A. Act.

This decision entitled non-white voters to become members of the Cape and Natal provincial councils.[61] And section 139 was amended to make all persons, instead merely of persons of European descent, who had been naturalized in any of the four colonies, deemed to have been naturalized throughout the Union.[62] Verbal amendments were adopted without opposition to fourteen other sections, most of them having been proposed by the Transvaal advisers to Smuts and moved by him in the convention.[63]

The following proposals were moved and either withdrawn or rejected without a division: the Cape Parliament's recommendation that a senator nominated to replace a retired or deceased nominated senator should only hold his seat for the unexpired part of the term, instead of for a further period of ten years (section 23);[64] Fitzpatrick's proposal that the property qualification for elected senators should be reduced from £500 to £250 (section 25);[65] Beck's proposal that the Union Government should bear the approved election expenses of candidates for the House of Assembly, subject to the forfeiture of deposits by candidates who received less than a fifth of the number of votes required to secure their election (section 37);[66] and Merriman's proposal that the duration of the provincial councils should be increased from three to five years (section 73).[67]

Towards the end of the sitting of 10 May Malan proposed that the preamble of the Constitution should include the phrase, 'trusting in the guidance and blessing of God Almighty'. He said that South Africans were a religious people and many of them wished the fact to be recognized in the Constitution. Steyn and others supported him, But, according to Malan, Smuts opposed the proposal 'because the grammar of the sentence was not quite correct', Fischer 'did not want such holy words to appear in an Act', Hertzog 'did not want to be accused of hypocrisy', and Merriman 'felt that he could not insert these words as a colour line was drawn in the constitution'. The result was that when a division was taken the proposal was defeated by sixteen votes to thirteen. The con-

---

[61] *Minutes*, p. 262; Malan, pp. 238–9. S. 70 of the draft Act has the same number in the S.A. Act.

[62] *Minutes*, p. 267. S. 139 of the draft Act became s. 138 of the S.A. Act.

[63] Ibid., pp. 251–4, 261–3, 266–7, 269, 271–2. The sections thus amended (with the corresponding sections of the S.A. Act in brackets where different) were 6, 23 (24), 26 (27), 33 (34), 35, 37, 38, 42, 46, 53, 75, 85, 130 (128), and 145 (144).

[64] Ibid., p. 253. S. 23 of the draft Act became s. 24 of the S.A. Act.

[65] Ibid., p. 271. S. 25 of the draft Act became s. 26 of the S.A. Act.

[66] Ibid.; Malan, pp. 246–7. S. 37 of the draft Act has the same number in the S.A. Act.

[67] *Minutes*, p. 262. S. 73 of the draft Act has the same number in the S.A. Act.

vention had been somewhat embarrassed by this debate and it decided that no reference should be made to it in the minutes.[68]

The convention also considered the questions, when should the delegates of the colonies go to England and what authority should the colonial parliaments vest in them? On 27 April Lord Selborne had written to de Villiers to explain that the Imperial Parliament had a very heavy programme during its current session, so that it was important that the time to be allotted to the South Africa Bill should be carefully arranged in advance. Selborne asked that the South African delegation should reach London by 17 July, 'to give time for the Secretary of State to discuss with it any modifications of the schedule which appear to His Majesty's Government to be necessary or any points of drafting which may have been raised'.[69] The four prime ministers conferred on this subject on the evening of 8 May. Since he was still anxious to ensure that the general election should not be held during the South African winter, Botha reiterated the proposal, which he had previously made by letter,[70] that the South Africa Bill should not be enacted until considerably later; but Merriman's views prevailed and the prime ministers agreed to meet the British request by having the delegates leave South Africa by the end of June.[71] De Villiers and the prime ministers also took care to draft a resolution to ensure that the delegation would not be authorized to consent to any substantial amendment to the draft Constitution. When this resolution was moved by de Villiers on 10 May, some members wanted the delegation to be debarred from consenting to the slightest departure from the words of the Constitution as approved in South Africa, but the majority realized that it would be wise to leave the door open for drafting amendments and the resolution was adopted without a division in the form recommended by the president. It provided

That the delegates to be appointed by the South African Governments to proceed to London to confer with the Secretary of State for the Colonies in reference to the passage of the South Africa Act through the British Parliament be authorized, *inter alia*:—

[68] Malan, pp. 246–9. A similar invocation is to be found in the preamble to the Australian Constitution; and s. 1 of the S.A. Act has subsequently (1925) been amended to read: 'The people of the Union acknowledge the sovereignty and guidance of Almighty God.'   [69] House of Assembly, National Convention Minutes, III.

[70] See above, pp. 324–5.

[71] Merriman to Mrs. Merriman, 9 May 1909: 'Yesterday after dinner I had a conference with Botha Moor and Fischer—the former looks and is very ill and seems to have lost all go. I had the greatest difficulty to get him to see the importance of pushing the Act along and getting it through in England. However if all goes well it is decided to leave the end of June.' Merriman Papers.

(i) To agree to any necessary amendments in the Act which do not involve alterations of any of its principles.

(ii) To confer with the Secretary of State for the Colonies as to the Royal Instructions to be issued to the Governor-General.

(iii) To draft for the guidance of the South African Governments rules and regulations for the first elections of senators, in accordance with the provisions of the Act.[72]

The convention sat for the last time on the morning of 11 May, when the members signed five English and five Dutch copies of their second and final report, comprising the amended draft Constitution and the resolution concerning the delegates who were to proceed to England.[73] They then dispersed, somewhat weary, to their homes. No doubt Merriman summed up the general feeling when he wrote to tell his mother: 'How glad I am that the whole business is over I cannot tell you. For a whole year it has occupied my mind to the exclusion of other things and the strain when one thought that ship wreck was possible was very great.'[74]

The remarkable fact is not so much that they contrived to devise a Constitution for South Africa, but rather that every one of them was able to sign it. Unanimity is rarely achieved in public affairs within the confines of a single homogeneous state; it was unprecedented to achieve it among representatives of four different states, speaking two different languages, within a decade of a bitter and devastating war. The unanimous signing of the final, as well as the first, report of the convention was indeed an act of courage and restraint on the part of every delegate, a vindication of the chairmanship of Sir Henry de Villiers, and, above all, a triumph for the statesmanship of Botha and Smuts—a realization of their political ideals on the grand scale.

4. SOUTH AFRICA APPROVES

The final report of the National Convention was well received by both the Dutch and the English press in the Transvaal, the Orange River Colony, and the Cape Colony. Some of the newspapers which supported the governing parties criticized the provision for the reservation of so many classes of constitutional Bills and expressed regret that section 40 was unchanged, and nearly all the newspapers which supported the

[72] *Minutes*, p. 272; Malan, pp. 248–9.

[73] Cd. 4721 (1909), *Second Report to the respective parliaments of the delegates to the South African Convention, 1908–1909; with copy of the Draft South Africa Constitution Bill as finally passed by the Convention*; *Minutes*, pp. 274, 349–54; Malan, pp. 250–1. The only absentees were the three Rhodesian delegates, who signed later.

[74] Merriman to Mrs. Julia Merriman, 12 May 1909, Merriman Papers.

opposition parties deplored the elimination of proportional representation; but not one of them contended that the revised draft Constitution was unacceptable. Consequently, as June approached nobody doubted that the revised draft Constitution would be approved by overwhelming majorities in the three parliaments. Nevertheless, there were complications of two sorts in the Cape Colony. Firstly, the appeal to Britain which was being organized by African and Coloured leaders had the support of prominent white inhabitants of the Colony; and, secondly, there were disturbing undercurrents within the South African Party.

Already, before the Bloemfontein session of the convention, African and Coloured congresses had accepted the principle of appealing to Britain and had given authority to their executive bodies to organize the appeals.[75] Members of these executives had consulted W. P. Schreiner and urged him to accompany their deputations and use his influence on their behalf in England. Moreover, a group of Cape Town Europeans had decided to make their own appeal to Britain in the same cause and they, too, had turned to Schreiner for leadership. After careful consideration Schreiner had decided to accept these responsibilities. In principle he was loath to solicit imperial intervention. Nevertheless, he considered that there were cases in which the imperial authority had an obligation to intervene; and that this was clearly such a case. As he explained to Sir Charles Dilke:

Some of us in South Africa, who have never favoured unnecessary or ill-informed . . . intervention in the internal affairs of self-governing Colonies or independent States, discern in these contrary days a very real risk that the doctrine of non-interference may be carried to a most dangerous extreme at a time when both the great political parties in the Mother Country appear to be united in a weary feeling that Africa is 'a Beast', and inclined towards handing over all trusts and responsibilities to the European section of our population on such terms as these may design. This is the 'elimination of the Imperial Factor' with a vengeance. . . . The whole scheme and all its parts must be the act of the Imperial Parliament. It must not abandon its trust.[76]

After the publication of the convention's final report, these plans were put into action. The A.P.O. raised money from its members and appointed Dr. Abdurahman, M. J. Fredericks, and D. J. Lenders to represent it in England.[77] The African committee also raised money and appointed J. T. Jabavu and the Rev. W. Rubusana. Meanwhile Schreiner took part

[75] See above, pp. 325–7.
[76] Quoted in Walker, *Schreiner*, p. 321.
[77] According to M. J. Fredericks, the general secretary of the A.P.O., 22,000 people contributed to the fund. *Cape Times*, 23 June 1909.

in drafting 'An Appeal to the Parliament and Government of Great Britain and Ireland'. In measured language the appeal called on Britain to ensure the preservation of the established rights of the non-European inhabitants of the Cape Colony; and it concluded as follows:

In all these matters it is not easy to forecast the future, or to provide efficient safe-guards against unforeseen contingencies and developments. But this, at any rate, should be clear—that the ruling principle should be the principle which has animated past policy—the principle of freedom of opportunity to all civilised citizens of whatever race or colour. The Imperial Power is the guardian of those constitutional rights which, having itself granted, itself only can take away.

We consider, therefore, that we should be untrue to South Africa, and untrue to our duty as citizens of South Africa, did we not urge upon the Imperial Parliament and Government to maintain and protect our fundamental rights and liberties. Only thus can we hope to overcome under Union those unwise and, as it seems to us, unjust and illiberal tendencies which contradict our traditional policy, conflict with all that is best and noblest in our history, and are opposed, as we believe, to the true principles of statesmanship, as well as to the highest dictates of humanity and religion.[78]

This appeal was eventually signed by W. P. Schreiner (Prime Minister, 1898–1900); Sir Gordon Sprigg (Prime Minister, 1878–81, 1886–90, and 1900–4); Sir Bisset Berry (Speaker of the House of Assembly, 1892–1908); Morris Alexander, M.L.A.; J. D. Cartwright, M.L.C.; William Carter, Archbishop of Cape Town; and sixteen other prominent citizens, lay and clerical, including a minister of the Dutch Reformed Church.

The undercurrents in the South African Party arose from its peculiar structure. Merriman had always been handicapped by the fact that he was not a member of its only effective extra-parliamentary organization, the Afrikaner Bond, and after a year of office his leadership was in jeopardy. His cabinet colleagues felt that he did not confide in them sufficiently—and in truth he had a poor opinion of most of them. Malan was flirting with the wine-farmers, who regarded Merriman as the main obstacle to the repeal of the brandy excise.[79] And outside the Cabinet there was always Hofmeyr, spinning a web of disaffection around the Prime Minister. Hofmeyr was very gloomy about the final work of the convention. He complained to Steyn that he was not convinced by his reasons for leaving the language section as it stood; that the provision for

---

[78] Merriman Papers, No. 285/1909; *The Times*, 6 July 1909.

[79] The wine-farmers had sent a petition to the National Convention in Bloemfontein asking for relief for their industry, but without avail. House of Assembly, National Convention Minutes, III.

the reservation of Bills would give the British Government the power to interfere in South Africa's internal affairs; and that the failure to amend section 40 meant 'that we now at best can expect a small majority over the jingo-party in the first Union Parliament—a majority which will vanish altogether when Rhodesia is incorporated'.[80] Nevertheless, he added, the draft Act would go through and he only hoped that it would not be amended in England, as he wanted its faults to be corrected in and by South Africa herself.[81] On 18 May he presided over a meeting of the Cape Town district committee of the Bond and persuaded it to adopt and publish a resolution criticizing the revised draft Act, but expressing the hope that 'unforeseen alterations will not be made in the draft in England without the concurrence of our Parliaments'.[82]

By that time it had been suggested to Merriman that he should invite Hofmeyr to become a member of the delegation to England. The suggestion was most distasteful to Merriman, but he realized that it might have the effects both of consolidating the South African Party and of thwarting Schreiner. On 14 May he asked Botha for his opinion.[83] Botha warned him that the Progressives would look on Hofmeyr's nomination with 'great suspicion' and that he considered that all the delegates should have been members of the convention.[84] Nevertheless, on 27 May Merriman swallowed his pride and sent Hofmeyr a written invitation.[85]

Before Hofmeyr had committed himself in reply an event took place which made Merriman even more determined that he should join the delegation. Speaking in the House of Commons on the motion for the Whitsun adjournment on 27 May, Colonel Seely, the Colonial Under-Secretary, made a loose and ambiguous reference to the procedure which would be followed for the enactment of the South Africa Bill, in which he said, *inter alia*:

As I understand it, the Draft Act cannot be brought in here in identical terms. A fresh Bill will have to be drafted. There will also be amendments proposed by His Majesty's Government. We have settled upon broad principles, but there are certain principles between this country and South Africa which will have to be discussed. After these discussions have proceeded for a little time a Bill will have to be brought in.[86]

---

[80] The original reads: 'dat wy nu op zyn best slechts 'n kleine meerderheid boven de jingo-party in het eerste Unie Parlement kunnen verwachten — eene meerderheid, die geheel zal verdwynen zoodra Rhodesia ingelyfd wordt.' Hofmeyr to Steyn, 14 May 1909, Steyn Papers. [81] Ibid.

[82] *Cape Times*, 19 May 1909.

[83] Transvaal Archives, Prime Minister, LX (ii).

[84] Botha to Merriman, 21 and 25 May 1909 (telegrams), Merriman Papers.

[85] Hofmeyr Papers. [86] *Parl. Deb.*, 5th Ser., Commons, v. 1421–2.

The next morning some South African newspapers published the following summary of Seely's statement:

Turning to the procedure to be observed in connection with the passage of the Bill, embodying the Constitution through Parliament, Colonel Seely said a fresh Bill would be necessary.

In this the Imperial Government would introduce amendments to which he was confident the Colonial Premiers would agree.

After their consent had been obtained, the Bill was likely to be introduced in the House of Lords, and after the passage through that House it was improbable that further amendments would be made in the House of Commons.[87]

To Merriman, who was alert to detect any revival of the policy which had been adopted by Joseph Chamberlain in 1900, when he had insisted on a substantial amendment in the draft Australian Constitution, this was a red rag to a bull.[88] It was also an opportunity for him to reassert his leadership. He therefore persuaded his Cabinet to endorse a stiff minute which was dispatched to the Secretary of State:

Ministers desire to state that they view with great concern the reported utterance of the Under Secretary of State for the Colonies in the House of Commons on the procedure to be adopted in regard to the passage of the South Africa Act, which is at variance with all the previous understandings on the subject. Before proceeding further, they would desire some explanation, as their Parliament will not be asked to give a free hand to delegates. The utterance is, in their opinion, calculated to seriously embarrass the cause of union and to arouse grave suspicions.[89]

Replying on 31 May, Lord Crewe took refuge in the assertion that the Reuter message was 'incorrect and misleading'. Seely, he claimed, had said that a new Bill would be necessary for technical reasons, since the draft Bill which had been published as a command paper did not incorporate the Bloemfontein amendments.[90]

---

[87] *South African News*, 28 May 1909.

[88] When the Australian delegates came to London in 1900 with a draft Constitution for the Commonwealth of Australia, already approved by referenda in five Australian colonies, Joseph Chamberlain, Secretary of State for the Colonies, sought to eliminate s. 74, which limited appeals as of right from Australian courts to the Privy Council and empowered the Australian Parliament to make laws limiting the power of the Queen to grant special leave of appeal. Eventually a compromise was reached. Its main feature was that Australian Bills limiting the power of the Queen to grant special leave of appeal to the Privy Council were to be reserved by the Governor-General for the Queen's pleasure. J. Quick and R. R. Garran, *The Annotated Constitution of the Australian Commonwealth* (Sydney, 1901), pp. 228–53, 748–50; J. L. Garvin, *The Life of Joseph Chamberlain*, iii (London, 1934), 557–67.

[89] 28 May 1909, Merriman Papers, No. 240/1909.

[90] The technical excuse was a poor one. The draft Bill as recommended by the conven-

You may assure your Ministers that His Majesty's Government have no intention of suggesting departures from general principles contained in Bill, but it may be necessary to discuss modifications of some detail provisions. These modifications are not likely to be of such a nature that His Majesty's Government anticipate any difficulty in obtaining the full concurrence of the delegates in any alterations proposed.[91]

This reply was supported by reassuring messages from the London agents-general of the Transvaal and Natal to their governments.[92] However, Merriman remained suspicious that the Imperial Government intended to coerce the South African delegates into accepting substantial amendments and in these circumstances the presence of Hofmeyr might be a boon, because he had an incomparable capacity for saying 'No'.[93]

Merriman and Hofmeyr had a long discussion on 29 May, and two days later Hofmeyr wrote a reply to the invitation. He said he was willing to join the delegation on three conditions. Firstly, no amendments were to be accepted which 'involve alterations in principle or changes in the intent or meaning of any clause or provision'. Secondly, if the Cape delegates were not unanimous in regard to any proposed amendment, 'including even those of a merely formal character', the Act was to be resubmitted to the Cape Parliament for its approval before it came into effect. And, thirdly, these points were to be included in the resolution which was to be introduced into the Cape Parliament during the next few days.[94]

By this time the three prime ministers had exchanged views on the terms of the resolutions to be submitted to their parliaments,[95] with the result that soon after the sessions started on 1 June similar resolutions were introduced into the three parliaments for the approval of the revised draft South Africa Act and for the preparation of addresses asking the King to cause the necessary steps to be taken to authorize the Union in accordance with the provisions of the draft Act, and the addresses which were then prepared by joint committees of both Houses

tion at its Bloemfontein session would have reached the Colonial Office by the end of May and could have been published at any time thereafter as a command paper. It was in fact published thus in July—Cd. 4271 (1909).

[91] 31 May 1909, Merriman Papers, No. 240/1909.

[92] Moor to Merriman, 29 May; Botha to Merriman, 2 June. Merriman Papers (telegrams).

[93] As regards this controversy, it may be remarked that: (a) Seely's statement was reasonably summarized by Reuter; and (b) the subsequent disclaimers by the Secretary of State were inaccurate as to the content of Seely's statement, but accurate as to the intentions of the British Government.

[94] Hofmeyr Papers (draft). It is possible that this letter was not dispatched: it is not to be found in the Merriman Papers.

[95] Fischer to Moor, Botha, and Merriman, 21 May 1909, Merriman Papers (telegram).

were substantially the same. Furthermore, in each case the resolutions concerning the delegates who were to go to England conformed with the recommendation of the convention that they were 'To confer with the Secretary of State for the Colonies as to the Royal Instructions to be issued to the Governor-General' and 'To draft for the guidance of the South African Government rules and regulations for the first elections of senators, in accordance with the provisions of the Act.' But they differed in their definitions of the delegates' powers to accept amendments to the draft Act. Since Botha was satisfied by Sir Richard Solomon's assurance that the British Government had no intention of suggesting substantial amendments, the Transvaal resolution adhered to the terms recommended by the convention and authorized the delegates 'To agree to any necessary amendments in the Act which do not involve alterations of any of its principles.' Fischer, however, shared Merriman's suspicions of the intentions of the British Government, and the Orange River Colony resolution added the somewhat ambiguous proviso that the delegates' authority should 'be confined only to such amendments as are not inconsistent with the provisions and principles laid down in the said Draft Act'. The Cape Colony resolution went further still and met Hofmeyr's wishes by authorizing the delegates only to accept 'such amendments in the Act which do not involve alterations in any of the principles of that Act as may be agreed in by all the delegates', so that a single member of the Cape delegation would be able to block any amendment.[96]

The three parliaments were formally opened on 1 June, and the next day the prime ministers moved the resolutions approving of the revised draft South Africa Act in the lower houses. Nothing arose to mar the harmony between the two main parties in the Transvaal Parliament.[97] Botha, who was still palpably unwell, said that the Transvaal delegates had tried to have the draft Act endorsed without any fundamental changes, but that they had had to yield because 'union was endangered'.[98] He concluded with a declaration of his hopes for the future:

It is expected of every man of authority that he shall do his utmost to co-operate, in order really to unify the two races. If ever, the time has now come to seize the hand of brotherhood and to bear with each other. . . . I expect tolerance from everybody, in order to make of South Africa what it should be. . . . I shall do my utmost to work along those lines in the future.[99]

[96] These resolutions and addresses are printed in Hofmeyr, *Minutes*, pp. 355–9.
[97] The debates on the revised draft South Africa Act are reported in *Transvaal Leg. Ass. Deb., 1909*, cols. 10–26, and *Transvaal Leg. Co. Deb., 1909*, cols. 9–17.
[98] *Transvaal Leg. Ass. Deb., 1909*, col. 10.   [99] Ibid., cols. 11–12.

These remarks were greeted with cheers, and Farrar, seconding the resolution, referred briefly and with moderation to the dropping of proportional representation. Criticism came from only three members— W. J. Wybergh (Nationalist), P. Whiteside (Labour), and H. W. Sampson (Labour). Wybergh taunted Farrar, reminding him of his assertion that proportional representation was an essential part of the Act, and Sampson announced that he would vote against the resolution, because, so he contended, the majority of the people in the Transvaal did not want union and no Member of Parliament had held a meeting of his constituents since the 'vital amendments' had been made at Bloemfontein.[1] Nevertheless, the resolution was carried without a division 'amid considerable applause'.[2] On the same day Smuts piloted the resolution through the Legislative Council. A. D. W. Wolmarans (Het Volk) said that he still objected to union as strongly as ever, but he refrained from restating the reasons for his opposition and the resolution was agreed to without a division. The address to the King and the resolutions conferring authority on the delegates were adopted by both Houses without opposition on 3 June and on the 25th Botha announced that the Transvaal delegation would consist of himself, Smuts, Hull, Farrar, and Fitzpatrick.

Making somewhat typically rambling speeches, Fischer moved the resolution approving of the revised Act in both Houses of the Orange River Colony Parliament.[3] In the assembly Sir John Fraser, the Leader of the Opposition, seconded the resolution, which was 'agreed to unanimously amid acclamation'[4] after only one more speech. In the council, on the other hand, D. W. Drew said that he was not prepared to endorse the amended draft Act before he knew the result of the Natal referendum. His opposition was prompted by Hertzog's recent dismissal of three English-speaking school inspectors. If Natal stayed out, Drew feared, 'a retrogressive majority' would rule the Union. 'The remschoen [brakeshoe; obscurantist] element in the Transvaal was held in check by the enlightened non-racial leadership of General Botha's government, but here it had leaders who pandered to it, and in the Cape there seemed to be nobody whose influence over it was at once permanent and wholesome.'[5] Members of both parties hastened to rebuke Drew for expressing such views. 'Thank God', said Fischer, 'there are not many in South

[1] Ibid., col. 24.
[2] Ibid., col. 26.
[3] The debates on the revised draft South Africa Act are reported in *O.R.C. Leg. Ass. Deb., 1909*, cols. 99–111, and *O.R.C. Leg. Co. Deb., 1909*, cols. 55–74.
[4] *O.R.C. Leg. Ass. Deb., 1909*, col. 111.
[5] *O.R.C. Leg. Co. Deb., 1909*, cols. 61–62.

Africa who would make a speech of that nature';[6] and the resolution was declared carried without a dissentient vote. Soon afterwards both Houses of the Orange River Colony Parliament adopted the address to the King and the resolution conferring authority on the delegation, and on 10 June Fischer announced that the Orange River Colony delegation would consist of himself, Steyn, Hertzog, and Browne.

When the Cape Parliament met the threatened disintegration of the South African Party did not take place.[7] Hofmeyr's influence was no doubt exerted in the direction of cohesion; the sheep-farmers did not support the grape-farmers in caucus; and the latter were eventually appeased by a reduction of the brandy excise from 6s. to 3s. a gallon.[8] After Merriman had moved the resolution of approval of the revised draft South Africa Act, Schreiner made a final attempt to persuade the Cape Parliament to insist upon amendments. He remarked that the Prime Minister seemed to regard the Imperial Parliament as a rubber stamp. While he (Schreiner) did not believe in 'undue or unnecessary interference', he considered the 'fundamental blots' on the Constitution to be so serious that he would not hesitate to bring them to the notice of the Imperial Parliament.[9] He prophesied that 'when the inwardness of what was proposed was thoroughly appreciated in England there would be such a wave of feeling there as would make it very difficult for the Imperial Parliament to do the injustice which that House was now asked to consecrate'. And he moved as an amendment that the House should only give its approval 'subject to the modifications necessary to safeguard the native and coloured inhabitants of this colony against discrimination on the grounds of race or colour in respect of political rights'.[10] These remarks evoked a stream of criticism from members of the South African Party. To appeal to Westminster would be 'dangerous' and 'contrary to the interests of the natives themselves', said H. E. S. Fremantle.[11] The Natives and Coloured people 'had been as liberally treated by the Governments of South Africa as any other section of the population', said A. S. du Plessis.[12] C. J. Levey declared that Schreiner had 'disturbed the native mind'.[13] Sauer reiterated his prophecy that after union there would be a progressive extension of rights to non-Europeans. A. C. A. van Rooy described the amendment as 'an insult and an accusation' to the white people of South Africa, who were 'determined not to tolerate

---

[6] *O.R.C. Leg. Co. Deb., 1909*, col. 69.

[7] The debates on the revised draft South Africa Act are reported in *Cape Hansard, 1909*, pp. 160–73, and *Cape Leg. Co. Deb., 1909*, cols. 19–27.

[8] This concession was made in the budget introduced by Merriman on 5 Oct. 1909.

[9] *Cape Hansard, 1909*, p. 163.   [10] Ibid., p. 164.

[11] Ibid.   [12] Ibid., p. 165.   [13] Ibid.

such interference with its own problems'.[14] And even Stanford (Independent) said that he thought the condition of the Natives 'would be worse if the position were forced'.[15] Not a single Unionist participated in the debate, but T. Searle (South African Party) said that he sympathized with Schreiner, though he considered that the amendment was unnecessary on the ground that the Cape non-European franchise had been secured absolutely by the reservation, while Cronwright Schreiner (South African Party) declared that he 'almost wholly' agreed with his brother-in-law.[16] On 3 June Schreiner called for a division on his amendment, but only Sir Gordon Sprigg (Independent) voted with him and the amendment was defeated by ninety-four votes to two. Sprigg then announced that he wished to address the House before the main question was put, but the Speaker ruled him out of order and the resolution approving of the revised draft Act was accepted without a further division. The next day the resolution was adopted without a division by the council. The address to the King was adopted by both Houses on the 7th and the resolution conferring authority on the delegates on the 8th, when the names of the Cape Colony delegation to England were also approved by both Houses. In moving these names—Merriman, de Villiers, Sauer, Jameson, and Hofmeyr—the Prime Minister went out of his way to explain that Hofmeyr had assured him: '"You must understand I will be a complete Unionist; I am for the Bill, the whole Bill, and nothing but the Bill."'[17]

In Natal there was a vigorous campaign leading to the referendum, which took place on 10 June. The most prominent of the anti-Unionists were men of conservative outlook and loyalist sentiments, whose endemic distrust of Afrikaner politicians had been stirred up by the Transvaal–Mozambique Convention and by the dismissal of the three English-speaking school inspectors in the Orange River Colony. Besides Yonge and Silburn, they included Sir David Hunter, J. J. Hillier, F. S. Tatham, and F. A. Laughton, all of whom were men of standing, and at the last moment Maydon also joined their ranks. A speech delivered by Silburn at Hillary on 25 May was a typical, if somewhat extreme, example of their oratory. The British Liberals, Silburn declared, having obtained power with the help of lying statements about South Africa, had hatched a conspiracy with General Botha to revive their prestige by rushing through a South African union. The Witwatersrand magnates had entered into an unholy alliance with their late enemies. The Natal Govern-

---

14 Ibid., p. 172.   15 Ibid., p. 168.
16 Ibid., p. 165.   17 Ibid., p. 193.

ment was treacherous and cowardly. The delegates had betrayed Natal in the convention by accepting the terms of Botha, Smuts, Merriman, Malan, and Hertzog. The Constitution would bring into power a Boer Government, which would tamper with the franchise and impose the Hertzog Education Act upon Natal—and 'he absolutely refused to be told in a British Colony, by a Dutchman or a German, that his children must learn Dutch'. Therefore the electorate must reject the Constitution and let the British people know that 'Natal, a British Colony, was anxious to become an integral portion, an original State, of United British South Africa, but refused to become an original Province of an embryo Republic.'[18] The Natal Labour Party, too, was anti-Unionist, following the lead which had been given by Palmer and Taylor in the Legislative Assembly. It issued a statement rejecting the revised draft Act owing to the elimination of proportional representation and to the Transvaal–Mozambique Convention.[19] Many of its members were railwaymen, whose strike against a proposal to introduce a system of piecework had been firmly dealt with by the Natal Government in April, with the result that they were inclined to oppose union because it was the policy of the Government.

Towards the end of May these two groups, Imperialist and Labour, coalesced to form a Natal League to oppose union. The league held successful meetings in several centres, notably in Pietermaritzburg, where an anti-Unionist resolution was carried by a large majority.[20] On 4 June the league issued a manifesto in which it called on the voters to reject the draft Act, and undertook at the next general election to put forward candidates pledged to promote the 'international development' of Natal and to work for her ultimate entry into the Union on 'fair, just, and equitable terms, securing the independence of Natal'.[21] The league, however, was a hasty improvisation. It lacked funds. It lacked cohesion. And its policy was nebulous beyond its opposition to the draft Act. Its main asset was the unremitting support of the *Natal Witness* and the *Natal Advertiser*, two of the leading newspapers in the colony.

The Unionist forces, in contrast, were powerful and well-organized, and their policy was more realistic. The Cabinet, the convention delegates, and most Members of Parliament exerted their influence on the side of union. The *Times of Natal* and the *Natal Mercury* were for acceptance. Moreover, the concessions which had been made to Natal at Bloemfontein and the publication of the letter from Botha to Moor on

18 *Natal Witness*, 28 May 1909.   19 *The Times*, 1 June 1909.
20 *Natal Witness*, 27 May 1909.
21 Ibid., 5 June 1909.

the Mozambique Convention[22] went some way towards soothing the Natal electorate; and so did the Transvaal loan of £500,000, the arrangements for which were completed towards the end of May.[23] Successful Unionist meetings were held in nearly every town and village in the colony. On 26 May the Natal Closer Union Society issued a manifesto which concentrated on the material aspects of the issue before the electorate. 'Isolation', it proclaimed, 'means no Customs Union, railway war, ruined industries, increased taxation, more unemployed, increase of public debt, and a decrease in the value of property'; whereas 'Union, on the other hand, means trade expansion, agricultural, financial, and industrial development, equal rights, reduced taxation, and a reduction of the public debt.'[24] Pressure was also brought to bear from outside Natal. Fitzpatrick and Feetham came down from the Transvaal and addressed public meetings. Botha and Fischer, in moving the resolutions for the acceptance of the revised draft Act in their parliaments, made it clear that the other three colonies would unite even if Natal stayed out. And *The Times* came out with a strong leading article urging Natal to join the Union in her own interests and in the interests of British influence in the Union.[25]

Nevertheless, the result of the referendum was by no means a foregone conclusion. On 24 May Watt was warning Smuts that he had grave doubts about the outcome.[26] On the 27th Maydon was assuring Botha that the voting would be against union.[27] And on the same day Merriman was considering what should be done if Natal stayed out. 'I suppose', he wrote to Botha, 'in the event of the referendum going against the Bill we shall denounce the Customs Union and that the Railway Agreement will fall through?'[28] During the final week, however, observers noted that opinion was swinging strongly in the direction of acceptance. On 4 June Sir Matthew Nathan, the Governor, predicted that there would be a 70 per cent. poll and that two-thirds of the votes cast would be in favour of union;[29] and on the 7th *The Times* correspondent reported that the railwaymen were no longer hostile and that 'the commercial and industrial interests are practically unanimous in favouring the Union, in spite of the strong prejudices against the Mozambique Treaty'.[30] This was a discern-

---

[22] See above, pp. 378–9.
[23] Botha to Merriman, 21 May 1909, Merriman Papers (telegram).
[24] *Natal Mercury*, 27 May 1909.   [25] *The Times*, 26 May 1909.
[26] Smuts Papers.
[27] Transvaal Archives, Prime Minister, LX (ii).   [28] Ibid.
[29] Nathan to Hely-Hutchinson, 4 June 1909 (telegram); copy enclosed in Hely-Hutchinson to Merriman, 8 June 1909, Merriman Papers.
[30] *The Times*, 8 June 1909.

ing comment. C. G. Smith, who supported union while continuing to deplore the Mozambique Convention, was more typical than Maydon, who sided with the anti-Unionists. When it came to the final decision very few commercial and industrial men in Natal were prepared to risk the prospect of isolation.

The referendum took place on 10 June amid considerable excitement. The result was announced on the 12th: in favour of the draft Act, 11,121; against, 3,701. Thus almost exactly three-quarters of the votes were in favour. Moreover, there was a decided majority for the draft Act in every constituency. Even in Pietermaritzburg, where the Natal League had held its most successful meetings, 1,122 voted in favour and only 722 against. The sole grain of comfort for the anti-Unionists was the smallness of the poll. Of 25,463 registered voters, only 58·2 per cent. cast their votes in the referendum and only 43·7 per cent. voted in favour of the draft Act.[31]

It then only remained for the Natal Parliament to endorse the will of the electorate.[32] In a brief session between 16 and 18 June both Houses approved a suitable address to the King and Moor announced that he would take with him to England the men who had represented Natal in the National Convention. It was Silburn who seconded the address to the King. He said that he and his colleagues who had fought against the draft Act would endeavour to make the Constitution 'as perfect an instrument for the future government of South Africa as it is possible for us to do'.[33]

Thus the draft South Africa Act, having been signed by every delegate in the convention, was endorsed to an overwhelming extent by the white electorates, or their parliamentary representatives, in each of the four colonies. The Transvaal and Orange River Colony parliaments, whose assemblies were elected by all the white male adults, approved it without a single dissentient vote. The two Houses of the Cape Parliament, whose members were returned by an 85 per cent. white electorate, approved it with only two dissentients. And the Natal electorate, which was 99 per cent. white, approved it by a three-quarters majority of the votes cast in a referendum. Compare with this the proceedings in North America, where in 1787–8 the Constitution of the United States was ratified by small majorities in several of the State conventions—by 187 to 168 in Massachusetts, by 54 to 46 in New Hampshire, by 87 to 79 in Virginia, and by 30 to 27 in New York.[34] Compare, too, the proceedings in Austra-

---

[31] Cd. 5099, pp. 8–10; *Natal Mercury* and *Natal Witness*, 14 June 1909.

[32] *Natal Leg. Ass. Deb.* xlviii. 1–6, 8–9, 32; *Natal Leg. Co. Deb.* xx. 1–13.

[33] *Natal Leg. Ass. Deb.* xlviii. 3.

[34] Carl van Doren, *The Great Rehearsal* (London, 1948), pp. 202, 206, 230, 235. It is

lia, where in 1899 the draft Constitution for the Commonwealth was carried by 107,420 votes to 82,741 in the final New South Wales referendum and by 38,488 votes to 30,996 in Queensland.[35] Seldom, if ever, has the adoption of a democratically drafted Constitution so clearly represented the will of an electorate.[36]

On the other hand, some of the most important provisions of the draft South Africa Act were opposed by nearly all the politically conscious non-whites, including the non-white voters in the Cape Colony, and it is significant that in the last resort the only opposition to the draft Act in the Cape Parliament was made on their behalf.

also of interest that, whereas every member of the South African Convention signed the draft South Africa Act, four members of the American Convention left Philadelphia before it had completed its work (Lansing and Yates of New York, and Martin and Mercer of Maryland) and three others who stayed to the end did not sign the Constitution (Randolph and Mason of Virginia, and Gerry of Massachusetts). Ibid., pp. 118, 139, 157, 175.

[35] Quick and Garran, op. cit., p. 225.

[36] Excluding from the reckoning dictatorial constitutions submitted for popular approval by plebiscite in the Napoleonic manner.

CHAPTER VII

THE CONSTITUTION ENACTED IN ENGLAND

1. THE BRITISH BACKGROUND

BY 1909 the affairs of South Africa no longer loomed large in the eyes of the British Government, Parliament, press, or people. The shadows of war were beginning to fall across Europe and in March there was a naval scare following the revelation that Germany might soon acquire a superiority in battleships of the *Dreadnought* class. This led in April to the introduction of a highly controversial budget by Lloyd George, and from then until the end of the session in November it was the budget—and the budget alone—which held the attention of the country. The South Africa Bill therefore attracted little interest.

Both the great political parties were nevertheless disposed to welcome any voluntary unification of the self-governing South African colonies in a British Dominion. The steps towards unification in South Africa had been reported by the more responsible British newspapers with interest and sympathy, and the draft South Africa Act was regarded by the Unionists as the coping-stone of the South African War and Milner's work of post-war reconstruction, and by the Liberals as the logical culmination of the policy of 'trusting the Boer', and a potential source of prestige to the Government.[1] There was, too, a general feeling that the auguries for the Union were propitious. Louis Botha had captured the imagination of the British public when he attended the colonial conference in 1907. The grant of responsible government seemed to have transformed him from a doughty foe into a willing partner, a loyal leader of a white colonial community of alien stock, a second Laurier. He seemed destined to exorcise anglophobia and krugerism from his people and to lead them along the more fruitful path of co-operation with British South Africans and the British Empire. Furthermore, the international situation made the consummation of the South African Union a matter of some urgency. In time of war the Suez Canal might be closed to the shipping of Britain and her allies, in which case the Cape route would reassume its former commercial and strategic importance and a friendly, self-sufficient, united South Africa would be a vital asset.

That this was the perspective in which the Government viewed the

---

[1] Members of the British Government made political capital out of the unification of South Africa. *The Times*, 3 July and 2 Aug. 1909.

draft South Africa Act is shown by the following passage in the autobiography of J. E. B. Seely, the Under-Secretary of State for the
Colonies:[2]

The matter [of South African Union] was urgent for many reasons. To my
mind, the two chief reasons were: Firstly, the devoted loyalty and friendship
of General Botha, a man of outstanding quality and overwhelming influence
with the Dutch in South Africa. George Wyndham[3] said to me soon after
I had taken office: 'I think you will succeed with your South African Settlement, because Botha happened to be born just at the right time.' The second
reason was that I had been forced to the conclusion that war with Germany
must come in the near future. If war came with a hostile population in South
Africa, not only would all chance of a settlement be postponed for a generation, but the Empire would be confronted with immense strategical difficulties.

Even in imperialist circles apprehensions about the future of South
Africa had greatly diminished by 1909. Milner, indeed, was still sceptical, if not of the motives of Botha and his colleagues, at least of their
capacity to instil faith in their proclaimed policy into the hearts of their
followers; and he feared that the unification of South Africa would pave
the way for the triumph of a resurgent Afrikaner nationalism throughout the country. But he no longer saw any purpose in giving expression
to his views in public. The grant of responsible government to the inland
colonies, which he had attacked so bitterly at the time, had cut the
ground from under his feet; and most of those who had previously supported him had become apathetic about South Africa, while others had
become downright optimistic. Lord Curzon, his fellow pro-consul,[4] had
toured South Africa early in 1909 and given his enthusiastic blessing to
the work of the National Convention;[5] and even the Imperial South
African Association, which had been founded at the end of the nineteenth century to support British supremacy in South Africa, declared in
its annual report published in May 1909 that its objects were 'nearer
accomplishment by the presentation of the draft Constitution', and that
the Constitution would promote 'the general fusion of races and the
growth of common purpose'.[6] Consequently it was apparent that there
would be no serious criticism of the draft South Africa Act from the
imperialist point of view. Liberals and Unionists alike seemed confident
that union would be followed by the disappearance of friction between

[2] Major-General J. E. B. Seely, *Adventure* (London, 1930), p. 133.
[3] George Wyndham (1863–1913) was a Unionist Member of Parliament and a prominent imperialist, who had been Chief Secretary for Ireland from 1900 to 1905.
[4] George Nathaniel Curzon, first Marquis of Kedleston (1859–1925), Viceroy of India
from 1899 to 1905.   [5] *The Times*, 23 March 1909.   [6] Ibid., 25 May 1909.

Boer and Briton and the evolution of a homogeneous white South African nation, which would be a loyal member of the British Empire.[7] Moreover, nearly all of them considered that this prospect should override all other factors in determining their approach to the draft Act.

Those people in Britain who gave any thought to the question disapproved of the colour-bar provisions of the draft Act and would have preferred that the door had been left open to 'civilized' non-whites to acquire full rights of citizenship; but the Government and the official Opposition were agreed that the Imperial Parliament should refrain from amending those provisions. It was common doctrine that the British Government, through the colonial governors, might advise, warn, or admonish colonial politicians when they were formulating policies and drafting Bills. This was what the Government had done, through Lord Selborne, when the National Convention was drafting the South Africa Bill—it had tried to persuade the convention to leave the door open to citizenship for civilized non-whites in all the provinces of the Union and it had used the South African desire for an early and effortless incorporation of the protectorates in the Union as a lever for that purpose; but the convention had not risen to the bait.[8] It was also common doctrine, however, that in the last resort Britain should acquiesce in the will of a self-governing colony in matters of internal policy, provided that the will of the colony had been expressed by a clear majority in a properly constituted legislature. For Britain to do otherwise would be to destroy the very basis of the second British Empire—the rule that self-governing colonies should be free to determine their own internal affairs. If the Imperial Parliament amended the colour-bar provisions of the draft South Africa Act, the official delegates of the South African colonies, bound as they were by instructions to accept no amendments of principle, would take their stand on the high ground of colonial liberty and unanimously declare that the amendments were unacceptable; their parliaments would agree with them by overwhelming majorities; the governments of Canada, Australia, and New Zealand would very likely rally to their support; and Britain would almost certainly be obliged to yield. Nothing would have been gained. But the goodwill of men like Louis Botha would have been weakened, if not destroyed, the negrophobic and anglophobic tendencies in South Africa would have been accentuated, and the other dominions would have been led to make a critical re-examination of their relationship with Britain. By 1909, indeed, all responsible British statesmen realized that it was too late for Britain to determine the distribution of

[7] The Times, 17 Dec. 1908, 18 Feb. 1909, 21 Apr. 1909, 24 May 1909, 17 June 1909.
[8] See above, pp. 217–18.

political power in South Africa. She had had her opportunity in 1902. But then, instead of using it, she had undertaken that 'The question of granting the franchise to natives [in the Transvaal and the Orange River Colony] will not be decided until after the introduction of self-government.'[9] The colour-bar provisions, first of the Transvaal and Orange River Colony constitutions, and now of the draft South Africa Act, were considered to flow logically from that commitment.[10] Consequently the British Government regarded it as being outside the range of practical politics to insist on any diminution of the colour-bar provisions of the draft Act; and it was a foregone conclusion that the Imperial Parliament would endorse the will of the South African parliaments.

There were, however, a few Liberal Members of Parliament who saw the problem in a different perspective—men who were imbued with the Wilberforce tradition and were so apprehensive that the white minority might abuse its powers over the non-white majority in South Africa that they believed that even at that late stage it was the duty of the Imperial Parliament to intervene. Foremost among them was Sir Charles Dilke, who had had a long experience of public affairs and commanded the respect of the House of Commons. In 1906 he had tried to secure some qualification of the colour-bar in the Transvaal Constitution and he was the man to whom Schreiner now entrusted the preparations for his campaign. Others, like Lord Courtney, were former pro-Boers who were critical of the draft South Africa Act for the same reason that they had formerly condemned the South African policy of the Unionists—because they considered that human rights were being violated. The Labour members of the House of Commons agreed with these dissident Liberals. Ramsay MacDonald, their parliamentary leader, had recently travelled in Africa and India and his book, *Labour and the Empire*,[11] following upon J. A. Hobson's forceful economic analysis of imperialism,[12] had crystallized the colonial policy of the young party into almost unqualified opposition to the control of non-white peoples by local white minorities. A few of the Irish members were of the same opinion; but most of them, being nationalists who regarded themselves as victims of British imperialism, sympathized with the national aspirations of the Afrikaner people and would support the policy of the Government.[13]

[9] Article 8 of the Treaty of Vereeniging. See above, pp. 11–12.

[10] Nevertheless, see above, p. 27, n. 65, where it is pointed out that Britain was not bound by the Treaty of Vereeniging to exclude Coloured and Indian men from the franchise in the Transvaal and Orange River Colony.

[11] J. Ramsay MacDonald, *Labour and the Empire* (London, 1907).

[12] J. A. Hobson, *Imperialism: a Study* (London, 1902).

[13] On the organization of British opposition to the colour-bar in the South Africa Bill

2. THE FAILURE OF THE SCHREINER MISSION

The High Commissioner, the official colonial delegates, and the members of the Coloured and African deputations arrived in England between 26 June and 17 July. The British press greeted the official delegates with a pæan of praise and the Government placed cars and office accommodation at their disposal. Special attention was paid to Louis Botha, who dined with the King on 22 July.[14] The high-water mark of the official hospitality came on the 24th, when all the delegates and their wives attended a state banquet at Buckingham Palace.

The only serious anxiety of the delegates was that Schreiner and the Coloured and African deputations might manage to arouse British public opinion to such an extent that the Government would feel obliged to insist upon amendments. Merriman, recalling Chamberlain's insistence on an amendment to the draft Australian Constitution,[15] was particularly anxious on that score and he had already taken steps to counteract Schreiner. He had hurried de Villiers off from South Africa in the same ship to keep an eye on him.[16] He had written a long letter to the Governor of the Cape Colony, assuring him that if Schreiner succeeded in his purpose the unification movement would collapse, the Imperial Government would be held responsible, and the white inhabitants of the Cape Colony would become as intolerant on the colour question as the northerners.

It is my firm conviction [he wrote] that no worse blow could have been struck at the cause of the sound relations between the races than this notion of attempting to induce the British Parliament to over-ride the almost unanimous wish of South Africa on a question of native policy which is after all technical rather than practical, and I venture to hope that the project may receive no encouragement from His Majesty's Government.[17]

see Stephen Gwynn and Gertrude M. Tuckwell, *The Life of the Rt. Hon. Sir Charles W. Dilke, 1843-1911* (London, 1917, 2 vols.), ii. 374–6; Walker, *de Villiers*, pp. 480–6; Walker, *Schreiner*, pp. 325–33; G. B. Pyrah, *Imperial Policy and South Africa, 1902–10* (Oxford, 1955), pp. 118–21.

[14] Agnes Merriman to Julia Merriman, 19 July 1909: 'Botha dines with Lord Crewe on Tuesday to meet the King! he is quite the *favoured* Premier. All these people are as keen about the Dutch now just as much as they *hated* them during the War—and it is a mercy Botha takes it all for what it is worth. . . . The more I see of Botha the more I like him—he goes his course utterly unmoved—and people are really quite silly about him.' Merriman Papers.   [15] See above, p. 388, n. 88.

[16] Merriman to de Villiers, 10 June 1909: 'I do hope *most earnestly* that you may find it convenient to go on 16th. It is of the utmost importance as I hear Schreiner and his deputation are going on that day to work mischief.' Merriman Papers (copy).

[17] Merriman to Hely-Hutchinson, n.d. [June 1909], Merriman Papers, No. 245/1909 (copy).

Merriman had also asked Stanford to call on Hely-Hutchinson and expound the views which he had expressed in the House of Assembly during its final debate on the draft Act. The interview took place on 28 June and Hely-Hutchinson sent the following telegram to Lord Crewe immediately afterwards:[18]

Colonel Stanford called on me to-day and said that although he shared Schreiner's objection to the inclusion of the restriction as to 'European descent' and regarded it as a blot on the Constitution he is strongly of opinion that the considered decision of the Convention on the subject, endorsed by the South African Parliaments, ought to be accepted. Further, he says that if the restriction were eliminated the danger of an attack on the existing franchise rights of the Cape Colony Natives would be great: and that the inclusion of the restriction will tend to minimise any probability there might be of an attempt being made in the Union Parliament to abolish or diminish those rights. He is also strongly of opinion that the settlement of this and cognate questions ought to be left to the people of South Africa whose lot, and that of their descendants, is cast here, and who will be the first and principal ones to suffer the evil consequences of any mistaken step that may be taken in the matter of the government and management of the Native population. He desires me to add that his experience of the discussions in the Convention assures him that there is a growing feeling and intention amongst the leading politicians in South Africa in favour of promoting the real interests of the Natives, and that, provided nothing (such as the elimination of the 'European descent' restriction) is done to arouse a contrary feeling, he is confident that in the end all will work out for their true interests.

This telegram provided the British Government with valuable arguments against amendments to the draft Act.

On reaching England the delegates sought to discredit Schreiner and the Coloured and African deputations in their private discussions with members of the Government, Members of Parliament, and officials of the colonial office, and in their public statements. Jameson, the first to arrive, informed *The Times* that the 'agitation' of the 'extreme negrophilists' was 'doing a great deal of harm to the native people'.[19] Merriman declared that Schreiner's mission was 'one of the most unkind things ever done to the natives'.[20] Sauer said:[21]

I fear that the growing feeling in favour of liberality of treatment will be arrested because of the attempt, first, to obtain what is now impossible,

[18] Copy enclosed in Hely-Hutchinson to Merriman, 29 June 1909, Merriman Papers.
[19] *The Times*, 28 June 1909.   [20] Ibid., 12 July 1909.
[21] Ibid.

namely equal rights, and secondly, because of the attempt to obtain interference from outside on a matter on which European people in South Africa
are united. . . . It is certain that if Mr. Schreiner were to succeed, which I
think is impossible, a strong reaction would set in against the continuance or
extension of the liberal native policy in South Africa.

Botha insisted that the question of political rights for non-whites would
'have to be solved in South Africa by the South Africans', who had
always 'shown a spirit of justice and fair play towards the native races'
in the past and could be trusted to do so in the future.[22]

Meanwhile Dilke had done what he could to prepare the way for
Schreiner. Already in March he had gone to see Seely to plead the cause
of the non-whites with an earnestness and an eloquence which left a
lasting impression on the Colonial Under-Secretary.[23] In May, after the
publication of the final report of the National Convention, he had led a
deputation of Liberal and Labour Members of Parliament to Lord Crewe
to protest against the colour-bar;[24] and at the annual meeting of the
Aborigines Protection Society on 19 May he had moved, and G. P.
Gooch, the historian, had seconded, a resolution, which was carried,
urging on the Government 'the grave importance of safeguarding the
existing native franchise in South Africa and its extension to duly qualified natives, and the abolition of the colour-bar in the Union Parliament'.[25] But the time had long passed since humanitarian organizations
were able to exert a decisive influence over policy and these protests had
no effect.

On 5 July Schreiner started his campaign with a statement to the press.
He declared that he had come to England

to try and get the blots removed from the Act, which makes it no Act of
Union, but rather an Act of Separation between the minority and the
majority of the people of South Africa. . . . The coloured inhabitants are
barred from the opportunity to rise and evolve naturally, which is the right
of every free man in a free country. We do not base our movement upon the
doctrine of the equality of all men, but upon the doctrine of the right to
freedom of opportunity—equality of opportunity. . . . The principles of
justice which are associated in our minds with Great Britain and her expansive policy are violated in the proposed Act of Union. We do not dream that
Union is to be wrecked if Great Britain resolves that injustice, which is
apparent, is to be removed. We know that the incentives towards Union are
so strong that none of the parties to the Convention would dream of reject-

[22] *The Times*, 19 July 1909.
[23] Gwynn and Tuckwell, ii. 378.
[24] Pyrah, p. 118   [25] *The Times*, 20 May 1909.

ing it merely because the offensive exclusion of persons of non-European descent might be removed.[26]

The next day *The Times* published the full text of the Appeal which he had brought from South Africa.[27]

Nevertheless, the British press almost unanimously opposed the suggestion that the British Parliament should tamper with the draft Act. The failure of the Schreiner mission may be followed in the columns of *The Times*. It published several reports from correspondents in South Africa, denying that Schreiner could properly claim to represent the views of the majority of the non-whites. One such report quoted a resolution which had been adopted by a 'coloured people's vigilance committee', which appears to have been created for the purpose, repudiating the appeal to Britain because 'We have confident trust in friends within South Africa who have consistently and steadily defended our cause, and whose efforts we believe will ultimately be crowned with success.'[28] Other reports emphasized the opposition of white South Africa to Schreiner's mission. Thus a Natal newspaper was quoted as saying that 'The arbitrary exercise of the authority of the Imperial Government against the opinion of the vast majority of the white colonists would wreck Union, which offers the best hope of an enlightened and consistent native policy.'[29] On 17 July *The Times* had a leading article predicting that there would be no serious opposition in Britain to any of the provisions of the draft Act, and asserting that 'Nothing could possibly be more unwise or more certain to prejudice it than any criticism from this country which would suggest that South African statesmen were indifferent to their responsibility towards the coloured races.' During the following month, indeed, *The Times* published several letters criticizing the colour-bar. On 17 July there was a letter from Sir Harry Johnston, who had played a major part in establishing British authority in East and Central Africa, and who objected to the provision giving power to the South African Parliament to disfranchise the Cape Province non-whites, since it would stand in the way of the creation of a larger Union, embracing all the British territories from Tanganyika to the Cape of Good Hope. On the 26th there was a letter from Sir Charles Bruce, who deplored the exclusion of non-whites from the franchise in the northern provinces of the Union, because it was a 'violation of that principle of equal opportunity, without distinction of race, colour, or creed, which was the faith of the Victorian era'. On 18 August, after the Bill had

---

[26] Ibid., 5 July 1909.   [27] See above, pp. 385–6.
[28] *The Times*, 23 June 1909.   [29] Ibid., 10 July 1909.

passed its second reading in the House of Commons, there was a strong letter from W. T. Stead, the editor of the *Review of Reviews*, in which he had already been supporting Schreiner. Stead compared the conduct of the Imperial Parliament with that of Pontius Pilate:

> But, like Pontius Pilate, they all agree to betray their trust, do what they admit to be a wrong thing—an unjust, and even a monstrous thing—under the same kind of pressure as that applied by the Sanhedrim. . . . If the South African male whites wish to brand themselves with the stigma of imposing a colour bar, let them do their own dirty work on their own responsibility.

There were also further letters from Schreiner, contending that the Imperial Parliament had a clear duty to the non-whites of South Africa, more especially as most of them had not been represented in the National Convention (27 July and 18 August); a letter from Dr. Abdurahman, the leader of the Coloured deputation, quoting remarks by Botha, Smuts, and Dr. Krause to show that there was a likelihood that the Union Parliament would use its power to obliterate the Cape non-white franchise (28 July); and a letter from J. T. Jabavu, of the African deputation, stressing 'the concern felt by the natives generally throughout South Africa, who are the unwilling victims of this measure', and saying that imperial sanction of the colour-bar provisions of the draft Act might become a precedent for legislation by the Union Parliament 'against all native advance' (19 August). But these letters did not evoke anything approaching a popular agitation, and in leading articles on 26 July and 20 August *The Times* steadily reiterated its opposition to the Schreiner amendments. Other British dailies adopted a similar attitude, or a still more hostile one, with the single exception of the *Manchester Guardian*, which supported Schreiner.

In these circumstances the Government had no reason to modify its policy. As will be seen, Crewe made no attempt to persuade the official South African delegates to accept any amendment of the colour-bar provisions when he conferred with them on 20 and 21 July. On the 22nd Crewe granted Schreiner and the Coloured and African deputations an interview, at which he adopted a 'sympathetic but necessarily non-committal' attitude.[30] During the following weeks, while the South Africa Bill was before Parliament, Schreiner even found it difficult to ensure that his amendments would be moved. On 27 July Schreiner, Abdurahman, Jabavu, Rubusana, and Dilke spoke at a meeting of the Anti-Slavery and Aborigines Protection Society and a resolution was adopted, expressing regret that the Bill excluded non-whites from the South African

Parliament and failed to safeguard the Cape franchise, and urging the Government to make sure that the inhabitants of the protectorates would remain as secure as before;[31] and two days later members of the deputations were given a hearing by forty Labour and Liberal members at the House of Commons.[32] But by the time the Bill reached the Commons Dilke warned Schreiner that there would not be a full House and that 'We shall not carry anything and therefore what we move (if anything) depends on how it looks.'[33]

3. THE COLONIAL SECRETARY'S CONFERENCE

Soon after Sir Henry de Villiers reached England on 3 July he had several discussions with the Colonial Secretary. In the light of these discussions Crewe and the colonial office officials drew up a draft South Africa Bill. Copies of the Bill were sent to the South African delegates on the 17th with a covering letter in which Crewe expressed the hope that the delegates would regard its variations from the draft South Africa Act as adopted in South Africa 'not as being definitely inserted in the Bill to be laid before the Imperial Parliament, but as being suggested for the purposes of friendly discussion'.[34] He proceeded to distinguish between the British proposals for amendments in the main body of the Bill and those for amendments in the schedule, which dealt with the administration of the so-called protectorates when and if they were transferred to the Union.

Those which appear in the Bill do not involve any change in principle; the Bill as a whole is perfectly satisfactory to His Majesty's Government, who are fully prepared to adopt and support it.

The amendments are inserted in part to adapt the form of the Bill to the Australian precedent (should the Delegates determine to adopt that model), and in part to remove ambiguities or to give effect to what is understood to be the real intention of the draft.

The suggested alterations in the Schedule are amplifications of the scheme contained therein, based, in some respects, on the analogy of the Indian Council, which has been cited as a precedent. They are not intended to affect the principles of the scheme, but to operate as the complement of it, and I recommend the amendments generally to the favourable consideration of the Delegates.

De Villiers was satisfied with the British draft Bill; but when the

---

[31] *The Times*, 28 July 1909. In May 1909 the Aborigines Protection Society and the British and Foreign Anti-Slavery Society had amalgamated.
[32] Ibid., 30 July 1909.   [33] Walker, *Schreiner*, p. 330.
[34] Brand Papers.

delegates met to discuss it under his chairmanship on the 19th he found that several of the British proposals, especially those concerning the schedule, were 'very unpalatable' to most of his colleagues and he feared that if they were insisted on there would be 'great difficulties in the way of agreement'.[35]

The formal conference between the delegates and Lord Crewe took place at the Foreign Office on 20 and 21 July.[36] Crewe explained that criticism in the Imperial Parliament would be confined to the provisions affecting the non-whites. In the main body of the Bill there were two important such provisions—those excluding them from the franchise, except in the Cape Province, and those excluding them from Parliament. Nevertheless, the policy of His Majesty's Government was one of co-operation:

It was the fixed conviction of His Majesty's Government that these matters must be settled in South Africa itself. It was of no use to express academic opinions, and His Majesty's Government feel that circumstances have not made it possible to adopt a different course than that adopted. His Majesty's Government were prepared to see the Bill through as it stands both as to franchise and as to representation.

The schedule, he continued, 'stood on a different footing'. His Majesty's Government was trustee for the protectorates, whose peoples had 'begged not to be handed over to the direct control of the Union Parliament', and since there was to be no Native representation in Parliament it was necessary to supply a buffer between it and the Natives when transfer took place. It was considered desirable to attach the schedule to the Bill so as to avoid the 'possible necessity' of detailed negotiations later on. The draft Bill contained certain amendments to the schedule as drawn up in South Africa, but none of these were amendments of principle, since it was recognized that the delegates were not able to consent to such amendments.

[35] De Villiers to Selborne, 19 July 1909; cited in Walker, *de Villiers*, pp. 482–3.

[36] The only records of the proceedings of the conference consist of two documents printed at the foreign office on 22 July. The first deals with the sitting of the 20th and the second with the sitting of the 21st. Both are headed: 'Printed for the use of the Imperial Conference. Secret. South Africa Bill. Conference between Delegates from South Africa and the Secretary of State for the Colonies.' De Villiers Papers. The documents contain a fairly full exposition of Crewe's opening remarks, a record of decisions taken, and a brief précis of the discussions on disputed points. De Villiers subsequently suggested to Crewe that if the documents were to have any binding effect, the précis of the discussions should be deleted as being too brief to be accurate. Ibid., 24 July 1909 (copy). The following account of the conference is based on those documents. The amendments which the conference made to the draft South Africa Act as adopted in South Africa are set out in Appendix K of G. R. Hofmeyr (ed.), *Minutes of Proceedings . . . of the South African National Convention*.

After Sir Henry de Villiers had replied on behalf of the delegates, the conference considered the form of the Bill. As prepared by the colonial office its form was similar to that of the Commonwealth of Australia Constitution Act, 1900—that is to say, there were seven preliminary sections and the Constitution itself was cast as sub-sections of section 8. De Villiers at once stated that the delegates would prefer to revert to the form in which the Bill had been drawn up and adopted in South Africa and Crewe agreed that this should be done.

The conference then worked through the British proposals for amendments to the main body of the Bill as adopted in South Africa.[37] Many of them were purely verbal—obvious improvements in most cases—and these were accepted by the delegates without objection.[38] Four British proposals were consequent on the fact that the Parliaments of all the four South African colonies had passed resolutions approving of the draft South Africa Act since the final session of the National Convention, so that it was no longer necessary to include phrases or sections providing for the contingency that one or more of them would not join the Union on its establishment. These, too, were accepted by the delegates without objection.[39] Three British proposals related to the name of the Union. In section 4 of the draft Act as adopted in South Africa the name had been given simply as 'South Africa'. The British draft Bill substituted the name 'The Union of South Africa' and Crewe explained to the delegates that the change was desirable 'to prevent ambiguity'. The delegates accepted this without objection and consequential amendments were made in two other sections of the Bill.[40] The following British proposals were also accepted by the delegates without objection: a new section, which became section 7, was inserted to provide that the Colonial Boundaries Act, 1895, and other Acts which applied to the self-governing South African colonies as self-governing colonies, should apply to the Union;[41] a provision was added to section 11 for the appointment of

[37] The numbers given to sections of the Bill in this chapter are those of the S.A. Bill as introduced into the British Parliament and of the S.A. Act as enacted.

[38] These amendments were to the fifth paragraph of the preamble, to the heading of part X of the Bill, and to ss. 1, 2, 18, 34, 51, 71, 75, 85 (xiii), 97, 103, 121, 127, 130, 133, 136, 151, and 152.

[39] These amendments were to the second paragraph of the preamble and to ss. 4 and 6 of the Bill, and for the deletion of s. 34 of the South African draft.

[40] Ss. 8 and 59. It is curious that the Union of South Africa should have acquired its official designation thus at the eleventh hour. The National Convention had adopted the designation 'South Africa' on 16 Oct. 1908: Sauer had proposed 'The Union of South Africa', Smartt 'British South Africa', Jagger 'The Commonwealth of South Africa', and Lindsay 'South Africa'; Sauer, Smartt, and Jagger had withdrawn their proposals; and Lindsay's had been accepted without a division. Hofmeyr, *Minutes*, pp. 10–12 and 15.

[41] S. 8 of the Commonwealth of Australia Constitution Act is similar.

a Deputy Governor-General during the temporary absence of the Governor-General from the Union;[42] new sentences were added to sections 26 and 44 to provide that residential and (in the case of the Senate) property qualifications acquired in any of the four self-governing colonies before union should be treated as qualifications acquired in the Union for the purposes of eligibility for membership of the Senate and House of Assembly; a new sentence was inserted in section 38 to empower the Delimitation Commission to regulate its own procedure; a proviso was added to section 106 to the effect that the section would not impair the right of appeal to the Privy Council from judgements given by the Appellate Division of the Supreme Court under or in virtue of the Colonial Courts of Admiralty Act, 1890; eight words were inserted in section 124 to provide that 'notwithstanding any other provisions contained in this Act' the Union's assumption of the debts and liabilities of the colonies should be subject to the conditions imposed by any law under which such debts or liabilities were raised or incurred;[43] words were deleted from section 149 so that the section would not empower Parliament to form a new province out of 'Territories', as distinct from provinces, within the Union;[44] and words were deleted from section 150 so that that section would provide means for the admission into the Union only of 'the territories administered by the British South Africa Company', and not other territories or colonies.[45] Two further amendments to the draft Act as adopted in South Africa emanated from de Villiers and were adopted without objection: words were inserted in section 103 to ensure that appeals from the full Eastern Districts Court at Grahamstown should go direct to the Appellate Division of the Supreme Court, and not to the Provincial Division in Cape Town;[46] and a sentence was added to sec-

[42] S. 126 of the Australian Constitution is similar.

[43] Crewe explained that the purpose of this insertion was to 'make it clear that the security of the [Transvaal] guaranteed loans under this clause was unimpaired by any other clause or clauses which might seem to conflict with it'.

[44] As previously worded, this section would have empowered parliament to tamper with the boundaries of the protectorates if they were incorporated in the Union.

[45] As previously worded, this section might have been applied to the protectorates and thus have provided a loophole of escape from the provisions of s. 151 and the schedule.

[46] This section had been amended by the National Convention at its Bloemfontein session in May 1909 in such a way that appeals from the Eastern Districts Court would in most instances have gone to Cape Town. J. G. Kotzé, the President of the Eastern Districts Court, and the Grahamstown Chamber of Commerce had protested to de Villiers, who had undertaken to insert the words 'by a single judge' as a drafting amendment 'to give effect to the undoubted intention of the Convention' that appeals from the Eastern Districts Court should go direct to the Appellate Division. These were the words which were inserted. Kotzé to de Villiers, 28 May 1909; Grahamstown Chamber of Commerce to de Villiers, 28 May 1909 (telegram); de Villiers Papers. De Villiers to Innes, 1 June 1909, Innes Papers.

tion 116 to provide that any appeals to the Privy Council which were pending at the establishment of the Union should be proceeded with as if the Act had not been passed.[47]

There were also two British proposals for amendments to section 147, which had been adopted in South Africa in the following form:

The control and administration of native affairs throughout the Union shall vest in the Governor-General-in-Council, who shall exercise all special powers in regard to native administration hitherto vested in the Governors of the Colonies or exercised by them as supreme chiefs.

One was for the insertion of words vesting the control and administration of 'matters specially or differentially affecting Asiatics', also, in the Governor-General-in-Council. Crewe explained that Lord Morley, Secretary of State for India, had asked him to secure the insertion, so that provincial governments would not be able to initiate discrimination against Asiatics. De Villiers and other delegates said that it was intended that Asiatic affairs should come under the control of the Union Government and that they saw no harm in accepting the proposal, which was agreed to. The other British proposal was for an addition to the section, explicitly giving the Governor-General-in-Council the powers over lands reserved for Natives which had previously been vested in the colonial governors or governors-in-council, and providing that such lands which could not previously be alienated without an act of a Colonial Parliament should not in future be alienated without an act of the Union Parliament. As Crewe explained, the purpose was to ensure that Native reserves should be as secure after Union as before. After some discussion this proposal, too, was accepted by the delegates with verbal changes.

None of the above proposals evoked opposition. The position was different, however, when the conference came to section 151. The British draft Bill included a proviso under which, so long as the protectorates were not included in the Union, the Union would pay them a fixed proportion of its customs revenue and would not impose differential customs duties nor railway rates on their produce. In promoting this proviso Crewe was anxious to ensure that the Union would be restrained from applying economic pressure on the protectorates. The delegates strongly objected. They assured Crewe that the protectorates would be treated fairly by the Union; but they said that so long as they remained outside the Union there was no justification for committing the Union to giving them better treatment than Rhodesia, and they complained that the

---

[47] De Villiers explained that he moved this addition on the suggestion of the registrar of the Privy Council.

pledge asked for was 'unilateral and not reciprocal'. Hofmeyr in particular was adamant in regarding the proposal as one which involved a new principle, and which the delegates consequently had no authority to accept.[48] But Crewe would not let the matter drop and it was still unresolved when the conference terminated on 21 July.

The South African delegates had come to the conference determined to resist the British proposals for amendments to the schedule, which they regarded as too numerous and too sweeping. Consequently, when the schedule was reached on the afternoon of the 20th de Villiers inquired whether it could not be dropped altogether; but Crewe replied that he regarded it as essential and that 'He did not think it would be possible to get the Bill through Parliament without the Schedule.' De Villiers then declared that the delegates 'were prepared to abide by the Schedule as it stands', that is to say, as drawn up in South Africa. Merriman went so far as to contend that it was unalterable. But Crewe was easily able to refute this argument, by referring to the letter which Lord Selborne had written to de Villiers on 15 December 1908 in which he had stated that the Secretary of State would still have the opportunity of proposing modifications to the schedule,[49] and by quoting from the letter which de Villiers had written to Selborne on 3 February 1909, when forwarding a copy of the convention's draft South Africa Act, in which he had written:[50]

The provisions relating to the Protectorates are dealt with in a Schedule to the Act. You will remember that these provisions were accepted by the Convention after prolonged informal negotiations between Your Excellency as High Commissioner and myself as President of the Convention and that, while the Schedule fairly represents the general principles on which the transfer of the Protectorates, whenever effected, should take place, it was clearly understood that it would be open to His Majesty's Government as well as to any delegation that may be appointed to confer with His Majesty's Government to suggest any modifications not inconsistent with these general principles.

In fact the British proposals for amendments to the schedule, though somewhat numerous, had for the most part been properly described by Crewe as 'amplifications' of the scheme agreed upon in South Africa and consistent with the principles of that scheme; and when they were discussed, clause by clause, many of them were agreed to by the delegates without opposition, either as they stood, or with minor verbal alterations,

[48] De Villiers to Crewe, 24 July 1909, de Villiers Papers (copy).
[49] See above, p. 274.
[50] House of Assembly, National Convention Minutes, V (copy).

while the omission of others was accepted by Lord Crewe. By the end of the conference the delegates had accepted amendments to eleven of the twenty-five clauses of the schedule;[51] but there were still several British proposals concerning the schedule (besides the British proposal concerning section 151 of the main body of the Bill) which had neither been withdrawn nor accepted, namely, a proposal for an insertion in clause 17, so that the Union would be unable to levy differential railway rates, as well as differential duties, on the produce of a transferred Protectorate; a proposal that in clauses 3 and 21 the amounts of the salaries and pensions of the members of the commission, which was to advise the Prime Minister on the administration of transferred protectorates, should be specified; and a proposal for an addition to clause 15. As drawn up in South Africa this clause read: 'The sale of liquor to natives shall be prohibited in the Territories.' In the British draft Bill it read:

The sale of intoxicating liquor to natives shall be prohibited in the Territories, and no provision giving facilities for introducing, obtaining, or possessing such liquor in any part of the Territories less stringent than those existing at the time of transfer shall be allowed.

Most of the delegates had been prepared to accept the British addition to this clause, but Hofmeyr and other Cape delegates had opposed it.

The questions which had been left undecided by the conference were settled by correspondence during the next few days. Crewe eventually dropped the proposed amendment to section 151 of the main body of the Bill after receiving a written assurance from de Villiers that 'the Delegates see no reason whatever to doubt that the liberal policy voluntarily pursued by the self-governing Colonies towards the territories in the past will under similar circumstances be continued by the Union even before the transfer of the territories'.[52] Crewe also dropped the proposed amendments to clauses 3, 17, and 21 of the schedule. On the other hand, Crewe warned de Villiers that if the delegates would not accept the proposed amendment to clause 15 of the schedule, it could be assumed that it would be moved when the Bill was before Parliament, in which case the Government would 'consider themselves at liberty to accept it'.[53] In discussing this most of the delegates preferred to accept the amendment rather than to risk its introduction during the passage of the Bill through Parliament, but Hofmeyr dug his toes in and (as he took pains to record), when the clause was put to the vote and de Villiers asked 'Is it agreed?'

[51] Clauses 1, 2, 3, 4, 10, 11, 13, 18, 19, 22, and 24.
[52] De Villiers to Crewe, 23 July 1909 (copy); reply, 27 July 1909. De Villiers Papers.
[53] Crewe to de Villiers, 22 July 1909, ibid.

Hofmeyr's last words were: 'No, *I* do not; I may submit, but *I do not agree.*'[54] De Villiers then informed Crewe that the delegates would accept the insertion so that 'nothing should be left undone which might prevent any further amendments being introduced by Parliament'.[55]

The result was that the South Africa Bill which was introduced into the British Parliament was in every detail accepted in advance by the South African delegation. Furthermore, it was essentially the same as the draft South Africa Act which had been approved by the South African parliaments in June. None of the alterations which had been made by the conference to the main body of the Bill had been disputed by critics as suspicious as Hertzog, Merriman, and Hofmeyr; and the only alteration to the Schedule to which Hofmeyr had objected was not, after all, a matter of very great moment.

The colonial office had also drafted Letters Patent for the creation of the office of Governor-General and Commander-in-Chief of the Union of South Africa and Royal Instructions to the Governor-General and Commander-in-Chief.[56] These documents followed the Canadian and Australian precedents except that they included the clause in the existing Instructions to the governors of the South African colonies relating to the exercise of the prerogative of pardon in capital cases. Under the draft Letters Patent a Governor-General and Commander-in-Chief of the Union was to be appointed under the royal Sign Manual and Signet, to perform his duties in accordance with the powers granted by the South Africa Act, by his commission, by such Instructions as might be given to him under the royal Sign Manual and Signet, or by royal order in the Privy Council or through a Secretary of State, and by the laws in force in the Union. They also provided for the creation of a Great Seal for the Union, and for the administration of the Government of the Union in the event of the absence of the Governor-General; they empowered the Governor-General to exercise the royal functions in respect of the summoning, proroguing, or dissolving of the Union Parliament; and they required the civil and military officers and ministers and all other inhabitants of the Union to obey the Governor-General or his deputy. The draft Royal Instructions provided that the Governor-General and his successors should publish the Letters Patent and take the Oaths of Allegiance and Office; that all persons holding offices of trust or profit in the Union should take the Oath of Allegiance; that the Instructions should

[54] Hofmeyr to de Villiers, 25 July 1909, de Villiers Papers.

[55] De Villiers to Crewe, 23 July 1909, ibid. (copy). In addition, a verbal amendment to the fourth paragraph of the preamble was agreed upon at the last minute without opposition from any delegate.

[56] Merriman Papers, No. 457/1909.

be communicated to the Executive Council; that information should be transmitted to the Secretary of State concerning laws assented to by him and Bills reserved for the royal pleasure; that the Governor-General should be able to exercise the prerogative of pardoning persons convicted of crimes after receiving the advice of at least one of his ministers in all cases except capital cases, when he was to consult the Executive Council; and that he should not leave the Union for more than one month, except for certain defined purposes, without the permission of the Secretary of State. They also provided that the Governor-General was to reserve for the King's pleasure any Bill which he was required to reserve by the South Africa Act, and any Bill which the Secretary of State had specially instructed him to reserve.

De Villiers and the four South African prime ministers conferred with Crewe on the subject on 26 July. The South Africans asked for a few changes, of which the most significant was that in the absence of the Governor-General the administration of the Government of the Union should be exercised by the Chief Justice, instead of by the senior military officer as provided in the draft Letters Patent.[57] All of their requests were incorporated in the revised drafts which Crewe sent to Merriman and Smuts at the end of August. The revised draft of the Royal Instructions also included a specific requirement that 'in particular' the Governor-General should reserve any Bill disqualifying any person in the Cape Province from being registered as a voter by reason of his race or colour only. By that time most of the delegates had left London, but Merriman and Smuts informed Crewe that they agreed that the documents in their final form were in accordance with the spirit of their discussion.[58]

The date of the inauguration of the Union was not settled at the conference on 26 July. Merriman, believing that delay would cause a 'feeling of insecurity' and 'great dissatisfaction', wished the Union to be inaugurated on 1 January 1910, and the election of the first Parliament to take place during April 1910; but Botha and Fischer wanted to have more time for party organization and Botha also feared that his party would be at a disadvantage unless the elections were held during the South African summer. Botha had previously contended that Merriman had accepted his request during a discussion in Bloemfontein in May, but Merriman had denied that this was so and had tried unavailingly to persuade Botha to consent to the immediate appointment of the members of the Delimitation Commission on an informal basis, so that the

---

[57] 'Meeting at Colonial Office, 26th July, 1909', Merriman Papers.
[58] Crewe to Merriman, 25 Aug. 1909; reply, 26 Aug. 1909 (copy). Ibid. *Union Gov. Gaz.* 1 of 1910.

parliamentary election would not be delayed by the unavailability of the commission's report.[59] On 25 July de Villiers and the prime ministers discussed the question in London, but they were unable to reach agreement.[60] Two days later, however, the question was settled at a full meeting of the delegates: the Union was to be inaugurated on 31 May 1910—the eighth anniversary of the Peace of Vereeniging—and the general election would follow in October or November. Botha had had his way.[61]

The delegates met for the last time on 30 July, to bid farewell to de Villiers, who sailed back to South Africa the next day because his wife had suffered a severe stroke. He left with the good wishes of all his fellow delegates, who presented him with a silver president's hammer with an ivory handle, carrying the engraved arms of the colonies in gold.[62] He also left with the knowledge that all was well with the Bill. It had already passed its second reading in the House of Lords and he had Crewe's assurance that

> The Bill is in quite smooth water, I am confident; and the demonstration which the very well-intentioned, but on this occasion unwise, advocates of native claims may make in the House of Commons will not in any way endanger it. We are all greatly indebted to you for your wise guidance and help during the negotiations here, the friendly character of which was the greatest possible satisfaction to me.[63]

4. THE SOUTH AFRICA BILL IN THE HOUSE OF LORDS[64]

Moving the second reading of the South Africa Bill in the House of Lords on 22 July, the Secretary of State, Lord Crewe, made an elaborate statement of the attitude of His Majesty's Government. He first sketched the efforts which had been made to federate South Africa in the second half of the nineteenth century, remarking that Carnarvon's scheme had failed because 'it was not home-made'.[65] The present legislation, he continued, had been facilitated by the decision of the Campbell-Bannerman Government to grant self-government to the former republics, and the historian of the future would give credit 'to the general political creed

---

[59] Telegrams and copies of telegrams between Merriman, Sauer, Fischer, and Botha, 22, 23, 24 June 1909, Transvaal Archives, Prime Minister, LX (ii). See above, pp. 324–5, 383.

[60] Merriman's Diary, 25 July 1909. The entry concludes: '*Mistrust Transvaal.*'

[61] Ibid., 27 July 1909; de Villiers to Crewe, 27 July 1909, de Villiers Papers (copy).

[62] Walker, *de Villiers*, pp. 482–6.

[63] Crewe to de Villiers, 30 July 1909, de Villiers Papers.

[64] *Parl. Deb.*, 5th Ser., Lords, ii. 753–97 (second reading), 855–70 (committee), 913 (third reading). [65] Col. 755.

held by the Government, to their more robust faith in the virtues of self-government as such than their predecessors probably held'.[66] Credit was also due to Selborne and the other South African governors, and to the 'remarkable band of statesmen in South Africa, representing all parties and both races, who have set to work and carried through this business'.[67] After expressing approval of the unitary form of the Constitution, he dwelt on three major aspects of the Bill which concerned the non-whites. Firstly, as regards the 'European descent' qualification for membership of the Union Parliament:[68]

I say frankly that there does seem to me to be a strong case against the insertion of such a provision in this Act or in any Act. There are men not of European descent who are of high standing, of high character, and of high ability. They regard this provision as a slight, and we regret that any loyal subjects of the King should consider themselves slighted.

On the other hand, the difficulties which have confronted those who have prepared this Bill were no doubt considerable. In the first place it is only in the Cape that the native has a vote; and therefore it would seem anomalous to allow a man to sit in an Assembly for which the class to which he belongs have not a vote in the greater part of the Union.

It is also fair to point out that in the Australian Commonwealth a similar restriction exists,[69] so that therefore, this cannot be said to be without precedent. It is also true that the grievance is probably not a practical one, because if it was the case that no coloured member was elected to the Cape Assembly in the past it is extremely improbable, at any rate for a long time to come, that any such would be elected to the Union Parliament. The fact which has decided us in not attempting to press this matter against the wishes of the South African delegates has been that this is undoubtedly one of those matters which represents a delicately balanced compromise between themselves. As a Government we cannot take—and personally I am not prepared to take—the responsibility for the possible wrecking of this Union measure altogether by a provision of this kind; and I am assured that such would be the result of any attempt to insert such a provision in the Bill. The cause of those who desire this change to be made has been pressed with deep feeling and much eloquence by some of the natives themselves, and by those who specially represent their cause. But I do feel that if this change is to be made it must be made in South Africa by South Africans themselves, and that it is not possible for us, whatever we may consider to be the special merits of the case, to attempt to force it upon the great representative body which with absolute unanimity demands that it should not appear.

Secondly, as regards the franchise, Crewe declared that there did not

---

[66] Col. 756.　　　　　　[67] Col. 757.　　　　　　[68] Cols. 759–60.

[69] Australian aborigines were excluded from the franchise and from membership of the State and Commonwealth parliaments.

seem to be much risk of a two-thirds majority being obtained in the Union Parliament for the elimination of the Cape franchise. He continued:[70]

It has also to be remembered that this is a matter on which we could not say that the power of disallowance which, of course, belongs to the Crown, would not be exercised. Certainly it is not too much to say that the disfranchisement of a class who had held this power of voting so long would be viewed here with very deep disappointment. Disfranchisement is always an odious thing in itself, and if it were to be applied in this particular manner I am bound to say that it would assume a somewhat specially odious form. Consequently I myself refuse to believe that there is any probability that this particular provision will be carried into effect. Looking at it as a purely abstract question, we could wish that the safeguard might be even stronger, but such as it is I am prepared to consider it strong enough. I may remind your Lordships also that there is a provision for the reservation of all constitutional Bills, and for reservation subject to instructions received from the Crown; and all Bills which desire to alter any provision in the Schedule are automatically reserved.

Thirdly, as regards the protectorates:[71]

... Clause 151 of the Bill ... enables what are known as the Protectorates possibly at some future time to be transferred to the care of the Union under regulations provided for in a Schedule. ... We felt bound to regard ourselves as trustees for these bodies of natives, and considering that it does not do for a trustee to hand over his trust to another man, however great his personal confidence may be in him, without a guarantee that the trust itself will be taken over, we decided to ask South Africa to accept the provisions embodied in the Schedule. Some opposition has been raised to the Schedule from two very different quarters. Some think that under no circumstances ought the native Protectorates to be handed over to the Union at all.

Here I may say that we have no desire, we are in no hurry, to hand over these areas to anyone. They are contented, they are not otherwise than prosperous, and we have no desire to part with them; in fact, they have expressed themselves as averse to passing from under the direct administration of the Crown. But we do feel that in any case that suggestion involves an impossibility. It does not seem conceivable that for an indefinite future these areas should remain administered from here and that the new South African Union should have no lot or part in their administration. Nor do I believe, in view of the varying circumstances of these districts, that it is possible to name a time limit and say, at any rate, we will not hand over a particular area for a fixed number of years. ...

On the other hand, there are those who contemplate the Protectorates

being handed over, but consider that it is not necessary to make any preliminary arrangement with regard to them, and that it would be better to
wait and deal with each case as it arises. To my mind there are strong
objections to that course. It is extremely advantageous to lay down, as we
have laid down in the Schedule, with the full concurrence of South African
opinion, certain general principles in order that continuity of administration
may exist, and in order that, above all, uncertainty may be avoided. By
introducing this Schedule we at any rate obtain a certain uniform and
agreed standard of administration. What weighs with me as much as anything is that the natives themselves are not anxious to be transferred, but,
admitting that they may be some day transferred, actively desire the incorporation of a charter such as this in the Act itself. To me those reasons seem
conclusive for the existence of this somewhat unusual form of provision in
the form of a Schedule.

Crewe then summarized the contents of the schedule and also explained
that, although the Bill did not guard against the imposition of differential duties or railway rates against the protectorates so long as they were
under British administration, he was satisfied with the delegates' assurance that they saw no reason to doubt that the liberal policy pursued by
the colonies, by which the protectorates had been admitted to the Customs Union, would be continued, 'first, because that opinion was freely
and willingly given; and, secondly, because any action of the kind
directed against a territory under the administration of the Crown would
be so grave from every point of view, would approach so nearly to what,
in the language of diplomacy, would be described as an unfriendly act,
that I do not for a moment contemplate the possibility of any such
occurrence'.[72]

In his peroration Crewe declared that the movement towards union
had already done much good in bringing leading South Africans together
in intimate contact and that the achievement of union would mark 'a
great advance in the fusion of the races which inhabit South Africa'.[73]
He hoped they would remain 'joined in a free union under the supremacy of the British Crown, with a guaranteed freedom, for as many
years in front of us as the imagination of man can venture to look'.[74] The
unification of South Africa would also, he said, place the self-governing
British dominions in something like their final form:[75]

There is the great American group, the great Pacific group, and the great
African group. There may be some re-arrangement and some modification,
but it is, I think, reasonable to say that for many years to come, longer than
the life of any of us here, these three great divisions will form the main

[72] Col. 766.   [73] Ibid.
[74] Ibid.   [75] Cols. 767–8.

self-governing parts of the British Empire outside these islands. This fact will enable the advisers of the Crown here and in the Colonies and Dominions abroad to deal with questions of Imperial defence with more certainty and with greater freedom than they have been able to deal with them hitherto. . . . If it should ever be the fact, as I hope it may, that it is found possible to solve the very difficult problem of co-operation all over the Empire in the policy of the Empire, to that achievement this Act of African Union is a necessary preliminary. I believe, therefore, that there will be no part of the Empire which will not give a most hearty welcome to the new South Africa, with earnest prayers that she may both merit and enjoy the rewards of prosperity and the blessings of peace.

Six other peers participated in the debate. Three of them were distinguished Unionists who had held the highest offices in the Empire. Lord Northcote, a former Governor-General of Canada, declared that 'the whole idea underlying the sentiments of the independent and yet inter-dependent members of the . . . British Empire', not only in South Africa, but also in Canada and Australia, was 'the determination to have white rule and white responsibility for the conduct of public affairs'.[76] Canada had recently been thrown into agitation by a threatened influx of Japanese immigrants; Australia was determined to preserve its whiteness; and he therefore had no difficulty in accepting the provisions in the Bill concerning the non-whites. Lord Curzon, a former viceroy of India, who had toured South Africa while the National Convention was in session, observed that the Bill was the indubitable expression of the will of white South Africa. He agreed with the conduct of the British Government on the issues affecting the non-whites. The protectorates would have to be transferred in due course, because there could not possibly be a permanent system of dual control in South Africa. The exclusion of Natives from the Union Parliament was to be regretted on abstract grounds, but it had to be accepted because insistence might wreck the Union. It was not in the least likely that public opinion in South Africa or in Britain would allow the Cape non-whites to be deprived of their voting rights. On the contrary, he hoped that public opinion in South Africa would 'steadily move in the opposite and more liberal direction in the future'.[77] Union would promote the development of a national conscience and 'produce large and broad-minded statesmen who will take a wide rather than the petty and narrower view both of local and Imperial affairs'.[78] Furthermore, the tensions between Boer and Briton in South Africa had already been 'submerged' and he looked forward to 'an increasing amalgamation of the white races'. The Bill, indeed, 'will be not

[76] Col. 769. [77] Col. 776. [78] Col. 777.

only the dawn of a new era in South Africa, but will prove a positive and most important landmark in the history of the civilised world [*sic*]'.[79] The Marquis of Lansdowne, who had held the offices of Governor-General of Canada, Viceroy of India, Secretary of State for War, and Foreign Secretary, and was the leader of the Unionist peers, declared that self-government having been granted to the South African colonies it was not for the British Parliament to question their decisions on matters of detail. The Bill was clearly for the good of the colonies and the Empire and so, although he regretted the exclusion of non-whites from Parliament and doubted whether the two-thirds majority was a sufficient safeguard for the Cape franchise, he accepted it as it stood. Lord Milner and Lord Selborne, who were sitting next to one another on the cross-benches, did not participate in the debate.

The only criticism of the Bill came from Lord Courtney, a Liberal peer who was President of the English Proportional Representation Society and had been an ardent pro-Boer during the South African War. He entirely agreed with the provisions concerning the relations between the different sections of the white population of South Africa. 'But when the representatives of the European communities there go further and lay down principles which shall govern the organisation of South Africa in the future with regard to the overwhelming black population, then I think we may be entitled to question their authority; and if we do not go to the length of pressing our opinions on their acceptance, we may at least state them and invite their consideration.'[80] The Government should have insisted on the removal of the European descent qualification for membership of the Union Parliament; and either the schedule should have been omitted, so that when the transfer of a protectorate was proposed the conditions could have been worked out in relation to the merits of the case, or the precautions laid down in the schedule should have been considerably stiffened, for as they stood they were 'very shadowy and unsubstantial'.[81] In conclusion, Courtney predicted that the Government of a large non-white majority by a relatively small white minority would lead to unrest, instability, and danger.

The Archbishop of Canterbury, R. T. Davidson, on the other hand, was willing for the Bill to pass without amendment. He regretted the colour-bar, but he would not oppose it, because that would wreck the Bill. He supposed that they should accept the 'principle' that for the present it was justifiable to impose on the South African Native restrictions and limitations 'which correspond to those which we impose on children', and he believed that 'the larger, sounder, and more

[79] Ibid. [80] Col. 779. [81] Col. 785.

Christian principles will in the long run prevail in South Africa as years advance'.[82]

Replying to the debate Lord Loreburn, the Lord Chancellor, a former pro-Boer, reiterated the attitude of the Government to the sections dealing with the non-whites. It was not possible to press for amendments, firstly, because the Bill was a compromise between different points of view in South Africa, secondly, because 'the doctrine of non-interference with the wishes of self-governing Colonies in regard to their own confines is thoroughly well established between both Parties',[83] and, thirdly, because the provisions in question affected the lives and business of people 6,000 miles away. Nevertheless, he hoped and believed that 'there will be in good time an admission of the native element in South Africa'.[84] The Bill was then read a second time without a division being called.

During the committee stage, which was taken on 3 August, four amendments were moved. In section 26 Lord Courtney moved an amendment to enable men not of European descent to become eligible for membership of the Union Senate as representatives of the Cape Province or Natal. He admitted that he would hesitate to press the amendment to a division, but he moved it, he said, 'for the purpose of eliciting, if possible, another chorus of agreement as to the painful character of this disqualification'.[85] Crewe agreed that there was 'something like a general concurrence of opinion that in itself this provision is an undesirable one', but, he added, 'there was an equally marked and declared concurrence that it would not be wise for your Lordships to attempt to amend that provision'.[86] To attempt to force such an amendment on white opinion in South Africa would defer rather than accelerate 'progress in the direction of equality between the white and the native races'.[87] The amendment was negatived without a division. In section 35 Lord MacDonnell moved the insertion of a time limit of ten years, within which no law should be passed to disqualify non-white voters on the ground of race. Crewe contended that the amendment would seem to invite reconsideration of the matter at the end of the ten years. He said that he was not so much afraid of what might happen in the early years, when the passing of the Act would be fresh in the minds of the South African delegates who had come to England, as he was of 'a sudden wave of feeling arising at some future and remote time'.[88] This amendment was then withdrawn. In section 151 Lord Courtney moved one amendment for the insertion of a time limit of ten years within which no protectorate

[82] Cols. 790–1.   [83] Col. 796.   [84] Col. 797.
[85] Col. 857.   [86] Cols. 858–9.   [87] Col. 860.
[88] Col. 865.

should be transferred, and another to prohibit the transfer of a protectorate 'until the terms and conditions of the transfer are made known to the Chiefs and inhabitants of such territory, and opportunity is given them to express their desires with respect to such transfer, or in support of any modification in its terms and conditions'.[89] Crewe denied Courtney's contention that the South African governments would agree to the omission of section 151 and the schedule, or to the insertion of a ten-year time limit. The first of these amendments, he said, would be tantamount to saying that no protectorate should be transferred for ten years and that then all three should be transferred; whereas he thought it was probable that a request for the transfer of Swaziland would be made within ten years and he could not say that such a request could be refused, and he declined to make any forecast as to if or when the others might or ought to be transferred to the Union. The second amendment

really only represents what is practically certain to occur if and when any transfer is proposed. My noble friend very rightly does not attempt to give the local chiefs an absolute veto on transfer; he merely desires that they should be consulted and their wishes should be considered. Of course, they will be consulted. I cannot imagine any High Commissioner or any Government in this country who would not consider most carefully the wishes of the chiefs and the natives in such a case as that; but I should not be prepared to say that the mere expression of a preference for remaining under the direct government of this country could be taken as an absolute bar to a transfer at some future time.[90]

Both amendments were then negatived without a division and the Bill was reported without amendment. The next day, 4 August, the Bill was read a third time and passed the House of Lords without further debate.

5. THE SOUTH AFRICA BILL IN THE HOUSE OF COMMONS[91]

Colonel J. E. B. Seely, the Colonial Under-Secretary, moved the second reading of the South Africa Bill in a thin House of Commons on 16 August. Mentioning Botha by name, he paid a tribute to the Boer leaders who had been 'foremost . . . in promoting that union of sentiment, that feeling of common nationality which has enabled this Bill to be introduced'.[92] Union would produce 'manifold advantages'[93] for the Natives of South Africa, because it would cause greater prosperity, in

[89] Col. 870. [90] Cols. 869–70.
[91] *Parl. Deb.*, 5th Ser., Commons, ix. 951–1058 (second reading), 1533–1656 (committee), 1656–60 (third reading). [92] Col. 952. [93] Col. 963.

which the Natives would share, and because Native affairs would come under the central government, which would have the best brains in South Africa at its disposal. He warned the house that any amendment of the principles in the Bill would 'smash the Union', since the delegates were bound by their instructions. .

Amendments of principle they cannot, they may not, they have not the power to accept. If we make any Amendment[s] of principle then they must go back to their Parliament[s] and ask that they be endorsed, and that whole long business will have to be gone over again. Whether we will be likely to get what we want, after having exacerbated feeling by interfering, is a very doubtful matter.[94]

Furthermore, although there were some provisions in the Bill which the Government regretted, there were none to which they could take over-riding objection. The constitutions which the Government itself had recently drawn up for the Transvaal and the Orange River Colony had included political colour-bars. The protection for the Cape franchise seemed to be perfectly adequate, for three reasons. He knew of no precedent for the disfranchisement of a great body of people 'in democratic times';[95] the Cape province would have fifty-nine representatives out of a total of 161 in a joint sitting of both Houses of the Union Parliament and four of the others would be senators specially nominated to look after Native interests; and even if a two-thirds majority was obtained in such a joint sitting there would still be the reservation safeguard, which was by no means illusory. The schedule was designed to protect the interests of the Native inhabitants of the protectorates. It was 'purely permissive'. It did not bring transfer any nearer; on the contrary, it made it 'somewhat more difficult'. Transfer might take place 'in the long distant years' and then it would probably be so gradual 'that the natives will never know from anything that occurs to them that the transition has been effected'; but if the question should arise during the life-time of the present Government, the House would certainly have the fullest opportunity of considering the matter before any territory was transferred.[96] Finally, Seely declared that 'This is a real and not a paper Union. It is a deep and lasting Union.'[97] Credit was due to many people, but above all to Campbell-Bannerman:

Without him Union might never have been, for without self-government Union was impossible. . . . Union is the will of the people, and without self-government the people's views cannot be heard. . . . To-day South Africa

---

[94] Col. 963.   [95] Col. 960.
[96] Cols. 957–8.   [97] Col. 964.

comes to us again bringing this Bill as a token of final reconciliation. Shall we not trust them again?[98]

The motion was seconded by Alfred Lyttelton, who had been Secretary of State for the Colonies from Chamberlain's resignation in 1903 until the fall of the Balfour Ministry in December 1905. He fully endorsed the Government's attitude to the Bill. While he recognized that W. P. Schreiner was a man of 'great ability and lofty character', he thought that the House should remember the Government's assurance that it was the will of South Africa that they should pass 'the Bill, the whole Bill, and nothing but the Bill'.[99] The United States of America was an example of what happened when a country was 'misled by rhetoricians'[1] into laying down absolute civic equality for non-whites in a constitution—the franchise thus granted had become useless to the Negroes in practice and had had disastrous effects upon the American people. Rather than follow such a precedent they should 'face the real facts and . . . acknowledge that the black races are not the equals of the white'.[2] Moreover, once responsible government had been granted to a colonial people, as in South Africa, they should trust them completely. Therefore they should not tamper with the Bill. Lyttelton also endorsed Seely's tribute to Botha and agreed that the grant of responsible government had won the goodwill of the Boer people; but he insisted that the South African war and the work of post-war reconstruction by Lord Milner had been necessary steps towards union.

Three critics of the colour-bar then came into the debate. Sir Charles Dilke (Liberal) admitted that the difficulties of the Government were enormous and that there was a great temptation to hope, even 'against our better reason', that things would come right in South Africa; but he could not but deplore the fact that the Bill entirely ignored the ultimate fate of the majority of the inhabitants of South Africa, who were 'to be governed by an absolute and permanent oligarchy'.[3] They had previously been told that one of the main objects of the South African War was to be the triumph of the Cape colonial principle of equal rights for all civilized men over the Boer republican principle of an absolute political colour-bar. Now they were being asked to allow the republican principle to predominate throughout South Africa.

I do not wish to be an alarmist, but I do not think it can be said that we are strengthening the Imperial fabric, in an Empire where there are 360

---

[98] Col. 965. [99] Col. 966. [1] Col. 967.
[2] Ibid. [3] Col. 974.

millions of coloured people under our rule, by this non-Federal Union in South Africa under such conditions.[4]

J. Keir Hardie (Labour) spoke much more strongly. He quoted statements by Botha, Smuts, and other South Africans, to show that they might be intending to destroy the Cape franchise. Economic competition, he contended, was causing white South African opinion to become less liberal rather than more liberal. No member of the House could justify the colour-bar and it was nonsense to maintain that amendments would wreck the Union. In its present form it was a Bill to unify the whites, to disfranchise the non-whites, and to embitter their relationship; and 'for the first time we are asked to write over the portals of the British Empire: "Abandon hope all ye who enter here."'[5] E. J. Griffith (Liberal) then pointed out that the Bill had been prepared by an all-white convention and had been opposed by many representative gatherings of non-whites. He predicted that in practice the imperial veto and the reservation of constitutional Bills would amount to nothing; and he concluded:

The security of South Africa, the security of white rule in South Africa, the security of Imperial supremacy in South Africa, depends to a large extent upon the willing and active loyalty of the subject races, and we must be careful not to strain that loyalty too far.[6]

The debate was then taken on to a more philosophical plane by the Leader of the Opposition, A. J. Balfour, who elaborated some of the assertions which had been made by Lyttelton. They were discussing 'one of the most important events in the history of the Empire, one of the great landmarks of Imperial policy, whose consequences I believe . . . will be felt long after the generation which assents to this Bill has passed away and been forgotten'.[7] The problem of relations between Europeans and Africans was entirely new and extremely complex; and no conclusive solution had yet been found. The United States of America had not solved it. After starting with 'a very crude *a priori* statement of the equality of mankind and a brutal application of the most rigid principles of slavery', they had later abolished slavery and come face to face with 'the immutable principles of their Constitution, which laid down, in true eighteenth century language, that all men were equal'.[8] Balfour continued:

All men are, from some points of view, equal; but, to suppose that the races of Africa are in any sense the equals of men of European descent, so

---

[4] Col. 977.   [5] Col. 994.   [6] Cols. 999–1000.
[7] Col. 1000.   [8] Col. 1001.

far as government, as society, as the higher interests of civilisation are concerned, is really, I think, an absurdity which every man who seriously looks
at this most difficult problem must put out of his mind if he is to solve the
problem at all.

   . . . If the races of Europe have really conquered, by centuries of difficulty
and travail, great rights and privileges for themselves, they have given some
of those rights and some of those privileges to men quite incapable, by themselves, of fighting for them at all, or obtaining them at all. That is the plain
historic truth of the situation, which it is perfect folly for us to attempt to
forget. It is that very fact of the inequality of the races which makes the
difficulty. If the races were equal the matter would be simple. Give them all
the same rights, put them on precise political equality, but if you think, as
I am forced to think, that there is an inequality, not necessarily affecting
every individual, but really affecting the two races . . . you cannot give them
equal rights without threatening the whole fabric of your civilisation. If that
is true, the problem comes up before us in this extraordinarily embarrassing
shape: how is a race, determined to have for itself equal rights and Constitutional freedom, who thinks that it ought to extend to every race justice,
equity, kindness, forbearance, everything that education and equality of
opportunity can give, to carry out that idea, if that is their idea, as I hope
it is, within the framework of any Constitution?[9]

Most of the critics of the Bill seemed to think that the best way to solve
the problem was for the Imperial Parliament to maintain a strict control
over the parliament which was being created in South Africa. But if that
were attempted, South Africans would feel that their most vital interests
were being decided by people who were not on the spot, who would not
suffer from any mistakes, and who knew nothing about the problem
except what they could get from emotional speeches. Collision between
the Imperial Parliament and the South African Parliament would then
be inevitable; and that would be no solution. The best hope of finding a
solution was to give the South African Parliament full control—'all the
duties, all the responsibilities of action, all the rewards if that action is to
be successful, and all the penalties if that action is to fail'[10]—even if that
meant that the South African Parliament would act illiberally, as would
very likely be the case. Consequently, although he disliked some of the
features of the Bill, he was prepared to accept it as it stood, in the light of
the Government's assurance that amendments of principle would wreck
it. For the most part he heartily approved of the Bill, which was 'the most
wonderful issue' out of all the divisions of the past between Boer and
Briton in South Africa. 'I do not believe the world shows anything like it
in its whole history.'[11] It had come about partly because all the members

---

[9] Cols. 1001–3.   [10] Col. 1004.   [11] Col. 1006.

of the House, however violently they may have differed about the war itself, were agreed that the white race should be dominant in South Africa and that there should be equal rights for all white men. He still had misgivings about the future, however, because the black population was likely to remain far in excess of the white population.

Darkness hangs over that problem. . . . All that we can do now is to make the best machinery we can for dealing with that problem, and I am convinced that . . . the only glimmer of hope of dealing successfully with the real race problem in South Africa, is not to attempt to meddle with it ourselves, but, having made this Union Parliament, to trust the men of a like way of thinking as ourselves to rise to the occasion . . . and . . . to meet this new problem . . . with all the courage, and, above all, with all the humanity and all the sympathy which is possible, unhampered by interference from this island, which, however well meant, may perhaps be ignorant, and whether it be ignorant or whether it be not, will undoubtedly be resented by those who may endeavour to control it.[12]

The Prime Minister, H. H. Asquith, followed Balfour, and his speech showed how close the two front benches had at last drawn in their attitude towards South Africa. He agreed that the problem of evolving free institutions in a community where two races in different stages of civilization were intermixed was essentially a modern problem, which was still unsolved; and that it was to be found in its most acute and complex form in South Africa, where the so-called inferior race vastly outnumbered the more advanced race alongside which it had been placed. He did not, however, take quite so strong a view as Balfour of the inherent and indelible differences between races; and he thought that the experience of the Cape Colony had shown that some at least of the non-whites of South Africa had a potentiality for progress which a wise Government should encourage and stimulate. Nevertheless, he was sure that South Africans should be left to determine their own future; and he believed that they would do so more wisely if they were united than if they were to remain divided between separate colonies.

Any control or interference from outside, particularly any interference from a distance, spasmodic interference . . . interference often ill-informed and sometimes sentimental . . . is the very worst in the interests of the natives themselves. . . . In my judgment, you are more likely to have a satisfactory . . . development of the native question . . ., when the problem is taken in hand, not by the several States individually and independently, but by a common body representing South Africa as a whole. . . . I anticipate that, as one of the many incidental advantages which the Union of

[12] Col. 1008.

South Africa is going to bring about, it will prove to be a harbinger of a native policy more consistent, and, as some of us may think, more enlightened than that which has been pursued by some communities in the past.[13]

Asquith then dealt specifically with the sections of the Bill which had been criticized, and he deliberately repeated Seely's assertion that if the House insisted on any amendment of principle 'for the time being at any rate, the prospects of Union in South Africa would be wrecked'.[14]

Three other members delivered polemics against the colour-bar. W. P. Byles (Liberal) described it as 'a poisonous principle which vitally effects the honour, character and reputation which England has built up for herself before the world';[15] G. H. Roberts (Labour) claimed that it would force non-whites to adopt unconstitutional methods and predicted a revival of krugerism; and A. Lupton (Liberal) considered that no case had been made for the Bill, that the House was being insulted in being told that it must not amend it, and that Britain should intervene before it was too late—while South Africa was still disunited and while there were still British troops there. On the other hand, eight more members spoke in support of the Bill, though practically every one of them said he regretted the colour-bar. They included two Liberals of South African origin—P. A. Molteno, a son of the first Prime Minister of the Cape Colony, and A. C. Beck—who based their case on the doctrine of non-intervention in the affairs of self-governing colonies.

The motion that the Bill be read a second time was then agreed to without a division being called.

Before the committee stage started the Government issued a whip to all Liberal members stating that it could not accept any amendment. Nevertheless, not only did the Labour Party attend in strength to support amendments, but nearly thirty Liberals decided to ignore the whip. There was a preliminary skirmish over section 24, to which two amendments were moved—one by Dilke, that four of the eight nominated senators should be nominated by the Governor-General instead of by the Governor-General-in-Council, in the hope that they would thereby be immune from party influence; and the other by George Greenwood (Liberal), for the deletion of the word 'reasonable' from the provision that four of the nominated senators were to be selected 'on the ground . . . of their thorough acquaintance . . . with the reasonable wants and wishes of the coloured races in South Africa'. Opposing the second of these amendments Seely said:

Amendments of principle cannot be accepted by the terms of the Instruction given to the delegates. Amendments in detail presumably may be, but the question of what is an Amendment of detail and what is an Amendment in principle may be one of some difficulty. Therefore if you accept Amendments in detail, and if the delegates afterwards find that in the view of their Parliaments they involve questions of principle, you may wreck the whole great scheme. . . . I ask the Committee to realise, for the reasons I have given, we cannot amend on points of detail without running the risk of losing this great Bill.[16]

E. J. Griffith and H. F. Luttrell (Liberal) and Keir Hardie protested that Seely was asking the House to abdicate its proper functions, but Balfour agreed with Seely, saying that it was best that the House, having unanimously agreed to the second reading, should accept the Bill 'graciously and without meticulous objections in points of detail or principle'.[17] Both amendments were then withdrawn. The critics of the colour-bar then made their main stand on an amendment to section 26, which was moved by G. N. Barnes (Labour) to entitle non-whites to become members of the Senate as representatives of the Cape Province and Natal. They contended that to exclude non-whites from Parliament was a negation of the British imperial tradition (Dilke); that an amendment could be negotiated with the colonial delegates, as had been done with the Australian delegates in 1900, without wrecking the prospects of union (Keir Hardie and Ramsay MacDonald); and that white South Africans would never of their own accord adopt a more liberal policy (Ramsay MacDonald). Others declared that to pass the amendment would be to wreck union (Asquith, Balfour, Seely); that the South African Parliament could be counted on to remove the colour-bar without unreasonable delay (Asquith); that it was now too late—the vital decisions had been made in the Treaty of Vereeniging and in the Transvaal and Orange River Colony Constitutions (H. Cox and J. A. Simon, Liberal, and A. Lyttelton); that the amendment could be distinguished from the one which had been made in the Australian Constitution (Simon); and that the new South African nation was 'plainly a nation of white men', which had 'the right, and even the duty, to maintain its European character'[18] (S. Gwynn, Irish Nationalist). Asquith concluded his remarks with an appeal 'with whatever authority and emphasis I can command to the Committee not to wreck this great work',[19] and Balfour supported him. Seely 'vehemently' repudiated the assertion that there was any retrogression of white opinion in South Africa—on the contrary, 'I have seen the most striking and enormous advance in generosity and in the humane treatment of the natives in South Africa'.[20] A division was called and the

[16] Col. 1547.   [17] Col. 1550.   [18] Col. 1576.   [19] Col. 1564.   [20] Col. 1598.

amendment was defeated by 157 votes to 57, the minority consisting of twenty-eight Labour members, twenty-six Liberals, and three Irish Nationalists.

Sixteen more amendments were moved. Two were amendments to section 34—for the division of the seats in the House of Assembly between the provinces to be based, not on the white male adult population, but on their total numbers of voters (Keir Hardie), and on their white male adults 'and other British subjects qualified to vote'[21] (Griffith). Six were to section 35 (i)—to open the way for female suffrage (P. Snowden, Labour); to provide the same protection for non-whites in Natal as for those in the Cape Province (Keir Hardie); to omit the means whereby the South African Parliament might pass a law disfranchising Cape voters on grounds of race (Griffith); to make such disfranchisement require the approval of two-thirds of the Cape Province members of both Houses (R. W. Essex, Liberal); to make it require the sanction of an Act of the Imperial Parliament (Lupton); and to ensure that any disfranchising Bill would be reserved for the signification of His Majesty's pleasure (G. Greenwood, Liberal). In section 64 G. N. Barnes (Labour) proposed the reservation of all Bills 'which in any way affect native territories'.[22] Dilke moved the omission of section 147, which vested the control of Native affairs in the Governor-General-in-Council. In section 151 Keir Hardie proposed to make the transfer of a protectorate impossible for ten years. C. Duncan (Labour) moved an addition to section 152, requiring any amendment to the schedule to be passed by the joint sitting, two-thirds majority procedure. Finally, Griffith and Keir Hardie each moved two amendments to the schedule. Both front benches steadfastly opposed these proposals and they were all withdrawn, except one of Griffith's amendments to the schedule, which was negatived without a division. The Bill was then reported without amendment.

Moving the third reading on 19 August, the Prime Minister made a solemn appeal to South Africa. The debates had shown, he said, that the House of Commons unanimously regretted the colour-bar provisions.

I wish, before this Bill leaves the Imperial Parliament, to make it perfectly clear that we here have exercised, and I think wisely and legitimately exercised, not only restraint of expression, but reserve of judgment in regard to matters of this kind, simply because we desire this great experiment of . . . complete self-government in South Africa to start on the lines and in accordance with the ideas which our fellow citizens there have deliberately and after long deliberation come to. . . .

[21] Col. 1612.   [22] Col. 1641.

Speaking for myself and for the Government, I venture to express not only the hope but the expectation . . . that the views which have been so strongly . . . given utterance to here, will be sympathetically considered by our fellow citizens there. For my part I think, as I have said throughout, that it would be far better that any relaxation of what many of us, almost all of us, regard as unnecessary restrictions from the electoral rights or rights of eligibility of our fellow subjects should be carried out spontaneously, and on the initiative of the South African Parliament, rather than they should appear to be forced upon them by the Imperial Parliament here. While we part from this measure without any . . . Amendment . . . I am sure our fellow subjects will not take it in bad part if we respectfully and very earnestly beg them at the same time that they, in the exercise of their un-doubted and unfettered freedom, should find it possible sooner or later, and sooner rather than later, to modify the provisions.[23]

On behalf of the Opposition, Walter Long endorsed the Prime Minister's remarks, declaring that he had spoken not for a party, but for the entire House. Keir Hardie then announced that the Labour Party would not divide the House against the third reading of the Bill, because to do so would diminish the effect of the Prime Minister's appeal; but it fervently hoped that the amendments which had been suggested would be enacted in South Africa at the first opportunity. Finally, A. Lupton (Liberal), seeking to gain a hearing amid cries of 'Agreed', insisted that no case had been made for the Bill, that the only 'conspicuous thing' it did was to establish a colour-bar, and that he would always feel ashamed of it. But he was shouted down and the third reading was agreed to without a division.[24]

[23] Cols. 1656–7.   [24] Col. 1660.

CHAPTER VIII

SOUTH AFRICA UNITED

1. A FRESH START *VERSUS* THE OLD PARTY LINES

AFTER the enactment of the South Africa Act, South African politics were dominated by the questions: Who was to be the first Prime Minister of the Union? What was to be the composition of his Cabinet, which was to assume power on 31 May 1910? What were to be the parties and the issues in the first general election which would be held towards the end of 1910?

Already during the National Convention these questions had been in the minds of many of the delegates. Fitzpatrick had argued that 'a fresh start' was needed. 'Complete and real co-operation' between Boer and Briton was 'the only course that promises success.' The old parties, with their racial bases, should be dissolved and a completely new Union-wide party should be formed, under Botha's leadership, to apply a policy of conciliation and rapid development of the country's resources. By this means, Fitzpatrick hoped, 'the old gang' of Afrikaner racialists would be reduced to impotence and the country would be freed from the racial tensions which had hitherto impeded its development. The Natal delegates agreed. Since their colony had been immune from any clear-cut party system and since they represented rural interests but had British sympathies, they disliked the prospect of having to choose between a rural-Afrikaner party and an urban-British party. To them, as to Fitzpatrick, government by a non-racialist central party was the natural consummation of the work of the convention; and they, too, had acquired confidence in Botha. Jameson, Smartt, and Walton, the Cape Unionist delegates, also agreed, and so did Lindsay, but Farrar was inclined to be sceptical and he realized that other Transvaal Progressives, notably Chaplin, would be opposed to the idea, because they were not prepared to trust Botha or any other Afrikaner leader.[1]

There was nothing Botha would have liked more than to be the leader of a great central party, supported by the overwhelming majority of Afrikaners and the overwhelming majority of British South Africans, and pledged to conciliation and material progress. But how could such

---

[1] Fitzpatrick to J. Wernher, 15 Nov. 1908; Fitzpatrick to Lord Milner, 15 Feb. and 14 Mar. 1908. Fitzpatrick Papers (copies).

a party be created and assured of victory at the polls? If he allied himself with Jameson and Fitzpatrick many British South Africans might rally to their support, but what of the Afrikaners? What of the powerful Bond, Unie, and Het Volk organizations? Would they trust Jameson and Fitzpatrick? Would they not regard it as a wanton waste of their victories in the last elections if the first Union Government was not formed exclusively from the governments of the four colonies? Botha thought he discerned a way of dealing with these questions. Het Volk, the Unie, and the South African Party (including the Bond) should be amalgamated, and the programme and leadership of the combined party should be completely non-racial and so progressive that all the 'moderate British' in South Africa would be able to join it. This was the broad strategy which Botha sought to apply. But it was an extremely dangerous strategy. The 'moderate British' would suspect him of a mere political manoeuvre unless he offered them substantial concessions in the form of seats in the Cabinet: and he would endanger his position with his own side if he made such concessions.

While they were in England during August Botha began to urge upon the English-speaking delegates that they should help him to get South African politics out of the old racial rut, but he also made it clear in a press statement that he believed in a strong Government and a strong Opposition, and that he was not in favour of 'a coalition government'.[2] Then early in September, after Merriman, Moor, and Smuts had sailed for South Africa, Botha took the cure at Bad Kissingen, where he managed to improve his physical condition by shedding no less than thirty pounds. From there he wrote to Steyn to assure him that he was preparing for the political battle that lay ahead: he had urged the Afrikaner members of the Natal Parliament to make sure that they elected Afrikaners to the Union Senate and he was planning to raise money to found an English-medium newspaper in Johannesburg to wean the moderates away from the Progressives.[3] He returned to London in time to see Fischer and Hertzog before they sailed for South Africa on the 11th. Fischer raised the question of provincial representation in the Union Cabinet, fearing that if Botha had his way the Unie might be excluded, but Botha was unwilling to commit himself because (so he explained to Steyn) he wanted a strong Government composed of the best men, irrespective of what part of the Union they came from. Fischer (he complained) seemed to be suspicious of him and even more of Smuts. What had he or Smuts done to warrant his suspicion? Moreover, Fischer

---

[2] Patrick Duncan to Lady Selborne, 29 Aug. 1909, Duncan Papers.
[3] Botha to Steyn, n.d. [c. 29 Aug. 1909] and 31 Aug. 1909, Steyn Papers.

had made an ambiguous press statement on the eve of his departure in which he had not endorsed his own forthright condemnation of a Coalition Government. Could it be that Fischer believed in coalition?[4]

Meanwhile, Jameson had decided to use his personal influence with Botha to try and set in train a completely new orientation of parties. The word 'coalition' was to be avoided. Botha had committed himself against it and, although it was being used by the English-medium press in South Africa, it did not properly express his intention. He did not want a coalition of all the major political parties in South Africa. He wanted a new party composed of like-minded people, excluding the extremists on both sides. If Botha was so enthusiastically soliciting the support of the 'moderate British', why should he not form the first Union Cabinet from 'the best men' in South Africa, irrespective of their previous party affiliations? Surely that was the only way of getting out of the old racial rut! Jameson therefore approached Botha and arranged to meet him on holiday at Nairn in Scotland. There in the second half of September the former Raider and the former Commandant-General of the South African Republic, whose friendship had started at the Colonial Conference in 1907 and flourished during the National Convention, warmed to the theme that together they would liberate South Africa from Anglo-Boer racialism; but while they were at one as to the broad objective, they were unable to reach agreement upon the means by which it was to be achieved.[5]

Soon after their meeting Botha returned to South Africa, where he soon realized that he would have to be careful if he was not to risk losing the support of the existing Afrikaner parties. When Jameson arrived in Cape Town in November, therefore, he received a letter which Botha had drafted in consultation with Smuts, inviting him to the Transvaal for further talks and carefully defining their scope:[6]

... I shall be very glad to continue the discussion we had at Nairn, and ... I am pleased that neither your party in the Cape Colony nor our party here has done anything so far yet to agitate or organise with a view to the Union elections. I am sorry that I cannot say the same of our Progressive friends in Johannesburg—they are remarkably active and busy organising on our party lines of today with a strong tendency to go along racial lines, which will probably postpone the attainment of harmonious relations. As I told

[4] Botha to Steyn, 12 and 17 Sept. 1909, ibid. Fischer's press statement was typically equivocal: 'I see many difficulties in the idea of coalition, but I am open to correction. The great thing is not to nail one's belief to one idea.' *The Times*, 13 Sept. 1909.

[5] Colvin, *Jameson*, ii. 287–8; Engelenburg, *Botha*, p. 190.

[6] Botha to Jameson, 4 Nov. 1909, Smuts Papers (copy). The fact that this copy or draft is in the Smuts Papers suggests that Smuts collaborated in its preparation.

you at Nairn I am absolutely against a Coalition Government, but I do hope that any programme of principles which I shall support will be on lines broad enough to be acceptable to English and Dutch, and I trust that you will be able to assist us in attaining this. We have both done our best to attain the Union of South Africa with the firm resolve to bring our politics in the future on a higher plane above racial strife. . . . One thing is certain, if I correctly understand our Progressive friends in Johannesburg, that they will do their utmost to persuade you not to co-operate with us. I am determined to use any influence that I may have along the broadest and most liberal lines possible. I do not know what your plans are now but we agreed to continue the discussion we had in Nairn. There is still much time no doubt but I wanted to make sure to see you if it is true, what is said here, that you intend coming up to the Transvaal soon, so that we can consult together what can best be done to steer matters in the right direction.

Jameson paid his visit to the Transvaal during the second half of December. He found that the Progressives were divided. Chaplin, with whom he stayed, regarded Botha's overtures as no more than an attempt to 'paralyse our organization' and Farrar was inclined to agree with him; but Fitzpatrick was so zealous for an arrangement with Botha that he had virtually severed his connexion with the Progressive Party. Jameson had several cordial talks with Botha in Pretoria, pressing him to go farther than he had been prepared to in his letter. Botha admitted that Jameson had made out a very strong case and he left Jameson under the impression that he would be willing to try to form a Cabinet including him and other British South Africans, provided he could be satisfied that a public could be found for such a scheme.[7]

Lady Selborne made a shrewd assessment of the complicated situation that ensued in a letter which she wrote to Patrick Duncan on 2 January:[8]

Botha is playing a very difficult diplomatic game. If he loses the Merriman Sauer Fischer support before he has secured that of the Progressives he may get a nasty tumble. At any rate they are pretty sure to hear of these negotiations and feel somewhat annoyed. If he has merely been trying to detach Jameson from the Progressive Party, he will have some difficulty in persuading the others that he meant nothing more. If Jameson stands firm and

---

[7] Colvin, ii. 289; Engelenburg, p. 191; B. K. Long, *Drummond Chaplin* (London, 1941), pp. 144–6; *Cape Times*, 12 Feb. and 15 June 1910 (speeches by Jameson and Botha). Colvin says: 'Botha, in fact, liked Jameson's ideas but was afraid they would not work. If, however, he could persuade the others that he was right Botha would go in with him: otherwise not.' Engelenburg says: 'Botha agreed to give the idea a chance, provided Jameson was able to convert the other men who counted.' By this time nearly everyone on both sides referred to Jameson's objective as 'coalition' but Jameson himself continued to insist on the phrase 'best-men Government'.

[8] Duncan Papers.

refuses to join without Farrar, and Botha takes him into his Cabinet on those terms, I suppose it would mean a definite break with Merriman and Sauer. . . . It seems to me very likely to break down and the whole pother may end in Fitzpatrick and Lindsay joining Het Volk which perhaps will change its name in compliment to them. If it does break down, Botha will have made a bad blunder, as it must sow distrust in Merriman and Fischer's minds. Perhaps however he means to get rid of them anyhow, and if he doesn't find any Progressive allies to fill his Government with good sound Dutchmen who fought in the war instead of only talking about it.

To the politicians of the South African Party and the Orangia Unie Botha steadfastly maintained that he was not contemplating anything like a Coalition Government, but that he was merely trying to confuse the opposition parties and to win over the moderate British, whose support was necessary to ensure success in the general election. On 31 December he assured D. P. de V. Graaff, a member of Merriman's Cabinet, that there was nothing in the rumour that he was contemplating a coalition and Graaff passed the information on to Merriman by telegram.[9] Two days earlier he had sent Merriman a letter elaborating his project of amalgamating the three governing parties:[10]

I believe [he wrote] that a great number of members of the 'Progressive Parties' would be willing and even anxious to subscribe to the principles and programmes of our parties if only the racial sentiment could be removed which they attach to the present parties. I have come to the conclusion that it would be best if a South African party could be organised with a new name and a programme as liberal and on as wide a basis as possible. In order to attain this I am of the opinion that an amalgamation should be arrived at of the South-African; Bond; Unie and Het Volk Parties and a new South African party be formed out of them the programme and principles of which will be acceptable to the moderate men amongst our present opponents. If we succeed in this the moderate section will be assured of the Government for a very long period.

He enclosed a draft manifesto as a basis for discussion and explained that he hoped to be in Cape Town in the middle of January to confer with Merriman, Fischer, and Malan. The manifesto declared that it was essential to the success of the Union that practical co-operation should be secured between the two white races and that racialism should be eliminated from all political questions, so that party divisions would rest on differences of principle and not on race.

It is believed that a great majority of men among both races are in favour of the formation of a political party, whose fundamental objects shall be to

[9] Merriman Papers.   [10] Ibid.

make the union a new and real force in the national development of South
Africa under the protection of the British flag.

A statement of the objects and principles of the new party followed. Its
objects were 'To emphasise the South African spirit and standpoint of
the party' and 'To make a success of Union'. Its principles included 'The
just and equal treatment of all Provinces of the Union, and the development in all of the same healthy national South African sentiment'; 'The
full . . . recognition of . . . racial equality and the open door for white
immigrants'; 'A resolute white policy which will promote the interests
and the increase of the white population'; 'A cautious native policy which
will avoid mere repression and exploitation of the natives and which will,
while uplifting the natives by all means suitable to their ideas and conditions, prevent as far as possible their political, social and industrial
mixture with the whites'; 'Determined resistance to all proposals for the
importation of Asiatic labour into any part of South Africa'; 'The establishment of an adequate system of national defence'; and the fostering of
agricultural and industrial expansion.

Merriman was in no mood to be sympathetic towards Botha's proposals. During October and November he had had a trying parliamentary session, in which the grape-farmers had renewed their agitation for
the removal of the brandy excise and eventually, opposed in Cabinet by
Malan and Graaff and outvoted in caucus, he had reluctantly consented
to a compromise under which the excise was reduced but not eliminated.
In the midst of this dispute he had sent Botha a memorandum, suggesting that they should appoint an Intercolonial Commission to visit
Pretoria and make recommendations for the provision of office accommodation for the civil servants of the Union. Botha, who intended to deal
with this question without the assistance of the Cape, had replied without
enthusiasm.[11] By now the press was full of speculation about the Botha–
Jameson negotiations and many of the English-medium newspapers
were advocating the formation of a Coalition Government under Botha.
Merriman was extremely suspicious. Not only did he resent the facts that
he had not been kept informed as to the nature of the negotiations and
that, if successful, they would frustrate his ambition to be the first Prime
Minister of the Union, but also he was opposed to a Coalition Government in principle. He considered that the first Union Cabinet should
consist exclusively of members of the governing parties in the colonial
parliaments, because he was not prepared to trust any of the Progressives
or Unionists with a share of power and because he believed that if they

[11] Merriman to Botha, 22 Oct. 1909 (copy) and reply, 1 Nov. 1909, Merriman Papers.

were brought in there would be friction and inefficiency. On 25 December he informed Fischer that he saw signs of 'a sort of intrigue to patch up an alliance with the people who call themselves "Moderates"!! ... We cannot have South Africa ruled by the Johannesburg Progressives under whatever fine sounding name they may choose to sail.' In America 'confusion and strife' had been the result of Washington's decision to include both Hamilton and Jefferson in his first Cabinet.[12]

On receiving Botha's letter and draft manifesto, Merriman consulted Sauer. They discussed the question whether Botha was being truthful in denying that he had any intention of forming a Coalition Government with Jameson. Sauer was satisfied with Botha's denial and insisted on going up to Pretoria to see Botha, who made a favourable impression on him. Merriman was not satisfied and he was hurt by Sauer's decision.[13] Replying to Botha on 5 January,[14] he complained of the coalition rumours and denounced 'the favourite Progressive nostrum of a "Coalition" Ministry'. He proceeded:

I therefore understand all your references to amalgamation to be solely to the drawing together of the different parties now existing under the names of 'The Bond', 'Het Volk' and 'Die Unie' in the Cape, Transvaal and Orange Free State respectively, under some designation which would enable English people to join the party without the fear, however groundless, of taking up a racial attitude. May I venture to point out that this is exactly what has been done in the Cape Colony where the South African Party embraces and is supported by the Bond, though more than one third of the members do not belong to that organisation. This party as you are aware has accepted an Englishman as its leader and has loyally supported him through a most trying time. In the Cabinet of seven three bear English names—almost exactly in proportion to the numbers of the two races in the Colony. . . . I should therefore see no reason why the same thing should not be repeated in the Union Parliament. A better name than the South African Party you could not have. It really embraces all we stand for, all we have accomplished. It would embrace 'Het Volk' and 'De Unie' as it has embraced the Bond, and it would, I think, attract many others who might not see their way clear to joining those organizations. To destroy them would be difficult and in the case of the Bond I think an impossible task. . . .

As for the proposed manifesto (which Merriman privately regarded as ridiculous and flabby) he wrote: 'written documents of that kind always seem to me singularly inconvenient. Either they are so broad as to be platitudinarian, or if they are specific they are often impracticable.' He

[12] Ibid. (copy).   [13] Merriman's Diary, 5–6 Jan. 1910.
[14] Merriman Papers (copy).

then explained that in his opinion they should indulge in no political manœuvres at all before the Governor-General arrived:

The constitutional course seems to be to wait until the Governor General calls on someone to form a cabinet. The man so selected will naturally call on his friends to join him and it will be his first duty to formulate a policy for submission to the electors. If the future Prime Minister is to be hampered either by the platitudes or the too specific pledges of a written programme he will start with a heavy handicap.

Finally, he said that he would be delighted to see Botha in Cape Town, but that he would be away visiting his constituency between 20 and 25 January.

As the parliamentary leader of the Afrikaner Bond, Malan, too, received a letter from Botha with a copy of the draft manifesto. His reactions were not complicated by distrust, for he had already fallen under Botha's spell. Considering the proposal on its merits, however, he feared that there might be a split in the Bond if they tried to amalgamate the Afrikaner parties before the general election. He therefore informed Botha that there were constitutional difficulties, as only a Bond Congress had the power to amend the Bond Constitution, and he suggested that they should come to an understanding, leaving each of the colonial parties a wide latitude until after the election, when the amalgamation should be effected.[15]

Meanwhile Jameson had been sounding out opinion. The Transvaal Progressives remained divided, but Farrar showed signs of coming over if he could be assured of a seat in the Cabinet. In Natal Jameson found that most of the politicians of both the Moor and the Smythe groups would support a 'best men government' led by Botha. Fraser and other members of the Constitutional Party in the Orange River Colony were also agreeable; and so were members of his own party in the Cape. By mid-January, therefore, Jameson was in a position to know that most British South Africans were behind him. On the other hand, he had tried and failed to win over Steyn.[16] Then on 17 January he made a guarded approach to Merriman, which confirmed Merriman's fear that Botha was still toying with coalition. Accordingly, on 22 January Merriman gave vent to his pent-up feelings in a speech at Carnarvon, denouncing 'the talk about coalition' as 'foolish and mischievous'. 'A Coalition was impossible. . . . A good Opposition and a good Parliament were as necessary as a good Government. . . . Existing parties formed the only basis for the parties of the future.'[17]

---

[15] Malan to Steyn, 12 Jan. 1910, Steyn Papers.
[16] Colvin, ii. 289–90; Engelenburg, p. 191.   [17] *Cape Times*, 23 Jan. 1910.

By the time Merriman returned to Cape Town, Fischer and Botha had arrived for the conference, which took place from 26 to 31 January. Malan, also, was present, on behalf of the Bond, at several of the meetings. Scarcely anything was achieved. Botha was not frank about his dealings with Jameson: Merriman feared the worst of them. Botha wanted the amalgamation scheme to be adopted and the draft manifesto to be revised and approved: Merriman wanted practical steps to be taken to ease the way for the administrative changes that were to take place on 31 May. Consequently they never got to grips with either problem. Merriman recorded in his diary that the talks were 'aimless and unpractical' and that the 'weak and obstinate' Botha initiated 'a long and wearisome discussion . . . on formation of some universal party'.[18] Soon afterwards he informed Sir James Rose Innes, the Chief Justice of the Transvaal, that it had been 'purgatory'—'a marked avoidance of real business—the Constitution of the new Government both as regards personnel and what is of far more importance as regards the practical details of Government', so that he expected there would be something like 'chaos' on 31 May.[19] Botha was just as exasperated. 'Mr. Merriman has no sympathy with my opinion as to re-organization on broad principles', he told Moor. 'He wishes to have no programme and no organization.'[20]

Merriman's next move was a public speech at Worcester on 5 February. Taking as his theme 'the future politics of South Africa', he again denounced coalition and declared that the existing line of division in South African politics was the only possible basis for the foreseeable future. He paid a tribute to the South African Party, Het Volk, and the Orangia Unie, but went on to deprecate any suggestion that they should be amalgamated forthwith. Commenting on this speech, the English-medium press came to the conclusion that Merriman had spoken on behalf of the other prime ministers and that they had considered and rejected coalition—the 'reactionary' Merriman and Fischer had triumphed over the 'progressive' Botha.[21]

Six days later Jameson addressed a crowded and enthusiastic meeting in the Cape Town city hall. He explained that he had had frank talks with Botha in Pretoria and that he had subsequently discovered that 'our party to a man' was 'completely in favour of accepting the best-men government'. He had seen Botha again since the prime ministers' conference and Botha had told him that he 'could not answer for all his party

[18] Merriman's Diary, 27 and 29 Jan. 1910.
[19] Merriman to Innes, 6 Feb. 1910, Innes Papers.
[20] Botha to Moor, 10 Feb. 1910 (telegram), Natal Archives, Prime Minister, cviii.
[21] *Cape Times*, 6 Feb. 1910.

in the other colonies', which meant that 'the negotiations have failed' and they must prepare for the electoral battle. Merriman had been the main obstacle, for it was he who 'had proclaimed that the work of the Union should not bear its intended fruit, and that the Government must be formed on the old miserable party lines'. Even now, however, the door was left open, and if Botha wished he would willingly co-operate with him in a best-men Government. This speech was given the widest publicity and the Opposition press portrayed Botha as being confronted with an embarrassing choice between abandoning his ideals and breaking with the 'reactionaries'. If only he would go in with Jameson, the two of them would 'win a tremendous verdict for coalition'.[22]

Soon afterwards Patrick Duncan, who had decided to enter South African politics, went to Cape Town from the Transvaal to find out from Jameson what the position between him and Botha was, and what he wished the Progressives to do. Duncan reported by letter to Farrar on the 17th.[23] Botha, he said, had left Jameson with the firm impression that he was still well disposed towards his ideas and that he was going to sound out his own Transvaal people to see whether he could be certain of enough support from them to enable him to defy the Cape opponents of coalition. He would have made up his mind by the time the Het Volk Congress met on 22 March. Jameson had undertaken to restrain his supporters from making polemical speeches until then. Duncan said that he was surprised to learn that Botha had 'offered to go as far with Jameson as he did' and that he was not sure of Botha's sincerity. On balance, however, he thought that Botha should be given reasonable time to reply to Jameson's 'open door' offer. His conclusion was as follows:

I think what we have to consider is not so much the merits or demerits of coalition as how to handle the situation which has grown up out of the negotiations which have taken place. On the merits of coalition we are all committed to the view and rightly so that given a fair division of power and an agreement on main principles we cannot refuse it. I must say I never thought till I heard of Botha's talks with Jameson that there was the slightest chance of such an agreement from his side but as he has gone so far with Jameson I think we are bound to give the thing a fair chance. If it does not come off it will not be our fault and we shall not suffer as a party for having gone as far as we could to meet the other side.

If the Progressives were unsure of Botha's real intentions, the same was true of Merriman. He was aghast at the revelations in Jameson's

22 *Transvaal Leader*, 12 Feb. 1910.   23 Duncan Papers (copy).

Cape Town speech, and on 17 February he delivered another public tirade against coalition, this time at Malmesbury.[24] His correspondence shows that at this time he inclined to the view that Botha was merely playing with Jameson, but that he was never quite sure of it. Thus he wrote to Innes on the 20th:[25]

That Botha and Jameson should coalesce may or may not be sound policy but to go behind my back and patch up something or even to talk about patching up something is not quite the sort of thing that gives me much hope for the future. My own belief is that Botha was quite sincere in what he told me and even if he changes his mind I have no right to complain but I do not like underhand work, nor do I see how it is possible . . . to sit down under the imputation that Jameson has cast on him in his revelations without making things plain. It savours of slimness [cunning] and of waiting to see how the cat jumps.

Fischer and Steyn were certain that Botha was merely trying to confuse the Progressives and delay their preparations for the election; but they were alarmed lest the rupture between Merriman and Botha should lead to a schism in the ranks of Afrikanerdom. Fischer wrote to Merriman on 18 February:[26]

You rightly assume that I was not honoured by the 'Best Men' with their confidence at any time, either in regard to negotiations in England or out here, on the subject of coalition or anything else in connection with Union politics in the present or for the future; and yet we survive! Of course the present game is by blackguarding some of the Cape and all the O.R.C. powers that be and praising the Transvaal and some at the Cape to cause a split in our camp; first divide and then dictate! if we are fools enough not to see and prevent the game. I have no reason to think that Botha has any idea of joining in a coalition, whatever some of his surroundings may intend, but he most probably thinks that he should keep the would be coalitionists in a fool's paradise for a while longer, before getting them plus their money bags on the warpath.

A few days later Steyn summed up this interpretation of Botha's conduct:[27] 'I also think', he informed Merriman, 'that he is only dangling this bait of coalition before their eyes in order to keep them quiet.'

On 22 February Smuts tried to reassure Merriman and Steyn. The

[24] *Cape Times*, 18 Feb. 1910. Jameson's Cape Town speech, and its enthusiastic reception, gave great offence to Merriman, who subsequently admitted to his wife (19 Apr. 1910): 'I get angry when I think of old Jagger in the chair and those 4000 fools howling themselves hoarse when Jameson advocated Botha. Well another crowd preferred Barabbas which was a good deal worse.' Merriman Papers.

[25] Innes Papers.   [26] Merriman Papers.

[27] Steyn to Merriman, 22 Feb. 1910, ibid.

whole business, he declared, had emanated from a Progressive Party
manœuvre to divide and weaken the governing parties. To Merriman he
wrote:[28]

I have never for a moment considered coalition possible—nor even advis·
able in the sense proposed by Jameson, that is to say, the entry of men like
Farrar and himself into the same Cabinet as yourself and Botha. But to me
it is as clear as daylight that the Progressive tactic is to use the failure to
bring about a Coalition Government as an argument of a racial character
against us. They would argue: 'We were so fair, asked for so little, but our
opponents—having obtained Union with our assistance—were determined
to play the top-dog and leave us in the cold. Hence coalition failed.' . . . The
Progressives are determined to steer the issue of the next elections in the
direction of racialism, as they expect in that way to prevent their moderate
followers from going over to us.

To Steyn he explained that they had to act with great circumspection to
be sure of getting a majority in the election. The Orange Free State and
Natal would balance one another, the prospects in the Cape were not
very promising, because of the unpopular fiscal policy of the Merriman
Government, and in the Transvaal the majority of the seats would be
urban seats, for all of which the English vote would be decisive. If the
Progressives got going too early, the moderates would become scared
and the election might be lost. That was why, wrote Smuts, he and
Botha talked of co-operation, although they had never thought of
coalition.[29]

Merriman was somewhat mollified as regards Smuts's role. A short
while earlier, after Smuts had made an ambiguous speech, he had begun
to have doubts about him. Now he admitted that one had to make
allowances for his 'surpassing intellect'.[30] But since Botha did not communicate with him directly, nor publicly disavow the coalition rumours,
he was more suspicious of him than ever. 'The whole noxious business is
inexpressibly distasteful', he confided to Innes on 1 March. 'The lying of
Jameson and the cowardly silence of Botha.'[31] Then on the 15th he
informed his wife: 'I see Botha is still going round letting off the most
amazing lot of platitudes. *He is going to humbug us* I am quite sure. If
he does I shall feel inclined to publish Johnnie's letter' (i.e. Smuts's letter
of 22 February).[32] And to Innes again, on 17 March: 'the question that
looms very large is whether Botha is humbugging us or humbugging
Jameson. Not perhaps a very dignified dilemma but there is a most

---

[28] Merriman Papers.   [29] Steyn Papers.
[30] Merriman to Steyn, 27 Feb. 1910, ibid.
[31] Innes Papers.   [32] Merriman Papers.

refreshing smack of slimness about it and at any rate it gives the Union a start on sound South African lines.'[33]

Botha did, however, keep in touch with Steyn, to whom he was always most anxious to justify himself. Writing to him on 28 February, he said that at the Cape Town Conference he had explained to Merriman and Fischer the exact purpose of the coalition negotiations, but apparently they did not trust him for they had criticized them in public. Moreover, at the Cape Town Conference they had rejected his proposals for the amalgamation of the governing parties. Merriman in particular had opposed him on all points and in his Worcester speech he had abused his confidence by referring to the amalgamation scheme. After this experience, wrote Botha, he could never deal with Merriman again. He was delaying his final reply to Jameson because the sooner the political battle began the greater would be the difficulty for the Afrikaner parties, since the other side had the money and the press. At present he was touring the Transvaal and seeing to the organization of Het Volk.[34]

In his letter to Steyn, Botha distinguished between the Bond (that is to say, Malan) and Merriman, saying that the Bond had been favourably disposed to the amalgamation scheme and that it was in friendly correspondence with him. Malan, indeed, was acting in harmony with Botha and Smuts. In his public speeches he, too, maintained a Delphic ambiguity. It was not yet possible, he said at Malmesbury on 10 February, to define how the parties would range themselves after union. 'The true friends of South Africa hoped that the old party lines would not be too sharply drawn in the early years.' 'The former distrust' must not be allowed to come to the surface.[35] Then on 28 February he wrote to assure Smuts that he agreed with him about the political situation. He was preaching the doctrine of a broad South African nationalism and hoped to gain the support of English-speaking people in the Cape Colony. He had advised Botha to reconsider the section in the draft manifesto dealing with Native policy, because it would have a great influence on the Native vote in the coming election. The first Union Cabinet should consist of men who were in sympathy with one another and able to follow a broad, constructive South African policy—which was as much as to say that he would support Botha, and not Merriman, for the premiership.[36]

Meanwhile the English-medium press had continued to cry for a radically fresh departure in politics. In the middle of March this campaign was given a new impetus by the publication of Fitzpatrick's

---

[33] Innes Papers.
[35] *Cape Times*, 11 Feb. 1910.
[34] Steyn Papers.
[36] Smuts Papers.

pamphlet, *The Union. A Plea for a Fresh Start.* The paramount question of the day, wrote Fitzpatrick, was 'whether we are to continue upon the old lines of parties whose origin and existence were due to racialism, or are to make an effort worthy of our opportunity to shed all that is undesirable in our past and make a fresh start'. In the National Convention the delegates had fallen into two groups, the broad-minded and the narrow-minded. Botha and Jameson stood in the forefront of the broad-minded. They both earnestly desired 'to lift South Africa out of the old rut' and have done for ever with the 'miserable old racial divisions'; they were incomparably 'the most distinguished, the most loved, and the most trusted representatives of their respective races'; both of them as prime ministers of colonies had proved their capacity to bury the past; and they had worked together in the National Convention and after in complete accord. The fresh start should therefore be initiated under their joint leadership. Finally, Fitzpatrick declared that he was convinced 'that we stand once more—for the last time—at a point where the roads diverge: one leading to long lasting differences between the two white races, the other to peace!'

Private appeals had also been made to Afrikaner politicians. Hyslop, the Natal Convention delegate, for example, had corresponded with Steyn,[37] Malan, and Smuts,[38] explaining to them the dilemma with which Natal would be confronted if the party divisions of the other colonies were continued after union. Only Hyslop's side of his correspondence with Smuts appears to have survived, but it is interesting because it indicates that Smuts tried hard to reassure him. In November 1909 Hyslop addressed his first appeal to Smuts to 'point out some way out of this racial tangle'. In December he thanked Smuts for his reply, which satisfied him 'that you at least have very much the same object in view that I have'. He was sure that 'The great majority of our leading men are not disposed to ally themselves to any of the parties in the other colonies but would I think support a party of moderates.' On 24 February he told Smuts that the leading Natal politicians 'are all with you and Botha in the work in which we understand you are engaged viz: the building up of a party of moderate men of both races'. He feared that the Orange River Colony was 'hopeless, judging from Hertzog's speeches'. 'If you fail, we in this poor colony will be placed in a very difficult position . . . we are all looking to Botha and you to save South Africa from relapsing into racialism.' And, finally, on 15 March Hyslop

[37] Hyslop to Steyn, 14 and 23 Feb. 1910, and reply (copy), 19 Feb. 1910, Steyn Papers.
[38] Hyslop to Smuts, 22 Nov. and 4 Dec. 1909, 24 Feb. and 15 Mar. 1910, Smuts Papers.

had cause to regret that 'the outlook is not as bright as it might be'. Steyn's replies to his letters had shown that he was wholly opposed to 'our views', but Malan 'should, I think, under certain circumstances, co-operate'. 'I shall be glad to hear', Hyslop concluded, 'how you propose forming the new party and how you intend to obviate the accusation that it is Het Volk under a new name.'

By that time it was obvious to Botha that it would be quite impossible for him to include any Progressive or Unionist politicians in the first Union Cabinet and he had to indulge in broad generalities in his address to the Het Volk Congress on 22 March.[39] Het Volk, he declared, had had four main objects: to bring about friendly relations with the neighbouring colonies, to obtain self-government, to secure equal rights for both the white races, and to unite South Africa. All of these objects had now been achieved. Never before had Boer and Briton been on such good terms. In granting them self-government Britain had fulfilled her promise, given in the Treaty of Vereeniging, in a manly way and they had to thank the late Sir Henry Campbell-Bannerman for this decision which had made racial amity and union possible. Het Volk had proved worthy of its trust and had never used its majority unfairly. The racial question was now buried and should remain buried.

Their organization must not fish in troubled waters; they must not destroy, but build up. . . . They must retain and promote friendship with Great Britain, whose sympathy they had, and whose protection they would need for a long time to come. They must see that a sound South African nation was born in which there was room for all whites. . . . Their nation must be built up of all sections. . . . They must reorganize on the broadest lines possible and form an association to which every man would be proud to belong. . . . To co-operate would solve all difficulties. . . . If South Africa were ruled as the Transvaal they would have peace and prosperity.

This speech was well received by the delegates and they proceeded unanimously to adopt a resolution instructing the Head Committee

to take all necessary steps in order to form from the now existing organization of Het Volk and other political organizations in South Africa on similar principles, as well as all whites in South Africa agreeing to those principles, a new political organization, and take all necessary steps regarding the name, programme, statutes and central committee of the organization.

The press deduced from these proceedings that coalition, a fresh start, or a Government of 'the best men' was dead, as indeed it was. The idea

---

[39] *Cape Times*, 23 Mar. 1910.

of carrying the bulk of the Afrikaners and the bulk of the British South Africans into a new middle of the road party led by Botha and Jameson had never had a chance of success and Botha must have realized this at an early stage in the negotiations. Had he, then, been deceiving Jameson in the calculating manner expounded by Smuts in his letters to Merriman and Steyn?. No precise answer can be given, for Botha, more than most men, was ruled by emotion rather than by logic and there can be no doubt that he passionately desired to assume the role of peacemaker between Boer and Briton. It seems probable that he embarked on the negotiations sincerely and that when he found that they could not succeed it was both politically and emotionally difficult for him to be frank. Jameson bore him no ill-will for the failure and believed that he would have broken with 'the old gang' if he had dared, and that he might still do so.[40] Consequently Botha succeeded in emerging without any significant loss of prestige with British South Africans, while Merriman, his only rival for the premiership, incurred their odium because he had not been prepared to pay lip-service to a plausible phantasy.

2. THE GOVERNOR-GENERAL, THE PRIME MINISTER, AND THE CABINET

While the South African delegates were in England several names were being mooted for the appointment of first Governor-General of the Union. There was a press report that Sir Wilfrid Laurier, the French Canadian Prime Minister of Canada, was under consideration 'in recognition of his services for the unification of races in Canada'.[41] There was a suggestion that Winston Churchill, then President of the Board of Trade, was an aspirant.[42] Some thought that it would be fitting if the appointment was offered to Sir Henry de Villiers as a sequel to his presidency of the National Convention.[43] These, however, were idle rumours.

[40] Jameson to his brother, 22 June 1910: 'I lunched with Botha at Pretoria last week and talked the whole thing out with him. It is the old story—he funked splitting up his own people at the start—hates most of his colleagues; but talks of getting rid of the old gang in a couple of years. I think he will probably come to grief in the process and told him so. Still he has been quite honest with me all through—only a much weaker vessel than I expected.' Colvin, ii. 295.

[41] *The Times*, 27 Aug. 1909.

[42] Sir Walter Hely-Hutchinson, Governor of the Cape Colony, to Merriman, 11 Aug. 1909: 'A friend just out from England tells me that Winston Churchill's candidature for the governor-generalship is by no means otherwise than serious—and that it is on the cards, though not likely, that he may be appointed. . . . The story is that Winston wants to form a Socialist-Radical party, but thinks that the time is not yet, and that he had better be out of politics for two or three years.' Merriman Papers.

[43] A. B. Marnham, M.P., to Merriman, 14 July 1909: 'Sauer had dinner with me at the

Asquith seems to have discussed the subject with Botha, but not with Merriman, and towards the end of September he approached Herbert Gladstone, telling him that Botha had asked for a Cabinet Minister and that the Dutch and the British in South Africa would like him to go. Herbert Gladstone, the fourth son of the great Liberal Prime Minister, had steered a middle course between the pro-Boers and the Liberal Imperialists during the war, and since 1906 he had been a conscientious Home Secretary. He was a mild man, he was not a strong debater, and he was reputed to be a weak link in the Cabinet. King Edward's biographer relates that when the Prime Minister unofficially suggested Gladstone's name to him for the South African appointment the King wrote at the bottom of Asquith's letter, 'Is there nobody better?' *The Times* agreed with the King. On 27 October it carried a news report that there was reason to believe that Gladstone would be appointed and three days later it took the Government to task in a leading article on imperial appointments. 'Ministers . . . must feel', it declared, 'that to impose upon India or upon the Dominions the failures of the Cabinet would be to do a grievous wrong to the Empire and to our race.' Nevertheless, Asquith stood his ground, and in so doing he showed a sound understanding of the needs of South Africa, which were for a man who, like Gladstone, would act with strict constitutional propriety, rather than for a pro-consul in the Milner–Curzon tradition. The appointment of Gladstone was announced in December and in February 1910 he was created a viscount.[44]

The British Government decided that Gladstone should arrive in Cape Town on 17 May and that Selborne should sail from Cape Town for England the next day. Merriman thought that Gladstone should reach South Africa several weeks earlier because, whereas in Canada in 1867 and in Australia in 1901 federal governments had been superimposed on existing colonial governments, in South Africa the colonial governments were due to disappear on 31 May, by which time the Cabinet had to be formed, the provincial administrators and the members of the Appellate Division of the Supreme Court had to be appointed, and complicated administrative arrangements had to be made. He raised the question

House last night, and we selected the future Governor-General for South Africa ! ! There is only one man in S. Africa who would command the esteem and affection of all parties, Sir Henry de Villiers. What a triumph this would be for your policy if de Villiers could be selected—a Dutchman to be the first Governor General of United South Africa. I intend to see Asquith and do all I can in this direction.' Ibid.

[44] Sir Sidney Lee, *King Edward VII: a Biography* (London, 1927, 2 vols.), ii. 492–3 ; Charles Mallet, *Herbert Gladstone: a Memoir* (London, 1932), pp. 226–9 ; *The Times*, 27 and 30 Oct. and 22 Dec. 1909.

with Botha and Fischer when they met in Cape Town at the end of January. They agreed with him and they all tried to expedite Gladstone's departure, but the original plan was adhered to and Gladstone had barely a fortnight in South Africa before Union Day. When he arrived, therefore, he had very little time in which to decide whom to invite to form the first Ministry.[45]

It had been argued in Natal that it would be improper for Gladstone to call on an active politician to form a Government before the general election had been held, and that he should ask Sir Henry de Villiers to form an interim Government from among the members of the National Convention.[46] But this suggestion was a variant of the 'fresh start' idea and it died with it. It is doubtful, indeed, whether de Villiers would have been a success as a Prime Minister, even of a short-lived administration, for his thirty-seven years as Chief Justice of the Cape Colony had made him lose touch with administration as well as with politics.

Another possibility for the premiership was Steyn, whose Free State background made him a likely *via media* between the Cape and the Transvaal and whose bearing and conduct in the convention had won general admiration from Afrikaners and British South Africans alike. He was the hero of the Free State. Botha, turning to him for advice and understanding, called him affectionately 'my voor os'.[47] Transvaalers like Beyers who were restive under Botha looked to him as a more reliable leader.[48] Merriman had confidence in him. And it was to him, amongst others, that Hyslop turned when he wanted to press his political views upon Afrikaners. It is conceivable, therefore, that Steyn would have become Prime Minister of a party administration, and that both Merriman and Botha would have served under him, had his health permitted it. But Steyn had never made a satisfactory recovery from his physical collapse at the end of the South African War. His eyes still gave him trouble, he did not have full control over his hands and his arms, and he lacked stamina. In August 1909 J. H. Hofmeyr had urged

[45] Merriman to P. A. Molteno, M.P., 31 Jan. 1910, Merriman Papers (copy). Fischer to Moor, 9 Feb. 1910 (telegram); Botha to Merriman, 18 Mar. 1910 (copy); Botha to Moor, 23 and 24 Mar. 1910 (telegrams). Natal Archives, Prime Minister, CVIII.

[46] *Natal Mercury*, 19 Mar 1910.

[47] Literal translation, 'my fore-ox'—i.e. one of the first pair in a span of oxen; a leader. Botha to Steyn, 4 Mar. 1910, Steyn Papers.

[48] C. F. Beyers, Speaker of the Transvaal Legislative Assembly, to Steyn, 9 Feb. 1910: 'Ik verlang al om een bietjie politiek van *mijn President* te hooren. Ik hoop net, dat wanneer wij een dag van die ou rooi vlag verlost zijn uwe gezondheid u weer zal toelaten de "voor-touw" te nemen. . . .' (Translation: 'I long to hear a little politics from *my President*. I only hope that one day when we are freed from the old red flag your health will again permit you to take the lead.') Ibid.

upon him that for the sake of Afrikaner unity it would be his duty to assume the premiership if he was fit to do so.[49] Steyn had therefore gone from England to Holland to consult Dr. Winkler, the specialist who had previously attended him, but after a thorough examination he had received an adverse report. Accordingly Steyn had informed Botha and Merriman that he would not be taking an active part in politics for two or three years, 'which definitely settles the question of my taking office'.[50] There was no other Free Stater in the running. The indecisive Fischer commanded little respect and Hertzog was regarded by Botha and Smuts, as well as by most British South Africans, as a narrow-minded and perhaps a dangerous man. That left the premiership between the Cape Colony and the Transvaal—between Merriman and Botha.

No politician in South Africa could match Merriman's forty-two years' parliamentary experience or his service in five cabinets. He was a recognized master of public finance in the strict Gladstonian tradition. His intellect, his unimpugnable integrity, and his courage were widely respected. He had a personal following in the Cape Colony. Steyn and other Free Staters tended to prefer him.[51] Smuts admired him. On the other hand, by 1910, at the age of 69, his outlook was pessimistic and his imagination was narrowing. Never an easy man to work with, he was becoming downright cantankerous, quick to expose the weaknesses in others and slow to applaud their better qualities. His quixotic determination to balance the accounts of the Cape Colony in its last financial year had made him unpopular among the grape-farmers, whose demands for the repeal of the excise he had resisted, and among the townsmen, who bitterly resented his 'ten bob tax' on small incomes.[52] Moreover, his services to Afrikanerdom were not generally recognized outside the Cape Colony, while most British South Africans, especially those in Natal and the Transvaal, whom he had frequently castigated with his mordant wit, regarded him as a reactionary and a renegade Englishman. His prospects were weakened, too, by the fact that he had neither the taste nor the talent for political intrigue. Nevertheless, as the Prime Minister of the largest, the most populous, and the mother colony he

[49] Hofmeyr to Steyn, 16 Sept. 1909, ibid.

[50] Steyn to Merriman, 14 Aug. 1909, Merriman Papers.

[51] The whole tenor of Steyn's correspondence in 1909 and 1910 shows that he would have preferred Merriman to Botha if it had been politically practicable. In Jan. 1910, for example, he asked Botha to declare that he would be willing to serve in the Cabinet under Merriman. Botha to Steyn, 21 Jan. 1910, Steyn Papers.

[52] J. E. Panther to Merriman, 28 May 1910: 'that awful "ten bob" tax of yours has bitten deep. No fewer than five men said to me last Saturday, when we heard the news, "Serve him right! Look at his ten shilling tax on incomes of £50!"' Merriman Papers.

might have surmounted these obstacles if he had had the support of a powerful political machine. But this he lacked. At a time when parties of the modern type had become established in three of the colonies, he had no real party behind him, for the South African Party had virtually no existence when the Cape Parliament was not in session. It was the Afrikaner Bond, of which he was not a member, which was deeply rooted in the Cape constituencies—and Malan, who had succeeded Hofmeyr[53] in its key office, the chairmanship of the *Kommissie van Toezicht*, preferred Botha.

Botha's lack of education, the brevity of his parliamentary and administrative experience, and his indifferent health would probably have disqualified him from the highest political office in a more mature society. These defects, however, were largely offset by his exceptional personal charm and by the presence of the indefatigable Smuts, while the forces which operated in favour of his candidature were powerful. Het Volk stood solidly behind him and many members of the Orangia Unie and the Bond preferred him because, whatever doubts may have been created by some of his more exuberant expressions of the conciliation policy, he was an Afrikaner, his war record was impressive, he was always ready to talk with farmers, Boer to Boer, in the Kruger manner, and in the last resort it was assumed that his direction could be controlled by a consolidated Afrikaner party. Furthermore, nearly all the British in South Africa preferred him to Merriman, at least as the lesser of two evils. Jameson and other Cape Unionists openly supported his claims, and so did Natal and the Transvaal Progressives.[54]

There would, of course, have been no problem if Botha and Merriman had been able to agree among themselves as to which of them should be Prime Minister, but that was quite impossible. Merriman disliked fools and schemers and he saw something of each in Botha. Above all, the long-drawn-out negotiations with Jameson alienated Merriman. Furthermore, he believed that it was of the first importance that the Union should be launched on Cape and not on Transvaal lines. Under Transvaal leadership he feared that the traditions of the Cape Parliament, which meant so much to him, would not become the traditions of the Parliament of the Union, that a heavy-handed Native policy would be applied, and that financial corruption would become endemic. Had not Botha boasted to him of the efficacy of the steam-roller?[55] Was not his simple

[53] Hofmeyr died in London on 16 Oct. 1909.

[54] e.g. Jameson in his Cape Town speech on 11 Feb. 1910, and Moor in a speech at Estcourt on 14 Apr. 1910. *Cape Times*, 12 Feb. and 15 Apr. 1910.

[55] Botha to Merriman, 24 July 1908, Merriman Papers.

paternalistic attitude towards all non-whites extremely dangerous?[56] Had not one of the last decisions of the Transvaal Legislative Assembly been a most discreditable job, declaring a brief extraordinary session to be an ordinary session, merely so that Members of Parliament would receive £300 each instead of the £42 to which they were legally entitled?[57] No, he could not possibly take office under such a man!

Botha was just as adamant. Already on 18 January he had declined to act on Steyn's advice that he should inform Merriman that he would be willing to serve under him.[58] Then, when Merriman abruptly dismissed his amalgamation proposals at the end of January, Botha finally decided that he would on no account accept his leadership. The prospects of South Africa could not be prejudiced for the sake of one caustic old man! 'I shall never deal with him again', he told Steyn.[59] It was his plain duty to become Prime Minister himself.

As the time for Gladstone's arrival approached supreme efforts were made to destroy any chances that Merriman may have had. Early in May several of the leading South African politicians, including Botha, Hull, Lionel Phillips, Sauer, Smartt, and D.\ P. de V. Graaff, gathered in Potchefstroom to attend an irrigation congress. There the claims of Botha were assiduously canvassed and, according to one who was present, 'it soon became clear that heaven and earth would be moved not to have Merriman as a leader or Premier of the first Union Government'.[60] Pressure was also brought to bear upon the Cape Town press to prepare the public to accept Botha. During 1909 F. J. Centlivres, the managing director of the *South African News*, an English-medium supporter of the South African Party, had sold Botha and Smuts a controlling interest in the paper without the knowledge of the other directors or the members of the staff.[61] In April 1910 Centlivres instructed the editor, R. Philipson-Stow, to refrain from pressing the claims of Merriman for the premiership and he reported to Smuts that 'It would be bad for the *News* just now if it were to become known in Cape Town that more than

[56] Referring to the convention debates on the Native franchise, Merriman informed Innes on 1 Mar. 1910 that 'Sauer and I had to sit and listen to things that made our blood boil.' Innes Papers.

[57] *Transvaal Debates of Both Houses of Parliament, 1910*, cols. 2, 680–3; *1910 Transvaal Supreme Court*, p. 372; *State*, iii. 990–6, iv. 297–306, 667–80; *Cape Times*, 19 May 1910; James Rose Innes, *Autobiography* (edited and with an introduction by B. A. Tindall) (London, 1949), pp. 210–11.

[58] Botha to Steyn, 21 Jan. 1910, Steyn Papers.

[59] Botha to Steyn, 28 Feb. 1910: 'Het is duidelik, President, met hem [Merriman] zal ik niet weer onderhandelen.' Van der Merwe, *Steyn*, ii. 245–6.

[60] P. Rabie to Merriman, 5 June 1910, Merriman Papers.

[61] F. J. Centlivres to Smuts, 8 Apr. and 12 May 1909, Smuts Papers.

half the voting power is in Pretoria ... and those who favour Mr. Merriman would be wild if they were to hear that the editor of the *News* had been told to stay his hand'.[62] Philipson-Stow disliked this policy but he submitted to the pressure until 31 May, when he resigned.[63] Even the *Cape*, the English-medium weekly which had previously taken an exceptionally strong anti-Botha and anti-Transvaal line, moderated its tone at the behest of J. G. van der Horst, one of the leading shareholders, and against the wishes of the editor, A. D. Donovan, and the cartoonist, D. C. Boonzaier, both of whom resigned in June.[64] Malan and Graaff went still farther. They considered that it was not enough to deny Merriman the premiership: either he must accept a portfolio in Botha's Cabinet, or he must be excluded from the Union Parliament lest he should become a focus of opposition to the Government. They therefore fomented a movement among Merriman's constituents to keep him out of Parliament if he refused to accept a place in the Ministry.[65]

On 15 May the Selbornes arrived in Cape Town at the end of their farewell tour of South Africa, during which they had been able to form an accurate impression of what was happening. Lady Selborne summed it up in a letter which she wrote from Cape Town:[66]

I really do feel sorry for Mr. Merriman. As far as one can gather in the midst of mendacity which enfolds the present doings of South African statesmen, his friends are all leaving him. The Unie has declared against him, the Bond are for Botha, led by Malan, and even Sauer is up for sale, if Botha thinks it worth while to buy him. Only Harry Currey is said to be faithful. ... Among many accomplished liars Fischer seems to have excelled. He was swearing fidelity to both leaders at the same time. Everybody else allowed a decent interval.

When Gladstone arrived on the 17th, Merriman, Sauer, and Malan, Botha and Smuts, Moor and Greene, Fischer and Hertzog, and Jameson and other Cape Colony politicians were gathered in Cape Town to welcome and advise him. Gladstone knew that Botha was the favourite of the British Government and people, but his hands were in no sense tied by instructions from the Colonial Office and he regarded it as his duty to select the man who could obtain the widest support.[67] Most of the first

[62] 24 Apr. 1910, Smuts Papers.

[63] Philipson-Stow to the Board of Directors, *South African News*, 31 May 1910, Merriman Papers (copy).

[64] Merriman Papers; the *Cape*, 27 May 1910, 17 and 24 June 1910.

[65] Letters to Merriman by J. D. de Ville (30 May 1910), J. A. Graaff, brother of D. P. de V. Graaff (3 June 1910), and J. H. Claassens (11 June 1910), Merriman Papers.

[66] Lady Selborne to Duncan, 15 May 1910, Duncan Papers.

[67] The late Sir Herbert Stanley, who was private secretary to Lord Gladstone in 1910,

two days he spent with Selborne, who sailed on the afternoon of the 18th. Then on the 19th and 20th he had long interviews with the colonial cabinet ministers as well as with Jameson. The Transvaal and Natal were for Botha. So were Malan[68] and Jameson. Fischer was probably indecisive, but Hertzog almost certainly recommended Merriman.[69] It was therefore obvious to Gladstone that there was only one possible decision and on 21 May he asked Botha to form a Cabinet.

If Merriman had been asked to form a Cabinet it is doubtful whether he would have succeeded. Fischer and Hertzog would have joined him. So, presumably, would Cape ministers. But what of the Transvaal and Natal? On 12 May Jacob de Villiers, the Transvaal Attorney-General, had told Steyn that he foresaw grave difficulties in Cape Town: 'Botha is determined to stand out if Merriman becomes Prime Minister. Smuts and Hull will follow him. This means the Transvaal stands out.'[70] On the other hand, on 6 September Smuts assured Merriman that 'when Sauer was here in Pretoria in March or April I told him that I would be perfectly willing to serve under you and I told General Botha the same'.[71] Natal would almost certainly have followed the Transvaal. If Jacob de Villiers was correct, therefore, Merriman would not have been able to form a Cabinet.

After seeing Gladstone Botha at once wrote a courteous letter to Merriman, asking him to do him the honour of joining his Ministry:[72]

Not only is it my strong personal wish that you may see your way clear to do so but I feel sure the people of South Africa who value your life-long public services and unique experience expect that you should continue to serve the country and assist in making a success of the Union in the establishment of which you have taken so distinguished a part.

Merriman declined:[73]

I do not think [he replied] that much good would be attained by my

assured the writer that the facts are as stated in the text. Merriman, Steyn, and Hertzog suspected that Gladstone had instructions from the Colonial Office to send for Botha. Merriman to Professor Goldwin Smith, 5 June 1910; Steyn to Merriman, 25 May 1910. Merriman Papers. Van den Heever, *Generaal Hertzog*, p. 277.

[68] According to his biographer, Malan told Gladstone that Botha would obtain more support than Merriman, but that he (Malan) would personally prefer someone with more experience of parliamentary government. Bettie Cloete, *Die Lewe van Senator F. S. Malan* (Johannesburg, 1946), pp. 222–4. However, the evidence cited above makes it quite clear that Malan advised Gladstone to ask Botha to form a Government.

[69] Van den Heever, pp. 274–7.

[70] 'Botha is getermineed om uit te staan als Merriman Eerste Minister wort. Smuts en Hull sal hem volg. Dit meen die Transvaal staat uit.' Steyn Papers.

[71] Merriman Papers.

[72] 21 May 1910, ibid.   [73] Ibid. (copy).

joining your Government and it is possible that I may do more by supporting it from outside.

Efforts were then made to persuade Merriman to change his mind, but
he stood firm. He had long been aware that the tide was flowing against
him and now, in a letter to Steyn, he set out his reasons for refusing to
take a subordinate office:[74]

> I have no respect for Botha's political knowledge. My experience in the
> Convention, and since, has shown me enough to convince me that we should
> constantly differ, and in this way weaken and render nugatory good govern-
> ment. Much as I like Botha as a man and admire him as a partisan in the
> field, that does not blind me to his political shortcomings. The whole of his
> tortuous intrigue with Jameson and the cowardly silence that he has kept in
> that matter, the extravagance of his administration and the discreditable job
> with which it terminated, to say nothing of the tactics of the steam roller and
> the caucus which dominate Transvaal politics all convince me that service
> under such a Chief would—holding the views that I do—be an act of politi-
> cal dishonesty. I am sure that inside a Cabinet I could do nothing to stay
> these tendencies. Outside particularly as an independent supporter I might
> exercise a restraining influence.

Merriman was particularly hurt by the conduct of Malan and Graaff
—'the two Judas' as he described them in his diary.[75] To fill his cup of
sorrow, on 25 May he received the news that his mother, who had followed his career with intense pride and had hoped to live to see him
Prime Minister of the Union, had died in Grahamstown at the age of 92.
There was, however, consolation in the stream of letters which he
received in the following weeks—from men like J. H. Conradie, who
wrote as 'a Dutchman to the core' to thank him for his services to his
people; C. J. Watermeyer, who hoped that Merriman would stay in
politics because 'they may not like you, but they fear you, and "what will
Merriman have to say?" will kill many a little job'; R. H. Lundie of
Uitenhage, who asked him to explain his attitude to the Botha Government because 'We all feel like sheep without a shepherd'; W. P. Schreiner
who wished he was at the Treasury to place the Union finances on a
sound footing; Olive Schreiner, who hoped he would now be free to act
as a leader of the small group who 'realise that only by treating the
South African natives with justice and binding them to us by affection
can we make the future of South Africa great'; J. A. Sishuba, who said
that his fellow Natives were 'awaiting the Union with a great deal of
anxiety'; Hertzog and Smuts; and, above all, Steyn, who assured him

[74] 22 May 1910, Steyn Papers.   [75] 27 May 1910.

that 'though you are not in the ministry you are in the hearts of all true South Africans who love straight-forward honest and clean statesmanship, and as far as Dutch South Africa is concerned I sincerely pray that they may never forget what you have been to them in the hour of their troubles'.[76] The general verdict, however, was that of *The Times*, which declared that Merriman had 'gone out of his way to spoil his own chances by his speeches since the National Convention'.[77]

Meanwhile Botha had been forming his Cabinet. One of his main problems was what to do with Hertzog, whose attempts to enforce the principles laid down in his Education Act had created a stir throughout South Africa. It had been impressed upon Botha that Hertzog's inclusion in the Cabinet might frighten away British voters in the forthcoming election,[78] and he therefore had Smuts and Malan interview Hertzog in Cape Town and try to persuade him to accept a place on the Appellate Division of the Supreme Court. Hertzog had been warned that an attempt might be made to remove him from politics, and he refused. On behalf of Botha, Smuts then offered him the Ministry of Justice, which he took.[79]

By the 23rd the Cabinet was almost complete. Eight men had accepted Botha's invitation to join him—Smuts and Hull from the Transvaal, Sauer, Malan, Burton, and Graaff from the Cape, and Fischer and Hertzog from the Orange River Colony. Sauer and Burton had consulted Merriman before they accepted and he had advised them to go in.[80] That appeared to leave only one place for Natal, for section 14 of the South Africa Act provided for a total of ten ministers in charge of departments. Botha offered Moor a place but he and Greene insisted that Natal should have another. Botha yielded, offering Natal an additional seat in the Cabinet, but without a portfolio. Still not content Moor and Greene then pressed Botha to move Sauer from the Ministry of Railways and Harbours, which had been provisionally allotted to him and which Greene seems to have coveted for himself, but at this stage Botha dug his heels in and threatened to inform Gladstone that he was unable to form a Government and to advise him to send for Jameson. This news alarmed Fischer so much that he sent a telegram to Steyn, at his farm

[76] Letters to Merriman from J. H. Conradie, 23 May; C. J. Watermeyer, 27 May; R. H. Lundie, 28 May; W. P. Schreiner, 26 May; Olive Schreiner, 26 May; J. A. Sishuba, n.d.; J. B. M. Hertzog, 1 June; J. C. Smuts, 9 June; and M. T. Steyn, 25 May. Merriman Papers.

[77] 23 May 1910.

[78] Jacob de Villiers to Steyn, 12 May 1910, Steyn Papers.

[79] Cloete, p. 227; van der Merwe, pp. 242–5; F. S. Crafford, *Jan Smuts: a biography* (Cape Town, 1945), p. 91; J. C. Smuts, *Jan Christian Smuts* (London, 1952), pp. 118–19.

[80] Merriman's Diary, 22 and 23 May 1910.

near Bloemfontein, in a code which had been specially arranged for such an emergency:[81]

This would be attended by fatal results for South Africans. Friends here think it imperative you should authorize us to say if Botha unable to form ministry or if he declines to save situation you would be prepared to act if called upon to form ministry by Gladstone. This will be used in last resort. Do not let considerations ill health stand in the way as we want you even if only for short time and will see state of health will not be affected. This request would not be made if not absolutely necessary.

To this appeal Steyn drafted a reply:[82]

I could only consent as a last resort to try to form a ministry if the prime ministers and their colleagues of the Transvaal Cape Colony and Free State and if possible Natal also should express a desire for me to do so.

The reply was not telegraphed, however, because Natal gave in and on the 24th Botha completed his Ministry. C. O'Grady Gubbins of Natal was to be a minister without portfolio, Sauer was to remain with the Ministry of Railways and Harbours, and Greene was to have a seat on the Railways and Harbours Board.[83]

Soon afterwards the members of the Cabinet-to-be moved to Pretoria, where the final distribution of the portfolios was determined. An attempt was made to shift Burton from the Ministry of Native Affairs, which had been provisionally allotted to him, and to give it to a northerner, but this did not succeed;[84] and at the last moment Botha took Agriculture from Malan and gave him Education instead.[85] The result was that the Ministry was announced on 31 May as follows:[86]

LOUIS BOTHA	Prime Minister and Minister of Agriculture.
J. W. SAUER	Minister of Railways and Harbours.
J. C. SMUTS	Minister of the Interior, Minister of Mines, and Minister of Defence.
J. B. M. HERTZOG	Minister of Justice.
F. S. MALAN	Minister of Education.
H. C. HULL	Minister of Finance.
A. FISCHER	Minister of Lands.
H. BURTON	Minister of Native Affairs.
F. R. MOOR	Minister of Commerce and Industries.

[81] Telegram, n.d., Steyn Papers.
[82] Draft telegram in Steyn's hand, n.d., ibid.
[83] Fischer to Steyn, 24 May 1910 (telegram), ibid.
[84] Burton to Merriman, 4 June; Sauer to Merriman, 6 June. Merriman Papers.
[85] Cloete, pp. 228–9.   [86] Union of S.A. Gov. Gaz. i. 4.

D. P. DE V. GRAAFF Minister of Public Works.
C. O'G. GUBBINS Minister without portfolio.

The names of the judges of the Appellate Division of the Supreme Court, the administrators of the provinces, and the Union High Commissioner in London were also gazetted on Union Day.[87] Sir Henry de Villiers was the automatic choice as Chief Justice of the Union and he was also created a baron—an exceptional honour for a born and bred colonial. Sir James Rose Innes, Chief Justice of the Transvaal, and Sir William Solomon, of the Transvaal bench, became the ordinary judges of appeal. J. A. J. (Jacob) de Villiers, the Transvaal Attorney-General, was appointed Judge President of the Transvaal Division of the Supreme Court and one of the two additional judges of appeal, and C. G. Maasdorp of the Cape bench became Judge President of the Cape Division and the other additional judge of appeal. There was some criticism of the appointment of J. A. J. de Villiers, who had been a politician and a barrister, but never a judge. Nevertheless, an Appeal Court was created which would set an extremely high standard of judicial ability and integrity and which would play an important part in the development and standardization of Roman Dutch law in the Union of South Africa.

There was a great wrangle between the ministers over the appointment of the Administrator of the Cape Province. Sauer and Burton pressed the claims of H. L. Currey, Merriman's candidate and a minister without portfolio in his Cabinet, and Malan and Graaff insisted on N. F. de Waal, the Cape Colonial Secretary and a member of the Bond.[88] It was de Waal who received the appointment. The other administratorships went to J. F. B. Rissik, the Transvaal Minister of Lands and Native Affairs, C. J. Smythe, the former Prime Minister of Natal, and Dr. A. E. W. Ramsbottom, the Treasurer of the Orange River Colony. Sir Richard Solomon, the Transvaal Agent-General, became High Commissioner for the Union in London, and Sir Somerset French, the Cape Agent-General, was retired on pension.

Owing to the death of King Edward VII on 6 May, the Union was inaugurated with a minimum of ceremony and festivity. In the Legislative Assembly building in Pretoria the royal commission appointing the Governor-General was read in English and in Dutch and the Chief Justice administered the oaths of office to Lord Gladstone and the members of the Cabinet, while the administrators were also sworn in in

---

[87] Ibid. The name of C. G. Maasdorp as Judge President of the Cape Division and an additional Judge of Appeal was gazetted eleven days later. Ibid., p. 101.

[88] Burton to Merriman, 4 June 1910; Sauer to Merriman, 6 June 1910. Merriman Papers. Also Cloete, p. 228.

the provincial capitals. The Union of South Africa was born. The Executive and the Judiciary had come into being. But there was still no Parliament.

3. THE GENERAL ELECTION

The general election which took place on 15 September 1910 was a curiously confused contest. It had the appearance of a struggle for power between the South African National Party, supporting the Botha Government, the Unionist Party of South Africa, led by Jameson, and the South African Labour Party, but the appearance was deceptive for three reasons. Firstly, although the press described the supporters of the Government as members of the South African National Party or Nationalists (and these terms will be used here for convenience), the party had not yet acquired any real organizational existence. Secondly, the differences between the policies advocated by Botha and by Jameson were few and insignificant, whereas there were profound differences between those policies and the views expressed by Botha's colleague, Hertzog. Thirdly, there were many independent candidates of various hues in every province.

The first pan-South African political party to come into existence was the Labour Party. A conference of representatives of trade unions and of the Transvaal Independent Labour Party met in Durban in October 1908, agreed in principle to the creation of a single party, and instructed C. H. Haggar, a former Australian who held a seat in the Natal Parliament, to tour South Africa and promote the idea of unity for political action. Haggar encountered great difficulties. There was a deep division between the leaders of the craft unions and their middle class sympathizers on the one hand and a small minority of doctrinaire socialists on the other, and there were personal antagonisms within each group. Nevertheless, after several further conferences the South African Labour Party was officially launched in Durban in January 1910 with H. W. Sampson, a member of the Transvaal Parliament, as president and Haggar as general secretary.[89]

Soon after Botha's speech to the Het Volk congress on 22 March 1910 had put an end to any hope that the first Union Government would be a Government of 'the best men', plans were made for the amalgamation

---

[89] C. H. Haggar, 'Organised Labour as a Political Factor', *State*, iii. 933–45 (June 1910); R. K. Cope, *Comrade Bill: the Life and Times of W. H. Andrews, Workers' Leader* (Cape Town, 1943), pp. 112–14.

of the Transvaal Progressives, the Cape Unionists, and the Orange River Colony Constitutionalists. Jameson had been anxious to draw out of his political commitments in South Africa. His health was deteriorating, he was weary of politics, and he wanted to concentrate on the affairs of the British South Africa Company. Nevertheless, he was persuaded to assume the leadership of the united Party, since nobody else could command the allegiance of its diverse elements. A hundred and twelve delegates from the three colonial parties met in Bloemfontein on 23 May. They included Jameson, Smartt, Crewe, and Walton from the Cape, Farrar, Fitzpatrick, Chaplin, Phillips, and Duncan from the Transvaal, and Fraser of Bloemfontein. Efforts had been made to obtain a representative delegation from Natal, but the leading Natal politicians were reluctant to commit themselves and the Natal attendance was limited to a few observers. At a public meeting on 24 May Jameson announced that the three colonial opposition parties had merged in the Unionist Party of South Africa, with himself as leader.[90] The coalition negotiations had caused hardly any defections. Fitzpatrick, for example, was back in the fold and in a pugnacious mood, believing that Botha's rejection of his *Plea for a Fresh Start* showed that he had fallen into the clutches of reactionaries.

The government forces, on the other hand, were curiously uncoordinated. In March the Het Volk congress had given full powers to the Head Committee to negotiate and conclude an amalgamation, but when the congress of the Afrikaner Bond met in April, while it authorized the *Kommissie van Toezicht* to convene a conference of delegates of friendly parties, it also insisted that the report of any such conference should be referred back to another congress for deliberation; and the congress of the Orangia Unie, which met later in April, passed a similar resolution.[91] After he had formed his Union Government Botha tried to take the matter farther. At a public meeting in the Pretoria opera house on 14 June, with Smuts, Fischer, Hertzog, Sauer, and Graaff on the platform, he expressed the hope that 'the old parties will not continue to exist on their old lines and that they will all fall into line to form one great party', to be called the South African National Party.[92] But nothing was done to translate his wishes into action. The Bond and the Unie preferred to preserve their separate identities until the election was over and the political situation had been clarified. Consequently the South African National Party was not actually constituted until 1911,

[90] *Cape Times*, 25 May 1910; Colvin, *Jameson*, ii. 292–3; Long, *Chaplin*, pp. 154–6.
[91] *Cape Times*, 23 Mar., 4 and 20 Apr. 1910.
[92] Ibid., 15 June 1910.

and in effect the government's election campaign was conducted by the three colonial parties.

When the Labour Party was still in embryo the left wing had succeeded in introducing into its constitution the statement that one of the objects of the party was 'The socialisation of the means of production, distribution and exchange.'[93] Nevertheless, as the election approached it was the craft union and middle class elements—men like H. W. Sampson, F. H. P. Creswell, and C. H. Haggar—that prevailed, and the party's election manifesto was their work.[94] It was strictly reformist: there was no mention of socialist objectives. The preamble declared, however, that

The South African Labour Party is absolutely non-racial, and will fight racialism wherever it shows its head. It seeks only the national interest, and by national interest we mean the interests of men and women living in the country, whether rich or poor, skilled or unskilled.

From this it might have been deduced that the party was advocating the abolition of the political, industrial, and social colour-bars: but that was far from the case. The manifesto opposed racial discrimination against white people, but it advocated severe discrimination against non-whites. There should be no extension of the Native parliamentary franchise. 'Kaffirs' should have 'separate representation' in an 'Advisory Council'. They should be prohibited from owning or occupying land 'in areas occupied by whites', but should be provided with 'suitable' reserves, where they should receive 'proper' educational facilities and 'agricultural training'. Furthermore, bonuses should be paid to mines and factories employing white labour, Asiatic immigration should be prohibited, and every effort should be made to repatriate the Asiatics who were already living in South Africa. The manifesto also contained demands for a comprehensive workmen's compensation act, a forty-eight-hour week, free education, and other things which appeared in the contemporary programmes of labour parties elsewhere; but it was clear that according to the South African Labour Party only white people should benefit from them. It was a party of the privileged, not the underprivileged.

The Unionist manifesto was published on 25 May.[95] It declared that the party's objects were:

[93] Haggar, op. cit., p. 941; Cope, *Andrews*, p. 113.
[94] *Manifesto of the South African Labour Party* (n.d. [1910]), South African Public Library.
[95] *Cape Times*, 25 May 1910.

(a) To bring to completion the Union of South Africa in accordance with the spirit and intention of the Constitution.

(b) To work for the advancement of every section of the People, for the promotion of agricultural, commercial and industrial prosperity, and for the settlement of a permanent, contented population.

(c) To build up in South Africa a strong and united nation, working out its own domestic problems according to its own needs and aspirations, and taking its share in the defence of the Empire and in all movements leading to more effective participation by the different portions of the Empire in its common benefits and obligations.

The party's programme was as follows. A scheme of national defence was to be adopted and the Royal Navy was to be supported. An efficient and impartial civil service was to be created and made free from political influence. There was to be 'a vigorous education policy, including provision for compulsory education wherever possible, and the extension of free education where required'. Further Asiatic immigration would be opposed, but 'fair treatment' was to be secured 'for those now lawfully settled in the country', and a commission would be appointed to study labour conditions in Natal 'in order to bring them into harmony at the earliest possible date with this principle without detriment to established industries'. The Natives were to be treated 'in accordance with the degree of civilisation attained by them, and with the different and local conditions under which they live and work'. Legislation would be passed to improve the conditions of employment of industrial workers. Land settlement would be encouraged, suitable immigrants would be attracted, and the Union's agricultural, industrial, and mining resources would be developed. There would be 'a moderate Customs Tariff primarily for revenue purposes, but providing for adequate encouragement of legitimate South African industries and products, together with the maintenance and extension of the principle of preferential tariffs within the Empire'.

The nearest approach to an authoritative statement of the policy of the Government was a manifesto, signed by Botha alone, which was read to the meeting which he addressed in Pretoria on 14 June.[96] It was based on the document which Botha had circulated to Merriman, Malan, Fischer, and others in December 1909, but several changes had been made in consequence of their criticisms. The preamble declared that the main need for South Africa was that 'the various peoples who have made this country their permanent home' should be welded into 'one South African

[96] Ibid., 15 June 1910. Botha's manifesto was read to the meeting by his private secretary, Dr. W. E. Bok.

nation'. For this it was 'essential to secure the co-operation of all South Africans of whatever race, and to eliminate racialism from all political and national questions', and to base political parties upon 'differences of principle on practical questions, and not upon differences of race'. The objects of the party would be:

(a) To use its utmost endeavours to make a success of Union, and to promote the spirit of Union throughout South Africa and among all sections of its people.
(b) To promote a healthy South African spirit in dealing with our political and national problems.

The following programme was then set out. All parts of the Union would receive 'just and equal treatment'. The 'equality provisions' of the South Africa Act would be maintained and 'all causes of estrangement and misunderstanding between the various sections of the people' would be avoided. The Native question would be placed 'above party politics' and the 'coloured races' would be treated in 'a broad and liberal spirit'. White immigration would be encouraged and Asiatic immigration pre-vented. There would be an 'expanding education policy to meet the growing requirements of South Africa'. Conditions of labour would be improved and white labour would be secured its 'proper' share in the industrial and agricultural expansion of South Africa. An adequate sys-tem of national defence would be created for South Africa as part of the Empire. The State departments would be efficiently reorganized with due regard to the vested rights of civil servants. Economic and railway policy would develop 'along lines which will give greater freedom of expansion to South African industries and commerce'. Stable conditions would be fostered in the mining industries to encourage capital invest-ment and vigorous development. And agricultural expansion and land settlement would be promoted by improved means of production, the diffusion of agricultural knowledge, and the opening up of foreign markets for South African produce.

The similarity between the Unionist manifesto and the Botha mani-festo was remarkable. Both laid the main emphasis on the idea of a single South African nation and both did it in much the same way, avoiding any explicit statement that it was a white nation that was envisaged, although that was clearly the case. Both professed a non-dogmatic Native policy.[97] Both advocated white immigration and

[97] The 'Native question' was not an election issue. In the Cape Province both sides strove to win the support of the non-white voters: in the other provinces both sides came out against any extension of the non-white vote.

opposed Asiatic immigration. Both gave unqualified support to material expansion. Neither made any provision for special protection for the Afrikaner. Perhaps the most striking difference was that the Unionist manifesto explicitly supported imperial preference and implicitly supported imperial federation, while the Botha manifesto did not touch on those issues; but even Botha's document treated South African defence as part of an imperial problem and in their election speeches Botha and Smuts continued to stress the imperial aspect of their conciliation policy. 'South Africa', said Smuts, 'should do everything possible to assist the Empire which had given the Transvaal freedom. There was not another nation in the world which would have done the same thing, and South Africans should never forget the great act.' Botha declared that 'He had heard that people were being stirred up to "vote British", but had not the Empire every reason to regard him and his party as her sons, as good as any other?'[98] There was, indeed, no policy dispute between Botha and Jameson. As Jameson said, he was 'absolutely at one' with the Prime Minister on policy.[99]

What, then, were the election issues between the Government and the Unionists? Jameson made his position clear in a speech at the Wanderers in Johannesburg on 3 August.[1] It was not his objective, he said, to replace the Botha Government with a Unionist Government. He still wanted a Government of the best men. Botha had agreed with him, but had lacked the moral courage to act accordingly, with the result that he had formed a Cabinet with a 'reactionary' majority, who were making it impossible for him to carry out his declared policy. 'And that is the root reason for the formation of our party—to help the prime minister to coerce his colleagues in order that the policy should be carried out.'

It was therefore Hertzogism that became the main election issue. Botha had had good reasons to be anxious about the effects of giving Hertzog a place in his Cabinet. The application of Hertzog's Education Act of 1908, with its principles of compulsory bilingualism both as regards the teaching of Dutch and English as languages and as regards the use of both languages as media of instruction, had created a storm in the Orange River Colony and beyond its borders. There was undoubtedly a strong emotional content in the opposition to the Act, for many British South Africans resented 'having Dutch rammed down our children's throats'. There was also, however, a practical content. In the crown colony period 240 teachers had been imported into the Orange River Colony from Britain and other parts of the Empire. By the end of 1909

---

[98] *The Times*, 11 Aug. 1910.   [99] *Cape Times*, 4 Aug. 1910.
[1] Ibid.

all but ninety of them had resigned and the Government found it difficult, if not impossible, to replace them with successors of equal professional competence. Moreover, in May 1909 Hertzog had found it necessary to dismiss three school inspectors on the ground that they had
been trying to make his Act 'unworkable, unpopular and ridiculous'.
Opposition to the Act steadily increased. A delegation of English-
speaking inhabitants of the colony went to London to appeal for British
aid, and questions were asked in the House of Commons, but the British
Government stood firm by the doctrine of non-intervention in the internal affairs of a self-governing colony. Negotiations took place between
Hertzog and representatives of the English-speaking community, but
they ended in a cloud of mutual recriminations. Then in April 1910
Hugh Gunn resigned from the Directorship of Education in the Orange
River Colony on the grounds that the Act was unworkable and was
causing a decline in standards, and soon afterwards an Educational
Council was formed to establish schools in which the principles of the
Smuts Act would be applied.[2] On 3 May, however, Hertzog declared
that

he wished it to be understood that South Africa would stick to the School
Act, and the sound and just educational principles contained therein. That
Act would be maintained not only in the Free State but by the South Afri-
cans throughout the whole of South Africa.[3]

The press construed this statement as meaning that Hertzog wished to
extend his Act to the other provinces of the Union. Consequently the
announcement that Hertzog had been included in Botha's Cabinet met
with criticism from the opposition press throughout the country.

Botha tried desperately to ward off this attack on his Government. On
14 June he said he hoped to bring education 'on a non-party line'. On
7 July he said that the idea of compulsion as regards the medium of
instruction was abhorrent to him and that he regarded the Smuts Act
as a model. On 12 July he announced that the educational policy of his
Government was: '1. Equal opportunities of language. 2. Medium in the
mother tongue—even if it costs the State a little more money. 3. No
compulsion.' Soon afterwards Smuts declared that the Cabinet 'were all
agreed that there should be no compulsion in education' and Botha said
that they were 'absolutely unanimous' on the point.[4] Jameson demanded

[2] For the literature on the educational dispute in the Orange River Colony, see above,
p. 19, n. 52.
[3] *Cape Times*, 4 May 1910.
[4] Ibid., 15 June, 8 and 13 July, 5 and 10 Aug. 1910.

that Botha should give effect to his policy by withholding financial grants from the Free State until it had amended the Hertzog Act, but Smuts very properly replied that school education was a provincial matter for at least five years, that the only body which could amend the Hertzog Act was the Free State Provincial Council, and that it would be contrary to the spirit and intention of the Constitution if the Central Government were to coerce a province by threatening to withhold subsidies.[5]

That was the situation on 19 August when Hertzog made his nomination speech at Smithfield.[6] On the point at issue he spoke with two voices. On the one hand, he denied that he had ever threatened to extend the compulsory principle to the other provinces of the Union. Botha's policy statement, including 'No compulsion', had his 'hearty support' and it was 'a pure fabrication' to say that the Cabinet was divided on the question. On the other hand, he went to great lengths to defend his conduct as Minister of Education in the Orange River Colony and to reaffirm his faith in the content of his Education Act. National unity in South Africa, he said, must be accompanied by the preservation of the language difference, for if the Afrikaners surrendered their language they would lose their 'character and existence as a people'. Moreover, the principle of compulsion was thoroughly sound, even if he was now prepared to waive its application:

I should ever consider it a great injustice by parents towards their children if they did not compel their children to learn the Dutch language, and, in my view, legal compulsion is in every way a justifiable way of stopping that injustice; but I have never considered it to be a matter of sufficient importance to force it upon my English-speaking fellow-citizens against their will.

Hertzog also went out of his way to explain that the Smuts Education Act did not provide equality, because it made English the medium of instruction after standard III and because while it compelled Dutch-speaking children to learn English it did not compel English-speaking children to learn Dutch. But that was not all. Hertzog also dealt with two other questions very differently from the Prime Minister. Firstly, Hertzog's reference to the imperial tie was ambiguous. Thanks to Campbell-Bannerman, he said, South Africa had been granted 'full and free self-government with the recognition of the status of equals within the Imperial State building'. This action had 'reconciled us to our loss suffered by the fortunes of war, and *if we are no longer permitted to be free republicans*,[7] we will be and remain free Britons' and carry out 'our

[5] Ibid., 4 and 5 Aug. 1910.   [6] Ibid., 20 Aug. 1910.
[7] My italics.

duties regarding Great Britain . . . so long as we are given the privilege of working out our national salvation through the recognised means of autonomy'. Secondly, whereas Botha had given his unqualified support to the encouragement of white immigration, Hertzog declared that 'There is nothing more detestable than the cry for immigration from outside.' It was a capitalist cry raised for the purpose of depressing the wages of South Africans. What was wanted was internal migration of white South Africans from the cities back to the land, but no immigration from outside the Union. There was, furthermore, a marked difference between the tone of Botha's speeches and the tone of Hertzog's. Botha had refrained from strong denunciations of his opponents. Hertzog made a vehement attack on Jameson and his party, who, he declared, 'by lies, distortion, and false representation, yes by direct incitement, are endeavouring to flood South Africa with racialism'. He recalled the Jameson Raid and Jameson's support of the 1902 agitation for the suspension of the Cape constitution—'a criminal effort to persuade the British Government to rob his adopted fatherland' of 'its existence as a self-governing colony'. Jameson's 'pretended conciliation policy' had never been genuine, for the Unionist press was calling on its readers to 'vote British'. The 'malice and hatred' of the Jameson party 'against the Dutch-speaking South African and his language' had been shown, above all, in the agitation against his Education Act. They had 'incited' the English-speaking people of the Free State 'in the most shameless way'. They had sent delegates on a 'criminal mission' to try and induce the British Government to intervene in Free State affairs. They seemed to spend most of their time 'inventing fiction' for the press. 'The Unionist method of fighting', he concluded, 'is that of the slanderer and the racialist.'

This speech was denounced by the Unionists as the speech of a fanatic. 'Obviously political discussion would be utterly impossible if the members of opposing parties were to resort to vulgar and insolent abuse of this kind', declared the *Cape Times*. Jameson's bona fides in his negotiations with Botha had been accepted by Botha himself, so why should Hertzog deny it? Even the pro-Hertzog press had construed Hertzog's earlier speech as meaning that he intended to apply his Education Act to the other parts of the Union, so why should he denounce the opposition press for reaching the same conclusion? How could he reconcile his fresh defence of the principle of compulsion with his claim to be a hearty supporter of Botha's principle of no compulsion? And how could he claim that the Cabinet was united? The deduction was drawn that Botha had admitted a 'political firebrand' into his

Cabinet and that he should repudiate 'the unpardonable outbreak at Smithfield'.[8]

Botha was dismayed by these developments, but he lacked the means to control Hertzog. He and his colleagues tried, however, to divert attention from Hertzogism to other issues. Much use was made, for example, of the revival of economic prosperity in South Africa during the period of Het Volk, Orangia Unie, and South African Party rule. The main counter-attack upon the Unionists was the allegation that they were a capitalist party. Hertzogism, said Sauer, was just an election cry. Every member of the Cabinet had said he was against compulsion, so why all this agitation? The Unionists were trying to divert attention from the real point at issue, which was 'whether capitalism should dominate our affairs'.[9] Fischer put the same argument more picturesquely. The capitalists, he said, were 'dirty aasvogels' (vultures), who had found a bit of carrion in the Witwatersrand and wanted to exhaust its wealth and then to seek other carrion elsewhere.[10] Here the Labour Party were useful allies. They produced election posters listing the directorships of mining companies held by leading Unionists—Jameson, Farrar, Phillips, Chaplin, and Bailey—and declaring: 'Every vote for a Unionist is a vote for Directors' Domination!'[11] Predikants also exerted their influence on the government side. On 11 September, the last Sunday before the election, for example, Ds. Broekhuizen exhorted a Pretoria congregation to stand together 'for the rights of our people' and to 'support the men whom God has placed over us'. The members of the Cabinet were the servants of God. They had been a blessing to the people. They might perhaps have done more, but would 'the others' have done as much? The predikant proceeded to remind his hearers of the bloodshed, the destruction, and the misery caused by the war and concluded with an eloquent appeal against the lure of nice-sounding words and the power of the money-bag. Special prayers were offered 'that our people may unanimously do their duty'.[12]

Thus, in spite of Botha's good intentions the election had many of the hallmarks of a racial conflict between Boer and Briton. On 8 September

---

[8] *Cape Times*, 22, 23, and 24 Aug. 1910.
[9] Ibid., 25 Aug. 1910.　　　　　　　　　　　　　　　[10] Ibid., 6 Sept. 1910.
[11] Examples of these election posters are in the South African Public Library.
[12] *The Times*, 13 Sept. 1910. On 22 Sept. the *Volksstem*, Pretoria, published a sermon which had been preached by Ds. Bosman, comparing the trials of the Boer people and those of the Jews in the days of Nehemiah. Nehemiah was also troubled 'by strangers and uitlanders'. He had to defend himself against a raid. Attempts were made to discredit him by offers of co-operation; his own people fell away, married wives from Ammon and Moab, and refused to speak their native language. In spite of all trials, however, Jerusalem was ultimately rebuilt and populated by the tribes of Judah and Benjamin. 'Similarly let Pretoria be converted into a strong fortress.' *The Times*, 23 Sept.

the *Cape Times* published a cartoon showing a policeman (South Africa) looking in through the window into the 'Convention Room' where a very miserable cat ('Convention Spirit') sits all alone. 'Poor devil!' says P.C. South Africa. 'The fuss they made of it! Call themselves "Nationalists", and leave the poor beast to starve.' The convention spirit was, indeed, very much starved during the campaign. Each side called the other racialist and protested its own innocence. Unionists, in crying Hertzogism, credited Hertzog with ambitions of Afrikaner domination which he, at any rate, did not possess. Nationalists, in crying capitalism, created an equally distorted picture of the purposes of the Unionist leaders.

The Delimitation Commission appointed under section 38 of the South Africa Act consisted of judges Sir Perceval Laurence (Cape Colony), W. H. Beaumont (Natal), Sir William Solomon (Transvaal), and A. W. Fawkes (Orange River Colony). They met for the first time on 1 November 1909, when Laurence was elected chairman, and, after they had toured the country and heard evidence from interested parties in the main centres, they signed their report on 10 May 1910, and it was published in the *Government Gazette* on 1 June.[13]

It was not necessary for the commissioners to determine how many seats in the first Union House of Assembly should be allotted to each province, for that had been laid down in the South Africa Act—the Cape Province was to have fifty-one, the Transvaal thirty-six, and Natal and the Orange Free State seventeen each. Their first task was to determine the provincial quotas, 'by dividing the total number of voters in the province, as ascertained at the last registration of voters, by the number of members of the House of Assembly to be elected therein'. In the Cape Colony and the Transvaal the 1909 registrations had been completed shortly before the commission started its work, but the Natal and Orange River Colony registrations were not complete and, rather than delay their proceedings, the commissioners decided to use the 1907 registrations in those colonies. The result was that the provincial quotas worked out as follows: Cape Province 2,791, Transvaal 2,715, Orange Free State 2,131, and Natal 1,647. The maxima and minima of voters to a division were then worked out by adding 15 per cent. to and deducting 15 per cent. from the quotas. The commissioners then discussed the rules laid down in section 40 (3) of the South Africa Act, according to which they were to give 'due consideration' to five factors. In their report they

---

[13] Also published separately, *Report of the Delimitation Commission under the South Africa Act, 1909* (Pretoria, 1910).

observed that the first four factors corresponded with the instructions which had been given to the Transvaal Delimitation Commission in 1906, but that those instructions had contained nothing corresponding to the fifth factor, 'sparsity or density of population'. 'It appeared obvious', they reported, 'though not specifically laid down, that the intention was, in sparsely populated areas, that the Commission should endeavour to frame divisions containing a number of voters less than, and in densely populated districts a number exceeding, the quota.' They had found, however, that it was 'practically impossible to arrive at any precise definition of sparsity or density'. Nevertheless, they reported, they had had no great difficulty in deciding into which category each division should be placed.

Their delimitation gave considerable stress to this fifth factor and a marked advantage to the rural voters. In the Cape Province Kimberley, Port Elizabeth, and East London were given a total of five seats with an average load of 9·2 per cent. above the quota and the Cape peninsula was given eight seats with an average load of 14·5 per cent., while eleven rural divisions had at least 8 per cent. fewer voters than the quota. In the Transvaal seventeen seats were given to the Witwatersrand and two to Pretoria town, with an average load of 5·3 per cent., and six rural divisions had at least 8 per cent. fewer voters than the quota. In Natal five seats were allotted to Durban and two to Pietermaritzburg, with an average load of 6·3 per cent., and three rural divisions had at least 8 per cent. fewer voters than the quota. In the Orange Free State the Bloemfontein urban seat had a load of 14·5 per cent. Thus the main urban areas of the Union were given forty seats and the rest of the country eighty-one: whereas if each province had been divided into equal constituencies those main urban areas would have had forty-three seats and the rest of the country seventy-eight.[14]

For the thirty-eight rural divisions in the Cape Province fifty-one Nationalist,[15] eleven Unionist, and two Independent candidates were nominated.[16] Eleven Nationalists were returned unopposed, including

[14] There is necessarily an arbitrary element in any distinction between urban and rural constituencies. Several constituencies which have been classified here as rural contained medium sized towns—e.g. Stellenbosch, Paarl, Albany (Grahamstown), King William's Town, and Queenstown. Nevertheless, the classification which has been adopted is reasonable. as all the towns mentioned in the previous sentence formed parts of constituencies which included large rural areas.

[15] Note that although supporters of the Botha Government were described as Nationalists in 1910, in 1913 Hertzog founded a party which took over that label.

[16] In the preparation of this account of the election, material generously supplied by Professor G. H. L. Le May and Mrs. Le May, based mainly on the *Star* reports, has

J. W. Sauer (Aliwal North), D. P. de V. Graaff (Namaqualand), J. X. Merriman (Victoria West), and H. C. van Heerden (Cradock); and so were five Unionists, including L. S. Jameson (Albany) and T. W. Smartt (Fort Beaufort).[17] There were straight fights between Nationalists and Unionists in only five rural divisions in the province. The Nationalists won two of them—Uitenhage and Somerset East—while the Unionists won Griqualand East, Queenstown, and Three Rivers (near Port Elizabeth).[18] At Barkly (near Kimberley) the Unionist had a clear victory over a Nationalist and an Independent, and at Ceres the Nationalist overwhelmed an Independent. There were thirty-four candidates in the fifteen other rural divisions in the Cape Province, and all of them were Nationalists.[19] In seven cases the candidate sponsored by the Bond defeated another Nationalist. They included Malmesbury, where F. S. Malan was the victor; and Albert, where H. Burton, the Minister of Native Affairs, defeated A. Coetsee, a leading local Bondsman who had appealed unsuccessfully to the *Kommissie van Toezicht* against the validity of the meeting which had selected Burton as the Bond candidate, although he was not a member of the Bond. At Clanwilliam, on the other hand, a non-Bond Nationalist defeated the Bond candidate. In two divisions—Piquetberg and Wodehouse—the Bond machinery for selecting candidates broke down and there were contests between rival Bondsmen.[20] In the other five divisions—George, Ladysmith, Oudtshoorn, Riversdale, and Swellendam—there were no branches of the Bond and, in the absence of Independent or Unionist candidates, there were free-for-alls between Nationalists.

In the thirteen urban divisions in the Cape Province the story was very different. There were twelve Unionist candidates, two Nationalists, two

been found most useful. It has been supplemented with the *Cape Times* and *South African News* reports and with M. P. A. Malan and M. C. van Rensburg. *Verkiesingsuitslae 1910–1943 met volledige naamlys van Volksraadslede vanaf 1910* (Bloemfontein, n.d.).

[17] Two of the Unionists who were returned unopposed were described as Independent Unionists on nomination day, but were regarded as Unionists by the time Parliament met.

[18] The unsuccessful candidate in Griqualand East was described as an Independent on nomination day, but on the eve of the poll the *South African News*, a pro-government newspaper, claimed him as a Nationalist.

[19] Some of these candidates were described in the press as Nationalists, others as Independent Nationalists, but without consistency. Twenty-one candidates in the entire province were officially sponsored by the Bond. Their names were published in *Ons Land* on 20 Aug.

[20] The findings of the *Kommissie van Toezicht* on the disputes connected with the selections of Bond candidates for Albert, Piquetberg, and Wodehouse are in *Zeven en twintigste Centrale Vergadering van de Afrikaander Bond en Boeren Vereniging* (Cape Town, 1911).

Labour, one Socialist, one 'Social Reform', and seven Independents. Two of the Unionists were returned unopposed—E. H. Walton for Port Elizabeth Central and H. S. Harris[21] for Beaconsfield (Kimberley)—and so was one Independent. That left Unionists facing opponents in East London, Kimberley, and the eight Cape peninsula seats. The Labour candidates and the Independents were supported by the pro-government press. On polling day the Unionists triumphed in all the ten contests. The closest result was in Woodstock, where J. Hewat defeated the Labour candidate by 951 to 926.[22]

In the Cape Province as a whole the Nationalists won twenty-nine seats (all rural), the Unionists twenty-one (twelve urban, nine rural), and an Independent one (urban). The Unionist territory fell into three separate blocks: the Cape peninsula (eight urban seats), the Kimberley area (two urban seats, one rural), and a large area in the eastern part of the province, which may broadly be described as the 1820 settler country, stretching from Three Rivers and Port Elizabeth Central eastwards to the Natal border (two urban seats, eight rural). The rest of the province was Nationalist. Most of the non-white voters appear to have preferred the Unionists, who won all the seven inter-party contests in which more than 20 per cent. of the voters were non-white.[23]

[21] Harris was described as an Independent Unionist on nomination day but was regarded as a Unionist by the time Parliament met.

[22] The victor in Cape Town Harbour was L. S. Jameson, who had already been returned unopposed for Albany. He subsequently chose to represent Albany and Cape Town Harbour went to another Unionist.

[23] The following were the divisions in which the non-white vote was most significant:

Division	Non-white % of the electorate	Result
Tembuland	49·2	Unionist unopposed
Namaqualand	30·8	Nationalist unopposed
Newlands	30·4	Unionist 1,083, Independent 643
Fort Beaufort	29·3	Unionist unopposed
King William's Town	29·1	Unionist unopposed
Stellenbosch	28·8	Bond Nationalist 1,134, Nationalist 976
Port Elizabeth S.-W.	28·5	Independent unopposed
Kimberley	26·0	Unionist 1,121, Labour 584
Cape Town Castle	24·0	Unionist 1,273, Independent 571, Social Reform 224
South Peninsula	23·4	Unionist 1,153, Independent Nationalist 754, Independent 68
Aliwal	21·9	Nationalist unopposed
Port Elizabeth Central	21·1	Unionist unopposed
Queenstown	20·1	Unionist 1,156, Nationalist 942
Griqualand East	20·0	Unionist 877, Independent Nationalist 675

The *Cape Province Official Gazette* for 26 July 1910 gives the racial composition of

The Orangia Unie organization was triumphant in the Free State. Nationalists stood in all the seventeen divisions. Eight of them were returned unopposed, including A. Fischer (Bethlehem) and J. B. M. Hertzog (Smithfield). In three divisions Nationalists won straight fights against Unionists, in three others Nationalists defeated Independents of Unionist leanings, in Kroonstad a Nationalist defeated an Independent of Nationalist leanings, and in Vredefort a Nationalist won a triangular contest against a Unionist and an Independent. Thus Nationalists won all the rural seats in the province. Their closest contest was in Bloemfontein District, where J. P. G. Steyl beat G. A. Falck by 897 to 828. In Bloemfontein Town, on the other hand, the Unionist candidate, C. L. Botha, won with 863 votes to 653 for the Nationalist and 146 for Labour. In the entire province the Unionists only succeeded in polling 2,662 votes and sympathetic Independents another 1,314.

The Nationalists made a clean sweep of the Transvaal rural divisions. Eleven were returned unopposed, three defeated Independents of Nationalist leanings, two defeated Unionists, and one won a triangular contest against Labour and Independent candidates. The only close contest was at Marico, which was won by 756 to 739 from an Independent. 971 votes were polled by the two Unionists.

The keenest fights in all South Africa were in the Transvaal urban divisions, where there were three well-organized parties in the field. The Unionists put up candidates for all the nineteen seats, but not one of them was returned unopposed. There were eleven Labour candidates, ten Nationalists, two Socialists, and three Independents. Notwithstanding the fact that the Transvaal Government had sided with the employers to suppress a strike on the Rand in 1907, some of the Labour leaders had come to an agreement with Het Volk that they would not contest the same seats, and in fifteen divisions the Unionist was confronted with either a Nationalist or a Labour opponent; but in Fordsburg, Georgetown, and Pretoria West the agreement broke down and both Nationalist and Labour candidates were nominated, while at Von Brandis the Unionists' only opponent was an Independent.[24] On the Witwatersrand eleven Unionists were successful. They included Sir George Farrar (who defeated H. C. Hull, the Minister of Finance, at Georgetown), Patrick Duncan, Drummond Chaplin, and Lionel Phillips. Labour were lucky to win four Witwatersrand seats by narrow majorities over Union-

the Cape Province electoral roll in each division according to the 1909 registration and the 1910 delimitation.

[24] The Nationalist–Labour negotiations are reflected in correspondence between Smuts and Haggar in June and July 1910. Smuts Papers.

ists.[25] The Nationalists won two Witwatersrand seats—Vrededorp, and Krugersdorp, where Abe Bailey was defeated by 1,094 to 981. They also won Pretoria West, where J. C. Smuts overwhelmed his Unionist, Labour, and Independent opponents. Many of these contests attracted considerable attention, but none of them captured the public imagination as much as the contest in Pretoria East, where Louis Botha and Sir Percy Fitzpatrick met in a straight fight. In 1907 Fitzpatrick had scored a notable victory over Sir Richard Solomon in the division which corresponded most closely with the Union division of Pretoria East and he had no hesitation in standing there in 1910. Pressure was put on the Prime Minister by members of his own party to contest the seat, rather than to take the safe rural seat of Standerton which he had held in the Transvaal Parliament, and he yielded—an unwise decision, for Fitzpatrick was a doughty electioneer and Botha's energies should have been spared for more important issues than the securing of his seat in Parliament. According to Fitzpatrick, who may have exaggerated, Botha had a secret meeting with him before nomination day and tried to bribe him not to go forward as a candidate for Pretoria East, offering him a safe seat elsewhere, or a railway commissionership at £3,000 a year, or a baronetcy, but these were contemptuously rejected.[26] The result of this poll was a Unionist triumph: Fitzpatrick won by 1,231 to 1,136. The total poll in the nineteen Transvaal urban divisions was divided between the parties as follows: Unionists 19,043 (twelve seats), Nationalists 8,344 (three seats), Labour 7,708 (four seats), Socialists 33, and Independents 951.

The campaign in Natal was more confused than in the other provinces because of the lack of an indigenous party system. During 1910 leaders of both the main parties in South Africa made strenuous efforts to build up local support, but they were not very successful. In January Jameson found the Natal British unco-operative—'still of the pure grocer variety', he informed his brother, 'ostensibly British but really in Botha's pocket as the dispenser of good things'[27]—and, as has been said, Natal was not properly represented in Bloemfontein when the Unionist Party was launched. Later, however, a number of Unionist committees were established and the Durban press veered towards the Unionist cause. Botha and Smuts also visited Natal and were well received, but their efforts to win over the British voters were offset by fears of Hertzogism and by a

---

[25] The successful Labour candidates included C. H. Haggar, who had quarrelled with the other Labour leaders and described himself as Independent Labour.

[26] Fitzpatrick, 'The Botha Election' (unpublished manuscript), Fitzpatrick Papers.

[27] Colvin, *Jameson*, ii. 290.

general reaction against the last Natal Government from which Botha had selected the Natal members of his Cabinet. The majority of the Natal British, indeed, were impervious to the blandishments of both parties and hoped to return a strong block of Independents to Parliament to watch the evolution of Union politics and, perhaps, to support Botha at a later stage, provided that he disciplined Hertzog or cast him off.

Nationalist candidates appeared in four northern divisions, two midland divisions, and (as a gesture more than anything else) two coastal divisions, Unionists took the field in five coastal divisions and in Weenen, Labour candidates contested six divisions, and a Socialist appeared in Pietermaritzburg South. Independents—in some cases two or more rival Independents—stood in every division except four. On polling day Nationalists won only the two northernmost divisions, where there was a large Afrikaner population—Vryheid, where two of them tied and the issue was decided by drawing lots,[28] and Newcastle. At Weenen a young Unionist, H. M. Meyler, defeated F. R. Moor, the Minister of Commerce and Industries, by 495 to 450; and the other Nationalist candidates were convincingly beaten. The Unionists won five of the six seats they contested. Besides Weenen they obtained three Durban seats and Victoria County, all by absolute majorities. Their successful candidates included P. A. Silburn, the imperialist,[29] and Sir David Hunter. At Umlazi, on the other hand, where there were six candidates including a Unionist and a Nationalist, it was an Independent, A. Fawcus, who was victorious, with the lowest winning poll in all South Africa—327. Ten seats in all were won by Independents, all of whom had English names. The Labour candidates and the Socialist were all beaten. These results were a rebuff not only to the Union Government but also to the last Natal Government. Only two of its members, Moor and W. A. Deane, had faced the electors and both were defeated, whereas three members of the previous Smythe Ministry were returned as Independents—T. Watt, J. G. Maydon, and W. F. Clayton—and a fourth, T. Hyslop, lost by only four votes to another Independent at Klip River. The results might also have been construed as a vote of no confidence in the last Natal Parliament, only six members of which were chosen to go to Cape Town.

The final position was as follows:

---

[28] There were two candidates at Vryheid—G. Rabe, who was described as Nationalist, and M. W. Myburgh, who was described as Independent Nationalist. Each polled 377 votes and it was Myburgh who was successful in the drawing of lots.

[29] P. A. Silburn, the victor at Durban Point, was described as an Independent Unionist, but by the time Parliament met he was regarded as a Unionist.

	Nationalist	Unionist	Labour	Independent	Total
Cape Province . .	29	21	0	1	51
Transvaal . . .	20	12	4	0	36
Orange Free State .	16	1	0	0	17
Natal. . . .	2	5	0	10	17
	67	39	4	11	121

There would be a clear government majority of thirteen over all other members in the House of Assembly.

The effect of the delimitation had been considerable but not decisive. Fifty seats won by Nationalists and nine seats won by non-Nationalists were in divisions with fewer voters than the provincial quotas: whereas seventeen seats won by Nationalists and forty-five seats won by non-Nationalists were in divisions with more voters than the provincial quotas. As the following table shows, the total number of quotas in the divisions won by Nationalists was 64·26 and the total number of quotas in the divisions won by non-Nationalists was 56·74, so that if each province had been divided into equal constituencies the government majority over all other members would probably have been seven instead of thirteen:

Number of quotas in divisions won by each party

	Nationalist	Unionist	Labour	Independent	Total
Cape Province . .	27·32	22·66	0	1·02	51
Transvaal . . .	19·13	12·70	4·17	0	36
Orange Free State .	15·86	1·14	0	0	17
Natal. . . .	1·95	5·04	0	10·01	17
	64·26	41·54	4·17	11·03	121

Ingenious attempts were made by the press to estimate the relative voting strengths of the different parties, but they varied immensely, as each newspaper was inclined to make its estimate as favourable as possible to the party which it supported. The *Cape Times*, for example, estimated the total Nationalist vote at between 90,000 and 95,000 and the total Unionist vote at between 80,000 and 85,000, while the *South African News* gave the Nationalists 115,544 and the Unionists 77,119.[30] In fact it was quite impossible to make an accurate estimate from an election in which thirty-nine members were returned unopposed, sixteen

[30] *Cape Times* and *South African News*, 21 Sept. 1910.

others had contests only with members of their own party, and there were so many Independent candidates.[31]

What the results did show was that, notwithstanding the 'non-racial' platforms of all the parties, there was a very close correspondence between 'race' and politics throughout the Union. Every division won by a Nationalist contained a large number of Afrikaners: every non-Nationalist division contained a large number of British South Africans. The overwhelming majority of the Afrikaner electorate had certainly voted Nationalist: the overwhelming majority of the British South African electorate had certainly voted non-Nationalist. All the Nationalist divisions were rural except three—one in Pretoria and two on the Witwatersrand, which reflected the beginning of a townward movement of Afrikaners: all the non-Nationalist divisions were urban except seventeen, which were in the only areas where British settlement had taken root on an effective scale.[32]

Thirty-two of the forty places in the Senate had been filled by the colonial parliaments in their final sessions. These senators had been elected by proportional representation in joint sittings of both Houses in accordance with section 24 (iii) of the South Africa Act. In the parliaments of the Cape Colony, the Transvaal, and the Orange River Colony the elections had been conducted on strict party lines, each party supporting a ticket arranged at a caucus meeting. All the elected senators were drawn from the colonial parliaments and most of them were somewhat elderly and unambitious politicians. For the Cape there were six members of the South African Party, including Dr. J. H. M. Beck, the Convention delegate, and two Unionists. For the Orange River Colony there were six members of the Orangia Unie and two Constitutionalists, including Sir John Fraser. For the Transvaal there were four members of Het Volk, including J. H. de la Rey and A. D. W. Wolmarans, a Nationalist Party member of the Transvaal Cabinet, E. P. Solomon, a Labour member of the Transvaal Parliament, P. Whiteside, and two Progressives. The Natal senators were the last Colonial Secretary of Natal, C. O'Grady Gubbins, who was minister without portfolio in the

[31] Mrs. Le May, who has gone into this question carefully, reaches the conclusion that all that can be said is that the Nationalists may be credited with something between 50 per cent. and 60 per cent. of the total vote.

[32] See above, p. 471, n. 14. The Nationalist urban divisions were Krugersdorp, Vrededorp, and Pretoria West. The non-Nationalist rural divisions were Albany, Barkly, Border, Fort Beaufort, Griqualand East, King William's Town, Queenstown, Tembuland, and Three Rivers (Cape Province), and Dundee, Klip River, Umlazi, Umvoti, Umzimkulu, Victoria County, Weenen, and Zululand (Natal).

Union Government, and seven other politicians of the old school, most of them supporters of the Moor administration.[33] The names of the nominated senators were announced on 13 October. Those nominated 'on the ground mainly of their thorough acquaintance . . . with the reasonable wants and wishes of the coloured races in South Africa' were W. P. Schreiner, W. E. M. Stanford, J. C. Krogh, and F. R. Moor. The choice of Schreiner and Stanford was above criticism. Krogh, too, had sound claims, having been a member of the South African Native Affairs Commission of 1903–5, but the appointment of the defeated assembly candidate for Weenen in this category was an unfortunate precedent. It is true that Moor had been Minister for Native Affairs for many years in Natal, but it was also well known that he was unsympathetic to African advancement. The other four nominated senators included F. W. Reitz, a former President of the Orange Free State.[34] The Government was thus assured of a large majority in the Senate, which was a particularly valuable asset since the composition of the Senate was unalterable for ten years, except for the filling of vacancies.

The results of the general election—and more particular the defeats of Botha, Hull, and Moor—were generally regarded as a rebuff to the Government. Botha himself was extremely depressed. He considered resignation and it was some time before he consented to take the safe rural seat of Losberg, while Hull was also slow in accepting the offer of Barberton. Moor, on the other hand, resigned from the Cabinet, where his place was filled by G. Leuchars, who had been elected as an Independent for the Natal division of Umvoti. Botha and Smuts were convinced that Hertzog had been the main cause of their failure to win British votes. Botha complained about it to Steyn;[35] and Smuts informed an English friend that 'the thing that knocked us badly was General Hertzog's Education policy in the Free State, which the English people resented as directed against their racial ideals. It is very hard that Botha and Hull should be punished for a policy which they have always stoutly resisted; but such is the logic of the crowd.'[36] Nevertheless, wrote Smuts, 'we shall continue our liberal South African policy'.[37] Conciliation had been the lodestar of Botha and Smuts in the creation of the South African Union: it would remain so now that the Union was in being.

[33] *The Times*, 31 May 1910.
[34] *Cape Times*, 14 Oct. 1910.
[35] Van der Merwe, ii. 241.
[36] Smuts to A. B. Gillett, 19 Sept. 1910, Smuts Papers (copy).
[37] Ibid.

4. CONCLUSION

The Union was launched on a wave of optimism. There was a wide-spread belief, in England and in South Africa, that Boer and Briton would spontaneously fuse into one nation. It was to be a prosperous nation, efficiently exploiting the natural resources of the country. It was to be an expansive nation, peacefully absorbing the High Commission Territories, Southern Rhodesia, and, perhaps, the other British colonies and protectorates in central and even east Africa. Like Canada, Australia, and New Zealand, it was to be an active partner in the British Empire.

How firmly based was this orthodox view? If the arguments that had been used by men like Smuts and Merriman in support of their prediction of an Anglo-Boer fusion are examined, they are found to be sweeping and insubstantial.[38] For example, the fact that most Britons as well as Boers were Protestants did not warrant the deduction that there was no religious obstacle to their fusion, for there were fundamental differences between the social teachings of the Dutch Reformed Churches and those of the other Christian Churches in South Africa (including even the Presbyterian Church). Nor did the fact that both Boer and Briton were mainly of Teutonic descent warrant the deduction that racial sentiment would not hold them apart. Racial sentiment is the product of historical as well as biological factors, and the historical experiences of Boer and Briton had been very dissimilar. The tensions of the period when the British imperialism was at its height, culminating in the war of 1899–1902, had left diverse deposits of remembered strivings and sufferings, and although most white South Africans professed the orthodox view in public, there were not very many like Botha, Smuts, and Merriman, to whom it was a reality and not a mask, a permanent way of life and not a stepping-stone towards another goal. From the British South African mind the aspirations which Milner had fostered had not been wholly deleted. Men like Fitzpatrick were still hoping that the tempo of economic development would be increased to such an extent that the British element would sooner or later outnumber the Afrikaners and the Afrikaners would sooner or later be denationalized, so that the South African nation would become essentially British in culture and feeling. In many an Afrikaner mind, on the other hand, an exclusive national ideal and a republican yearning were still present. The belief that the preservation of the Afrikaners as a distinct people was an object of the divine will was deeply engrained and persistently propagated by predikants. Many Afrikaners who had hitherto supported, or at least not

[38] See above, pp. 104, 330.

actively opposed, the policy of Botha and Smuts had done so in the realization that it was sound tactics—a means of obtaining concessions from Britain. But now that South Africa was united and the imperial factor was virtually eliminated, were not different tactics called for? Would not the conciliation policy, if persisted in, produce the very results which Fitzpatrick desired?

Of these two deviations from the orthodox view, it was the Afrikaner one which was the more formidable. Even under the propitious circumstances of the period immediately after the war, British immigration had not reached a decisive scale, British South Africans had not acted in unison, and Afrikaner national consciousness had not been undermined. In the 1910 election a significant proportion of the English-speaking voters preferred labour or independent candidates to Unionists and there was still no sign of a *British* South African national spirit. Afrikaner nationalism, on the other hand, had a powerful institutional basis in the Dutch Reformed Churches, a vigorous cultural basis in the language movement, and a potential leader in Hertzog. In these circumstances the short-term prospects of the Union would hinge upon the relations between Botha and Hertzog. Perhaps regular contact in the Cabinet would allay their mutual suspicions and yield some compromise between the policy of conciliation and the policy of protection for the Afrikaner. Alternatively, their differences might become accentuated to breaking-point, as Jameson had predicted. In that event the stage would be set for the creation of an avowedly nationalist Afrikaner party—and once such an organization existed there could be no knowing what its ultimate character would be, for a party which is nourished by racial fervour generates its own dynamics.

Ultimately, however, the fate of the Union and its prospects of peaceful territorial expansion would depend mainly upon the capacity of white South Africans to establish satisfactory relations with their Coloured, Indian, and African fellow countrymen. So preoccupied had they been with other issues for more than a decade that they had not paid much attention to this question, save when it had been forced upon them by the Natal Native Rebellion and by the need to devise the franchise sections of the Union Constitution. It remained to be seen whether the British hope that white South Africans would become increasingly liberal was justified, or whether, as more and more non-whites acquired western skills and western aspirations, the whites, outnumbered as they were, would seek to maintain their supremacy at all costs—even at the cost of denying any non-white an effective say in the Government of the country. Already there were signs that the liberal tradition of the Cape

Colony might be overwhelmed. Negrophobic views had been expressed in the Cape Parliament as well as the other colonial parliaments, and the crude ideas of the Labour Party had attracted many of the Witwatersrand voters.[39] What if such a policy were to be adopted by one of the major parties? Might it not be a perfect prescription for victory at the polls? Moreover, it was being claimed that there was moral justification for racial discrimination. The 'kafir', it was said, was 'naturally' inferior to the white man—'something between a child and an animal'.[40] He was being spoilt by contact with whites and it was therefore in his own interest that the contact should cease. He should be 'separated' from the whites and allowed to develop 'along his natural lines'.[41] Such writers did not explain what they meant by the 'natural lines' of African development; nor did they explain how white South Africans, who had been dependent on non-white labour ever since the time of Van Riebeeck, were to be persuaded to do without it; nor did they define the positions which were to be occupied by the Coloured and Indian peoples of South Africa. Nevertheless, few white South Africans agreed with Schreiner that the orthodox ideal of a white South African nation was incomplete on the ground that the Coloured, the Indian, and the African, as well as the white inhabitants of the Union, should be regarded as parts of the new nation and potential citizens of the new State.[42]

The founders of the Union believed that a Sovereign Parliament would be the best constitutional instrument for the handling of these difficult problems.[43] They had buttressed this belief with many arguments, of which some were dubious interpretations of history,[44] others were false prophecies,[45] and none was conclusive. In following the British example,[46]

[39] See above, pp. 339, 462.

[40] L. E. de Payre, 'Should we Civilise the Kafir?', *State*, iii. 548.

[41] F. W. Bell, *A Suggested Solution of the South African Native Problem* (Johannesburg, 1909).

[42] Trevor Fletcher in 'The Native Problem', *State*, iii. 773, did so: 'We have to realise that he [the Native] is a potential citizen, and as such our responsibilities demand that he be trained and given the opportunity to undertake effectively the duties of citizenship. . . . The kafir is a human being: he will advance in the same way that all human beings have advanced and just as we ourselves have advanced. And the manner of that advance has not been brought about by segregation but by a process which is the opposite of it.'

[43] Note, however, the 'unorthodox' views of Olive Schreiner (pp. 108–9) and J. G. Kotzé (p. 101).

[44] e.g. the argument that in America federalism had 'caused' the civil war (see above, p. 187).

[45] e.g. the argument that the federal Commonwealth of Australia was 'a bundle of jangling and wrangling States, whose only salvation was to unite', i.e. to establish a unitary Constitution (see above, p. 104).

[46] The South African Constitution was fully flexible from the outset, except for the

they had ignored the fact that in so far as the flexible character of the British Constitution met the needs of the British people, that was because they had become a comparatively homogeneous people, and their respect for constitutional conventions, for political compromise, and for personal liberty was strong enough to form an effective barrier against arbitrary action by the Government of the day; whereas the essence of the problem confronting South Africa was that her peoples were extremely heterogeneous, and the colour consciousness of most of the whites and the national exclusiveness of most of the Afrikaners were potent enough to override any feelings they may have had for conventions, for compromise, and for the liberties of others. Since a flexible Constitution provides no legal safeguards against arbitrary government, it was the very worst prescription for such a country. So long as Afrikaners remained in a political majority they would have the opportunity, and therefore the temptation, to stand together, to obtain control of Parliament, and to impose their will on the other inhabitants. A division of powers, territorially between the centre and the regions, and within the centre between the Legislature, the Executive, and the Judiciary, would have provided the only sound basis for concord in South Africa. The Constitution of the United States of America would have been a better model than the British Constitution.

provisions embodying the remnant of imperial authority (ss. 7–9, 64–66, 106) and the restrictions laid down in the amending section (s. 152), which only limited the power of a bare majority of the members of both Houses of Parliament in a few fields (see above, pp. 282–3).

APPENDIX A

STATISTICS

I. POPULATION

1904 CENSUS

Numbers	Cape Colony	Natal	Transvaal	Orange River Colony	Total
White . . .	579,741	97,109	297,277	142,679	1,116,806
Native . . .	1,424,787	904,041	937,127	225,101	3,491,056
Coloured . . .	395,034	6,686	24,226	19,282	445,228
Asiatic . . .	10,242	100,918	11,321	253	122,734
	2,409,804	1,108,754	1,269,951	387,315	5,175,824

Percentage of the total population belonging to each race

White . . .	24·06	8·76	23·41	36·84	21·58
Native . . .	59·12	81·54	73·79	58·12	67·45
Coloured . . .	16·39	0·60	1·91	4·98	8·60
Asiatic . . .	0·43	9·10	0·89	0·06	2·37

1911 CENSUS

Numbers	Cape Province	Natal	Transvaal	Orange Free State	Union of South Africa
White . . .	582,377	98,114	420,562	175,189	1,276,242
Native . . .	1,519,939	953,398	1,219,845	325,824	4,019,006
Coloured . . .	454,985	9,111	34,793	27,054	525,943
Asiatic . . .	7,664	133,420	11,012	107	152,203
	2,564,965	1,194,043	1,686,212	528,174	5,973,394

Percentage of the total population belonging to each race

White . . .	22·70	8·22	24·94	33·17	21·37
Native . . .	59·26	79·85	72·34	61·69	67·28
Coloured . . .	17·74	0·76	2·06	5·12	8·80
Asiatic . . .	0·30	11·17	0·65	0·02	2·55

Note: In the 1904 census each of the four colonies used a category 'European or White', but they divided the rest of their populations in different ways. In the 1911 census three main ethnic categories were used: 'European', 'Bantu', and 'Mixed and other Coloured'. No further ethnic information was obtained from Europeans, but 'Bantu' were required to add the name of a tribe and 'Mixed and other Coloured' were required to state the sub-group to which they belonged. Some parts of the 1911 census report were based on the three main categories mentioned above; but others merely distinguished 'Europeans' and 'Others'.

The lines of division between the main categories were not clear. The directors of the censuses did not lay down standard rules, the laws contained several different definitions, and practice varied from one part of South Africa to another. Consequently the ethnic categories in both the 1904 and the 1911 census reports are imprecise and inconsistent.

Subsequently, directors of census and statistics have divided the people of the

Union into four main ethnic categories: 'European (white)', 'Natives (Bantu)' 'Asiatics', and 'Mixed and other Coloured'.

The following terms have been used in this appendix:

'White', meaning people of (or reputed to be of) exclusively European descent, including Jews.

'Native', meaning Bantu-speaking Africans.

'Coloured', including people descended from Hottentots and Bushmen, and people descended from the slaves who were imported into the Cape Colony from West Africa, East Africa, Madagascar, and Asia in the seventeenth and eighteenth centuries. Many Coloured people were partly, and some were largely, of European descent.

'Asiatic', meaning people who came to South Africa from Asia (mainly from India) in the second half of the nineteenth century and in the twentieth century, and their descendants.

Sources: Census of 17 April 1904: Cape of Good Hope, G. 19 (1905); Natal (Pietermaritzburg, 1905); Transvaal and Swaziland (London, 1906); Orange River Colony (Bloemfontein, n.d.). Census of 7 May 1911: U.G. 32 (1912) (11 vols.).

II. BIRTHPLACES

1911 CENSUS

Percentage of the total population born in different areas

	Cape Province	Natal	Trans- vaal	Orange Free State	Union of South Africa
WHITE					
Union of South Africa . .	86·19	61·33	70·40	90·12	79·62
United Kingdom . . .	9·59	30·13	19·91	7·34	14·26
Elsewhere in the British Empire .	0·69	3·47	2·16	0·58	1·35
Foreign countries . . .	3·50	4·99	7·47	1·90	4·72
At sea, unknown or unspecified .	0·03	0·08	0·06	0·06	0·05
NATIVE					
Union of South Africa . .	98·89	99·64	86·93	84·81	94·30
High Commission Territories .	0·93	0·30	3·01	14·78	2·54
Portuguese East Africa . .	0·06	0·04	9·24	0·32	2·86
Others	0·12	0·02	0·82	0·09	0·30
COLOURED AND ASIATIC					
Union of South Africa . .	97·73	46·95	80·81	97·61	85·91
Elsewhere in Africa . . .	0·89	1·25	1·82	2·03	1·08
India	1·04	51·53	15·00	0·18	12·56
Others	0·34	0·27	2·37	0·18	0·45

Union of South Africa: any of the territories which formed part of the Union in 1911. High Commission Territories: Basutoland, Bechuanaland Protectorate, and Swaziland.

Source: U.G. 32*f* (1912).

III. RELIGIONS

1911 Census

Percentage of the total population belonging to different religions

	Cape Province	Natal	Trans-vaal	Orange Free State	Union of South Africa
WHITE					
Dutch Reformed Churches . .	58·31	12·54	48·52	78·75	54·37
Other Protestants . . .	33·95	75·65	38·25	16·93	36·34
Roman Catholics . . .	3·87	7·49	5·01	1·62	4·22
Other Christians . . .	0·34	0·58	0·77	0·22	0·37
TOTAL CHRISTIANS . . .	96·47	96·26	92·55	97·52	95·30
Jews	2·87	1·51	6·16	1·60	3·68
Others	0·66	2·23	1·29	0·88	1·02
NATIVE					
Dutch Reformed Churches . .	1·14	0·25	1·64	9·74	1·78
Other Protestants . . .	29·28	13·14	20·88	37·61	23·58
Roman Catholics . . .	0·35	1·17	0·42	0·75	0·60
Other Christians . . .	0·31	0·23	0·21	0·40	0·26
TOTAL CHRISTIANS . . .	31·08	14·79	23·15	48·50	26·22
'No Religion'	68·90	85·21	76·66	51·36	73·70
Others	0·02	0·00	0·19	0·14	0·08
COLOURED AND ASIATIC					
Dutch Reformed Churches . .	26·57	0·08	10·15	20·66	19·65
Other Protestants . . .	58·24	4·54	41·15	55·94	45·73
Roman Catholics . . .	1·62	2·86	2·84	1·09	1·94
Other Christians . . .	0·82	0·04	0·80	0·38	0·63
TOTAL CHRISTIANS . . .	87·25	7·52	54·94	78·07	67·95
Hindus	0·51	76·40	9·74	0·04	17·06
Mohammedans	5·22	9·44	13·77	0·15	6·48
'No Religion'	6·40	4·63	18·57	21·52	7·45
Others	0·62	2·01	2·98	0·22	1·06

Source: U.G. 32*e* (1912).

IV. OCCUPATIONS (MALES)
1911 CENSUS
Percentage of the total male population in different occupations

	Cape Province	Natal	Trans-vaal	Orange Free State	Union of South Africa
ALL RACES					
Professions	1·64	1·51	1·98	2·70	1·84
Commerce	2·00	1·72	2·39	1·62	2·04
Transport	2·14	1·72	1·57	0·96	1·78
Manufacturing Industries . .	7·54	6·24	7·43	6·05	7·11
Mining	3·07	2·21	28·33	5·53	11·13
Agriculture	42·43	39·81	22·61	37·28	35·21
Domestic	2·16	4·77	5·17	7·84	4·10
Dependants	38·47	41·61	30·15	37·07	36·29
Others	0·55	0·41	0·37	0·95	0·50
WHITE					
Professions	5·27	10·26	6·79	7·11	6·40
Commerce	6·31	8·97	6·63	4·13	6·32
Transport	5·20	9·99	3·82	1·92	4·64
Manufacturing Industries . .	11·31	17·15	14·05	7·90	12·27
Mining	3·05	4·17	14·20	2·45	6·91
Agriculture	27·43	14·60	18·48	36·13	24·56
Domestic	1·25	1·24	1·63	0·82	1·32
Dependants	38·96	31·80	33·53	38·25	36·44
Others	1·22	1·82	0·87	1·29	1·14
NATIVE					
Professions	0·53	0·58	0·45	0·42	0·50
Commerce	0·36	0·38	0·47	0·32	0·40
Transport	0·58	0·70	0·68	0·42	0·63
Manufacturing Industries . .	2·67	3·07	5·06	4·83	3·76
Mining	3·27	1·17	33·71	7·36	13·80
Agriculture	52·26	44·02	24·30	38·38	39·60
Domestic	1·65	4·70	5·88	10·70	4·53
Dependants	38·48	45·28	29·26	36·81	36·56
Others	0·20	0·10	0·19	0·76	0·22
COLOURED AND ASIATIC					
Professions	0·36	0·75	0·47	0·26	0·47
Commerce	1·52	3·98	14·65	0·35	3·10
Transport	3·04	1·74	4·79	1·14	2·79
Manufacturing Industries . .	17·81	15·52	10·47	8·12	16·30
Mining	2·47	6·13	12·38	4·42	4·18
Agriculture	31·31	34·29	15·15	31·87	30·75
Domestic	4·91	7·27	17·06	20·45	7·06
Dependants	37·81	29·25	24·15	32·32	34·49
Others	0·77	1·07	0·88	1·07	0·86

The occupational categories used in the 1911 census were not altogether satisfactory, as the following notes indicate:

Commerce: 'Persons who buy, sell, exchange or insure, keep, or lend money, property or goods of all kinds.'

Transport: Includes posts and telegraphs.

Industries: Including persons engaged in the construction or repair of buildings, railways, docks, and roads; dealers in as well as manufacturers of textiles, clothing, food, drinks, tobacco, and timber; dealers in hides, skins, wool, and ostrich feathers; and undefined engineers, mechanics, contractors, and general labourers.

Mining: Including persons working or dealing in minerals, stone, gas, light, and energy, salt, &c.

Domestic: Includes provision of board and lodging, as well as rendering of personal service.

Dependants: Including, as well as scholars and children, convicts and other persons supported by the community.

Source: U.G. 32d (1912).

V. DISTRIBUTION OF THE LAND AND OF THE NATIVE POPULATION

(c. 1913)

The percentage of the total land area in different categories

	Urban areas	Farms owned by Whites	Farms owned by Whites but occupied by Natives only	Native reserves, mission reserves, and farms owned by Natives	Crown lands occupied by Natives	Unoccupied Crown lands
Cape Province .	1·3	78·1	0·1	9·3	0·1	11·2
Natal . .	0·9	48·4	9·5	30·4	3·2	7·5
Transvaal . .	1·2	61·0	9·1	4·4	1·6	22·5
O.F.S. . .	1·4	97·0	0·0	1·5	0·0	0·0
The Union .	1·2	74·0	2·9	8·9	0·7	12·4

The percentage of the total Native population on the different categories of land

Cape Province .	8·0	15·0	0·5	75·7	0·8	
Natal . .	3·5	33·1	7·9	52·0	3·4	
Transvaal . .	23·3	29·6	16·8	25·1	5·2	
O.F.S. . .	14·0	79·4	0·0	6·6	0·0	
The Union .	12·2	29·1	7·4	48·6	2·7	

Source: The above tables are derived from tables in the U.G. 19 (1916), *Report of the Natives Land Commission, 1913–16*, i, appendix iii, p. 9, and appendix iv, p. 9. It will be observed that they make no allowance for the ownership or occupation of land by Coloured people or by Asiatics. Not much land was owned privately by Coloured people. The principal Coloured reserves—Leliefontein, Komaggas, Steinkopf, Concordia, and Richtersveld in Namaqualand in the Cape Province, extensive but arid areas with a very small population—were included in the category of Native reserves (appendix iii, p. 3). It is not clear in what category the commission placed the somewhat small proportion of the land in Natal which was owned by Asiatics.

VI. ORDINARY REVENUE, ORDINARY EXPENDITURE, AND BALANCES OF THE CAPE COLONY

1 JULY 1902–30 MAY 1910

The financial years 1902–9 started on 1 July and ended on 30 June. The period shown as 1909–10 is an eleven-month period terminating on 30 May 1910

	Ordinary revenue			Ordinary expenditure			Deficit	Surplus
	Customs	Railway receipts	Total	Railway working and maintenance	Interest &c. on Public debt	Total		
	£	£	£	£	£	£	£	£
1902–3	3,503,479	5,617,867	11,701,150	4,365,242	1,627,153	11,197,970	..	503,180
1903–4	2,396,584	5,120,261	9,913,855	4,307,713	1,687,045	10,862,866	949,011	..
1904–5	1,925,879	4,033,039	8,472,303	3,111,988	1,625,478	9,149,498	677,195	..
1905–6	1,870,956	3,940,788	8,236,880	2,704,862	1,656,454	8,231,719	..	5,161
1906–7	1,763,400	3,662,533	7,701,192	2,760,975	1,743,463	8,349,316	648,124	..
1907–8	1,543,088	3,094,444	6,981,873	2,448,457	1,818,769	7,973,727	991,854	..
1908–9	1,253,051	3,065,379	7,312,112	2,164,390	1,927,020	7,681,305	369,193	..
1909–10	1,248,534	3,143,468	7,747,332	1,980,550	1,800,128	7,611,298	..	136,034
	£15,504,971	£31,677,779	£68,066,697	£23,844,177	£13,885,510	£71,057,699	3,635,377	£644,375
							644,375	
							£2,991,002	

Sources: *Statistical Register of the Province of the Cape of Good Hope for the Year 1909* (Cape Town, 1910); G. 39 (1910), 'Cape of Good Hope. Finance Accounts for the Period 1st July, 1909, to 30th May, 1910' (in *Printed Annexures to the Votes and Proceedings of the Union House of Assembly, 1910–11, iv*).

VII. ORDINARY REVENUE, ORDINARY EXPENDITURE, AND BALANCES OF NATAL

1 JULY 1902–30 MAY 1910

The financial years 1902–9 started on 1 July and ended on 30 June. The period shown as 1909–10 is an eleven-month period terminating on 30 May 1910

	Ordinary revenue			Ordinary expenditure			Deficit	Surplus
	Customs	Railway receipts	Total	Railway working and maintenance	Interest &c. on Public debt	Total		
	£	£	£	£	£	£	£	£
1902–3	1,032,049	2,286,963	4,334,175	1,646,326	499,360	5,102,007	767,832	..
1903–4	770,705	2,499,323	4,160,145	1,740,950	502,500	4,071,439	..	88,706
1904–5	579,718	1,884,408	3,384,849	1,354,369	608,082	3,814,599	429,750	..
1905–6	569,603	2,085,958	3,665,089	1,333,225	760,404	3,673,972	8,883	..
1906–7	539,900	1,881,551	3,471,932	1,385,620	805,382	3,681,914	209,982	..
1907–8	482,144	2,019,527	3,510,350	1,391,186	865,775	3,689,752	179,402	..
1908–9	477,211	1,989,173	3,569,275	1,311,083	898,742	3,530,577	..	38,698
1909–10	459,314	2,409,322	4,293,728	1,372,511	725,785	3,530,349	..	763,379
	£4,910,644	£17,056,225	£30,389,543	£11,535,270	£5,666,030	£31,094,609	1,595,849	£890,783
							890,783	
							£705,066	

Sources: *Natal Government Gazette*, 1903–6; *Statistical Year Books for the Colony of Natal*, 1902–9; 'Natal. Finance Accounts for the Period 1st July, 1909, to 30th May, 1910' (in *Printed Annexures to the Votes and Proceedings of the Union House of Assembly, 1910–11*, vii).

VIII. ORDINARY REVENUE, ORDINARY EXPENDITURE, AND BALANCES OF THE TRANSVAAL*

1 JULY 1902–30 MAY 1910

The financial years 1902–9 started on 1 July and ended on 30 June. The period shown as 1909–10 is an eleven-month period terminating on 30 May 1910

	Ordinary revenue			Ordinary expenditure		Surplus
	Customs	Mines	Total	Public debt	Total	
	£	£	£	£	£	£
1902–3	2,176,658	508,730	5,427,509	139,637	4,273,421	1,154,088
1903–4	1,759,644	720,758	5,333,341	750,000	4,318,539	1,014,802
1904–5	1,590,783	791,383	4,411,990	831,208	4,018,268	393,722
1905–6	1,699,052	983,003	4,670,230	661,022	4,236,537	433,693
1906–7	1,638,140	1,236,623	4,651,532	713,497	4,415,476	236,056
1907–8	1,546,444	1,068,642	4,670,218	350,000	4,118,848	551,370
1908–9	1,548,826	1,436,452	5,735,524	627,465	4,553,492	1,182,032
1909–10	1,680,203	1,340,432	5,585,637	598,916	4,792,861	792,776
	£13,639,750	£8,086,023	£40,485,981	£4,671,745	£34,727,442	£5,758,539

* See also the C.S.A.R. accounts, p. 496 below.

Sources: T.G. 25 (1908), Statistics of the Transvaal Colony for the Years 1902–07; T.G. 28 (1909), Statistics of the Transvaal Colony for the Years 1903–08; 'Finance Accounts of the Transvaal for the Financial Year 1909–10' (in Printed Annexures to the Votes and Proceedings of the Union House of Assembly, 1910–11, v).

IX. ORDINARY REVENUE, ORDINARY EXPENDITURE, AND BALANCES OF THE ORANGE RIVER COLONY*

1 JULY 1902–30 MAY 1910

The financial years 1902–9 started on 1 July and ended on 30 June. The period shown as 1909–10 is an eleven-month period terminating on 30 May 1910

	Ordinary revenue		Ordinary expenditure		Deficit	Surplus
	Customs	Total	Public debt	Total		
	£	£	£	£	£	£
1902–3	288,805	956,536	5,777	839,923	..	116,613
1903–4	419,235	875,137	105,468	807,300	..	67,837
1904–5	298,738	786,050	181,163	780,536	..	5,514
1905–6	305,535	759,307	118,808	759,178	..	129
1906–7	310,713	787,328	120,250	774,586	..	12,742
1907–8	285,077	740,453	74,040	727,626	..	12,827
1908–9	283,379	915,286	132,666	952,513	37,227	..
1909–10	342,337	952,860	134,539	957,741	4,881	..
	£2,533,819	£6,772,957	£872,711	£6,599,403	£42,108	215,662
						42,108
						£173,554

* See also the C.S.A.R. accounts, p. 496 below.

Source: *Orange River Colony, Colonial Treasurer's Annual Accounts, 1902–10.*

X. NET PUBLIC DEBT OF EACH COLONY ON 31 MAY 1910, AT THE ESTABLISHMENT OF THE UNION

Service	Cape Colony	Natal	Transvaal	O.R.C.	Total
	£	£	£	£	£
Railways . . .	29,416,758	13,978,154	15,618,448	4,991,119	64,004,479
Harbours . . .	6,480,977	3,595,445	..	..	10,076,422
War and Defence .	7,788,697	1,170,775	1,579,175	..	10,538,647
Repatriation . .	..	..	5,305,101	1,279,413	6,584,514
Sundry . . .	8,586,071	2,933,107	8,385,357	1,900,144	21,804,679
TOTAL . . .	£52,272,503	£21,677,481	£30,888,081	£8,170,676	£113,008,741

Net debt per head

	£ s. d.	£ s. d.	£ s. d.	£ s. d.	£ s. d.
Total population . .	20 7 8	18 3 1	18 6 4	15 9 5	18 18 4
White population . .	89 15 2	220 18 10	73 8 9	46 12 9	88 11 0

Note: The net debts per head have been calculated from the population figures in the 1911 census.
Source: *Official Year Book of the Union of South Africa* . . ., i. 636.

XI. THE SOUTH AFRICAN RAILWAY SYSTEMS

C.G.R. Cape Government Railways.
N.G.R. Natal Government Railways.
C.S.A.R. Central South African Railways, owned jointly by the governments of the Transvaal and the Orange River Colony.
C.F.L.M. Caminho de Ferro de Lourenço Marques.

Mileages of new lines constructed

	C.G.R.	C.S.A.R.	N.G.R.	Total
1901 mileages open . .	2,134	1,331	591	4,056
1902 new mileage . .	183	21	45	249
1903 ,, . .	197	56	105	358
1904 ,, . .	149	91	37	277
1905 ,, . .	321	262	42	625
1906 ,, . .	206	254	29	489
1907 ,, . .	65	390	41	496
1908 ,. . .	11	155	97	263
1909 ,, . .	54	13	12	79
1910 (to 30 May) new mileage	8	137	..	145
31 May 1910 mileages open	3,328	2,710	999	7,037

Source: *Official Year Book of the Union of South Africa* . . ., i. 570.

Mileages from the ports to Germiston in the competitive zone in 1908

	C.G.R.	C.S.A.R.	N.G.R.	C.F.L.M.	Total
Cape Town . . .	695	270	..	..	965
Port Elizabeth . . .	328	374	..	..	702
East London . . .	286	369	..	..	655
Durban	..	166	307	..	473
Lourenço Marques . .	..	301	..	55	356

Source: House of Assembly, National Convention Minutes, II, Annexure 91a, Statement 17B.

*Tonnage and percentage of tonnage of the principal classes of traffic
from the ports to the competitive zone, comprising all stations between
Pretoria, Springs, Klerksdorp, and Vaal River*

	Tonnage				Percentage of tonnage		
	Cape Ports	Durban	Lourenço Marques	Total	Cape Ports	Durban	Lourenço Marques
1903 (approx.)	..	..	..	..	24·0	42·0	34·0
1904 . .	88,109	196,764	208,290	493,163	17·9	39·9	42·2
1905 . .	79,350	219,669	309,459	608,478	13·0	36·1	50·9
1906 . .	68,016	152,152	244,641	464,809	14·6	32·7	52·7
1907 . .	53,824	118,097	221,534	393,455	13·7	30·0	56·3
1908 . .	49,898	90,422	238,527	378,847	13·2	23·8	63·0
1909 . .	62,926	103,828	308,006	474,760	13·3	21·9	64·8
1910 Jan.–May (approx.)	..	..	..	..	12·0	20·0	68·0

Source: Reports of the General Managers of the C.G.R. and the C.S.A.R. for 1909
(in *Printed Annexures to the Votes and Proceedings of the Union House of
Assembly, 1910–11*, iv and vii).

Railway earnings and expenditure

For the earnings and working and maintenance expenditure of the C.G.R. and
N.G.R. see Statements VI and VII above.

	Central South African Railways		
	Earnings	Ordinary working expenditure*	Surplus
	£	£	£
1902 (6 months)	2,438,295	1,139,295	1,299,000
1903 . .	5,374,735	3,500,949	1,873,786
1904 . .	4,587,779	2,813,628	1,774,151
1905 . .	5,364,619	2,554,466	2,810,153
1906 . .	4,782,049	2,198,003	2,584,046
1907 . .	4,294,144	2,083,264	2,210,880
1908 . .	4,218,297	1,993,807	2,224,490
1909 . .	5,064,421	1,778,818	3,285,603
	£36,124,339	£18,062,230	£18,062,109

* Ordinary working expenditure, classified under the following headings: traffic
and running; maintenance of way, works, and telegraphs; maintenance equipment;
and general expenses. The total working expenditure during this period was
£20,212,892, the additional sum consisting of £113,747 spent on special works
during 1902–4 and £2,036,915 contributed to the Renewals Fund which was started
on 1 July 1905.

Source: Report of the General Manager of the C.S.A.R. for 1909 (in *Printed Annexures
to the Votes and Proceedings of the Union House of Assembly, 1910–11*, vii),
pp. 33 and 49.

XII. THE GOLD- AND DIAMOND-MINING INDUSTRIES

Gold output of the Transvaal

	Fine ounces	£	Percentage of world output
1901	258,032	1,096,051	2·04
1902	1,718,921	7,301,501	11·97
1903	2,972,897	12,628,057	18·75
1904	3,773,517	16,028,883	22·46
1905	4,909,541	20,854,440	26·69
1906	5,792,823	24,606,336	29·75
1907	6,450,740	27,400,992	32·32
1908	7,056,266	29,973,115	33·01
1909	7,295,108	30,987,650	33·05
1910	7,531,386	31,973,123	34·20

Source: Annual Report of the Transvaal Government Mining Engineer for 1909–10 (in *Printed Annexures to the Votes and Proceedings of the Union House of Assembly, 1910–11,* v), p. 12.

Diamond output of South Africa

	Cape Colony	Transvaal	O.R.C.	Total	
	£	£	£	Carats	£
1902	4,949,808	2,402	No records	Records incomplete	
1903	4,833,040	239,752			
1904	5,191,661	1,150,873	866,111	3,683,157	7,208,645
1905	4,428,383	922,330	853,834	3,368,789	6,204,547
1906	6,992,811	1,563,141	1,040,691	4,136,236	9,596,643
1907	6,310,796	2,268,075	1,407,055	5,170,812	9,985,926
1908	3,085,352	1,549,815	771,414	4,091,121	5,406,581
1909	4,690,478	1,176,680	1,332,201	5,169,871	7,199,359
1910	5,267,659	1,416,464	1,505,074	5,456,558	8,189,197

Source: *Official Year Book of the Union of South Africa* . . ., i. 451.

Employees in the Transvaal gold-mining industry

	Average number of employees				Average monthly wages		
	White	Native*	Chinese†	Total	White	Native*	Chinese†
					s.	s. d.	s. d.
1901–2	4,090	18,887	..	22,977	409	26 8	..
1902–3	10,285	48,653	..	58,938	444	38 6	..
1903–4	12,665	74,139	1,004	87,808	491	48 10	..
1904–5	15,371	89,846	22,890	128,107	485	52 0	33 6
1905–6	18,089	95,599	47,639	161,327	505	51 11	39 9
1906–7	17,513	102,420	53,062	172,995	515	52 3	41 6
1907–8	17,655	131,931	36,044	185,630	469	49 1	44 3
1908–9	19,891	166,845	12,206	198,942	465	46 4	47 3
1909–10	23,341	180,283	2,245	205,869	456	48 7	55 2

* These were described as 'Coloured' in the mining records. Nearly all of them were Bantu-speaking Africans.
† The first Chinese arrived in June 1904. The last left in March 1910.

Source: Annual Report of the Transvaal Government Mining Engineer for 1909–10, Tables 2, 10, and 11.

Sources of Native labour employed in the Transvaal gold- and coal-mining industries: percentage from each source

	1904	1905	1906	1907	1908	1909	1910
Transvaal	7·0	5·8	4·0	6·1	9·1	8·0	7·5
Cape Colony . . .	12·7	6·1	13·7	14·5	24·4	24·3	26·0
Natal	3·5	2·6	4·8	4·4	5·1	6·3	6·7
Orange River Colony . .	0·3	0·2	0·3	0·4	0·5	0·3	0·4
	23·5	14·7	22·8	25·4	39·1	38·9	40·6
Basutoland	2·9	1·9	2·6	2·3	3·1	2·5	3·2
Bechuanaland Protectorate .	0·7	0·7	0·4	0·2	0·8	0·6	0·4
Swaziland	0·6	0·8	0·7	1·8	1·0	0·9	1·4
	4·2	3·4	3·7	4·3	4·9	4·0	5·0
British Tropical Colonies &c. .	5·9	8·7	2·5	1·0	0·9	2·7	2·4
Portuguese East Africa . .	66·2	73·2	71·0	69·4	55·0	54·3	52·0

Source: Sheila T. van der Horst, *Native Labour in South Africa* (London, 1942), p. 216.

XIII. OVERSEAS TRADE

Value of imports through Cape ports, Durban, and Lourenço Marques
(excluding specie)

	Cape ports	Durban	Total	Lourenço Marques	Grand total
	£	£	£	£	£
1902	32,109,605	13,317,445	45,427,050	Records not	
1903	33,761,831	14,999,204	48,761,035	available	
1904	21,824,309	10,651,451	32,475,760		
1905	19,760,970	10,552,548	30,313,518		
1906	18,102,872	8,869,932	26,972,804	3,654,120	30,626,924
1907	15,586,792	7,552,326	23,139,118	3,395,923	26,535,041
1908	13,739,878	6,709,422	20,449,300	3,916,993	24,366,293
1909	14,610,981	7,624,598	22,235,579	4,826,371	27,061,950

Value of exports through Cape ports, Durban, and Lourenço Marques
(excluding specie)

	Cape ports	Durban	Total	Lourenço Marques	Grand total
	£	£	£	£	£
1902	16,381,279	3,372,790	19,754,069	Records not	
1903	22,502,282	2,446,566	24,948,848	available	
1904	27,470,627	2,273,522	29,744,149		
1905	33,769,216	2,508,337	36,277,553		
1906	40,048,693	3,000,266	43,048,959	237,749	43,286,708
1907	44,504,450	3,580,571	48,085,021	296,839	48,381,860
1908	42,011,582	3,624,957	45,636,539	243,850	45,880,389
1909	46,573,223	4,482,036	51,055,259	253,996	51,309,255

Analysis of exports through Cape ports (excluding specie)

	Gold	Diamonds	Wool and mohair	Ostrich feathers	Hides and skins	Others
	£	£	£	£	£	£
1902	5,915,207	5,427,360	2,700,286	895,005	483,605	959,816
1903	11,979,658	5,472,690	2,470,447	945,001	470,211	1,164,275
1904	15,554,665	6,422,488	2,407,691	1,058,988	478,293	1,548,502
1905	20,731,159	6,758,623	2,455,939	1,081,187	563,686	2,178,622
1906	24,398,208	9,257,531	2,969,483	1,406,119	688,701	1,328,651
1907	28,226,185	8,973,148	3,404,894	1,814,210	794,833	1,291,180
1908	30,969,024	4,796,655	2,767,941	1,738,389	627,306	1,112,267
1909	32,159,603	6,370,301	3,663,905	2,091,207	860,685	1,427,522

Source: *Official Year Book of the Union of South Africa . . .*, i. 510–12.

Destinations of exports through Cape ports (excluding specie)

	South African produce		Imported goods re-exported	Total
	United Kingdom	Elsewhere		
	£	£	£	£
1906	38,400,304	1,229,375	419,014	40,048,693
1907	42,884,549	1,207,666	412,235	44,504,450
1908	40,208,216	1,532,198	271,168	42,011,582
1909	44,161,536	2,083,054	328,633	46,573,223

Source: *Statistical Register of the Province of the Cape of Good Hope for the Year 1909*, Part XIII, No. 5.

APPENDIX B

THE MEMBERS OF THE NATIONAL CONVENTION

CAPE COLONY

JOHANNES HENDRICUS MEIRING BECK (South African Party)

Born 28 November 1855 at Worcester, Cape Colony.

Educated at Worcester School, the South African College, and Edinburgh University.

Occupations: Medical doctor and farmer.

Public Life: 1898–1910: Member of the House of Assembly for Worcester. 1910–19: Elected Senator for the Cape Province (South African Party). 1916–19: Minister of Posts and Telegraphs.

Honours: Kt. 1911.

Died 15 May 1919.

SIR JOHN HENRY DE VILLIERS

Born 15 June 1842 at Paarl, Cape Colony.

Educated at the South African College and in Utrecht, Berlin, and London.

Occupation: Lawyer.

Public Life: 1867–73: Member of the House of Assembly for Worcester. 1872–3: Attorney-General. 1873–1910: Chief Justice and President of the Legislative Council. 1881: Member of the Transvaal Royal Commission. 1896: Member of the Judicial Committee of the Privy Council. 1908–9: President of the National Convention. 1910–14: Chief Justice of the Union of South Africa.

Honours: Kt. 1877, K.C.M.G. 1882, P.C. 1896, Baron 1910 (Baron de Villiers of Wynberg).

Died 2 September 1914.

JOHN WILLIAM JAGGER (Unionist)

Born 20 September 1859 at Northowram, Yorkshire, England.

Educated at Burnsall Grammar School.

Migrated to South Africa 1880.

Occupation: Merchant—founder of J. W. Jagger & Co.

Public Life: 1899–1904: President of the Association of Chambers of Commerce of South Africa. 1902–10: Member of the House of Assembly for Cape Town. 1910–29: Member of the House of Assembly for Cape Town Central (Unionist Party, South African Party). 1921–4: Minister of Railways and Harbours.

Died 20 June 1930.

LEANDER STARR JAMESON (Unionist)

Born 9 February 1853 in Edinburgh, Scotland.

Educated at Godolphin School, Hammersmith, and University College, London.

Migrated to South Africa 1878.

Occupations: Medical doctor, colonial administrator, and director of the British South Africa Co. and De Beers Consolidated Mines.

Public Life: 1889: Visited Matabeleland as agent of Cecil Rhodes. 1890: Rhodes's representative with the Southern Rhodesian pioneers. 1891–6: Administrator of Mashonaland. 1894–6: Administrator of Matabeleland. 1895–6: Invaded the South African Republic with an armed force, surrendered, was handed over to Britain for trial, and sentenced to 15 months' imprisonment, but released in December 1896. 1899–1902: On active service. 1900–10: Member of the House of Assembly for Kimberley and Grahamstown. 1903–10: Leader of the Progressive (Unionist) Party. 1904–8: Prime Minister.

1910–12: Member of the House of Assembly for Albany, Leader of the Unionist Party and of the Opposition. 1912: Settled in England. 1913–17: President of the British South Africa Co.

Honours: C.B. 1894, P.C. 1907, Bt. 1911.

Died 26 November 1917.

GYSBERT HENRY MAASDORP (South African Party)

Born 3 July 1845 at Malmesbury, Cape Colony.

Educated at Graaff Reinet, Cape Colony, and University College, London. Did not graduate.

Occupation: Farmer.

Public Life: 1898–1903: Member of the Legislative Council for the Midland division. 1904–10: Member of the House of Assembly for Graaff Reinet.

1910–15: Member of the House of Assembly for Graaff Reinet (South African Party).

Died 23 October 1919.

FRANÇOIS STEPHANUS MALAN (South African Party)

Born 12 March 1871 near Wellington, Cape Colony.

Educated at Paarl High School, Victoria College, Stellenbosch, and Cambridge University.

Occupations: Lawyer and journalist.

Public Life: 1895–1908: Editor of *Ons Land*. 1901: Sentenced to 12 months' imprisonment for publishing a defamatory libel on General French. 1900–10: Member of the House of Assembly for Malmesbury. 1908–10: Secretary for Agriculture. May 1908: Delegate to Intercolonial Conference, Pretoria and Cape Town. 1909–11: Chairman of the *Kommissie van Toezicht* of the Afrikaner Bond.

1910–24: Member of the House of Assembly for Malmesbury (South African Party). 1910–21: Minister of Education and Minister of Agriculture. 1912: Minister of Mines. 1927–41: Elected Senator for the Cape Province (South African Party, United Party). 1940–1: President of the Senate.

Honours: P.C. 1920; and honorary degrees.

Died 31 December 1941.

JOHN XAVIER MERRIMAN (South African Party)

Born 15 March 1841 at Street, Somerset, England.

Migrated to South Africa 1848.

Educated at the Diocesan College, Rondebosch, and Radley College, England.

Occupations: At various times a land surveyor, diamond dealer, wine merchant, mining estate manager, farmer, and director of the South African Mutual Assurance Co.

Public Life: 1869–1910: Member of the House of Assembly for Aliwal North, Wodehouse, Namaqualand, and Victoria West. 1875–8 and 1881–4: Commissioner of Crown Lands and Public Works. 1890–3 and 1898–1900: Treasurer. 1908–10: Prime Minister and Treasurer. May 1908: Delegate to Intercolonial Conference, Pretoria and Cape Town.

1910–24: Member of the House of Assembly for Victoria West and Stellenbosch (South African Party).

Honours: P.C. 1909; and honorary degrees.

Died 1 August 1926.

JACOBUS WILHELMUS SAUER (South African Party)

Born 1850 at Burghersdorp, Cape Colony.

Educated at the South African College.

Occupations: Solicitor and farmer.

Public Life: 1874–1903 and 1905–10: Member of the House of Assembly for Aliwal North and George. 1881–4: Secretary for Native Affairs. 1890–3: Colonial Secretary. 1898–1900 and 1908–10: Commissioner of Public Works. May 1908: Delegate to Intercolonial Conference, Pretoria and Cape Town.

1910–13: Member of the House of Assembly for Aliwal (South African Party). 1910–12: Minister of Railways and Harbours. 1912: Minister of Agriculture. 1912–13: Minister of Justice and Minister of Native Affairs.

Died 24 July 1913.

THOMAS WILLIAM SMARTT (Unionist)

Born 22 February 1858 at Trim, County Meath, Ireland.

Educated at Trinity College, Dublin.

Migrated to South Africa 1880.

Occupations: Medical doctor and farmer.

Public Life: 1893–1910: Member of the House of Assembly for Wodehouse, Cathcart, East London, and Fort Beaufort. 1896–8: Colonial Secretary. 1900 and 1904–8: Commissioner of Public Works.

    1910–29: Member of the House of Assembly for Fort Beaufort (Unionist and South African Party). 1911–21: Leader of the Unionist Party. 1921–4: Minister of Agriculture.

Honours: K.C.M.G. 1911, P.C. 1921.

Died 17 April 1929.

WILLIAM ERNEST MORTIMER STANFORD (Independent)

Born 2 August 1850 at Alice, Cape Colony.

Educated at Lovedale, Cape Colony.

Occupation: Civil servant.

Public Life: 1863–1907: Cape Colony Civil Service. 1880–2: Member of the Native Laws and Customs Commission. 1877–8, 1880–1, and 1899–1902: On active service—Colonel. 1899–1902 and 1904–7: Secretary for Native Affairs. 1902–7: Chief Magistrate, Transkeian Territories. 1903–5: Member of the South African Native Affairs Commission. 1908–10: Member of the House of Assembly for Tembuland.

    1910–29: Nominated Senator under section 24 (ii) of the South Africa Act.

Honours: C.M.G. 1892, C.B. 1901, O.B.E. 1918, K.B.E. 1919.

Died 9 September 1933.

HERCULES CHRISTIAN VAN HEERDEN (South African Party)

Born 2 September 1862 near Tarkastad, Cape Colony.

Educated at Victoria College, Stellenbosch.

Occupation: Farmer.

Public Life: 1898–1910: Member of the House of Assembly for Cradock. 1909–11: Chairman of the Afrikaner Bond.

    1910–20: Member of the House of Assembly for Cradock (South African Party). 1913–20: Minister of Agriculture. 1920–9: Nominated Senator (South African Party). 1921–9: President of the Senate.

Died 16 July 1933.

EDGAR HARRIS WALTON (Unionist)

Born 25 July 1856 in Ceylon.

Educated at Clevedon College, Northampton, England.

Migrated to South Africa 1879.

Occupation: Proprietor and editor of the *Eastern Province Herald*.

Public Life: 1898–1910: Member of the House of Assembly for Port Elizabeth. 1904–8: Treasurer.

1910–20: Member of the House of Assembly for Port Elizabeth Central (Unionist). 1920–4: High Commissioner for the Union of South Africa in London.

Honours: K.C.M.G. 1911.

Publication: *The Inner History of the National Convention of South Africa* (Cape Town, 1912).

Died 12 April 1942.

NATAL

EDWARD MACKENZIE GREENE

Born 18 November 1857 in Pietermaritzburg, Natal.

Educated at Lancing College, Sussex, England.

Occupations: Lawyer and farmer.

Public Life: 1879–80: On active service (Zulu War). 1899–1902: On active service—Lt.-Col. in command of the Natal Carbineers. 1897–1910: Member of the Legislative Assembly for Lion's River. 1908–10: Minister of Railways and Harbours.

Honours: C.M.G. 1909; Honorary Colonel in British Army.

Died 22 August 1944.

THOMAS HYSLOP

Born 9 October 1859 at New Cumnock, Ayrshire, Scotland.

Educated at Ayr Academy.

Migrated to South Africa 1882.

Occupation: Farmer.

Public Life: 1899–1903: President Natal Farmers' Conference. 1902–10: Member of the Legislative Assembly for Umgeni. 1903 and 1905–6: Treasurer.

Honours: Kt. 1911.

Died December 1919.

FREDERICK ROBERT MOOR

Born 12 May 1853 at Estcourt, Natal.

Educated at Hermannsburg School, Natal.

Occupations: Diamond digger (1872–9) and farmer.

Public Life: 1886–1910: Member of the Legislative Assembly for Weenen County. 1893–7 and 1899–1903: Minister of Native Affairs. 1906–10: Prime Minister and Minister of Native Affairs. May 1908: Delegate to Intercolonial Conference, Pretoria and Cape Town.

1910–20: Nominated Senator under section 24 (ii) of the South Africa Act. 1910: Minister of Commerce and Industries.

Honours: P.C. 1907, K.C.M.G. 1911; and honorary degrees.

Died 18 March 1927.

WILLIAM BOASE MORCOM

Born 9 October 1846 at Redruth, Cornwall, England.
Educated privately.
Migrated to South Africa 1861.
Occupations: Lawyer and civil servant.
Public Life: 1880–1: Attorney-General of the Transvaal Colony. 1889–93: Attorney-General of Natal. 1897–1910: Member of the Legislative Assembly for Pietermaritzburg City. 1903: Minister of Justice.
Died 24 April 1910.

> *Resigned from the National Convention before it reassembled in Cape Town on 11 January 1909.*

CHARLES JOHN SMYTHE

Born 21 April 1852 at Methven Castle, Perthshire, Scotland.
Educated at Glenalmond College, Perthshire.
Migrated to Natal 1872.
Occupation: Farmer.
Public Life: 1893–1910: Member of the Legislative Assembly for Lion's River. 1897–9: Speaker. 1899–1903: Colonial Secretary. 1905–6: Prime Minister and Colonial Secretary.

1910–18: Administrator of the Province of Natal.
Died 15 May 1918.

THOMAS WATT

Born 20 January 1857 at Shawlands, near Glasgow, Scotland.
Educated privately and at Glasgow University.
Migrated to Natal 1883.
Occupation: Lawyer.
Public Life: 1900–1: On active service—Captain. 1901–10: Member of the Legislative Assembly for Newcastle. 1903–6: Minister of Justice and Minister of Education.

1910–29: Member of the House of Assembly for Dundee (Independent and South African Party). 1912–16: Minister of Posts and Telegraphs. 1912–20: Minister of Public Works. 1916–21: Minister of the Interior. 1919–21: Minister of Public Health. 1921–4: Minister of Posts and Telegraphs and Minister of Public Works.
Honours: C.MG. 1906, K.C.M.G. 1912.
Died 11 September 1947.

> *Joined the National Convention in succession to W. B. Morcom when it resumed in Cape Town on 11 January 1909.*

TRANSVAAL

Louis Botha (Het Volk)

Born 27 September 1862 near Greytown, Natal.

Education: Scarcely any formal education.

Occupation: Farmer.

Public Life: 1898–1902: Member of the South African Republic Volksraad for Vryheid. 1899–1902: On active service. 1900–2: Commandant-General of the South African Republic. 1902: Signed Treaty of Vereeniging. 1905–10: Chairman of Het Volk. 1907–10: Member of the Legislative Assembly for Standerton, Prime Minister and Minister of Agriculture. May 1908: Delegate to the Intercolonial Conference, Pretoria and Cape Town.

1910–19: Prime Minister, Leader of the South African Party and Member of the House of Assembly for Losberg. 1910–12 and 1912–13: Minister of Agriculture. 1913–19: Minister of Native Affairs. 1914–15: In command of Union forces in South-west Africa. 1919: Signed the Treaty of Versailles.

Honours: P.C. 1907; and honorary degrees.

Died 26 August 1919.

Schalk Willem Burger (Het Volk)

Born October 1862 in Lydenburg, South African Republic.

Education: Scarcely any formal education.

Occupation: Farmer.

Public Life: 1881–96: Member of the Volksraad of the South African Republic for Lydenburg. 1896–1902: Member of the Executive Council. 1900–2: Acting President. 1902: Signed Treaty of Vereeniging. 1907–10: Member of the Legislative Assembly for Lydenburg South.

1915–18: Elected Senator for the Transvaal (South African Party).

Died 18 December 1918.

Jacobus Herculaas de la Rey (Het Volk)

Born 22 October 1847 in the Winburg District.

Education: Scarcely any formal education.

Occupation: Farmer.

Public Life: 1893–1902: Member of the South African Republic Volksraad for Lichtenburg. 1899–1902: On active service. 1900–2: Assistant Commandant-General of the South African Republic. 1902: Signed Treaty of Vereeniging. 1902: With Botha and de Wet on mission to Europe. 1907–10: Member of the Legislative Assembly for Ventersdorp.

1910–14: Elected Senator for the Transvaal (South African Party).

Died 15 September 1914—shot by a policeman while travelling by car through Langlaagte with General Beyers, who was trying to compromise him in the Rebellion.

SIR GEORGE HERBERT FARRAR (Progressive)

Born 17 June 1859 at Bedford, England.
Educated at the Modern School, Bedford.
Migrated to South Africa in 1879.
Occupations: Chairman, East Rand Proprietary Mines; and farmer.
Public Life: 1896: As a member of the Reform Committee, sentenced to death after the Jameson Raid, but sentence commuted on payment of £25,000. 1899–1900: On active service—Major. 1903: President of the Transvaal Chamber of Mines. 1903–7: Member of the Legislative Council. 1907–10: Leader of the Opposition and member of the Legislative Assembly for Boksburg East.

    1910–11: Member of the House of Assembly for Georgetown (Unionist).
Honours: D.S.O. 1900, Kt. 1902, Bt. 1911.
Died 19 May 1915 on active service in South-west Africa.

SIR JAMES PERCY FITZPATRICK (Progressive)

Born 24 July 1862 at King William's Town, Cape Colony.
Educated at Downside School, Bath, England.
Occupations: 1892–8: Head of Intelligence Department and 1898–1907 partner in H. Eckstein & Co., branch of Wernher, Beit & Co., financiers. Also writer and farmer.
Public Life: 1896: As secretary of the Reform Committee, sentenced to two years' imprisonment after the Jameson Raid, but released in May 1896. 1899–1900: An official adviser on South African affairs to the British Government. 1902: President of the Transvaal Chamber of Mines. 1903–7: Member of the Legislative Council. 1907–10: Member of the Legislative Assembly for Pretoria South Central.

    1911–20: Member of the House of Assembly for Pretoria East (Unionist).
Honours: Kt. 1902, K.C.M.G. 1911.
Publications: *Through Mashonaland with Pick and Pen* (Johannesburg, 1892); *The Outspan. Tales of South Africa* (London, 1897); *The Transvaal from Within* (London, 1899); *Jock of the Bushveld* (London, 1907); *The Union. A Plea for a Fresh Start* (Johannesburg, 1910); *South African Memories* (edited and introduced by G. H. Wilson, London, 1932).
Died 24 January 1931.

HENRY CHARLES HULL (Nationalist)

Born 21 November 1860 at Caledon, Cape Colony.
Educated by private study.
Occupation: Solicitor.
Public Life: 1896: As a member of the Reform Committee, imprisoned

after the Jameson Raid. 1899–1902: On active service. 1903–7: Member of the Legislative Council. 1907–10: Treasurer and Member of the Legislative Assembly for Georgetown. May 1908: Delegate to the Intercolonial Conference, Pretoria and Cape Town.

1910–15: Member of the House of Assembly for Barberton (South African Party). 1910–12: Minister of Finance.
Died 9 October 1932.

HENRY LILL LINDSAY (Progressive)

Born 5 April 1860 at Somerset West, Cape Colony.
Educated at Burghersdorp and Victoria College, Stellenbosch.
Occupation: Solicitor.
Public Life: 1907–10: Member of the Legislative Assembly for Troyeville.
Died 9 June 1947.

JAN CHRISTIAAN SMUTS (Het Volk)

Born 24 May 1870 near Riebeeck West, Cape Colony.
Educated at Riebeeck West School, Victoria College, Stellenbosch, and Christ's College, Cambridge. Double first in the law tripos.
Occupations: Lawyer and farmer.
Public Life: 1898–1902: State Attorney of the South African Republic. 1899–1902: On active service. 1901–2: In command of South African Republic commando in the Cape Colony. 1902: Signed Treaty of Vereeniging. 1905: A founder of Het Volk. 1907–10: Colonial Secretary and Member of the Legislative Assembly for Wonderboom. May 1908: Delegate to the Intercolonial Conference, Pretoria and Cape Town.

1910–50: Member of the House of Assembly for Pretoria West, Standerton, and Pretoria East (South African Party and United Party). 1910–12: Minister of Mines and Minister of the Interior. 1910–19: Minister of Defence. 1912–13: Minister of Finance. 1915: South-west African campaign. 1916–17: In command, East African campaign. 1917–18: Member of British War Cabinet. 1919: Signed Treaty of Versailles. 1919–24: Prime Minister and Minister of Native Affairs. 1924–33: Leader of the Opposition. 1925: President of the British Association. 1933–9: Minister of Justice. 1938: Minister of Mines. 1939–48: Prime Minister, Minister of Defence, and Minister of External Affairs. 1940–5: G.O.C., Union Defence Forces in the Field. 1948–50: Leader of the Opposition.
Honours: P.C. 1917, C.H. 1917, F.R.S. 1930, O.M. 1947. 1931–4: Rector of St. Andrews University. 1937– : Chancellor of the University of Cape Town. 1941– : Field Marshal in the British Army. 1948– : Chancellor of Cambridge University. Many other honours.
Publications: *Een Eeuw van Onrecht, A Century of Wrong* (editor) (pub-

lished anonymously in Dutch and English, Dordrecht, 1900); *The League of Nations: a Practical Plan* (London, 1919); *Wartime Speeches* (London, 1919); *Holism and Evolution* (London, 1926); *Africa and Some World Problems* (London, 1930); *Plans for a Better World* (London, 1942).
Died 11 September 1950.

ORANGE RIVER COLONY

ALBERT BROWNE (Constitutionalist)

Born 1860 at Bury St. Edmunds, England.
Educated at Bury St. Edmunds and King's College, London.
Migrated to South Africa 1891.
Occupation: Civil servant 1877–1907.
Public Life: 1891–1900: Assistant Imperial Secretary, South Africa. 1901–7: Colonial Treasurer, Orange River Colony. 1907–10: Member of the Legislative Council.
Honours: I.S.O. 1903, C.M.G. 1911, O.B.E. 1918, C.B.E. 1919, K.B.E. 1920.
Died 20 December 1923.

CHRISTIAAN RUDOLF DE WET (Orangia Unie)

Born 7 October 1854 in the Smithfield District, Orange Free State.
Education: No formal education except for a brief period of schooling in 1865–6.
Occupation: Farmer.
Public Life: 1880–1: On active service with South African Republic forces. 1885: Member of the South African Republic Volksraad for Lydenburg. 1891–8: Member of the Orange Free State Volksraad for Upper Modder River. 1899–1902: On active service. 1900–2: Chief Commandant of the Orange Free State. 1902: Signed Treaty of Vereeniging. 1902: With Botha and de la Rey on mission to Europe. 1907–10: Minister of Agriculture and Member of the Legislative Assembly for Vredefort.
    1914: Participated in the Rebellion. 1915: Sentenced to 6 years' imprisonment but released in December.
Publication: *Three Years' War* (London, 1902).
Died 3 February 1922.

ABRAHAM FISCHER (Orangia Unie)

Born 9 April 1850 in Cape Town.
Educated at the South African College.
Occupation: Lawyer.
Public Life: 1878–96: Member of the Orange Free State Volksraad. 1896–1902: Member of the Executive Council. 1900–2: Member of the Joint

Republican Deputation to Europe. 1906–10: Chairman of the Orangia Unie. 1907–10: Prime Minister, Colonial Secretary, and Member of the Legislative Assembly for Bethlehem. May 1908: Delegate to the Intercolonial Conference, Pretoria and Cape Town.

1910–13: Member of the House of Assembly for Bethlehem (South African Party) and Minister of Lands and Irrigation. 1912–13: Minister of the Interior.

Honours: P.C. 1911.

Died 16 November 1913.

JAMES BARRY MUNNIK HERTZOG (Orangia Unie)

Born 3 April 1866 near Wellington, Cape Colony.

Educated at Victoria College, Stellenbosch, and Amsterdam University.

Occupations: Lawyer and farmer.

Public Life: 1895–9: Judge of the High Court, Orange Free State. 1899–1902: On active service. 1900–2: Assistant Chief Commandant of the Orange Free State. 1902: Signed Treaty of Vereeniging. 1906: A founder of the Orangia Unie. 1907–10: Attorney-General and Minister of Education, and Member of the Legislative Assembly for Smithfield. May 1908: Delegate to the Intercolonial Conference, Pretoria and Cape Town.

1910–41: Member of the House of Assembly for Smithfield and Smithfield-Rouxville (South African Party, Nationalist Party, United Party, Reunited Nationalist Party (H.N.P.)). 1910–12: Minister of Justice. 1912: Minister of Native Affairs. 1914–33: Leader of the Nationalist Party. 1933–9: Leader of the United Party. 1924–39: Prime Minister. 1924–9: Minister of Native Affairs. 1927–39: Minister of External Affairs. 1939–41: Leader of the Reunited Nationalist Party (H.N.P.).

Died 21 November 1942.

MARTHINUS THEUNIS STEYN (Orangia Unie)

Born 2 October 1857 near Winburg, Orange Free State.

Educated at Grey College, Bloemfontein, Wevente, Holland, and the Inner Temple, London.

Occupations: Lawyer and farmer.

Public Life: 1889–96: Judge of the High Court, Orange Free State. 1896–1902: President of the Orange Free State. 1899–1902: In the field throughout the War. 1908–9: Vice-President of the National Convention.

Died 28 November 1916.

SOUTHERN RHODESIA

CHARLES PATRICK JOHN COGHLAN

Born 24 June 1863 at King William's Town, Cape Colony.
Educated at St. Aidan's College, Grahamstown, and the South African
    College.
Occupation: Solicitor.
Public Life: 1908–23: Member of the Southern Rhodesian Legislative
    Council and Leader of the unofficial members. 1923–7: Prime Minister.
Honours: Kt. 1910, K.C.M.G. 1925.
Died 28 August 1927.

SIR LEWIS LLOYD MICHELL

Born 11 August 1842 in Plymouth, England.
Educated at Christ's Hospital, England.
Migrated to South Africa 1864.
Occupations: 1864–1904: Banker. 1895–1904: General Manager of the
    Standard Bank of South Africa. 1902–28: Director of the British South
    Africa Company.
Public Life: 1899–1902: President of the Martial Law Board, Cape Colony.
    1902–5: Member of the House of Assembly for Cape Town and Wyn-
    berg. 1904–5: Minister without Portfolio, Cape Colony. May 1908:
    Rhodesian delegate to the Intercolonial Conference, Pretoria and Cape
    Town.
Honours: Kt. 1902, C.V.O. 1910.
Died 29 October 1928.

SIR WILLIAM HENRY MILTON

Born 3 December 1854 in England.
Educated at Marlborough College, England.
Migrated to South Africa 1878.
Occupation: Civil servant.
Public Life: 1878–96: Cape Colony civil service. 1894–6: Head of the Prime
    Minister's Department and Department of Native Affairs. 1896: Chief
    Secretary, Rhodesia. 1898–1914: Administrator of Southern Rhodesia
    and President of the Executive and Legislative Councils.
Honours: C.M.G. 1900, K.C.M.G. 1903, K.C.V.O. 1910.
Died 6 March 1930.

APPENDIX C

BIBLIOGRAPHY

I. *UNPUBLISHED PRIMARY SOURCES*

A. Official

Cape Archives, Prime Minister, CCXXVII–CCXLII, CCCI–CCCIII, CDXXIX.
Natal Archives, Prime Minister, C–CX, CXXI–CXXV.
Transvaal Archives, Prime Minister, LVIII–LX.
Orange Free State Archives, Colonial Secretary, DCCCXXVI.
Union of South Africa House of Assembly, Annexures, 1910–11, CCCLVIII–CCCLXII (National Convention, Minutes of Proceedings, Annexures, Correspondence, &c., I–V).

B. Private

Brand Papers; by kind permission of Lord Brand.
De Villiers Papers; by kind permission of the Dowager Lady de Villiers.
Duncan Papers; by kind permission of Mr. Patrick Duncan and Mr. John Duncan.
Fitzpatrick Papers; by kind permission of Mrs. Niven.
Hofmeyr Papers; in the South African Public Library, Cape Town.
Innes Papers; in the South African Public Library, Cape Town.
Kilpin Papers; in the Library of Parliament, Cape Town.
Merriman Papers; in the South African Public Library, Cape Town.
Michell Papers; in the Cape Archives.
Milner Papers; in the library of New College, Oxford.
Silburn Papers; by kind permission of Mr. R. Silburn.
Smuts Papers; by kind permission of Mr. J. C. Smuts and the Trustees of the Smuts Archive; at present in the Jagger Library, University of Cape Town.
Stanford Papers; by kind permission of Mrs. Ruffel.
Steyn Papers; in the Orange Free State Archives.
Draft of the Selborne Memorandum; in the library of Rhodes House, Oxford.
Richard Feetham, 'Some Problems of South African Federation and Reasons for Facing them' (unpublished paper, 1906); by kind permission of the Hon. Richard Feetham.

II. *PUBLISHED PRIMARY SOURCES*

A. OFFICIAL

British

Parliamentary Debates, 1906–10.

Parliamentary Papers:

1640 (1853), Cape of Good Hope Constitution Ordinance, 1853.

C. 7013 (1893), *Further Correspondence Relating to the Proposal to Establish Responsible Government in Natal.*

Cd. 528, 546, 663 (1901), Papers *re* Negotiations between Louis Botha and Lord Kitchener, 1901.

Cd. 1096 (1902), *Correspondence Respecting Terms of Surrender of the Boer Forces in the field.*

Cd. 1162 (1902), *Petition for the Temporary Suspension of the Cape Constitution and Reply of His Majesty's Government.*

Cd. 1599 (1903), *Draft Customs Union Convention Agreed to by Representatives of the British Colonies and Territories in South Africa at a Conference at Bloemfontein in March, 1903.*

Cd. 1894, 1896, 1897, 1945, 2025, 2183, 2401, 2786, 2788, 2819, 3025 (1904–6), Papers *re* Labour in the Transvaal mines.

Cd. 2399 (1905), *Report of the South African Native Affairs Commission, 1903–1905.*

Cd. 2400, 2479, 2823 (1905–6), Papers *re* Constitutional changes in the Transvaal.

Cd. 2905, 2927, 3027, 3247, 3563, 3888, 3889, 3998, 4001, 4194, 4195, 4328, 4403, 4404, 4585 (1906–9), Papers *re* Native Affairs in Natal.

Cd. 2977 (1906), *Customs Union Convention Provisionally Agreed to by the Representatives of the South African Colonies at a Conference Held at Pietermaritzburg in March, 1906.*

Cd. 3250 (1906), *Transvaal Constitution, 1906. Letters Patent and Instructions Relating to the Transvaal; and Swaziland Order in Council.*

Cd. 3526 (1907), *Letters Patent and Instructions Relating to the Orange River Colony.*

Cd. 3564 (1907), *Papers Relating to a Federation of the South African Colonies.*

Cd. 4525 (1909), *Report to the Respective Parliaments of the Delegates to the South African Convention, 1908–1909; with Copy of the Draft South Africa Constitution Bill.*

Cd. 4587 (1909), *Convention (Dated 1st April, 1909) Between the Governor of the Transvaal and the Portuguese Province of Mozambique.*

Cd. 4721 (1909), *Second Report to the Respective Parliaments of the Delegates to the South African Convention, 1908–1909; With Copy of the*

Draft South Africa Constitution Bill as Finally Passed by the Convention.

Cd. 5099 (1909), *Correspondence Respecting an Act for a Referendum in Natal on the Draft South Africa Union Act.*

South African

Debates, Minutes, and *Votes and Proceedings* of the Parliaments of the Cape of Good Hope, Natal, the Transvaal and the Orange River Colony, and of the Legislative Council of Southern Rhodesia.

Results of the Census of 17 April 1904: Cape Colony, G. 19 (1905); Natal (Pietermaritzburg, 1905); Transvaal and Swaziland (London, 1906); Orange River Colony (Bloemfontein, n.d.).

South African Native Affairs Commission, 1903–5, Report and Appendices (Cape Town, 1905, 5 vols.).

Minutes of the Intercolonial Conference, Pretoria and Cape Town, May 1908 (Pretoria, 1908).

Statistical Registers for the Colony of the Cape of Good Hope, 1903–9.

Statistical Year Books for the Colony of Natal, 1902–9.

Natal Native Affairs Commission, 1906–7, Report and Evidence (Pietermaritzburg, 1907, 2 vols.).

T.G. 2 (1908), *Report and Minutes of Evidence of the Transvaal Mining Industry Commission.*

T.G. 13 (1908), *Report of the Transvaal Indigency Commission.*

T.G. 25 (1908), *Statistics of the Transvaal Colony for the Years 1902–1907.*

T.G. 28 (1909), *Statistics of the Transvaal Colony for the Years 1903–1908.*

Orange River Colony, Colonial Treasurer's Annual Accounts, 1902–10.

Union of South Africa Government Gazette, 1910.

Printed Annexures to the Votes and Proceedings of the Union House of Assembly, 1910–11 (7 vols.).

U. 17 (1911), *Blue Book on Native Affairs, 1910.*

U.G. 32 (1912), *Census of the Union of South Africa, 1911* (11 vols.).

Reports of Union Delimitation Commissions: First (Pretoria, 1910); Second, U.G. 15 (1913); Third, U.G. 58 (1919); Fourth, U.G. 27 (1923); Fifth, U.G. 21 (1928).

U.G. 19, 22, 25 (1916), *Report of the Natives Land Commission, 1913–16.*

U.G. 54 (1937), *Report of Commission of Inquiry Regarding the Cape Coloured Population of the Union.*

Official Year Books of the Union of South Africa and of Basutoland, Bechuanaland Protectorate and Swaziland, Nos. 1–28.

B. Contemporary Books and Pamphlets

Afrikaner Bond, *Drie en twintigste — Zeven en twintigste Centrale Vergadering van de Afrikaander Bond en Boeren Vereniging* . . . (Cape Town, 1907–11, 5 vols.).

A. W. Alderson, *The Worst Tax of All* (London, 1909).

L. S. Amery (editor), *The Times History of the War in South Africa, 1899–1902* (London, 1900–9, 7 vols.).

Anonymous, *A Question of Colour: A Study of South Africa* (Edinburgh, 1906).

—— *The Government of South Africa* (Cape Town, 1908, 2 vols.).

Brigadier-General G. G. Aston, *The Defence of United South Africa as a Part of the British Empire* (Cape Town, 1910).

F. W. Bell, *The Native as a Political Factor and the Native Franchise* (Johannesburg, 1908).

—— *The South African Native Problem: A Suggested Solution* (Johannesburg, 1909).

M. J. Bonn, *Die Eingeborenenpolitik im britischen Südafrika* (Berlin, 1908).

—— *Nationale Kolonialpolitik* (Munich, 1910).

R. H. Brand, *Proportional Representation* (Johannesburg, n.d. [1908]).

—— *The Union of South Africa* (Oxford, 1909).

O. F. Brothers, *The First Transvaal Parliament* (Johannesburg, 1907).

J. H. B. Browne, *South Africa: A Glance at Current Conditions and Politics* (London, 1905).

Sir William Butler, *From Naboth's Vineyard: Being Impressions Formed During a Fourth Visit to South Africa Undertaken at the Request of the 'Tribune' Newspaper* (London, 1907).

Frank R. Cana, *South Africa from the Great Trek to the Union* (London, 1909).

C. C. Clark, *Closer Union* (Durban, 1909).

Cape Town Closer Union Society, *The Framework of Union* (Cape Town, 1908).

Closer Union Societies, *Proceedings of the Annual Meeting of the Association of Closer Union Societies at Johannesburg, March 3rd, 4th and 5th, 1909* (Johannesburg, n.d. [1909]).

E. M. O. Clough, *The South African Parliamentary Manual* (London, 1909).

A. R. Colquhoun, *The Africander Land* (London, 1906).

H. J. Crocker, *The South African Race Problem: The Solution of Segregation* (Johannesburg, 1909).

L. G. Curtis, *Some Suggestions as to how Certain Obstacles to South African Union may be Overcome* (Johannesburg, 1908).

Joseph J. Doke, *M. K. Gandhi: An Indian Patriot in South Africa* (London, 1909).

PATRICK DUNCAN, *Closer Union: Stirring Speech on Unification* (Durban, n.d. [1908]).

J. EDGAR, *Closer Union* (Cape Town, 1908).

E. J. EDWARDS, *The Amalgamation of the Transvaal and Natal* (Johannesburg, 1906).

M. S. EVANS, *The Native Problem in Natal* (Durban, 1906).

SIR J. PERCY FITZPATRICK, *The Union: A Plea for a Fresh Start* (Johannesburg, 1910).

H. E. S. FREMANTLE, *Closer Union: The Financial Aspect* (Cape Town, 1908).

—— *The New Nation: A Survey of the Condition and Prospects of South Africa* (London, 1909).

A. R. GOLDING, *Notes on the Labour Position in the Transvaal* (London, 1904).

H. GUNN, *The Language Question in the Orange River Colony, 1902–1910* (Johannesburg, 1910).

CECIL HARMSWORTH, *Pleasure and Profit in South Africa* (London, 1908).

J. A. HOBSON, *Imperialism: A Study* (London, 1902).

GIJS R. HOFMEYR, *Closer Union of South African Colonies* (Pretoria, 1908).

E. B. IWAN-MÜLLER, *The Future of South Africa* (Oxford, 1903).

RICHARD JEBB, *Studies in Colonial Nationalism* (London, 1905).

DS. J. D. KESTELL and D. E. VAN VELDEN, *De Vredesonderhandelingen tusschen de regeeringen der twee Zuid-Afrikaansche republieken en de vertegenwoordigers der Britische regeering ... 1902 ...* (Pretoria, 1909) (English translation, London, 1912).

D. KIDD, *Kafir Socialism and the Dawn of Individualism: An Introduction to the Study of the Native Problem* (London, 1908).

SIR GODFREY LAGDEN, *The Basutos* (London, 1909, 2 vols.).

PAUL LEDERER, *Die Entwicklung der südafrikanischen Union auf verkehrspolitischer Grundlage* (Leipzig, 1910).

J. RAMSAY MACDONALD, *Labour and the Empire* (London, 1907).

ALGERNON M. S. METHUEN, *The Tragedy of South Africa* (London, 1905).

PERCY ALPORT MOLTENO, *A Federal South Africa* (London, 1896).

ORANGIA UNIE, *Verrichtingen van het derde Jaarlijksch Congres der Orangia Unie ...* (Bloemfontein, 1908).

—— *Verrichtingen van het Buitengewoon Congres der Orangia Unie ... en van het Vierde Jaarlijksch Congres ...* (Bloemfontein, 1909).

JOSEPH MILLERD ORPEN, *The Native Question in Connection with the South African Bill ...* (Cape Town, 1909).

E. J. PAYNE, *Colonies and Colonial Federations* (London, 1904).

LIONEL PHILLIPS, *Transvaal Problems: Some Notes on Current Politics* (London, 1905).

H. E. V. PICKSTONE, *A Reply to Lord Selborne's Questions* (Cape Town, 1909).

J. REYNOLDS-TAIT and M. KANTROVITCH, *The Fallacy of Federation* (Durban, 1909).

P. SAMASSA, *Das neue Südafrika* (Berlin, 1905).

V. SAMPSON, *Closer Union—A Union Constitution. Scheme of Government. The Franchise Question* (Cape Town, 1908).

R. C. A. SAMUELSON, *Native Question. Rules of Policy. Past Shortcomings. The White Man's Burden* (Pietermaritzburg, 1906).

EDGAR SANDERSON, *Great Britain in Modern Africa* (London, 1907).

OLIVE SCHREINER, *Closer Union: A Letter on the South African Union and the Principles of Government* (London, 1909).

ANDRÉ SIEGFRIED, *The Race Question in Canada* (London, 1907).

P. A. SILBURN, *The Constitutional Crisis in South Africa* (Durban, n.d. [1908]).

THE UNIONIST PARTY OF SOUTH AFRICA, *Constitution and Rules . . ., 1910* (1910).

'RIP VAN WINKLE' (pseudonym of I. D. Colvin), *The Parliament of Beasts and other Verses* (Cape Town, 1905).

R. V. WYNNE, *South African Confederation* (Cape Town, 1908).

C. CONTEMPORARY ARTICLES

A BRITISH COLONIST, 'British Rule in the Transvaal', *Contemporary Review*, lxxxv. 329–51 (March 1904).

ANONYMOUS, 'Liability for Defamation of Legislative Body', *Cape Law Journal*, xv. 1–10 (January 1898).

—— 'South African Politics', *Round Table*, i. 84–102 (November 1910).

—— 'The Closer Union Movement', *State*, i. 19–29 (January 1909).

—— 'The Closer Union Societies', ibid., pp. 104–12, 233–4, 391–2 (January–March 1909).

—— (some signed 'Philip Kerr'), 'The Month', ibid., pp. 7–17, 117–35, 259–82, 359–78, 477–501, 595–617; ii. 1–24, 121–40, 241–69, 365–87, 509–30, 669–88; iii. 3–14, 179–90, 355–66, 523–32, 691–702, 987–96; iv. 118–32, 284–306, 461–72, 613–27, 787–97, 947–59 (January 1909–December 1910).

—— 'Union and the Native Protectorates', ibid. i. 45–54 (January 1909).

SIR BISSET BERRY, 'The Pretoria Resolutions, 1908, and After', ibid., pp. 82–91, 196–207 (January–February 1909).

LOUIS BOTHA, 'The Boers and the Empire', *Contemporary Review*, lxxxix. 609–16 (November 1902).

R. H. BRAND, 'Proportional Representation', *State*, Spec. Cons. No., pp. 19–32 (12 February 1909).

LADY VIOLET CECIL, 'The Johannesburg Voter', *National Review*, xlvii. 100–4 (March 1906).

Rev. William Cunningham, 'Impressions of South Africa', ibid., pp. 228–41 (April 1906).

Lord Curzon of Kedleston, 'Reflections on South African Union', *State*, i. 503–11 (May 1909).

L. E. de Payre, 'Should we Civilise the Kafir?' ibid. iii. 542–9 (April 1910).

Charles D. Don, 'The Asiatic Question in Natal', ibid. iv. 713–22 (November 1910).

P. Duncan, 'Analysis and Explanation of the Constitution', ibid. Spec. Cons. No., pp. 1–18 (12 February 1909).

—— 'The Asiatic Question in the Transvaal', ibid. i. 159–74 (February 1909).

—— 'The Labour Question in the Transvaal', ibid. iii. 912–20 (June 1910).

H. A. L. Fisher, 'Political Unions', ibid. i. 295–314, 380–94, 525–38 (March–May 1909).

Trevor Fletcher, 'The Native Problem', ibid. iii. 766–78 (May 1910).

G. Seymour Fort, 'The Situation in South Africa', *Fortnightly Review*, new ser., lxxviii. 854–65 (November 1905).

C. S. Goldmann, 'South Africa and her Labour Problem', *Nineteenth Century*, lv. 848–62 (May 1904).

Rev. W. Greswell, 'Federalism in South Africa', *Fortnightly Review*, new ser., lxi. 617–31 (April 1897).

C. H. Haggar, 'Organised Labour as a Political Factor', *State*, iii. 933–45 (June 1910).

R. F. A. H[oernlé], 'A German Appreciation of South African Native Policy', ibid. i. 347–55, 402–11 (March–April 1909).

Sir Walter Hely-Hutchinson, 'The South African Outlook', *United Empire*, new ser., i. 161–82 (March 1910).

J., 'Lord Milner in South Africa', *Monthly Review*, xxvii. 54–63 (April 1907).

Johannesburger, 'The Question of the Capital', *State*, i. 182–8 (February 1909).

M. Kantrovitch, 'Natal and the Draft Constitution', ibid., pp. 418–24 (April 1909).

A. Berriedale Keith, South African Union', *Journal of Comparative Legislation*, new ser., x. 40–92 (1909).

Sir Godfrey Lagden, 'The Native Question in South Africa', *The Empire and the Century: A Series of Essays on Imperial Problems and Possibilities by Various Writers* (London, 1905), pp. 539–56.

C. J. Langenhoven, 'The Female Franchise and the Native Franchise', *State*, ii. 58–65 (July 1909).

—— 'The Problem of the Dual Language in South Africa', ibid. iii. 403–15 (March 1910).

Sir Perceval Laurence, 'Problems of Closer Union', ibid. i. 63–81 (January 1909).

ALFRED LYTTELTON, 'The Government and South Africa', *National Review*, xlvii. 219–27 (April 1906).

F. S. MALAN, 'Het Burgerschap in de Unie van Zuid-Afrika', *State*, iii. 906–11 (June 1910).

SIR LEWIS MICHELL, 'Greater South Africa', *Proceedings of the Royal Colonial Institute*, xl. 261–86 (1909).

J. SAXON MILLS, 'Towards Union in South Africa', *Fortnightly Review*, new ser., lxxxiv. 285–95 (August 1908).

LORD MILNER, 'Greater Britain and South Africa', *National Review*, xlvii. 209–18 (April 1906).

LORD MONK BRETTON, 'South African Loyalty', *Nineteenth Century*, lxi. 727–35 (May 1907).

ARTHUR W. NOON, 'Socialism and United South Africa', *State*, iii. 805–16 (May 1910).

F. PERRY, 'Portuguese East Africa and South African Union', ibid. i. 549–58 (May 1909).

HOWARD PIM, 'The Native Franchise', ibid. ii. 75–83, 170–80 (July–August 1909).

GUSTAV S. PRELLER, 'Union and the Boer. Why are the Boers so very unanimously in favour of Union?', ibid. i. 627–38 (June 1909).

G. G. ROBINSON, 'The Prospects of a United South Africa', *The Empire and the Century: A Series of Essays on Imperial Problems and Possibilities by Various Writers* (London, 1905), pp. 521–38.

MARCEL SAUVÉ, 'L'Union Sud-Africaine', *Questions Diplomatiques et Coloniales*, xxx. 609–18 (November 1910).

LORD SELBORNE, 'South Africa's Great Problem', *State*, iii. 859–63 (June 1910).

F. J. SEWARD, 'Parties under Union', *African Monthly*, vi. 361–71 (September 1909).

P. A. SILBURN, 'Federation of the South African Colonial Forces', *Empire Review*, viii. 378–86 (November 1904).

—— 'The Political Element in Imperial Defence', ibid. ix. 36–43 (February 1905).

—— 'Colonial Defence', *African Monthly*, i. 3–12 (December 1906).

TRANSVAALER, 'Political Parties in the Transvaal', *National Review*, xlv. 461–88 (May 1905).

X, 'Industrial and Economic Reform in South Africa', *State*, ii. 293–303 (September 1909).

—— 'The £300 Incident', ibid. iv. 667–80 (November 1910).

W. WYBERGH, 'The Transvaal and the New Government', *Contemporary Review*, lxxxix. 313–23 (March 1906).

—— 'Native Policy: Assimilation or Segregation', *State*, i. 322–36, 455–64 (March–April 1909).

D. Primary Material Subsequently Published

G. W. Eybers (editor), *Select Constitutional Documents illustrating South African History, 1795–1910* (London, 1918).

Cecil Headlam (editor), *The Milner Papers (South Africa) 1897–1905* (London, 1931–3, 2 vols.).

G. R. Hofmeyr (editor), *Minutes of Proceedings with Annexures (selected) of the South African National Convention held at Durban, Cape Town and Bloemfontein, 12th October, 1908, to 11th May, 1909* (Cape Town, 1911).

Alfred Viscount Milner, *The Nation and the Empire: Being a Collection of Speeches and Addresses: With an Introduction by Lord Milner, G.C.B.* (London, 1913).

Arthur Percival Newton (editor), *Select Documents Relating to the Unification of South Africa* (London, 1924, 2 vols.).

Johann F. Preller (editor), *Die Konvensie-Dagboek van sy edelagbare François Stephanus Malan, 1908–1909* (with an English translation by A. J. de Villiers) (Cape Town, 1951).

Sir Edgar H. Walton, *The Inner History of the National Convention of South Africa* (Cape Town, 1912).

Basil Williams (editor), *The Selborne Memorandum: a Review of the Mutual Relations of the British South African Colonies in 1907* (Oxford, 1925).

III. *SECONDARY SOURCES*

A. Biographical (in alphabetical sequence of subjects' surnames)

R. K. Cope, *Comrade Bill: The Life and Times of W. H. Andrews, Workers' Leader* (Cape Town, 1943).

Herbert Henry Asquith, 1st Earl of Oxford and Asquith, *Memoirs and Reflections, 1852–1927* (London, 1928, 2 vols.).

J. A. Spender and Cyril Asquith, *Life of Herbert Henry Asquith, Lord of Oxford and Asquith* (London, 1932, 2 vols.).

W. Duncan Baxter, *Turn Back the Pages* (Cape Town, 1954).

W. C. Scully, *Sir J. H. Meiring Beck: A Memoir* (Cape Town, n.d. [1921]).

G. D. Scholtz, *Generaal Christiaan Frederik Beyers, 1869–1914* (Johannesburg, 1941).

Harold Spender, *General Botha: The Career and the Man* (London, 1916).

Earl Buxton, *General Botha* (London, 1924).

F. V. Engelenburg, *General Louis Botha* (London, 1929).

Basil Williams, *Botha, Smuts and South Africa* (London, 1946).

J. A. Spender, *The Life of the Right Hon. Sir Henry Campbell-Bannerman* (London, 1923, 2 vols.).

J. L. Garvin, *The Life of Joseph Chamberlain* (London, 1932–4, vols. i–iii).

JULIAN AMERY, *The Life of Joseph Chamberlain* (London, 1951, vol. iv).

B. K. LONG, *Drummond Chaplin: His Life and Times in Africa* (London, 1941).

J. P. R. WALLIS, *One Man's Hand: The Story of Sir Charles Coghlan and the Liberation of Southern Rhodesia* (London, 1950).

ERIC A. WALKER, *Lord de Villiers and His Times: South Africa 1842–1914* (London, 1925).

J. H. H. DE WAAL, *My Herrinerings van ons Taalstryd* (Cape Town, 1932).

C. R. DE WET, *Three Years' War* (London, 1902).

J. D. KESTELL, *Christiaan de Wet: 'n Lewensbeskrywing* (Cape Town, 1920).

ERIC ROSENTHAL, *General de Wet: A Biography* (Cape Town, 1946).

STEPHEN GWYNN and GERTRUDE M. TUCKWELL, *The Life of the Rt. Hon. Sir Charles W. Dilke, 1843–1911* (London, 1917, 2 vols.).

SIR SIDNEY LEE, *King Edward VII: A Biography* (London, 1927, 2 vols.).

SIR J. PERCY FITZPATRICK, *South African Memories* (London, 1932) (prepared for the press by G. H. Wilson).

J. P. R. WALLIS, *Fitz: The Story of Sir Percy Fitzpatrick* (London, 1955).

SIR GEORGE FRASER, *Episodes in My Life* (Cape Town, 1922).

CHARLES MALLET, *Herbert Gladstone: A Memoir* (London, 1932).

G. A. L. GREEN, *An Editor Looks Back* (Cape Town, 1947).

GUSTAVE HALLÉ, *Mayfair to Maritzburg: Reminiscences of Eighty Years* (London, 1933).

L. E. NEAME, *General Hertzog* (London, 1930).

C. M. VAN DEN HEEVER, *Generaal J. B. M. Hertzog* (Johannesburg, 1943).

—— *General J. B. M. Hertzog* (Johannesburg, 1946).

J. H. HOFMEYR, in collaboration with F. W. REITZ, *The Life of Jan Hendrik Hofmeyr (Onze Jan)* (Cape Town, 1913).

JAMES ROSE INNES, *Autobiography* (London, 1949) (edited and with an introduction by B. A. Tindall).

G. SEYMOUR FORT, *Dr. Jameson* (London, 1908).

IAN COLVIN, *The Life of Jameson* (London, 1922, 2 vols.).

J. C. G. KEMP, *Die Pad van die Veroweraar* (Cape Town, 1942).

SIR GEORGE ARTHUR, *Life of Lord Kitchener* (London, 1920, 3 vols.).

C. J. LANGENHOVEN, *U Dienswillige Dienaar* (Cape Town, 1932).

BETTIE CLOETE, *Die Lewe van Senator F. S. Malan* (Johannesburg, 1946).

SIR PERCEVAL LAURENCE, *The Life of John Xavier Merriman* (London, 1930).

W. BASIL WORSFOLD, *The Reconstruction of the New Colonies under Lord Milner* (London, 1913, 2 vols.).

LIONEL CURTIS, *With Milner in South Africa* (Oxford, 1951).

VLADIMIR HALPÉRIN, *Lord Milner et l'évolution de l'impérialisme britannique* (Paris, 1950) (English translation, with a foreword by L. S. Amery, London, 1952).

EDWARD CRANKSHAW, *The Forsaken Idea: A Study of Viscount Milner* (London, 1952).

SIR JAMES TENNANT MOLTENO, *Further South African Recollections* (London, 1926).

JOHN VISCOUNT MORLEY, *Recollections* (London, 1917, 2 vols.).

G. G. MUNNIK, *Memoirs* (Cape Town, n.d. [1934]).

LIONEL PHILLIPS, *Some Reminiscences* (London, 1924).

VISCOUNT SAMUEL, *Memoirs* (London, 1945).

R. C. A. SAMUELSON, *Long, Long Ago* (Durban, 1929).

ERIC A. WALKER, *W. P. Schreiner: A South African* (London, 1937).

MAJOR-GENERAL J. E. B. SEELY, *Adventure* (London, 1930).

N. LEVI, *Jan Smuts* (London, 1917).

SARAH GERTRUDE MILLIN, *General Smuts* (London, 1936, 2 vols.).

H. C. ARMSTRONG, *Grey Steel (J. C. Smuts): A Study in Arrogance* (London, 1937).

RENÉ KRAUS, *Old Master: The Life of Jan Christian Smuts* (New York, 1944).

F. S. CRAFFORD, *Jan Smuts: A Biography* (London, 1945).

B. K. LONG, *In Smuts's Camp* (London, 1945).

J. C. SMUTS, *Jan Christian Smuts* (London, 1952).

N. J. VAN DER MERWE, *Marthinus Theunis Steyn: 'n Lewensbeskrywing* (Cape Town, 1921, 2 vols.).

G. H. WILSON, *Gone Down the Years* (Cape Town, n.d. [1947]).

B. SELECT GENERAL PUBLICATIONS

M. A. BASSON, *Die Voertaalvraagstuk in die Transvaalse Skoolwese* (Johannesburg, 1944).

K. N. BELL and W. P. MORRELL (editors), *Select Documents on British Colonial Policy, 1830–60* (Oxford, 1928).

GEORGE BENNETT (editor), *The Concept of Empire: Burke to Attlee, 1774–1947* (London, 1953).

E. BOTES, *Die Taalmediumvraagstuk* (Johannesburg, 1941).

ALEXANDER BRADY, *Democracy in the Dominions: A Comparative Study in Institutions* (Toronto, 1947).

CARNEGIE COMMISSION, *Report on the Poor White Problem in South Africa* (Stellenbosch, 1932, 5 vols.).

J. A. COETZEE, *Politieke Groepering in die wording van die Afrikanernasie* (Johannesburg, 1941).

J. C. COETZEE, *Onderwys in Transvaal, 1838–1937* (Pretoria, 1941).

D. V. COWEN, *Parliamentary Sovereignty and the Entrenched Sections of the South Africa Act* (Cape Town, 1951).

C. W. DE KIEWIET, *A History of South Africa: Social and Economic* (Oxford, 1941).

M. H. DE KOCK, *Selected Subjects in the Economic History of South Africa* (Cape Town, 1924).

G. DEKKER, *Afrikaanse Literatuurgeskiedenis* (4th ed., Cape Town, 1947).

GILBERT W. F. DOLD and C. P. JOUBERT, *The Union of South Africa: The Development of its Laws and Constitution* (London, 1955).

HUGH EDWARD EGERTON, *Federations and Unions within the British Empire* (2nd ed., Oxford, 1924).

—— *A Short History of British Colonial Policy 1606–1909* (9th ed., revised by A. P. Newton, London, 1932).

R. C. K. ENSOR, *England, 1870–1914* (Oxford, 1936).

S. H. FRANKEL, *Capital Investment in Africa: Its Course and Effects* (London, 1938).

E. GITSHAM and J. F. TREMBATH, *A First Account of Labour Organisation in South Africa* (Durban, 1926).

MALCOLM HAILEY, 1ST BARON HAILEY, *Native Administration in the British African Territories*, Part V, *The High Commission Territories: Basutoland, the Bechuanaland Protectorate and Swaziland* (London, 1953).

—— *An African Survey* (revised ed., London, 1957).

ELIE HALÉVY, *Imperialism and the Rise of Labour* (2nd ed., London, 1951).

—— *The Rule of Democracy, 1905–1914* (2nd ed., London, 1952).

W. K. HANCOCK, *Survey of British Commonwealth Affairs* (London, 1937–42, 2 vols.).

J. H. HOFMEYR AND OTHERS, *Coming of Age: Studies in South African Citizenship and Politics* (Cape Town, 1930).

—— and J. P. COPE, *South Africa* (2nd ed., London, 1952).

SIR IVOR JENNINGS and C. M. YOUNG, *Constitutional Laws of the Commonwealth* (2nd ed., Oxford, 1952).

ARTHUR BERRIEDALE KEITH, *Responsible Government in the Dominions* (2nd ed., Oxford, 1928, 2 vols.).

W. P. M. KENNEDY and H. J. SCHLOSBERG, *The Law and Custom of the South African Constitution* (London, 1935).

RALPH KILPIN, *The Old Cape House* (Cape Town, n.d. [1918]).

—— *The Romance of a Colonial Parliament* (London, 1930).

—— *Parliamentary Procedure in South Africa* (3rd ed., Cape Town, 1955).

PAUL KNAPLUND, *British Commonwealth and Empire, 1901–1955* (London, 1956).

I. D. MACCRONE, *Race Attitudes in South Africa: Historical, Experimental and Psychological Studies* (London, 1937).

M. P. A. MALAN and M. C. VAN RENSBURG, *Verkiesingsuitslae 1910–43* (Bloemfontein, n.d.).

E. G. MALHERBE, *Education in South Africa, 1652–1922* (Cape Town, 1925).

J. S. MARAIS, *The Cape Coloured People, 1652–1937* (London, 1939).

L. MARQUARD, *The Peoples and Policies of South Africa* (London, 1952).

—— *The Story of South Africa* (London, 1955).

GEOFFREY MARSHALL, *Parliamentary Sovereignty and the Commonwealth* (Oxford, 1957).

A. C. MARTIN, *The Concentration Camps 1900–1902 (Facts, Figures and Fables)* (Cape Town, 1957).

HENRY JOHN MAY, *The South African Constitution* (3rd ed., Cape Town, 1955).

M. NATHAN, *The South African Commonwealth: Constitution—Problems —Social Conditions* (Johannesburg, 1919).

A. P. NEWTON and E. A. BENIANS (editors), *South Africa, Rhodesia and the Protectorates* (*The Cambridge History of the British Empire*, vol. viii) (Cambridge, 1936).

G. S. NIENABER and P. J. NIENABER, *Die Geskiedenis van die Afrikaanse Beweging* (Pretoria, 1941).

MARGERY PERHAM and LIONEL CURTIS, *The Protectorates of South Africa: the Question of their Transfer to the Union* (London, 1935).

E. C. PIENAAR, *Die triomf van Afrikaans* (2nd ed., Cape Town, 1946).

G. B. PYRAH, *Imperial Policy and South Africa, 1902–10* (Oxford, 1955).

J. QUICK and R. R. GARRAN, *The Annotated Constitution of the Australian Commonwealth* (Sydney, 1901).

A. A. ROBERTS, *A South African Legal Bibliography* (Pretoria, 1942).

H. M. ROBERTSON, *South Africa: Economic and Political Aspects* (Durham, North Carolina, and Cambridge, 1957).

EDWARD ROUX, *Time Longer than Rope* (London, 1948).

G. D. SCHOLTZ, *Die Rebellie, 1914–15* (Johannesburg, 1942).

C. G. W. SCHUMANN, *Structural Changes and Business Cycles in South Africa, 1806–1936* (London, 1938).

J. STUART, *A History of the Zulu Rebellion, 1906, and of Dinizulu's Arrest, Trial and Expatriation* (London, 1913).

L. M. THOMPSON, *The Cape Coloured Franchise* (Johannesburg, 1949).

C. M. VAN DER HEEVER and P. DE V. PIENAAR (editors), *Kultuurgeskiedenis van die Afrikaner* (Cape Town, 1945–50, 3 vols.).

SHEILA T. VAN DER HORST, *Native Labour in South Africa* (London, 1942).

JEAN VAN DER POEL, *Railway and Customs Policies in South Africa, 1885–1910* (London, 1933).

A. J. H. VAN DER WALT, J. A. WIID, and A. L. GEYER (editors), *Geskiedenis van Suid-Afrika* (Cape Town, 1951, 2 vols.).

CARL VAN DOREN, *The Great Rehearsal: The Story of the Making and Ratifying of the Constitution of the United States* (London, 1948).

J. J. VAN ROOYEN, *Die Nasionale Party: sy opkoms en oorwinning — Kaaplandse aandeel* (Cape Town, 1956).

ERIC A. WALKER, *A History of Southern Africa* (3rd ed., London, 1957) (first published 1928 under title *A History of South Africa*).

JOHN H. WELLINGTON, *Southern Africa: A Geographical Study* (Cambridge, 1955, 2 vols.).

K. C. WHEARE, *Federal Government* (London, 1946).

W. B. WORSFOLD, *The Union of South Africa* (London, 1912).

C. SELECT ARTICLES

B. BEINART, 'Parliament and the Courts', *Butterworths South African Law Review, 1954*, pp. 134–81.

—— 'The Legal Relationship between the Government and its Employees', ibid., *1955*, pp. 21–72.

—— 'The South African Appeal Court and Judicial Review', *Modern Law Review*, xxi. 587–608 (November 1958).

G. L. BEER, 'Lord Milner and British Imperialism', *Political Science Quarterly*, xxx. 301–8 (June 1915).

I. D. BOSMAN, 'Die Grondwet en die Staatsregterlike Ontwikkeling van die Unie sedert 1910', *Geskiedenis van Suid-Afrika* (Cape Town, 1951, 2 vols.), ii. 99–128.

D. V. COWEN, 'Legislature and Judiciary: Reflections on the Constitutional Issues in South Africa', *Modern Law Review*, xv. 277–96; xvi. 273–98 (July 1952, July 1953).

—— 'The Entrenched Sections of the South Africa Act: Two Great Legal Battles', *South African Law Journal*, lxx. 1–28 (August 1953).

RALPH KILPIN, 'South Africa: National Convention, Before and After', *Parliamentary Government in the Commonwealth* (London, 1951), pp. 159–65.

PAUL KNAPLUND, 'The Unification of South Africa: A Study in British Colonial Policy', *Transactions of the Wisconsin Academy of Sciences, Arts and Letters*, xxi. 1–21 (July 1924).

H. J. MANDELBROTE, 'The Royal Prerogative in the Union', *South African Law Journal*, liii. 426–40 (November 1936).

—— 'The Union Constitution and its Working', *The Cambridge History of the British Empire*, viii. 676–93.

WALTER NASH, 'Parliamentary Government in New Zealand', *Parliamentary Government in the Commonwealth* (London, 1951), pp. 42–60.

EARL OF SELBORNE, 'The South African Protectorates', *Journal of the African Society*, xiii. 353–64 (July 1914).

DS. B. SPOELSTRA, 'Die Bewindsaanvaarding van die Botha-Regering oor Transvaal as Selfregerende Britse Kolonie in 1907', *Archives Year Book for South African History, 1953*, ii. 307–88.

L. M. THOMPSON, 'Constitutionalism in the South African Republics', *Butterworths South African Law Review, 1954*, pp. 49–72.

—— 'The Colony of Natal and the "Closer Union Movement"', ibid., *1955*, pp. 81–106.

—— 'The Non-European Franchise in the Union of South Africa', *Parliamentary Government in the Commonwealth* (London, 1951), pp. 166–77.

D. Unpublished Theses and Research Essays

Joan Bradley, 'Section 137 of the South Africa Act' (University of Cape Town, 1955).

Norman Bromberger, 'General Botha and the Conciliation Policy, 1902–1910' (University of Cape Town, 1957).

P. Cuthbert, 'The Premiership of L. S. Jameson, 1904–08' (University of Cape Town, 1950).

D. A. Etheredge, 'The Grant of Responsible Government to the Transvaal in 1906' (University of the Witwatersrand, 1946).

J. Kirstein, 'Some Foundations of Afrikaner Nationalism' (University of Cape Town, 1956).

E. Mamkile, 'African Public Opinion and the Unification of South Africa' (University of Cape Town, 1954).

B. K. Ross, 'A Study of Politics in the Cape Colony from January 1908 to May 1910' (University of Cape Town, 1950).

A. E. G. Trollip, 'The First Phase of Hertzogism' (University of the Witwatersrand, 1947).

F. Vermooten, 'Transvaal en die Totstandkoming van die Unie van Suid-Afrika, 1906–10' (Potchefstroom University, 1955).

INDEX

Abdurahman, Dr., 326, 341, 385, 406.
Acts of Parliament (British):
British North America Act (1867),
269, 270, 271 n. 69, 288–9, 346.
Colonial Boundaries Act (1895), 409.
— Courts of Admiralty Act (1890),
410.
— Laws Validity Act (1865), 87,
99 n. 7, 100, 284 & n. 13.
Commonwealth of Australia Consti-
tution Act (1900), 409 & n. 41.
South Africa Act (1877), 3 & n. 3.
Statute of Westminster (1931), 284
n. 13.
See also South Africa Act (1909).
— — — (Colonial). See also under
Education.
Cape Colony: Additional Represen-
tation Act (1904), 129; Cape Act
32 (1895), 265 n. 53; Representa-
tion Acts, 127 & n. 78.
Natal: Natal Act 21 (1894), 265 n. 53;
Referendum Act (1909), 360–1,
362 n. 82.
Transvaal: Public Service and Pensions Act (1908), 268; Transvaal
Acts Nos. 2 and 15 (1907), 27 n. 65;
Transvaal Act No. 19 (1908), 265
n. 53.
African Political Organization, 214 &
n. 19, 326 f., 340–1, 375, 385 &
n. 77.
Africans, 1, 4, 42 & n. 99, 51, 65 f., 113,
132, 481; appeal to Britain, 385 f.;
Bantu-speaking, 2, 50, 214, 269,
325, 486 f., 498; in Cape Colony,
214–15; criticism of draft Constitution, 325–7; deputation to England, 402 f., 406; Kaffirs, 11, 462,
482; Milner's policy, 6, 12, 17;
political rights, 108 f., 110 & n. 34,
111–16, 375. See also Franchise,
Labour, and Native question.
Afrikaans, see Language.
Afrikaansche Christelijke Vrouwen
Vereeniging, 195 n. 55.
Afrikaners, 1 & n. 1, 2, 4, 7 f., 15 ff.,
30, 35, 64, 80, 82, 126, 128 f., 139,
143 f., 147, 150, 165, 236, 256, 310,

319, 328, 343 f., 355–6, 401, 433 ff.,
445 ff., 450, 465, 467, 478, 480 f.;
Bond, see under Political Parties;
divisions, 17, 81; domination
feared, 350 f., 355, 362, 366, 393,
399, 470; isolationism, 33, 41, 80,
483; in National Convention,
176 ff., 186, 193 f., 196–9, 236, 239,
254, 266, 296; and Natives, 119;
revival and cultural movement,
17–28, 36, 39, 135, 269; suspicions
of Smuts, 32 n. 73. See also under
Natal and Orange River Colony.
Albany (Grahamstown), 471 n. 14, 472,
473 n. 22, 478 n. 32.
Albert, Cape Province, 472 & n. 20.
Alden, P., 124.
Alexander, Morris, 339, 386.
Alfred County, Natal, 127.
Aliwal, Cape Province, 473 n. 23.
— North, 472.
Anglo-Boer co-operation, 35–38, 41,
132, 144 f., 177, 196, 390, 398,
420 f., 433, 437, 447.
— feud, v, 4, 16–17, 64, 139, 143, 319,
366, 435, 437, 469–70, 478, 480 f.
— nationhood, 31, 66, 82, 96, 98, 102,
104, 126, 143, 168, 307–8, 311, 314,
330, 350, 355–6, 400, 445, 463 f.,
480.
Anglo-German agreement, 4; conflict,
301 & n. 75, 398 f.
Anti-Slavery and Aborigines Protection
Society, 404, 406, 407 n. 31.
Armstrong, G. S., 351 n. 48.
Asiatics, 27 & n. 65, 111, 411, 438,
462–5, 486–9; meaning of term,
487; occupation of land, 490.
Asquith, H. H., 24, 428–32, 449 &
n. 43.
Attorney-General, 330, 333.
Australia, 77, 123, 294, 400, 420; capital,
304; Constitution, 71, 85, 97,
101–4, 106–9, 155, 170, 187, 190,
199 f., 211 f., 242 f., 244 n. 9, 245,
247, 283–4, 346, 482 n. 45, British
Government and, 265, 388 & n. 88,
402; electoral system, 25, 132, 323;
settlers from, 14.

438–9, 441 ff., 445 f., 448 & n. 40, 468; Transvaal Ministry (1908–10), 28, 139, 266, 391.

Brand, R. H., v, 61 & n. 1, 84, 107 n. 26, 133–4 & n. 94, 149, 157 & n. 65, 162 ff., 179, 183, 186, 192, 222, 239, 241, 266, 281, 283, 287, 309, 364, 367 n. 1, 369 f. & n. 13, 373.

Brandfort, O.F.S., *see under* Conferences, &c.

Bredasdorp, Cape Province, 307 n. 99.

Britain and National Convention, 173–4, 217, 220, 226, 380–1; proportional representation in, 133; self-governing dominions, 419–20.

British:
Constitution, 97, 105, 109, 163 f., 187, 199, 207, 252, 482–3; electoral system, 128, 323.
Forces, 223, 225, 231, 246, 429.
Loans, 13.
Mining companies, 3.
Native policy, 51, 67 & n. 15, 120 f., 124 f., 214, 217 f., 271, 276, 326, 334, 385, 402, 405, 408, 420, 425–6.
Policy towards South Africa, 1, 64, 82, 400, 466–8; in relation to South Africa Act, 389 f., 403, 416. *See also* South Africa Act (1909).
Settlers, 1 f., 7 f., 14 ff., 35, 41, 51, 63 f., 79, 126, 138, 165, 176, 236, 310, 314, 343, 364, 366, 433, 436 f., 439 f., 444, 448, 450 ff., 457, 465, 475–6, 478–81; fear of Afrikaner domination, 82–83, 176, 236; in National Convention, 176 & n. 10, 194 ff., 198, 236, 254, 266, 268.
See also Parliaments.
— South Africa Company, 3 f., 49 f., 150 f., 269 ff. & n. 69, 278, 461; charter, 51, 84, 269, 410.

Broekhuizen, Ds., 469.

Browne, A., 145, 174 n. 4, 175 nn. 5, 9, 176 n. 10, 190, 197, 207, 229, 287, 299, 335, 367, 369, 392, 510.

Bruce, Sir Charles, 405.

Brunner, E. A., 41, 353.

Burger, S. W., 21, 144, 174, 175 nn. 5, 9, 182, 189, 219, 276, 299, 311, 368, 507.

Burton, H., 29, 37, 457 ff., 472.

Byles, W. P., 429.

Campbell-Bannerman, Sir Henry, 23 f., 26, 33, 82, 416, 424, 447, 467.

Canada, Federation of, 66, 85, 97, 101–4, 106 f. & n. 26, 108 f., 123, 136 f., 150, 155, 199, 294, 400; French Canadians, 8; precedents, 269, 279, 306, 330, 449; race question, 77 f., 420; settlers in South Africa, 14.

Cape Colony:
Civil Service, 265 & n. 53.
Constitutional: Constitutional Ordinance (1853), 127; electoral system, 127 f., 130, 134 n. 95, franchise, 109–10, 112 f., 115–17, 120, 123, 138, *see also* Cape Native franchise *under* Native question, voters, 228 & n. 55, 235 & n. 83; self-government, 4; suspension of Constitution attempted, 8–9, 16, 38. Draft Constitution, amendments, 336–48, 362–74, 379 ff., 389, Cape coloured franchise, 337, 339, 341–2, 345, delegation to England, 393, Parliamentary debates and resolutions, 336–48, 382, 389 f., 392 f., 396 f., reactions to, 310, 315–20.
Division into provinces suggested, 153, 255.
Dutch Reformed Church, 17 n. 48.
Economic: customs and railways, 54–59, 92–93, 285–7, 491, 495; diamonds, 3, 54, 497, 500; occupations, 489; population, 2, 54, 226 f. & nn. 53, 54, 231 n. 64, 233, 235 n. 82, 486–90; taxation, revenue, expenditure, 39, 54, 140, 286–7, 345, 451, 491, 495; brandy excise, 386 & n. 79, 392, 438, 451.
Education, 289.
Judicial system, 260–1.
Land distribution, 490.
Language question, 135, 138.
National Convention: capital, 295–304; delegates, 142, (named) 146, 175, 177–80 & n. 18, 215, 243, 256, 289, 291, 293, 302, 316, 325, 368 ff., 389; franchise, 218 f.; Governor, 202 n. 80; railways and harbours, 291.
Native question, 112–16, 214–15, 315, 333, 339, 481–2; African Political Organization, 214; land, 490.
Parliament, Senate, 205 n. 91, 243; unitary Constitution supported, 189–90.

PRINTED IN GREAT BRITAIN
AT THE UNIVERSITY PRESS, OXFORD
BY VIVIAN RIDLER
PRINTER TO THE UNIVERSITY